MOONLIGHT SERENADE

A Bio-discography
of the Glenn Miller Civilian Band

MOONLIGHT

SERENADE

A Bio-discography

of the Glenn Miller Civilian Band

by

JOHN FLOWER

ARLINGTON HOUSE New Rochelle, N.Y.

All photographs from Arsene Studios except those credited to Glenn Miller Estate or 20th Century-Fox.

Library of Congress Catalog Card Number 74–179717

ISBN 0–87000–161–2

MANUFACTURED IN THE UNITED STATES OF AMERICA

DEDICATION

To the members of The Glenn Miller Society

FOREWORD

This discography of the Glenn Miller civilian orchestra is truly a magnificent tribute to a giant in the field of popular music. In an extremely short period of time Glenn rose from obscurity to world-wide fame but never lost the common touch. He travelled all over the country with his orchestra, playing in many, many places, but somehow managed to find sufficient time to arrange in his own inimitable way and to perpetuate on phonograph records a tremendous amount of music--music that was highly popular all over the world during his lifetime and that remains so to this day.

John Flower and his associates have compiled in this book a highly accurate listing of the recordings of the Glenn Miller orchestra, together with personnel and other pertinent data. These men, working over a period of years and on their own time, have assembled, checked and re-checked a multitude of facts, have corrected many long-existing errors with respect to names, dates and places, and have now produced what is unquestionably one of the most complete and accurate discographies of a popular dance orchestra ever published.

Every Glenn Miller fan--indeed everyone who ever heard of Glenn Miller and had any interest in the Glenn Miller music--will, I am sure, be delighted to join with me in extending to the indefatigable John Flower and his loyal associates heartfelt thanks for a job well done.

New York, New York
June 15, 1971

David Mackay
Executor, Glenn Miller Estate

This work has two purposes. The first is to catalogue all commercial recordings made by Glenn Miller and His Orchestra whether issued or unissued, and to list all non-commercial recordings (broadcasts) made by him. The second is to give a running commentary as to his whereabouts, his engagements (with crowd drawn where known),his films, the changing personnel of his band outside of the recording sessions, and his accomplishments during the period 1935 to 1942. Note that outside of the recording session in 1935 the actual period is from 1937 to 1942. We hope to be able to publish in the near future a discography on his earlier years as a sideman and arranger, as well as a discography on the Army Air Forces Orchestra 1943 to 1945 (which is already in preparation).

The overall format of this work is a chronological progression. Three type faces are used to differentiate among the several classes of information contained herein. The type style used in this paragraph is employed throughout the text for factual data and descriptive matter.

This type face is used to identify commercial recordings, whether issued or unissued.

All broadcast material is shown in this type face.

We realize that there will inevitably be errors and omissions in this work but we have done our best with the information available. It must be noted that information from the Miller Estate, RCA Victor, and other sources, has led us to change facts and figures that were shown in the original discography published by The Glenn Miller Appreciation Society.

We must also mention that in some of the quotations from various magazines and newspapers the words are mispelled, punctuation is incorrect, and language is poor. However, since these are quotations we have not attempted to make any corrections.

Finally, we must apologize for the long delay in getting this work published. It has been in the "works" for over ten years and we are pleased to see the final result. However, due to the delay, the final result is much more complete than it would otherwise have been.

PHYSICAL LAYOUT OF THE RECORDING SESSIONS

The first entry is the date followed by the studio location.

The second entry is the personnel for the recording session. If the personnel of the next recording session is the same as previously shown then the personnel is not repeated but reference is made to the last complete listing of personnel. Personnel changes are emphasized by listing replacements in CAPITALS. Most of the information on the personnel is from the Glenn Miller Payroll Records and RCA Victor. Prior to October 1938 no records for G.M.P.R. are available and we have had to rely on various magazine articles in Down Beat, Metronome, etc., as well as the recording companies of Columbia, Decca, Brunswick, and RCA Victor, for information.

Next, in the left-hand margin, are the matrix numbers, followed by the take number, when known (e.g. 043973-1). Our take information has come directly from the record companies. The fact that RCA Victor indicate there were only one, two or three takes of a tune does not mean that these were the only takes made at the recording session. All it means is that out of perhaps five or six takes made at a recording session only one, two or three takes were "processed" and kept, and are now in RCA Victor's files.

To the right of the matrix number(s) are the catalogue numbers of the issued records with the first issue underlined (e.g. BB 10536-A, HMVAu EA-2436, etc.) showing the side number (e.g. In this case it is Side A). We had hoped to indicate which releases were LP's, 45's, 78's, etc. but due to a constant addition of new releases this was not possible.

Below the catalogue numbers, in bold face type, are the tune titles; a code indicating the name of the arranger, where known (see explanation of code in "Abbreviation" section); and the name(s) of the vocalist(s), if any.

Below the tune titles are the show credits, film credits, where known.

Below this section in brackets, are the names of the lyricists and composers. Where we do not know this information open brackets (   ) indicate this lack of information.

Finally, below the lyricist and composer credits are the soloists, where known. In order to shorten this last listing we refer only to the last name of the musician (e.g. Ts, Beneke) with the code for the instrument played.

The first entry is the date; followed by the hotel, theater, night club, or dance hall; then followed by the town or city; then followed by the state or province; and then followed by the type of show (e.g. SUNSET SERENADE) in capital letters, where known.

The next entry is the network, followed by the time on the air, where known.

On the next line is the name of the announcer, where known.

Finally, we show the tunes, where known. We tried to get the correct order of the tunes as broadcast but since we were not able to listen to all of the broadcasts (and some are unavailable), the order may be out in some cases. Where a tune has been released on record the catalogue numbers are shown in exactly the same way as for a recording session. Note that we also show matrix numbers for LP's etc. (even though they do not show any sequence) so that the issued tune stands out. Matrix numbers shown in these cases are for the first LP, etc. issued. For tunes that have been issued on record or where we have an aircheck we show the timing of the aircheck. When a timing is shown as thus (2:40) the dash on the last bracket indicates that our copy of the aircheck, or the recorded aircheck, is incomplete at the end. The following symbol is shown where the beginning of the tune is incomplete (2:40). The times shown are for music only and do not include announcements (and applause) unless the announcement is said after the tune has started. These timings do not always correspond with RCA Victor who are including applause, and announcements (in some instances) in their timings. All timings of broadcasts were timed by the author and may not be the same as stated by RCA Victor or else-where. Naturally, the timings of home recordings are out if they were off speed or re-taped many times.

There are some broadcasts where we have no details but out-side of the Chesterfield Shows we have not, as a rule, shown "NO DETAILS AVAILABLE" to avoid repetition. Although we have al-most a complete listing of all the Chesterfield Shows, many are in rough shape and many of the original discs were cracked and broken before final transfer to tape. This has made our checking job re dates almost impossible as some of the discs were broken after the issuance of the First Limited Edition and the final tapes (in RCA Victor's files) do not contain these programs.

We have not listed details of vocalists, arranger credits, etc. in the listing of broadcasts due to the fact that we have not heard all of the broadcasts (and the vocalists were often changed on broadcast versions of a recorded tune), but mainly to save space. We decided to only show all of the details where we have the air-check, or where the aircheck has been released on record, or where it is the only listing in the discography of the tune. Also, if the tune is unreleased we have not shown the complete tune title. Therefore, "I Do, Do You? (Do You Believe In Love)" is shown as "I Do, Do You?" In some cases where we have heard the aircheck at RCA Victor (but do not have the tune in our collection) we show vocalist(s) and   solo credits.

Where we have an introduction of a tune by Glenn Miller or a known announcer this is shown (e.g. Int GM).

TGM - THIS IS GLENN MILLER   LPM 1190

N - THE NEARNESS OF YOU   CAS 2128

OR - ORIGINAL RECORDINGS   CAS 829

OO - ONE AND ONLY GLENN MILLER   CAS 2267

BGM - BEST OF GLENN MILLER #2   LPM 3564

FFT - FOR THE FIRST TIME   LPM 6100

GGM - THE GREAT GLENN MILLER   CAL -751

GMC-1 - GLENN MILLER CONCERT   LPM 1193

GMC-2 - GLENN MILLER CONCERT #2   LPT 30

GMC-3- GLENN MILLER CONCERT #3   LPT 3001

GDB - GREAT DANCE BANDS OF THE 30 & 40's   LPM - 2080

LE #1 - LIMITED EDITION   VOL 1   LPT 6700

LE #2 - LIMITED EDITION   VOL 2   EPOT 6701

OA - ON THE AIR   LPM - 6101

BM - BLUE MOONLIGHT   LPM   3657

C-1   CHESTERFIELD BROADCASTS #1 LSP 3873

C-2   CHESTERFIELD BROADCASTS #2 LSP 3981

E   GLENN MILLER ON EPIC   LN 3236

SIW   SPIRIT IS WILLING   EPAT 428

45E   GLENN MILLER VOL II   EPIC EG 7034

GMM   GLENN MILLER MEMORIAL 1944-1969   VPM -6019

SP   STRING OF PEARLS   ADL2 -048 0168

OW   ORCHESTRA WIVES   LPT 3065

SVS   SUN VALLEY SERENADE   EPBT 3064

ALP   A LEGENDARY PERFORMER   CPM2 0693

CGM-1   COMPLETE GLENN MILLER #1

CGM-2   COMPLETE GLENN MILLER #2   AXM2 - 5514

RD -   READERS DIGEST RD 25-K

GML-   GLENN MILLER LIVE 1940

TAPE - CASETTE TAPE TIMELESS TREASURES

ABBREVIATIONS

ARRANGER CREDIT ABBREVIATIONS:

Eddie Barefield	(EB)	Joe Lippman	(JL)
Carl Biesecker	(CB)	Chummy MacGregor	(ChM)
Roland Bundock	(RB)	Jack Maisel	(JM)
Benny Carter	(BC)	Billy May	(BM)
Bill Challis	(BCh)	Hal McIntyre	(HM)
H.G. Chapman	(HGC)	Glenn Miller	(GM)
Charles Dixon	(CD)	Harold Mooney	(HMo)
Eddie Durham	(ED)	Bill Moore	(BMo)
E.G. Eberhard	(EE)	Wheeler Moran	(WM)
Fred Van Eps	(FVE)	Freddy Norman	(FN)
Bill Finegan	(BF)	William Schulz	(WS)
Jerry Gray	(JG)	George Siravo	(GS)
Bill Grey	(BG)	Buddy Stanton	(BS)
A. Guenther	(AG)	George Williams	(GW)
Fletcher Henderson (FH)		Henri Woode	(HW)
Gabe Julien?	(GJ?)	Al Young	(AY)
Dean Kincaide	(DK)		

INSTRUMENTAL ABBREVIATIONS:

as	alto saxophone	g	guitar
bar	baritone (saxophone)	harp	harp
b	bass	maraccas	maraccas
b-clt	Bass clarinet	p	piano
cello	cello	tbn	trombone
celeste	celeste	ts	tenor saxophone
clt	clarinet	tpt	trumpet
cnt	cornet	vla	viola
d	drums	vln	violin

LABEL ABBREVIATIONS: Following are the abbreviations used in the text for the labels on which Glenn Miller's recordings, tapes, and transcriptions were issued. All labels are of U.S. origin if they are not qualified by a notation in parentheses following them. Note that Canadian Bluebird (and Victor) records are the same numbers as the American issue and are not shown unless they are a different take.

AFR	Armed Forces Record	Cam	Camden
AFRS	Armed Forces Radio Service	Cl	Clave (Spain)
AH	Ace Of Hearts (England)	Co	Columbia
Ar	Ariola	CoAu	Columbia (Australia)
BB	Bluebird	CoAus	Columbia (Austria)
Bert.	Bertelsmann	CoE	Columbia (England)
Schall.	Schallplattenring (Germany)	CoG	Columbia (Germany)
Bilt	Biltmore	CoIr	Columbia (Ireland)
Br.	Brunswick	CoJ	Columbia (Japan)
BrE	Brunswick (England)	Cq	Conqueror
BrG	Brunswick (Germany)	De	Decca

DeArg	Decca (Argentina)	Vi	Victor
DeC	Decca (Canada)	ViArg	Victor (Argentina)
DeF	Decca (France)	Vi Braz	Victor (Brazil)
DeI	Decca (Italy)	ViJ	Victor (Japan)
DeSp	Decca (Spain)	VD	V-Disc
El	Electrola (Germany)	Vo	Vocalion
Epic	Epic	VoE	Vocalion (England)
Emb	Ember (England)	VdP	Voce Del Padrone
Fe Au	Festival (Australia)		(Italy HMV)
GMMS	Glenn Miller Moonlight	WRC	World Record Club
	Serenade		
GrF	Gramophone (France HMV)		
Ha	Harmony		
Hall	Hallmark (Britain)		
HMV	His Master's Voice (England)		
HMVAu	His Master's Voice (Australia)		
HMVAus	His Master's Voice (Austria)		
HMVHu	His Master's Voice (Hungary)		
HMVIn	His Master's Voice (India)		
HMVIr	His Master's Voice (Ireland)		
HMVN	His Master's Voice (Norway)		
HMVSc	His Master's Voice (Scandinavia)		
HMVSp	His Master's Voice (Spain)		
HMVSw	His Master's Voice (Switzerland)		
Lu	Lucky (Japan)		
LW	Longine(s)		
MT	Movietone		
MT G	Movietone (Germany)		
MW	Montgomery Ward		
OK	Okeh		
Ph Arg	Philips (Argentina)		
PhAu	Philips (Australia)		
PhE	Philips (England)		
Pick Int.	Pickwick International (Britain)		
Polyd	Polydor (France)		
Poly	Polygon		
RCA	Rca (England)		
RCA Arg	Rca (Argentina)		
RCA Au	Rca (Australia)		
RCA Cam G	Rca Camden (Germany)		
RCA G	Rca (Germany)		
RCA F	Rca (France)		
RCA It	Rca (Italy)		
RCA Int.	Rca (International)		
RD	Reader's Digest		
RD Br.	Reader's Digest (Britain)		
RZ	Regal Zonophone (England)		
RZ Au	Regal Zonophone (Australia)		
TCF	Twentieth Century-Fox		
RCFArg	Twentieth Century-Fox (Argentina)		
TCF Au	Twentieth Century-Fox (Australia)		
TCF Int.	Twentieth Century-Fox (International)		
TR	Top Rank (England)		

MISCELLANEOUS ABBREVIATIONS:

arr	arranger
BB	Billboard (magazine)
B. & O. RR	Baltimore & Ohio Railroad
C.B. & Q. RR	Chicago, Burlington & Quincy Railroad
CBS	Columbia Broadcasting System
DB	Down Beat (magazine)
D.S.T.	Daylight Saving Time
E.D.T.	Eastern Daylight Time
E.S.T.	Eastern Standard Time
EP	Extended Play (record)
G.M.C.	Glenn Miller Contracts
G.M.D.	Glenn Miller Diary
G.M.P.R.	Glenn Miller Payroll Records
Int	Introduction
Int LB	Introduction by Larry Bruff
Int PD	Introduction by Paul Douglas
Int EH	Introduction by Ed Herlihy
Int GM	Introduction by Glenn Miller
LP	Long Play (record)
Met.	Metronome (magazine)
NBC	National Broadcasting Corporation
RR	Railroad
voc	vocal, vocalist(s)

ACKNOWLEDGMENTS

This book is not the result of one person's work. Without the help, guidance and constructive criticism of many others it could not have been completed.

There are always certain collectors whose interest and efforts surpass others in obtaining information for a discography and it is to them that I wish to pay special tribute here:

To Ed Polic who set up his own notes, checked my notes, supplied a great deal of the information on record releases, discovered alternate takes and private airchecks which were checked out for duplication, did the groundwork on sorting out the GMMS Transcriptions, evaluating new information, correcting my mistakes, etc.

To David Mackay, Executor of the Glenn Miller Estate, who permitted us to examine his files on the Miller band and gave us unstintingly the guidance that has produced this book. His help has been invaluable.

To Don Whyte, who gave encouragement when zeal was lacking, looked into the problems involved in publishing a book and provided us with new aircheck material and information.

To Ralph Monsees, who discovered new airchecks, made arrangements for meetings with the Executor in New York City, and provided constant encouragement and enthusiasm for the book.

To these collectors, enthusiasts, musicians, and record company representatives, without whose contributions this work would have been less than complete: The Glenn Miller Society, of London, England, Dr. Michael Arie, Stephen Bedwell, Ed Burke, Geoffrey Butcher, Joel Feigenbaum, Bobby Hackett, Bill Holland, Dick March, Brad McCuen, Francis Mitchell, John Mickolas, H. E. Pettingell, the Ransom Brothers, Al Samet, Fred Skinner, Henry Whiston, Tom Zak, and many, many more too numerous to mention here. A big vote of thanks to all!

John Flower

INTRODUCTION

FROM THE AUTHOR OF "THE BIG BANDS" AND "SIMON SAYS: THE SIGHTS AND SOUNDS OF THE SWING ERA"

This book offers an amazing mass of factual data. That's obvious. What is less obvious, and what you don't realize until you're really into it, is the wonderful memories it evokes. For, even though this is primarily a Miller discography -- a seemingly cold listing of what the band did, when and where -- it serves as a great reminder of so many aspects of the band's career. That's why, when John Flower was showing me his manuscript, I kept reacting with remarks like, "Oh yeah, I remember that night!" or "Hey, I never realized he was with the band at that time!" or "This is one arrangement I'd forgotten all about!"

John and his associates have given us a wonderful overview, impersonal perhaps, but doggedly detailed, of the music that enthralled so many millions of listeners for -- come to think of it -- not a terribly long time. They focus first on some intriguing portions of the band's early struggles, when just a few of us friends and maybe a couple of couples here and there were listening to guys like Fazola and his round-toned clarinet, or to Johnny Austin and his seering trumpet -- or ogling Kathleen Lane with her gorgeous figure that housed her attractive vibrato. And then they zero in on the parts of Glenn's career that create the most nostalgia for the most people: those day-to-day and night-to-night activities, with their complete coverage of one-night stands, radio broadcasts, steady locations, theatre dates and, of course, recording sessions -- so many of them shared by so many of you who will be looking through this book.

All of this reveals, in toto, the impressively large amount of playing and traveling that the Miller orchestra did in a relatively short time. But this book also reveals something just as impressive: John Flower's refreshing combination of devotion, accuracy and honesty. There's no bull here. When John isn't quite certain about some detail, either because the information is nowhere available, or because two bits of it turn out to be contradictory, he tells us so. Such diligence, coupled with such non-phoniness, are qualities of which Glenn, himself, would have approved very much, indeed. But then, of course, Glenn would have been equally proud of, and impressed by, this entire work, and, I'm sure, would have had just as much fun perusing it and remembering and reliving all the details and highlights as undoubtedly you and so many other Miller enthusiasts are going to have.

Right now, I'm working on my own book about Glenn Miller -- a biography about the man, about the people around him, and what he and they were all really like. I hope that when I'm finished, I will be able to be just as proud of my efforts as I'm certain John Flower must be of his. For all of this, thank you very much, John!

GEORGE T. SIMON

MOONLIGHT SERENADE

A Bio-discography
of the Glenn Miller Civilian Band

April 1935

> While Glenn was with the Ray Noble Orchestra he
> decided to record a few tunes with a group of side-
> men from the Noble crew plus a few others that were
> currently in the New York area. Many of these side-
> men later became bandleaders themselves.

25 April, 1935 (THUR): Columbia Studios, New York City, New York

Trombones	Glenn Miller, Jack Jenney
Trumpets	Bunny Berigan, Charlie Spivak
Reeds	Johnny Mince, Clt & as; Eddie Miller,ts
Strings	Harry Bluestone, Vladimir Slodinsky, vlns; Harry Waller, vla; Bill Schuman, cello
Rhythm	Claude Thornhill, p; Larry Hall, g; Delmar Kaplan, b; Ray Bauduc, d
Vocalist	Smith Ballew

17379
    Co 3051-D, Bilt 1022, Epic LN-3236, Epic LA 16002,
       PhE BBR 8092, CoE 33 SX 1462, ·CoG C 83404
LP-E   A Blues Serenade-voc Smith Ballew
TAPE   (Mitchell Parish-Frank Signorelli)
CD   Tbn, Miller; tpt, Berigan; tbn, Miller;
      ts, Miller; tbn, Miller

17380
    Co 3051-D, Bilt 1022, Epic LN-3136, Epic LN-3236,
       Epic LA 16002, PhE BBR 8092, CoE 33 SX 1462,
       CoG C 83404
LP-E   Moonlight On The Ganges-voc Smith Ballew
TAPE   (Chester Wallace-Sherman Myers)
CD   Tbn, Miller; tpt, Berigan

17381
    Co 3058-D, Bilt 1045, Co 35881, CoE FB-1150,
       Epic LN-3236, Epic LA 16002, PhE BBR 8092,
       CoE 33 SX 1462, CoG C 83404, Ph Arg P 23588 H
LRE   In A Little Spanish Town (arr GM)
TAPE   (Sam M. Lewis-Joe Young-Mabel Wayne)
      Ts, Miller; clt, Mince; p. Thornhill;
      tpt, Berigan; ts, Miller

> For this next tune, same personnel except that
> Jack Jenney, tbn, and the strings are omitted.

17382
    Co 3058-D, Bilt 1045, Co 35881, CoE FB-1150,
       Epic EG-7005, Epic LN-3236, Epic LG-3109,
       Epic LA 16002, Epic LA 16006, PhE BBR 8092,
       PhE BBL 7086, CoE SEG 8309, CoE 33 SX 1462,
       CoE 33 SX 1491, CoG C 83404, Ph Arg P 23588 H
LP-E   Solo Hop (arr GM)
TAPE   (Glenn Miller)
      Tpt, Berigan; ts, Miller; clt, Mince;
      tpt, Berigan

It is interesting to note that years later Harry
Bluestone (vln) took over Glenn's "I Sustain The
Wings" show over N.B.C. when the Miller band went
overseas.

Epic EG-7005, Epic LG-3109, Epic LA 16006, PhE
BBL 7086, CoE SEG 8309 and CoE 33 SX 1491 were
issued under Bunny Berigan's name.

The above session was just a pick-up date and the
records were not commercially successful. Glenn recorded as a sideman for almost two years before he
was ready to attempt leading a band on a full time
basis. Glenn's career as a sideman will be covered
in another book.

January 1937

Miller started looking for men. Found Hal McIntyre
leading a band in Meriden, Connecticut. Hired him
as hot clarinetist but this changed when Irving
"Fazola" came in later on. Miller spent six weeks
finding men for his new band. Found tenor saxist
Johnny Harrell in a 42nd Street spot in New York.
(It was here that Glenn and George Simon were tossed
out for not drinking.) Found trumpeter Sterling
Bose. (Met. March 1937 & Dec. 1939)

March 1937

Band being booked by Rockwell-O'Keefe while the group
was in its rehearsal stages. (Met. March 1937)

Started rehearsals at the Haven Studios on West 54th
Street, New York City. Charlie Spivak led the brass
while Toots Mondello led the saxes at rehearsals.
(Met. Dec. 1939)

Miller realized that some of his uncovered "stars"
wouldn't star on a record date and so the band was
supplemented with several star sidemen for the upcoming Decca date. George Siravo played lead while
the hot tenor was divided between Jerry Jerome and
Carl Biesecker. Hal McIntyre played third sax and
clarinet. The band cut six sides in three hours.
Until about his third session for Bluebird Glenn
considered them the best his band had ever made.
(Met. Dec. 1939)

George Siravo did some arranging while with the band.

22 March, 1937 (MON): Decca Studios, New York City, New York

Trombones	Glenn Miller, Jesse Ralph, Harry Rodgers
Trumpets	Charlie Spivak, Manny Klein, Sterling Bose
Reeds	George Siravo, as; Hal McIntyre, clt & as; Jerry Jerome, ts; Carl Biesecker, ts
Rhythm	Howard Smith, p; Dick McDonough, g; Ted Kotsoftis, b; George Simon, d
Vocalists	Doris Kerr, Sterling Bose, the Tune Twisters (trio including Jack Lathrop)

62058 A   De 1342 A, De 25075, De 9-25075, BrE 03807, DeC 10113,
DeF BM-03807, DeSp RB-45014, BrG 82414,
LW/LWS 265, AH 143, BrEOE 9169, Longine Stereo Tape
TAPE 78 P Peg O' My Heart (arr GM)
(Alfred Bryan-Fred Fisher)
Ts, Biesecker; clt, McIntyre

62059 A   De 1284 B, BrG 82574, AH 143, BrE OE 9169
TAPE Wistful And Blue-voc Doris Kerr
(Julian Davidson-Ruth Etting)
Ts, Biesecker

62060 A   De 1239 B, BrE 02831, AH 143
TAPE How Am I To Know? (arr GM)-voc Doris Kerr
From the MGM Production "Dynamite"
(Jack King-Dorothy Parker)

62061 A   De 1284 A, AH 143, BrE OE 9169, BrG 87079, Br 12" LP
TAPE Anytime, Anyday, Anywhere-voc Sterling Bose (And the
Tune Twisters)
(Louis Weslyn-Max Kortlander)
Tpt, Bose

62062 A   De 1239 A, De 25075, De 9-25075, BrE 02831, BrE 03807,
DeF BM-03807, DeSp RB-45014, De DL 8399,
BrG 82414, AH 143, BrG 87079, BrE LAT 8167,
DeI BM 1136, AFRS "America's Pop Music" 67,
De DL 78384
78P Moonlight Bay (arr GM)-voc the Band
(Edward Madden-Percy Wenrich)
Clt, McIntyre; tpt, Bose

62063 A   De 1342 B, DeC 10113, BrG 82574, AH 143, BrE OE 9169
TAPE I'm Sitting On Top Of The World (arr HM)
(Sam M. Lewis-Joe Young-Ray Henderson)
Ts, Jerome; clt, McIntyre; ts, Jerome; tpt, Klein

Several magazine articles have indicated that Miller
did not play on this session but acted as leader
and arranger only: "Another trombonist started a
band about this time, but he didn't play trombone

(continued on next page)

with it."   (Met. Oct. 1943) "Hal McIntyre was the
only present Millerian heard, for at that time Glenn
refused to play trombone, fearing he'd be labelled an
inferior Tommy Dorsey." (Met. May 1941)

Simon on drums later became editor of Metronome
magazine. He became one of Glenn's closest friends
and was one of the first to boost Glenn's new band
by his articles in Metronome.

Mid-April 1937

Trombones	Glenn Miller, Jesse Ralph, Pete Skinner
Trumpets	Tweet Peterson, Jimmy Troutman, Sterling "Bozo" Bose
Reeds	George Siravo, as; Hal McIntyre, clt & as; Jerry Jerome, ts; Carl Biesecker, ts
Rhythm	John Chalmers "Chummy" MacGregor, p; Ted Kotsoftis, b; Emery "Eak" Kenyon, d

May 1937

Band played a one-nighter (a Friday substituting for
Gus Arnheim) at the New Yorker Hotel, New York City.
Only Klein and rhythm section different. Ralph Hitz
(the hotel owner) was present and liked the band so
much that he arranged a tour of the band to his other
hotels during the coming summer. (Met. Dec. 1939)

15 May, 1937 (SAT)

Glenn Miller and His Orchestra opened at the Raymor
Ballroom, (253 Huntington Avenue) Boston, Massachu-
setts. Vi Mele was the girl vocalist. Off Sundays -
8:00-1:00 A.M.; 8:00-12:00 Midnight Sat. (Boston Post,
May 15, 1937; BB May 22, 1937; Variety, May 19, 1937;
Met. June 1937; GMC.)
Note: the Miller band did not play on May 29th as Phil
Emerson and His Band played. (Boston Post, May 29,
1937)

30 May, 1937 (SUN)

Glenn Miller and His Orchestra played at the Colonial
Casino, Onset, Massachusetts. (Boston Post, May 29,
1937)

31 May, 1937 (MON)

        Glenn Miller and His Orchestra at the Raymor Ball-
        room, Boston, Massachusetts, for six more days
        (closed, Saturday, June 5th). (Boston Post, May
        31 & June 5, 1937)

6 June, 1937 (SUN)

        Glenn Miller's crew supplemented Hudson-De Lange at
        the Playland Casino in Rye, New York. (BB June 12,
        1937) The Miller orchestra was composed of 14
        musicians for this date and the band received $200.00.
        The manager of Playland Casino was Michael Badolato.
        The terms of the contract were as follows: "Money is
        to be paid at the end of the engagement. Band to
        rehearse and play show sometime between hours of
        8:00 PM to 3:00 AM" (The Big Bands by George T. Simon)

9 June, 1937 (WED): Brunswick Studios, New York City, New York

        Trombones   Glenn Miller, Jesse Ralph, Harry Rodgers
        Trumpets   Charlie Spivak, Manny Klein, Sterling Bose
        Reeds   George Siravo, as; Hal McIntyre, clt & as;
                     Jerry Jerome, ts; Carl Biesecker, ts
        Rhythm   Howard Smith, p; Dick McDonough, g;
                     Ted Kotsoftis, b; George Simon, d

B 21234-3   Br 7915, Bilt 1046, CoE SCM 5086, CoE DB 3416, Cq 9488,
          OK 5051, Vo 5051, Epic EG-7012, Epic LG-1008,
          CoE D269, PhE BBR 8072, Epic LN 1101, CoIR IDB
          488, Epic EG-1008, CoAus SV 149, Co XLP-114353,
          Co D 404, Lu LX5, Lu 60526 (take 1? on Lu)
TAPE 78 B I Got Rhythm (arr GM)
CD   From the musical production "Girl Crazy"
          (Ira Gershwin-George Gershwin)
          Clt, McIntyre; ts, Jerome; tpt, Klein; d, Simon

B 21235-1   Br 7923, CoE DB 3416, CoE SCM 5086, OK 5051, Poly
          6002, Vo 5051, VoE S.127, CoJ M 164, Epic
          Eg-7012, Epic EG-1008, Epic LG-1008, PhE
          BBR 8072, Epic LN 1101, CoAus SV 149, CoIr
          IDB 488, PhAu B 21543
TAPE   Sleepy Time Gal (arr GM)
TAPE   (Joseph R. Alden-Raymond B. Egan-Ange Lorenzo-
CD   Richard A. Whiting)
          Clt, McIntyre

B 21236-1   Br 7923, Poly 6002, Epic EG-7034, Epic LG-1008,
          PhE BBR 8072, VoE S.127, Epic LN 1101,
          Epic EG-1008, Lu 60514
TAPE 45E Community Swing (arr GM)
CD   (Glenn Miller)
          Tpt, Klein; clt, McIntyre; d, Simon

(Session continued on next page)

[6]

B 21240-1   Br 7915, ~~Bilt 1046~~, Epic EG-7012, Epic EG 7102,
                  Epic LG-1008, PhE BBR 8072, Epic EG-1008,
                  Epic LN 1101, Lu LX5, Lu 60526
TAPE 78B ➤ ~~Time On My Hands~~ (You In My Arms) (arr CB)
  CD   (Harold Adamson-Mack Gordon-Vincent Youmans)
                  Muted tbn, Miller

> There is some indication that Johnny Harrell played
> tenor sax instead of Biesecker but in view of
> Biesecker's arrangement being used on "Time On My
> Hands" as well as information from various LP's and
> other discographies we've listed Biesecker.

> Matrices 21237/8 are by the harpist, Mildred
> Drilling; 21239 was never used.

> Before departing for his upcoming Hotel Roosevelt,
> New Orleans spot, Glenn Miller added very fine (and
> higher than usual pitched) gal warbler Kathleen Lane
> to his entourage. (Met. July 1937)

> Sterling Bose was fired for "non-musical conditions"
> but rehired within twenty-four hours because his
> successor's "non-musical conditions" were much
> worse. (Met. July 1937)

11 June, 1937 (FRI)

> Glenn Miller and His Orchestra played at the Hunt
> Club, Cleveland, Ohio, from 8:30-1:30 A.M. (G.M.C.)

17 June, 1937 (THUR)

> Glenn Miller and His Orchestra opened at the Blue
> Room of the Hotel Roosevelt, New Orleans. (Variety,
> July 9, 1937)
>   "Originally booked for two weeks into the Hotel
> Roosevelt here, Glenn Miller had his contract renewed
> for another duo. At the end of the first month,
> Miller was again renewed for one more month at this
> Ralph Hitz swank hostelry." (Met. Aug. 1937)
> The band eventually played a record-breaking 10 week
> engagement at this hotel winding up August 26th.
> While at this hotel the band broadcast over WSMB
> (320 KW) nightly, except Sunday and Wednesday, at
> 12:30 A.M. and over WWL (850 KW) nightly at 1:30 A.M.
> (DB, Aug. 1937)

Mid-June 1937

Miller having rhythm section problems--drummers
changing rapidly. Two of the drummers were Emery
Kenyon and Buddy Schutz. Spivak out--Miller
couldn't afford him. (Met. Dec. 1939)

27 August, 1937 (FRI)

Glenn Miller and His Orchestra opened at the Century
Room of the Hotel Adolphus, Dallas, Texas. (Met.
Sept. 1937 & BB, Aug. 14, 1937) The length of this
engagement is not known.
    "Down in Dallas it was a pleasure to bump into
Glenn Miller leading a good band at the Adolphus
hotel and doing swell business. The rhythm section
is still giving Glenn some trouble but he should
straighten out his difficulties in short order."
(DB, Oct. 1937, article by John Hammond)

3 October, 1937 (FRI)

Glenn Miller and His Orchestra opened at the Hotel
Nicollet, Minneapolis, Minnesota. The band played
for four weeks (7 days a week--Luncheon 12:30-2:00
P.M. weekdays) with a 2 weeks option, but closed
October 30th.

Doc Carney (from Detroit) taken on as drummer; Ardell
Garrett replaced Sterling Bose on third trumpet,
while the first brass chair was taken over by Bob
Price. (Met. Nov. 1937)

5 November, 1937 (FRI)

Glenn Miller and His Orchestra opened at the Raymor
Ballroom, Boston, Massachusetts (no Sundays).
(G.M.C. & Boston Post, 5 November, 1937)
Miller decided on five sax styling during this date
and added Irving "Fazola" (clarinet and alto sax)
and dropped the guitar. (Met. Dec. 1939)
The following were in the band at the beginning of
this date:

Trombones	Glenn Miller, Jesse Ralph, Bud Smith
Trumpets	Bob Price, Tweet Peterson, Ardell Garrett
Reeds	George Siravo, as; Hal McIntyre, as; Irving "Fazola" Prestopnick, clt & as; Jerry Jerome, ts; Carl Biesecker, ts

(continued on next page)

```
              Rhythm        J. Chalmers "Chummy" MacGregor, p;
                            Rowland Bundock, b; Doc Carney (Cenardo),d
              Vocalist      Kathleen Lane
```

This date gave Miller his first coast-to-coast air-
shots (a WJZ Network line via WBZ Boston, Variety,
Dec. 15, 1937) over NBC. (Met. Dec. 1939)

Later Tony Viola replaced George Siravo.

A couple of the tunes played while at the ballroom
were "Swannee River" and "Basin Street" (with a vocal
by Kathleen Lane. (Met. Dec. 1937)

Miller also tried to hire Brad Gowans (in Frankie
Ward's Orchestra) while in Boston. (DB, Dec. 1937)

Glenn Miller signed Arthur Michaud of Rockwell O'Keefe
as personal manager. (Met. Dec. 1937)

24 November, 1937 (WED): Raymor Ballroom, Boston, Massachusetts
                         NBC 12:00-12:30 A.M.

29 November, 1937 (MON): Brunswick Studios, New York City, New York

```
              Trombones     Glenn Miller, Jesse Ralph, BUD SMITH
              Trumpets      GEORGE "PEE WEE" ERWIN, BOB PRICE,
                            ARDELL GARRETT
              Reeds         Hal McIntyre, as; TONY VIOLA, as;
                            IRVING "FAZOLA" PRESTOPNICK, clt & as;
                            Jerry Jerome, ts; Carl Biesecker, ts
              Rhythm        JOHN CHALMERS "CHUMMY" MACGREGOR, p;
                            CARMEN MASTREN, g; ROWLAND BUNDOCK, b;
                            DOC CARNEY (CENARDO), d
              Vocalist      KATHLEEN LANE
```

B 22079-1   Br 8034, BrG 81468, Epic LN-3236, Epic LA 16002,
                  PhE BBR 8092, CoE 33 SX 1462, CoE SEG 8237,
                  CoG C 83404
          — My Fine Feathered Friend (arr CB)-voc Kathleen Lane
                  From the Universal film "You're A Sweetheart"
                  (Harold Adamson-Jimmy McHugh)
                  clt, Fazola; ts. Jerome

B 22080-1   Br 8062, Cq 9488, OK 4449, Poly 6001, Vo 4449,
                  Epic EG-7034, Epic LG-1008, PhE BBR 8072,
                  Epic EG-1008, Epic LN 1101, CoE DB 8072
          — Humoresque (arr GS)
                  (Anton Dvorak)

(Session continued on next page)

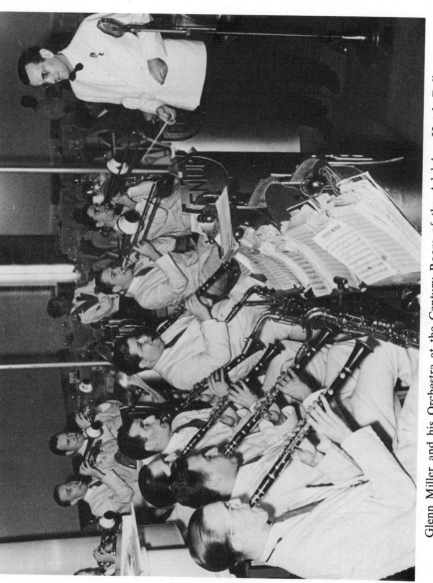

Glenn Miller and his Orchestra at the Century Room of the Adolphus Hotel, Dallas, Texas, August–October 1937. Left to right, front row: Carl Biesecker, Jerry Jerome, Hal McIntyre, George Siravo, Irving "Fazola" Prestopnick (clarinets); Jesse Ralph, Bud Smith (trombones). Back row: Sterling Bose, Tweet Peterson, Bob Price (trumpets). (*Photo courtesy Glenn Miller Estate*)

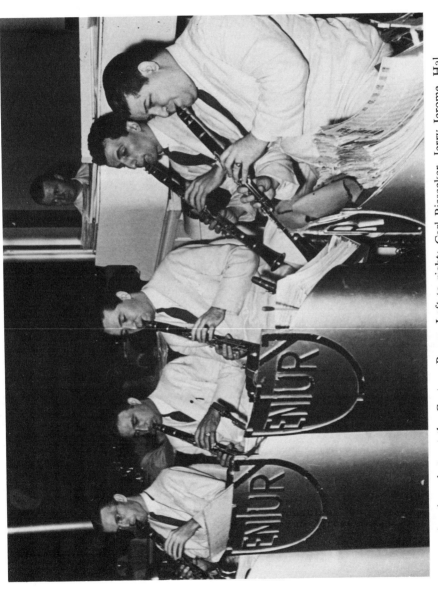

Another photo at the Century Room. Left to right: Carl Biesecker, Jerry Jerome, Hal McIntyre, George Siravo, Irving "Fazola" Prestopnick. Chummy MacGregor is at the piano. (*Photo courtesy Glenn Miller Estate*)

                         P, MacGregor; tpt, Price; clt, Fazola;
                         ts, Jerome; p, MacGregor

B 22081-1   Br 8062, Cq 9489, OK 5131, Poly 6001, Vo 5131,
                         Epic EG-7034, Epic LG-1008, PhE BBR 8072,
                         Epic EG-1008, CoE DB 8072
TAPE   45E —   Doin' The Jive (arr GM)-voc Kathleen Lane (and Band--
  CD   dialogue, Glenn Miller and Chummy MacGregor)
                         (Glenn Miller-John Chalmers MacGregor)
                         Ts, Jerome; clt, Fazola

B 22082-1   Br 8034, BrG 81468, Epic LN-3236, Epic LA 16002,
                         PhE BBR 8092, CoE 33 SX 1462, CoE SEG 8237,
                         CoG C 83404
TAPE   LPE —   Silhouetted In The Moonlight (arr GM)-voc Kathleen
  CD   Lane.
                         From the Warner Bros.' film "Hollywood Hotel"
                         (Johnny Mercer-Richard E. Whiting)
                         Clt, Fazola

30 November, 1937 (TUES): Raymor Ballroom, Boston, Massachusetts
                          NBC 11:30-12:00 Midnight

1 December, 1937 (WED):   Raymor Ballroom, Boston, Massachusetts
                          NBC 12:00-12:30 A.M.

3 December, 1937 (FRI)

              Glenn Miller and His Orchestra played at the Parker
              House Roof, Boston, Massachusetts, for the Sophomore
              Dance of Technology from 8:00 P.M. to 2:00 A.M.
              (G.M.C.) The Clyde Morgan Orchestra played at the
              Raymor Ballroom this evening. (Boston Post, Dec. 3,
              1937)

5 December, 1937 (SUN)

              Glenn Miller and His Orchestra played at Hamilton
              Park, Waterbury, Connecticut from 8:30-1:30 A.M.
              (G.M.C.)

6 December, 1937 (MON)

              The Raymor Ballroom was closed this night. (Boston
              Post, November 30, 1937)

[10]

13 December, 1937 (MON)

      The Raymor Ballroom was closed this night. (Boston
Post, Dec. 13, 1937)

13 December, 1937 (MON): Brunswick Studios, New York City, New York

      Same personnel as for the November 29th recording
session.

B 22135-1   Br 8041, Bilt 1047, BrG 81457, Epic LN-3236,
          Epic LA 16002, PhE BBR 8092, CoE 33 SX 1462,
          CoE SEG 8237, CoG C 83404

TAPE LP-E — Every Day's A Holiday (arr CB)-voc Kathleen Lane
  CD   (Sam Coslow-Barry Trivers)
          Ts, Jerome

B 22136-1   Br 8041, Bilt 1047, BrG 81457, Epic LN-3236,
          Epic LA 16002, PhE BBR 8092, CoE 33 SX 1462,
          CoG C 83404

TAPE LP-E — Sweet Stranger (arr GM)-voc Kathleen Lane
  CD   (Ned Wever-Milton Ager-Jerry Livingston)
          Clt, Fazola

      This Brunswick session took five hours to make the
two sides. (Met. Dec. 1939)

17 December, 1937 (FRI)

      Glenn Miller and His Orchestra close at the Raymor
Ballroom, Boston, Massachusetts. (Variety, Dec. 1,
1937; Boston Post, Dec. 17, 1937)

18 December, 1937 (SAT)

      Glenn Miller and His Orchestra played at Ricker
Gardens, Portland, Maine, from 8:00-12:00 Midnight.
(G.M.C.)
      "Fazola's clarinet and Jerry Jerome's tenor
along with the swell vocals by Kathleen Lane of Glenn
Miller's band gave the local cats a boot." (Met.
Feb. 1938)

20 December, 1937 (MON)

      Glenn Miller and His Orchestra played at Brunswick,
Maine. (G.M.C.)

Late December 1937

> The band was in a state of flux during the following
> one-nighters:
>
>> Bowdoin College, Maine--one of Frat houses
>> for pre-holiday house party. (Met. Jan. 1938)
>> Pennsylvania--lots of car and bus breakdowns in
>> heavy snows--morale low--Miller's wife sick.
>> (Met. Dec. 1939)
>> Maurice "Moe" Purtill replaced Doc Carney but
>> only for one night--Tommy Dorsey called Miller
>> next day for Purtill as he needed a replace-
>> ment for Dave Tough. Vic Angle, former
>> drummer with Red Nichols and Joe Venuti, re-
>> placed Purtill late in December. (Met. Jan.
>> 1938)
>> Les Biegel, hot trumpet, replaced Tweet
>> Peterson. (Met. Jan. 1938) Les Biegel stated
>> in "Down Beat" (July 27, 1951) that he joined
>> the band at the Nicollet Hotel in Minneapolis
>> which is contrary to the above information.

25 December, 1937 (SAT)

> Glenn Miller and His Orchestra played at Brookline
> Country Club, Brookline, Pennsylvania from 10:00-
> 3:00 A.M. (G.M.C.)

27 December, 1937 (MON)

> Glenn Miller and His Orchestra played at Berkshire
> Country Club, Reading, Pennsylvania from 10:00-
> 3:00 A.M. (G.M.C.)

28 December, 1937 (TUES)

> Glenn Miller and His Orchestra played at the Osborne
> Hotel, Auburn, New York from 10:00-3:00 A.M. (G.M.C.)

30 December, 1937 (THUR)

> Glenn Miller and His Orchestra played at the Armory,
> Easton, Maryland from 9:30-2:00 A.M. (G.M.C.)

31 December, 1937 (FRI)

> Glenn Miller and His Orchestra played at Valencia
> Ballroom, York, Pennsylvania from 9:00-2:00 A.M. (G.M.C.)

Miller gave the band notice on New Year's Eve.
Miller lost over $18,000.00 in 1937, was having
managerial problems, his wife was sick, Henry Okun
was suing Kathleen Lane for breach of contract,
some of the band members were heavy drinkers and
prima-donnas, and morale in the band was very low.
(DB, July 27, 1951; Met. Dec. 1939)

2 January, 1938 (SUN)

Glenn Miller and His Orchestra played at Ritz Ballroom, Bridgeport, Connecticut from 9:30-12:30 A.M.
(G.M.C.) Tommy "Butch" Di Carlos (lead tpt) replaced Garrett. (Met. Feb. 1938) After this date
the band returned to New York and disbanded. (DB,
July 27, 1951; Met. Dec. 1939)

Kathleen Lane joined Isham Jones; Jerry Jerome joined
Red Norvo; Les Biegel went home to Milwaukee; Fazola
went back to Ben Pollack and then to Bob Crosby.
(Met. Dec. 1939)

January 1938

Miller spent time making new arrangements and looking
for men for his new band.

February 1938

Miller played trombone on several Tommy Dorsey
broadcasts. (Met. Dec. 1939)

March 1938

Miller started rehearsals at the Haven Studios on
West 54th Street, New York City. Glenn had just
turned down a $250. a week job with Vincent Lopez.
No more prima-donnas. Glenn started Edition #3 with
only four hold-overs from the 1937 band (McIntyre,
MacGregor, Rowland Bundock and Bob Price). Two men
from Gene Krupa's band, Claude Lakey and Dave Schultz,
recommended a saxophonist who was in Detroit with Ben
Young's band. Two weeks later Tex Beneke joined the
band and was paid $52.50 a week. Glenn hired Gail
Reese, who had worked for Carl Ravazza and Bunny
Berigan, and Ray Eberle who he met at a Jimmy Dorsey
program. Eberle was hired at $35 a week. (Met.
Dec. 1939; Met. March 1954; DB, July 27, 1951)

April 1938

Rehearsal Personnel:

Trombones	Glenn Miller, Brad Jenney, Al Mastren (Alex Mastandrea)
Trumpets	Johnny "Zulu" Austin, Bob Price, Gasparre Rebito
Reeds	Hal McIntyre, as; "Wee Willie" Wilbur Schwartz, as & clt; Bernie Billings, as & bar; Gordon "Tex" Beneke, ts; Sol Kane, ts
Rhythm	John Chalmers "Chummy" MacGregor, p; Rowland Bundock, b; Bob Spangler, d
Vocalists	Gail Reese, Ray Eberle (Vocal quartet add Kane and Schwartz)

Changes in personnel from early April until Raymor Ballroom date: Stanley "Moose" Aronson, as & bar replaced Bernie Billings.

16 April, 1938 (SAT)

Glenn Miller and His Orchestra open at the Raymor Ballroom, Boston Massachusetts. The band did not play on Sundays and Mondays (except April 18th). (Boston Post, April 16, 1938) The band broadcast several times a week for NBC: NBC Blue-Wednesdays 12:30 A.M. and Saturdays 11:00 P.M. EDT. (DB, June 1938)

6 May, 1938 (FRI)

Glenn Miller and His Orchestra did not play at the Raymor Ballroom this evening but played at Wellesley College. (Boston Post, May 6, 1938)

23 May, 1938 (MON): Brunswick Studios, New York City, New York

Trombones	Glenn Miller, BRAD JENNEY, AL MASTREN
Trumpets	JOHNNY "ZULU" AUSTIN, Bob Price, GASPARRE REBITO
Reeds	Hal McIntyre, as & clt; STANLEY "MOOSE" ARONSON, as & bar; WILBUR "WEE WILLIE" SCHWARTZ, clt & as; GORDON "TEX" BENEKE, ts; SOL KANE, ts
Rhythm	Chummy MacGregor, p; Rowland Bundock, b; BOB SPANGLER, d
Vocalists	GAIL REESE, RAY "JIM" EBERLE

(Session continued on next page)

B 22972-1   Br 8152, Bilt 1048, ~~Epic LN-3236~~, Epic LA 16002,
                    PhE BBR 8092, CoE 33 SX 1462, CoE SEG 8237,
                    CoG C 83404
TAPE/LP-E - ~~Don't Wake Up My Heart~~-voc Ray Eberle
CD   (Sam Lewis-George W. Meyer-Pete Wendling)
                    Clt, Schwartz

B 22973-1   Br 8152, Bilt 1048, ~~Epic LN-3236~~, Epic LA 16002,
                    PhE BBR 8092, CoE 33 SX 1462, CoG C 83404
TAPE/LP-E   ~~Why'd Ya Make Me Fall In Love~~-voc Gail Reese
CD   (Walter Donaldson)
                    P, MacGregor; ts, Beneke

B 22974-1   Br 8173, Bilt 1108, CoAu DO-2783, OK 4449, Vo 4449,
                    BrG 81677, Epic EG-7012, Epic LG-1008,
                    PhE BBR 8072, Epic LN 1101, Epic EG-1008,
                    PhAu B 21543, Lu 60514
TAPE LP-E - ~~Sold American~~ (arr GM)-Chant by the Orchestra
CD   (Glenn Miller-John Chalmers MacGregor)
                    Tbn, Miller; ts, Beneke; tpt, Austin

B 22975-1   Br 8173, Bilt 1108, CoAu DO-2783, Cq 9489, OK 5131,
                    Vo 5131, BrG 81677, ~~Epic EG-7034~~, Epic LG-1008,
                    PhE BBR 8072, Epic EG-1008, Lu 60440
LRE *TAPE* - ~~Dipper Mouth Blues~~ (arr GM)-Chant by the Orchestra
CD   (Joe Oliver-Louis Armstrong)
                    Clt, Schwartz; tbn, Miller

28 May, 1938 (SAT)

          Glenn Miller and His Orchestra close at the Raymor
          Ballroom, Boston, Massachusetts. (Boston Post,
          May 28, 1938)

29 May, 1938 (SUN)

          Glenn Miller and His Orchestra played at Kimballs
          Starlight Ballroom (Route 128), South Lynfield.
          Dance started at midnight. (Boston Post, May 28,
          1938)

3 June, 1938 (FRI)

          Glenn Miller and His Orchestra played at Canobie
          Lake. (G.M.C.)

10 June, 1938 (FRI)

          Glenn Miller and His Orchestra played at Bristol,
          Connecticut. (G.M.C.)

12 June, 1938 (SUN)

        Glenn Miller and His Orchestra played a one-nighter
at Roton Point Park, South Norwalk, Connecticut.
(Variety, June 8, 1938; G.M.C.)

14 June, 1938 (TUES)

        Glenn Miller and His Orchestra opened at the
Paradise Restaurant, New York City, playing both
dance music and a lengthy show. The orchestra was
there for two weeks--closed June 27th. Freddie
Fisher's Schnicklefritzers were on with Miller during
the show. Broadcast on NBC Blue Monday June 20th at
11:30 P.M.; Monday June 27th at 11:30 P.M.; Saturday
June 18th at 9:30 P.M. and Saturday June 25th at
9:30 P.M. Eastern Daylight Time. (DB, July 1938; Met.
July 1938; BB June 18, 1938; G.M.C.) The Paradise
Restaurant was located at 1619 Broadway, New York
City.

18 June, 1938 (SAT): Paradise Restaurant, New York City, New York
*   NBC-Blue 9:30-10:00 P.M. EDT.*

                Moonlight Serenade (Theme)
                Butcher Boy-voc GR
                        (Rudy Vallee-Paolo Citoroello)
                Don't Wake Up My Heart
                Cowboy From Brooklyn-voc TB & GM
                My Best Wishes
                I Know That You Know

PPRM-5333   Vi LPM/LSP-2767 (Vi LPM/LSP-6101), RCA RD/SF-7610
    OA   — (3:20) On The Sentimental Side-voc Ray Eberle
                        From the Paramount film "Doctor Rhythm"
                        (Johnny Burke-James Monaco)
                        Tbn, Miller; clt, Schwartz

                On The Alamo
                The Dipsey Doodle-Chant by the Orchestra
                Moonlight Serenade (Theme)

20 June, 1938 (MON): Paradise Restaurant, New York City, New York
*   NBC-Blue 11:30-12:00 Midnight EDT.*

                Moonlight Serenade (Theme)
                  Why'd Ya Make Me Fall In Love
                You Leave Me Breathless-voc RE
                        From "Cocoanut Grove"
                        (Ralph Freed-Fred Hollander)

(Broadcast continued on next page)

E4VP 8208   <u>Vi LPT 6701</u>, <u>Vi EPOT 6701</u> (947-0186), HMV RLS 598,
                RCA G EPOT-6701
   LE-2   - (3:11) Doin' The Jive (arr GM)-voc Gail Reese, Tex
                        Beneke, Glenn Miller and The Band
                        (Glenn Miller-John Chalmers MacGregor)
                        Clt, Schwartz; ts, Beneke

                  I Fall In Love Every Day-voc RE
                      From the Paramount Film "College Swing"
                      (Manning Sherwin-Frank Loesser)
                  Honeysuckle Rose
                      (Andy Razaf-Thomas "Fats" Waller)
                  How Can You Forget?-voc GR
                      From the Warner Bros. film "Fools For
                      Scandal"
                      (Lorenz Hart-Richard Rodgers)

E4VP 8208   <u>Vi LPT 6701</u>, <u>Vi EPOT 6701</u> (947-0184), HMV RLS 598,
                RCA G EPOT-6701
   LE-2   - (2:44) So Little Time-voc Ray Eberle
                    (Peter DeRose-William Hill)

                  Dipper Mouth Blues
                  Moonlight Serenade (Theme)

   25 June, 1938 (SAT): Paradise Restaurant, New York City, New York
               NBC-Blue 9:30-10:00 P.M. EDT.

                  Moonlight Serenade (Theme)
                  Why'd Ya Make Me Fall In Love
                  Cathedral In The Pines-voc RE
                    (Charles & Nick Kenny)

E4VP 8208   <u>Vi LPT 6701</u>, <u>Vi EPOT 6701</u> (947-0184), HMV RLS 598,
                RCA G EPOT-6701
   LE-2   - (3:21) Down South Camp Meetin'
                  (Fletcher Henderson-Irving Mills)
                  Tpt, Austin; ts, Beneke

                  At Your Beck And Call-voc GR
                    (Eddie DeLange-Buck Ram)

PPRM-5341   <u>Vi LPM/LSP-2769</u> (<u>Vi LPM/LSP-6101</u>), RCA RD/SF-7612
   OA   - (0:41) Moonlight Serenade (Theme)
                  (Mitchell Parish-Glenn Miller)

PPRM-5341   <u>Vi LPM/LSP-2769</u> (<u>Vi LPM/LSP-6101</u>), RCA RD/SF-7612
         (3:38) MEDLEY:
   OA   -   Why Do I Love You?
                      From the musical production "Show Boat"
                      (Oscar Hammerstein, 2nd-Jerome Kern)

(Broadcast continued on next page)

OA - Can't Help Lovin' Dat Man
                    From the musical production "Show Boat"
                    (Oscar Hammerstein, 2nd-Jerome Kern)
                    Tbn, Miller
OA - Make Believe
                    From the musical production "Show Boat"
                    (Oscar Hammerstein, 2nd-Jerome Kern)
OA - Ol' Man River
                    From the musical production "Show Boat"
                    (Oscar Hammerstein, 2nd-Jerome Kern)
                    Tbn, Miller; tpt, Austin

PPRM-5334   Vi LPM/LSP-2767 (Vi LPM/LSP-6101), RCA RD/SF-7610
   OA - (3:13) Moonshine Over Kentucky-voc Gail Reese
                    (Sydney D. Mitchell-Lew Pollack)
                    Tpt, Austin

           Bugle Call Rag
           Moonlight Serenade (Theme)

*27 June, 1938 (MON): Paradise Restaurant, New York City, New York
           NBC-Blue 11:30-12:00 Midnight EDT.*

           Moonlight Serenade (Theme)

           MEDLEY:
               Butcher Boy-voc GR
               Marie-voc RE and the Band

           Lovelight In The Starlight-voc RE
               From "Cocoanut Grove"
               (Ralph Freed-Fred Hollander)

E4VP 8208   Vi LPT 6701, Vi EPOT 6701 (947-0185), HMV RLS 598,
   LE-2   RCA G EPOT-6701
            (2:53) Humoresque (arr GS)
                    (Anton Dvorak)
                    P, MacGregor; tpt, Austin, clt, Schwartz;
                    ts, Beneke; p, MacGregor

PPRM-5334   Vi LPM/LSP-2767 (Vi LPM/LSP-6101), RCA RD/SF-7610
   OA   (2:38) My Best Wishes-voc Ray Eberle
                    (Ted Koehler-Sam Pokrass)

PPRM-5337   Vi LPM/LSP-2768 (Vi LPM/LSP-6101), RCA RD/SF-7611
   OA - (2:25) I Know That You Know
                    From the musical production "Oh, Please"
                    (Anne Caldwell-Vincent Youmans)
                    Tpt, Austin; ts, Beneke; as, ??;
                    d, Spangler

(Broadcast continued on next page)

How'dja Like To Love Me?-voc GR
   From the Paramount film "College Swing"
   (Frank Loesser-Burton Lane)

PPRM-5334   Vi LPM/LSP-2767 (Vi LPM/LSP-6101), RCA RD/SF-7610
   ○ ↶   (3:25)   Don't Wake Up My Heart-voc Ray Eberle
         (Sam Lewis-George W. Meyer-Pete Wendling)
         Clt, Schwartz

   By The Waters Of Minnetonka
   Moonlight Serenade *(Theme)*

2 July, 1938 (SAT)

   Glenn Miller and His Orchestra played at Roseland
   State Ballroom (Loew's State Theatre Building),
   Boston, Massachusetts. (Boston Post, July 2, 1938)

3 July, 1938 (SUN)

   Glenn Miller and His Orchestra open at Reed's Casino,
   Asbury Park, New Jersey for about six weeks. Here
   they made their debut over the Mutual Broadcasting
   System (MBS). During this period Bill Stegmeyer,
   ts & as, replaced Sol Kane. (Met. July 1938; Met.
   Aug. 1938; BB July 9, 1938; BB July 23, 1938) The
   information about the six weeks stand is doubtful
   due to the fact that we have a listing of one night
   stands from mid-July on.

15 July, 1938 (FRI)

   Glenn Miller and His Orchestra played at Canobie
   Lake Park Ballroom, Salem, New Hampshire. (Boston
   Post, July 15, 1938)

18 July, 1938

   Glenn Miller and His Orchestra played at Shelbourne
   Inn Pavillion, Shelbourne, New Hampshire. (Boston
   Post, July 17, 1938)

19 July, 1938 (TUES)

   Glenn Miller and His Orchestra played at Fieldston
   on the Atlantic, Marshfield, Massachusetts.
   (Boston Post, July 19, 1938)

20 July, 1938 (WED)

> Glenn Miller and His Orchestra played at North
> Shore Gardens (under the auspices of Peabody
> Firemen's Relief Association), Salem-Peabody Line,
> Massachusetts. (Boston Post, July 19, 1938;
> G.M.C.)

31 July, 1938 (SUN)

> Glenn Miller and His Orchestra played at Pleasure
> Beach, Bridgeport, Connecticut from 8:00-12:00
> midnight. (G.M.C.)

August 1938

> During the summer the female vocalist position had
> a turnover: Virginia Vonne replaced Gail Reese
> (Met. Sept. 1938) and Linda Keane replaced Virginia
> Vonne.

5 August, 1938 (FRI)

> Glenn Miller and His Orchestra played at Geo. F.
> Pavillion, Johnson City, New York from 9:00-1:00
> A.M. (G.M.C.)

6 August, 1938 (SAT)

> Glenn Miller and His Orchestra played at Manhasset
> Bay Yacht Club, Manhasset Bay, Long Island from
> 9:00-2:00 A.M. (G.M.C.)

11 August, 1938 (THUR)

> Glenn Miller and His Orchestra played at the
> Crystal Ballroom, Cumberland, Maryland from 8:30-
> 1:15 A.M. (G.M.C.)

12 August, 1938 (FRI)

> Glenn Miller and His Orchestra played at Gwynn Oak
> Park, Baltimore, Maryland from 9:00-1:00 A.M.
> (G.M.C.)

13 August, 1938 (SAT)

       Glenn Miller and His Orchestra played at the Beach
Point Club, Mamaroneck, Long Island from 9:00-
2:00 A.M. (G.M.C.)

14 August, 1938 (SUN)

       Glenn Miller and His Orchestra played at Pleasure
Beach, Bridgeport, Connecticut from 8:30-12:30 A.M.
(G.M.C.)

15 August, 1938 (MON)

       Glenn Miller and His Orchestra played at Lakewood
Park, Mahanoy City, Pennsylvania from 8:30-1:00 A.M.
(G.M.C.)

16 August, 1938 (TUES)

       Glenn Miller and His Orchestra played at Roseland
State Ballroom, Boston, Massachusetts. (Boston
Post, Aug. 16, 1938)

18 August, 1938 (THUR)

       Glenn Miller and His Orchestra played at Shelbourne
Inn Pavillion, Shelbourne, New Hampshire. (Boston
Post, Aug. 14, 1938)

20 August, 1938 (SAT)

       Glenn Miller and His Orchestra played for one week
(closed Friday, August 26th) at Hamid's Million
Dollar Pier, Atlantic City, New Jersey. Sat & Sun.
matinee 3:00-5:00 P.M. (BB Aug. 13, 1938; G.M.C.)

       From a picture of the band taken on Hamid's Million
Dollar Pier the following personnel were present:

Trombones	Glenn Miller, Brad Jenney, Al Mastren
Trumpets	Johnny Austin, Louis Mucci, Bob Price
Reeds	Hal McIntyre, as; Stanley Aronson, as & bar; Wilbur Schwartz, clt & as; Tex Beneke, ts; Unsigned (probably Bill Stegmeyer, ts)

(Continued on next page)

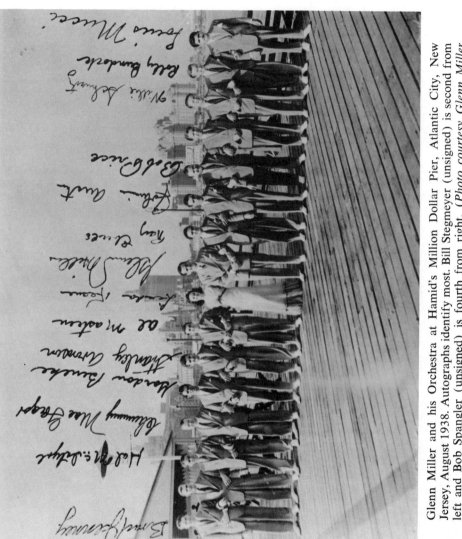

Glenn Miller and his Orchestra at Hamid's Million Dollar Pier, Atlantic City, New Jersey, August 1938. Autographs identify most. Bill Stegmeyer (unsigned) is second from left and Bob Spangler (unsigned) is fourth from right. (*Photo courtesy Glenn Miller Estate*)

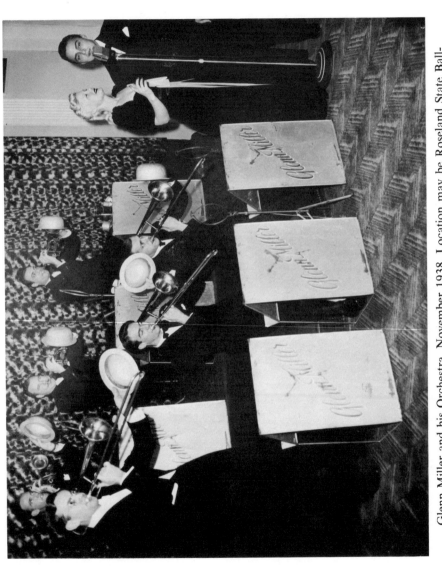

Glenn Miller and his Orchestra, November 1938. Location may be Roseland State Ball-room, Boston. Left to right, front row: Miller, Tanner, Mastren, Hutton, Eberle. Back row: Kimble, Price, Austin. (*Photo courtesy Glenn Miller Estate*)

Rhythm   Chummy MacGregor, p; Rowland Bundock, b;
                Unsigned (probably Bob Spangler, d)
Vocalists   Linda Keane, Ray Eberle

27 August, 1938 (SAT)

Glenn Miller and His Orchestra played for one week
(closed Friday, September 2nd) at Guy Hunt's Ocean
Pier, Wildwood, New Jersey. (BB, Aug. 6, 1938;
BB, Aug. 13, 1938; G.M.C.)

September 1938

Sometime during this month Glenn signed a recording
contract with RCA Victor on their 35¢ Bluebird
label.

Also during this month Marion Hutton joined the band
replacing Linda Keane as vocalist.
    "It was while playing Boston that he heard two
sisters with Lopez: Betty and Marion Hutton. The
talk was all about Betty, but Glenn much preferred
Marion's more mature work. And so one morning, just
an hour before the band left on a southern tour, a
well built lass with an even better built grin
joined the band. She made an immediate hit.
Southerners knew her as Sissy Jones, but upon a
return to the North, she was re-assigned her more
dignified moniker." (Met. Dec. 1939)

Miller was in Boston July 2nd and August 16th. It
might be the latter date when he heard Marion. However, Linda Keane was vocalist with the band during
the date at Hamid's Million Dollar Pier, so it must
be assumed that Marion joined the band some time
after this date. A short tour of the southern
states began in early September.

Finally, during the period September to October Bob
Barker played 2nd trumpet with Bob Price on 1st
trumpet and Johnny Austin on 3rd (hot) trumpet.
(Met. Nov. 1938)

4 September, 1938 (SUN)

Glenn Miller and His Orchestra played at the Wardman
Park Hotel (Connecticut Avenue and Woodley Road,
N.W.) Washington, D.C. from 9:00-1:00 A.M. (G.M.C.)

9 & 10 September, 1938 (FRI & SAT)

        Glenn Miller and His Orchestra played at Memorial
        Auditorium (5 Elks Club Bldg.), Raleigh, North
        Carolina. (G.M.C.)

13 September, 1938 (TUES)

        Glenn Miller and His Orchestra played at the
        Jewish Progressive Club (525 Healy Bldg.),
        Atlanta, Georgia from 9:00-1:00 A.M. (G.M.C.)

14 September, 1938 (WED)

        Glenn Miller and His Orchestra played at the Twin
        City Club (West Fourth Street), Winston-Salem,
        North Carolina from 10:00-2:00 A.M. (G.M.C.)

16 September, 1938 (FRI)

        A swing battle was staged by WNEW's Martin Block
        between the bands of Artie Shaw, Tommy Dorsey,
        Claude Hopkins and Merle Pitt. This benefit was
        held at New York's 105th Regiment Armory. Guest
        artists included Ozzie Nelson (who sang one song)
        and Glenn Miller, "who played some swell jazz
        trombone before Tommy's band". (Met. Oct. 1938)

17 September, 1938 (SAT)

        Glenn Miller and His Orchestra played at the
        Beach Point Club, Mamaroneck, Long Island from
        9:00-2:00 A.M. (G.M.C.)

23 September, 1938 (FRI)

        Glenn Miller and His Orchestra played at Cedar-
        brook Country Club (Ogonta Ave.), Philadelphia,
        Pennsylvania from 7:00-12:00 Midnight. (G.M.C.)

24 September, 1938 (SAT)

        Glenn Miller and His Orchestra played at Philmont
        C.C. (G.M.C.)

27 September, 1938 (TUES): Victor Studios, New York City, New York

Trombones	Glenn Miller, Al Mastren, PAUL TANNER
Trumpets	Johnny Austin, Louis Mucci, Bob Price
Reeds	Hal McIntyre, as; Stanley Aronson, as & bar; Wilbur Schwartz, clt & as; Tex Beneke, ts; Bill Stegmeyer, ts & as
Rhythm	Chummy MacGregor, p; Rowland Bundock, b; Bob Spangler, d
Vocalist	Ray Eberle

027410-1   BB 7853-A, MW 7519, Poly 6005, Vi PR-114, Cam Cal/Cas-
           829 AFRS P-8995, RCA G Cas-829, Pick Int. CDS
           1004, RCA Cam Arg Cal-3138, RCA Cam Fr 900.028
  OA   My Reverie (arr GM)-voc Ray Eberle
           Arrangement based on Debussy's Melody "Reverie"
           (Larry Clinton)
           Tbn, Miller

027411-1   BB 7870-A, MW 7531, Poly 6004, Vi 447-0034,
           Vi LPT-3036, Vi EPBT-3036 (947-0091), Vi LPT-
           3067, Vi EPBT-3067 (947-0200), HMV DLP 1062,
           Vi LPM/LSP-3564, Vi TP3-5044, RCA G EPBT-3067,
           Vi P8S-5061, RCA F 130210, RCA G LPT-3067,
           ViJ 1190, Vi Arg LPM-3564
           By The Waters Of Minnetonka (arr GM) (Part 1)-Chant
           by the Orchestra
           (Indian Love Song)
           (J.M. Cavanass-Thurlow Lieurance)
           Ts, Beneke; clt, Beneke

027412-1   BB 7870-B, MW 7531, Poly 6004, Vi 447-0034, Vi LPT-
           3036, Vi EPBT-3036 (947-0091), Vi LPT-3067,
           Vi EPBT-3067 (947-0200), HMV DLP 1062,
           Vi LPM/LSP-3564, Vi TP3-5044, RCA G EPBT-3067,
           Vi P8S-5061, RCA F 130210, RCA G LPT-3067,
           ViJ 1190, Vi Arg LPM 3564
           By The Waters Of Minnetonka (arr GM) (Part 2)
           (Indian Love Song)
           (J.M. Cavanass-Thurlow Lieurance)
           Tbn, Miller; tpt, Austin; as, Stegmeyer

027413-1   BB 7853-B, MW 7519, Poly 6005, HMVAu EA-2541
           King Porter Stomp
           (Ferdinand "Jelly-Roll" Morton)
           Tbn, Miller; ts, Beneke; tpt, Austin; as,
           Stegmeyer

           The label on "My Reverie" shows lyrics and arrange-
           ment by Larry Clinton. This means the interpretation
           from Debussy. The actual arrangement of this

(Session continued on next page)

version is by Glenn Miller. According to the
November 1938 issue of "Metronome" the arrangement
was made for Tommy Dorsey.

The original 78 issue of "By The Waters of
Minnetonka" was a two-sided 10" disc. Later EP
and LP reissues (through splicing) have made it a
continuous number.

All tunes 1 take. (RCA Victor)
This session lasted from 2:00 P.M. to 4:14 P.M.
(RCA Victor)

30 September, 1938 (FRI)

Glenn Miller and His Orchestra opened at Roseland
State Ballroom, Boston, Massachusetts, with two CBS
weekly coast to coast hookups (Tuesday, 11:30 P.M.
and Saturday, 11:00 P.M.--DB, Dec. 1938)(Variety,
Sept. 28, 1938) The local station (CBS) for these
broadcasts was WABC. (BB, Dec. 24, 1938; Boston
Post, Sept. 30, 1938)

The Miller band also played a number of one-nighters
during its stay at the Roseland State Ballroom and
used Boston as its base of operations. The band
usually played at the Roseland State Ballroom on
Tuesday, Friday and Saturday nights.

1 October, 1938 (SAT)

Glenn Miller and His Orchestra played at Roseland
State Ballroom, Boston, Massachusetts. (Boston Post,
Oct. 1, 1938)

2 October, 1938 (SUN)

Open. (G.M.P.R.)

This date marks the beginning of the Glenn Miller
Payroll Records (G.M.P.R.). At this stage they were
rather rough and did not indicate the date when a
musician joined or left the band. These records
begin on a Sunday and end on a Saturday (eg. October
2nd to October 8th) All we can assume is that a
musician was there for the entire week as the
salaries were all the same and there is no pro rata
breakdown (as the later payrolls in 1940, 1941 and
1942 show) to indicate that a musician may have only
been with the band for part of the week. The payroll

(Continued on next page)

records also show where the band was playing but
does not always give a complete description of the
location so that in some cases we know the town
but not the name of the ballroom etc.

Trombones	Glenn Miller, Al Mastren, Paul Tanner
Trumpets	Johnny Austin, BOB PECK, Bob Price
Reeds	Hal McIntyre, as; Stanley Aronson, as & bar; TONY VIOLA, clt & as; Tex Beneke, ts; Bill Stegmeyer, ts & as
Rhythm	Chummy MacGregor, p; Rowland Bundock, b; Bob Spangler, d
Vocalists	Marion Hutton, Ray Eberle
Band-Boy	Warren "Jetter" Jordan

3 October, 1938 (MON)

Glenn Miller and His Orchestra played at Hotel
Statler (for Dodge Dealers), Boston, Massachusetts.
(G.M.P.R.)

4 October, 1938 (TUES)

Glenn Miller and His Orchestra played at Roseland
State Ballroom, Boston, Massachusetts. (G.M.P.R. &
Boston Post, Oct. 4, 1938)

5 October, 1938 (WED)

Glenn Miller and His Orchestra played at the
Auditorium, Lowell, Massachusetts. (G.M.P.R. &
Boston Post, Oct. 2, 1938) Note: The Boston Post
stated that the band would be playing at the
Commodore Ballroom while G.M.P.R. listed the
Auditorium.

6 October, 1938 (THUR)

Glenn Miller and His Orchestra played at Brookline
Country Club, Brookline, Pennsylvania from 10:00-
4:00 A.M. (G.M.C. & G.M.P.R.)

7 October, 1938 (FRI)

Glenn Miller and His Orchestra played at Roseland
State Ballroom, Boston, Massachusetts. (G.M.P.R.
& Boston Post, Oct. 7, 1938)

8 October, 1938 (SAT)

> Glenn Miller and His Orchestra played at Roseland
> State Ballroom, Boston, Massachusetts. (G.M.P.R.
> & Boston Post, Oct. 8, 1938)

9 October, 1938 (SUN)

> Glenn Miller and His Orchestra played at Ritz Ball-
> room, Bridgeport, Connecticut from 9:00-2:00 A.M.
> (G.M.P.R. & G.M.C.)

Trombones	Glenn Miller, Al Mastren, Paul Tanner
Trumpets	Johnny Austin, Bob Peck, Bob Price
Reeds	Hal McIntyre, as; Stanley Aronson, as & bar; WILBUR SCHWARTZ, clt & as; Tex Beneke, ts; Bill Stegmeyer, ts & as
Rhythm	Chummy MacGregor, p; Rowland Bundock, b; Bob Spangler, d
Vocalists	Marion Hutton, Ray Eberle
Band-Boy	Warren Jordan

10 October, 1938 (MON)

> Open. (G.M.P.R.)

11 October, 1938 (TUES)

> Glenn Miller and His Orchestra played a double date
> this evening. From 8:30-12:00 Midnight the band
> played at Roseland State Ballroom, Boston,
> Massachusetts. From 1:00-4:00 A.M. the band played
> at The New Weymouth Tent (Nantasket Road), Weymouth,
> Massachusetts. (G.M.P.R. & Boston Post, Oct. 11,
> 1938)

12 October, 1938 (WED)

> Glenn Miller and His Orchestra played in Manchester,
> New Hampshire. (G.M.P.R.)

13 October, 1938 (THUR)

> Glenn Miller and His Orchestra played in Dover, New
> Hampshire. (G.M.P.R.)

14 October, 1938 (FRI)

>Glenn Miller and His Orchestra played at Roseland
>State Ballroom (battle of bands with Erskine
>Hawkins), Boston, Massachusetts. (G.M.P.R. &
>Boston Post, Oct. 14, 1938)

15 October, 1938 (SAT)

>Glenn Miller and His Orchestra played at Roseland
>State Ballroom, Boston, Massachusetts. (G.M.P.R.
>& Boston Post, Oct. 15, 1938)

16 October, 1938 (SUN)

>Glenn Miller and His Orchestra played at the Wilcox
>Dance Pavilion at Savin Rock, Connecticut, to 596
>followers at 65¢ each for his take of $386.00.
>(BB, Nov. 5, 1938 & G.M.P.R.)

17 October, 1938 (MON)

>Open. (G.M.P.R.)

18 October, 1938 (TUES)

>Glenn Miller and His Orchestra played at Roseland
>State Ballroom, Boston, Massachusetts. (G.M.P.R.
>& Boston Post, Oct. 18, 1938)

19 October, 1938 (WED)

>Glenn Miller and His Orchestra played at The New
>Weymouth Tent, Weymouth, Massachusetts. (G.M.P.R.
>& Boston Post, Oct. 19, 1938)

20 October, 1938 (THUR)

>Glenn Miller and His Orchestra played at Ricker
>Gardens, Portland, Maine. (G.M.P.R.)

21 October, 1938 (FRI)

>Glenn Miller and His Orchestra played at Adams
>House, Harvard University, Cambridge, Massachusetts
>from 9:00-2:00 A.M. (G.M.P.R. & G.M.C.)

22 October, 1938 (SAT)

        Glenn Miller and His Orchestra played at Roseland
State Ballroom, Boston, Massachusetts. (G.M.P.R. &
Boston Post, Oct. 22, 1938)

23 October, 1938 (SUN)

        Open. (G.M.P.R.) G.M.C. indicates that the band
was at Capitol Park, Hartford, Connecticut but we
believe that the payroll record would be more
accurate since the "contract" would have been signed
well in advance and could have been changed.

Trombones	Glenn Miller, Al Mastren, Paul Tanner
Trumpets	Johnny Austin, Bob Peck, Bob Price
Reeds	Hal McIntyre, as; Stanley Aronson, as & bar; TONY VIOLA, as & clt; Tex Beneke, ts; Bill Stegmeyer, ts & as
Rhythm	Chummy MacGregor, p; Rowland Bundock, b; Bob Spangler, d
Vocalists	Marion Hutton, Ray Eberle
Band-Boy	Warren Jordan

24 October, 1938 (MON)

        Open. (G.M.P.R.)

25 October, 1938 (TUES)

        Glenn Miller and His Orchestra played at Roseland
State Ballroom, Boston, Massachusetts. (G.M.P.R. &
Boston Post, Oct. 25, 1938)

26 October, 1938 (WED)

        Open. (G.M.P.R.)

27 October, 1938 (THUR)

        Open. (G.M.P.R.)

28 October, 1938 (FRI)

        Glenn Miller and His Orchestra played at Hotel
Statler (M.I.T. Prom), Boston, Massachusetts, from
9:00-3:00 A.M. (G.M.P.R. & G.M.C.)

29 October, 1938 (SAT)

> Glenn Miller and His Orchestra played at Algonquin
> Club, Boston, Massachusetts. (G.M.P.R. & G.M.C.)

30 October, 1938 (SUN)

> Open. (G.M.P.R.)

Trombones	Glenn Miller, Al Mastren, Paul Tanner
Trumpets	Johnny Austin, JACK KIMBLE, Bob Price
Reeds	Hal McIntyre, as; Stanley Aronson, as & bar; WILBUR SCHWARTZ, clt & as; Tex Beneke, ts; Bill Stegmeyer, ts & as
Rhythm	Chummy MacGregor, p; Rowland Bundock, b; Bob Spangler, d
Vocalists	Marion Hutton, Ray Eberle
Band-Boy	Warren Jordan

31 October, 1938 (MON)

> Glenn Miller and His Orchestra played at The New
> Weymouth Tent, Weymouth, Massachusetts. (G.M.P.R.
> & Boston Post, Oct. 31, 1938)

1 November, 1938 (TUES)

> Glenn Miller and His Orchestra played at Roseland
> State Ballroom, Boston, Massachusetts. (G.M.P.R. &
> Boston Post, Nov. 1, 1938)

2 November, 1938 (WED)

> Open. (G.M.P.R.)

3 November, 1938 (THUR)

> Open. (G.M.P.R.)

4 November, 1938 (FRI)

> Glenn Miller and His Orchestra played in White Plains,
> New York. (G.M.P.R.)

5 November, 1938 (SAT)

> Glenn Miller and His Orchestra played at Exeter
> Academy (Academy Gymnasium), Exeter, New Hampshire.
> Matinee: 5:00-6:00 P.M. Evening: 8:30-12:00 Mid-
> night. (G.M.P.R. & G.M.C.)

6 November, 1938 (SUN): Roseland State Ballroom, Boston,
*   Massachusetts*

> *(1:11) Moonlight Serenade (Theme)*
> *   (Mitchell Parish-Glenn Miller)*
> *(3:13) Rug Cutter's Swing (arr BF)*
> *   (Horace Henderson)*
> *   Tpt, ??; ts, Beneke; tbn, Miller; clt,*
> *   Schwartz?; tbn, Miller; tpt, Austin*
> *(2:46) I've Got A Pocketful Of Dreams-voc Ray Eberle*
> *   From Paramount film "Sing, You Sinners"*
> *   (Johnny Burke-Jimmy Monaco)*
> *   Ts, Beneke; tpt, Austin*
> *(2:50) Wait Until My Heart Finds Out-voc Marion*
> *   Hutton*
> *   (Sammy Cahn-Saul Chaplin)*
> *   Tbn, Miller; as, ?? (Stegmeyer?)*
> *(2:23) My Own-voc Ray Eberle*
> *   From the Universal film "That Certain Age"*
> *   (Harold Adamson-Jimmy McHugh)*
> *(4:38) Oh, Baby*
> *   From "Rain or Shine"*
> *   (Owen Murphy)*
> *   Tbn, Miller; ts, Beneke; tpt, Austin;*
> *   as, ??*

> NOTE: If all these programs were on Tuesday and
> Saturday nights then this date is incorrect. Band
> at Waterbury on this date.

6 November, 1938 (SUN)

> Glenn Miller and His Orchestra played at Hamilton
> Park (Hop sponsored by The Supreme Market Fellow-
> ship Association), Waterbury, Connecticut.
> (G.M.P.R. & Boston Post, Nov. 6, 1938)

7 November, 1938 (MON)

> Glenn Miller and His Orchestra played at Hotel
> Bradford, Boston, Massachusetts from 8:30-1:00 A.M.
> (G.M.P.R. & G.M.C.)

8 November, 1938 (TUES)

>Glenn Miller and His Orchestra played at Roseland State Ballroom, Boston, Massachusetts. (G.M.P.R. & Boston Post, Nov. 8, 1938)

9 November, 1938 (WED)

>Glenn Miller and His Orchestra played at Hotel Bradford, Boston, Massachusetts from 8:30-1:00 A.M. (G.M.P.R. & G.M.C.)

10 November, 1938 (THUR)

>Glenn Miller and His Orchestra played at Ricker Gardens, Portland, Maine. (G.M.P.R.)

11 November, 1938 (FRI)

>Glenn Miller and His Orchestra played at Roseland State Ballroom, Boston, Massachusetts. (G.M.P.R. & Boston Post, Nov. 11, 1938)

12 November, 1938 (SAT)

>Glenn Miller and His Orchestra played at Roseland State Ballroom, Boston, Massachusetts. (G.M.P.R. & Boston Post, Nov. 12, 1938)

13 November, 1938 (SUN)

>Glenn Miller and His Orchestra played in New London, Connecticut. (G.M.P.R.) The paycheck records mention A.F. of M. Local 802 was paid for a date at Ocean Beach, New Jersey. There is an Ocean Beach, Connecticut, which is near New London, Connecticut, so there is some confusion as to where the band played this evening.

14 November, 1938 (MON)

>Open. (G.M.P.R.)

15 November, 1938 (TUES)

>Glenn Miller and His Orchestra played at Roseland
State Ballroom (St. Francis Xavier Association),
Boston, Massachusetts from 8:00-1:00 A.M. (G.M.P.R.
& Boston Post, Nov. 14, 1938)

16 November, 1938 (WED)

>Glenn Miller and His Orchestra played at King
Phillip Ballroom, Lake Pearl, Wrentham, Massachusetts.
(G.M.P.R. & Boston Post, Nov. 13, 1938)

17 November, 1938 (THUR)

>Open. (G.M.P.R.)

18 November, 1938 (FRI)

>Glenn Miller and His Orchestra played at the
Auditorium (St. Patrick's Parish), Lowell, Massachusetts from 8:00-1:00 A.M. (G.M.P.R. & G.M.C.)

19 November, 1938 (SAT)

>Glenn Miller and His Orchestra played at Roseland
State Ballroom, Boston, Massachusetts. (G.M.P.R. &
Boston Post, Nov. 19, 1938)

20 November, 1938 (SUN)

>Glenn Miller and His Orchestra played in Waterbury,
Connecticut. (G.M.P.R.)

21 November, 1938 (MON)

>Glenn Miller and His Orchestra played in Dover
(Knights of Columbus dance), New Hampshire. (G.M.
P.R. & Boston Post, Nov. 20, 1938)

22 November, 1938 (TUES)

>Glenn Miller and His Orchestra played at Roseland
State Ballroom (The Great Waltz Contest), Boston,
Massachusetts. (G.M.P.R. & Boston Post, Nov. 22,
1938)

23 November, 1938 (WED)

        Glenn Miller and His Orchestra played at the
        Municipal Auditorium (Chapter Order of De Molay),
        Worcester, Massachusetts from 9:00-2:00 A.M.
        (G.M.P.R. & G.M.C.)

24 November, 1938 (THUR)

        Glenn Miller and His Orchestra played at Broadwood
        Hotel, Philadelphia, Pennsylvania. (BB, Nov. 5,
        1938 & G.M.P.R.)

25 November, 1938 (FRI)

        Glenn Miller and His Orchestra played at the Armory,
        Hingham, Massachusetts. (G.M.P.R. & G.M.C.)

26 November, 1938 (SAT)

        Glenn Miller and His Orchestra played in Portland,
        Maine. (G.M.P.R.)

27 November, 1938 (SUN)

        Glenn Miller and His Orchestra played at the Ritz
        Ballroom, Bridgeport, Connecticut, from 8:30-
        12:30 A.M., and drew 1,000 dancers with a gross of
        $475.00 (55¢ gents, 40¢ ladies). (BB, Dec. 10,
        1938, G.M.P.R. & G.M.C.)

Trombones	Glenn Miller, Al Mastren, Paul Tanner
Trumpets	Johnny Austin, CLAUDE BOWEN, Bob Price
Reeds	Hal McIntyre, as; Stanley Aronson, as & bar; Wilbur Schwartz, clt & as; Tex Beneke, ts; Bill Stegmeyer, ts & as
Rhythm	Chummy MacGregor, p; Rowland Bundock, b; Bob Spangler, d
Vocalists	Marion Hutton, Ray Eberle
Band-Boy	Warren Jordan

28 November, 1938 (MON)

        Open. (G.M.P.R.)

29 November, 1938 (TUES)

      Glenn Miller and His Orchestra played at Roseland
      State Ballroom (The Big Jitterbug Contest), Boston,
      Massachusetts. (G.M.P.R. & Boston Post, Nov. 29,
      1938)

30 November, 1938

      Glenn Miller and His Orchestra played at Rockingham
      Ballroom, Newmarket, New Hampshire. (G.M.P.R. &
      Boston Post, Nov. 27, 1938)

1 December, 1938 (THUR)

      Open. (G.M.P.R.)

2 December, 1938 (FRI)

      Glenn Miller and His Orchestra played at Amherst
      College (Alumni Gym), Amherst, Massachusetts, from
      8:30-1:00 A.M. (G.M.P.R. & G.M.C.)

3 December, 1938 (SAT): Roseland State Ballroom, Boston, Massachusetts
                    CBS 11:00-11:30 P.M. (WABC New York)

Announcer: Hugh Sargent

      What Have You Got That Gets Me?-voc M.H.

(0:25) Unknown Tune
      Tpt, Austin
(3:09) When Paw Was Courtin' Maw- voc Tex Beneke
      (Talking Glenn Miller and Tex Beneke)
      (Jack Manus-Leonard Joy)
      Ts, Beneke
(2:31) What Goes On Here In My Heart?-voc Marion Hutton
      From the Paramount film "Give Me A Sailor"
      (Leo Robin-Ralph Rainger)
      Ts, Beneke; tpt, Austin)
(3:28) With You On My Mind-voc Ray Eberle
      From "Straight, Place and Show"
      (Lew Brown-Lew Pollack)
(2:56) King Porter Stomp
      (Ferdinand "Jelly-Roll" Morton)
      Tbn, Miller; ts, Beneke; tpt, Austin;
      as, McIntyre (?)
(1:21) Moonlight Serenade (Theme)
      (Mitchell Parish-Glenn Miller)

4 December, 1938 (SUN)

>   Glenn Miller and His Orchestra played at the Y.M.H.A.
>   (Broad & Pine Streets), Philadelphia, Pennsylvania,
>   from 8:30-1:00 A.M.   (G.M.P.R. & G.M.C.)

5 December, 1938 (MON)

>   Glenn Miller and His Orchestra played in Pottsville,
>   Pennsylvania.   (G.M.P.R.)

6 December, 1938 (TUES)

>   Glenn Miller and His Orchestra played at Roseland
>   State Ballroom (New England States Great Waltz Contest),
>   Boston, Massachusetts.   (G.M.P.R. & Boston Post, Dec.
>   6, 1938)

7 December, 1938 (WED)

>   Glenn Miller and His Orchestra played at Ricker
>   Gardens, Portland, Maine.   (G.M.P.R.)

8 December, 1938 (THUR)

>   Glenn Miller and His Orchestra played at the Deck,
>   Worcester, Massachusetts.   (G.M.P.R.)

9 December, 1938 (FRI)

>   Glenn Miller and His Orchestra played at Hotel Statler
>   (Imperial Ballroom--for R.O.T.C. Military Ball of
>   Boston University), Boston, Massachusetts, from 9:00-
>   2:00 A.M.   (G.M.P.R. & G.M.C.)

10 December, 1938 (SAT)

>   Glenn Miller and His Orchestra played at Roseland
>   State Ballroom, Boston, Massachusetts.   (G.M.P.R. &
>   Boston Post, Dec. 10, 1938)

11 December, 1938 (SUN)

>   Glenn Miller and His Orchestra played in Waterbury,
>   Connecticut.   (G.M.P.R.)

(continued on next page)

Trombones	Glenn Miller, Al Mastren, Paul Tanner
Trumpets	Johnny Austin, ?????????, Bob Price
Reeds	Hal McIntyre, aś; Stanley Aronson, as & bar; Wilbur Schwartz, clt & as; Tex Beneke, ts; CLAUDE LAKEY, ts
Rhythm	Chummy MacGregor, p; Rowland Bundock, b; CODY SANDIFER (SANDERFORD), d
Vocalists	Marion Hutton, Ray Eberle
Band-Boy	Warren Jordan

There are problems deciding upon the personnel for the week December 11th to December 17th. The above names are shown for full payroll but under a section on G.M.P.R. shown as "Expenses" there are extra salaries indicated for Harder (instrument unknown), Knowles (trumpet), and Howlett (instrument unknown). Legh Knowles (trumpet) came from Red Norvo. (Met. Feb. 1939) He was certainly in the trumpet section for part of this week and probably one (or both) of the men (Harder and Howlett) were in for the other part of the week. It is also possible that Lakey or Sandifer did not join at the beginning of the week and the two unknown instrumentalists might have been their temporary substitutes, but the payroll records do not go into enough detail to determine this. Bob Spangler (drums) left the band to join Jan Savitt. (Met. Jan. 1939) It was rumored that Cliff Leeman (who was ill and had been replaced by Buddy Rich in the Artie Shaw band), upon recovery, might join Miller but this never happened. (Met. Feb. 1939)

12 December, 1938 (MON)

Open. (G.M.P.R.)

13 December, 1938 (TUES): Roseland State Ballroom, Boston, Massachusetts
CBS 11:30-12:00 Midnight. (WABC New York)

(2:09) Sugar Foot Stomp (Dipper Mouth Blues)(arr GM)-
Chant by the Band
(Joe Oliver-Louis Armstrong)
Clt, Schwartz; tbn, Miller

(4:20) Mutiny In The Nursery-voc Marion Hutton,
Ray Eberle, Tex Beneke and the Band
From the Warner Brothers' film "Going Places"
(Johnny Mercer-Harry Warren)
Tpt, Austin

(Broadcast continued on next page)

(3:23) My Reverie (arr GM)-voc Ray Eberle
Arrangement based on Debussy's Melody
"Reverie"
(Larry Clinton)
Tbn, Miller

14 December, 1938 (WED)

Glenn Miller and His Orchestra played in Newmarket, New Hampshire. (G.M.P.R.)

15 December, 1938 (THUR)

Glenn Miller and His Orchestra played in Portland, Maine. (G.M.P.R.)

16 December, 1938 (FRI)

Glenn Miller and His Orchestra played at Roseland State Ballroom, Boston, Massachusetts. (G.M.P.R. & Boston Post, Dec. 16, 1938)

17 December, 1938 (SAT)

Glenn Miller and His Orchestra played at Roseland State Ballroom, Boston, Massachusetts. (G.M.P.R. & Boston Post, Dec. 17, 1938)

Note that we do not have a payroll listing for the next week. During this period Johnny Austin left the band (he returned for a short period in January) and was replaced by Claude Bowen. It is quite possible that there were other changes (temporary).

20 December, 1938 (TUES)

Glenn Miller and His Orchestra closed at Roseland State Ballroom, Boston, Massachusetts. (Boston Post, Dec. 20, 1938)

21 December, 1938 (WED)

Glenn Miller and His Orchestra played at Bancroft Hotel, Worcester, Massachusetts, from 9:00-2:00 A.M. (G.M.C.)

23 December, 1938 (FRI): Paradise Restaurant, New York City, N.Y.
NBC   11:30-12:00 Midnight.

Glenn Miller and His Orchestra opened at the Paradise
Restaurant, New York City, N.Y. (BB. Dec. 24, 1938;
Variety, Dec. 21, 1938; G.M.C.)
"Glenn Miller cut short his New England
sojourn to re-enter the Paradise in N.Y. with NBC
wires." (Met. Jan. 1939)

> *Moonlight Serenade (Theme)*
> *MEDLEY:*
> > *Why Do I Love You?*
> > *Can't Help Lovin' Dat Man*
> > *Make Believe*
> > *Ol' Man River*

E4VP 8208   Vi LPT 6701, Vi EPOT 6701 (947-0186), HMV RLS 598,
                   RCA G EPOT-6701
         (2:20)   This Can't Be Love (arr GM)-voc Ray Eberle
                        From the musical production "The Boys
                        From Syracuse"
                        (Lorenz Hart-Richard Rodgers)

> *What Have You Got That Gets Me?*
> *With You On My Mind*
> *King Porter Stomp*
> *Wait Until My Heart Finds Out*
> *Simple And Sweet-voc RE*
> > *(Bud Green-Abel Baer)*
> *By The Waters Of Minnetonka*
> *Moonlight Serenade (Theme)*

26 December, 1938 (MON)

Glenn Miller and His Orchestra played at Iona
School, New Rochelle, New York, from 10:00-3:00
A.M. (G.M.C.) According to G.M.C. the Paradise
employer let Glenn off for this night as this
private engagement was already signed.

29 December, 1938 (THUR)

We have a paycheck record for the week ending
December 29th so that the following personnel is
definite. Note that the last payroll record
ended the week of December 17th which was a Saturday. Now the week ending falls on a Thursday so

(continued on next page)

that the missing payroll would appear to cover
over a week (December 18th to December 29th.) but
since we've no proof of this we can not safely
say that the following personnel was present
during that period and we could only assume that
this personnel was set from December 23rd to
December 29th.

Trombones	Glenn Miller, Al Mastren, Paul Tanner
Trumpets	CLAUDE BOWEN, ??????????, Bob Price
Reeds	Hal McIntyre, as; Stanley Aronson, as & bar; Wilbur Schwartz, clt & as; Tex Beneke, ts; Claude Lakey, ts
Rhythm	Chummy MacGregor, p; Rowland Bundock, b; Cody Sandifer, d
Vocalists	Marion Hutton, Ray Eberle
Band-Boy	Warren Jordan
Arranger	Bill Finegan

We're not sure who the third trumpeter was but
Legh Knowles is on the week of December 30th to
January 5th and might have been with the band on
this date (but there is no paycheck issued to
him on December 29th). For the week December 11th
to December 17th Legh Knowles is shown for being
there part of the week but he may not have joined
the band full time until later.

30 December, 1938 (FRI): Paradise Restaurant, New York City, N.Y.
NBC 11:30-12:00 Midnight

Trombones	*Glenn Miller, Al Mastren, Paul Tanner*
Trumpets	*Claude Bowen, LEGH KNOWLES, Bob Price*
Reeds	*Hal McIntyre, as; Stanley Aronson, as & bar; Wilbur Schwartz, clt & as; Tex Beneke, ts; Claude Lakey, ts*
Rhythm	*Chummy MacGregor, p; Rowland Bundock, b; Cody Sandifer, d*
Vocalists	*Marion Hutton, Ray Eberle*
Band-Boy	*Warren Jordan*

PPRM-5338   Vi LPM/LSP-2768 (Vi LPM/LSP-6101), RCA RD/SF-7611
(3:12) When Paw Was Courtin' Maw-voc Tex Beneke
                    and Glenn Miller
              (Jack Manus-Leonard Joy)
              Ts, Beneke

Why Doesn't Somebody Tell Me These Things-
          voc Marion Hutton (   )
With You On My Mind
Down South Camp Meetin'
Moonlight Serenade (Theme)

31 December, 1938 (SAT): Paradise Restaurant, New York City, N.Y.
NBC   10:00-10:15 P.M.

> *Moonlight Serenade (Theme)*
> *King Porter Stomp*
> *Please Come Out Of Your Dream*
> *FDR Jones*
> *One O'Clock Jump*
> *Moonlight Serenade (Theme)*

6 January, 1939 (FRI): Paradise Restaurant, New York City, N.Y.
NBC   11:30-12:00 Midnight

> *Moonlight Serenade (Theme)*
> *Dipper Mouth Blues*
> *Please Come Out Of Your Dream*

PPRM-5333   Vi LPM/LSP 2767 (Vi LPM/LSP 6101), RCA RD/SF 7610
(4:19) Mutiny In The Nursery-voc Marion Hutton,
                Ray Eberle, Tex Beneke and the Band
                From the Warner Brothers' Film "Going
                Places"
                (Johnny Mercer-Harry Warren)
                Tpt, ??

> *My Reverie*
> *Blue Skies*
> *What Have You Got That Gets Me?*
> *A Room With A View*
> *One O'Clock Jump*
> *Moonlight Serenade (Theme)*

13 January, 1939 (FRI)

> Glenn Miller and His Orchestra played at the State
> Armory, Haverhill, Massachusetts. Concert, 8:30-
> 9:00 P.M. and dancing, 9:00-1:00 A.M. (G.M.C.)
> Note that G.M.C. did not mention this as one of
> the dates that the Paradise management let Glenn
> off so this contract may not have been fulfilled.

16 January, 1939 (MON)

> Glenn Miller and His Orchestra played at Nevins
> Hall, Framingham, Massachusetts, from 8:00-1:00
> A.M. for the Framingham Catholic Women's Club.
> (G.M.C.) According to G.M.C. the Paradise manage-
> ment let Glenn off for this night as this private
> engagement was already signed.

18 January, 1939 (WED): Paradise Restaurant, New York City, N.Y.
             NBC WJZ 11:30 - 12:00 Midnight EST.

    (1:16) <u>*Moonlight Serenade*</u> *(Theme)*
        (Mitchell Parish-Glenn Miller)
    (3:08) <u>*Blue Skies*</u> *(arr BF)*
        (Irving Berlin)
        Tpt, ??; ts, Beneke; clt, Schwartz;
        tbn, Miller
    (3:20) <u>*A Room With A View*</u> *(arr GJ?)-voc Ray Eberle*
        (Al Stillman-Einar Swan)
    (2:42) <u>*Could Be*</u> *(arr BF)-voc Marion Hutton*
        (Johnny Mercer-Walter Donaldson)
        Tbn, Miller;ts, Beneke
    (2:26) <u>*This Can't Be Love*</u> *(arr GM)-voc Ray Eberle*
        From the musical production "The Boys
        From Syracuse"
        (Lorenz Hart-Richard Rodgers)
    (2:11) <u>*Dipper Mouth Blues*</u> *(arr GM)-Chant by the*
        Orchestra
        (Joe Oliver-Louis Armstrong)
        Clt, Schwartz; tbn, Miller
    (2:50) <u>*What Have You Got That Gets Me*</u>*?-voc Marion*
        Hutton
        From the Paramount film "Artists and
        Models Abroad"
        (Leo Robin-Ralph Rainger)
        Ts, Beneke; tbn, Miller
    (2:37) <u>*Please Come Out Of Your Dream*</u>*-voc Ray Eberle*
        (Carl Sigman)
    (4:16) <u>*One O'Clock Jump*</u>
        (Lee Gaines-Count Basie)
        P. MacGregor; ts, Beneke; tbn, Miller;
        as, ??; tpt, ??; p, MacGregor
    (1:34) <u>*Moonlight Serenade*</u> *(Theme)*
        (Mitchell Parish-Glenn Miller)

20 January, 1939 (FRI)

    Glenn Miller and His Orchestra played at the Town
Hall, Southbridge, Massachusetts for the American
Optical Firemen's Association. Concert, 8:30-
9:00 P.M. and dancing, 9:00-2:00 A.M. (G.M.C.)
According to G.M.C. the Paradise management let
Glenn off for this night as this private engage-
ment was already signed.

24 January, 1939 (TUES)

> This was the last day for two Miller sidemen:
>
> Claude Bowen was replaced by Johnny Austin. The paycheck records show that Bowen was paid for the week ending January 12th and 3 days ending January 24th. There is no mention of Bowen being paid for the week ending January 19th but this might have been missed in our research. Bowen joined Harry James.
>
> Claude Lakey was replaced by Al Klink. The paycheck records show that Lakey was paid for the period up to January 24th. Lakey also joined Harry James.

25 January, 1939 (WED)

> | | |
> |---|---|
> | Trombones | Glenn Miller, Al Mastren, Paul Tanner |
> | Trumpets | JOHNNY AUSTIN, Legh Knowles, Bob Price |
> | Reeds | Hal McIntyre, as; Stanley Aronson, as & bar; Wilbur Schwartz, clt & as; Tex Beneke, ts; AL "MOSE" KLINK, ts |
> | Rhythm | Chummy MacGregor, p; Rowland Bundock, b; Cody Sandifer, d |
> | Vocalists | Marion Hutton, Ray Eberle |
> | Band-Boy | Warren Jordan |
>
> The paycheck records for the week ending January 26th show that Johnny Austin was paid for 2 1/2 days at the Paradise and for two club dates. This might mean that Austin re-joined the band on the night of January 24th or it might mean that Austin worked part of the 27th. Austin eventually joined Jan Savitt. There was a story (see Met. Dec. 1939) that Miller had to let Austin go because he was a poor reader of music but this story was denied by Miller (see Met. Jan. 1940).
>
> The paychecks show that Jack Maisel was paid for arranging "Wrappin' It Up" on January 26th.

26 January, 1939 (THUR)

> Glenn Miller and His Orchestra closed at the Paradise Restaurant, New York City, New York. (G.M.P.R.)

27 January, 1939 (FRI)

Trombones	Glenn Miller, Al Mastren, Paul Tanner
Trumpets	CHARLIE HILL, Legh Knowles, Bob Price
Reeds	Hal McIntyre, as; Stanley Aronson, as & bar; Wilbur Schwartz, clt & as; Tex Beneke, ts; Al Klink, ts
Rhythm	Chummy MacGregor, p; Rowland Bundock, b; Cody Sandifer, d
Vocalists	Marion Hutton, Ray Eberle
Band-Boy	Warren Jordan

29 January, 1939 (SUN)

Glenn Miller and His Orchestra played a one-nighter at the Ritz Ballroom, Bridgeport, Connecticut and drew 1,200. The gross take was $780.00. Prices were set at 65¢. (BB, Feb. 11, 1939)

1 February, 1939 (WED)

Glenn Miller and His Orchestra played a one-nighter at the Ocean Pier Ballroom, Old Orchard Beach, Maine.

6 February, 1939 (MON): Victor Studios, New York City, N.Y.

Trombones	Glenn Miller, Al Mastren, Paul Tanner
Trumpets	Charlie Hill, Legh Knowles, Bob Price
Reeds	Hal McIntyre, as; Stanley Aronson, as & bar; Wilbur Schwartz, clt & as; Tex Beneke, ts; Al Klink, ts
Rhythm	Chummy MacGregor, p; ALLAN REUSS, g; Rowland Bundock, b; Cody Sandifer, d
Vocalists	Marion Hutton, Ray Eberle

033607-1   BB 10139-A, RZ MR 3028
(Gotta Get Some) Shut-Eye (arr BF)-voc Marion
        Hutton
        (Johnny Mercer-Walter Donaldson)
        Ts, Beneke

033608-1   BB 10139-B
How I'd Like To Be With You In Bermuda-voc Ray
        Eberle
        (Bickley Reichner-Clay Boland)
        P, MacGregor; tbn, Miller; p, MacGregor;
        ts, Beneke; tbn, Miller; tpt, ??

(Session continued on next page)

033609-1   BB 10145-A, HMVAu EA 2378
             Cuckoo In The Clock(arr BF)-voc Marion Hutton
               (Johnny Mercer-Walter Donaldson)
               Tbn, Miller; ts, Beneke

033610-1   BB 10145-B
             Romance Runs In The Family(arr BF)-voc Marion
               Hutton
               (Al Hoffman-Al Goodhart-Manny Kurtz)
               Tbn, Miller; tpt, Price; ts, Beneke; tbn,
               Miller

             Allan Reuss, guitar, was hired only for this
             recording session. (G.M.P.R.)

             All tunes 1 take. (RCA Victor)
             This session lasted from 1:30 P.M. to 4:45 P.M.
             (RCA Victor)

10 February, 1939 (FRI)

             Glenn Miller and His Orchestra played at
             Massachusetts State College, Massachusetts.
             (G.M.P.R.)

11 February, 1939 (SAT)

             Glenn Miller and His Orchestra played at Vassar
             College, Massachusetts. (G.M.P.R.)

12 February, 1939 (SUN)

             Glenn Miller and His Orchestra played in Waterbury,
             Connecticut. (G.M.P.R.)

13 February, 1939 (MON)

             Glenn Miller and His Orchestra played in Sanford,
             Maine,from 8:00-1:00 A.M. (G.M.P.R. & G.M.C.)

14 February, 1939 (TUES)

             Glenn Miller and His Orchestra played at the
             Roseland Ballroom, Taunton, Massachusetts.
             (G.M.P.R. & Boston Post, Feb. 14, 1939)

15 February, 1939 (WED)

>Glenn Miller and His Orchestra played at Ricker
>Gardens, Portland, Maine. (G.M.P.R. & Boston
>Post, Feb. 14, 1939)

16 February, 1939 (THUR)

>Glenn Miller and His Orchestra played at
>McCullough Gym, Middlebury College, Middlebury,
>Vermont, from 9:00-2:00 A.M. (G.M.P.R. & G.M.C.)

17 February, 1939 (FRI)

>Glenn Miller and His Orchestra played at University
>Gym, University of Vermont, Burlington, Vermont,
>from 9:00-2:00 A.M. (G.M.P.R. & G.M.C.)

>The payroll records for the week February 17th to
>February 24th show that a Robert Brinker (instru-
>ment unknown) played with the band. However, it is
>not known how he fitted into the band as all the
>musicians (with the exception of Reuss) as listed
>on the recording session of February 6th were
>present.

18 February, 1939 (SAT)

>Glenn Miller and His Orchestra played at Winslow
>Hall, La Salle Junior College (117 Woodland Road),
>Auburndale, Massachusetts, from 8:00-12:00 Mid-
>night. (G.M.P.R. & G.M.C.)

19 February, 1939 (SUN)

>Glenn Miller and His Orchestra played at Ocean
>Beach, New London, Connecticut. (G.M.P.R.)

20 February, 1939 (MON)

>Glenn Miller and His Orchestra played at the City
>Auditorium, Nashua, New Hampshire. Concert,
>8:00-9:00 P.M. and dancing, 9:00-1:00 A.M.
>(G.M.P.R. & G.M.C.)

21 February, 1939 (TUES)

> Glenn Miller and His Orchestra played at the State
> Armory, Haverhill, Massachusetts. (G.M.P.R. &
> Boston Post, Feb. 21, 1939) This might be the date
> that is shown for January 13, 1939.

22 February, 1939 (WED)

> Glenn Miller and His Orchestra played at King
> Philip Ballroom, Lake Pearl Park, Wrentham,
> Massachusetts. (G.M.P.R. & Boston Post, Feb. 22,
> 1939)

23 February, 1939 (THUR)

> Glenn Miller and His Orchestra played at the
> Armory, Norwich University, Norwich, Vermont,
> (G.M.P.R. & G.M.C.)

24 February, 1939 (FRI)

> Glenn Miller and His Orchestra played at Mount
> Holyoke College, South Hadley, Massachusetts.
> (G.M.P.R. & G.M.C.)

Trombones	Glenn Miller, Al Mastren, Paul Tanner
Trumpets	LEE CASTALDO (CASTLE), Legh Knowles, Bob Price
Reeds	Hal McIntyre, as; Stanley Aronson, as & bar; Wilbur Schwartz, clt & as; Tex Beneke, ts; Al Klink, ts
Rhythm	Chummy MacGregor, p; Rowland Bundock, b; Cody Sandifer, d
Vocalists	Marion Hutton, Ray Eberle
Band-Boy	Warren Jordan
Instrument Unknown	Robert Brinker

> According to G.M.P.R. this was Brinker's last day
> with the band.

25 February, 1939 (SAT)

> Glenn Miller and His Orchestra played at the
> University of Buffalo, Buffalo, New York, and drew
> 2,100 people. (G.M.P.R.)

26 February, 1939 (SUN)

>Glenn Miller and His Orchestra played at Ritz
>Ballroom, Bridgeport, Connecticut. (G.M.P.R.)

27 February, 1939 (MON)

>Open. (G.M.P.R.)

28 February, 1939 (TUES)

>Open. (G.M.P.R.) Haven Studios, New York City.
>(G.M.P.R.)

1 March, 1939 (WED)

>While Glenn was rehearsing the band this afternoon
>in its usual spot, the Haven studio on West 54th
>Street, Mike Nidorf of G.A.C. brought him news that
>the band would open at the Glen Island Casino on
>May 17th. It was Glenn's thirty-fourth birthday.
>Apparently the managers of the Casino hired the band
>on the basis of what they had heard it do during
>the Paradise engagement, considered by Glenn to have
>been the band's all-time performing low. And Frank
>Dailey, after hearing of the pick, decided to book
>the band into the Meadowbrook prior to the Glen
>Island Casino job. (Met. Dec. 1939; DB July 27,
>1951; Met. March 1954)

2 March, 1939 (THUR)

>Open. (G.M.P.R.)

3 March, 1939 (FRI)

>Glenn Miller and His Orchestra played at the
>University of Pennsylvania, Philadelphia,
>Pennsylvania. (G.M.P.R.)

4 March, 1939 (SAT)

>Glenn Miller and His Orchestra played at Lehigh
>University, Easton, Pennsylvania. (G.M.P.R.)

>According to G.M.P.R. this was Lee Castaldo's last
>day with the band. He was replaced the next day
>by R.D. McMickle.

5 March, 1939 (SUN)

Trombones	Glenn Miller, Al Mastren, Paul Tanner
Trumpets	Bob Price, Legh Knowles, R. DALE "MICKEY" MCMICKLE
Reeds	Hal McIntyre, as; Stanley Aronson, as & bar; Wilbur Schwartz, clt & as; Tex Beneke, ts; Al Klink, ts
Rhythm	Chummy MacGregor, p; Rowland Bundock, b; Cody Sandifer, d
Vocalists	Marion Hutton, Ray Eberle
Band-Boy	Warren Jordan

McMickle came in from Mal Hallett. There were rumors that Miller would also bring in drummer, Cliff Leeman, trumpeter Lee Castaldo (he was with the band), and clarinetist Hank D'Amico, but outside of Castaldo, who was with the band from February 24th to March 4th, these changes never came about. (Met. April 1939) In early March guitarist Bobby Darra was offered a spot with the Miller band but his brother, Wally Darra, who led a 14-piece band, refused to let his younger brother go. (DB, April 1939)

5 March, 1939 (SUN): Meadowbrook Ballroom, Cedar Grove, New Jersey

> *Moonlight Serenade (Theme)*
> *Blue Skies*
> *Sometime-voc RE*
> *By The Waters Of Minnetonka*
> *Could Be-voc MH*
> *King Porter Stomp*
> *My Blue Heaven*
> *Shut-Eye-voc MH*
> *Let's Stop The Clock-voc RE*
> *(Haven Gillespie-J. Fred Coots)*
> *One O'Clock Jump*
> *Moonlight Serenade (Theme)*

The date of broadcast would appear to be wrong since the Miller band opened at the Meadowbrook on March 7th. On close checking at RCA Victor this was found to be a Meadowbrook broadcast and March 5th is the date that RCA Victor supplied. However, we still believe the date to be incorrect but shall leave it as shown above until further information is available. One final problem: the Harry Smith recording studio recorded a broadcast on March 5, 1939 (G.M.P.R.)

7 March, 1939 (TUES)

        Glenn Miller and His Orchestra opened at Meadow-
brook Ballroom, Cedar Grove, New Jersey. (BB,
Feb. 11, 1939; Variety, Feb.8, 1939)

        Broadcast schedule:
           NBC Blue--Sunday at 12 midnight.
           NBC Blue--Thursday and Friday at 11:30 P.M.
           Mutual----Tuesday, Thursday and Saturday at
                  10:30 P.M.
           Above E.S.T. (DB, March 1939)

        Miller started the Meadowbrook job with a four week
contract which was extended to seven weeks after
the band had played there for one week! (Met.
April 1939) This means that approximately 35-37
broadcasts were made from the Meadowbrook. Miller
closed at the Meadowbrook on April 20th.

*8 March, 1939 (WED): Meadowbrook Ballroom, Cedar Grove,
New Jersey WOR 9:15 - 9:30 P.M. EST.*

    *(3:13) Sold American (arr GM)-Chant by Marion
Hutton, Ray Eberle and the Orchestra
(Glenn Miller-John Chalmers MacGregor)
Tbn, Miller; ts, Beneke; tpt, ??*
    *(2:41) Please Come Out Of Your Dream-voc Ray
Eberle
(Carl Sigman)*
    *(3:53) Poinciana
(Buddy Bernier-Nat Simon)
Tbn, Miller; ts, Beneke; tpt, ??;
ts, Beneke; tbn, Miller*

*9 March, 1939 (THUR): Meadowbrook Ballroom, Cedar Grove,
New Jersey
Mutual (WJZ) 10:30 P.M. EST.*

    *(2:21) I Get Along Without You Very Well (arr HM)
-voc Ray Eberle
(Hoagy Carmichael)*
    *(4:04) Oh, Baby
From "Rain or Shine"
(Owen Murphy)
Tbn, Miller; ts, Beneke; tbn, Miller;
as, ??*
    *(2:35) My Heart Belongs To Daddy-voc Marion Hutton
From the musical production "Leave It
To Me" (Cole Porter)
Tbn, Miller
Hallelujah!*

23 March, 1939 (THUR)

        G.M.P.R. show that Gabe Julian (pianist and
arranger) was with the band from March 23rd to
April 8th as an arranger.

        G.M.P.R. show that Andy Picciano substituted one
night (date unknown) at the Meadowbrook. This
might be Andy Picardi who played drums with Bobby
Hackett in November 1938. Since there appears to
be a gap between Sandifer leaving the band and
Purtill joining the band this would appear to
justify our assumption that Picciano was a drummer.

*23 March, 1939 (THUR): Meadowbrook Ballroom, Cedar Grove,
                    New Jersey
                    NBC-Blue 11:30-12:00 Midnight EST.*

        Moonlight Serenade (Theme)

PPRM-5341   Vi LPM/LSP-2769 (Vi LPM/LSP-6101), RCA RD/SF-7612
              (2:39) Don't Worry 'Bout Me-voc Ray Eberle
                    (Ted Koehler-Rube Bloom)

PPRM-5338   Vi LPM/LSP-2768 (Vi LPM/LSP-6101), RCA RD/SF-7611
              (4:01) Oh, Baby
                    From "Rain or Shine"
                    (Owen Murphy)
                    Tbn, Miller; ts, Beneke; tbn, Miller;
                    p, MacGregor; as, ??

        Shut-Eye

E4VP 8206   Vi LPT 6701, Vi EPOT (947-0192), HMV RLS 598,
                RCA G EPOT-6701, RD 3/4-64,
                AFRS "America's Pop Music" 72
              (2:46) Deep Purple-voc Ray Eberle
                    (Mitchell Parish-Peter DeRose)

        My Blue Heaven
        Sticks And Stones-voc MH
                    (Al Hoffman-Al Goodhart-Manny Kurtz)

E4VP 8205   Vi LPT 6701, Vi EPOT (947-0190), HMV RLS 598
                RCA G EPOT-6701
              (2:21) Get Out Of Town-voc Ray Eberle
                    From the musical production "Leave It
                    To Me"
                    (Cole Porter)

(Broadcast continued on next page)

Pagan Love Song
Moonlight Serenade (Theme)

The Victor album LPT 6701 showed the incorrect
date of May 23rd (but the right location) for
both "Deep Purple" and "Get Out Of Town". The
above date for these two tunes has been verified
by Brad McCuen of R.C.A. Victor.

26 March, 1939 (SUN): Meadowbrook Ballroom, Cedar Grove,
New Jersey
NBC Blue 12:00 Midnight EST.

Moonlight Serenade (Theme)
Pagan Love Song
Don't Worry 'Bout Me
Romance Runs In The Family

E4VP 8205   Vi LPT 6701, Vi EPOT 6701 (947-0190), HMV RLS 598,
                 RCA G EPOT-6701
                 (1:48) We've Come A Long Way Together (arr WS)-
                        voc Ray Eberle
                        (Sam Stept-Ted Koehler)
                        Ts, Beneke

Dipper Mouth Blues
The Moon Is A Silver Dollar

E4VP 8205   Vi LPT 6701, Vi EPOT 6701 (947-0191), HMV RLS 598,
                 RCA G EPOT-6701
                 (2:33) Heaven Can Wait-voc Ray Eberle
                        (Edgar DeLange-Jimmy Van Heusen)

Bugle Call Rag
Sometime
Moonlight Serenade (Theme)

The Victor album LPT 6701 showed the incorrect
date of May 26th (but the right location) for
both "We've Come A Long Way Together" and "Heaven
Can Wait". The above date for these two tunes
has been verified by Brad McCuen of R.C.A.
Victor.

30 March, 1939 (THUR): Meadowbrook Ballroom, Cedar Grove,
New Jersey
NBC Blue 11:30-12:00 Midnight EST.

Moonlight Serenade (Theme)

(Broadcast continued on next page)

                   Little Brown Jug
(2:02) *I Get Along Without You Very Well* (arr HM)-
               voc Ray Eberle
               (Hoagy Carmichael)
(2:12) *Could Be* (arr BF)-voc Marion Hutton
               (Johnny Mercer-Walter Donaldson)
               Tbn, Miller;ts, Beneke
(2:09) *How I'd Like To Be With You In Bermuda*-
               voc Ray Eberle
               (Bickley Reichner-Clay Boland)
               P, MacGregor; tbn, Miller; p, MacGregor;
               ts, Beneke; tbn, Miller;tpt, ??
(3:45) *My Blue Heaven* (arr BF)
               (George Whiting-Walter Donaldson)
               Tbn, Miller; ts, Beneke; d, Sandifer?
(1:12+) *I Want My Share Of Love* (arr BF)-voc
               Marion Hutton
               (Sammy Cahn-Saul Chaplin)
               Clt, ??; tbn, Miller
(1:38) *The Masquerade Is Over*-voc Ray Eberle
               (Herb Magidson-Allie Wrubel)
(2:32) *King Porter Stomp*
               (Ferdinand "Jelly-Roll" Morton)
               Tbn, Miller; ts, Beneke; tpt, ??;
               ts, Klink?
(0:45) *Moonlight Serenade* (Theme)
               (Mitchell Parish-Glenn Miller)

31 March, 1939 (FRI): Meadowbrook Ballroom, Cedar Grove, New Jersey
              NBC-Blue 11:30-12:00 Midnight EST.

              Moonlight Serenade (Theme)
              Blue Skies
              Deep Purple

PPRM-5341   Vi LPM/LSP-2769 (Vi LPM/LSP-6101), RCA RD/SF-7612
            (2:42) *The Moon Is A Silver Dollar*-voc Marion
               Hutton
               (Mitchell Parish-Sammy Fain)
               Clt, Schwartz

              Don't Worry 'Bout Me

PPRM-5333   Vi LPM/LSP-2767 (Vi LPM/LSP-6101), RCA RD/SF-7610
            (4:40) *Song Of The Bayou* (arr BF)
               (Rube Bloom)
               P, MacGregor; tbn, Miller; ts, Beneke;
               p, MacGregor; clt, Schwartz

(Broadcast continued on next page)

E4VP 8206   Vi LPT 6701, Vi EPOT 6701 (947-0192), HMV RLS 598
                  RCA G EPOT-6701,
                  AFRS "America's Pop Music" 72
               (2:35) My Heart Belongs to Daddy-voc Marion Hutton
                        From the musical production "Leave It
                        To Me"
                  (Cole Porter)
                  Tbn, Miller

               Heaven Can Wait
               Runnin' Wild

The Victor album LPT 6701 showed the incorrect date
of May 31st (but the right location) for "My Heart
Belongs to Daddy". The above date for this tune
has been verified by Brad McCuen of R.C.A. Victor.

1 April, 1939 (SAT)

               According to G.M.P.R. Cody Sandifer was paid (with
               the rest of the sidemen) up to April 1st and a
               separate cheque was issued on April 2nd which might
               represent an extra day's employment but G.M.P.R.
               does not make this clear. We do not know who the
               drummer was for April 2nd (this is a Sunday and was
               probably a day off), April 3rd, April 4th (Carlson
               was on the recording date only), and April 5th.
               Purtill joined on the 6th (G.M.P.R.)

4 April, 1939 (TUES): Victor Studios, New York City, New York

               Trombones   Glenn Miller, Al Mastren, Paul Tanner
               Trumpets   Bob Price, Legh Knowles, Dale
                           McMickle
               Reeds   Hal McIntyre, as; Stanley Aronson, as
                           & bar; Wilbur Schwartz, clt & as; Tex
                           Beneke, ts; Al Klink, ts
               Rhythm   Chummy MacGregor, p; ALLAN REUSS, g;
                           Rowland Bundock, b; FRANK CARLSON, d
               Vocalists   Marion Hutton, Ray Eberle, Tex Beneke,
                           Glenn Miller

035699-1   BB 10201-B, MW 7965, Cam Cal/Cas-751, RCA G Cas-
                  751, Pick. Int. CDS 1004
               The Chestnut Tree ('Neath The Spreading Chestnut
                  Tree)-voc Marion Hutton and Band
                  (Jimmy Kennedy-Hamilton Kennedy-Tommie
                  Connor)
                  Ts, Beneke; tpt, McMickle; tbn, Miller

(Session continued on next page)

035700-1   BB 10201-A, MW 7965, Cam Cal/Cas-829, Vi PRM-181,
       AFRS P-8995, RCA G Cas-829, Pick. Int.
       CDS 1004, RCA Cam Arg Cal-3138, RCA Cam
       Fr 900.028
     And The Angels Sing-voc Ray Eberle
       (Johnny Mercer-Ziggy Elman)
       Muted tbn, Miller

035701-1   BB 10214-B, GrF K-8644, HMV BD 5942, RZ MR 3090,
       MW 7967, HMVSw JK-2396, Polyd 10214,
       Vi 20-1566 (Vi P-148), Vi 42-0028, Vi 27-
       0028, Vi 44-0007, ViJ 1020, Vi PR-111,
       Vi 420-0045, Vi 447-0045, VD 39, Navy VD 160,
       El EG-7465, Vi LPT-3036, Vi EPBT 3036
       (947-0091), Vi LPT-3057, Vi EPBT 3057
       (947-0136), Vi EPA-5032, Vi EPA 733, Vi LPT
       6700, Vi EPNT 6700 (947-0016), Vi SPD-18
       (599-9103), HMV DLP 1021, HMV DLP 1024,
       Vi SP 33-90, RCA RD-27068, RCA RCX 1003,
       Vi PRM-181, Vi 45 Special-1953, Vi LPM/LSP-
       1192, HMVAus GA 5010, Vi EPB-1192 (547-0809),
       RCA It EPA 30-159, Vi LPC-101, RCA It LJ
       50012, RCA It LPM 10011, RCA It 45N 0978,
       Vi LPM/LSP-3564, AFRS "America's Pop Music"
       67, RCA G 447-0045, RCA G EPC-1192, RCA G
       LPM/LSP-1192, RCA F 230201, RCA F 530243,
       HMV Ir I.M. 1189, VdP 7E PQ 518, Vi P8S-
       5061, VdP HN 2253, RCA G LPT 6700, AFRS P-
       2463, RD 3/4-64, HMVAus VDLP 302, HMV F
       7MF195, HMV 3-20516, RCA Int. 11008, HMV
       RLS 599, Vi 7" Special 45, El WDLP 1021,
       El WDLP 1024, El 7MW 644, Vi TP3-5044,
       RCA G EPA 5032, RCA G LPM 9801, RCA G LSP-
       9901, HMVHu HUC 131, Vi EPBT-1192, Vi Arg
       LPM 3564, HMV F M33090, HMV F BD 5942,
       RCA G SRS 560, Vi Arg LPM/LSP-1192, Vi VPM-
       6019, Vi Arg 3AE-3286, RCA F 740.515
     Moonlight Serenade (arr GM)
       (Mitchell Parish-Glenn Miller)
       Clt, Schwartz

035702-1   BB 10229-B, MW 7947, RZ MR 3091, Vi LPM-2080,
       RD 3/4-64 (Test albums only) RZ Au G 23821
     The Lady's In Love With You-voc Tex Beneke
       (Dialogue: Glenn Miller and Tex Beneke)
       From the Paramount film "Some Like It Hot"
       (Frank Loesser-Burton Lane)
       Ts, Beneke; d, Carlson

(Session continued on next page)

```
"Moonlight Serenade" 2 takes; all other tunes
1 take.  (RCA Victor)
This session lasted from 1:30 P.M. to 5:00 P.M.
(RCA Victor)
```

Carlson and Reuss were hired for this recording
date only. (G.M.P.R.) Carlson was on loan from
Woody Herman.

Previous titles to Miller's theme, "Moonlight
Serenade", were "Gone With The Dawn" and "Now I
Lay Me Down To Weep". There is no difference
between the Victor 20-1566 issue and the Bluebird
issue.

4 April, 1939 (TUES): Meadowbrook Ballroom, Cedar Grove,
New Jersey
NBC-Blue 11:30-12:00 Midnight EST.

Moonlight Serenade (Theme)

E4VP 8205   Vi LPT 6701, Vi EPOT 6701 (947-0191), HMV RLS 598,
Vi It LPM 10141, Vi It LJ 50020, RCA G
LSP-9901, RCA G EPOT-6701, RCA G SRS 560,
Vi It LPM-50020,
AFRS "America's Pop Music" 67
(3:32) Blue Skies (arr BF)
(Irving Berlin)
Tpt, McMickle; ts, Beneke; clt,
Schwartz; tbn, Miller

Don't Worry 'Bout Me
Romance Runs In The Family

PPRM-5342   Vi LPM/LSP-2769 (Vi LPM/LSP-6101), RCA RD/SF-7612
(3:32) The Masquerade Is Over-voc Ray Eberle
(Herb Magidson-Allie Wrubel)

The Chestnut Tree
Sticks And Stones

PPRM-5342   Vi LPM/LSP-2769 (Vi LPM/LSP-6101), RCA RD/SF-7612
(3:13) Our Love (arr AG)-voc Ray Eberle
Larry Clinton adaptation of a theme
from "Romeo and Juliet" by
Tchaikovsky
(Larry Clinton-Buddy Bernier-Bob
Emmerich)
Muted tbn, Miller

(Broadcast continued on next page)

By The Waters of Minnetonka
Moonlight Serenade (Theme)

6 April, 1939 (THUR)

Trombones	Glenn Miller, Al Mastren, Paul Tanner
Trumpets	Bob Price, Legh Knowles, Dale McMickle
Reeds	Hal McIntyre, as; Stanley Aronson, as & bar; Wilbur Schwartz, clt & as; Tex Beneke, ts; Al Klink, ts
Rhythm	Chummy MacGregor, p; Rowland Bundock, b; MAURICE "MOE" PURTILL, d
Vocalists	Marion Hutton, Ray Eberle
Band-Boy	Warren Jordan

Purtill joined the band on this date. (G.M.P.R.)
His position with the band was to be temporary until
Cliff Leeman (formerly with Shaw) recovered from his
illness. (Met. May 1939) Leeman never did join the
Miller band.

7 April, 1939 (FRI): Meadowbrook Ballroom, Cedar Grove,
New Jersey
NBC-Blue 11:30-12:00 Midnight EST.

Moonlight Serenade (Theme)
(0:36) *Unknown Tune*
(2:27) *Don't Worry 'Bout Me*-voc Ray Eberle
    (Ted Koehler-Rube Bloom)
(2:10) *My Heart Belongs To Daddy*-voc Marion Hutton
    From the musical production "Leave It
    To Me"
    (Cole Porter)
    Tbn, Miller
(2:12) *East Side Of Heaven*-voc Ray Eberle
    From the Universal Film "East Side Of
    Heaven"
    (James V. Monaco-Johnny Burke)
(2:29) *When Paw Was Courtin' Maw*-voc Tex Beneke
    and Glenn Miller
    (Jack Manus-Leonard Joy)
    Ts, Beneke
(3:46) *I Want My Share Of Love*(arr BF)-voc Marion
    Hutton
    (Sammy Cahn-Saul Chaplin)
    Clt, ??; tbn, Miller
(2:49) *Our Love* (arr AG)-voc Ray Eberle
    (Larry Clinton adaptation of a theme
    from"Romeo and Juliet" by Tschaikowsky)
    (Larry Clinton-Buddy Bernier-Bob
    Emmerich)
    Muted tbn, Miller

(Broadcast continued on next page)

(3:16) Pagan Love Song
        From the MGM film "The Pagan"
        (Arthur Freed-Nacio Herb Brown)
        Tbn, Miller;as, ??; muted tpt, ??;
        ts, Beneke;d, Purtill
(0:58) Sometime
        (Glenn Miller-John Chalmers MacGregor)
(0:10) Moonlight Serenade (Theme)
        (Mitchell Parish-Glenn Miller)

10 April, 1939 (MON): Victor Studios, New York City, New York

Trombones   Glenn Miller, Al Mastren, Paul Tanner
Trumpets   Bob Price, Legh Knowles, Dale McMickle
Reeds   Hal McIntyre, as; Stanley Aronson, as & bar; Wilbur Schwartz, clt & as; Tex Beneke, ts; Al Klink, ts
Rhythm   Chummy MacGregor, p; ALLAN REUSS, g; Rowland Bundock, b; Maurice Purtill
Vocalists   Marion Hutton, Ray Eberle, Tex Beneke

035729-1   BB 10219-B, MW 7968, RZ MR 3117, Vi EPA 527, Vi LPM-3181, Vi LPT 6700, Vi EPNT 6700 (947-0128), HMV RLS 599, Vi SPD-18 (599-9107), HMV DLP 1049, RCA Int. CT20122, RCA G LPT 6700
Wishing (Will Make It So)-voc Ray Eberle
From the RKO film "Love Affair"
(Buddy G. DeSylva)
Ts, Beneke

035730-1   BB 10219-A, MW 7968, Vi 20-1572, Cam Cas-2267, RCA G Cas-2267
Three Little Fishies (Itty Bitty Poo)-voc Marion Hutton,
Tex Beneke and Band
(Saxie Dowell)
Ts, Beneke

035731-1   BB 10214-A, HMVAu EA-3318, MW 7967, Polyd 10214, RZ MR 3090, Vi 20-1753, Vi 42-0028, Vi 27-0028, ViJ 1020, Vi 420-0045, Vi 447-0045, Vi EPA-527, Vi LPM-3181, Vi LPT-3036, Vi EPBT 3036 (947-0090), Vi LPT-3067, Vi EPBT 3067 (947-0199), HMV DLP 1062, Vi LM 6074, Vi LPM 2775, Vi EPA-5032, Cam Cal/Cas-829, AFRS P-8995, Cam SPC-33-9, Vi LPM/LSP-3377, RCA RCX 1003, Vi TP3-5044, RD 3/4-64, RCA Int. 11008, Vi P8S-5061, RCA Int. CT 20122, RCA G EPA 5032, RCA G LPM/LSP-3377, RCA G EPBT-3067, Vi LPC-101,

(Session continued on next page)

RCA G 447-0045, RCA F 130210, RCA G Cas-829,
Pick. Int. CDS 1004, RCA Cam Arg Cal-3138,
Vi VPM-6019, RCA G Cas 10231, HMV F M33090,
RCA Cam Fr 900.028, AFRS "America's Pop
Music" 72, RCA G LPT-3067

Sunrise Serenade
(Frankie Carle)
Ts, Beneke

035732-1   BB 10286-A, HMV B10622, HMV 7M195, Vi 20-1566
(Vi P-148), Vi 47-2853 (Vi WP-148), Vi 420-
0031, Vi 447-0031, Vi EPA-148, Vi EPA-5049,
Vi LPM-31, HMV DLP 1024, Vi SP 33-90,
RD 3/4-21, RCA 1096 (78), RCA RCX 1024,
El (Test), Vi PRM-181, HMVIn NE 757, AFRS
P-NAV-2, RDS 6174, AFRS P-1542, Vi 7" 33 1/3,
EL WDLP 1024, El 7MW 117, HMVAus VDLP 302,
RCA 1096(45), AFRS P-8706, HMVIr I.P. 887,
RD 3/4-64 (Production albums only), Vi P8S-
1253, RCA G 447-0031, RCA Int. 20003,
RCA G EPA 148, AFRS "Jukebox USA" 199,
RCA F 85243, AFRS G.I. Jive H-12-1054,
Vi LSP-4125, AFRS H-62-43, HMV 3-20516,
RCA Int. INTS 1002, Vi P8S-1432, Vi VPM-6019,
ViJ S-18

Little Brown Jug (arr BF)
(Traditional)
Ts, Beneke; tpt, McMickle; tbn, Miller

"Three Little Fishies" 2 takes; all other tunes
1 take. (RCA Victor)
This session lasted from 1:30 P.M. to 5:00 P.M.
(RCA Victor)

The label on "Little Brown Jug" erroneously shows
Glenn Miller as the arranger.

Reuss was hired for this recording date only.
(G.M.P.R.)

14 April, 1939 (FRI)

Trombones   Glenn Miller, Al Mastren, Paul Tanner
Trumpets   Bob Price, Legh Knowles, Dale McMickle
Reeds   Hal McIntyre, as; Stanley Aronson, as
             & bar; Wilbur Schwartz, clt & as; Tex
             Beneke, ts; Al Klink, ts

(Continued on next page)

```
Rhythm        Chummy MacGregor, p; ARTHUR ENS, g;
              Rowland Bundock, b; Maurice Purtill, d
Vocalists     Marion Hutton, Ray Eberle
Band-Boy      Warren Jordan
```

G.M.P.R. show that Arthur Ens joined the band on
this date.

18 April, 1939 (TUES): Victor Studios, New York City, New York

Same personnel as for April 14th.

035764-1   BB 10229-A, CoE DS1354, MW 7947, Vi EPA-5094
            My Last Goodbye-voc Ray Eberle
              (Eddy Howard)

035765-1   BB 10269-A, Vi 20-2972, Vi LPM-2080, HMVAu EA 2409
            But It Didn't Mean A Thing-voc Marion Hutton
              (Mack David-Jerry Livingston)

035766-1   BB 10286-B, HMV BD 5805, HMV MH 136, Vi 20-2411
              (Vi P-189), Vi 420-0042, Vi 447-0042, Vi LPT-
              3002, Vi It LJ 50020, Vi EPBT-3002 (947-0039),
              Vi LPM-1190, HMV DLP 1081, RCA RCX 1063,
              Vi It LPM-10141, HMVIn NE 757, RD 3/4-64,
              RCA F 130210, RCA G LPM-1190, Vi It LPM-50020,
              RCA Int. B-21040, RCA G EPC-1190, HMV 3-20516,
              RCA Int. T-21040, AFRS "Jukebox USA" 140
            Pavanne (arr BF)
              (Morton Gould)
              Ts, Beneke; tbn, Miller

035767-1   BB 10269-B, HMV BD 5805, HMV MH 136, Vi 20-2413
              (Vi P-189), Vi 420-0038, Vi 447-0038, Vi 47-
              2877, Vi LPT-3036, Vi EPBT-3036 (947-0091),
              Vi LPT-3067, HMV DLP 1062, Vi EPBT-3067
              (947-0200), Vi PRM-181, AFRS P-1118, Cam Cal/
              Cas-829, RCA Int. 10010, AFRS P-8996, AFRS
              "Jukebox USA" 308, RCA F 130211, HMV 3-20516,
              RCA G Cas-829, RCA G EPBT-3067, RCA G LPT-3067,
              HMVIn NE 771, Pick Int. CDS 1004, RCA Cam Arg
              Cal-3138, RCA Cam Fr 900.028
            Runnin' Wild (arr BF)
              (Joe Grey-Leo Wood-Harrington Gibbs)
              Ts, Beneke; tpt, McMickle; ts, Beneke;
              d, Purtill

          "Runnin' Wild" 2 takes; all other tunes 1 take.
          (RCA Victor)
          This session lasted from 1:30 P.M. to 4:30 P.M.
          (RCA Victor)
```
```

18 April, 1939 (TUES): Meadowbrook Ballroom, Cedar Grove,
New Jersey
Mutual 10:30-11:00 P.M. EST.

Moonlight Serenade (Theme)
The Lady's In Love With You
Wishing
Pavanne
And The Angels Sing
King Porter Stomp
The Moon Is A Silver Dollar

PPRM-5342   Vi LPM/LSP 2769 (Vi LPM/LSP 6101), RCA RD/SF 7612
(3:05) Sometime-voc Ray Eberle
(Glenn Miller-Chummy MacGregor)

Hold Tight
Moonlight Serenade (Theme)

20 April, 1939 (THUR)

Glenn Miller and His Orchestra closed at
Meadowbrook Ballroom, Cedar Grove, New Jersey.
(G.M.P.R.)

21 April, 1939 (FRI)

Glenn Miller and His Orchestra played for one week
(closed Thursday, April 27th) at the Paramount
Theater, Newark, New Jersey. (BB, April 29, 1939;
Variety, April 12, 1939; G.M.P.R.) "Ray Eberle
and Marion Hutton handle their vocal assignments
with finesse. Both were called back for extra
encores. Glenn's trombone playing and his arrangements are not to be slighted. He does a swell job
on the slide horn and his arrangements always draw
applause. His production number Danny Boy was
particularly well received." (Review of Friday
afternoon show April 21st by Bruno M. Kern in BB,
April 29, 1939)

April 21st was Aronson's last day with the band
and on April 22nd Gabriel Gelinas joined the band
from Jan Savitt's band. (G.M.P.R. & Met. May 1939)

22 April, 1939 (SAT)

Trombones   Glenn Miller, Al Mastren, Paul Tanner
Trumpets   Bob Price, Legh Knowles, Dale McMickle

(Continued on next page)

```
Reeds         Hal McIntyre, as; GABRIEL GELINAS,
              as & bar; Wilbur Schwartz, clt & as;
              Tex Beneke, ts; Al Klink, ts
Rhythm        Chummy MacGregor, p; Arthur Ens, g;
              Rowland Bundock, b; Maurice Purtill, d
Vocalists     Marion Hutton, Ray Eberle
Band-Boy      Warren Jordan
```

27 April, 1939 (THUR)

"Glenn Miller and Orchestra playing their first
theater date at the local Paramount theater turned
in a profitable week by pulling $14,200. gross last
week. Ray Eberle and Marion Hutton, Miller's
vocalists met the theater audience for the first
time and impressed." (BB, May 6, 1939)

28 April, 1939 (FRI)

Glenn Miller and His Orchestra played at Holy Cross
College Prom, Worcester, Massachusetts. (G.M.C.)

29 April, 1939 (SAT)

Glenn Miller and His Orchestra played at Cornell
University, Ithaca, New York. (Variety, March 29,
1939; G.M.P.R.)

30 April, 1939 (SUN)

Glenn Miller and His Orchestra played at the Arena,
New Haven, Connecticut. (G.M.C.) "Mal Hallett and
Glenn Miller feature billing at New Haven Arena
April 30 for another big show at this spot with
Andrews Sisters and 8-act Broadway revue." (Met.
May 1939) Note: The Andrews Sisters travelled with
Glenn Miller on college dates this week. (BB,
April 29, 1939)

1 May, 1939 (MON)

Glenn Miller and His Orchestra played at Nuttings
on the Charles, Waltham, Massachusetts. (Boston
Post, May 1, 1939; G.M.P.R.)

2 May, 1939 (TUES)

        Glenn Miller and His Orchestra played at North
        Shore Gardens, Salem, Massachusetts. (Boston
        Post, May 2, 1939; G.M.P.R.)

3 May, 1939 (WED)

        Glenn Miller and His Orchestra played at George
        Clarey's Bayside Pavilion on Mollett's Bay,
        Burlington, Vermont. (Boston Post, April 30,
        1939; G.M.P.R.)

4 May, 1939 (THUR)

        Glenn Miller and His Orchestra played at the
        University of Pennsylvania, Philadelphia,
        Pennsylvania. (G.M.P.R.)

5 & 6 May, 1939 (FRI & SAT)

        Glenn Miller and His Orchestra played at the
        Georgetown University Senior Prom, Wardman Park
        Hotel, Washington, D.C. (evening of May 5th and
        afternoon of May 6th). (G.M.P.R.)

6 May, 1939 (SAT)

        Glenn Miller and His Orchestra played at the John
        Hopkins Junior Prom, Alcazar, Baltimore, Maryland,
        and drew 2,500. (Met. June 1939; G.M.P.R.)

7 May, 1939 (SUN)

        Glenn Miller and His Orchestra played at Lake
        Compounce, Bristol, Connecticut. (G.M.P.R.)

8 May, 1939 (MON)

        Glenn Miller and His Orchestra played at the
        Biltmore Hotel for Providence College, Providence,
        Rhode Island, from 9:00-2:00 A.M. (G.M.C.)

9 May, 1939 (TUES): Victor Studios, New York City, New York

        Same personnel as for April 22nd.

036877-1   BB 10276-B, HMVAu EA-2446, MW 8371, HMV 7EG 8067,
                Vi EPAT-427, Vi LPT-1031, Cam Cal/Cas-829,
                AFRS P-8995, RCA G Cas-829, RCA G LPT-1031,
                AFRS "America's Pop Music" 72, Pick Int.
                CDS 1004, Vi VPM-6019, RCA Cam Fr 900.028
        To You (arr GM)-voc Ray Eberle
                (Tommy Dorsey-Ted Shapiro-Benny Davis)

036878-1   BB 10276-A, MW 8371, RZ MR 3117, Vi 20-3561
                (Vi P-255), HMV DLP 1049, Vi LPM-6702,
                Vi LPM/LSP-3377, Vi PRM-181, AFRS P-1445,
                RD 3/4-64, RCA G LPM/LSP-3377, Vi TP3-5044,
                HMVAu EA 2407, Vi VPM-6019, RCA G Cas 10231,
                Vi VLP 3377
        Stairway To The Stars-voc Ray Eberle
                Melody based on a Theme from "Park Avenue
                Fantasy"
                (Mitchell Parish-Matty Malneck-Frank
                Signorelli)
                Ts, Beneke; tbn, Miller

        "To You" 2 takes; "Stairway To The Stars" 1 take.
        (RCA Victor)
        This session lasted from 9:15 P.M. to 12:15 A.M.

10 May, 1939 (WED)

        Glenn Miller and His Orchestra played at King
        Phillip Ballroom on Lake Pearl, Wrentham,
        Massachusetts. (G.M.P.R.)

11 May, 1939 (THUR)

        Glenn Miller and His Orchestra played at the
        Armory, North Adams, Massachusetts, from 8:30-
        1:00 A.M. (G.M.C.)

        During the band's tour through Massachusetts
        Miller offered Worcester musician Oakie Menard
        a job. (Met. June 1939)

12 May, 1939 (FRI)

        Glenn Miller and His Orchestra played at the
        Garfield Club, Williams College, Williamstown,
        Massachusetts, from 11:30-4:30 A.M. (G.M.C.)

13 May, 1939 (SAT)

        Glenn Miller and His Orchestra played at Old
Orchard Pier, Old Orchard Beach, Maine. (Boston
Post, May 11, 1939; Met. June 1939; G.M.P.R.)

14 May, 1939 (SUN)

        Glenn Miller and His Orchestra returned to New
York City to do a broadcast from the studios of
CBS, 8:00-9:00 P.M. (G.M.P.R.)

Mid-May, 1939

        During this period the band is supposed to have
played at the World's Fair in New York City but
this is unconfirmed.

        Advertisements at this time pointed out that
Miller used a Bach Deluxe Model 6 trombone.
(DB, May 1939)

17 May, 1939 (WED): Glen Island Casino, New Rochelle, New York

        Glenn Miller and His Orchestra opened at the Glen
Island Casino in New Rochelle, New York, broadcasting over both the NBC and MBS Networks. This
was the big break that the band needed to launch
it on its way and Miller delivered his music to a
highly enthusiastic opening night crowd of eighteen
hundred people, which broke all existing day
records for the Casino. (Swing, June 1939;
G.M.P.R.)

        Moonlight Serenade (Theme)

E4VP 8203   Vi LPT 6701, Vi EPOT 6701 (947-0184), HMV RLS 598,
              RCA G EPOT-6701
       (4:19) At Sundown
              (Walter Donaldson)
              Ts, Beneke; tpt, Hurley; ts, Beneke;
              clt, Schwartz

E4VP 8204   Vi LPT 6701, Vi EPOT 6701 (947-0187), HMV RLS 598,
              Vi CR 156, Vi It LPM 10011, Vi It LJ 50012,
              RCA G EPOT-6701, AFRS "America's Pop Music"
              67
       (2:51) And The Angels Sing-voc Ray Eberle
              (Johnny Mercer-Ziggy Elman)
              Tbn, Miller

(Broadcast continued on next page)

ALP

The Chestnut Tree
Sunrise Serenade
King Porter Stomp
I Want My Share Of Love
Stairway To The Stars
Runnin' Wild
Moonlight Serenade (Theme)

"Highlight of Glenn's opening day included
the introduction of his theme song, 'Moonlight
Serenade', as a popular song with original lyrics
by Mitchell Parish, writer of lyrics to 'Deep
Purple' and 'Stardust'. Highly successful also
with the Glen Island dancers was Glenn's novel
medley idea of 'Something Old', 'Something New',
'Something Borrowed', 'Something Blue'. Take-offs
of Tommy Dorsey's 'Marie', Larry Clinton's
'Dipsey Doodle', Blue Barron's theme song and
several others were used in the medley. Another
novel idea of Glenn's used at the Casino is a
series of songs made popular at Glen Island.
Numbered among these are many of the first songs
popularized by Tommy and Jimmy Dorsey, Glen Gray,
Larry Clinton and Ozzie Nelson. . . . Lockwood
Conkling, manager of the Casino, arranged for a
minimum of five early evening broadcasts every
week for Miller's radio programs." (Swing, June
1939)

Clyde Hurley is heard on trumpet during "At Sundown" and according to G.M.P.R. he did not join
the band until May 19th. Since most of the dates
in Vi LPT 6701 are incorrect we can only assume
that this version of "At Sundown" is from a later
date since we have been unable to check this date
with RCA Victor. To support G.M.P.R. we offer
this quote: "Once he got into Glen Island, Miller
sent to the coast for hot trumpet star Clyde
Hurley, whom he'd heard on a Ben Pollack record."
(Met. Dec. 1939)

19 May, 1939 (FRI)

Trombones	Glenn Miller, Al Mastren, Paul Tanner
Trumpets	CLYDE HURLEY, Legh Knowles, Dale McMickle
Reeds	Hal McIntyre, as; Gabriel Gelinas, as & bar; Wilbur Schwartz, clt & as; Tex Beneke, ts; Al Klink, ts

(Continued on next page)

```
                    Rhythm          Chummy MacGregor, p; Arthur Ens, g;
                                    Rowland Bundock, b; Maurice Purtill, d
                    Vocalists       Marion Hutton, Ray Eberle
                    Band-Boy        George Durgom
```

25 May, 1939 (THUR): Victor Studios, New York City, New York

Same personnel as for May 19th.

037152-1   BB 10290-B, MW 8370, Vi 20-2889, Vi 420-0037,
            Vi 447-0037, Vi EPAT-429, Vi LPT-1016,
            Cam Cal/Cas-829, AFRS P-8996, RCA G Cas-829,
            RCA G EPAT-429, RCA G LPT 1016, AFRS P-1118,
            Pick. Int. CDS 1004, Vi DJ-339, RCA Cam Fr
            900.028
            Blue Evening (arr JL)-voc Ray Eberle
            (Gordon Jenkins-Joe Bishop)
            Muted tpt, McMickle; ts, Beneke

037153-1   BB 10290-A, MW 8370, RD 3/4-25, RD Br. RDS 6097
            The Lamp Is Low-voc Ray Eberle
                    Melody based on a Theme from Maurice Ravel's
                    Pavane
                    (Mitchell Parish-Peter DeRose-Bert Shefter)

037154-1   BB 10309-A
            Rendezvous Time In Paree-voc Ray Eberle
                    From the Shubert musical production "Streets
                    of Paris"
                    (Al Dubin-Jimmy McHugh)
                    Ts, Beneke

037155-1   BB 10309-B
            We Can Live On Love (We Haven't Got A Pot To
            Cook In)
                    (arr CD)-voc Marion Hutton
                    From the Shubert musical production "Streets
                    of Paris"
                    (Al Dubin-Jimmy McHugh)
                    Tpt, Hurley; tbn, Miller; ts, Beneke

037156-1   BB 10303-A, MW 8368, Vi Arg 26964
            Cinderella (Stay In My Arms)-voc Ray Eberle
                    (Jimmy Kennedy-Michael Carr)
                    Tbn, Miller

037157-1   BB 10303-B, MW 8368, HMV BD 5854, HMV MH 147,
            Vi EPA-5133, Cam Cal/Cas-751, RCA G Cas-751,
            El G EG 7736, RD 3/4-64, Pick. Int. CDS 1040,
            Vi Arg 26964

(Session continued on next page)

Moon Love-voc Ray Eberle
                Adapted from Tschaikowsky's 5th Symphony,
                2nd Movement
                (Mack David-Mack Davis-Andre Kostelanetz)
                Tbn, Miller; ts, Beneke

"The Lamp Is Low" 1 take; all other tunes 2 takes.
(RCA Victor)
This session lasted from 12:30 P.M. to 4:30 P.M.
(RCA Victor)

29 May, 1939 (MON): Glen Island Casino, New Rochelle, New York
                NBC-Blue 11:30-12:00 Midnight

                Moonlight Serenade (Theme)
                The Lady's In Love With You
                Wishing
                We Can Live On Love

E4VP 8203   Vi LPT 6701, Vi EPOT 6701 (947-0184), HMV RLS 598,
                RCA G EPOT-6701
                (2:43) My Last Goodbye-voc Ray Eberle
                        (Eddy Howard)

                King Porter Stomp
                I Want My Share Of Love
                In The Middle Of A Dream-voc RE
                        (Al Stillman-Elmer Swann-Tommy Dorsey)

E4VP 8203   Vi LPT 6701, Vi EPOT 6701 (947-0185), HMV RLS 598,
                Vi SPA-7-4, RCA G EPOT-6701
                (3:33) Hallelujah! (arr BF)
                        From the musical production "Hit The
                        Deck"
                        (Leo Robin-Clifford Grey-Vincent
                        Youmans)
                        Ts, Beneke; clt, Schwartz; tbn, Miller;
                        tpt, Hurley; tbn, Miller; d, Purtill

                (2:27) Stairway To The Stars-voc Ray Eberle
                        Melody based on a Theme from "Park
                        Avenue Fantasy"
                        (Mitchell Parish-Matty Malneck-Frank
                        Signorelli)
                        Muted tbn, Miller; ts, Beneke; muted
                        tbn, Miller
                (1:20) Moonlight Serenade (Theme)
                        (Mitchell Parish-Glenn Miller)

2 June, 1939 (FRI): Victor Studios, New York City, New York

Trombones	Glenn Miller, Al Mastren, Paul Tanner
Trumpets	Clyde Hurley, Legh Knowles, Dale McMickle
Reeds	Hal McIntyre, as; Gabriel Gelinas, as & bar; Wilbur Schwartz, clt & as; Tex Beneke, ts; Al Klink, ts
Rhythm	Chummy MacGregor, p; RICHARD FISHER, g; Rowland Bundock, b; Maurice Purtill, d
Vocalists	Marion Hutton, Tex Beneke, Glenn Miller

037179-1　　BB 10317-A, Vi LPM 2080
Guess I'll Go Back Home (This Summer) (arr BCh)-
　　　voc-Tex Beneke
　　　　(Willard Robison-Ray Mayer)
　　　　Ts, Beneke

037180-1　　BB 10299-A, MW 8369, RZ MR 3130, Vi LPM 6702
I'm Sorry For Myself (arr CD)-voc Marion Hutton and
　　　　Tex Beneke (Dialogue: Glenn Miller and Tex
　　　　Beneke)
　　　　From the 20th Century-Fox film "Second Fiddle"
　　　　(Irving Berlin)
　　　　Ts, Beneke; tpt, Hurley

037181-1　　BB 10299-B, MW 8369
Back To Back (arr EE)-voc Marion Hutton
　　　　From the 20th Century-Fox film "Second Fiddle"
　　　　(Irving Berlin)
　　　　Ts, Beneke; tpt, Hurley; ts, Beneke; tpt,
　　　　Hurley

037182-1　　BB 10317-B, HMV BD 5829, HMV 7EG 8204, Vi LPT 6700,
　　　　Vi EPNT 6700 (947-0118), Vi SPD-18 (599-9112),
　　　　HMV RLS 599, RCA G LPT 6700, HMVAus GA 5028,
　　　　VdP HN 2494, VdP 7E PQ 542, Vi LSP-4125,
　　　　HMVHu HUC 114, RCA Int. INTS 1002, Vi P8S-1432
Slip Horn Jive (arr ED)
　　　　(Eddie Durham)
　　　　Ts, Beneke; tpt, Hurley; tbn, Miller; ts,
　　　　Beneke; tpt, Hurley

　　　　"Slip Horn Jive" 2 takes; all other tunes 1 take.
　　　　(RCA Victor)
　　　　This session lasted from 1:30 P.M. to 4:30 P.M.
　　　　(RCA Victor)

2 June, 1939 (FRI): Glen Island Casino, New Rochelle, New York

> *In The Middle Of A Dream*
> *Stairway To The Stars*

9 June, 1939 (FRI)

Trombones	Glenn Miller, Al Mastren, Paul Tanner	
Trumpets	Clyde Hurley, Legh Knowles, Dale McMickle	
Reeds	Hal McIntyre, as; HAROLD A. TENNYSON, as & bar & clt; Wilbur Schwartz, clt & as; Tex Beneke, ts, Al Klink, ts	
Rhythm	Chummy MacGregor, p; Richard Fisher, g; Rowland Bundock, b; Maurice Purtill, d	
Vocalists	Marion Hutton, Ray Eberle	
Band-Boy	George Durgom	

13 June, 1939 (TUES): Glen Island Casino, New Rochelle, New York

> *Moonlight Serenade* (Theme)
> *At Sundown*
> *Cinderella*

PPRM-5338

> Vi LPM/LSP-2768 (Vi LPM/LSP-6101), RCA RD/SF-7611
> (2:41) Back To Back (arr EE)-voc Marion Hutton
> From the 20th Century-Fox film "Second
> Fiddle"
> (Irving Berlin)
> Ts, Beneke; tpt, Hurley; ts, Beneke;
> tpt, Hurley

> *To You*
> *Slip Horn Jive*

E4VP 8203

> Vi LPT 6701, Vi EPOT 6701 (947-0186), HMV RLS 598,
> RCA G EPOT-6701
> (5:00) The Hour Of Parting (arr BF)
> (Michael Spoliansky-Gus Kahn)
> Ts, Beneke; tbn, Miller; clt, Tennyson;
> tpt, Hurley; ts, Beneke

> *Moon Love*
> *Pagan Love Song*
> *Moonlight Serenade* (Theme)

17 June, 1939 (SAT)

> G.M.P.R. show that Clyde Hurley did not play with
> the band on June 17th and June 18th due to illness.
> There is no mention of a substitute.

18 June, 1939 (SUN)

G.M.P.R. show that Legh Knowles did not play with the band from June 18th to (and including) June 25th. His replacement was John McGhee.

Trombones	Glenn Miller, Al Mastren, Paul Tanner
Trumpets	????????????, JOHN MCGHEE, Dale McMickle
Reeds	Hal McIntyre, as; Harold Tennyson, as & bar & clt; Wilbur Schwartz, clt & as; Tex Beneke, ts; Al Klink, ts
Rhythm	Chummy MacGregor, p; Richard Fisher, g; Rowland Bundock, b; Maurice Purtill, d
Vocalists	Marion Hutton, Ray Eberle
Band-Boy	George Durgom

19 June, 1939 (MON)

Trombones	Glenn Miller, Al Mastren, Paul Tanner
Trumpets	CLYDE HURLEY, John McGhee, Dale McMickle
Reeds	Hal McIntyre, as; Harold Tennyson, as & bar & clt; Wilbur Schwartz, clt & as; Tex Beneke, ts; Al Klink, ts
Rhythm	Chummy MacGregor, p; Richard Fisher, g; Rowland Bundock, b; Maurice Purtill, d
Vocalists	Marion Hutton, Ray Eberle
Band-Boy	George Durgom

G.M.P.R. on this date show that Eddie Durham was paid for arranging "Concert In The Park", "St. Louis Blues", and "I Want To Be Happy".

19 June, 1939 (MON): Glen Island Casino, New Rochelle, New York

Moonlight Serenade (Theme)
The Lady's In Love With You
Rendezvous Time In Paree
I'm Sorry For Myself
Cinderella
Moonlight Serenade (Theme)

19 June, 1939 (MON): Glen Island Casino, New Rochelle, New York

Moonlight Serenade (Theme)
King Porter Stomp
To You
Back To Back

(Broadcast continued on next page)

A New Moon And An Old Serenade-voc Ray
        Eberle
        (Block-Silver-Coslow)
Moonlight Serenade-voc Ray Eberle
One O'Clock Jump
Guess I'll Go Back Home
Wishing
By The Waters Of Minnetonka
Moonlight Serenade (Theme)

It is rather surprising to see "Moonlight Serenade"
with a vocal. Since this tune was always treated
as an instrumental and since Eberle sang on the
previous tune we suspect that this might be the
theme (instrumental only) to mark the halfway point
in the program along with station identification.
Outside of the fact that we have not heard this
broadcast the only indication (outside of our
listing) that this might be a vocal version is the
following: "Highlight of Glenn's opening day included the introduction of his theme song, 'Moonlight
Serenade', as a popular song with original lyrics
by Mitchell Parish..." (Swing, June 1939) This
article referred to the band's May 17th opening at
the Glen Island Casino.

20 June, 1939 (TUES): Glen Island Casino, New Rochelle, New York

        Moonlight Serenade (Theme)
        Farewell Blues
        Moon Love

E4VP 8204   Vi LPT 6701, Vi ~~EPOT 6701~~ (947-0189), HMV RLS 598,
               RCA F EPOT-6701
               (2:22) ~~We Can Live On Love~~ (We Haven't Got A Pot
                      ~~To Cook In)~~
                      (arr CD)-voc Marion Hutton
                      From the Shubert musical production
                      "Streets of Paris"
                      (Al Dubin-Jimmy McHugh)
                      Tpt, Hurley; tbn, Miller; ts, Beneke

        Hold Tight

22 June, 1939 (WED): Victor Studios, New York City, New York

        Same personnel as for June 19th.

037675-1   BB 10329-A, MW 8367, Vi EPA-5133, Vi LPM 6702,
                   RD 3/4-64
  CGM   Oh, You Crazy Moon-voc Ray Eberle
               (Johnny Burke-Jimmy Van Heusen)
               Ts, Beneke; tbn, Miller

037676-1   BB 10329-B, MW 8367
  CGM   Ain't Cha Comin' Out?-voc Marion Hutton and Tex
               Beneke
               (Bert Kalmar-Harry Ruby)
               Ts, Beneke

               Both tunes 1 take. (RCA Victor)
               This session lasted from 12:15 P.M. to 2:15 P.M.
               (RCA Victor)

26 June, 1939 (SUN)

          Trombones   Glenn Miller, Al Mastren, Paul Tanner
          Trumpets   Clyde Hurley, LEGH KNOWLES, Dale
                       McMickle
          Reeds   Hal McIntyre, as; Harold Tennyson, as
                       & bar & clt; Wilbur Schwartz, clt & as;
                       Tex Beneke, ts; Al Klink, ts
          Rhythm   Chummy MacGregor, p; Richard Fisher, g;
                       Rowland Bundock, b; Maurice Purtill, d
          Vocalists   Marion Hutton, Ray Eberle
          Band-Boy   George Durgom

          G.M.P.R. on this date show that Eddie Durham was
          paid for arranging "Royal Garden Blues", "Shout",
          and "Moten Swing".

          During the week of June 23rd to June 29th Tommy
          Mack joined the band as road manager. (G.M.P.R.)

27 June, 1939 (MON): Victor Studios, New York City, New York

        Same personnel as for June 26th.

037699-1   BB 10344-B, RZ MR 3129
  CGM   The Day We Meet Again-voc Ray Eberle
               (Campbell-Hunter-Grosz)
               Ts, Beneke

(Session continued on next page)

```
038200-1        BB 10344-A
    CGM         Wanna Hat With Cherries-voc Marion Hutton
                        (Larry Clinton-Joe Carringer-Betty Lynn)

038201-1        BB 10352-A, GrF K-8644, HMV BD 5854, HMV MH 147,
                        MW 8366, Vi LPM 2080, El G EG 7736
    CGM         Sold American (arr GM)-Chant by the Orchestra
                        (Glenn Miller-Chummy MacGregor)
                        Tbn, Miller; ts, Beneke; tpt, Hurley

038202-1        BB 10352-B, HMV BD 5839, HMVSp GY-620, MW 8366,
                        ViJ 1165, Cam Cal/Cas-829, RCA G Cas-829,
                        AFRS P-8995, Pick Int. CDS 1004, RCA Cam
                        Arg Cal-3138, RCA Cam Fr 900.028
    CGM         Pagan Love Song
                        From the MGM film "The Pagan"
                        (Arthur Freed-Nacio Herb Brown)
                        Tbn, Miller; ts, Klink; muted tpt, Hurley;
                        ts, Beneke; d, Purtill
```

"The Day We Meet Again" and "Sold American"
1 take; "Wanna Hat With Cherries" and "Pagan Love
Song" 3 takes each. (RCA Victor)
This session lasted from 1:30 P.M. to 4:00 P.M.
(RCA Victor)

30 June, 1939 (FRI): Glen Island Casino, New Rochelle, New York

Moonlight Serenade (Theme)

```
PPRM-5342       Vi LPM/LSP-2769 (Vi LPM/LSP-6101), RCA RD/SF-7612
                (3:15) Beer Barrel Polka
                        (Lew Brown-Wladimir A. Timm-Jaromir
                        Vejvoda)
                        Ts, Beneke; tbn, Miller

                        Cinderella
                        Back To Back
                        Pagan Love Song
                        Moonlight Serenade (Theme)
                        Moonlight Serenade (Theme)
                        Dipper Mouth Blues
                        Moon Love
                        Guess I'll Go Back Home

E4VP 8203       Vi LPT 6701, Vi EPOT 6701 (947-0185), Vi SPA-7-4,
                        HMV RLS 598, RCA G EPOT-6701
                (2:55) I'm Sorry For Myself (arr CD)-voc Marion
                        Hutton and Tex Beneke (Dialogue:Glenn
                        Miller and Tex Beneke)
```

(Broadcast continued on next page)

From the 20th Century-Fox film "Second
Fiddle"
(Irving Berlin)
Ts, Beneke; tpt, Hurley

Moonlight Serenade (Theme)

6 July, 1939 (THUR)

G.M.P.R. for the week ending July 6th show that
Eddie Durham was paid for arranging "White Star",
"Well, All Right", and "Weary Blues".

10 July, 1939 (MON): NBC Studios, New York City, New York
Magic Key of Radio Program

The announcer for this program is Roy Miller

(2:32) *Ain't Cha Comin' Out?-voc Marion Hutton and*
Tex Beneke
(Bert Kalmar-Harry Ruby)
Ts, Beneke

(1:49) *Moon Love-voc Ray Eberle*
Adapted from Tschaikowsky's 5th
Symphony, 2nd Movement
(Mack David-Mack Davis-Andre
Kostelanetz)

(3:24) *Moonlight Serenade (arr GM)*
(Mitchell Parish-Glenn Miller)
Clt, Schwartz

(2:36) *Runnin' Wild (arr BF)*
(Joe Grey-Leo Wood-Harrington Gibbs)
Ts, Beneke; tpt, McMickle; ts, Beneke;
d, Purtill

The band travelled by Greyhound Bus Line from the
Glen Island Casino to NBC Studios in New York City
and then returned to the Glen Island Casino.
Miller had to pay for the services of a stand-by
Orchestra from 7:30 P.M. to 11:00 P.M. (G.M.P.R.)

12 July, 1939 (WED): Victor Studios, New York City, New York

      Same personnel as for June 26th.

038261-1   BB 10366-B, HMV BD 5546, HMVSp GY-455, MW 8364,
              HMVIn BD 5546
CGM   Ding-Dong! The Witch Is Dead-voc Marion Hutton
              From the MGM film "The Wizard of Oz"
              (E.Y. Harburg-Harold Arlen)
              Ts, Beneke

038262-1   BB 10366-A, HMV BD 5546, HMVSp GY-455, MW 8364,
              Vi PR-114, HMV 7EG 8135, Vi LPM 2080,
CGM   HMVIn BD 5546, RCA G EPA-9019, HMVSc X7607
     Over The Rainbow-voc Ray Eberle
              From the MGM film "The Wizard of Oz"
              (E.Y. Harburg-Harold Arlen)

038263-1   BB 10358-B, MW 8365, HMV 7EG 8097
CGM   The Little Man Who Wasn't There-voc Tex Beneke
              (Dialogue: Glenn Miller and Tex Beneke)
              (Harold Adamson-Bernard Hanighen)
              Ts, Beneke

038264-1   BB 10358-A, MW 8365, RZ MR 3129, Cam Cas-2267,
              RCA G Cas-2267
CGM   The Man With The Mandolin-voc Marion Hutton
              (James Cavanaugh-John Redmond-Frank Weldon)
              P, MacGregor; Mandolin, Fisher; ts, Beneke

      "Ding-Dong! The Witch Is Dead" and "The Little
      Man Who Wasn't There" 2 takes each; "Over The
      Rainbow" and "The Man With The Mandolin" 1 take
      each. (RCA Victor)
      This session lasted from 1:30 P.M. to 4:30 P.M.
      (RCA Victor)

13 July, 1939 (THUR)

      G.M.P.R. for the week ending July 13th show that
      Eddie Durham was paid for arranging "Careless
      Love" and an untitled tune.

14 July, 1939 (FRI): Glen Island Casino, New Rochelle, New York

      Moonlight Serenade (Theme)
      Beer Barrel Polka
      The Lamp Is Low
      The Jumpin' Jive

(Broadcast continued on next page)

PPRM-5341   Vi LPM/LSP 2769 (Vi LPM/LSP 6101), RCA RD/SF 7612
                 (3:58) Hold Tight-voc Marion Hutton and the Band
                       (Kent Brandow-Robinson Ware Spotswood)
                       Ts, Beneke; ts, Klink; tbn, Miller;
                       ts, Beneke; d, Purtill; tpt, ??

                 Moonlight Serenade (Theme)

14 July, 1939 (FRI): Glen Island Casino, New Rochelle, New York

                 Moonlight Serenade (Theme)
                 I Want To Be Happy
                 My Last Goodbye
                 The Little Man Who Wasn't There
                 Dipper Mouth Blues
                 Moonlight Serenade (Theme)

16 July, 1939 (SUN)

                 Glenn Miller and Benny Carter attended a benefit
                 concert by Jimmy Dorsey and his Orchestra at the
                 outdoor gardens of Frank Dailey's Meadowbrook,
                 Cedar Grove, New Jersey. More than 2,000 people
                 attended. The benefit was for Charley Levine, a
                 Meadowbrook waiter who was hospitalized as a
                 result of being struck by a Jersey "safety patrol"
                 car as he crossed the road in front of the Meadow-
                 brook. (Met. August 1939)

20 July, 1939 (THUR): Glen Island Casino, New Rochelle, New York

                 Moonlight Serenade (Theme)
                 The Lady's In Love With You
                 Rendezvous Time In Paree

E4VP 8203   Vi LPT 6701, Vi EPOT 6701 (947-0186), HMV RLS 598,
                       RCA G EPOT-6701
                 (2:28) The Jumpin' Jive-voc Marion Hutton
                       (Cab Calloway-Frank Froeba-Jack Palmer)
                       Tpt, Hurley; ts, Beneke

                 Farewell Blues
                 Moonlight Serenade (Theme)

20 July, 1939 (THUR)

                 G.M.P.R. for the week ending July 20th show that
                 Eddie Durham was paid for arranging "Baby Me" and
                 an untitled tune.

22 July, 1939 (SAT)

        Marion Hutton collapsed on the bandstand at Glen
        Island Casino. Doctors blamed nervous indigestion
        and exhaustion. Marion Hutton underwent a minor
        sinus operation before returning August 1st.
        (Met. August 1939)

        Kay Starr (16-years-old) was flown in from Memphis,
        Tennessee, to replace Marion Hutton for this period.
        This was Kay Starr's "first break". She took over
        on the bandstand at the Glen Island Casino and also
        did a record session with the Miller orchestra.

24 July, 1939 (MON): Glen Island Casino, New Rochelle, New York
*   NBC   WJZ   5:00 - 5:30 P.M.*

*   (1:24) Moonlight Serenade (Theme)*
*   (Mitchell Parish-Glenn Miller)*
*   (3:06) I Want To Be Happy (arr ED)*
*   From the musical production "No, No,*
*   Nanette"*
*   (Irving Caesar-Vincent Youmans)*
*   Tpt, Hurley; ts, Beneke; tbn, Miller;*
*   d, Purtill*
*   (3:33) Oh, You Crazy Moon-voc Ray Eberle*
*   (Johnny Burke-Jimmy Van Heusen)*
*   Ts, Beneke; tbn, Miller*
*   (2:39) Baby Me (arr ED)-voc Kay Starr*
*   (Lou Handman-Harry Harris-Archie*
*   Gottler)*
*   Tpt, Hurley; ts, Beneke*
*   (3:03) My Isle Of Golden Dreams (arr BF)*
*   (Gus Kahn-Walter Blaufuss)*
*   Ts, Beneke*

26 July, 1939 (WED): Victor Studios, New York City, New York

        Same personnel as for June 26th except that KAY
        STARR, vocalist, replaces Marion Hutton.

038138-1   BB 10553-B, HMV BD 5929, HMV MH 145, Vi 20-3562
             (Vi P-255), El G EG 7788, AFRS P-1445,
             HMVIn NE. 771, AFRS "America's Pop Music"
             72
CGM   Starlit Hour (arr GM)-voc Ray Eberle
             From "Earl Carroll Vanities"
             (Mitchell Parish-Peter DeRose)

(Session continued on next page)

038139-1 BB 10372-A, HMV MH 104, MW 8363, AFRS "America's
       Pop Music" 72
 C G M Blue Orchids-voc Ray Eberle
       (Hoagy Carmichael)
       Ts, Beneke

038140-1 BB 10388-B, HMV BD 5839, HMVSp GY-620, HMVSw
       JK-2232, MW 8361, HMV 7EG 8204, Vi LPT 6700,
       Vi EPNT 6700 (947-0125), Vi SPD-18 (599-9112),
       HMV RLS 599, Vi LPM/LSP-3564, RCA It EPA
       30-078, Vi TP3-5044, RD 3/4-64, RCA G LPT 6700,
       AFRS P-9980, Vi Arg LPM-3564
 C G M Glen Island Special (arr ED)
       (Eddie Durham)
       Tpt, Hurley; ts, Beneke; ts, Klink

038141-1 BB 10383-B, HMVSp GY-584, MW 8362, Vi EPNT 6700
       (947-0129), Vi LPT 6700, Vi SPD-18 (599-9103),
       HMV RLS 599, RCA G LPT 6700
 C G M Love With A Capital "You"-voc Kay Starr
       From the Paramount film "$1000 A Touchdown"
       (Leo Robin-Ralph Rainger)
       Ts, Beneke; tpt, Hurley

038142-1 BB 10372-B, MW 8363, Vi EPNT 6700 (947-0128),
       Vi LPT 6700, Vi SPD-18 (599-9108), HMV RLS 599,
       Vi 45 Special-1953, RCA G LPT 6700, RD 3/4-64
 C G M Baby Me (arr ED)-voc Kay Starr
       (Lou Handman-Harry Harris-Archie Gottler)
       Tpt, Hurley; ts, Beneke

038143-? BB Unissued
       My Isle Of Golden Dreams (arr BF)
       (Gus Kahn-Walter Blaufuss)
       Ts, Beneke

       "Starlit Hour" 2 takes; all other tunes 1 take.
       (RCA Victor)
       This session lasted from 12:00 Noon to 4:00 P.M.
       (RCA Victor)

       According to Brad McCuen of RCA Victor "My Isle
       Of Golden Dreams" was not issued from this session
       although it is shown on the RCA recording sheets
       for this date. It is not clear whether a take was
       made.

26 July, 1939 (WED): Glen Island Casino, New Rochelle, New York

E4VP 8204   Vi LPT 6701, Vi EPOT 6701 (947-0188), HMV RLS 598,
                  RCA G EPOT-6701
                  (2:48) Blue Orchids-voc Ray Eberle
                          (Hoagy Carmichael)
                  Ts, Beneke

                  Since most of the dates in Vi LPT 6701 are in-
                  correct it is quite possible that this date is in-
                  correct and, if so, we suspect that this tune might
                  be from the July 28th broadcast, but have been
                  unable to verify with RCA Victor.

28 July, 1939 (FRI): Glen Island Casino, New Rochelle, New York

                  Moonlight Serenade (Theme)
                  Little Brown Jug
                  Moon Love

E4VP 8204   Vi LPT 6701, Vi EPOT 6701 (947-0188), HMV RLS 598,
                  RCA G EPOT 6701
                  (3:14) Sunrise Serenade
                        (Frankie Carle)
                  Ts, Beneke

                  Dipper Mouth Blues
                  Moonlight Serenade (Theme)

28 July, 1939 (FRI): Glen Island Casino, New Rochelle, New York

                  In The Mood
                  Blue Orchids
                  By The Waters Of Minnetonka
                  Moonlight Serenade (Theme)

1 August, 1939 (TUES): Victor Studies, New York City, New York

                  Same personnel as for June 26th and MARION HUTTON,
                  vocalist replaces Kay Starr.

038170-1   BB 10416-A, Vi 82943-A, GrF K-8487, HMV BD 5565,
                  MW 8358, Vi Arg 3AE-3286, Vi Arg LPM/LSP-
                  1192, HMVAu EA-2685, HMVSw JK-2047, Vi 20-
                  1565 (Vi P-148), Vi 47-2853 (Vi WP-148),
                  Vi 20-1753, Vi 20-4086, Vi 47-4086, Vi 420-
                  0043, Vi 447-0043, ViJ 1044, VD 123, Vi EPA-
                  148, Vi EPA-528, Vi EPA-5032, Vi EPA-733,

(Session continued on next page)

Vi LPM 31, Vi LPT 3057, Vi EPBT-3057
(947-0136), Vi LOC-1011, Vi EOD-1011
(519-0010), Vi LPC 101, USA RS HO7H-1760,
RCA RCX 1003, HMV DLP 1024, El WDLP 1024,
Vi LPM/LSP-1192, Vi EPB-1192 (547-0810),
Vi SP 33-90, RCA RD 27068, Vi LPM 2774,
Vi LM 6088, Vi PR-112, Vi LPM 3182, Vi LPM/
LSP-3377, Vi It LPM 10043, RD 3/4-21, RD R/
SYM, RCA It LPM 10011, El G EG 7485, RCA It
EPA 30-152, RCA It 45N 0899, AFRS P-NAV-2,
AFRS Swingtime 53, AFRS H-62-1 Phonograph
Album No. 1, RD Br. RDS 6172, Vi It LJ
50015, Vi It LJ 50012, RD 3/44-1, VdP 7E
PQ 518, HMV 3-20516, VdP AV-707, HMVIr I.M.
1019, RCA G LPM 1071, El 7MW 642, HMVAus
VDLP-302, Vi LPM 1071, Vi EPB 1071, Vi EPBT-
1192, AFRS H-12-1000 G.I. Jive, AFRS P-1542,
AFRS P-S-15, Vi VLP 3377, HMVAus GA 5020,
RCA G LPM/LSP-1192, HMV F 7MF195, RCA Int.
10004, RCA Int. 20003, RCA G EPA 148, RCA G
EPA 5032, RCA G LPM 9801, AFRS "Jukebox USA"
180, AFRS "Jukebox USA" 263, AFRS "America's
Pop Music" 67, GrF K-8480, RCA G EPC-1192,
Vi P8S-5061, RCA G LPM/LSP-3377, Vi TP3-
5044, RCA G 447-0043, RCA F 85243, RCA F
230201, RCA F 530243, HMVSc X7106, RCA Int.
CT20124, Navy VD 132, HMVHu HUC 115, Vi VPM-
6019, RCA G Cas 10231, RCA G SRS 560

CGM   In The Mood
(Andy Razaf-Joe Garland)
Ts, Beneke; ts, Klink; tpt, Hurley

038171-1   BB 10399-B, HMVSw JK-2309, MW 8360, HMV MH 181, HMV
7EG 8097, Vi LPM 2080, HMVSc X.6538
CGM   Wham (Re-Bop-Boom-Bam) (arr ED)-voc Marion Hutton
and Band
(Eddie Durham-"Taps" Miller)
Ts, Beneke; tbn, Miller; ts, Beneke;
tpt, Hurley

038172-1   BB 10383-A, MW 8362, HMVAu EA 2478
CGM   An Angel In A Furnished Room-voc Ray Eberle
(Al Dubin-Ted Fiorito)
Ts, Beneke

038173-1   BB10388-A, HMV MH 158, HMVSw JK-2232, MW 8361,
El G (Test)
CGM   Twilight Interlude-voc Ray Eberle
(Peter Tinturin-Al Jacobs)
Muted tbn, Miller; ts, Beneke

(Session continued on next page)

038174-1   BB 10416-B, HMV BD 5585, Vi 82943-B, MW 8358,
                ViJ A-1044, RD 3/4-64 (Test albums only),
                HMVAu EA 2511
 CGM   I Want To Be Happy (arr ED)
                From the musical production "No, No, Nanette"
                (Irving Caesar-Vincent Youmans)
                Tpt, Hurley; ts, Beneke; tbn, Miller; d, Purtill

038175-1   BB 10495-B, HMV BD 5602, HMV MH 149, HMVSw JK-2326,
                Vi EPA-5094, HMVIn BD 5602, RD 3/4-64 (Test
                albums only)
 CGM   Farewell Blues
                (Elmer Schoebel-Paul Mares-Joseph Leon Rappolo)
                Ts, Beneke; tpt, Hurley; tbn, Miller; tpt, ??

           All tunes 1 take. (RCA Victor)
           This session lasted from 1:30 P.M. to 4:30 P.M.
           (RCA Victor)

           We have no definite arranger credits for "In The
           Mood" but the musical score published by Shapiro,
           Bernstein & Co. indicates that the tune was
           "arranged by Joe Garland as suggested by Glenn
           Miller". In a recent radio interview on station
           WHO, Des Moines, Iowa, Chummy MacGregor, reading
           from his forthcoming book "Moonlight Serenade Re-
           visited", stated that the band bought an arrange-
           ment of "In The Mood" from Eddie Durham for five
           dollars. All they used of the original arrangement
           were the two front saxophone strains and another
           part that occurred later on in the arrangement.
           MacGregor mentioned that additional solos were
           added to the original arrangement and he wrote the
           finishing coda. Miller probably edited some of
           the arrangement along with MacGregor (and others?).

1 August, 1939 (TUES): Glen Island Casino, New Rochelle, New York

                Moonlight Serenade (Theme)
                The Lady's In Love With You

E4VP 8204 Vi LPT 6701, Vi EPOT 6701 (947-0187), HMV RLS 598,
                RCA G EPOT-6701
           (2:59)Twilight Interlude-voc Ray Eberle
                (Peter Tinturin-Al Jacobs)
                Muted tbn, Miller; ts, Beneke

                We Can Live On Love
                I Want To Be Happy
                Moonlight Serenade (Theme)

3 August, 1939 (THUR)

      Glenn Miller auditioned clarinetist Jerry Yelverton
      (who was playing in the Barry Wood band) after work
      at the Glen Island Casino. One of the tunes played
      was _Star Dust_. Larry Binyon (NBC saxman) also sat
      in. Glenn Miller's mother was at the Casino this
      night. (Met. Sept. 1939)

4 August, 1939 (FRI): Glen Island Casino, New Rochelle, New York

      Moonlight Serenade (Theme)
      Slip Horn Jive

PPRM-5334   Vi LPM/LSP 2767 (Vi LPM/LSP 6101), RCA RD/SF 7610
      (2:26) The Lamp Is Low-voc Ray Eberle
                Melody based on a Theme from Maurice
                Ravel's Pavane
                (Mitchell Parish-Peter DeRose-Bert
                Shefter)

      My Isle Of Golden Dreams
      King Porter Stomp
      Moonlight Serenade (Theme)

11 August, 1939 (FRI)

Trombones	Glenn Miller, Al Mastren, Paul Tanner
Trumpets	Clyde Hurley, Legh Knowles, Dale McMickle
Reeds	Hal McIntyre, as; GERALD YELVERTON, as & bar & clt; Wilbur Schwartz, clt & as; Tex Beneke, ts; Al Klink, ts
Rhythm	Chummy MacGregor, p; Richard Fisher, g; Rowland Bundock, b; Maurice Purtill, d
Vocalists	Marion Hutton, Ray Eberle

15 August, 1939 (TUES): Glen Island Casino, New Rochelle, New York

      Moonlight Serenade (Theme)
      Ain't Cha Comin' Out?
      The Lamp Is Low
      My Isle Of Golden Dreams

E4VP 8204   Vi LPT 6701, Vi EPOT 6701 (947-0189), HMV RLS 598,
            Vi SPA-7-4, RCA G EPOT-6701, Vi PRM-181
      (3:26) Pagan Love Song
                From the MGM film "The Pagan"
                (Arthur Freed-Nacio Herb Brown)
                Tbn, Miller; ts, Al Klink; muted tpt,
                Hurley; ts, Beneke; d, Purtill

      Moonlight Serenade (Theme)

17 August, 1939 (THURS)

> G.M.P.R. for the week ending August 17th show that
> Art Gunther was paid for arranging "A Man And His
> Dream".

18 August, 1939 (FRI) Victor Studios, New York City, New York

> Same personnel as for August 11th.

041586-1   BB 10486-B, HMV BD 5697, HMV MH 144, Vi LPM 6702,
                RD 3/4-64, Vi LPM/LSP-3564, Vi TP3-5044,
                Vi P8S-5061, Vi Arg LPM-3564
      CGM   Who's Sorry Now?-voc Ray Eberle
                (Bert Kalmar-Harry Ruby-Ted Snyder)
                Ts, Beneke

038143-1   BB 10399-A, HMV BD 5842, HMVSw JK-2309, MW 8360,
                Vi 20-2412 (Vi P-189), Vi 420-0032,
                Vi 447-0032, Vi LPT-3002, Vi EPBT-3002 (947-0038),
                RCA RCX 1062, HMV DLP 1081, Vi LPM 1190, Vi EPB-
                1190 (547-0828), HMVSc X.6538, RCA Int.B-21040,
                RCA Int. T-21040, RCA G EPC-1190, RCA G LPM-1190
      CGM   My Isle Of Golden Dreams (arr BF)
                (Gus Kahn-Walter Blaufuss)
                Ts, Beneke

041587-1   BB 10404-B, HMV BD 5850, HMV MH 142, HMVSw JK-2354,
                MW 8359, ViJ 1158, Vi LPM 2080, Vi VPM-6019
      CGM   My Prayer-voc Ray Eberle
                (Jimmy Kennedy-George Boulanger)
                Tbn, Miller

041588-1   BB 10404-A, HMV BD 5822, HMV MH 139, HMVSw JK-2422,
                ViJ 1165, ViJ 1158, Vi LPM/LSP-3657, RCA RD/SF-
                7842, MW 8359, RCA G LPM/LSP-3657, El G EG
                7720, HMVAus GA 5102, HMVAu EA 3539,
                RCA F 440.727
      CGM   Blue Moonlight-voc Ray Eberle
                (Dana Suesse)
                B-clt, Klink; clt, Schwartz; ts, Beneke;
                clt, Schwartz

041589-1   Vi 20-1585-A
      CGM   Basket Weaver Man-voc Ray Eberle
                (Joe McCarthy-Walter Donaldson)

> "Blue Moonlight" 2 takes; all other tunes 1 take.
> (RCA Victor)   This session lasted from 1:00 P.M.
> to 4:30 P.M. (RCA Victor)

(Session continued on next page)

According to the RCA file and Brad McCuen of RCA
Victor the issued take of "My Isle Of Golden
Dreams" is from this session. Note that the matrix
number is the one that was assigned for the July
26th session.

"Basket Weaver Man" has also been released with
just the title "Basket Weaver". This tune was
never released on the Bluebird label and was finally
released on the Victor label in 1944.

Summer, 1939: Glen Island Casino, New Rochelle, New York

> *Moonlight Serenade* (Theme)
> *Runnin' Wild*
> *Pavanne*
> *Stairway To The Stars*
> *Pagan Love Song*

Summer, 1939: Glen Island Casino, New Rochelle, New York

> *Moonlight Serenade* (Theme)
> *The Lady's In Love With You*
> *Twilight Interlude*
> *Ding-Dong! The Witch Is Dead*
> *Bugle Call Rag*
> *Moonlight Serenade* (Theme)

23 August, 1939 (WED): Glen Island Casino, New Rochelle, New York

Glenn Miller and His Orchestra closed at the Glen
Island Casino after a record-breaking season,
including an overflow crowd of 1,200 on the final
evening. Woody Herman's band followed Miller into
Glen Island, opening August 24th. (Met. Sept.
1939; G.M.P.R.)

The announcer for this program is Al Robinson.

(1:15) *Moonlight Serenade* (Theme)
        (*Mitchell Parish-Glenn Miller*)
(3:28) *St. Louis Blues* (arr ED)
        (*William C. Handy*)
        Tpt, Hurley; ts, Beneke; p, MacGregor;
        tbn, Miller; tpt, Hurley
Wham
(2:55) *My Isle Of Golden Dreams* (arr BF)
        (*Gus Kahn-Walter Donaldson*)
        Ts, Beneke

(Broadcast continued on next page)

TALK AND PRESENTATION TO MARION HUTTON, RAY EBERLE
AND GLENN MILLER

> *In The Mood*
> *Oh, You Crazy Moon*
> *Moonlight Serenade* *(Theme)*

Shortly after leaving the Casino Miller decided to
augment his brass to four trumpets and four
trombones. "Three part harmony in the trumpet and
trombone sections sounds too thin. By adding two
men, I'll have two more full-sounding sections."
Glenn added trumpeter Johnny Best (from Artie Shaw)
on August 27th, and put his road manager, Tommy
Mack, (On Sept. 1st) on the third trombone chair
(until Miller could find a permanent replacement).
(Met. Sept. 1939)

25 August, 1939 (FRI)

Glenn Miller and His Orchestra played for one week
(closed Thursday, August 31st) at Loew's Capitol
Theatre, Washington, D.C. The theater did its best
business in three years with a take of $22,500.00.
(Evening Star, Washington, D.C. Aug. 25, 1939; Met.
Oct. 1939; G.M.P.R.)

27 August, 1939 (SUN): Washington, D.C.

Trombones	Glenn Miller, Al Mastren, Paul Tanner
Trumpets	Clyde Hurley, Legh Knowles, Dale McMickle, JOHNNY BEST
Reeds	Hal McIntyre, as; Gerald Yelverton, as & bar & clt; Wilbur Schwartz, clt & as; Tex Beneke, ts; Al Klink, ts
Rhythm	Chummy MacGregor, p; Richard Fisher, g; Rowland Bundock, b; Maurice Purtill, d
Vocalists	Marion Hutton, Ray Eberle

1 September, 1939 (FRI)

Glenn Miller and His Orchestra played for one week
(closed Thursday, September 7th) at the Hippodrome
Theater, Baltimore, Maryland. The band did the best
theater business in the city's history with a take
of $19,000.00. (Sun, Baltimore, Md.,Sept. 1 & 7,
1939; Met. Oct. 1939; G.M.P.R.)

(continued on next page)

Trombones	Glenn Miller, Al Mastren, Paul Tanner, TOMMY MACK
Trumpets	Clyde Hurley, Legh Knowles, Dale McMickle, Johnny Best
Reeds	Hal McIntyre, as; Gerald Yelverton, as & bar & clt; Wilbur Schwartz, clt & as; Tex Beneke, ts; Al Klink, ts
Rhythm	Chummy MacGregor, p; Richard Fisher, g; Rowland Bundock, b; Maurice Purtill, d
Vocalists	Marion Hutton, Ray Eberle

Throughout this period G.M.P.R. show that 15 men and leader are present on the one nighters etc. (except for the week Sept. 1st to Sept. 7th) and we wonder if Mack played all the time. For example, there are two broadcasts on WFBR, one on Sept. 5th and one on Sept. 6th which Mack does not get paid for while the rest of the band does receive payment. Also note that Miller hires Walter Barrow for the recording session of September 11th.

5 September, 1939 (TUES): Baltimore, Maryland
                        NBC-WFBR

(1:20) Moonlight Serenade (Theme)
            (Mitchell Parish-Glenn Miller)
(2:54) Glen Island Special (arr ED)
            (Eddie Durham)
            Tpt, Hurley; ts, Beneke; ts, Klink
(0:19) The Lamp Is Low-no vocal as tune is
            partial Melody based on a Theme from
            Maurice Ravel's Pavane
            (Mitchell Parish-Peter DeRose-Bert
            Shefter)
(1:32) The Jumpin' Jive-voc Marion Hutton
            (Cab Calloway-Frank Froeba-Jack Palmer)
            Tpt, Hurley; ts, Beneke
(3:11) My Blue Heaven (arr BF)
            (George Whiting-Walter Donaldson)
            Tbn, Miller; ts, Beneke; d, Purtill
(0:25) Moonlight Serenade (Theme)
            (Michell Parish-Glenn Miller)

8 September, 1939 (FRI)

Glenn Miller and His Orchestra played at the New York State Fair, Syracuse, New York. The band set the record for the largest dancing crowd in the city's history with a take of $5,089.00.
(Variety, Aug. 23, 1939; G.M.P.R.--15 men and leader)

9 September, 1939 (SAT)

>   Glenn Miller and His Orchestra played at the
>   Hershey Park Ballroom, Hershey, Pennsylvania, and
>   drew 4,807 people. The band broke Guy Lombardo's
>   record of $3,800.00 (with 4,370 people) set in
>   1931, with $4,300.00. (BB, Sept. 23, 1939; Met.
>   Oct. 1939; Variety, Aug. 23, 1939; G.M.P.R.--15
>   men and leader; The Patriot, Harrisburg, Pa., Sept.
>   9, 1939)

10 September, 1939 (SUN)

>   Glenn Miller and His Orchestra played at Lake
>   Compounce, Bristol, Connecticut, and broke Kay
>   Kyser's record with $3,500.00. (Met. Oct. 1939;
>   G.M.P.R.--15 men and leader)

11 September, 1939 (MON): Victor Studios, New York City, N.Y.

Trombones	Glenn Miller, Al Mastren, Paul Tanner, WALTER BARROW
Trumpets	Clyde Hurley, Legh Knowles, Dale McMickle, Johnny Best.
Reeds	Hal McIntyre, as; Gerald Yelverton, as & bar & clt; Wilbur Schwartz, clt & as; Tex Beneke, ts; Al Klink, ts
Rhythm	Chummy MacGregor, p; Richard Fisher, g; Rowland Bundock, b; Maurice Purtill, d
Vocalist	Ray Eberle

042662-1   BB 10423-A, HMV BD 5822, HMV MH 139, HMVSw JK-2281,
                 MW 8645, Cam Cal/Cas-829, RCA G Cas-829,
                 AFRS P-8996, El G EG.7720, Pick Int. CDS
CGM   1004, RCA Cam Fr 900.028
            Melancholy Lullaby-voc Ray Eberle
                 (Edward Heyman-Benny Carter)
            Ts, Beneke

042663-1   BB 10423-B, HMVSw JK-5822, MW 8645, RZ MR 3198
CGM   (Why Couldn't It Last) Last Night-voc Ray Eberle
                 (Nick & Charles Kenny-Austen Croom-Johnson)

            Both tunes 1 take. (RCA Victor)
            This session lasted from 8:30 P.M. to 11:00 P.M.
            (RCA Victor)

            Walter Barrow was hired for this record session
            only. (G.M.P.R.)

            G.M.P.R. indicates that there was also a 3 hour
            audition on this date but does not state what the
            audition was about.

12 September, 1939 (TUES)

>Glenn Miller and His Orchestra played at King
>Phillip Ballroom on Lake Pearl, Wrentham,
>Massachusetts. The band broke attendance records
>and drew over 3,200. (Met. Oct. 1939; Boston Post,
>Sept. 12, 1939; G.M.P.R.--15 men and leader)

13 September, 1939 (WED)

>Glenn Miller and His Orchestra played at Canobie
>Lake Park Ballroom, Salem, New Hampshire. The
>band broke attendance records and drew over 3,200.
>(Met. Oct. 1939; Boston Post, Sept. 13, 1939;
>G.M.P.R.--15 men and leader)

14 September, 1939 (THUR)

>Glenn Miller and His Orchestra played at Ocean
>Pier Ballroom, Old Orchard Beach, Maine, and did
>capacity. (Met. Oct. 1939; Boston Post, Sept. 13,
>1939; G.M.P.R.--15 men and leader)

15 September, 1939 (FRI)

>Glenn Miller and His Orchestra played for five days
>(closed Tuesday, September 19th) at the State
>Theater, Hartford, Connecticut, and broke the
>theater record. The band was featured exclusively
>on the marquee. (Met. Oct. 1939; Variety, Aug. 30,
>1939)
>   "Miller tooters have a book of popular faves
>mostly for the jitterbug traffic. Pleasing to the
>more conservative is his superb arrangement of
>Londonderry Aire. Bandleader trombones consider-
>ably - only time he directs is when Marion Hutton
>steps to the mike. Vocalist does nicely with
>Jumpin' Jive - FDR Jones - Hold Tight. Uses
>Weekend of a Private Secretary as a beg off. Bands
>other chirper, Ray Eberle, was restricted to one
>number at the last show Friday Sept. 15, 1939, night,
>Moon Love. He was held down because of half hour
>broadcast over WTIC from the stage. Ordinarily he
>does several tunes." (G.M.P.R.--15 men and leader)

>The October issue of Metronome also mentioned that
>Glenn Miller, Tommy Dorsey, and Glen Gray made
>personal appearances at Geo. F. Pavilion, Bing-
>hampton, New York, and drew heavily. The exact date
>of this appearance is not known.

20 September, 1939 (WED)

      Glenn Miller and His Orchestra played for three
weeks (closed Tuesday, October 10th) at the
Paramount Theater, New York City, New York. (New
York Daily News, Sept. 20 & Oct. 10th, 1939;
Variety, Sept. 13, 1939) While Miller was at the
Paramount with the Ink Spots, Artie Shaw opened
at the Strand the same week. The first week the
Miller band grossed $59,500; the second week
$53,000; third week gross unknown.

      G.M.P.R. show that Tommy Mack played trombone at
the Paramount (we have photos taken by Arsene
Studios to support this statement) on September
20th, 21st, 22nd, 23rd and 24th but not on
September 25th and 26th. From September 29th to
October 5th Mack is paid for 4 days less one show
but the days are not listed by G.M.P.R. G.M.P.R.
is not too clear about the period October 6th to
October 10th regarding Mack but since there is no
mention of him missing days or shows we must
assume he was present for these last 5 days.

25 September, 1939 (MON): Victor Studios, New York City, N.Y.

Trombones	Glenn Miller, Al Mastren, Paul Tanner, TOBY TYLER
Trumpets	Clyde Hurley, Legh Knowles, Dale McMickle, Johnny Best
Reeds	Hal McIntyre, as; JIMMY ABATO, as & bar; Wilbur Schwartz, clt & as; Tex Beneke, ts; Al Klink, ts
Rhythm	Chummy MacGregor, p; Richard Fisher, g; Rowland Bundock, b; Maurice Purtill, d
Vocalist	Ray Eberle

042729-1   BB 10438-A, GrF K-8487, HMV BD 5565, HMVSw JK-2047,
         El G EG-7485, Vi LPM-6702, El 7MW 642,
CGM   VdP AV-707, HMVIr I.M. 1019, HMVHu HUC 115
     Out Of Space-voc Ray Eberle
       (Winky Tharp-Gene Gifford-Joe Bishop)

042730-1   BB 10438-B, Cam Cal/Cas-751, RCA G Cas-751, Pick.
         Int. CDS 1040
CGM   So Many Times-voc Ray Eberle
       (Don DeVito-Jimmy Dorsey)
       Ts, Beneke; tbn, Miller

     Both tunes 1 take. (RCA Victor)
This session lasted from 11:30 P.M. to 3:30 A.M.
(RCA Victor)

     Toby Tyler was hired for this record session
only. (G.M.P.R.)

3 October, 1939 (TUES): Victor Studios, New York City, N.Y.

Trombones	Glenn Miller, Al Mastren, Paul Tanner, TOMMY MACK
Trumpets	Clyde Hurley, Legh Knowles, Dale McMickle, Johnny Best
Reeds	Hal McIntyre, as; Jimmy Abato, as & bar; Wilbur Schwartz, clt & as; Tex Beneke, ts; Al Klink, ts
Rhythm	Chummy MacGregor, p; Richard Fisher, g; Rowland Bundock, b; Maurice Purtill, d
Vocalists	Marion Hutton, Ray Eberle

042780-1   BB 10486-A, HMV BD 5927, HMVSw JK-2412, Vi 20-1536,
             El G EG-7562, HMV 7EG 8043, Vi EPAT-426,
             Vi LPT 1031, RD 3/4-25, RD Br. RDS 6092,
             HMVAus GA 5102, RCA G LPT-1031, HMVIr I.P. 923,
             RD 8-5013

CGM   Blue Rain-voc Ray Eberle
             (Johnny Mercer-Jimmy Van Heusen)

042781-1   BB 10448-A
CGM   Can I Help It?-voc Ray Eberle
             (Eddie DeLange-Jimmy Van Heusen)

042782-1   BB 10448-B
CGM   I Just Got A Letter-voc Marion Hutton
             (Dave Franklin)
             As, McIntyre

             All tunes 1 take. (RCA Victor)
             This session lasted from 11:30 A.M. to 2:30 P.M.
             (RCA Victor)

3 October, 1939 (TUES)

             Glenn Miller, along with Benny Goodman, Al Donahue,
             and Dinah Shore attended the opening of the new
             Carl Fischer record store. (Met. Nov. 1939)

4 October, 1939 (WED)

             Glenn Miller and Bill Finegan attended the Benny
             Goodman opening at the Waldorf. Other musical
             personalities present included Artie Shaw, Larry
             Clinton, Henry Busse, Will Bradley, Eddie Sauter,
             Helen Ward, John Hammond, Johnny Mercer to name
             a few. (Met. Nov. 1939)

             The October 21st issue of The Billboard reported
             that on October 4th the Miller band drew 2,000
             people at Mason's Temple, Scranton, Pennsylvania.

(continued on next page)

First date at Paramount Theater, New York, September–October 1939. Left to right, front row: Tanner, Mack, Mastren, Miller. Back row: Best (hidden), Knowles, Mc-Mickle, Hurley, Purtill.

Paramount Theater, New York, September–October 1939. Klink (at left) and Beneke exchange solos.

We fail to see how Miller could be in two places
at once in this instance and suspect that the
Scranton date is incorrect.

The October 4th issue of Variety (1939) reported
that:
    "Glenn Miller will replace Paul Whiteman on
Chesterfield's Wednesday night (8:30-9:00) spot
on CBS Dec. 27, 1939. It's Miller's first
commercial. His program will include the Andrews
Sisters. Miller's contract stipulates that he
remain in New York City for his broadcasts during
the first 13 weeks and after that he has traveling privileges. Deal was set up between G.A.C.,
Miller's representative, and Newell-Emmett Agency."

4 October, 1939 (WED): New York City, New York (GLENN MILLER'S
*   NBC 11:45 P.M.   HAYRIDE SERENADE)*

Stunt of driving through New York City streets
on a hayride.

6 October, 1939 (FRI): Carnegie Hall, New York City, New York

Glenn Miller and His Orchestra took part in a
special swing concert at Carnegie Hall, New York
City. As part of Music Festival Week it was
given gratis by ASCAP (the American Society of
Composers, Authors and Publishers) to the public
in appreciation of its twenty-five years of
support. The Miller band was the final band on
the bill, the others being Paul Whiteman, Fred
Waring and Benny Goodman.

The Miller band was introduced by Gene Buck,
master of ceremonies and President of ASCAP.
For this concert the Miller band personnel is
the same as for the October 3rd recording
session.

H2PP-6679   Vi LPM-1506, Vi EPC-1506 (547-1100), RCA RD 27057,
                  Vi TP3-5020, RCA G LPM 1506, RCA F 430261,
                  Vi Arg LPM-1506
             (0:42) Moonlight Serenade (Theme)
                   (Mitchell Parish-Glenn Miller)

H2PP-6679   Vi LPM-1506, Vi EPC-1506 (547-1100), RCA RD 27057,
                  Vi TP3-5020, RCA G LPM 1506, RCA F 430261,
                  Vi Arg LPM-1506

(Session continued on next page)

                 (2:43) Runnin' Wild (arr BF)
                     (Joe Grey-Leo Wood-Harrington Gibbs)
                     Ts, Beneke; tpt, Hurley; ts, Beneke;
                     d, Purtill

H2PP-6679   Vi LPM-1506, Vi EPC-1506 (547-1102), RCA RD
                 27057, Vi TP3-5020, RCA G LPM 1506,
                 RCA F 430261, Vi Arg LPM-1506
                 (3:33) Sunrise Serenade
                     (Frankie Carle)
                     Ts, Beneke

H2PP-6679   Vi LPM-1506, Vi EPC-1506 (547-1101), RCA RD
                 27057, Vi TP3-5020, RCA G LPM 1506,
                 RCA F 430261, Vi Arg LPM-1506
                 (3:01) Little Brown Jug (arr BF)-Chant by Band
                     (Traditional)
                     Ts, Beneke; tpt, Hurley; tbn, Miller

H2PP-6679   Vi LPM-1506, Vi EPC-1506 (547-1101), RCA RD
                 27057, Vi TP3-5020, Vi PR-114, RCA G LPM
                 1506, RCA F 430261, Vi Arg LPM-1506
        Int GM (1:45) Stairway To The Stars-voc Ray Eberle
                     Melody based on a Theme from "Park
                     Avenue Fantasy"
                     (Mitchell Parish-Matty Malneck-Frank
                     Signorelli)
                     Tbn, Miller

H2PP-6679   Vi LPM-1506, Vi EPC-1506 (547-1101), RCA RD
                 27057, Vi TP3-5020, RCA G LPM 1506,
                 RCA F 430261, Vi Arg LPM-1506
                 (1:40) To You (arr GM)-voc Ray Eberle
                     (Tommy Dorsey-Ted Shapiro-Benny Davis)

H2PP-6679   Vi LPM-1506, Vi EPC-1506 (547-1100), RCA RD
                 27057, Vi TP3-5020, RCA G LPM 1506,
                 RCA F 430261, Vi Arg LPM-1506
        Int GM (5:01) One O'Clock Jump-Chant by Band
                     (Lee Gaines-Count Basie)
                     P, MacGregor; ts, Beneke; tbn, Miller;
                     ts, Klink; tpt, Hurley; tpt, Best

H2PP-6680   Vi LPM-1506, Vi EPC-1506 (547-1100), RCA RD
                 27057, Vi TP3-5020, Vi PR-114, RCA G LPM
                 1506, RCA F 430261, Vi Arg LPM-1506
        Int GM (1:47) Londonderry Air (Danny Boy) (arr GM & JCM)
                     (Fred E. Weatherly)
                     Tbn, Miller

(Session continued on next page)

H2PP-6680   Vi LPM-1506, Vi EPC-1506 (547-1101), RCA RD 27057,
                  Vi TP3-5020, RCA G LPM 1506, RCA F 430261,
                  Vi Arg LPM-1506
      Int GM (1:42) The Jumpin' Jive-voc Marion Hutton
                        (Cab Calloway-Frank Froeba-Jack
                        Palmer)

H2PP-6680   Vi LPM-1506, Vi EPC-1506 (547-1101), RCA RD 27057,
                  Vi TP3-5020, RCA G LPM 1506, RCA F 430261,
                  Vi Arg LPM-1506
              (1:53) FDR Jones-voc Marion Hutton and Band
                        (Harold J. Rome)

H2PP-6680   — Vi LPM-1506, Vi EPC-1506 (547-1101), RCA RD 27057,
                  Vi TP3-5020, RCA G LPM 1506, RCA F 430261,
                  Vi Arg LPM-1506
      Int GM (1:30) Hold Tight-voc Marion Hutton and Band
                        (Kent Brandow-Robinson Ware Spotswood)

H2PP-6680   Vi LPM-1506, Vi EPC-1506 (547-1102), RCA RD 27057,
                  Vi TP3-5020, RCA G LPM 1506, RCA F 430261,
                  Vi Arg LPM-1506
      Int GM (3:20) In The Mood
                        (Andy Razaf-Joe Garland)
                        Ts, Beneke; ts, Klink; tpt, Hurley

H2PP-6680   Vi LPM-1506, Vi EPC-1506 (547-1102), RCA RD 27057,
                  Vi TP3-5020, RCA G LPM 1506, RCA F 430261,
                  Vi Arg LPM-1506
      Int GM (3:35) Bugle Call Rag (arr GM)
                        (Jack Pettis-Billy Meyers-Elmer
                        Schoebel)
                        D, Purtill; tbn, Miller; ts, Beneke;
                        tpt, ??; tbn, Miller; tpt, ??, ts,
                        Beneke; d, Purtill

H2PP-6680   Vi LPM-1506, Vi EPC-1506 (547-1102), RCA RD 27057,
                  Vi TP3-5020, RCA G LPM 1506, RCA F 430261,
                  Vi Arg LPM-1506
              (0:41) Moonlight Serenade (Theme)
                        (Mitchell Parish-Glenn Miller)

            "Sharing honors with Swing's King was
      Glenn Miller, whose band, playing a mixed
      program, killer-dillers and beautifully-scored
      ballads, without using music, caused the
      greatest furor among the assembled jitterbugs.
      His stuff had most of them indulging in their
      usual 'can-anybody-find-the-beat' clapping."
      (Met. Nov. 1939)

(continued on next page)

The band also played a concert at the 34th
Street Armory, New York City, New York the same
evening. Tommy Mack played at both concerts.
(G.M.P.R.)

7 October, 1939 (SAT)

G.M.P.R. show that on this date Art Gunther was
paid for arranging "At Least You Could Say Hello"
and "On A Little Street In Singapore".

9 October, 1939 (MON): Victor Studios, New York City, New York

Same personnel as for October 3rd recording
session.

042923-1   BB 10455-A, MW 8644, HMV DLP 1145
                  Bless You-voc Ray Eberle
                          (Eddie Lane-Don Baker)

042924-1   BB 10465-B, HMVAu EA-2436, HMVSw JK-2281 or
                          HMVSw JK-2280
                  Bluebirds In The Moonlight (Silly Idea)
                          (arr BC)-voc Marion Hutton
                          From Paramount's Technicolor Cartoon
                          "Gulliver's Travels"
                          (Leo Robin-Ralph Rainger)
                          P, MacGregor, tpt, Hurley

042925-1   BB 10465-A, HMV 7EG 8135, Cam Cal/Cas-2128,
                          RCA G Cas-2128
                  Faithful Forever-voc Ray Eberle
                          From Paramount's Technicolor Cartoon
                          "Gulliver's Travels"
                          (Leo Robin-Ralph Rainger)
                          As, McIntyre

042926-1   BB 10455-B, MW 8644
                  Speaking Of Heaven-voc Ray Eberle
                          (Jimmy Van Heusen-Mack Gordon)
                          As, McIntyre

                  All tunes 1 take. (RCA Victor)
                  This session lasted from 11:30 A.M. to 4:00 P.M.
                  (RCA Victor)

10 October, 1939 (TUES)

                  Eddie Sauter and Jimmie Bracken (George Simon)
                  stopped by to say goodbye to Miller before the
                  band left town on an Eastern tour. (Met. Nov. 1939)

11 October, 1939 (WED)

> Glenn Miller and His Orchestra played at Masonic
> Temple, Scranton, Pennsylvania. The promoter was
> Max Kearson. Most of the dancers were disappoint-
> ed because the music was too fast. Miller
> attempted to pace his music to satisfy a minority
> of jitterbugs. (Met. Nov. 1939)
> Perhaps this is the Billboard date which was
> listed as October 4th. (G.M.P.R.--15 men and
> leader)

12 October, 1939 (THUR)

> Glenn Miller and His Orchestra played at the
> George F. Pavilion, Johnson City, New York. Tex
> Beneke stole the show with "The Little Man Who
> Wasn't There". The crowd often applauded Maurice
> Purtill's drumming and Beneke's tenoring. (Met.
> Nov. 1939; G.M.P.R.--15 men and leader)

13 October, 1939 (FRI)

> Glenn Miller and His Orchestra played for one
> week (closed Thursday, October 19th) at Shea's
> Theater, Buffalo, New York. The band drew a good
> quota of Torontonians and played to capacity.
> (Met. Nov. 1939; BB Oct. 7, 1939; Variety, Oct. 4,
> 1939; Buffalo Courier Express, Oct. 13 & 19, 1939;
> G.M.P.R.--16 men and leader; Four stage shows a
> day: 1:39 P.M., 4:19 P.M., 7:09 P.M., 9:39 P.M.
> with Eunice Healy, John Gallus, Grace & Nikko.)

20 October, 1939 (FRI)

> Glenn Miller and His Orchestra played for one
> week, except Sunday (closed Thursday, October
> 26th) at the Earle Theater, Philadelphia,
> Pennsylvania. The band broke Benny Goodman's
> opening day record, and on Saturday smashed Kay
> Kyser's record for that day. Their take for that
> week was $31,700.00. (Met. Nov. 1939; BB Nov. 4,
> 1939; G.M.P.R.--16 men and leader)
>   "The most tumultuous audiences since Benny
> Goodman's appearance here two years ago are
> jamming their way into the Earle this week to
> gander at Glenn Miller's Orchestra and the be-
> spectacled maestro doesn't disappoint. A varied
> program ranging from the latest jive to the
> sweet melodic Danny Boy satisfies everyone. Well

(continued on next page)

arranged 45 minute show is aided by tasteful back
drops and okay lighting effects. Show opens with
Miller gang jamming through a medley including
Sunrise Serenade and Moonlight Serenade. Ray
Eberle pleasingly tenors Over the Rainbow encoring
To You. The band pace gets hot again with Jumpin'
Jive. Miller soloing on his horn. Stage then is
darkened with faint light on Miller as he introduces Danny Boy. Band separates into voice units
and as each section goes into action different
colored spots play them up. It's very effective
and brings plenty of plaudits. The 5 saxes
especially click during this number. Marion
Hutton, zippy blonde eyeful with the band, does a
good job with vocals of Jumpin' Jive and FDR
Jones. In an encore she teams with saxophonist
Tex Beneke in Little Man Who Wasn't There. Band
bows out with In the Mood and Runnin' Wild."
(Friday night review in Variety, Oct. 25, 1939)

22 October, 1939 (SUN)

The band crossed the river for this one day
(Pennsylvania Blue Law) to play in Camden, New
Jersey, and broke the five-year record of Blanche
Calloway. (Met. Nov. 1939)

27 October, 1939 (FRI)

Glenn Miller and His Orchestra played for one
week (closed Thursday, November 2nd) at the
Stanley Theater, Pittsburg, Pennsylvania. (Swing,
Oct. 1939; DB Oct. 15, 1939; BB Sept. 23, 1939;
G.M.P.R.--16 men and leader)
        "Heavy rains at getaway held Glenn Miller
with "They Shall Have Music" (United Artist) down
at Stanley but he's finishing strong. Picture
hasn't been doing much around here, so Miller
hotter than a firecracker at the moment can take
practically all of the credit." (Variety, Nov.
1, 1939)

3 November, 1939 (FRI)

Glenn Miller and His Orchestra played at the
Fairmount Fair Grounds, Philadelphia, Pennsylvania,
in the afternoon. This was the first time in the
history of this annual fair that the Fairmount
Park Guards featured a name band. (Met. Nov. 1939)

(continued on next page)

Later that evening Glenn Miller and His Orchestra
played at the University of Pennsylvania Junior
Prom, Philadelphia, Pennsylvania. (Variety, Oct.
4, 1939; BB Oct. 7, 1939; BB Nov. 18, 1939;
G.M.P.R.--15 men and leader)

4 November, 1939 (SAT)

Glenn Miller and His Orchestra played at the
Sunnybrook Ballroom, Pottstown, Pennsylvania, and
drew 4,002. (BB, Nov. 18, 1939; BB Oct. 7, 1939;
Variety, Oct. 4, 1939; G.M.P.R.--15 men and
leader)

5 November, 1939 (SUN): Victor Studios, New York City, New York

Same personnel as for October 3rd recording
session.

043354-1
BB 10495-A, HMV BD 5569, HMV DLP 1049, HMVIr
I.P. 1163, Vi LSP-4125, RCA Int. INTS 1002,
Vi P8S-1432, Vi VPM-6019
Indian Summer-voc Ray Eberle
(Al Dubin-Victor Herbert)
Ts, Beneke

043355-1
BB 10498-A, HMV MH 158, HMVAu EA-3345, HMVSw
JK-2241, El G (Test)
It Was Written In The Stars-voc Ray Eberle
From the musical production "Dubarry Was A
Lady"
(Cole Porter)
Tpt, Hurley; muted tbn, Miller

043356-1
BB 10498-B, HMV BD 5683, HMV MH 140, HMVSw
JK-2241, Vi 20-2410 (Vi P-189), Vi 420-0041,
Vi 447-0041, Vi LPT-3002, Vi EPBT-3002
(947-0038), Vi EPA-5008, RCA RCX 1040, HMV
DLP 1081, Vi LPM-1190, Vi VPM-6019, Vi EPB-
1190 (547-0829), Vi PRM-181, Vi LPM/LSP-
3377, RD 3/4-45, HMVAus GA 5082, RCA Int.
B-21040, RCA Int. T-21040, RCA F 130210,
AFRS "Jukebox USA" 151, RCA G LPM/LSP-3377,
Vi TP3-5044, RCA G LPM-1190, RCA G EPA 5008,
RCA G EPC-1190, Vi P8S-5061, RCA G Cas
10231, HMVIn BD 5683, HMVAu EA 2511, RCA G
LPM/LSP-9944, Vi VLP 3377
Johnson Rag (arr BF)
(Henry Kleinkauf-Guy Hall)
Ts, Beneke; ts, Klink; tbn, Miller;
tpt, Hurley

(Session continued on next page)

"Indian Summer" 1 take; all other tunes 2 takes.
(RCA Victor)
This session lasted from 3:00 P.M. to 7:45 P.M.
(RCA Victor)

5 November, 1939 (SUN)

Glenn Miller attended Bobby Byrne's opening night
at the Hotel New Yorker, New York City, New York.
(Met. Dec. 1939)

6 November, 1939 (MON)

Glenn Miller and His Orchestra played at the
Springfield Auditorium, Springfield, Massachusetts. (Boston Post, Nov. 6, 1939; G.M.P.R.--
15 men and leader)

7 November, 1939 (TUES)

Glenn Miller and His Orchestra played at Rhodes,
Providence, Rhode Island. (Boston Post, Nov. 6,
1939; G.M.P.R.--16 men and leader)

8 November, 1939 (WED)

Glenn Miller and His Orchestra played at the
Valencia Ballroom, York, Pennsylvania. (BB,
Oct. 7, 1939; The York Dispatch, York, Pa.,
Nov. 8, 1939; G.M.P.R.--15 men and leader)

9 November, 1939 (THUR)

Glenn Miller and His Orchestra played at the
Ritz Ballroom, Pottsville, Pennsylvania.
(Variety, Oct. 4, 1939; BB, Oct. 7, 1939;
Pottsville Pa. Evening Republican, Nov. 9, 1939;
G.M.P.R.--16 men and leader)

10 November, 1939 (FRI)

Frank D'Annolfo joined the band as permanent
fourth trombonist replacing Tommy Mack who was
also the roadmanager for the band. (G.M.P.R.)

(continued on next page)

Trombones	Glenn Miller, Al Mastren, Paul Tanner, FRANK D'ANNOLFO
Trumpets	Clyde Hurley, Legh Knowles, Dale McMickle, Johnny Best
Reeds	Hal McIntyre, as; Jimmy Abato, as & bar; Wilbur Schwartz, clt & as; Tex Beneke, ts; Al Klink, ts
Rhythm	Chummy MacGregor, p; Richard Fisher, g; Rowland Bundock, b; Maurice Purtill, d
Vocalists	Marion Hutton, Ray Eberle
Band-Boy	Raul Hidalgo

Glenn Miller and His Orchestra played at Symphony
Hall (corner of Huntington Ave. & Mass. Ave.),
Boston, Massachusetts, for a gala Armistice Eve
dance. (Boston Post, Nov. 10, 1939; G.M.P.R.)

11 November, 1939 (SAT)

Glenn Miller and His Orchestra played at White
Plains, Westchester, New York. (Variety, Nov. 8,
1939)

12 November, 1939 (SUN)

Glenn Miller and His Orchestra played at the
Roseland Ballroom, Brooklyn, New York. (Variety,
Oct. 25, 1939; New York Daily News, Nov. 12, 1939;
G.M.P.R.)

On this same date the band played a Fitch Band-
wagon program (30 minutes). (G.M.P.R.)

13 November, 1939 (MON)

Glenn Miller and His Orchestra played at the Hecla
Park Ballroom, Bellefonte, Pennsylvania.
(Variety, Oct. 4, 1939; BB, Oct. 7, 1939; The
Sentinel, Lewistown, Pa., Nov. 11, 1939; G.M.P.R.)

14 November, 1939 (TUES)

Glenn Miller and His Orchestra played at the
Coliseum, Greensburg, Pennsylvania, for promoter
Fred Luther. The band drew 1,587 but failed to
come close to the all-time record held by Hal
Kemp of 2,743. The band gave their all to a
receptive throng who applauded more for the slower,

(continued on next page)

more melodic tempos. (Met. Dec. 1939; Variety,
Oct. 4, 1939; Greensburg Daily Tribune, Greensburg,
Pa., Nov. 14, 1939; G.M.P.R.)

15 November, 1939 (WED)

Glenn Miller and His Orchestra played at Mealey's
Auditorium, Allentown, Pennsylvania. (Variety, Oct.
25, 1939; The Morning Call, Allentown, Pa., Nov. 15,
1939; G.M.P.R.)

16 November, 1939 (THUR): Meadowbrook Ballroom, Cedar Grove, N.J.
NBC 11:30-12:00 Midnight WJZ

Glenn Miller and His Orchestra opened at the Meadowbrook Ballroom, Cedar Grove, New Jersey. This was
the band's second engagement at the Meadowbrook
within a year. (Met. Nov. 1939; Variety, Nov. 8,
1939; G.M.P.R.)

Moonlight Serenade (Theme)

E4VP 8205   Vi LPT 6701, Vi EPOT 6701 (947-0192), HMV RLS 598,
               RCA G EPOT-6701
(2:59) I Want To Be Happy (arr ED)
                    From the musical production "No, No,
                    Nanette"
                    (Irving Caesar-Vincent Youmans)
                    Tpt, Hurley; ts, Beneke; tbn, Miller;
                    d, Purtill

(3:04) Indian Summer-voc Ray Eberle
*   (Al Dubin-Victor Herbert)*
*   Ts, Beneke; tpt, Best*
*   I Just Got A Letter*
(2:43) (Why Couldn't It Last) Last Night-voc
*   Ray Eberle*
*   (Nick & Charles Kenny-Austen Croom-*
*   Johnson)*
(3:29) Blue Moonlight-voc Ray Eberle
*   (Dana Suesse)*
*   B-clt, Klink; clt, Schwartz; ts, Beneke;*
*   clt, Schwartz*
(2:26) Runnin' Wild (arr BF)
*   (Joe Grey-Leo Wood-Harrington Gibbs)*
*   Ts, Beneke; tpt, Hurley; ts, Beneke;*
*   d, Purtill*
(0:06) Moonlight Serenade (Theme)
*   (Mitchell Parish-Glenn Miller)*

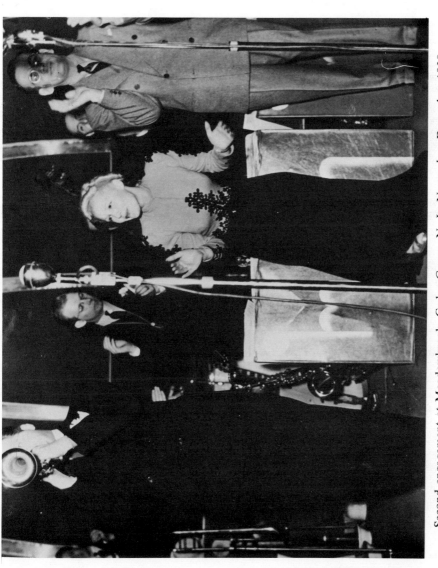

Second engagement at Meadowbrook, Cedar Grove, N. J., November–December 1939. Clyde Hurley is the trumpet soloist. The rest of the band add encouragement by clapping in time with the music. (*Photo courtesy Glenn Miller Estate*)

The Andrews Sisters with Miller and unknown announcer rehearsing for Chesterfield show, early 1940. (*Photo courtesy Glenn Miller Estate*)

17 November, 1939 (FRI): Meadowbrook Ballroom, Cedar Grove, N.J.

(0:10) Wham (Re-Bop-Boom-Bam) (arr ED) no vocal as
            tune is partial
            (Eddie Durham-"Taps" Miller)
(3:01) Careless-voc Ray Eberle
            (Lew Quadling-Eddy Howard-Dick Jurgens)
            P. MacGregor; muted tbn, Miller
(0:06) St. Louis Blues (arr ED)
            (William C. Handy)
(2:37) Bluebirds In The Moonlight (Silly Idea)
            (arr BC)-voc Marion Hutton
            From Paramount's Technicolor Cartoon
            "Gulliver's Travels"
            (Leo Robin-Ralph Rainger)
            P, MacGregor; tpt, Hurley
(3:36) In The Mood
            (Andy Razaf-Joe Garland)
            Ts, Beneke; ts, Klink; tpt, Hurley
            (Five endings)

18 November, 1939 (SAT): Victor Studios, New York City, New York

Same personnel as for November 10th.

043390-1   BB 10507-B, HMV BD 5842, Vi 82944-B, MW 8641,
                  RCA Cam Arg Cal-3138, RCA Cam Fr 900.028,
                  Cam Cal/Cas-829, AFRS P-8996, RCA G Cas-829,
                  Pick. Int. CDS 1004
              Ciri-Biri-Bin (arr BF)-voc Ray Eberle
                  (Harry James-Jack Lawrence-A. Pestalozza)

043391-1   BB 10520-A, HMV BD 5569, Vi LPT 6700, Vi EPNT 6700
                  (947-0121), Vi SPD-18 (599-9106), HMV RLS
                  599, RCA G LPT 6700, HMVIr I.P. 1163
              Careless-voc Ray Eberle
                  (Lew Quadling-Eddy Howard-Dick Jurgens)
                  P, MacGregor

043392-1   BB 10507-A, Vi 82944-A, MW 8641
              Oh Johnny, Oh Johnny, Oh!-voc Marion Hutton
                  (Ed. Rose-Abe Olman)
                  Ts, Beneke

              All tunes 1 take. (RCA Victor)
              This session lasted from 1:30 P.M. to 4:30 P.M.
              (RCA Victor)

22 November, 1939 (WED): Victor Studios, New York City, New York

Same personnel as for November 10th.

043909-1 BB 10553-A, HMVAu EA-2525, HMV DLP 1145
    In An Old Dutch Garden (By An Old Dutch Mill)-voc
      Ray Eberle
      (Mack Gordon-Will Grosz)
      Ts, Beneke

043910-1 BB 10526-B, HMVAu EA-3484
    This Changing World-voc Ray Eberle
      (Harold Adamson-Dana Suesse)
      Tpt, Hurley or Best; tbn, Miller

043911-1 BB 10526-A, Vi 20-1585, Vi LPT 6700, Vi EPNT
      6700 (947-0127), Vi SPD-18 (599-9106),
      Vi 45 Special-1953, HMV RLS 599,
      RCA G LPT 6700
    On A Little Street In Singapore (arr AG)-voc
      Ray Eberle
      (Billy Hill-Peter DeRose)

043912-1 BB 10520-B, HMV BD 5585, HMV 7EG 8043, Vi EPAT-
      426, Vi LPT-1031, RCA G LPT-1031
    Vagabond Dreams-voc Ray Eberle
      (Jack Lawrence-Hoagy Carmichael)
      As, McIntyre; tpt, Hurley or Best

    All tunes 1 take. (RCA Victor)
    This session lasted from 1:15 P.M. to 4:15 P.M.
    (RCA Victor)

24 November, 1939 (FRI): Meadowbrook Ballroom, Cedar Grove, N.J.

Part 1

Moonlight Serenade (Theme)

E4VP 8206 Vi LPT 6701, Vi EPOT 6701 (947-0191), HMV RLS
      598, RCA G EPOT-6701
    (4:47) St. Louis Blues (arr ED)
      (William C. Handy)
      Tpt, Hurley;ts, Beneke; p. MacGregor;
      tbn, Miller; tpt, Hurley

    Blue Moonlight
    Oh Johnny, Oh Johnny, Oh!
    My Isle Of Golden Dreams

(Broadcast continued on next page)

Part 2

Moonlight Serenade (Theme)
Slip Horn Jive

E4VP 8206   Vi LPT 6701, Vi EPOT 6701 (947-0190), HMV RLS 598,
                RCA G EPOT-6701
              (3:20) Indian Summer-voc Ray Eberle
                     (Al Dubin-Victor Herbert)
                     Ts, Beneke; tpt, Best

               Love With A Capital "You"
               Bugle Call Rag
               Moonlight Serenade (Theme)

A good example in the difference between the recording and the broadcast is this version of "Indian
Summer". Johnny Best's trumpet solo is not on the
recorded version.

25 November, 1939 (SAT)

     G.M.P.R. show that on this date lawyer, David
     Mackay was paid for professional services rendered.
     This was the beginning of a long association be-
     tween the Miller band and David Mackay which con-
     tinues to this day.

25 November, 1939 (SAT): Meadowbrook Ballroom, Cedar Grove, N.J.

               Moonlight Serenade (Theme)
               Ain't Cha Comin' Out?
               Speaking Of Heaven
               Little Brown Jug
               This Changing World
               Glen Island Special
               In An Old Dutch Garden

E4VP 8205   Vi LPT 6701, Vi EPOT 6701 (947-0192), HMV RLS 598,
                RCA G EPOT-6701
              (2:45) Bluebirds In The Moonlight (Silly Idea)
                     (arr BC)-voc Marion Hutton
                     From Paramount's Technicolor Cartoon
                     "Gulliver's Travels"
                     (Leo Robin-Ralph Rainger)
                     P, MacGregor; tpt, Hurley

               Farewell Blues
               Moonlight Serenade (Theme)

26 November, 1939 (SUN): Meadowbrook Ballroom, Cedar Grove, N.J.

> *Moonlight Serenade (Theme)*
> *Oh Johnny, Oh Johnny, Oh!*
> *Indian Summer*
> *My Isle Of Golden Dreams*

E4VP 8206   Vi LPT 6701, Vi EPOT 6701 (947-0190), Vi SPA-7-4,
HMV RLS 598, RCA G EPOT-6701
(3:47) *Tiger Rag (arr ED)*
(Tony Sbarbaro-Eddie Edwards-Henry
Ragas-Larry Shields-Nick LaRocca-
Harry DeCosta)
Ts, Klink; d, Purtill

> *Moonlight Serenade (Theme)*

The composer credits for "Tiger Rag" are for
members of "The Original Dixieland Jazz Band"
with the one exception being DeCosta.

27 November, 1939 (MON)

Glenn Miller and His Orchestra played for New
York's Local 802 annual Medical Fund benefit at
Madison Square Garden. According to the December
issue of Metronome "top shouting honors, awarded
by the thousands assembled, going to Glenn Miller
and his lads, whose five brilliant selections
busted the show wide open long about 1:30 in the
morning." Other name bands there that evening
were the following: Woody Herman, Bob Crosby, Benny
Goodman, Charlie Barnet, Teddy Wilson, Jan Savitt
and Andy Kirk. (Met. Dec. 1939; BB Oct. 7, 1939)

28 November, 1939 (TUES)

G.M.P.R. show that on this date Eddie Durham was
paid for arranging "Tiger Rag" and "I Know".

3 December, 1939 (SUN): Meadowbrook Ballroom, Cedar Grove, N.J.

> *Moonlight Serenade (Theme)*
> *Little Brown Jug*
> *Can I Help It?*
> *Wham*

5 December, 1939 (TUES): Meadowbrook Ballroom, Cedar Grove, N.J.
12:30-1:00 A.M. WEAF

        Moonlight Serenade (Theme)
        Little Brown Jug
        Blue Rain
        Oh Johnny, Oh Johnny, Oh!
        In An Old Dutch Garden
        Moonlight Serenade (Theme)
        Moonlight Serenade (Theme)
        Slip Horn Jive
        Faithful Forever
        The Man With The Mandolin
        Tiger Rag
        Moonlight Serenade (Theme)

6 December, 1939 (WED): Victor Studios, New York City, New York

        Same personnel as for November 10th.

043973-1   BB 10561-B
            I Beg Your Pardon-voc Ray Eberle
                (Mack Gordon-J. Fred Coots)

043974-1   BB 10536-A, HMVAu EA-2436, HMV 7EG 8067, Vi EPAT-
               427, Vi LPT-1031, RCA G LPT-1031
            Faithful To You-voc Ray Eberle
                (Martin Block-Harold Green-Mickey Stoner)
                Clt, Abato?

043975-1   BB 10536-B, HMV BD 5587, Vi LPM/LSP-3657, RCA
               RD/SF-7842, RCA G LPM/LSP-3657, AFRS P-
               10071, RCA F 440.727
            It's A Blue World-voc Ray Eberle
                From the Columbia film "Music In My Heart"
                (Bob Wright-Chet Forrest)
                Clt, Schwartz;as, McIntyre

043976-1   BB 10561-A
            Ooh! What You Said-voc Marion Hutton
                From the musical comedy "Three After Three"
                (Johnny Mercer-Hoagy Carmichael)
                Ts, Beneke

            All tunes 1 take. (RCA Victor)
            This session lasted from 1:30 P.M. to 5:00 P.M.
            (RCA Victor)

            The idea for the song "I Beg Your Pardon" is sup-
            posedly the result of composer Mack Gordon's
            difficulty in getting in and out of elevators.
            (Swing, Nov. 1939)

6 December, 1939 (WED): Meadowbrook Ballroom, Cedar Grove, N.J.

Glenn Miller and His Orchestra closed at the Meadowbrook Ballroom, Cedar Grove, New Jersey. The
Miller band was followed by Larry Clinton into the
Meadowbrook. (Variety, Oct. 25, 1939; BB, Oct. 21,
1939; G.M.P.R.)

Moonlight Serenade (Theme)
King Porter Stomp

E4VP 8206   Vi LPT 6701, Vi EPOT 6701 (947-0191), HMV RLS 598,
RCA G EPOT-6701
(2:35) After All (arr JG)-voc Ray Eberle
(Guy Wood-Bud Green)

I Just Got A Letter
On A Little Street In Singapore
In The Mood
Faithful To You
Bluebirds In The Moonlight
Farewell Blues
Moonlight Serenade (Theme)

G.M.P.R. indicates that Jerry Gray joined the band
as arranger for the week beginning December 22nd
but note that "After All" was arranged by Jerry
Gray, so he must have joined the band around this
time.

7 December, 1939 (THUR)

Glenn Miller and His Orchestra played in New Elms,
Youngstown, Ohio, and drew 2,005. Ray Eberle and
Marion Hutton were knockouts. (Met. Jan. 1940;
G.M.P.R.)

8 December, 1939 (FRI)

Glenn Miller and His Orchestra played for one
week (closed Thursday, December 14th) at Loew's
State Theatre, Cleveland, Ohio. (Cleveland Plain
Dealer, Dec. 8 & 14, 1939; Met. Dec. 1939; Variety,
Oct. 4, 1939; G.M.P.R.)
      "The Glenn Miller stage show, re-opening the
combination of vaudeville and films this week in
Loew's State, seems to have been arranged solely
for the Glenn Miller fans. These, I fancy from
the crowded house and the whistles and stomps of
approval together with the type of music given them,
add up to a legion of jitterbugs.

(continued on next page)

It seemed to me the more rhythmic noise from the
stage, the louder the cheers and applause from
the audience, and when the brasses and the
drummer began to work on the emotion of the crowd,
I began to question both its sanity and mine.
The different tempos and arrangements of
"Sunrise Serenade" was the first smash hit. The
second came with "One O'Clock Jump," but "In The
Mood" created a kind of frenzy which made me a
little fearful of the outcome of the show. The
only piece he played which I really understood
was his version of "Londonderry Air," and that was
"sweet." The others are done in what must be the
typical Glenn Miller style, blasting brasses,
wailing saxophones, and a drummer with six hands
and "two left feet."
If this is "music" as you know you want it,
then Glenn Miller is one of the season's high
lights for you. The show is all Miller's too.....
Ray Eberle has a voice for popular melodies.
Marion Hutton is the only member with a personality strong enough to get across the footlights and
get to the jitterbugs and us old fossils alike.
There was madness in the air when she sang "Jim
Jam Jumpin' Jives."....
But it's Miller's show, and judging from the
crowd yesterday, that's all the crowd wants--
Miller and more of him." (Reviewed by W. Ward
Marsh in The Cleveland Plain Dealer, Dec. 9, 1939.
The Glenn Miller radio orchestra-revue was on
stage at: 12:40, 3:05, 5:30, 8:00, 10:25, approxi-
mately 45 minute stage shows)

15 December, 1939 (FRI)

Glenn Miller and His Orchestra played at the
Memorial Hall, Columbus, Ohio. (Variety, Nov. 15,
1939; G.M.P.R.)

16 December, 1939 (SAT)

Glenn Miller and His Orchestra played at Castle
Farm, Cincinnati, Ohio. (Variety, Oct. 25, 1939;
G.M.P.R.)

17 December, 1939 (SUN)

Glenn Miller and His Orchestra played at Moonlight
Ballroom, Canton, Ohio. (G.M.P.R.)

18 December, 1939 (MON)

> Glenn Miller and His Orchestra played at
> Charleston, West Virginia. (G.M.P.R.)

19 December, 1939 (TUES)

> Glenn Miller and His Orchestra played at the
> Trianon Ballroom, Toledo, Ohio. (G.M.P.R.)

20 December, 1939 (WED)

> Glenn Miller and His Orchestra played at the
> Auditorium, Erie, Pennsylvania. (G.M.P.R.)

> Miller against Bob Hope (Tues), Kay Kyser (Wed),
> Bing Crosby (Thur) and Bob Burns on his new
> Chesterfield Show debuting at 8:30 P.M. Wednesday,
> December 27th over 93 stations. Begins 15 minute
> segment Tuesday, January 2nd, 1940. (Variety,
> Dec. 20, 1939)

21 December, 1939 (THUR)

> Glenn Miller and His Orchestra played in
> Washington, D.C. for the Solgrave Club. (G.M.P.R.)

22 December, 1939 (FRI)

> Glenn Miller and His Orchestra played at the
> Buffalo Country Club, Buffalo, New York. (Variety,
> Oct. 4, 1939; G.M.P.R.)

23 December, 1939 (SAT)

> Glenn Miller and His Orchestra played at the
> Mohawk Armory, Mohawk, New York, and drew 1,500.
> (Variety, Nov. 29, 1939; BB, Jan. 6, 1940; Met.
> Jan. 1940; G.M.P.R.)

24 December, 1939 (SUN)

> Glenn Miller and His Orchestra played at Harlem's
> famed Savoy Ballroom, New York City, to over
> 4,000. The band pulled more persons into the

(continued on next page)

place than it had ever held before and broke Guy
Lombardo's nine-year-old all-time attendance
record. (Met. March 1940; DB, May 15, 1940)
Later the same evening the Miller band presented
Glenn with a new Buick Roadmaster in the lobby of
the Pennsylvania Hotel. The car, which the band
had pooled their money ($2,000.00) and traded in
Miller's old car, was bedecked with signs bearing
such inscriptions as "To Our Old Pal Glenn".
(DB, Jan. 15, 1940; DB, Feb. 1, 1940; G.M.P.R.)

25 December, 1939 (MON)

Glenn Miller and His Orchestra played at the
Pennsylvania Athletic Club, Philadelphia,
Pennsylvania. (Variety, Oct. 25, 1939; G.M.P.R.)

26 December, 1939 (TUES)

Glenn Miller and His Orchestra played at the Rose-
land Ballroom, New York City, New York. (New York
Daily News, Dec. 26, 1939; Variety, Oct. 25, 1939;
G.M.P.R.)

*27 December, 1939 (WED): New York City, New York (CHESTERFIELD
                 SHOW) CBS 8:30-9:00 P.M., West Coast
                 Rebroadcast 11:30-12:00 Midnight*

Glenn Miller and His Orchestra began the first of
many broadcasts sponsored by Chesterfield
cigarettes over the CBS Network. This series ran
until September 24th, 1942. The Miller band had
replaced Paul Whiteman's band on the once-a-week
half hour Wednesday night spot. For the first
thirteen weeks (including this week) the Miller
band shared the program with the Andrews Sisters
(who had signed for only thirteen weeks because of
previous commitments). These programs became
known as Chesterfield's "Moonlight Serenade" and
after the first week they were aired three times
weekly (15 minutes each show). The staff
announcers for this show were either Paul Douglas
(usually New York City as in this case) and Larry
Bruff.

*(0:44) Moonlight Serenade (Theme)
              (Mitchell Parish-Glenn Miller)*

(Broadcast continued on next page)

ALP

(3:00) ~~Little Brown Jug~~ (arr BF)-Chant by band
~~(Traditional)~~
~~Ts,~~ Beneke; tpt, Hurley; tbn, Miller
(0:45) *To You* (arr GM)-voc Ray Eberle
(Tommy Dorsey-Ted Shapiro-Benny Davis)
Bei Mir Bist Du Schon-voc Andrews Sisters
(Jacob Jacobs-Sammy Cahn-Saul Chaplin-
Sholom Secunda)

ALP ~~*Danny Boy*~~
~~*Ciri-Biri-Bin*~~-voc Andrews Sisters

MEDLEY:
Star Dust
Blue Orchids
Sunrise Serenade
Mood Indigo

In The Mood
Moonlight Serenade (Theme)

The medley is the first of the now famous "Something Old, Something New, Something Borrowed, and
Something Blue" medleys that Glenn Miller was to
use throughout the rest of his career.

"Miller's initial program for the smoke
account not only provided swell music in the modern
idiom but reflected a smart hand at the routining
of this type of show. Miller started off on his
right foot by giving 'em those very items that have
clicked best on his recording test. Every number
served either to highlight Miller's sizzling brass
or to furnish some rich samples of those instrumental ensemble effects that have done much to
make the Miller unit what it is. The over all
impression was that Miller not only had a unique
knack for blending rhythm and melody but that he
has struck a telling balance between swing and
sweet music.

The Andrews Sisters were deftly fitted into
the proceedings, giving it plenty of bounce and
crack harmony. As an aid to identification they
opened with Bei Mir Bist Du Schoen. The trio's
other contribution Ciri-Biri-Bin turned out the
top sock of the occasion. It's one of the
choicest things that the sisters have in their
repertoire. Ray Eberle, Miller's staff vocalist,
also filled in with a chorus here and there."
(Variety, Jan. 3, 1940)

(Continued on next page)

On this date the AFM ruled that Eli Oberstein, owner of U.S. Records, would have to sue Glenn Miller in civil court if he expected to hold him to an alleged contract (signed some time in September). Oberstein said that "he will obtain an injunction restraining Miller from making records for that company (Victor-Bluebird) and will try to force the leader, through civil court action, to go through with the contract." (Met. Jan. 1940)

28 December, 1939 (THUR)

Glenn Miller and His Orchestra played at the Blackstone Hotel, Chicago, Illinois. (Swing Jan. 1940; Variety, Nov. 15, 1939; G.M.P.R.)
"Hill Blackett of the firm Blackett-Sample-Hummert, Thursday, December 28, 1939 imported the Glenn Miller Orchestra from New York to supply dansapation at the Blackstone Hotel for the debut of his daughter Patricia.
Miller almost failed to make it, due to faulty train connections." (Variety, Jan. 3, 1940)

29 December, 1939 (FRI)

Glenn Miller and His Orchestra played at the Trianon Ballroom, Toledo, Ohio. (Cleveland Plain Dealer, Sun. Dec. 24, 1939; Met. Dec. 1939; G.M.P.R.)

30 December, 1939 (SAT)

Glenn Miller and His Orchestra played at the Arena, New Haven, Connecticut. (G.M.P.R.)

31 December, 1939 (SUN)

Glenn Miller and His Orchestra played at the Mechanic's Building, Boston, Massachusetts. (Boston Post, Dec. 30, 1939; G.M.P.R.)

According to ex-leader Frank Dailey, owner of the Meadowbrook, the top bands to play his spot in 1939 in the following order were Jimmy Dorsey, Glenn Miller, Larry Clinton, and Tommy Dorsey. (Met. Jan. 1940)

[112]

January, 1940

The Glenn Miller radio series sponsored by
Chesterfield cigarettes was changed to three times
weekly starting the first week of January. The
change was probably brought about in order to provide competition with Bob Crosby and His Orchestra
who replaced Benny Goodman and His Orchestra on
the Camel cigarettes program on Saturday nights
(beginning January 6th). Miller broadcast from the
CBS Playhouse (first located on Broadway and 53rd
Street, later on West 45th Street) while in New
York City. The series' producer was Jean Warren
Hight.

With the addition of the three Chesterfield Shows a
week Miller also broadcasted from the Cafe Rouge of
the Hotel Pennsylvania in New York City beginning
January 4th. The band's radio schedule was as
follows:

          MONDAY   12:00-12:30 A.M. NBC-Blue (Cafe Rouge)
          TUESDAY   10:00-10:15 P.M. CBS-Chesterfield Show
          WEDNESDAY 10:00-10:15 P.M. CBS-Chesterfield Show
          THURSDAY   10:00-10:15 P.M. CBS-Chesterfield Show
          FRIDAY   11:30-12:00 P.M. NBC-Red (Cafe Rouge)
          SATURDAY   12:00-12:30 A.M. NBC-Blue (Cafe Rouge)

The one exception to the above rule appears to have
been on the band's opening night broadcast from the
"Cafe Rouge" (January 4th) as this was a Thursday
night and the radio time for this night was 12:00-
12:30 A.M. NBC-Blue (Swing, Jan. 1940 & Feb. 1940;
DB, Feb. 1, 1940)

Sometime in January Miller, Sammy Kaye and Claude
Thornhill appeared on Gene King's radio program on
station WEVD. (Met. Feb. 1940)

2 January, 1940 (TUES): New York City, New York (CHESTERFIELD SHOW)
CBS 10:00-10:15 P.M. EST.

NO DETAILS AVAILABLE

3 January, 1940 (WED): New York City, New York (CHESTERFIELD SHOW)
CBS 10:00-10:15 P.M. EST.

The announcer for this show is Paul Douglas.

(Broadcast continued on next page)

Moonlight Serenade (Theme)

K2PP-0043   Vi LPM-6100, RCA RD 27145, RCA G LPM 6100,
             RD 3/4-64
             (3:33) MEDLEY:
             Int PD I Cried For You
                          (Gus Arnheim-Abe Lyman-Arthur Freed)
             Int GM This Changing World-voc Ray Eberle
                          (Harold Adamson-Dana Suesse)
             Int PD Marie-voc The Band (Borrowed from Tommy
                          Dorsey)
                          (Irving Berlin)
             Int PD Blue Skies
                          From "Blue Skies"
                          (Irving Berlin)
                          Ts, Beneke

             Careless
             Say "Si Si"-voc AS
             Farewell Blues
             Moonlight Serenade (Theme)

4 January, 1940 (THUR): New York City, New York (CHESTERFIELD SHOW)
             CBS 10:00-10:15 P.M. EST.

             Moonlight Serenade (Theme)
             The Yodelin' Jive-voc AS
                     (Hughie Prince-Don Raye)
             My Isle Of Golden Dreams
             My Prayer-voc RE

At this point in the program Dave Dexter presented
Glenn Miller with a golden trophy.

             In The Mood
             Moonlight Serenade (Theme)

4 January, 1940 (THUR): Cafe Rouge, Hotel Pennsylvania,
             New York City, N.Y.
             NBC-Blue 12:00-12:30 A.M.

             Glenn Miller and His Orchestra opened at the "Cafe
             Rouge" of the Hotel Pennsylvania, New York City,
             New York. The announcer for this program is Hugh
             James. No Sundays. (G.M.P.R.)

             (1:27) *Moonlight Serenade* (Theme)
                     (Mitchell Parish-Glenn Miller)

(Broadcast continued on next page)

      (5:05) *St. Louis Blues* (arr ED)
                (William C. Handy)
                Tpt, Hurley; ts, Beneke; tbn, Miller;
                tpt, Hurley
      (3:03) *Faithful Forever*-voc Ray Eberle
                From Paramount's Technicolor Cartoon
                "Gulliver's Travels"
                (Leo Robin-Ralph Rainger)
                As, McIntyre?
      (2:32) *Oh Johnny, Oh Johnny, Oh!*-voc Marion Hutton
                (Ed. Rose-Abe Olman)
                Ts, Beneke
      (1:47) *Sunrise Serenade* (PARTIAL)
                (Frankie Carle)
      (0:38) *Moonlight Serenade* (Theme)
                (Mitchell Parish-Glenn Miller)
      (2:52) *Slip Horn Jive* (arr ED)
                (Eddie Durham)
                Ts, Beneke; tpt, Hurley; tbn, Miller;
                Ts, Klink; tpt, Hurley
      (3:12) *Speaking Of Heaven*-voc Ray Eberle
                (Jimmy Van Heusen-Mack Gordon)
                As, McIntyre
      (2:43) *Ooh! What You Said*-voc Marion Hutton
                From the musical comedy "Three After
                Three"
                (Johnny Mercer-Hoagy Carmichael)
                Ts, Beneke
      (3:50) *Pagan Love Song*
                From the MGM film "The Pagan"
                (Arthur Freed-Nacio Herb Brown)
                Tbn, Miller; ts, Klink; muted tpt,
                Hurley; ts, Beneke; d, Purtill
      (0:22) *Moonlight Serenade* (Theme)
                (Mitchell Parish-Glenn Miller)

5 January, 1940 (FRI): Cafe Rouge, Hotel Pennsylvania,
                  New York City, N.Y.
                  NBC-Red 11:30-12:00 P.M. EST.

    The announcer for this program is Hugh James.

      (1:27) *Moonlight Serenade* (Theme)
                (Mitchell Parish-Glenn Miller)
      (2:27) *Johnson Rag* (arr BF)-voc The Band
                (Henry Kleinkauf-Guy Hall)
                Ts, Beneke; ts, Klink; tpt, Hurley
      (3:17) *Faithful To You*-voc Ray Eberle
                (Martin Block-Harold Green-Mickey
                Stoner)
                Clt, Abato

(Broadcast continued on next page)

     (2:53) I Just Got A Letter-voc Marion Hutton
               (Dave Franklin)
               Ts, Beneke
     (3:22) In An Old Dutch Garden-voc Ray Eberle
               (Mack Gordon-Will Grosz)
               Ts, Beneke
     (2:58) I Want To Be Happy (arr ED)
               From the musical production "No, No, Nanette"
               (Irving Caesar-Vincent Youmans)
               Tpt, Hurley; ts, Beneke; tbn, Miller; d, Purtill
     (2:43) Bless You-voc Ray Eberle
               (Eddie Lane-Don Baker)
     (3:14) The Little Man Who Wasn't There-voc Tex Beneke
               (Dialogue: Marion Hutton and Tex Beneke)
               (Harold Adamson-Bernard Hanighen)
               Ts, Beneke
     (4:13) Tiger Rag (arr ED)
               (Tony Sbarbaro-Eddie Edwards-Henry Ragas-Larry Shields-Nick LaRocca-Harry DeCosta)
               Ts, Klink; d, Purtill
     (0:48) Moonlight Serenade (Theme)
               (Mitchell Parish-Glenn Miller)

The 'vocal' by the Band on "Johnson Rag" amounts to a few shouts of "Hey!", "Hey Johnson!", "Hey Johnson Rag!" and similar shouting was done on "Little Brown Jug" at the beginning of the tune (but only on broadcast versions)

Note that Marion Hutton is on the dialogue instead of Glenn Miller (who was on the recording of "The Little Man Who Wasn't There").

6 January, 1940 (SAT): Victor Studios, New York City, New York

     Same personnel as for November 10th.

046082-1   BB 10570-B, HMVAu EA-3556
             The Gaucho Serenade (arr JG)-voc Ray Eberle
                 (James Cavanaugh-John Redmond-Nat Simon)
                 Clt, Schwartz

046083-1   BB 10580-B
             The Sky Fell Down (arr BF)
                 (Edward Heyman-Louis Alter)
                 Tbn, Miller

(Session continued on next page)

046084-1   BB <u>10570</u>-A, Vi 20-3562 (Vi P-255), HMV 7EG 8135,
            AFRS P-1445
      <u>When You Wish Upon A Star</u>-voc Ray Eberle
            From the Walt Disney Motion Picture
            "Pinocchio"
            (Ned Washington-Leigh Harline)
            Ts, Beneke

      "The Sky Fell Down" 2 takes; all other tunes 1 take.
      (RCA Victor)
      This session lasted from 2:00 P.M. to 5:30 P.M.
      (RCA Victor)

6 January, 1940 (SAT): Cafe Rouge, Hotel Pennsylvania,
*   New York City, N.Y.*
*   NBC-Blue 12:00-12:30 A.M.*

      <u>Moonlight Serenade</u> (Theme)
      <u>Glen Island Special</u>
      <u>Last Night</u>
      <u>Wham</u>
      <u>Indian Summer</u>
      <u>King Porter Stomp</u>
      <u>It's A Blue World</u>
      <u>Wanna Hat With Cherries</u>
      <u>My Blue Heaven</u>
      <u>Moonlight Serenade</u> (Theme)

9 January, 1940 (TUES): New York City, New York (CHESTERFIELD SHOW)
*   CBS 10:00-10:15 P.M. EST.*

      <u>Moonlight Serenade</u> (Theme)
      <u>Annie Laurie</u>
      *   (Alicia Ann Spottiswoode)*
      <u>South Of The Border</u>-voc AS
      *   (Jimmy Kennedy-Michael Carr)*
      <u>Faithful Forever</u>
      <u>I Just Got A Letter</u>
      <u>King Porter Stomp</u>
      <u>Moonlight Serenade</u> (Theme)

10 January, 1940 (WED)

      Glenn Miller, Benny Goodman, Paul Whiteman, and
      Teddy Powell were invited to lead their bands at
      the President's Ball at Madison Square Garden on
      this date (President Roosevelt's birthday). It
      is not known if Miller actually played. (Swing,
      Dec. 1939)

10 January, 1940 (WED): New York City, New York (CHESTERFIELD SHOW)
CBS 10:00-10:15 P.M. EST.

The announcer for this program is Paul Douglas.

Moonlight Serenade (Theme)

E3VP 5242   Vi LPT 6700, Vi EPNT 6700 (947-0126), Vi SPD-18
               (599-9105), HMV RLS 599, RCA RD 27090,
               Vi LOP 1005, Vi LPM-1973, RCA G LPT 6700,
               AFRS P-6717, RCA Vi Arg 3AE-3342
               (3:38) MEDLEY:
               Int GM   My Melancholy Baby
                        (Geo. A. Norton-Ernie Burnett)
               Int GM   Moon Love-voc Ray Eberle
                        Adapted from Tschaikowskys'
                        5th Symphony, 2nd Movement
                        (Mack David-Mack Davis-Andre
                        Kostelanetz)
               Int GM   Stompin' At The Savoy (borrowed from
                        Benny Goodman)
                        (Benny Goodman-Chick Webb-Edgar
                        Sampson-Andy Razaf)
                        Tpt, Hurley
               Int PD   Blue Moon
                        (Lorenz Hart-Richard Rodgers)
                        Ts, Beneke

               Beer Barrel Polka-voc AS

E3VP 5244   Vi LPT 6700, Vi EPNT 6700 (947-0120), Vi SPD-18
               (599-9103), HMV RLS 599, RCA G LPT 6700
               (2:19) Bless You-voc Ray Eberle
                      (Eddie Lane-Don Baker)

               Slip Horn Jive
               Moonlight Serenade (Theme)

               Victor album LPT 6700 showed "Bless You" as being
               broadcast on March 10th, 1940 (which is a Sunday)
               but correct information from the Miller Estate has
               provided us with the above date.

11 January, 1940 (THUR): New York City, New York (CHESTERFIELD SHOW)
CBS 10:00-10:15 P.M. EST.

Moonlight Serenade (Theme)

(Broadcast continued on next page)

        (1:46) Ciri-Biri-Bin (arr BF)-voc Ray Eberle
                (Harry James-Jack Lawrence-
                A. Pestalozza)
        (2:15) South American Way-voc Andrews Sisters
                From the musical production "Streets
                of Paris"
                (Al Dubin-Jimmy McHugh)
        Sunrise Serenade
        My Blue Heaven
        Moonlight Serenade (Theme)

15 January, 1940 (MON): Victor Studios, New York City, New York

Same personnel as for November 10th.

046431-1   BB 10580-A, HMV 7EG 8135
            Give A Little Whistle-voc Marion Hutton
                From the Walt Disney Motion Picture
                "Pinocchio"
                (Ned Washington-Leigh Harline)
                Ts, Beneke; p, MacGregor

046432-1   BB 10587-A, Vi 83046-A, HMV BD 5644, HMVSw JK-2146,
            VD 352, Vi 20-2411 (Vi P-189), Vi 420-0036,
            Vi 447-0036, RCA RCX 1040, Vi EPAT-405,
            Vi EPA-5008, Vi LPT 1016, Cam Cal/Cas-2128,
            RCA G Cas-2128, RCA G EPA-5008, RCA G
            EPAT-405, RCA G LPT 1016, Navy VD 132,
            RCA Cam Arg Cal-3138, RCA G LPM/LSP-9944
            Missouri Waltz
                (James Royce Shannon-Frederic Knight Logan)
                As, McIntyre

046433-1   BB 10587-B, Vi 83046-B, HMV BD 5644, HMVSw
            JK-2146, Vi 420-0036, Vi 447-0036, RCA RCX
            1063, Vi EPA-727, HMV DLP 1081, Vi LPT-3002,
            Vi EPBT-3002 (947-0039), Vi LPM-1190,
            Vi EPB-1190 (547-0828), RCA G EPC-1190,
            RCA G LPM-1190, RCA Int. B-21040, RCA Int.
            T-21040
            Beautiful Ohio (arr JG)
                (Ballard MacDonald-Mary Earl)
                Ts, Beneke; p, MacGregor

046434-1   BB 10657-B
            What's The Matter With Me-voc Marion Hutton
                (Sam M. Lewis-Terry Shand)
                Tpt, Hurley; ts, Beneke

(Session continued on next page)

"Missouri Waltz" and "Beautiful Ohio" 2 takes;
all other tunes 1 take. (RCA Victor)
This session lasted from 1:00 P.M. to 4:30 P.M.
(RCA Victor)

15 January, 1940 (MON): *Cafe Rouge, Hotel Pennsylvania,*
                        New York City, N.Y.
                        NBC-Blue 12:00-12:30 A.M.

        (2:23) *King Porter Stomp*
                        (Ferdinand "Jelly-Roll" Morton)
                        Tbn, Miller; ts, Beneke; tpt, Hurley;
                        ts, Klink
        (0:55) *It's A Blue World* no vocal as tune is partial
                        (From the Columbia film "Music In My
                        Heart"
                        (Bob Wright-Chet Forrest)
                        Clt, Schwartz
                        Drink To Me Only With Thine Eyes

16 January, 1940 (TUES): *New York City, N.Y. (CHESTERFIELD SHOW)*
                        CBS 10:00-10:15 P.M. EST.

                        Moonlight Serenade (Theme)
                        Johnson Rag
                        Indian Summer
                        Chico's Love Song-voc AS
                                (Lester Lee-Dan Shapiro-Jerry Seelan)

K2PP-0042   Vi LPM-6100, RCA RD 27145, RCA G LPM-6100
    FFT   (1:21) Sweet And Low
                                (J. Barnby-Alfred Tennyson)
                                P. MacGregor

                        Tiger Rag
                        Moonlight Serenade (Theme)

17 January, 1940 (WED): *New York City, N.Y. (CHESTERFIELD SHOW)*
                        CBS 10:00-10:15 P.M. EST.

                        Moonlight Serenade (Theme)
                        Baby Me-voc Marion Hutton
                        Blue Rain
                        Little Sally Waters-voc AS
                                (
                        Pagan Love Song
                        Moonlight Serenade (Theme)

18 January, 1940 (THUR): New York City, N.Y. (CHESTERFIELD SHOW)
               CBS 10:00-10:15 P.M. EST.

> *Moonlight Serenade* (Theme)
> *Pavanne*
> *The Little Red Fox*-voc AS
>   *(Johnny Lange-Hy Heath-Lew Porter-*
>   *Kerth)*
> *Speaking Of Heaven*
> *In The Mood*
> *Moonlight Serenade* (Theme)

19 January, 1940 (FRI)

> The payroll records for the week January 19th to
> January 25th are missing and it is during this
> period that Al Mastren (trombonist) left the band
> and was replaced by Howard Gibeling. A number of
> reasons are given for Mastren leaving the band.
> Down Beat (Feb. 15th) said that he was "taken
> sick late in January". Metronome (March 1940)
> said that it was due to an "injury to his arm".
> Swing (March 1940) just said that he was "out
> with an ailment".
>
> The payroll records for the week January 26th to
> February 1st are of some help in that they show
> the following:
>
> Mastren was paid for the Chesterfield Show of
> January 23rd; he was not paid for the record date
> of January 26th (or the 29th); he was paid for 5
> days out of 7. The big question here is which 5
> days? We can only assume that he was with the
> band up until January 23rd.
>
> Tommy Mack was paid for the record session of
> January 26th but not the record session of January
> 29th; he was also paid for the Chesterfield Shows
> of January 31st and February 1st.
>
> Gibeling was not paid for the record date of
> January 26th but he was paid for the record date
> of January 29th; he was also paid for the Chester-
> field Show of January 30th; and he was paid for 4
> days out of 7. The big question here is which 4
> days?
>
> To sum up what we do know and what we don't know:

(continued on next page)

```
Jan. 19th (Fri)--?????
Jan. 20th (Sat)--?????
Jan. 21st (Sun)--?????
Jan. 22nd (Mon)--?????
Jan. 23rd (Tues)-MASTREN (on Chesterfield Show);
                 Hotel Pennsylvania job ?????
Jan. 24th (Wed)--?????
Jan. 25th (Thur)-?????
Jan. 26th (Fri)--MACK (on record session);
                 Hotel Pennsylvania job ?????
Jan. 27th (Sat)--?????
Jan. 28th (Sun)--?????
Jan. 29th (Mon)--GIBELING (on record session);
                 Hotel Pennsylvania job ?????
Jan. 30th (Tues)-GIBELING (on Chesterfield Show);
                 Hotel Pennsylvania job ?????
Jan. 31st (Wed)--MACK (on Chesterfield Show);
                 Hotel Pennsylvania job ?????
Feb.  1st (Thur)-MACK (on Chesterfield Show);
                 Hotel Pennsylvania job ?????
```

23 January, 1940 (TUES): New York City, N.Y. (CHESTERFIELD SHOW)
CBS 10:00-10:15 P.M. EST.

Ed Herlihy (announcer) replaced Paul Douglas on this date. Douglas was in the hospital for an operation.

Moonlight Serenade (Theme)
Little Brown Jug
Careless
Ciri-Biri-Bin-voc AS

K2PP-0046   Vi LPM-6100, RCA RD 27147, RCA G LPM-6100
(1:29) Silver Threads Among The Gold
            (Eben E. Rexford-Hart Pease Danks)

I Want To Be Happy
Moonlight Serenade (Theme)

24 January, 1940 (WED): New York City, N.Y. (CHESTERFIELD SHOW)
CBS 10:00-10:15 P.M. EST.

The announcer for this program is Ed Herlihy.

E3VP 5237   Vi LPT 6700, Vi EPNT 6700 (947-0120), Vi LOP-
            1005, Vi SPD-18 (599-9105), Vi LPM-1973,
            HMV RLS 599, RCA RD 27090, RCA G LPT 6700,
            AFRS P-6720

(Broadcast continued on next page)

                    (0:14) Moonlight Serenade (Theme)
                           (Mitchell Parish-Glenn Miller)

E3VP 5237   Vi LPT 6700, Vi EPNT 6700 (947-0120), Vi LOP-
                         1005, Vi SPD-18 (599-9105), Vi LPM-1973,
                         HMV RLS 599, RCA RD 27090, RCA G LPT 6700,
                         AFRS P-6720
                    (3:02) MEDLEY:
                    Int EH   Japanese Sandman
                               (Raymond B. Egan-Richard A. Whiting)
                    Int GM   What's The Matter With Me-voc Marion
                             Hutton
                               (Sam M. Lewis-Terry Shand)
                    Int GM   Let's Dance (borrowed from Benny Goodman)
                               (Baldridge-Gregory Stone-Bonime)
                               Tpt, Hurley; ts, Beneke
                    Int GM   Blue Room
                               (Lorenz Hart-Richard Rodgers)

                             I Want My Mama-voc AS
                                 (Al Stillman-Emilio de Torre-
                                 Jararaca Paiva-Vicente Paiva)
                             It's A Blue World
                             Glen Island Special
                             Moonlight Serenade (Theme)

25 January, 1940 (THUR): New York City, N.Y. (CHESTERFIELD SHOW)
                         CBS 10:00-10:15 P.M. EST.

                             Moonlight Serenade (Theme)
                             The Rumba Jumps!
                             In An Old Dutch Garden
                             Well, All Right-voc AS
                                 (Frances Faye-Don Raye-Dan Howell)
                             Runnin' Wild
                             Moonlight Serenade (Theme)

26 January, 1940 (FRI): Victor Studios, New York City, New York

                    Trombones   Glenn Miller, TOMMY MACK, Paul
                                 Tanner, Frank D'Annolfo
                    Trumpets   Clyde Hurley, Legh Knowles, Dale
                                 McMickle, Johnny Best
                    Reeds   Hal McIntyre, as; Jimmy Abato, as &
                                 bar; Wilbur Schwartz, clt & as; Tex
                                 Beneke, ts; Al Klink, ts
                    Rhythm   Chummy MacGregor, p; Richard Fisher,
                                 g; Rowland Bundock, b; Maurice
                                 Purtill, d
                    Vocalists   Marion Hutton, Tex Beneke
(Session continued on next page)

046727-1   <u>BB 10622-B</u>, HMV BD 5602, HMV MH 149, HMV 7EG
        8254, Vi P8S-1432, Vi LPT 6700, Vi EPNT 6700
        (947-0119), HMV RLS 599, Vi SPD-18 (599-9107),
        Vi 45 Special-1953, Vi LSP-4125, HMVIn BD
        5602, RCA G LPT 6700, RCA Int. INTS 1002
    Say "Si Si"(Para Vigo Me Voy)-voc Marion Hutton
        (Al Stillman-Francia Luban-Ernesto Lecuona)
        Ts, Beneke

046728-1   <u>BB 10673-A</u>, VdP GW-2023, HMV 7EG 8055, Vi Arg 68-
        0881
    The Rumba Jumps!-voc Marion Hutton and Tex Beneke
        From the musical production "Three After
        Three"
        (Johnny Mercer-Hoagy Carmichael)
        D, Purtill; ts, Beneke

    Both tunes 2 takes. (RCA Victor)
    This session lasted from 2:00 P.M. to 5:15 P.M.
    (RCA Victor)

27 January, 1940 (SAT): Cafe Rouge, Hotel Pennsylvania,
                      New York City, N.Y.
                      NBC-Blue 12:00-12:30 A.M. WJZ

       (2:08) Say "Si Si" (Para Vigo Me Voy)-voc Marion
             Hutton
             (Al Stillman-Francia Luban-Ernesto
             Lecuona)
             Ts, Beneke
       (0:38) Faithful To You no vocal as tune is partial
             (Martin Block-Harold Green-Mickey
             Stoner)
       (2:12) What's The Matter With Me-voc Marion Hutton
             (Sam M. Lewis-Terry Shand)
             D, Purtill; tpt, Hurley; ts, Beneke
      (1:20) Pagan Love Song
             From the MGM film "The Pagan"
             (Arthur Freed-Nacio Herb Brown)
             Tbn, Miller; ts, Klink

29 January, 1940 (MON): Victor Studios, New York City, New York

        Trombones   Glenn Miller, HOWARD GIBELING, Paul
                        Tanner, Frank D'Annolfo
        Trumpets   Clyde Hurley, Legh Knowles, Dale
                        McMickle, Johnny Best

(Session continued on next page)

Reeds	Hal McIntyre, as; Jimmy Abato, as & bar; Wilbur Schwartz, clt & as; Tex Beneke, ts; Al Klink, ts
Rhythm	Chummy MacGregor, p; Richard Fisher, g; Rowland Bundock, b; Maurice Purtill, d
Vocalists	Marion Hutton, Tex Beneke

046735-1   BB 10665-A, HMV BD 5612, HMV MH 11, HMVSw JK-2279, ViJ 1092, El G (Test), Vi 20-1567 (Vi P-148), Vi 20-1754, Vi 47-2854 (Vi WP-148), Vi 420-0047, Vi 447-0047, Vi EPAT-405, Vi LPM-31, Vi LPT 3067, HMV DLP 1062, AFRS H-62-70 Phonograph Album No. 70, AFRS P-NAV-2, RD 3/4-44-2, HMVAus GA 5011, AFRS P-1542, AFRS P-S-15, AFRS "America's Pop Music" 72, RCA F 130210, RD 3/4-64, Vi LPM-2246, HMVIr I.M. 737, HMVSc X6535, HMVHu HUC 116, RCA G EPAT-405, RCA G LPM 9801, AFRS "Jukebox USA" 220, RCA G LPT 3067, RCA G LSP-9901, RCA G 447-0047, HMVAu EA-2780, Vi VPM-6019, RCA G SRS 560, Vi Braz 27132, RCA Br. RD-8094
Star Dust (arr BF & GM)
(Mitchell Parish-Hoagy Carmichael)
Ts, Beneke; tpt, Hurley; ts, Beneke; clt, Schwartz

046736-1   BB 10665-B, HMV BD 5697, HMV MH 144, HMVSw JK-2279, VD 39, ViJ 1099, AFRS H-62-70 Phonograph Album No. 70, Cam Cal/Cas-2128, RCA G Cas-2128, HMVSc X6535, RCA Cam Arg Cal-3138, Vi Braz 27132
My Melancholy Baby (arr BF)-voc Tex Beneke
(Geo. A. Norton-Ernie Burnett)
Ts, Beneke

046737-1   BB 10598-B, VdP GW-2077
Let's All Sing Together (arr JG)-voc Marion Hutton
(Joe Audino-Nick DiRocca-Bill Keeshan)
Ts, Beneke; tpt, Hurley; d, Purtill

046738-1   BB 10754-B, HMV BD 5618, HMVAu EA-2780, HMVSw JK-2125, Vi LPT 6700, Vi EPNT 6700 (947-0128), HMV RLS 599, Vi SPD-18 (599-9110), RD 3/4-64, RCA G LPT 6700, HMVIr I.P. 931
Rug Cutter's Swing (arr BF)
(Horace Henderson)
Tpt, Hurley; ts, Beneke; tbn, Miller; tpt, Hurley

(Session continued on next page)

046739-1   BB 10598-A, HMV BD 5587, HMVAu EA-2552, VdP GW-
            2077, HMV 7EG 8055, Vi EPA 528, Vi LPM
            3182, Vi PR-114, RD 3/4-25, RD Br. RDS
            6099, RCA Int. CT20124
            The Woodpecker Song-voc Marion Hutton
                (Harold Adamson-Eldo di Lazzaro)
                Ts, Beneke

            "Let's All Sing Together" and "The Woodpecker
            Song" 2 takes each; all other tunes 1 take.
            (RCA Victor)
            This session lasted from 1:00 P.M. to 5:15 P.M.
            (RCA Victor)

29 January, 1940 (MON): *Cafe Rouge, Hotel Pennsylvania,*
                        New York City, N.Y.
                        NBC-Blue   12:00-12:30 A.M.   WJZ

        Tunes not in correct order.

        (2:12) *Let's All Sing Together (arr JG)-voc*
                        Marion Hutton
                        (Joe Audino-Nick DiRocca-Bill Keeshan)
                        Ts, Beneke; tpt, Hurley; d, Purtill
        (2:11) *On A Little Street In Singapore (arr AG)-*
                        voc Ray Eberle
                        (Billy Hill-Peter DeRose)
        (1:23) *Glen Island Special (arr ED)*
                        (Eddie Durham)
                        Tpt, Hurley; ts, Beneke
        (2:29) *The Rumba Jumps! voc Marion Hutton and Tex*
                        Beneke
                        From the musical production "Three
                        After Three"
                        (Johnny Mercer-Hoagy Carmichael)
                        D, Purtill; ts, Beneke
        (1:25) *In The Mood*
                        (Andy Razaf-Joe Garland)
                        Ts, Beneke; ts, Klink; tpt, Hurley

30 January, 1940 (TUES): *New York City, N.Y. (CHESTERFIELD SHOW)*
                        CBS   10:00-10:15 P.M. EST.

                Moonlight Serenade (Theme)
                Rug Cutter's Swing
                I Love You Much Too Much-voc Patty Andrews
                        (Don Raye-Alex Olshey-C. Towber)
                Wanna Hat With Cherries-voc MH
                Sweet And Low

(Broadcast continued on next page)

[126]

K2PP-0042   Vi LPM 6100, RCA RD 27145, RCA G LPM 6100,
             RCA G LPM 9852, RCA G LPM/LSP-9944
             (2:06) Hallelujah! (arr BF)
                           From the musical production "Hit the
                           Deck"
                           (Leo Robin-Clifford Grey-Vincent
                           Youmans)
                           Ts, Beneke; clt, ??; d, Purtill

             Moonlight Serenade (Theme)

             Impending marriages of Patty Andrews to Vic Schoen
             and Maxene Andrews to Lou Levy threatened to break
             up the Andrews Sisters' trio during this period.
             "And when Patty appeared solo on Glenn Miller's
             Chesterfield show one night, when the trio couldn't
             get together because of parental interference, fan
             mail jumped to 10 times its normal proportions."
             (DB, Feb. 15, 1940)

             According to the same issue of Down Beat Vic Schoen
             made the arrangements that the Miller band played
             for the Andrews Sisters.

31 January, 1940 (WED): New York City, New York (CHESTERFIELD SHOW)
*   CBS   10:00-10:15 P.M. EST.*

       The announcer for this show is Ed Herlihy.

       Trombones   Glenn Miller, TOMMY MACK, Paul Tanner,
       *   Frank D'Annolfo*
       Trumpets   Clyde Hurley, Legh Knowles, Dale
       *   McMickle, Johnny Best*
       Reeds   Hal McIntyre, as; Jimmy Abato, as &
       *   bar; Wilbur Schwartz, clt & as;*
       *   Tex Beneke, ts; Al Klink, ts*
       Rhythm   Chummy MacGregor, p; Richard Fisher,
       *   g; Rowland Bundock, b; Maurice*
       *   Purtill, d*

             Moonlight Serenade (Theme)

K2PP-0044   Vi LPM-6100, RCA RD 27146, RCA G LPM 6100
             (3:23) MEDLEY:
                    Whispering
                           (Malvin Schonberger-Richard Coburn-
                           Vincent Rose)
             Int GM Ooh! What You Said-voc Marion Hutton
                           From the musical comedy "Three
                           After Three"
                           (Johnny Mercer-Hoagy Carmichael)

(Broadcast continued on next page)

Int EH ~~The Dipsey Doodle~~ (borrowed from Larry
                 Clinton)
                 (Larry Clinton)
                 ~~Tbn, Miller~~
Int GM ~~The Birth Of The Blues~~
                 From the musical production "George
                 White's Scandals"
                 (B.G. De Sylva-Lew Brown-Ray Henderson)
                 Tpt, Hurley

> *Begin The Beguine-voc AS*
> *From the musical production "Jubilee"*
> *(Cole Porter)*
> *Faithful Forever*
> *My Blue Heaven*
> *Moonlight Serenade (Theme)*

1 February, 1940 (THUR): New York City, New York (CHESTERFIELD SHOW)
*   CBS 10:00-10:15 P.M. EST.*

> *Moonlight Serenade (Theme)*
> *Missouri Waltz*
> *South Of The Border-voc AS*
> *Speaking Of Heaven*
> *Tuxedo Junction*
> *Moonlight Serenade (Theme)*

2 February, 1940 (FRI): Cafe Rouge, Hotel Pennsylvania,
*   New York City, N.Y.*
*   NBC-Red 11:30-12:00 P.M.*

> *The Gaucho Serenade*

3 February, 1940 (SAT): Ambassador Hotel, New York City, New York
*   WNEW 5:30 P.M.*

        MARTIN BLOCK 5th ANNIVERSARY SHOW

> *Moonlight Serenade (Theme)*
> *Tiger Rag*
> *Faithful To You*
> *Ciri-Biri-Bin-voc AS*
> *Star Dust*
> *The Rumba Jumps!*
> *Indian Summer*
> *Beer Barrel Polka-voc AS*
> *Tuxedo Junction*
> *In The Mood*
> *Moonlight Serenade (Theme)*

5 February, 1940 (MON): Victor Studios, New York City, New York
          Same personnel as for January 31st broadcast.

046784-1   BB 10605-B, HMV BD 5596, HMVSw JK-2183, HMV 7EG
                  8055
                  Sweet Potato Piper (arr JG)-voc Marion Hutton and
                       Tex Beneke
                       From the Paramount film "The Road to Singapore"
                       (Johnny Burke-James V. Monaco)
                       Ts, Beneke

046785-1   BB 10605-A, HMV BD 5596, HMVSw JK-2183
                  Too Romantic-voc Ray Eberle
                       From the Paramount film "The Road to Singapore"
                       (Johnny Burke-James V. Monaco)

046786-1   BB 10612-A (gold label) (Not known if this take on
                       silver label also), HMV BD 5595, HMVIr I.M.
                       1021, HMVIr I.P. 922, HMVAu EA-2541, HMVSw
                       JK-2200, HMV DLP 1024, HMVAus GA 5137, HMVAus
                       VDLP 302, El WDLP 1024
                  Tuxedo Junction (arr JG)
                       (William Johnson-Julian Dash-Erskine Hawkins-
                       Buddy Feyne)
                       Muted tpt, McMickle; open tpt, Hurley;
                       muted tpt, McMickle; p, MacGregor

046786-2   BB 10612-A (silver label) (Not known if this take
                       on gold label also),Vi 20-1552 (Vi P-146),
                       Vi 20-1565 (Vi P-148), Vi 20-1754, Vi 27-0085
                       (Vi WPT-12), Vi 420-0047, Vi 447-0047, Vi EPA-
                       528, Vi EPBT-3029,Vi EPA-5081, Vi LPT-3036,
                       Vi EPBT-3036 (947-0090), Vi LPT-3057, Vi EPBT-
                       3057 (947-0137), Vi EPA-733, Vi LPM/LSP-1192,
                       Vi EPB-1192, Vi EPB-1192 (547-0810), Vi LPT-
                       12, Vi SP-33-90, Vi LPM 3182, Vi LPM/LSP-3377,
                       RD 3/4-21, RD Br.RDS 6176, RCA RCX 1035, RCA
                       RD 27068, ViJ LM-5, Vi It LPM 10011, Vi It LJ
                       50012, RCA G LPM/LSP-1192, AFRS "America's
                       Pop Music" 72, RCA G EPC-1192, RCA G LPM/LSP-
                       3377, RCA G LPM 9801, AFRS P-2412, RCA G LSP-
                       9901, Vi 83035, Vi TP3-5044, Vi LPM-1071,
                       RCA G LPM 1071, RD 3/4-64 (Production albums
                       only), RCA G 447-0047, RCA F 230201, RCA F
                       530243, Vi VPM-6019, Vi P8S-5061, Vi EPBT-
                       1192, RCA Int. CT20124, Vi Arg LPM/LSP-1192,
                       RCA G Cas 10231, RCA G SRS 560, RCA F 740.515,
                       RCA Br. RD-8094 (unissued)

(Session continued on next page)

Tuxedo Junction (arr JG)
    (William Johnson-Julian Dash-Erskine Hawkins-
    Buddy Feyne)
    Muted tpt, McMickle; open tpt, Hurley;
    muted tpt, McMickle; p, MacGregor

046787-1   BB 10612-B, HMV BD 5595, HMVSw JK-2200, HMVIr
    I.M. 1021, Vi 83035-B, Vi 420-0040, Vi 447-
    0040, RCA RCX 1063, Vi EPA-5149, Vi LPT 3002,
    Vi EPBT-3002 (947-0039), Vi SP-33-90, Vi LPM
    1190, HMV DLP 1081, ViJ LM-5, Vi It LPM-10141,
    Vi It LJ 50020, Vi It LPM 50020, HMVIr I.P.
    922, RCA Int. B-21040, RCA Int. T-21040, RCA
    F 130211, RCA G EPC-1190, RCA G LPM-1190,
    HMV 3-20516, RD 3/4-64, Vi VPM-6019, RCA Br.
    RD-8094 (unissued)

Danny Boy (Londonderry Air) (arr GM & ChM)
    (Fred E. Weatherly)
    Celeste, MacGregor; muted tbn, Miller

"Tuxedo Junction" 2 takes; all other tunes 1 take.
(RCA Victor)
This session lasted from 1:00 P.M. to 4:45 P.M.
(RCA Victor)

In a recent radio interview on station WHO, Des
Moines, Iowa, Chummy MacGregor, reading from his
forthcoming book "Moonlight Serenade Revisited",
stated that when the Miller band was at the Savoy
(December 24, 1939) along with the Erskine
Hawkins Orchestra it picked up the arrangement of
"Tuxedo Junction." It was a different arrangement
from the final Miller product. Hal McIntyre got a
lead sheet from one of Hawkins' sax men. Jerry
Gray wrote it up and at a rehearsal the band added
brass figures, plungers and pedal note pauses for
the trombones and the build up at the finish.

5 February, 1940 (MON): Cafe Rouge, Hotel Pennsylvania,
    New York City, N.Y.
    NBC-Blue 12:00-12:30 A.M.

The announcer for this program is Hugh James.

(1:29) Moonlight Serenade (Theme)
    (Mitchell Parish-Glenn Miller)
(3:30) Symphony In Riffs
    (Benny Carter-I. Mills)
    Ts, Beneke; tpt, Hurley; ts, Beneke

(Broadcast continued on next page)

(3:08) <u>When You Wish Upon A Star</u>-voc Ray Eberle
From the Walt Disney Motion Picture
"Pinocchio"
(Ned Washington-Leigh Harline)
Ts, Beneke
(2:54) <u>The Rumba Jumps</u>!-voc Marion Hutton and
Tex Beneke
From the musical production "Three
After Three"
(Johnny Mercer-Hoagy Carmichael)
D, Purtill; ts, Beneke
(3:30) <u>Star Dust</u>(arr BF & GM)
(Mitchell Parish-Hoagy Carmichael)
P, MacGregor; ts, Beneke; tpt, Hurley;
ts, Beneke; clt, Schwartz
(2:59) <u>Slip Horn Jive</u> (arr ED)
(Eddie Durham)
D, Purtill; ts, Beneke; tpt, Hurley;
tbn, Miller; ts, Klink; tpt, Hurley
(3:04) <u>Starlit Hour</u> (arr GM)-voc Ray Eberle
From "Earl Carroll Vanities"
(Mitchell Parish-Peter DeRose)
(3:16) <u>The Little Man Who Wasn't There</u>-voc Marion
Hutton and Tex Beneke
(Harold Adamson-Bernard Hanighen)
Ts, Beneke
(3:55) <u>Tiger Rag</u> (arr ED)
(Tony Sbarbaro-Eddie Edwards-Henry
Ragas-Larry Shields-Nick LaRocca-
Harry DeCosta)
Ts, Klink; d, Purtill
(0:55) <u>Moonlight Serenade</u> (Theme)
(Mitchell Parish-Glenn Miller)

6 February, 1940 (TUES): New York City, New York (CHESTERFIELD SHOW)
CBS 10:00-10:15 P.M. EST.

<u>Moonlight Serenade</u> (Theme)
<u>The Woodpecker Song</u>
<u>On A Little Street In Singapore</u>
<u>Three O'Clock In the Morning</u>-voc AS
(Dorothy Terris-Julian Robeldo)
<u>Danny Boy</u>
<u>Farewell Blues</u>
<u>Moonlight Serenade</u> (Theme)

7 February, 1940 (WED): New York City, New York (CHESTERFIELD SHOW)
CBS   10:00-10:15 P.M. EST.

The announcer for this show is Ed Herlihy. Paul
Douglas was "recovering in okay fashion after an
operation for gallstones in Philly". (DB, Feb.
15, 1940)

Moonlight Serenade (Theme)

K2PP-0042		Vi LPM-6100, RCA RD 27145, RCA G LPM 6100
		(3:08) MEDLEY:
FFT	Int EH	I Never Knew (arr JG)
		(Tom Pitts-Ray Egan-Roy Marsh)
FFT	Int EH	Let's All Sing Together (arr JG)-voc
		Marion Hutton
		(Joe Audino-Nick DiRocca-Bill
		Keeshan)
FFT	Int GM	Thinking Of You (arr JG) (borrowed from
		Kay Kyser)
		From the musical production "Five
		O'Clock Girl"
		(Bert Kalmar-Harry Ruby)
		P, MacGregor
FFT	Int GM	Alice Blue Gown (arr JG)
		From the RKO film "Irene"
		(Joseph McCarthy-Harry Tierney)
		Ts, Beneke

This Changing World-voc RE
Let's Have Another One-voc AS
(Don Raye-Hughie Prince)
King Porter Stomp
Moonlight Serenade (Theme)

8 February, 1940 (THUR): New York City, New York (CHESTERFIELD SHOW)
CBS   10:00-10:15 P.M. EST.

Moonlight Serenade (Theme)
My Isle Of Golden Dreams
Oh Johnny, Oh Johnny, Oh!-voc AS
The Gaucho Serenade
ALP   (3:05) *Tuxedo Junction (arr JG)*
(William Johnson-Julian Dash-
Erskine Hawkins-Ruddy Feyne)
Muted tpt, McMickle; open tpt,
Hurley; muted tpt, McMickle;
p, MacGregor
Moonlight Serenade (Theme)

9 February, 1940 (FRI): Cafe Rouge, Hotel Pennsylvania,
New York City, N.Y.
NBC-Red 11:30-12:00 Midnight

Moonlight Serenade (Theme)
First tune unknown
Faithful Forever
The Woodpecker Song
Indian Summer
In The Mood
In An Old Dutch Garden
What's The Matter With Me
Bugle Call Rag
Moonlight Serenade (Theme)

12 February, 1940 (MON)

Trombones	Glenn Miller, JIMMY PRIDDY, Paul Tanner, Frank D'Annolfo
Trumpets	Clyde Hurley, Legh Knowles, Dale McMickle, Johnny Best
Reeds	Hal McIntyre, as; Jimmy Abato, as & bar; Wilbur Schwartz, clt & as; Tex Beneke, ts; Al Klink, ts
Rhythm	Chummy MacGregor, p; Richard Fisher, g; Rowland Bundock, b; Maurice Purtill, d
Vocalists	Marion Hutton, Ray Eberle
Band-Boy	Raul Hidalgo

13 February, 1940 (TUES): New York City, New York (CHESTERFIELD SHOW)

The announcer for this show is Ed Herlihy.

Moonlight Serenade (Theme)
The Rumba Jumps!-voc MH & TB
Starlit Hour-voc RE
I've Got No Strings-voc AS
From the Walt Disney Motion Picture
"Pinocchio"
(Ned Washington-Leigh Harline)
Tpt, Hurley
Tuxedo Junction
Moonlight Serenade (Theme)

14 February, 1940 (WED): New York City, New York (CHESTERFIELD SHOW)
                        CBS   10:00-10:15 P.M. EST.

        The announcer for this show is Ed Herlihy.

                    Moonlight Serenade (Theme)

K2PP-0042   Vi LPM-6100, RCA RD 27145, RCA G LPM 6100
                 (3:24)   MEDLEY:
    FFT   Int EH   My Gal Sal
                         (Paul Dresser)
                       Ts, Beneke
    FFT   Int EH   You're A Lucky Guy-voc Marion Hutton
                         (Saul Chaplin-Sammy Cahn)
    FFT   Int GM   When Summer Is Gone (borrowed from Hal
                         Kemp)
                         (Monte Wilhite-Charles Harrison)
                       Ts, Beneke
    FFT   Int EH   Wabash Blues
                         (Dave Ringle-Fred Meinken)
                       Tpt, Hurley

                 Down By The Ohio-voc AS
                         (Jack Yellen-Abe Olman)
                 It's A Blue World
                 Pagan Love Song
                 Moonlight Serenade (Theme)

15 February, 1940 (THUR): New York City, New York (CHESTERFIELD SHOW)
                         CBS   10:00-10:15 P.M. EST.

                 Moonlight Serenade (Theme
                 Star Dust
                 The Little Red Fox-voc AS
                 In An Old Dutch Garden
                 Tiger Rag
                 Moonlight Serenade (Theme)

16 February, 1940 (FRI): Cafe Rouge, Hotel Pennsylvania,
                         New York City, N.Y.
                         12:01 A.M.

        Glenn Miller and His Orchestra participated in a
        V.F.W. Hello America Radio Hour in which the music
        of several bands was heard from 11:30-12:30. Guy
        Lombardo was heard from the "Cocoanut Grove" in
        the Hotel Ambassador, Los Angeles "live" as well
        as a number lesser known bands. The Glenn Miller
        band was heard for three minutes "live" at
        12:01 A.M. (G.M.P.R.)

17 February, 1940 (SAT)

Trombones	Glenn Miller, Jimmy Priddy, Paul Tanner, Frank D'Annolfo
Trumpets	Clyde Hurley, Legh Knowles, Dale McMickle, Johnny Best
Reeds	Hal McIntyre, as; ERNIE CACERES, as, bar & clt; Wilbur Schwartz, clt & as; Tex Beneke, ts; Al Klink, ts
Rhythm	Chummy MacGregor, p; Richard Fisher, g; Rowland Bundock, b; Maurice Purtill, d
Vocalists	Marion Hutton, Ray Eberle
Band-Boy	Raul Hidalgo

"Ernie Caceres, brilliant Mexican clarinetist, who played with Bobby Hackett and Jack Teagarden, has left Bob Zurke and joined Glenn Miller's band. He replaces young Jimmy Abato, who has signed a contract with Paul Whiteman." (Met. March 1940)

G.M.P.R. for the week ending February 22nd show that Caceres had one day deducted from his pay so we must assume that he joined the band on this date and not the 16th. The only problem here is that Abato is paid up for the week ending February 15th and we wonder who played with the band on February 16th. Perhaps Abato stayed on for one more day.

19 February, 1940 (MON): Victor Studios, New York City, New York

Same personnel as for February 17th.

047067-1   BB 10622-A, HMV BD 5612, Vi LPT 6700, Vi EPNT 6700
            (947-0122), Vi SPD-18 (599-9109), HMV RLS 599,
            RCA G LPT 6700, HMVIr I.M. 737, HMVSc X7607,
            HMVHu HUC 116
            Imagination-voc Ray Eberle
            (Jimmy Van Heusen-Johnny Burke)

047068-1   BB 10689-A, Vi 20-3563 (Vi P-255), HMV DLP 1145,
            RD 3/4-64, AFRS P-1445
            Shake Down The Stars-voc Ray Eberle
            (Eddie DeLange-Jimmy Van Heusen)

047069-1   BB 10673-B, HMV BD 1216, VdP GW-2023, HMV 7EG
            8254, Vi Arg 68-0881
            I'll Never Smile Again (arr JG)-voc Ray Eberle
            (Ruth Lowe)

(Session continued on next page)

Glenn Miller and his Orchestra at the Cafe Rouge of the Hotel Pennsylvania, New York, February–April 1940. Left to right, front row: Tanner, Priddy, D'Annolfo, Miller (trombones); Klink, Schwartz, McIntyre, Caceres, Beneke (saxophones). Back row: Knowles, Best, McMickle, Hurley (trumpets); Purtill (drums); Bundock (bass). Seated at left front is singer Eberle.

Cafe Rouge, February–April 1940. The entire band gets together for a vocal treatment of a tune. Since Ernie Caceres is in the saxophone section these photos from the Cafe Rouge would date from after February 17.

A good side view of the band in action with trumpet soloist Clyde Hurley standing.

Glenn Miller relaxing after a set at the Cafe Rouge with Tommy Dorsey (second from left). Others unknown.

```
047070-1        BB 10684-B, HMVAu EA-3337, Cam Cas-2267,
                   RCA G Cas-2267
                Starlight And Music (arr JG)-voc Ray Eberle
                   (Hoffman-Kent-Hart)
                   Ts, Beneke; clt, ??

                All tunes 1 take.  (RCA Victor)
                This session lasted from 1:00 P.M. to 4:30 P.M.
                (RCA Victor)
```

19 February, 1940 (MON): *Cafe Rouge, Hotel Pennsylvania,*
                        New York City, N.Y.
                        NBC-Blue 12:00-12:30 A.M. EST.

   (2:35) Tiger Rag (arr ED)
                   (Tony Sbarbaro-Eddie Edwards-
                   Henry Ragas-Larry Shields-Nick
                   LaRocca-Harry DeCosta)
                   Tpt, Best; ts, Beneke; d, Purtill

20 February, 1940 (TUES): *New York City, New York (CHESTERFIELD*
                                                SHOW)
                        CBS 10:00-10:15 P.M. EST.

                Moonlight Serenade (Theme)
                Johnson Rag
                The Sky Fell Down-voc RE
                The Woodpecker Song-voc AS
                Old Black Joe
                Wham-voc MH & Band
                Moonlight Serenade (Theme)

21 February, 1940 (WED): *New York City, New York (CHESTERFIELD*
                                                SHOW)
                        CBS 10:00-10:15 P.M. EST.

   The announcer for this show is Paul Douglas.

                Moonlight Serenade (Theme)

```
K2PP-0045       Vi LPM-6100, RCA RD 27146, RCA G LPM 6100
                (3:48) MEDLEY:
                Int GM   If I Had My Way (arr JG)
                         (Lou Klein-James Kendis)
                         Ts, Beneke
```

(Broadcast continued on next page)

```
Int PD    All The Things You Are (arr JG)
          From the musical production
          "Very Warm for May"
          (Oscar Hammerstein, 2nd-Jerome
          Kern)
Int GM    Oh Johnny, Oh Johnny, Oh! (arr JG)-
          voc Marion Hutton
          (borrowed from Orrin Tucker)
          (Ed. Rose-Abe Olman)
Int GM    Blue (And Brokenhearted) (arr JG)
          (Grant Clarke-Edgar Leslie-
          Lou Handman)
          Tpt, Hurley
```

          The Gaucho Serenade-voc RE
          Joseph, Joseph-voc AS
                (Sammy Cahn-Saul Chaplin-Samuel
                Steinberg-Nellie Casman)
          Runnin' Wild
          Moonlight Serenade (Theme)

22 February, 1940 (THUR): New York City, New York
                (CHESTERFIELD SHOW)
                CBS   10:00-10:15 P.M. EST.

          Moonlight Serenade (Theme)
          Little Brown Jug
Int GM   (2:04) When You Wish Upon A Star-voc Ray Eberle
                From the Walt Disney Motion Picture
                "Pinocchio"
                (Ned Washington-Leigh Harline)
                Ts, Beneke
          (3:55) Say "Si Si"-voc Andrew Sisters
                (Al Stillman-Francia Luban-
                Ernesto Lecuona)
          In The Mood
          Moonlight Serenade (Theme)

24 February, 1940 (SAT): Victor Studios, New York City, New York

          Same personnel as for February 17th.

(Session continued on next page)

047093-1   BB 10657-A, HMV DLP 1145, Vi LPM/LSP-3657,
              RCA RD/SF-7842, RD 3/4-64, AFRS P-10071,
              RCA G LPM/LSP-3657, RCA F 440.727
           Polka Dots And Moonbeams (arr JG)-voc Ray Eberle
              (Johnny Burke-Jimmy Van Heusen)
              As, McIntyre; ts, Beneke

047094-1   BB 10631-A, HMV BD 5606
           My! My! (arr JG)-voc Marion Hutton
              From the Paramount film "Buck Benny Rides
              Again"
              (Frank Loesser-Jimmy McHugh)
              As, Caceres

047095-1   BB 10631-B, HMV BD 5606
           Say It (arr BF)-voc Ray Eberle
              From the Paramount film "Buck Benny Rides
              Again"
              (Frank Loesser-Jimmy McHugh)
              As, McIntyre

047096-1   BB 10638-B, Vi LPM/LSP-3657, RCA RD/SF-7842
              RCA G LPM/LSP-3657, RCA F 440.727
           Moments In The Moonlight-voc Ray Eberle
              (Richard Himber-Irving Gordon-
              Al Kaufman)
              Ts, Beneke

047097-1   BB 10684-A, HMV BD 5664, HMV 7EG 8055, HMV DLP
              1049, Vi LPM/LSP-3657, RCA RD/SF-7842,
              AFRS P-10071, RCA G LPM/LSP-3657, RCA F
              440.727
           Hear My Song, Violetta-voc Ray Eberle
              (Buddy Bernier-Bob Emmerich-Klase-Lukesch)

047098-1   BB 10638-A, HMV BD 5626, HMVAu EA-2625,
              RD 3/4-25, RD Br. RDS 6099, RD Br. RDS
              6176, AFRS "America's Pop Music" 72
           Sierra Sue (arr JG)-voc Ray Eberle
              (Joseph B. Carey)
              As, McIntyre

           All tunes 1 take. (RCA Victor)
           This session lasted from 2:00 P.M. to 5:15 P.M.
           (RCA Victor)

26 February, 1940 (MON): Cafe Rouge, Hotel Pennsylvania,
New York City, N.Y.
NBC-Blue 12:00-12:30 A.M. EST.

    The announcer for this program is Hugh James.

(1:36) <u>Moonlight Serenade</u> (Theme)
    (Mitchell Parish-Glenn Miller)
(3:25) <u>Little Brown Jug</u> (arr BF)-voc The Band
    (Traditional)
    Ts, Beneke; tpt, Hurley; tbn, Miller
(3:23) <u>When You Wish Upon A Star</u>-voc Ray Eberle
    From the Walt Disney Motion Picture
    "Pinocchio"
    (Ned Washington-Leigh Harline)
    Ts, Beneke
(2:45) <u>Say "Si Si"</u>-voc Marion Hutton
    (Al Stillman-Francia Luban-Ernesto
    Lecuona)
    Ts, Beneke
(2:43) <u>The Sky Fell Down</u> (arr BF)-voc Ray Eberle
    (Edward Heyman-Louis Alter)
    Muted tbn, Miller
(4:06) <u>My Blue Heaven</u> (arr BF)
    (George Whiting-Walter Donaldson)
    Tbn, Miller; ts, Beneke; d, Purtill
(2:55) <u>Starlit Hour</u> (arr GM)-voc Ray Eberle
    From "Earl Carroll Vanities"
    (Mitchell Parish-Peter DeRose)
(2:51) <u>Let's All Sing Together</u> (arr JG)-voc
    Marion Hutton
    (Joe Audino-Nick DiRocca-Bill Keeshan)
    Ts, Beneke; tpt, Hurley; d, Purtill
(4:32) <u>Tuxedo Junction</u> (arr JG)
    (William Johnson-Julian Dash-Erskine
    Hawkins-Buddy Feyne)
    Muted tpt, McMickle; open tpt, Hurley
(1:31) <u>Moonlight Serenade</u> (Theme)
    (Mitchell Parish-Glenn Miller)

27 February, 1940 (TUES): New York City, New York (CHESTERFIELD SHOW)
CBS 10:00-10:15 P.M. EST.

The announcer for this show is Paul Douglas. Miller
does not announce on this program: "On the eve of
his opening at the Paramount Theatre Glenn Miller
was rushed to Mount Sinai Hospital with grippe
complicated by sinus infection." (Variety, March 6,
1940)

(Broadcast continued on next page)

Moonlight Serenade (Theme)
Let's All Sing Together-voc MH
Too Romantic-voc RE
Hold Tight-voc AS
Tuxedo Junction
Moonlight Serenade (Theme)

28 February, 1940 (WED): New York City, New York (CHESTERFIELD SHOW)
CBS 10:00-10:15 P.M. EST.

The announcer for this show is Paul Douglas.

Moonlight Serenade (Theme)

K2PP-0045 Vi LPM-6100, RCA RD 27146, RCA G LPM 6100
           (3:08) MEDLEY:
           Int PD If You Were The Only Girl In The World
                     (arr JG)
                   Later introduced in film: "The
                   Vagabond Lover"
                   (Clifford Grey-Nat D. Ayer)
           Int PD Sweet Potato Piper (arr JG)-voc Marion
                   Hutton
                   (From the Paramount film "The Road
                   to Singapore"
                   (Johnny Burke-James V. Monaco)
           Int PD Song Of The Islands (arr JG) (borrowed
                   from Ben Pollack)
                   (Charles E. King)
           Int PD Bye Bye Blues (arr JG)
                   (Bert Lown-Chauncey Gray-Dave Bennett-
                   Fred Hamm)
                   Tpt, Hurley

           I Want My Mama-voc AS
           Indian Summer-voc RE
           Farewell Blues
           Moonlight Serenade (Theme)

28 February, 1940 (WED)

           Glenn Miller and His Orchestra played for two weeks
           (closed Tuesday, March 12th) at the Paramount
           Theater, New York City, New York. (BB, March 9,
           1940; Variety, March 6, 1940; Variety, March 13,
           1940)

           The band opened without Glenn who was in Mount Sinai
           Hospital with grippe complicated by a sinus infection.

(Continued on next page)

His own band members led the first show, Dick
Stabile led the 2nd show, and Tommy Dorsey led the
next three shows. Gene Krupa led the last show
Wednesday night. Bob Weitman, managing director of
the house "called Tommy Dorsey at his home and pre-
vailed upon him as a personal favor to pinch hit for
Miller. Dorsey accepted quickly but was unable to
play all shows." (BB, March 9, 1940; Variety, March
6, 1940)

"Glenn Miller's crew opened its date at the
Paramount last Wednesday February 29, 1940 minus Glenn
Miller. Subbing for the maestro, who was afflicted
with sinus trouble was Tommy Dorsey whose own band is
currently at the Meadowbrook, Cedar Grove, New Jersey,
and is booked to follow Miller into the Paramount.
This made for an odd bit of business for immediately
following the Paramount trailer announcing Dorsey's
coming, up popped the elevator stage with Dorsey
aboard it.
At the evening show it made little difference
because adult audiences apparently wouldn't know
Dorsey from Miller if he sat in their laps. Even the
jitterbugs didn't get it at first. For Dorsey and
Miller have many similar physical characteristics and
both toot trombones. With Dorsey's announcement of
Miller's absence and introducing himself, however he
drew a heavy salvo of applause at this catching.
During Miller's hospitalization, until Sunday, Charlie
Barnet, Dick Stabile and Gene Krupa substitute at the
baton.
Show as a whole is rather short and heavy
orchestrally. Crew offers no novelty turns on its
own, only vocalizing of its 2 warblers, Marion Hutton
and Ray Eberle. Added are the Andrew Sisters (3) and
a novelty act, Frank and Jean Hubert.
The Orchestra gets underway with Tiger Rag.
After that the orchestra sticks pretty much to slow
ones and plays even those more leisurely than usual.
It's plenty listenable, however, all the way through
characterized principally by Miller's nifty arrangements. Each shows unique originality and particularly
outstanding on this score is Tuxedo Junction that's
followed by another Miller favorite Londonderry Aire
in which the stage is darkened and colored lights play
on the instrumentalists who are tooting. Dorsey
tromboned in with the brass section on several numbers
and took one short solo. Standing out about Miller's
16 piece current combination is its general appearance. Lads are all nice lookers, clean cut and neatly

(Continued on next page)

groomed. Marion Hutton's piping on the other hand,
might be bolstered. Perhaps it is her choice of
numbers but it seems more like a distinct lack of
voice which becomes too apparent after the novelty
of her jitterbuggish presentation has worn off.
Opener Boog-it is distinctly bad for an evening
audience. Registers as very pointless. Others
following are so so. Ray Eberle upholds the male
end of the warbling much better. He does Indian
Summer, Careless, and Blue World, all good and counting for solid returns." (Variety, March 6, 1940)

29 February, 1940 (THUR): Paramount Theater, New York City, New York

Thursday's first 3 shows were led by Tommy Dorsey,
Paul Douglas M.C. subbed for Miller at the 4th show,
while Gene Krupa led the last 2 shows. (BB, March 9,
1940; Variety, March, 1940)

*29 February, 1940 (THUR): New York City, New York (CHESTERFIELD SHOW)
CBS 10:00-10:15 P.M. EST.*

The announcer for this show is Paul Douglas.

Moonlight Serenade (Theme)
Sunrise Serenade
Chico's Love Song-voc AS
Careless
One O'Clock Jump
Moonlight Serenade (Theme)

1 March, 1940 (FRI): Paramount Theater, New York City, New York

Friday's shows were led by Tommy Dorsey (3 shows)
followed by Gene Krupa (2 shows) and Charlie Barnet
the last show. (BB, March 9, 1940)

2 March, 1940 (SAT): Paramount Theater, New York City, New York

Saturday Tommy Dorsey led the first show followed by
Gene Krupa for the next show. (BB, March 9, 1940)
Paul Douglas, M.C.'d the next four shows. (Variety,
March 1940)

"Every band I go with, the leader gets sick!"
So says Jerry Gray, ex-Shaw arranger who had to take
over direction of Glenn Miller's band for the

(Continued on next page)

commercial when Miller's sinus trouble landed him
in hospital during the band's busiest week. Others
who pinch-hit as leader of the Miller men for the
commercials and the Paramount Theater included Dick
Stabile, Tommy Dorsey and Gene Krupa. Glenn was
recovering okay at press time, but still weak and
walking with 'pins' in his legs." (DB, March 15,
1940) This article failed to mention Charlie
Barnet.

This was to have been the band's busiest week.
    "Glenn Miller will break all records for hard
labor during the week of Feb. 28. That week he and
his band will do a total of 36 shows at the Paramount
Theater, two nightly sessions six nights a week at
the Pennsylvania, and three broadcasts on his Chesterfield show, plus three rehearsals for same. Totals
54 sessions in the same week--and on top of it, he'll
have to find time to cut records for Bluebird!"
(DB, March 1, 1940)

While Miller did his theater and radio stints, Charlie
Spivak's band took over at the Hotel Pennsylvania.
(Met. March 1940) However, the January 13th issue of
"The Billboard" stated that Claude Thornhill "subs
for Glenn Miller at Hotel Pennsylvania". The
February 14th issue of "Variety" stated that "Charlie
Spivak debut last night (Tuesday) as relief band for
Glenn Miller at the Pennsylvania Hotel while Miller
was at CBS Playhouse 3 nights a week. Thornhill did
the same earlier on the Pennsylvania schedule."

According to Variety, March 6, 1940, Miller was due
back on the stand on Saturday, but since all shows on
this date were led as shown above it must be assumed
that Miller did not return until Monday (4th). For
the first show that day Dorsey, Barnet, Krupa, and
Stabile welcomed Miller back. (Met. April 1940)

4 March, 1940 (MON): Cafe Rouge, Hotel Pennsylvania,
*   New York City, N.Y.*
*   NBC-Blue 12:00-12:30 A.M.*

The announcer for this program is Al Robinson.

(1:30) Moonlight Serenade (Theme)
*   (Mitchell Parish-Glenn Miller)*
(3:40) Symphony In Riffs
*   (Benny Carter-I. Mills)*
*   Ts, Beneke; tpt, Hurley; ts, Beneke*

(Broadcast continued on next page)

```
    (3:21) Careless-voc Ray Eberle
                (Lew Quadling-Eddy Howard-Dick Jurgens)
                P, MacGregor
    (2:44) Let's All Sing Together (arr JG)-voc Marion
                Hutton
                (Joe Audino-Nick DiRocca-Bill Keeshan)
                Ts, Beneke; tpt, Hurley; d, Purtill
Int. GM (3:01) I'll Never Smile Again (arr JG)-voc Ray Eberle
                (Ruth Lowe)
    (3:42) In The Mood
                (Andy Razaf-Joe Garland)
                Ts, Beneke; ts, Klink; tpt, Hurley
    (3:46) Indian Summer-voc Ray Eberle
                (Al Dubin-Victor Herbert)
                Ts, Beneke; tpt, Best
    (3:50) Tiger Rag (arr ED)
                (Tony Sbarbaro-Eddie Edwards-Henry Ragas-
                Larry Shields-Nick LaRocca-Harry DeCosta)
                Ts, Klink; d, Purtill
    (1:37) Moonlight Serenade (Theme)
                (Mitchell Parish-Glenn Miller)
```

Miller introduced "I'll Never Smile Again" by saying: "We're presenting this tune for the first time on the air."

On this version of "In The Mood" there are four ride-outs before the coda (instead of the usual three).

5 March, 1940 (TUES): New York City, New York (CHESTERFIELD SHOW)
            CBS   10:00-10:15 P.M. EST.

```
            Moonlight Serenade (Theme)
            Flow Gently, Sweet Afton
                (Robert Burns-James E. Spilman)
            Beer Barrel Polka-voc AS
            Sweet Potato Piper
            Starlit Hour
            Slip Horn Jive
            Moonlight Serenade (Theme)
```

6 March, 1940 (WED): New York City, New York (CHESTERFIELD SHOW)
            CBS   10:00-10:15 P.M. EST.

The announcer for this show is Paul Douglas.

```
            Moonlight Serenade (Theme)
```

(Broadcast continued on next page)

        (3:18) MEDLEY:
             Japanese Sandman
             (Raymond B. Egan-Richard A. Whiting)
    Int GM What's The Matter With Me-voc Marion Hutton
             (Sam M. Lewis-Terry Shand)
    Int GM Let's Dance (borrowed from Benny Goodman)
             (Baldridge-Gregory Stone-Bonime)
             Tpt, Hurley; ts, Beneke
    Int GM Blue Room
             (Lorenz Hart-Richard Rodgers)

Int GM (2:52) The Donkey Serenade-voc Andrews Sisters
             From the MGM film "The Firefly"
             (Bob White-Chet Forrest-Rudolph Friml-
             Herbert Stothart)
Int GM (2:42) The Sky Fell Down (arr BF)-voc Ray Eberle
             (Edward Heyman-Louis Alter)
             Muted tbn, Miller
Int GM (2:59) I Want To Be Happy (arr ED)
             From the musical production "No, No,
             Nanette"
             (Irving Caesar-Vincent Youmans)
             Tpt, Hurley; ts, Beneke; tbn, Miller;
             d, Purtill
             Moonlight Serenade (Theme)

7 March, 1940 (THUR): New York City, New York (CHESTERFIELD SHOW)
             CBS 10:00-10:15 P.M. EST.

             Moonlight Serenade (Theme)
             Pavanne
             When You Wish Upon A Star
             Do I Love You?-voc AS
             From the musical production "DuBarry
             Was A Lady"
             (Cole Porter)
             Bugle Call Rag
             Moonlight Serenade (Theme)

     "Glenn Miller's sizzling dansapation Thursday night
     (March 7, 1940) for Chesterfields was notable for
     two things: one, nifty arrangement, two, the whistl-
     ing, stomping, screaming, studio audience. What a
     politician wouldn't give." (Variety, March 13, 1940)

11 March, 1940 (MON): Cafe Rouge, Hotel Pennsylvania,
             New York City, N.Y.
             NBC-Blue 12:00-12:30 A.M. EST. Station WJZ

(Broadcast continued on next page)

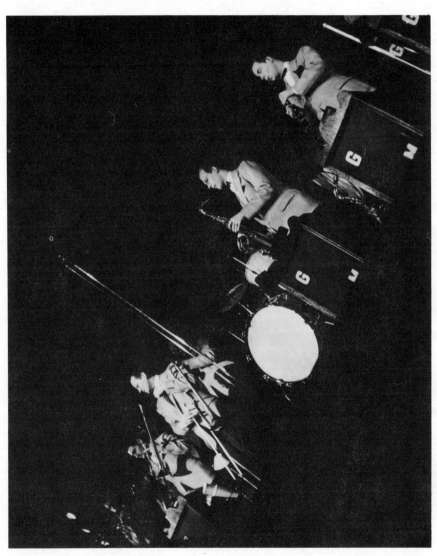

Second date at the Paramount, March 1940. Left to right: Priddy, D'Annolfo, Miller, Klink, Schwartz.

Marion Hutton mugging during a number at the Paramount. Glenn hired her over her sister Betty because of her showmanship.

(2:53) _Too Romantic-voc Ray Eberle_
From the Paramount film "The Road to
Singapore"
(Johnny Burke-James V. Monaco)

12 March, 1940 (TUES): New York City, New York (CHESTERFIELD SHOW)
CBS   10:00-10: 15 P.M. EST.

Moonlight Serenade (Theme)
Boog-It-voc MH & Band
It's A Blue World
Ciri-Biri-Bin-voc AS
Drink To Me Only With Thine Eyes

E3VP 5241   Vi LPT 6700, Vi EPNT 6700 (947-0127), Vi SPD-18
(599-9110), HMV RLS 599, Vi LPM/LSP-1192,
RCA RD 27068, RCA G LPT 6700, RCA G EPC-
1192, RCA G LPM/LSP-1192, RCA F 530243,
Vi Arg LPM/LSP-1192, RCA F 740.515
(2:32) King Porter Stomp
(Ferdinand "Jelly-Roll" Morton)
Tbn, Miller; ts, Beneke; tpt, Hurley;
ts, Klink

Moonlight Serenade (Theme)

12 March, 1940 (TUES): Paramount Theater, New York City, New York

This was Glenn Miller's last day at the Paramount.
The band grossed $55,000. the first week and
$43,000. for the second week. (Variety, March 13,
1940)

"Glenn Miller who concluded a 2 week engagement at the Paramount N.Y.C. last (Tuesday) has
signed to replay the house, date to be set later.
It may be in six months or so. Deal with Miller
was set in his dressing room in a few minutes flat
with Bob Weitman, managing director of the theater,
and Harry Kalcheim, head of Paramount booking
department.
In consequence of the fact that Tommy Dorsey,
Dick Stabile, Gene Krupa, and Charlie Barnet subbed
for him the first four days of his New York
Paramount engagement when he was sick Miller will
appear on the first show today (Wednesday) with
Tommy Dorsey who opens at the house.
Weitman sent the pinch hitting conductors
Dunhill pipes in personal appreciation of their
coming to the theater's rescue." (Variety, March
13, 1940)

13 March, 1940 (WED): New York City, New York (CHESTERFIELD SHOW)
CBS   10:00-10:15 P.M. EST.

Moonlight Serenade (Theme)

K2PP-0047   Vi LPM-6100, RCA RD 27147, RCA G LPM 6100
               (3:11) MEDLEY:
                        When Irish Eyes Are Smiling (arr JG)
                          (Chauncey Olcott-George Graff-
                          Ernest R. Ball)
          Int GM   Confucius Say (arr JG)-voc Marion Hutton
                          (Cliff Friend-Carmen Lombardo)
          Int GM   Rose Room (arr JG) (borrowed from Phil
                          Harris)
                          (Harry Williams-Art Hickman)
                          Tpt, Best?; ts, Beneke
          Int GM   The Wang, Wang Blues (arr JG)
                          (Gus Mueller-"Buster" Johnson-
                          Henry Busse-Leo Wood)
                          Tpt, Hurley

               Run, Rabbit, Run-voc AS
                   From "The Little Dog Laughed"
                   (Noel Gay-Butler)
               Sierra Sue
               My Blue Heaven
               Moonlight Serenade (Theme)

14 March, 1940 (THUR): New York City, New York (CHESTERFIELD SHOW)
CBS   10:00-10:15 P.M. EST.

               Moonlight Serenade (Theme)
               Wham
               Faithful To You
               Let's Have Another One-voc AS
               Tuxedo Junction
               Moonlight Serenade (Theme)

18 March, 1940 (MON): Cafe Rouge, Hotel Pennsylvania,
New York City, N.Y.
NBC-Blue   12:00-12:30 A.M. EST.

          (2:40) *Rug Cutter's Swing(arr BF)*
                    (Horace Henderson)
                    Tpt, Best; ts, Beneke; tbn, Miller;
                    tpt, Hurley

          (2:12) *Faithful To You-voc Ray Eberle*
                    (Martin Block-Harold Green-
                    Mickey Stoner)

(Broadcast continued on next page)

(4:35) Tuxedo Junction (arr JG)
        (William Johnson-Julian Dash-
        Erskine Hawkins-Buddy Feyne)
        Muted tpt, McMickle; open tpt, Hurley;
        clt, ??; muted tpt, McMickle; p, MacGregor

Note that this is the only version we have of
"Tuxedo Junction" that included a clarinet solo.
This was the full arrangement of this tune.

19 March, 1940 (TUES): New York City, New York (CHESTERFIELD SHOW)
        CBS   10:00-10:15 P.M. EST.

The announcer for this show is Paul Douglas.

        Moonlight Serenade (Theme)
        Rug Cutter's Swing
        I'll Never Smile Again-voc RE
        Say "Si Si"-voc AS
        Jeannie With The Light Brown Hair

E2VL 4545   Vi LPT-3001, Vi EPBT-3001 (947-0054), HMV DLP-1021,
             Vi LPM-1193, AFRS P-2666, El WDLP 1021,
             Vi TP3-5020, RCA G EPB 3001, RCA G LPM-1193
        (2:04) Dipper Mouth Blues (arr GM)
               (Joe Oliver-Louis Armstrong)
               Clt, Caceres; tbn, Miller

        Moonlight Serenade (Theme)

20 March, 1940 (WED): New York City, New York (CHESTERFIELD SHOW)
        CBS   10:00-10:15 P.M. EST.

The announcer for this show is Paul Douglas.

        Moonlight Serenade (Theme)

        MEDLEY:
          Linger Awhile (arr JG)
             (Harry Owens-Vincent Rose)
          Ooh! What You Said (arr JG)-voc
             Marion Hutton
             (From the musical comedy "Three After
             Three"
             (Johnny Mercer-Hoagy Carmichael)
          The Perfect Song (arr JG) (borrowed from
             Amos 'n' Andy)
             From the motion picture "The Birth of
             a Nation"
             (Clarence Lucas-Joseph Carl Breil)

(Broadcast continued on next page)

The Blues My Sweety Gave To Me (Naughty
    Sweetie Blues) (arr JG)
    (Meyer)
    Tpt, Hurley

The Woodpecker Song-voc AS
Too Romantic-voc RE
In The Mood
Moonlight Serenade (Theme)

21 March, 1940 (THUR): New York City, New York (CHESTERFIELD SHOW)
    CBS   10:00-10:15 P.M. EST.

Moonlight Serenade (Theme)
My! My!
Polka Dots And Moonbeams
(2:46) *The Donkey Serenade-voc Andrews Sisters*
        From the MGM film "The Firefly"
        (Bob White-Chet Forrest-Rudolph Friml-
        Herbert Stothart)
St. Louis Blues
Moonlight Serenade (Theme)

This was the last show that the Andrews Sisters were on as it completed their thirteen weeks.

"Andrews Sisters drop off the Glenn Miller Chesterfield show after tomorrow night's broadcast (Thursday) the last in the program's initial 13 weeks. Sponsor would have looked to renew the trio but Miller leaves his current Pennsylvania Hotel stand the first week of April and heads for a road tour. Girls do likewise on a theater tour and General Amusement Company which books both found it too tough to rearrange bookings so that the trio could work along a route similar to Miller's enabling them to join him 3 nights a week for the airways.
The renewal then would have meant that the sisters would have to cancel out of the theater bookings which were made before they were committed to Chesterfields. Under that arrangement a prohibitive salary would have had to be paid them for the money lost on the cancelled theater dates."
(Variety, March 20, 1940)

24 March, 1940 (SUN)

Glenn Miller and His Orchestra played at the Mosque Theater, Newark, New Jersey. (G.M.P.R.)

26 March, 1940 (TUES): New York City, New York (CHESTERFIELD SHOW)
CBS   10:00-10:15 P.M. EST.

Moonlight Serenade (Theme)

V-4086 RR-17356 GMMS 3/103
       (2:35) Pennsylvania Six-Five Thousand (arr JG)
              (Carl Sigman-Jerry Gray)
              Tpt, Best; ts, Beneke

Indian Summer

V-4086 RR-17356 GMMS 3/103, GMMS 42/90
    Int GM (2:11) Let's All Sing Together (arr JG)-voc
                  Marion Hutton
                  (Joe Audino-Nick DiRocca-Bill Keeshan)
                  Ts, Beneke; tpt, Hurley; d, Purtill

V-4086 RR-17356 GMMS 3/103
    Int GM (2:32) Moonlight Serenade (arr GM)
                  (Mitchell Parish-Glenn Miller)
                  Clt, Schwartz

V-4086 RR-17356 GMMS 3/103, GMMS 41/89
    Int GM (2:40) Slip Horn Jive (arr ED)
                  (Eddie Durham)
                  D, Purtill; ts, Beneke; tpt, Hurley;
                  tbn, Miller; ts, Klink; tpt, Hurley

Moonlight Serenade (Theme)

In this early version of "Pennsylvania Six-Five
Thousand" there is no shouting of the title by
the band.

27 March, 1940 (WED): New York City, New York (CHESTERFIELD SHOW)
CBS   10:00-10:15 P.M. EST.

Moonlight Serenade (Theme)
Boog-It
MEDLEY:
    Sweet Leilani
    Faithful To You
    Smoke Rings
    Under A Blanket Of Blue
By The Waters Of Minnetonka
Moonlight Serenade (Theme)

28 March, 1940 (THUR): New York City, New York (CHESTERFIELD SHOW)
CBS   10:00-10:15 P.M. EST.

The announcer for this show is Paul Douglas.

Moonlight Serenade (Theme)

V-4086 WR-963 GMMS 15/63, GMMS 45/93, AFRS P-2240
           (3:36) Star Dust (arr BF & GM)
                        (Mitchell Parish-Hoagy Carmichael)
                        Ts, Beneke; tpt, Hurley; ts, Beneke;
                        clt, Schwartz

V-4086 WR-963 GMMS 15/63, AFRS P-2252
      Int GM (2:52) Sweet Potato Piper (arr JG)-voc
                        Marion Hutton and Tex Beneke
                        From the Paramount film "The Road
                        to Singapore"
                        (Johnny Burke-James V. Monaco)
                        Ts, Beneke

V-4086 WR-960 GMMS 12/60, GMMS 40/88, GMMS 46/94, AFRS P-2244
      Int GM (2:36) When You Wish Upon A Star-voc
                        Ray Eberle
                        From the Walt Disney Motion Picture
                        "Pinocchio"
                        (Ned Washington-Leigh Harline)
                        Ts, Beneke

V-4086 WR-963 GMMS 15/63, GMMS 52/100, AFRS P-2240
      Int GM (2:36) Pagan Love Song
                        From the MGM film "The Pagan"
                        (Arthur Freed-Nacio Herb Brown)
                        Muted tpt, Hurley; ts, Beneke;
                        d, Purtill

Moonlight Serenade (Theme)

30 March, 1940 (SAT): Victor Studios, New York City, New York

      Same personnel as for February 17th.

048482-1   BB 10689-B, HMV BD 5626
              Boog-It (arr JG)-voc Marion Hutton
                        (and the Band)
                        (Cab Calloway-Jack Palmer-Buck Ram)
                        As, McIntyre; tpt, Hurley

(Session continued on next page)

Next six photos show band at Cafe Rouge without their tuxedos, February–April 1940.

Good showmanship by the band. When brass hats were fanned in front of trumpets and trombones, they gave an "ooh-wah" sound that helped identify the band.

Mutes were often employed by the brass section to give different tonal effects.

When the brass hats were not used for creating aural effects they could be worn like hats for visual effects.

Tex Beneke at the microphone. Miller appears to be looking right at the camera. Richard Fisher is on guitar, Rolly Bundock on bass.

Moe Purtill takes off on a drum solo.

048483-1   BB 10728-B, HMV BD 5664, HMV DLP 1049
            (HMV labelled as "You Are My Heart's
            Delight"), RD 3/4-64
            Yours Is My Heart Alone (arr BF)
            (Ludwig Herzer-Fritz Lohner-Franz
            Lehar-English words by Harry Bache
            Smith)
            Ts, Beneke

048484-1   BB 10717-B, HMV BD 5617, VdP GW-2000
            I'm Stepping Out With A Memory Tonight-voc
            Ray Eberle
            (Herb Magidson-Allie Wrubel)
            Ts, Beneke

048485-1   BB 10701-A, HMV BD 5654, HMVSw JK-2169, VD 352,
            Vi 420-0032, Vi 447-0032, Vi EPAT-
            405, HMV DLP 1049, Vi LPT 1016,
            Vi SP-33-90, Cam Cal/Cas-2128,
            RD 3/4-64, RCA G EPAT-405, RCA G
            LPT 1016, RCA G Cas-2128, HMVIr
            I.P. 1036, Navy VD 132
            Alice Blue Gown (Waltz) (arr BF)
            From the RKO film "Irene"
            (Joseph McCarthy-Harry Tierney)
            Ts, Beneke

048486-1   BB 10701-B, HMV BD 5654, HMVSw JK-2169, HMV
            RLS 599, Vi LPT 6700, Vi EPNT 6700
            (947-0116), RCA G LPT 6700,
            Vi SPD-18 (599-9103), HMVIr I.P.
            1036
            Wonderful One (Waltz) (arr JG)
            Adapted from a theme by Marshall
            Neilan
            (Dorothy Terris-Paul Whiteman-
            Ferde Grofe)
            As, McIntyre

048487-1   BB 10717-A, HMV BD 5617, Vi EPNT 6700 (947-
            0123), Vi LPT 6700, Vi SPD-18
            (599-9111), HMV RLS 599, RCA G
            LPT 6700
            Devil May Care-voc Ray Eberle
            (Johnny Burke-Harry Warren)
            Muted tbn, Miller

(continued on next page)

[152]

"Devil May Care" 2 takes; all other tunes
1 take. (RCA Victor)
This session lasted from 1:00 P.M. to 5:00
P.M. (RCA Victor)

31 March, 1940 (SUN): Victor Studios, New York City, New York

Same personnel as for February 17th.

048488-1   BB 10694-A, HMV 7EG 8043, Vi EPAT-426, Vi LPT
                1031, Cam Cal/Cas-751, Cam Cal/Cas-2128,
                RCA G LPT-1031, RCA G Cas-751, RCA G
                Cas-2128, Pick. Int. CDS 1040
            April Played The Fiddle (arr BF)-voc Ray
                Eberle
                From the Universal film "If I Had
                My Way"
                (Johnny Burke-James V. Monaco)
                As, McIntyre

048489-1   BB 10728-A, Vi LPT 6700, Vi EPNT 6700 (947-
                0122), Vi SPD-18 (599-9106), HMV RLS
                599, Cam Cal/Cas-2128, RCA G LPT 6700,
                RD 3/4-64, RCA G Cas-2128, RCA Cam
                Arg Cal-3138
            Fools Rush In (Where Angels Fear To Tread)-
                voc Ray Eberle
                (Johnny Mercer-Rube Bloom)

048490-1   BB 10694-B, HMV 7EG 8241
            I Haven't Time To Be A Millionaire (arr JG)-
                voc Tex Beneke
                From the Universal film "If I Had
                My Way"
                (Johnny Burke-James V. Monaco)
                As, Caceres

048491-1   BB 10740-A, HMV BD 5633, Vi LPM 2080, El
                G EG 7620, RD 3/4-64, HMVIr I.P. 993,
                HMVIn BD 5633
            Slow Freight (arr BF)
                (Mills-Lupin Fien-Buck Ram)
                Muted tpt, McMickle; open tpt, Hurley;
                muted tpt, McMickle

(Continued on next page)

"Fools Rush In" and "I Haven't Time To Be
A Millionaire" 2 takes; other two tunes 1
take. (RCA Victor)
This session lasted from 2:00 P.M. to 6:30
P.M. (RCA Victor)

1 April, 1940 (MON): Cafe Rouge, Hotel Pennsylvania,
New York City, N.Y.
NBC-Blue 12:00-12:30 A.M. EST.

Wanna Hat With Cherries

2 April, 1940 (TUES): New York City, New York
(CHESTERFIELD SHOW)
CBS 10:00-10:15 P.M. EST.

The announcer for this show is Paul Douglas.

Moonlight Serenade *(Theme)*

V-4086 RR-17356 GMMS 4/104
      (2:18) Johnson Rag (arr BF)-Chant by the
          Band
          (Henry Kleinkauf-Guy Hall)
          Ts, Beneke; ts, Klink; tpt,
          Hurley

V-4086 RR-17356 GMMS 4/104
   Int GM (2:09) I'll Never Smile Again (arr JG)-
          voc Ray Eberle
          (Ruth Lowe)

V-4086 RR-17356 GMMS 4/104, GMMS 24/72
   Int GM (3:04) Wham (Re-Bop-Boom-Bam) (arr ED)-voc
          Marion Hutton and Band
          (Eddie Durham-"Taps" Miller)
          Ts, Beneke; tbn, Miller; ts,
          Beneke; tpt, Hurley

Old Black Joe

(Broadcast continued on next page)

V-4086 RR-17356 GMMS 4/104
        Int GM (2:14) Fanhat Stomp
                    (Eddie Barefield)
                    Tbn, Miller; tpt, Hurley; ts,
                    Beneke;as, Caceres

V-4086 RR-17356 GMMS 4/104, GMMS 3/103, Vi LPT 6700, Vi 45
                    Special-1953, Vi EPNT 6700 (947-0116),
                    HMV RLS 599, RCA G LPT 6700, Vi SPD-18
                    (599-9112)
                (0:13) Moonlight Serenade (Theme)
                        (Mitchell Parish-Glenn Miller)

"Fanhat Stomp" was featured on the air for
the first time on this broadcast and Glenn
announced it by saying: "We're breaking one
in for the first time, romantically entitled
'Fanhat Stomp'."

3 April, 1940 (WED): New York City, New York
                    (CHESTERFIELD SHOW)
                    CBS 10:00-10:15 P.M. EST.

The announcer for this program is Paul Douglas.

(0:44) Moonlight Serenade (Theme)
            (Mitchell Parish-Glenn Miller)
(2:27) The Woodpecker Song-voc
            Marion Hutton
            (Harold Adamson-Eldo di Lazzaro)
            Ts, Beneke
(6:45) MEDLEY:
Int PD Sweet And Lovely (arr JG)
            From the MGM film "Two Girls
            And A Sailor"
            (Gus Arnheim-Harry Tobias-
            Jules Lemare)
            Ts, Beneke
Int GM Sierra Sue (arr JG)-voc Ray Eberle
            (Joseph B. Carey)
Int GM The Very Thought Of You (arr JG)
            (borrowed from Ray Noble)
            (Ray Noble)
            P, MacGregor
Int GM Blue Evening (arr JG)
            (Gordon Jenkins-Joe Bishop)
            Ts, Beneke

(Broadcast continued on next page)

(3:02) *Tiger Rag* (arr ED)
                    (Tony Sbarbaro-Eddie Edwards-Henry
                    Ragas-Larry Shields-Nick LaRocca-
                    Harry DeCosta)
                    D, Purtill

        Moonlight Serenade (Theme)

"Tiger Rag" was, as Glenn put it, "a real stick
breaker for drummer man Purtill" on this show.
The Klink tenor solo was cut out of this performance, probably because of the time left on the
program.

4 April, 1940 (THUR): New York City, New York (CHESTERFIELD SHOW)
               CBS   10:00-10:15 P.M. EST.

        Moonlight Serenade (Theme)

E4VP-8209   Vi LPT 6701, Vi EPOT 6701 (947-0182), HMV RLS 598,
                RCA G EPOT-6701
       (2:50) The Rumba Jumps! -voc Marion Hutton and Tex
                  Beneke
                  From the musical production "Three
                  After Three"
                  (Johnny Mercer-Hoagy Carmichael)
                  D, Purtill; ts, Beneke

        Polka Dots And Moonbeams
   ALP   *My Melancholy Baby*

V-4086 WR-960 GMMS 12/60, GMMS 40/88, Vi LPT 6700, Vi EPNT 6700
                (947-0124), HMV RLS 599, Vi SPD-18
                (599-9111), AFRS P-2239, Vi It LPM 10141,
                Vi It LJ 50020, Vi It LPM 50020, RCA G
                LPT 6700
       (3:46) One O'Clock Jump
                  (Lee Gaines-Count Basie)
                  P, MacGregor; ts, Beneke; tbn, Miller;
                  Ts, Klink; tpt, Hurley

        Moonlight Serenade (Theme)

On Vi LPT 6701 "The Rumba Jumps!" was incorrectly
listed as being broadcast on May 10, 1940.

4 April, 1940 (THUR): Cafe Rouge, Hotel Pennsylvania,
New York City, N.Y.

Glenn Miller and His Orchestra closed at the
"Cafe Rouge" of the Hotel Pennsylvania, New York
City, New York, after a record-breaking three
month engagement. (G.M.P.R.)
Jimmy Dorsey followed Miller into the Hotel
Pennsylvania. At the end of this week Miller
began a road trip that lasted through October
7th when he reopened at the Hotel Pennsylvania
for a six-month engagement.

Moonlight Serenade (Theme)
Johnson Rag
The Gaucho Serenade
Boog-It
The Sky Fell Down
I Want To Be Happy

PPRM-5342   Vi LPM/LSP-2769 (Vi LPM/LSP-6101), RCA RD/SF-7612
(2:44) Starlit Hour (arr GM)-voc Ray Eberle
From "Earl Carroll Vanities"
(Mitchell Parish-Peter DeRose)

Too Romantic
My! My!
Tuxedo Junction
Moonlight Serenade (Theme)

5 April, 1940 (FRI)

Glenn Miller and His Orchestra played at Bucknell
University, Lewisburg, Pennsylvania, from 9:00-
2:00 A.M. The dance was held in the Davis
Gymnasium. (Sunbury Daily Item, April 6, 1940,
Sunbury, Pa.; G.M.P.R.)

6 April, 1940 (SAT)

Glenn Miller and His Orchestra played at Sunny-
brook Ballroom (G.M.P.R. says Sunnyside Park),
Pottstown, Pennsylvania, from 8:30-12:30 A.M.
(The Reading Times, Reading, Pa., April 4, 1940;
G.M.P.R.)

7 April, 1940 (SUN)

Glenn Miller and His Orchestra played at the
Roseland Ballroom, New York City, New York, from
9:00-1:00 A.M. (New York Daily News, New York,
April 7, 1940; Variety, March 27, 1940; G.M.P.R.)

Glenn helps Mal Hallett (right) celebrate his 20th anniversary in the band business at a party at Roseland Ballroom, New York, early April 1940. (*Photo courtesy Glenn Miller Estate*)

Miller band at Roseland, April 7, 1940. Left to right: Miller, Purtill, Schwartz, Klink, McIntyre. (*Photo courtesy Glenn Miller Estate*)

8 April, 1940 (MON)

       Glenn Miller and His Orchestra drew 6,500 at the
Coliseum (2200 Monroe St.) in Baltimore, Maryland,
from 9:00-1:00 A.M., and broke all records for a
one-nighter. Erskine Hawkins and His Orchestra
also were scheduled to appear in town on the same
date, but because of the Miller opposition the
Hawkins date was cancelled and he was rebooked
for a date later in the month. (Met. May 1940;
Baltimore News Post, Baltimore, Md., April 8, 1940;
Variety, March 20, 1940; G.M.P.R.)

9 April, 1940 (TUES)

       "Glenn Miller is now making Washington the
base of musical operations at near-by colleges
and dances. Broadcasts are being originated from
WJSV, which picks up the music at the little theater
of the Wardman Park Hotel. Tickets for the broadcasts on three nights each week are being distributed by the local Columbia outlet, with SRO for each
show so far. Miller will hover in this vicinity
until June 6." (BB, April 20, 1940)

9 April, 1940 (TUES): Wardman Park Hotel, Washington, D.C.
               CBS 10:00-10:15 P.M. EST. (CHESTERFIELD
                                        SHOW)

               Moonlight Serenade (Theme)
               Slow Freight
               It's A Blue World
               My! My!
               Danny Boy
               Runnin' Wild
               Moonlight Serenade (Theme)

10 April, 1940 (WED): Wardman Park Hotel, Washington, D.C.
               CBS 10:00-10:15 P.M. EST. (CHESTERFIELD
                                          SHOW)

               Moonlight Serenade (Theme)

V-4086 WR-964 GMMS 16/64
            (2:38) Say "Si Si" (Para Vigo Me Voy)-voc Marion
                      Hutton
                      (Al Stillman-Francia Luban-Ernesto
                      Lecuona)
                      Ts, Beneke

(Broadcast continued on next page)

WPRS-0976   Vi LSP-3981, RCA RD/SF-7982
             (6:53) MEDLEY:
             Int GM Coquette (arr JG)
                        (Gus Kahn-Carmen Lombardo-John W.
                        Green)
             Int GM Say It (arr BF)-voc Ray Eberle
                        From the Paramount film "Buck Benny
                        Rides Again"
                        (Frank Loesser-Jimmy McHugh)
             Int GM Does Your Heart Beat For Me? (arr JG)
                        (borrowed from Russ Morgan)
                        (Mitchell Parish-Russ Morgan-
                        Arnold Johnson)
                        P, MacGregor
             Int GM Blue Hawaii (arr JG)
                        From the Paramount film "Waikiki
                        Wedding"
                        (Leo Robin-Ralph Rainger)
                        Ts, Beneke

V-4086 WR-964 GMMS 16/64, GMMS 44/92, AFRS P-2240
             (2:48) Bugle Call Rag (arr GM)
                        (Jack Pettis-Billy Meyers-Elmer
                        Schoebel)
                        D, Purtill; tbn, Miller; ts, Beneke;
                        tpt, Hurley; tbn, Miller;tpt, Best?;
                        ts, Beneke; d, Purtill

                 Moonlight Serenade (Theme)

*11 April, 1940 (THUR): Wardman Park Hotel, Washington, D.C.
            CBS 10:00-10:15 P.M. EST. (CHESTERFIELD
                                         SHOW)*

                 Moonlight Serenade (Theme)
                 My Isle Of Golden Dreams

V-4086 WR-966 GMMS 18/66, GMMS 45/93
          Int GM (2:06) Wanna Hat With Cherries-voc Marion Hutton
                        (Larry Clinton-Jo Carringer-Betty Lynn)

                 Too Romantic

V-4086 WR-966 GMMS 18/66
          Int GM (3:58) St. Louis Blues (arr ED)
                        (William C. Handy)
                        Tpt, Hurley; ts, Beneke; p, MacGregor;
                        tbn, Miller; tpt, Hurley

                 Moonlight Serenade (Theme)

11 April, 1940 (THUR)

> G.M.P.R. are missing for the week April 5th to April 11th but since there are no changes in personnel for the next week (April 12th to April 18th) we can only assume that the personnel remained stable.

12 April, 1940 (FRI)

> Glenn Miller and His Orchestra played for two days (12th & 13th April) at the Virginia Military Institute, Lexington, Virginia, from 9:30-2:00 A.M. (G.M.P.R.)

14 April, 1940 (SUN)

> Day off. (G.M.P.R.)

15 April, 1940 (MON)

> Glenn Miller and His Orchestra played at Valencia Ballroom, York, Pennsylvania, from 8:30-12:30 A.M. (York Dispatch, York, Pa., April 15, 1940; G.M.P.R.)

16 April, 1940 (TUES): Wardman Park Hotel, Washington, D.C.
CBS 10:00-10:15 P.M. EST. (CHESTERFIELD SHOW)

The announcer for this show is Larry Bruff.

> *Moonlight Serenade (Theme)*

V-4086 WR-965 GMMS 17/65, GMMS 43/91
> (2:30) Rug Cutter's Swing (arr BF)
> (Horace Henderson)
> Ts, Beneke; tbn, Miller; tpt, Hurley

> *When You Wish Upon A Star-voc RE*
> *Sweet Potato Piper*
> *Long, Long Ago*
> *(Thomas Haynes Bayly)*
> *Dipper Mouth Blues*
> *Moonlight Serenade (Theme)*

17 April, 1940 (WED): Wardman Park Hotel, Washington, D.C.
(CHESTERFIELD SHOW)
CBS 10:00-10:15 P.M. EST.

Moonlight Serenade *(Theme)*

V-4086 WR-985 GMMS 25/73, GMMS 43/91, AFRS P-2248
(2:11) Boog-It (arr JG)-voc Marion Hutton and the
Band
(Cab Calloway-Jack Palmer-Buck Ram)
As, Caceres; tpt, Hurley

MEDLEY:
Goodnight, Sweetheart
I'm Stepping Out With A Memory Tonight
When My Baby Smiles At Me
A Blues Serenade
By The Waters Of Minnetonka
Moonlight Serenade *(Theme)*

18 April, 1940 (THUR): Wardman Park Hotel, Washington, D.C.
(CHESTERFIELD SHOW)
CBS 10:00-10:15 P.M. EST.

The announcer for this show is Larry Bruff.

Moonlight Serenade *(Theme)*

V-4086 WR-983 GMMS 23/71, AFRS P-2241
(2:05) Anchors Aweigh
(Alfred H. Miles-R. Lovell-Charles A.
Zimmerman)
Clt, Caceres; muted tpt, Hurley

V-4086 WR-983 GMMS 23/71, GMMS 50/98, Vi LPT 6700, Vi EPNT 6700
(947-0117), HMV RLS 599, Vi SPD-18 (599-
9104), AFRS P-2248, RCA G LPT 6700
Int GM (3:05) Weekend Of A Private Secretary-voc Marion
Hutton
(Bernard Hanighen-Johnny Mercer)
D, Purtill; tpt, Hurley

V-4086 WR-983 GMMS 23/71, GMMS 50/98
Int GM (1:41) Fools Rush In (Where Angels Fear To Tread)-
voc Ray Eberle
(Johnny Mercer-Rube Bloom)

(Broadcast continued on next page)

V-4086 WR-983 <u>GMMS 23/71</u>, AFRS P-2241
<u>(3:59) Tuxedo Junction</u> (arr JG)
(William Johnson-Julian Dash-Erskine
Hawkins-Buddy Feyne)
Muted tpt, McMickle; open tpt, Hurley;
muted tpt, McMickle; p, MacGregor

Moonlight Serenade *(Theme)*

On the commercial issues of "Weekend Of A Private
Secretary" the beginning of the tune and Miller's
introduction have been cut out.

19 April, 1940 (FRI)

Glenn Miller and His Orchestra played for two
nights (19th & 20th) at the University of Virginia,
Charlottesville, Virginia. The band played from
10:30-3:00 A.M. on April 19th and from 9:00-12:00
Midnight on April 20th. (G.M.P.R.)

21 April, 1940 (SUN)

Glenn Miller and His Orchestra played at Duke
University, Durham, North Carolina.

22 April, 1940 (MON)

Glenn Miller and His Orchestra played at Planter's
Warehouse (Jane St.), Wilson, North Carolina.
(Variety, March 20, 1940; G.M.P.R.)

Late April, 1940

While in Washington, Glenn Miller held a personal
demonstration of instruments and mouthpieces at
the Charles Miller store in company with Vincent
Bach and Irving Sax. (Met. May 1940)

Miller played a Bach trombone and during his band
career Bach featured Miller in their advertise-
ments.

23 April, 1940 (TUES): Wardman Park Hotel, Washington, D.C.
(CHESTERFIELD SHOW)
CBS   10:00-10:15 P.M. EST.

The announcer for this show is Larry Bruff.

Moonlight Serenade (Theme)
Pennsylvania Six-Five Thousand
Moments In The Moonlight
What's The Matter With Me

E2VL 4419   Vi LPT-30, HMV MH 172, Vi 42-0155 (PT-39), Vi 27-0155
(WPT-39), Vi EPBT-3026 (947-0026), HMV DLP
1012, Vi LPM-1189, RCA F 430228, RCA G EPC-
1189, El WDLP 1012, RCA G EPBT-3026
(1:57) Jeannie With The Light Brown Hair (arr JG)
(Stephen Foster)

King Porter Stomp
Moonlight Serenade (Theme)

24 April, 1940 (WED): Wardman Park Hotel, Washington, D.C.
(CHESTERFIELD SHOW)
CBS   10:00-10:15 P.M. EST.

The announcer for this show is Larry Bruff.

(0:46) *Moonlight Serenade (Theme)*
(Mitchell Parish-Glenn Miller)
(3:01) *Wham (Re-Bop-Boom-Bam) (arr ED)-voc Marion*
Hutton and Band
(Eddie Durham-"Taps" Miller)
Ts, Beneke; tbn, Miller; ts, Beneke;
tpt, Hurley
(4:32) MEDLEY:
Peg O' My Heart (arr JG)
(Alfred Bryan-Fred Fisher)
Int GM *Polka Dots And Moonbeams (arr JG)-voc*
Ray Eberle
(Johnny Burke-Jimmy Van Heusen)
Int LB *Mood Indigo (arr JG) (borrowed from Duke*
Ellington)
(Duke Ellington-Irving Mills-Albany
"Barney" Bigard)
Ts, Beneke
Int GM *Blue Orchids (arr JG)*
(Hoagy Carmichael)
Ts, Beneke
My Blue Heaven
Moonlight Serenade (Theme)

25 April, 1940 (THUR): Wardman Park Hotel, Washington, D.C.
                      (CHESTERFIELD SHOW)
                      CBS   10:00-10:15 P.M. EST.

   The announcer for this show is Larry Bruff.

            Moonlight Serenade (Theme)

WR-979 GMMS 19/67, AFRS P-2240
        (3:41) On The Alamo (arr JG)
                    (Gus Kahn-Isham Jones)
                    Tpt, Best

WR-979 GMMS 19/67
Int GM (2:12) Let's All Sing Together (arr JG)-
                    voc Marion Hutton
                    (Joe Audino-Nick DiRocca-Bill Keeshan)
                    Ts, Beneke; tpt, Hurley, d, Purtill

WR-979 GMMS 19/67, AFRS P-2252
Int GM (2:47) Say It (arr BF)-voc Ray Eberle
                    From the Paramount film "Buck Benny
                    Rides Again"
                    (Frank Loesser-Jimmy McHugh)
                    As, McIntyre

WR-979 GMMS 19/67, GMMS 42/90, Vi LPT-3001, HMV DLP-1013,
                    Vi EPBT-3001 (947-0055), Vi LPM-1189, El
                    WDLP 1013, AFRS P-2240, RCA G EPC-1189,
                    RCA F 430228, RCA G EPB-3001, Vi LPM-1070,
                    Vi EPB-1070, RCA G LPM-1070, RCA G EPB-
                    1070, RCA F 130243
Int GM (2:17) Fanhat Stomp
                    (Eddie Barefield)
                    Tbn, Miller; tpt, Hurley; ts, Beneke;
                    as, Caceres

            Moonlight Serenade (Theme)

        On the GMMS transcriptions the word "Larry" is
        left out (edited out) when Glenn introduces
        "Fanhat Stomp".

26 April, 1940 (FRI)

            Trombones   Glenn Miller, Jimmy Priddy, Paul
                         Tanner, Frank D'Annolfo
            Trumpets   Clyde Hurley, Legh Knowles, REUBEN
                         "ZEKE" ZARCHY, Johnny Best

(continued on next page)

```
Reeds          Hal McIntyre, as; Ernie Caceres, as,
               bar & clt; Wilbur Schwartz, clt & as;
               Tex Beneke, ts; Al Klink, ts
Rhythm         Chummy MacGregor, p; JACK LATHROP, g;
               Rowland Bundock, b; Maurice Purtill, d
Vocalists      Marion Hutton, Ray Eberle, JACK LATHROP
Band-Boy       Raul Hidalgo
```

Glenn Miller and His Orchestra played at the George
F. Pavilion, Johnson City, Pennsylvania from 9:00-
1:00 A.M. (G.M.D.)

27 April, 1940 (SAT)

Glenn Miller and His Orchestra played at Hofstra
College (the gym), Hempstead, Long Island, New
York, from 10:30 A.M. to 2:30 P.M. (G.M.D.;
Variety, March 27, 1940)

28 April, 1940 (SUN): Victor Studios, New York City, New York

Same personnel as for April 26th.

048963-1   BB 10754-A, HMV BD 5618, HMVSw JK-2125, VdP GW-
                2000, Vi 20-1567 (Vi P-148), Vi 47-2854
                (Vi WP-148), Vi 420-0046, Vi 447-0046, Vi
                EPAT-405, Vi EPA-5049, Vi LPM-31, Vi LPT-
                3057, Vi EPBT-3057 (947-0136), Vi LPM/LSP-
                1192, Vi EPB-1192 (547-0810), El G EG 7965,
                RCA It LPM 10011, RCA It EPA 30-159, RCA It
                45N 0978, Vi It LJ 50012, RCA RCX 1024, RCA
                RD 27068, RD 3/4-21, AFRS P-NAV-2, AFRS
                H-62-1 Phonograph Album No. 1, HMV DLP-1024,
                HMVAus GA 5046, HMVAus GA 5137, HMVAus
                VDLP 302, AFRS P-S-15, AFRS P-1542, VdP 7E
                PQ 518, RD 3/4-64, (Production albums only),
                RCA G EPAT-405, RCA G LPM 9801, AFRS "Jukebox
                USA" 306, AFRS "Take A Record Please" 23,
                EL WDLP 1024, AFRS "America's Pop Music" 67,
                HMVIr I.P. 931, RCA G EPC-1192, RCA G LPM/
                LSP-1192, RCA G LSP-9901, RCA G 447-0046,
                RCA F 230201, RCA F 530243, Vi EPBT-1192,
                Vi Arg LPM/LSP-1192, Vi VPM-6019, RCA G SRS
                560, RCA F 740.515, RCA Br. RD-8094 (unissued)
                Pennsylvania Six-Five Thousand (arr JG)-Chant by
                Band
                (Carl Sigman-Jerry Gray)
                (Telephone number of the Cafe Rouge, Hotel
                Pennsylvania, New York City, New York)
                Tpt, Best; ts, Beneke

(Session continued on next page)

(Session continued on next page)

048964-1   BB 10740-B, HMV BD 5633, Vi 20-2413 (Vi P-189)
Vi 420-0038, Vi 447-0038, Vi 47-2877, Vi EPA-727, Vi EPA-5103, Vi LPT-3036, Vi EPBT-3036 (947-0090), HMV DLP 1062, Vi LPT-3067, Vi EPBT-3067 (947-0199), Vi LPM-1190, Vi EPB-1190 (547-0829), El G EG 7620, RCA Int. 10010, AFRS "Jukebox USA" 209, HMVIn BD 5633, RCA G LPT-3067, RCA G EPBT-3067, RCA G EPC-1190, RCA F 130210, RCA G LPM-1190, HMVAus GA 5028, HMVIr I.P. 993
Bugle Call Rag (arr GM)
(Jack Pettis-Billy Meyers-Elmer Schoebel)
D, Purtill; tbn, Miller; ts, Beneke; clt, Caceres; tbn, Miller; ts, Beneke; d, Purtill

048965-1   BB 10745-A, HMV BD 5632, HMV MH 92, HMVAu EA-2736, El G EG 7567, Vi EPAT-427, HMV 7EG 8067, Vi LPT-1031, Cam Cal/Cas-2128, RCA G LPT-1031, RD 3/4-64, RCA G Cas-2128, AFRS "America's Pop Music" 72, RCA Cam Arg Cal-3138
The Nearness Of You (arr BF)-voc Ray Eberle
(Ned Washington-Hoagy Carmichael)
Ts, Beneke

048966-1   BB Unissued
W.P.A. (arr BF)-voc Tex Beneke and Band
(Jesse Stone)

048967-1   BB 10745-B, Vi LPT 6700, Vi EPNT 6700 (947-0117), Vi SPD-18 (599-9107), HMV RLS 599, RCA G LPT 6700
Mister Meadowlark (arr JG)-voc Jack Lathrop
(Johnny Mercer-Walter Donaldson)
P, MacGregor; ts, Beneke

048968-1   BB 10994-B, HMV BD 5678, HMVSw JK-2323, ViJ 1092, Cam Cal/Cas-2128, RD 3/4-64, RCA G Cas-2128, HMVIn BD 5678, RCA Cam Arg Cal-3138, Vi Arg 68-0691
My Blue Heaven (arr BF)
(George Whiting-Walter Donaldson)
Tbn, Miller; ts, Beneke; d, Purtill

"Mister Meadowlark" 2 takes; all other tunes 1 take.
(RCA Victor)
This session lasted from 1:00 P.M. to 5:45 P.M.
(RCA Victor)

"W.P.A." was never issued because of the stand
the AFM took on the lyrics of the tune. The words

(continued on next page)

were considered "Un-American". (DB, July 15, 1940)
The initials "W.P.A." stand for "Works Project
Administration." No master was ever made of
"W.P.A."

28 April, 1940 (SUN)

Glenn Miller and His Orchestra played at the Savoy
Ballroom (140th St. & Lenox Avenue), Harlem, New
York City, New York, from 8:00-10:00 P.M. and 12:00
Midnight-2:00 A.M. (New York Daily News, April 28,
1940; G.M.D.)
    "Glenn Miller played to a mob of over 4,000
at the Savoy." (DB, May 15, 1940)
    "Glenn Miller's date at the Savoy was plain
murder. The mob couldn't get enough. Phil Harris,
from the coast, and Joe Bernard were among those
present." (DB, May 15, 1940)

29 April, 1940 (MON)

Glenn Miller and His Orchestra played at the
Masonic Temple (Buddy Club), Scranton, Pennsylvania,
from 9:00 P.M. to 1:00 A.M. (Variety, March 27, 1940;
BB,May 11, 1940; The Scranton Times, Scranton, Pa.,
April 29, 1940; G.M.D.)

30 April 1940 (TUES): Wardman Park Hotel, Washington, D.C.
                (CHESTERFIELD SHOW)
                CBS 10:00-10:15 P.M. EST.

The announcer for this program is Larry Bruff.

Moonlight Serenade (Theme)

V-4086 WR-987 GMMS 27/75, GMMS 52/100
        (2:56) Slow Freight (arr BF)
                (Mills-Lupin Fein-Buck Ram)
                Muted tpt, McMickle; open tpt, Hurley;
                muted tpt, McMickle

V-4086 WR-987 GMMS 27/75
        Int GM (1:49) Fools Rush In (Where Angels Fear to Tread)-
                voc Ray Eberle
                (Johnny Mercer-Rube Bloom)

V-4086 WR-987 GMMS 25/75, AFRS P-2251
        Int GM (1:56) The Woodpecker Song-voc Marion Hutton
                (Harold Adamson-Eldo di Lazzaro)
                No Beneke solo

(Broadcast continued on next page)

Int LB (1:50) <u>Drink To Me Only With Thine Eyes</u>
(Ben Jonson)
(1:06) <u>Pagan Love Song</u>
From the MGM film "The Pagan"
(Arthur Freed-Nacio Herb Brown)
Muted tpt, Hurley
<u>Moonlight Serenade</u> (Theme)

1 May, 1940 (WED): Wardman Park Hotel, Washington, D.C.
(CHESTERFIELD SHOW)
CBS 10:00-10:15 P.M. EST.

The announcer for this program is Larry Bruff

<u>Moonlight Serenade</u> (Theme)
<u>My! My!</u>-voc MH
MEDLEY:
<u>You Tell Me Your Dream</u> (<u>I Had A Dream,</u>
<u>Dear</u>)
<u>Devil May Care</u>
<u>Sleep</u>
<u>Alice Blue Gown</u>
<u>Tiger Rag</u>
<u>Moonlight Serenade</u> (Theme)

2 May, 1940 (THUR): Wardman Park Hotel, Washington, D.C.
(CHESTERFIELD SHOW)
CBS 10:00-10:15 P.M. EST.

The announcer for this program is Larry Bruff.

<u>Moonlight Serenade</u> (Theme)
<u>Sunrise Serenade</u>

V-4086 WR-1030 <u>GMMS 28/76</u>, AFRS P-2251
Int LB <u>(2:44)</u>Cowboy From Brooklyn-voc Marion Hutton and
Tex Beneke
From the Warner Brothers' film
"Cowboy From Brooklyn"
(Johnny Mercer-Harry Warren)
Ts, Beneke

V-4086 WR-1030 <u>GMMS 28/76</u>, AFRS P-2251
Int GM <u>(1:36)</u>Sierra Sue (arr JG)-voc Ray Eberle
(Joseph B. Carey)
No alto sax solo

(Broadcast continued on next page)

V-4086 WR-1030 <u>GMMS 28/76</u>, AFRS P-2245
    Int GM <u>(3:39)</u> In The Mood
                            (Andy Razaf-Joe Garland)
                            Ts, Beneke; ts, Klink; tpt, Hurley
                            (There are four endings to this
                            version)

                    <u>Moonlight Serenade</u> (Theme)

3 May, 1940 (FRI)

            Glenn Miller and His Orchestra played at Pennsyl-
            vania State College, State College, Pennsylvania,
            from 10:00-2:00 A.M. (G.M.D.)

4 May, 1940 (SAT)

            Glenn Miller and His Orchestra played at Dartmouth
            University (Alumini Gym), Hanover, New Hampshire,
            from 10:00-2:00 A.M. (G.M.D.)

5 May, 1940 (SUN)

            Glenn Miller and His Orchestra played at Lake
            Compounce, Bristol, Connecticut. (Variety, April
            10, 1940)

6 May, 1940 (MON)

            Glenn Miller and His Orchestra played at Temple
            University (Broad & Berks St.), Philadelphia,
            Pennsylvania, from 10:00-2:00 A.M. (G.M.D.)

7 May, 1940 (TUES): Pittsburgh, Pennsylvania (CHESTERFIELD SHOW)
                    CBS   10:00-10:15 P.M. EST.

        The announcer for this program is Larry Bruff.

                    <u>*Moonlight Serenade*</u> *(Theme)*
                    <u>*Oh, Lady Be Good*</u>
                    <u>*April Played The Fiddle*</u>*-voc RE*
                    <u>*Say "Si Si"*</u>
                    <u>*Old Black Joe*</u>

(Broadcast continued on next page)

V-4086 WR-1030 GMMS 28/76
>   (2:10) I Want To Be Happy (arr ED)
>   From the musical production
>   "No, No, Nanette"
>   (Irving Caesar-Vincent Youmans)
>   Tpt, Hurley; ts, Beneke; tbn, Miller;
>   d, Purtill

>   *Moonlight Serenade* (Theme)

8 May, 1940 (WED): Pittsburgh, Pennsylvania (CHESTERFIELD SHOW)
>   *CBS   10:00-10:15 P.M. EST.*

>   *Moonlight Serenade* (Theme)
>   *Boog-It*
>   *MEDLEY:*
>   *Shine On, Harvest Moon*
>   *Imagination*
>   *Rose Room*
>   *Blue Room*

E1LVB 3200   Vi LPT-16, Vi 42-0107 (Vi PT-25), Vi 27-0107
>   (Vi WPT-25), Vi EPBT-3025 (947-0024), HMV
>   DLP-1021, Vi LPM-1193, El G EG 7861, El
>   WDLP 1021, Vi TP3-5020, RCA G LPM-1193,
>   RCA Int. B-21032, RCA Int. T-21032
>   Int GM (3:34) One O'Clock Jump
>   (Lee Gaines-Count Basie)
>   P, MacGregor; ts, Beneke; tpt,
>   Hurley

>   *Moonlight Serenade* (Theme)

9 May, 1940 (THUR): Hotel William Penn, Pittsburgh, Pennsylvania
>   *(CHESTERFIELD SHOW)*
>   *CBS   10:00-10:15 P.M. EST.*

>   *The announcer for this program is Larry Bruff.*

>   *Moonlight Serenade* (Theme)
>   *Time On My Hands* (arr JG)
>   *I Just Got A Letter-voc MH*
>   *I'm Stepping Out With A Memory Tonight-*
>   *voc RE*
>   *Tuxedo Junction*
>   *Moonlight Serenade* (Theme)

The Tuesday and Wednesday night programs may have
been broadcast from the Hotel William Penn as well
but this is the only program of the three in which
the Hotel is mentioned on the broadcast.

9 May, 1940 (THUR)

> Glenn Miller and His Orchestra played at Carnegie
> Tech, Pittsburgh, Pennsylvania, from 10:45-2:00
> A.M. (G.M.D.)

10 May, 1940 (FRI)

> Glenn Miller and His Orchestra played at the 174th
> Armory (Niagara & Connecticut Street), Buffalo,
> New York,from 9:00-1:00 A.M. (Buffalo Courier
> Express, May 10, 1940; G.M.D.)

11 May, 1940 (SAT)

> Glenn Miller and His Orchestra played at Union
> College, Schenectady, New York, from 10:00-
> 2:00 A.M. (G.M.D.)

12 May, 1940 (SUN)

> Glenn Miller and His Orchestra played at the State
> Theater, Hartford, Connecticut. (DB, May 15, 1940;
> G.M.D.)

13 May, 1940 (MON)

> Glenn Miller and His Orchestra played at the
> Worcester Auditorium, Worcester, Massachusetts.
> (Boston Post, May 13, 1940)

> Clyde Hurley "handed in his notice the middle of
> May, planning to return to native Texas for a
> vacation". (Met. June 1940) Hurley's last day
> with the band was May 30th. Later it was reported
> that he was "tired of stylized arrangements" and
> joined Tommy Dorsey about June 16.

14 May, 1940 (TUES): Wardman Park Hotel, Washington, D.C.
> *(CHESTERFIELD SHOW)*
> *CBS 10:00-10:15 P.M. EST.*

The announcer for this program is Larry Bruff.

(Broadcast continued on next page)

Moonlight Serenade (Theme)
Little Brown Jug
Devil May Care
What's The Matter With Me
Sweet Genevieve (arr JG)
        (George Cooper-Henry Tucker)
Anchors Aweigh
Moonlight Serenade (Theme)

15 May, 1940 (WED): New Indoor Gymnasium of Duke University at Durham, North Carolina (CHESTERFIELD SHOW) CBS 10:00-10:15 P.M. EST.

Moonlight Serenade (Theme)
Wham
MEDLEY:
    Sweet Leilani
    Faithful To You
    Smoke Rings
    Under A Blanket Of Blue

E1LVB 3200   Vi LPT-16, Vi 42-0109 (Vi PT-25), Vi 27-0109
              (Vi WPT-25), Vi LPT-3057, Vi EPBT-3057
              (947-0137), Vi EPA-5092, Vi EPBT-3025
              (947-0024), Vi LPM/LSP-1192, Vi EPB-1192
              (547-0809), Vi LPM-1193, HMV DLP-1021,
              Vi EPB-1193 (547-0823), RCA RD 27068, Vi
              TP3-5020, Vi It LPM 10011, Vi It LJ 50012,
              El G EG 7795, El WDLP-1021, RCA Int.
              B-21032, RCA Int. T-21032, RCA G EPC-1192,
              RCA F 530243, RCA G LPM/LSP-1192, RCA G
              LPM-1193, RCA F 230201, Vi EPBT-1192,
              Vi Arg LPM/LSP-1192, RCA F 740.515, RCA
              F A 75.240
    Int GM (3:35) St. Louis Blues (arr ED)
              (William C. Handy)
              Tpt, Hurley; ts, Beneke; tpt, Hurley

Moonlight Serenade (Theme)

The band also played a dance this evening at Duke
University from 8:30-1:00 A.M. (G.M.D.)

16 May, 1940 (THUR): Wardman Park Hotel, Washington, D.C. (CHESTERFIELD SHOW) CBS 10:00-10:15 P.M. EST

Moonlight Serenade (Theme)

(Broadcast continued on next page)

E4VP 8209   <u>Vi LPT 6701</u>, Vi EPOT 6701 (947-0183), HMV RLS 598,
               Vi It LPM 10141, Vi It LJ 50020, Vi It LPM
               50020, RCA G EPOT-6701, RCA G LSP-9901,
               RCA G SRS 560
               (2:44) Body And Soul
                        From the musical revue "Three's A
                        Crowd"
                        (Edward Heyman-Robert Sour-Frank Eyton-
                        John W. Green)
                        Ts, Beneke; tpt, Best

               Sweet Potato Piper
               I'll Never Smile Again
               Farewell Blues
               Moonlight Serenade (Theme)

               On Vi LPT 6701 "Body And Soul" was incorrectly
               listed as being broadcast on May 10, 1940.

               The band also played a dance this evening at the
               Riverside Stadium, Washington, D.C., from 10:00-
               2:00 A.M. (G.M.D.)

               Tommy Mack left the band on this date as road
               manager and was replaced by Glenn's brother,
               Herbie Miller. (G.M.P.R.) Mack retired because
               he was "tired of the heavy duties his job called
               for". (Met. June 1940)

17 May, 1940 (FRI)

               Trombones   Glenn Miller, Jimmy Priddy, Paul
                              Tanner, Frank D'Annolfo
               Trumpets   Clyde Hurley, Zeke Zarchy, DALE
                              McMICKLE, Johnny Best
               Reeds   Hal McIntyre, as; Ernie Caceres,
                              as, bar & clt; Wilbur Schwartz,
                              clt & as; Tex Beneke, ts; Al Klink, ts
               Rhythm   Chummy MacGregor, p; Jack Lathrop, g;
                              Rowland Bundock, b; Maurice Purtill, d
               Vocalists   Marion Hutton, Ray Eberle, Jack Lathrop
               Band-Boy   Raul Hidalgo

               Glenn Miller and His Orchestra played at the
               Wardman Park Hotel, Washington, D.C., for a
               Georgetown University dance, from 9:00-1:00 A.M.
               (G.M.D.)

                   "Zeke Zarchy, trumpeter who has been sub-
               stituting for Mick McMickle, will remain with
               the band after Mick returns. Zeke takes over
               Freddie Knowles' chair." (DB, June 1, 1940)

18 May, 1940 (SAT)

      Glenn Miller and His Orchestra played at Hershey
      Park, Hershey, Pennsylvania, from 8:30-12:30 A.M.
      (G.M.D.)

19 May, 1940 (SUN)

      Glenn Miller and His Orchestra played at Pleasure
      Beach, Bridgeport Park, Bridgeport, Connecticut,
      and drew 3,650 dancers. (Variety, May 15, 1940;
      BB, June 1, 1940)

20 May, 1940 (MON)

      Glenn Miller and His Orchestra played at Rhodes,
      Providence, Rhode Island. (Boston Daily Record,
      May 20, 1940; Boston Post, May 17, 1940)

21 May, 1940 (TUES): Boston, Massachusetts. (CHESTERFIELD SHOW)
         CBS 10:00-10:15 P.M. EST.

           Moonlight Serenade (Theme)
           Pennsylvania Six-Five Thousand
           The Nearness Of You
           FDR Jones
           Jeannie With The Light Brown Hair
           Dipper Mouth Blues
           Moonlight Serenade (Theme)

21 May, 1940 (TUES)

      Glenn Miller and His Orchestra played at the
      Quincy Armory, Quincy, Massachusetts. (Boston
      Daily Record, May 21, 1940; Boston Post, May
      21, 1940) Mal Hallett plays from 8:30-10:45
      P.M. until Miller finished his Chesterfield
      program and then Miller played from 10:45-
      2:00 A.M. (Boston Post, May 22, 1940)

22 May, 1940 (WED): Boston, Massachusetts (CHESTERFIELD SHOW)
         CBS 10:00-10:15 P.M. EST.

      The announcer for this program is Larry Bruff.

         Moonlight Serenade (Theme)

(Broadcast continued on next page)

V-4086 WR-982 <u>GMMS 22/70</u>
<u>(1:48)</u> The Woodpecker Song-voc Marion Hutton
(Harold Adamson-Eldo Di Lazzaro)
No Beneke sax solo

V-4086 WR-982 <u>GMMS 22/70</u>, GMMS 51/99, AFRS P-2247
<u>(5:54)</u> MEDLEY:
Int GM   <u>Poor Butterfly</u> (arr JG)
From the stage production "The
Big Show"
(John L. Golden-Raymond Hubbell)
Ts, Beneke
Int GM   <u>The Sky Fell Down</u> (arr BF)-voc Ray
Eberle
(Edward Heyman-Louis Alter)
Int LB   <u>I'm Gettin' Sentimental Over You</u> (arr
JG) (borrowed from Tommy Dorsey)
(Ned Washington-George Bassman)
Ts, Beneke
Int LB   <u>Black And Blue</u> (arr JG)
(Harry Brooks-Andy Razaf-Thomas
"Fats" Waller)
Tpt, Best

V-4086 WR-982 <u>GMMS 22/70</u>, AFRS P-2241
Int GM   <u>(3:38)</u> <u>By The Waters of Minnetonka</u> (arr GM)-
Chant by the Orchestra
(Indian Love Song)
(J.M. Cavanass-Thurlow Lieurance)
Ts, Beneke; clt, Caceres; tbn,
Miller; tpt, Hurley; d, Purtill

Moonlight Serenade (Theme)

22 May, 1940 (WED)

Glenn Miller and His Orchestra played at North
Shore Gardens, Salem, Massachusetts. (Boston
Daily Record, May 22, 1940; Boston Post, May
22, 1940) Mal Hallett plays from 8:30-10:45
P.M. until Miller finished his Chesterfield
program and then Miller played from 10:45-
2:00 A.M. (Boston Post, May 22, 1940)

23 May, 1940 (THUR): Boston Massachusetts (CHESTERFIELD SHOW)
CBS   10:00-10:15 P.M. EST.

The announcer for this program is Larry Bruff.

(Broadcast continued on next page)

Moonlight Serenade *(Theme)*
Moonglow
        (Eddie DeLange-Irving Mills-
        Will Hudson)
The Rumba Jumps!
Say It-voc RE
Runnin' Wild
Moonlight Serenade *(Theme)*

23 May, 1940 (THUR)

        Glenn Miller and His Orchestra played at the
        Mechanics Building (presented by the Esquire
        Club of Boston), Boston, Massachusetts. (Boston
        Daily Record, May 23, 1940; Boston Post, May 23,
        1940)

24 May, 1940 (FRI)

        Glenn Miller and His Orchestra played at Cornell
        University (Navy Day Ball), Ithaca, New York,
        from 10:30-3:30 A.M. (G.M.D.; Variety, May 1,
        1940)

25 May, 1940 (SAT)

        Glenn Miller and His Orchestra played at the
        Armory, Albany, New York, from 9:00-1:00 A.M.
        (G.M.D.)

26 May, 1940 (SUN)

        Glenn Miller and His Orchestra played at Dance-
        land, Sylvan Beach, New York, from 8:30-12:30 A.M.,
        and drew 3,000 dancers. (G.M.D.; BB, May 4, 1940;
        BB, June 29, 1940)

27 May, 1940 (MON)

        Glenn Miller and His Orchestra played at the
        Empire Ballroom, Allentown, Pennsylvania, from
        9:00-1:00 A.M. (G.M.D.)

28 May, 1940 (TUES): Wardman Park Hotel, Washington, D.C.
          (CHESTERFIELD SHOW)
          CBS   10:00-10:15 P.M. EST.

          The announcer for this program is Larry Bruff.

               Moonlight Serenade (Theme)

V-4086 WR-966 GMMS 18/66, GMMS 46/94, Vi LPM-6100, RCA RD 27146,
               RCA G LPM-6100
               (3:06) Conversation Piece (arr BF)
                    (Bill Finegan)
                    As, McIntyre; as, Caceres; tpt, Best;
                    ts, Beneke; ts, Klink

V-4086 WR-966 GMMS 18/66
     Int GM (1:40) Polka Dots And Moonbeams (arr JG)-voc
                    Ray Eberle
                    (Johnny Burke-Jimmy Van Heusen)
                    As, McIntyre

V-4086 WR-1008 GMMS 31/79, GMMS 49/97, AFRS P-2249
     Int GM (1:36) My! My! (arr JG)-voc Marion Hutton
                    From the Paramount film "Buck Benny
                    Rides Again"
                    (Frank Loesser-Jimmy McHugh)
                    As, Caceres

               Carry Me Back To Old Virginny
                    (James A. Bland)
               King Porter Stomp
               Moonlight Serenade (Theme)

29 May, 1940 (WED): Wardman Park Hotel, Washington, D.C.
          (CHESTERFIELD SHOW)
          CBS   10:00-10:15 P.M. EST.

          The announcer for this program is Larry Bruff.

               Moonlight Serenade (Theme)

UPRM-6315   Vi LPM/LSP-3873, RCA G LSP-3873, RCA RD/SF-7932
               (2:42) Yours Is My Heart Alone (arr BF)
                    (Ludwig Herzer-Fritz Lohner-Franz
                    Lehar-English words by Harry Bache
                    Smith)
                    Ts, Beneke

(Broadcast continued on next page)

V-4086 WR-958 <u>GMMS 10/58</u>, AFRS P-2243
    Int GM <u>(1:50)</u> <u>Let's All Sing Together</u> (arr JG)-voc
                    Marion Hutton
                    (Joe Audino-Nick DiRocca-Bill Keeshan)
                    Ts, Beneke; tpt, Hurley; d, Purtill

                April Played The Fiddle

V-4086 WR-965 <u>GMMS 17/65</u>, GMMS 51/99, AFRS P-2239
    Int LB & GM <u>(2:51)</u> <u>Slip Horn Jive</u> (arr ED)
                    (Eddie Durham)
                    Ts, Beneke; tpt, Hurley; tbn, Miller;
                    ts, Klink; tpt, Hurley

                Moonlight Serenade (Theme)

         This is the first program in which the medley was
         not featured on Wednesday evening. Instead it
         was played on Thursday night.

30 May, 1940 (THUR): Wardman Park Hotel, Washington, D.C. (CHESTERFIELD
              CBS   10:00-10:15 P.M. EST.   *SHOW)*

                Moonlight Serenade (Theme)
                A Cabana In Havana
                MEDLEY:
                    A Pretty Girl Is Like A Melody
                        From the Ziegfeld Follies of 1919
                        (Irving Berlin)
                    Shake Down The Stars
K2PP-0046   <u>Vi LPM-6100</u>, RCA RD 27147, RCA G LPM-6100
         (1:05) <u>Some Of These Days</u> (borrowed from Sophie
                    Tucker)
                    (Shelton Brooks)
                    Ts, Beneke
K2PP-0046   <u>Vi LPM-6100</u>, RCA RD 27147, RCA G LPM-6100
    Int GM (0:55) <u>Memphis Blues</u>
                    (William C. Handy-Robinson)
                    Tbn, Miller?; clt, Caceres
                Tiger Rag
                Moonlight Serenade (Theme)

         RCA Victor have added the name Robinson to the
         composer credits on "Memphis Blues" but most
         books show only Handy.

31 May, 1940 (FRI)

         Trombones   Glenn Miller, Jimmy Priddy, Paul
                        Tanner, Frank D'Annolfo

(Continued on next page)

Trumpets	CHARLES FRANKHAUSER, Zeke Zarchy, Dale McMickle, Johnny Best
Reeds	Hal McIntyre, as; Ernie Caceres, as, bar & clt; Wilbur Schwartz, clt & as; Tex Beneke, ts; Al Klink, ts
Rhythm	Chummy MacGregor, p; Jack Lathrop, g; Rowland Bundock, b; Maurice Purtill, d
Vocalists	Marion Hutton, Ray Eberle, Jack Lathrop
Band-Boy	Raul Hidalgo

Miller, while playing in Washington, D.C., hired former Krupa musician Charles Frankhauser as Hurley's replacement.

Glenn Miller and His Orchestra played at William and Mary College, Williamsburg, Virginia, for two nights (31st May and 1st June). On May 31st the band played from 10:00-2:00 A.M. and on June 1st the band played from 4:30-5:30 P.M. and 9:00-12:00 Midnight. (G.M.D.)

2 June, 1940 (SUN)

Glenn Miller and His Orchestra played at the Coliseum, Baltimore, Maryland, from 10:00-2:00 A.M. (G.M.D.)

3 June, 1940 (MON)

Glenn Miller and His Orchestra played at the Memorial Hall, Annapolis, Maryland, from 9:00-12:00 Midnight. (G.M.D.)

4 June, 1940 (TUES): Wardman Park Hotel, Washington, D.C. (CHESTERFIELD SHOW) CBS 10:00-10:15 P.M. EST.

The announcer for this program is Larry Bruff.

Moonlight Serenade (Theme)

V-4086 WR-959   GMMS 11/59, Vi LPT 6700, Vi EPNT 6700 (947-0123) Vi SPD-18 (599-9107), HMV RLS 599, RCA G LPT 6700, AFRS P-2238, RCA Vi It LJ 50012, RCA It LPM 10011, RCA It AlOV 0007, Vi LPM 6000, RCA G LPM 6000, Vi EPF 6000?
(2:20) Oh, Lady Be Good (arr BF)
From the musical production "Lady Be Good"

(Broadcast continued on next page)

          (Ira Gershwin-George Gershwin)
          Ts, Beneke; ts, Klink; d, Purtill

Hear My Song, Violetta

V-4086 WR-959 GMMS 11/59
    Int GM (1:55) Say "Si Si" (Para Vigo Me Voy)-voc
               Marion Hutton
               (Al Stillman-Francia Luban-Ernesto
               Lecuona)
               Ts, Beneke

V-4086 WR-963 GMMS 15/63, GMMS 47/95
    Int GM (1:20) Can't You Heah Me Callin', Caroline?
               (William H. Gardner-Caro Roma)

V-4086 WR-959 GMMS 11/59, Vi LPT-16, Vi 42-0107 (Vi PT-25),
               Vi TP3-5020, Vi 27-0107 (Vi WPT-25), Vi
               EPBT-3025 (947-0025), Vi LPM-1193, Vi EPB-
               1193 (547-0822), HMV DLP-1013, Vi It LPM-
               10141, AFRS P-2238, RCA Vi It LJ 50020,
               RCA F 130243, Vi It LPM 50020, RCA G LPM-
               1193, El WDLP 1013, RCA Int. B-21032, RCA
               Int. T-21032, El G EG 7861
   Int LB & GM (3:17) My Blue Heaven (arr BF)
               (George Whiting-Walter Donaldson)
               Tbn, Miller; ts, Beneke; ts, Klink;
               d, Purtill

Moonlight Serenade (Theme)

4 June, 1940 (TUES)

        Glenn Miller and His Orchestra played at Alcazar
        Ballroom (for John Hopkins University), Baltimore,
        Maryland, from 10:45-2:45 A.M. (G.M.D.)

5 June, 1940 (WED): Wardman Park Hotel, Washington, D.C.
             (CHESTERFIELD SHOW)
             CBS 10:00-10:15 P.M. EST.

     The announcer for this program is Larry Bruff.

          Moonlight Serenade (Theme)
          I Haven't Time To Be A Millionaire
          MEDLEY:
             Sweet And Lovely
             Sierra Sue
             The Very Thought Of You
             Blue Evening
          Wham-voc MH & Band
          Moonlight Serenade (Theme)

6 June, 1940 (THUR)

>   Glenn Miller and His Orchestra played at the
>   University of Tennessee Auditorium (Smokey Mountain
>   Festival "Wildflower Coronation Ball"), Knoxville,
>   Tennessee, from 9:00-1:00 A.M., and drew 7,500
>   dancers (Cab Calloway and His Orchestra played also).
>   (G.M.D.; BB, June 29, 1940)

6 June, 1940 (THUR): Knoxville, Tennessee (CHESTERFIELD SHOW)
            CBS   10:00-10:15 P.M. EST.
            Moonlight Serenade (Theme)
            Sophisticated Lady
            Devil May Care
            Be Happy-voc MH
            On Brave Old Army Team
            Moonlight Serenade (Theme)

7 June, 1940 (FRI)

>   Glenn Miller and His Orchestra played at the
>   University of North Carolina, Chapel Hill, North
>   Carolina, from 4:30-6:30 P.M. and 9:00-1:00 A.M.
>   (G.M.D.)

8 June, 1940 (SAT)

>   Glenn Miller and His Orchestra played at the
>   Coliseum, Parkersburg, West Virginia, from 9:30-
>   1:30 A.M.   (G.M.D.)

9 June, 1940 (SUN)

>   Glenn Miller and His Orchestra played at Meyers
>   Lake Park, Canton, Ohio, from 8:30-12:30 A.M.
>   (G.M.D.)

10 June, 1940 (MON)

>   Glenn Miller and His Orchestra played at The Bells,
>   East Lansing, Michigan, from 9:00-1:00 A.M. (G.M.D.)

11 June, 1940 (TUES): Chicago Civic Theater, Chicago, Illinois
                    (CHESTERFIELD SHOW)
                    CBS   10:00-10:15 P.M. EST.

Glenn Miller and His Orchestra arrived in Chicago
this day for the first of 21 broadcasts to be made
for Chesterfield. (DB, July 1, 1940) Before
going into the Sherman Hotel's Panther Room July
5th the band was scheduled to tour around the
Chicago area after the Thursday night program.

The announcer for this program is Larry Bruff.

Moonlight Serenade (Theme)

V-4086 WR-953 GMMS 6/54, GMMS 44/92, Vi LPM-6100, RCA RD 27147,
              RCA G LPM 6100
              (2:30) T'Ain't No Use At All (arr BF)
                    (Hill-Johnson)
                    As, Caceres; tpt, Best

Fools Rush In-voc RE

V-4086 WR-931 GMMS 2/102
       Int GM (2:06) Boog-It (arr JG)-voc Marion Hutton and Band
                    (Cab Calloway-Jack Palmer-Buck Ram)
                    As, Caceres; tpt,??

Drink To Me Only With Thine Eyes

V-4086 WR-953 GMMS 6/54
   Int LB & GM (2:40) Runnin' Wild (arr BF)
                    (Joe Grey-Leo Wood-Harrington Gibbs)
                    Ts, Beneke; clt, Caceres; ts, Beneke;
                    d, Purtill

Moonlight Serenade (Theme)

12 June, 1940 (WED): Chicago Civic Theater, Chicago, Illinois
                    (CHESTERFIELD SHOW)
                    CBS   10:00-10:15 P.M. EST.

The announcer for this program is Larry Bruff.

Moonlight Serenade (Theme)

V-4086 WR-952 GMMS 5/53, AFRS P-2243
              (1:55) Outside Of That I Love You (arr JG)-voc
                    Marion Hutton and Tex Beneke

(Broadcast continued on next page)

From the musical comedy "Louisiana
Purchase"
(Irving Berlin)
Ts, Beneke; tpt, Best

Medley:
   Coquette
   Say It
   Does Your Heart Beat For Me?
   Blue Hawaii

V-4086 WR-956 GMMS 9/57, AFRS P-2237, GMMS 48/96
   Int GM & LB (3:10) St. Louis Blues (arr ED)
                     (William C. Handy)
                     Tpt, ??; ts, Beneke; tpt, ??

   Moonlight Serenade (Theme)

13 June, 1940 (THUR): Victor Studios, Chicago, Illinois

   Same personnel as for May 31st.

053130-1   BB 10776-A, HMV MH 99, Vi LPM 2080
           When The Swallows Come Back To Capistrano (arr BF)-
                     voc Ray Eberle
                     (Leon Rene)

053131-1   BB 10768-B, HMV BD 5929, HMV MH 145, VdP GW-1984,
                     El G EG 7788
           A Million Dreams Ago (arr BF)-voc Ray Eberle
                     (Lew Quadling-Eddy Howard-Dick Jurgens)
                     Ts, Beneke

053132-1   BB 10768-A, HMV BD 5632, HMV MH 92, HMVAu EA-2723,
                     Vi 447-0444, RD 3/4-25, El G EG 7567,
                     HMVSc X7524, RD Br. RDS 6098, RD Br. RDS 6171
           Blueberry Hill (arr BF)-voc Ray Eberle
                     (Al Lewis-Larry Stock-Vincent Rose)

053133-1   BB 10776-B, HMV MH 104, HMVAu EA-3351
           A Cabana In Havana (arr BF)-voc Marion Hutton
                     (Tot Seymour-Mabel Wayne)
                     Ts, Beneke

053134-1   BB 10796-B, VdP GW-1984
           Be Happy (arr BF)-voc Marion Hutton
                     (Nemo-Prima-Battle)
                     Ts, Beneke

(Session continued on next page)

053135-1   BB 10796-A, Vi LPT 6700, Vi EPNT 6700 (947-0127),
Vi SPD-18 (599-9109), HMV RLS 599, RCA G
LPT 6700
Angel Child (arr BF)-voc Ray Eberle
(George Price-Abner Silver-Benny Davis)

"A Million Dreams Ago", "Blueberry Hill" and
"Angel Child" 2 takes each; all other tunes 1 take.
(RCA Victor)
This session lasted from 1:00 P.M. to 5:25 P.M.
(RCA Victor)

13 June, 1940 (THUR): Chicago Civic Theater, Chicago, Illinois
(CHESTERFIELD SHOW)
CBS   10:00-10:15 P.M. EST.

The announcer for this program is Larry Bruff.

Moonlight Serenade (Theme)

K2PP-0043   Vi LPM-6100, RCA RD 27145, Vi It LPM-10141, Vi It
LPM 50020, RCA Vi It LJ 50020, RCA G LPM
9852, RCA G LPM 6100, RCA G LPM/LSP-9944
(3:06) Solitude
(Eddie DeLange-Irving Mills-Duke
Ellington)
Ts, Beneke; tpt, Best

The Rumba Jumps!
I'm Stepping Out With A Memory Tonight
Everybody Loves My Baby
Moonlight Serenade (Theme)

14 June, 1940 (FRI)

Glenn Miller and His Orchestra played at the
University of Michigan, Ann Arbor, Michigan, from
10:00-2:00 A.M. (G.M.D.)

15 June, 1940 (SAT)

Glenn Miller and His Orchestra played at the I.M.A.
Auditorium, Flint, Michigan, from 9:00-1:00 A.M.
(G.M.D.; Variety, May 1, 1940)

16 June, 1940 (SUN)

Glenn Miller and His Orchestra drew 3,000 on a
Columbus date at Valley Dale, Ohio, from 9:00-
1:00 A.M. (G.M.D.)

(Continued on next page)

"He played a good session all evening, giving
a good show and spotting Beneke, Caceres, Klink,
Johnny Best, and Purtill on solos often. Marion
Hutton knocked herself out for the mob, who really
went for her jive. Beneke and Caceres' alto gave
the best kicks." (Met. July 1940)

17 June, 1940 (MON)

Glenn Miller and His Orchestra played at the
Coliseum, Evansville, Indiana, from 9:00-1:00 A.M.
C.S.T. (G.M.D.)

18 June, 1940 (TUES)

Glenn Miller and His Orchestra played for 3 nights
(18th, 19th, 20th June) at Castle Farms,
Cincinnati.

18 June, 1940 (TUES): Cincinnati, Ohio (CHESTERFIELD SHOW)
CBS 10:00-10:15 P.M. CST.

The announcer for this program is Larry Bruff.

Moonlight Serenade (Theme)
The Nearness Of You-voc RE
Be Happy-voc MH
Dipper Mouth Blues
Moonlight Serenade (Theme)

If this program is like the other Tuesday night
programs then we are missing information on two
tunes.

19 June, 1940 (WED): Cincinnati, Ohio (CHESTERFIELD SHOW)
CBS 10:00-10:15 P.M. C.S.T.

Moonlight Serenade (Theme)
The Woodpecker Song
MEDLEY:
    The Touch Of Your Hand (arr JG)
        From the film "Roberta"
        (Otto Harbach-Jerome Kern)
    Basket Weaver Man
    The Waltz You Saved For Me (arr JG)
        (borrowed from Wayne King)
        (Gus Kahn-Wayne King-Emil Flindt)
    Blue Danube (arr JG)
        (Johann Strauss)
One O'Clock Jump
Moonlight Serenade (Theme)

20 June, 1940 (THUR): Cincinnati, Ohio (CHESTERFIELD SHOW)
CBS   10:00-10:15 P.M.   C.S.T.

NO DETAILS AVAILABLE.

21 June, 1940 (FRI)

Glenn Miller and His Orchestra played for one
week (closed Thursday, June 27th) at the Fox
Theater, Detroit, Michigan. (BB, June 22, 1940;
Variety, April 17, 1940: Variety, June 5, 1940)
        "Glenn Miller closes Detroit's Fox Theater
Thursday, June 27, 1940 with $33,000. gross."
(BB, July 6, 1940)

25 June, 1940 (TUES)

The Chesterfield Show was not on the air because
of the political convention.

26 June, 1940 (WED): Stage of Masonic Auditorium, Detroit,
Michigan (CHESTERFIELD SHOW)
CBS   10:00-10:15 P.M. EST.

Moonlight Serenade (Theme)

V-4086 WR-965 GMMS 17/65
        (1:57) Outside Of That I Love You (arr JG)-voc
                Marion Hutton and Tex Beneke
                From the musical comedy "Louisiana
                Purchase"
                (Irving Berlin)

        MEDLEY:
          My Darling
          Blueberry Hill
          I Can't Get Started
          Blue
        Bugle Call Rag
        Moonlight Serenade (Theme)

27 June, 1940 (THUR)

The Chesterfield Show was not on the air because
of the political convention.

28 June, 1940 (FRI)

> Glenn Miller and His Orchestra played at Ideal
> Beach Resort, Monticello, Indiana, from 9:00-
> 1:00 A.M. C.S.T. (G.M.D.)

29 June, 1940 (SAT)

> Glenn Miller and His Orchestra played at Playland
> Park, South Bend, Indiana, from 9:00-1:00 A.M.
> D.S.T. (G.M.D.)

30 June, 1940 (SUN)

> Glenn Miller and His Orchestra played at the Rink
> Ballroom, Waukegan, Illinois, from 9:00-1:00 A.M.
> Chicago Time. (G.M.D.)

July 1940

> "Herbie Miller, for the last six weeks
> business manager of Glenn Miller's band, left his
> brother's outfit in July to join Charlie Spivak's
> newly-formed crew as a trumpeter. Herbie, fresh
> out of Colorado, where he taught school, decided
> he would rather play than manage.
> Miller replaced young Herbie with Eke Kenyon,
> the drummer who for several years starred with Hal
> Kemp's outfit. Eke will be in charge of all Miller
> road matters in the future." (DB, Aug. 1, 1940)
> Kenyon was Glenn's second drummer with the band
> during its formative stages. (Met. Aug. 1940)
>
> We should mention here that the payroll records
> are missing from June 28, 1940 until September 21st
> and the only record we have of the personnel is a
> law firm's interpretation of the Miller personnel
> from October 27, 1939 to September 27, 1942 which
> was done for the Miller Estate in 1951. Unfortunate-
> ly they did not take into consideration the pro rata
> salary figures which indicated that a sideman was
> not with the band for an entire week.
>
> Ray Eberle's marriage to Janet Young of East
> Orange, N.J., was revealed while the Miller band was
> playing at the Chicago Civic Theater. (DB, Aug. 1,
> 1940)

(Continued on next page)

Alec Fila, young trumpeter with Bob Chester
planned to join Miller in Chicago but this did not
occur and it was a year later when he finally
joined the band. (DB, July 15, 1940)

1 July, 1940 (MON)

        Glenn Miller and His Orchestra played at the
        Coliseum Ballroom, Oelwein, Iowa, from 9:00-1:00
        A.M. C.S.T., and drew 1861. (G.M.D.; BB, July 20,
        1940)

2 July, 1940 (TUES): University of Nebraska Coliseum, Lincoln,
                    Nebraska (CHESTERFIELD SHOW)
                    CBS   10:00-10:15 P.M.

            Moonlight Serenade (Theme)

UPRM-6314   Vi LPM/LSP-3873, RCA G LSP-3873, RCA Br. RD/SF-7932
              (2:07) Chicken Reel (arr BF)-Chant by Band
                    (Joseph M. Daly)
                    Tpt, Best

            Sierra Sue-voc RE
            Sweet Potato Piper-voc MH & TB
            Goin' Home
            Anchors Aweigh
            Moonlight Serenade (Theme)

        "4,000 mob Miller at Nebraska U. for his weekly
broadcast. Less than an hour later, Glenn was set
up for the dance at the Turnpike (eight miles away)
where he broke all house records, proving that corn
isn't everything out in Nebraska." (Met. Aug. 1940)
The Turnpike mentioned in this article was the
Turnpike Casino owned by R.H. Parley. According to
the July 13th, 1940 issue of The Billboard a crowd
of 8,000 free guests were jammed into The Nebraska
Coliseum.

3 July, 1940 (WED): Omaha City Auditorium, Omaha, Nebraska
                    (CHESTERFIELD SHOW)
                    CBS   10:00-10:15 P.M.

            Moonlight Serenade (Theme)
            Boog-It

(Broadcast continued on next page)

MEDLEY:
  S'posin'
      (Andy Razaf-Paul Denniker)
  When The Swallows Come Back To Capistrano
  Thanks For The Memory (borrowed from Bob
      Hope)
      From the film "Big Broadcast of 1938"
      (Leo Robin-Ralph Rainger)
  Blues In My Heart
      (Irving Mills-Benny Carter)
  I Want To Be Happy
  Moonlight Serenade (Theme)

"At Omaha, Miller packed the city auditorium
for both the broadcast and dance. Glenn and his
trombone, as well as Tex Beneke, took all honors as
far as the crowd was concerned." (Met. Aug. 1940)
The Miller band drew 3,108. (BB, July 20, 1940)

4 July, 1940 (THUR): Shrine Auditorium, Des Moines, Iowa
              (CHESTERFIELD SHOW)
              CBS 10:00-10:15 P.M.

The announcer for this program is Larry Bruff.

Moonlight Serenade (Theme)

V-4086 WR-958   GMMS 10/58, AFRS P-2238
            (3:05) My Isle Of Golden Dreams (arr BF)
                  (Gus Kahn-Walter Blaufuss)
                  Ts, Beneke

Cowboy From Brooklyn

V-4086 WR-958   GMMS 10/58, AFRS P-2243
    Int GM   (1:41) Devil May Care-voc Ray Eberle
                  (Johnny Burke-Harry Warren)

V-4086 WR-958   GMMS 10/58, AFRS P-2238
    Int GM   (3:00) Everybody Loves My Baby (But My Baby
                  Don't Love Nobody But Me) (arr JG)
                  (Jack Palmer-Spencer Williams)
                  Tpt, Best?;ts, Beneke;d, Purtill;
                  ts, Klink

Moonlight Serenade (Theme)

Later that evening Glenn Miller and His Orchestra
played at Val-Air in Des Moines and drew 4,439.
(BB, July 20, 1940)

5 July, 1940 (FRI)

> Glenn Miller and His Orchestra opened at the
> "Panther Room" of the Hotel Sherman in Chicago
> for a two week engagement.
>
> "Considering the season and the drawback
> (yes) of the Democratic convention, the town's
> been pretty much on the jump the past couple
> of weeks; at least in point of transient jazz
> nobility. Most eye-popping single incident was
> probably the queue of Glenn Miller-mad
> youngsters who, two Friday nights ago, formed
> an impatient line from the Panther room door,
> upstairs through the Clark street entrance to
> the hotel and half way down the street to the
> alley toward Lake street. The joint was that
> packed." (DB Aug. 1, 1940).

8 July, 1940 (MON)

> Glenn Miller and His Orchestra played at Ramona
> Park, Grand Rapids, Michigan, from 9:30-1:30
> E.S.T. (no Hotel date) (G.M.D.)

9 July, 1940 (TUES): Chicago Civic Theater, Chicago Illinois
(CHESTERFIELD SHOW)
CBS   10:00-10:15 P.M.

> *Moonlight Serenade (Theme)*
> *T'Ain't No Use At All*
> *Imagination-voc RE*

V-4086 WR-960 GMMS 12/60, GMMS 46/94, AFRS P-2244, Vi LPT 6701,
            Vi EPOT 6701 (947-0189), HMV RLS 598,
            RCA G EPOT-6701
      Int GM (1:23) Be Happy (arr BF)-voc Marion Hutton
                (Nemo-Prima-Battle)
                No saxophone solo

> *Carry Me Back To Old Virginny*

V-4086 WR-960 GMMS 12/60, GMMS 47/95, AFRS P-2239
      Int GM (2:58) On Brave Old Army Team (arr JG)
                (West Point Football Song)
                (Philip Egner)
                D, Purtill; ts, Klink; tpt, Best;
                d, Purtill; clt. Caceres

(Broadcast continued on next page)

Moonlight Serenade (Theme)

On Vi LPT 6701 "Be Happy" was incorrectly listed
as being broadcast on March 22,1940. On the
GMMS releases of "Be Happy" Glenn announces the
vocalist after the music had begun, but the
beginning of the tune and announcement are cut
from the Victor releases.

*10 July, 1940 (WED): Chicago Civic Theater, Chicago, Illinois
(CHESTERFIELD SHOW)
CBS   10:00-10:15 P.M.*

The announcer for this program is Larry Bruff.

Moonlight Serenade (Theme)

V-4086 WR-956   GMMS 9/57, GMMS 40/88, AFRS P-2251
             (2:30) A Cabana In Havana (arr BF)-voc
                     Marion Hutton
                     (Tot Seymour-Mabel Wayne)
                     Ts, Beneke

V-4086 WR-953   GMMS 6/54, GMMS 16/64, GMMS 44/92, Vi LPM-6100,
             RCA RD 27147, RCA G LPM 6100, AFRS P-2247,
             RD 3/4-64
             (5:30) MEDLEY:
             Int GM Goodnight, Sweetheart (arr JG)
                     Introduced in: "Earl Carroll's
                     Vanities"
                     (Ray Noble-James Campbell-Reg.
                     Connelly)
                     Clt, ??
             Int GM I'm Stepping Out With A Memory Tonight
                     (arr JG)-voc Ray Eberle
                     (Herb Magidson-Allie Wrubel)
             Int LB When My Baby Smiles At Me (arr JG)
                     (borrowed from Ted Lewis)
                     (Andrew B. Sterling-Ted Lewis-
                     Bill Munro)
                     Ts, Beneke
             Int GM A Blues Serenade (arr JG)
                     (Mitchell Parish-Frank Signorelli)
                     P, MacGregor

V-4086 WR-936   GMMS 1/101, GMMS 43/91
    Int GM   (2:45) My Blue Heaven (arr BF)
                     (George Whiting-Walter Donaldson)
                     Tbn, Miller; ts, Beneke; d, Purtill

Moonlight Serenade (Theme)

11 July, 1940 (THUR): Chicago Civic Theater, Chicago, Illinois
(CHESTERFIELD SHOW)
CBS   10:00-10:15 P.M.

Moonlight Serenade (Theme)

V-4086 WR-956   GMMS 9/57, GMMS 26/74, GMMS 47/95, Vi LPT-30,
                Vi 42-0153 (Vi PT-39), Vi 27-0153 (Vi WPT-
                39), Vi EPBT-3026 (947-0027), Vi LPT 6701,
                HMV RLS 598, Vi EPOT-6701 (947-0180),
                Vi EPA-726, HMV DLP-1012, Vi LPM-1189,
                Vi EPB-1189 (547-0800), El WDLP 1012, HMVSw
                JK-2804, RCA F 430228, RCA G EPBT-3026,
                RCA G EPC-1189, RCA G EPOT-6701
        (2:34) On The Alamo (arr JG)
                    (Gus Kahn-Isham Jones)
                Tpt, Best

The Gentleman Needs A Shave

V-4086 WR-956   GMMS 9/57, GMMS 11/59, AFRS P-2244, Vi LPT 6701,
                Vi EPOT 6701 (947-0178), HMV RLS 598,
                RCA G EPOT-6701
   Int GM (2:20) I'll Never Smile Again (arr JG)-voc
                Ray Eberle
                (Ruth Lowe)

Pagan Love Song
Moonlight Serenade (Theme)

        On Vi LPT 6701 "I'll Never Smile Again" was in-
        correctly listed as being broadcast on March 19,
        1940. On the GMMS releases of "I'll Never Smile
        Again" Glenn announces the vocalist but this
        announcement has been omitted from the Victor
        releases.

15 July, 1940 (MON)

        Glenn Miller and His Orchestra played at Bay
        Beach, Green Bay, Wisconsin, from 9:00-1:00 A.M.
        C.S.T. (G.M.D.)

16 July, 1940 (TUES): Chicago Civic Theater, Chicago, Illinois
(CHESTERFIELD SHOW)
CBS   10:00-10:15 P.M.

        The announcer for this program is Larry Bruff.

            Moonlight Serenade (Theme)

(Broadcast continued on next page)

V-4086 WR-954 <u>GMMS 7/55</u>, AFRS P-2237
          <u>(2:17)</u> <u>Rug Cutter's Swing</u> (arr BF)
               (Horace Henderson)
               Ts, Beneke; tbn, Miller; tpt, Best

V-4086 WR-954 <u>GMMS 7/55</u>, GMMS 39/87
  Int GM <u>(1:58)</u> <u>Polka Dots And Moonbeams</u> (arr JG)-voc
               Ray Eberle
               (Johnny Burke-Jimmy Van Heusen)
               As, McIntyre

V-4086 WR-954 <u>GMMS 7/55</u>, GMMS 39/87
  Int GM <u>(2:03)</u> <u>FDR Jones</u>-voc Marion Hutton and Band
               (Harold J. Rome)

V-4086 WR-954 <u>GMMS 7/55</u>, AFRS P-2237
  Int LB <u>(1:48)</u> <u>Drink To Me Only With Thine Eyes</u>
               (Ben Jonson)

V-4086 WR-954 <u>GMMS 7/55</u>, AFRS P-2237
  Int GM <u>(2:31)</u> <u>Runnin' Wild</u> (arr BF)
               (Joe Grey-Leo Wood-Harrington Gibbs)
               Ts, Beneke; clt, Caceres; ts, Beneke;
               d, Purtill

               Moonlight Serenade (Theme)

17 July, 1940 (WED): Chicago Civic Theater, Chicago, Illinois
                (CHESTERFIELD SHOW)
                CBS 10:00-10:15 P.M.

     The announcer for this program is Larry Bruff.

               Moonlight Serenade (Theme)
               I Haven't Time To Be A Millionaire

UPRM-6314   Vi LPM/<s>LSP-3873</s>, RCA G LSP-3873, RCA Br. RD/SF-
                  7932
          (6:33) MEDLEY:
               <u>Poor Butterfly</u> (arr JG)
               From the stage production "The Big
               Show"
               (John L. Golden-Raymond Hubbell)
               Ts, Beneke
          Int GM <u>The Sky Fell Down</u> (arr BF)-voc Ray Eberle
               (Edward Heyman-Louis Alter)
          Int LB <u>I'm Gettin' Sentimental Over You</u> (arr JG)
               (borrowed from Tommy Dorsey)
               (Ned Washington-George Bassman)
               Ts, Beneke

(Broadcast continued on next page)

```
Int LB   Black And Blue (arr JG)
              (Harry Brooks-Andy Razaf-Thomas
              "Fats" Waller)
         Tpt, Best
```

Farewell Blues
Moonlight Serenade (Theme)

18 July, 1940 (THUR)

The Chesterfield Show was not on the air because
of the political convention.

Glenn Miller and His Orchestra closed at the
"Panther Room" of the Hotel Sherman in Chicago,
Illinois.

"Glenn Miller's recent 2-weeker at the
Sherman Hotel's Panther Room (the old College Inn)
was the biggest in the hotel's history, including
the old days when Ben Bernie and Buddy Rogers
used to jam 'em in.
Patrons stood in line nightly, after 8 p.m.,
trying to get in. Even those with reservations
had difficulty getting through crowds around the
entrances. Head waiters said they had 'never seen
the like' as they madly scrambled around trying to
make room. At least 100 extra tables were
utilized." (DB Aug. 1, 1940).

19 July, 1940 (FRI)

Glenn Miller and His Orchestra played for one week
(closed Thursday, July 25th) at the Chicago
Theater, Chicago, Illinois. (Chicago Times, July
19 & 25, 1940)

23 July, 1940 (TUES): Chicago Civic Theater, Chicago, Illinois
(CHESTERFIELD SHOW)
CBS   10:00-10:15 P.M.

The announcer for this program is Larry Bruff.

Moonlight Serenade (Theme)

```
V-4086 WR-961   GMMS 13/61, GMMS 48/96
       Int GM   (2:04) Jeannie With The Light Brown Hair (arr JG)
                       (Stephen Foster)
```

(Broadcast continued on next page)

V-4086 WR-961 GMMS 13/61, Vi LPM/LSP-3873, RCA G LSP-3873,
                    RCA Br. RD/SF-7932
       Int GM (2:20) Outside Of That I Love You (arr JG)-
                     voc Marion Hutton and Tex Beneke
                     From the musical comedy "Louisiana
                     Purchase"
                     (Irving Berlin)

V-4086 WR-961 GMMS 13/61, GMMS 47/95, AFRS P-2244
       Int GM (3:13) A Handful Of Stars (arr BF)-voc Ray Eberle
                     From the MGM film "Hullabaloo"
                     (Jack Lawrence-Ted Shapiro)
                     Tpt, Best; ts, Beneke

V-4086 WR-961 GMMS 13/61, GMMS 27/75, AFRS P-2239
    Int LB & GM (3:16) King Porter Stomp
                       (Ferdinand "Jelly-Roll" Morton)
                       Tbn, Miller; ts, Beneke; tpt, Best;
                       ts, Klink

                 Moonlight Serenade (Theme)

          The Tuesday night programs (including this one)
          had their format changed to four tunes.

*24 July, 1940 (WED): Chicago Civic Theater, Chicago, Illinois
                    (CHESTERFIELD SHOW)
                    CBS 10:00-10:15 P.M.*

      The announcer for this program is Larry Bruff.

                 Moonlight Serenade (Theme)

V-4086 WR-955 GMMS 8/56, AFRS P-2243
            (3:18) Wham (Re-Bop-Boom-Bam) (arr ED)-voc
                   Marion Hutton and Band
                   (Eddie Durham-"Taps" Miller)
                   Ts, Beneke; tbn, Miller; ts, Beneke;
                   tpt, Best

V-4086 WR-955 GMMS 8/56, GMMS 48/96, AFRS P-2246
            (4:50) MEDLEY:
            Int GM Peg O' My Heart (arr JG)
                        (Alfred Bryan-Fred Fisher)
            Int GM Polka Dots And Moonbeams (arr JG)-voc
                        Ray Eberle
                        (Johnny Burke-Jimmy Van Heusen)
            Int LB Mood Indigo (arr JG) (borrowed from
                        Duke Ellington)
                        (Duke Ellington-Irving Mills-
                        Albany "Barney" Bigard)
                        Ts, Beneke

(Broadcast continued on next page)

```
Int LB    Blue Orchids (arr JG)
                (Hoagy Carmichael)
              Ts, Beneke
```

V-4086 WR-955 GMMS 8/56, Vi LPT 6700, Vi EPNT 6700 (947-0120),
                  AFRS P-2237, Vi SPD-18 (599-9103), HMV RLS
                  599, RCA G LPT 6700
   Int LB & GM (3:01) Down For The Count (arr BF)
                  (Bill Finegan)
                Tpt, Best; ts, Klink; tpt, Best;
                ts, Beneke

            Moonlight Serenade (Theme)

        The introduction to "Down For The Count" is cut
        from the Victor releases.

25 July, 1940 (THUR)

        The Chesterfield Show was not on the air because
        of the political convention.

26 July, 1940 (FRI)

        Glenn Miller and His Orchestra played at the St.
        Louis Municipal Auditorium and drew 5,000 people.
        It was Miller's first appearance in St. Louis,
        Missouri, with his own band. He was booked by
        the Casa-Loma ballroom management and played from
        9:00-1:00 A.M. (G.M.D.; Met. Sept. 1940; St.
        Louis Dispatch, July 26, 1940; Variety, July 24,
        1940; Variety, July 31, 1940)

27 July, 1940 (SAT)

        Glenn Miller and His Orchestra played at the
        Municipal Auditorium, Kansas City, Missouri, from
        9:30-1:30 A.M. C.S.T. Miller drew 11,300 dancers
        and broke the city record. The promoter was
        Barney Joffee. (G.M.D.; Variety, July 24, 1940;
        DB, Aug. 15, 1940)

28 July, 1940 (SUN)

        Glenn Miller and His Orchestra played at the Shore
        Acres Ballroom, Sioux City, Iowa, from 9:00-1:00
        A.M. C.S.T., and drew 3,200 people. (G.M.D.;
        BB, Aug. 10, 1940; Variety, July 24, 1940)

29 July, 1940 (MON)

        Glenn Miller and His Orchestra played at the Surf
        Ballroom, Clear Lake, Iowa, from 9:00-1:00 A.M.,
        and drew 3,000 people. (G.M.D.; BB, Aug. 10, 1940;
        Variety, July 24, 1940)

30 July, 1940 (TUES): Chicago Civic Theater, Chicago, Illinois
                (CHESTERFIELD SHOW)
                CBS 10:00-10:15 P.M.

       The announcer for this program is Larry Bruff.

          Moonlight Serenade (Theme)
          Goin' Home

V-4086 WR-952 GMMS 5/53, GMMS 14/62, AFRS P-2243
   Int GM (3:05) The Gentleman Needs A Shave (arr JG)-
                    voc Marion Hutton and Tex Beneke
                    (Kim Gannon-Guy Wood)
                    D, Purtill; ts, Beneke

V-4086 WR-952 GMMS 5/53, GMMS 43/91
   Int GM (2:36) When The Swallows Come Back To Capistrano
                    (arr BF)-voc Ray Eberle
                    (Leon Rene)

V-4086 WR-952 GMMS 5/53
  Int LB & GM (3:05) Everybody Loves My Baby (But My Baby
                    Don't Love Nobody But Me) (arr JG)
                    (Jack Palmer-Spencer Williams)
                    Tpt, Best?; ts, Beneke; d, Purtill;
                    ts, Klink

          Moonlight Serenade (Theme)

31 July, 1940 (WED): Chicago Civic Theater, Chicago, Illinois
                (CHESTERFIELD SHOW)
                  CBS 10:00-10:15 P.M.

       The announcer for this program is Larry Bruff.

          Moonlight Serenade (Theme)

V-4086 WR-936 GMMS 1/101, GMMS 41/89, Vi LPT 6700, Vi EPNT
             6700 (947-0125), Vi SPD-18 (599-9107),
             HMV RLS 599, RCA G LPT 6700

(Broadcast continued on next page)

(2:35) I Guess I'll Have To Change My Plan
           (arr BF)-voc Marion Hutton and
           Tex Beneke
           From the review "First Little Show"
           (Howard Dietz-Arthur Schwartz)
           Ts, Beneke

V-4086 WR-936   GMMS 1/101, GMMS 31/79, GMMS 41/89, Vi LPT 6700,
              HMV RLS 599, Vi EPNT 6700 (947-0126),
              Vi SPD-18 (599-9109), AFRS P-2247, RCA G
              LPT 6700
           (5:37) MEDLEY:
           Int GM My Darling
                  (Williams-Kelly-Kahn)
                  Ts, Beneke; muted tbn, Miller
           Int GM Blueberry Hill (arr BF)-voc Ray Eberle
                  (Al Lewis-Larry Stock-Vincent Rose)
           Int GM I Can't Get Started (borrowed from
                  Bunny Berigan)
                  (Ira Gershwin-Vernon Duke)
                  Tpt, Best
V-4086 WR-936   GMMS 1/101, GMMS 31/79, GMMS 41/89, AFRS P-2247
           Int LB Blue (And Brokenhearted)
                  (Grant Clarke-Edgar Leslie-Lou Handman)
                  Ts, Beneke

           By The Waters Of Minnetonka
           Moonlight Serenade (Theme)

           The Victor releases of the medley omitted the
           Miller introduction to "My Darling" and the
           last tune "Blue" was omitted in its entirety.

1 August, 1940 (THUR): Chicago Civic Theater, Chicago, Illinois
                  (CHESTERFIELD SHOW)
                  CBS 10:00-10:15 P.M.

           The announcer for this program is Larry Bruff.

           Moonlight Serenade (Theme)

V-4086 WR-931   GMMS 2/102
           (2:38) Sophisticated Lady
                  (Mitchell Parish-Irving Mills-
                  Duke Ellington)
                  Tpt, Best

           A Cabana In Havana

(Broadcast continued on next page)

V-4086 WR-931   GMMS 2/102, GMMS 42/90
    Int GM (2:54) <u>April Played The Fiddle</u> (arr BF)-voc
                   Ray Eberle
                   From the Universal film "If I Had
                   My Way"
                   (Johnny Burke-James V. Monaco)
                   Ts, Beneke

V-4086 WR-931   GMMS 2/102, AFRS P-2246
    Int GM (2:05) <u>Tiger Rag</u> (arr ED)
                   (Tony Sbarbaro-Eddie Edwards-Henry
                   Ragas-Larry Shields-Nick LaRocca-
                   Harry DeCosta)
                   D, Purtill

                   Moonlight Serenade *(Theme)*

2 August, 1940 (FRI)

        Glenn Miller and His Orchestra played at Indian
        Lake (Sandy Beach), Russells Point, Ohio, from
        9:00-1:00 A.M. (G.M.D.; BB, July 20, 1940)

3 August, 1940 (SAT)

        Glenn Miller and His Orchestra played at Iroquois
        Gardens, Louisville, Kentucky, from 10:00-2:00 A.M.
        (G.M.D.; BB, July 20, 1940)

4 August, 1940 (SUN)

        Glenn Miller and His Orchestra played at the
        Crystal Ballroom, Buckeye Lake, Ohio, from 9:00-
        1:00 A.M. E.S.T. (G.M.D.; BB, July 20, 1940)
            "Miller shatters record at Buckeye Lake
        Danceteria on his third date in this territory.
        The crowd, which bettered Glenn's 3,500 mark set
        at Valley Dale last June, was so immense that
        they were moved over to the skating rink in order
        to permit ticket-holders in. The date also set
        an all-time mark for the entire park." (Met.
        Sept. 1940)

5 August, 1940 (MON)

        Glenn Miller and His Orchestra played at the
        Sunset Ballroom, Carrolltown, Pennsylvania, from
        9:00-1:00 A.M. E.S.T. (G.M.D.; BB, July 20,
        1940; The Altoona Mirror, Aug. 3, 1940)

Summer 1940

> Miller band booked for New York World Fair--
> Dancing Campus (Michael Todd enterprise in the
> Great White Way). Admission 25¢. (Met. June
> 1940) We have no further details on whether
> the Miller band actually performed.

6 August, 1940 (TUES): New York City, New York (CHESTERFIELD SHOW)
CBS   10:00-10:15 P.M.

> *The announcer for this program is Paul Douglas.*

> *Moonlight Serenade (Theme)*

V-4086 WR-1006   GMMS 29/77, AFRS P-2245
    Int GM   (2:17) I'll Take You Home Again, Kathleen
                   (Thomas P. Westendorf)

V-4086 WR-1006   GMMS 29/77, AFRS P-2251
    Int GM   (2:14) I Haven't Time To Be A Millionaire
                   (arr JG)-voc Tex Beneke and
                   Marion Hutton
                   From the Universal film "If I Had
                   My Way"
                   (Johnny Burke-James V. Monaco)
                   Ts, Beneke

V-4086 WR-1006   GMMS 29/77
    Int GM   (2:38) I'll Never Smile Again (arr JG)-voc
                   Ray Eberle
                   (Ruth Lowe)

V-4086 WR-1006   GMMS 29/77
  Int GM & LB   (3:05) Down For The Count (arr BF)
                   (Bill Finegan)
                   Tpt, Best; ts, Klink; tpt, Best;
                   ts, Beneke

> *Moonlight Serenade (Theme)*

7 August, 1940 (WED): New York City, New York (CHESTERFIELD SHOW)
CBS   10:00-10:15 P.M.

> *Moonlight Serenade (Theme)*
> *I Never Took A Lesson In My Life*

(Broadcast continued on next page)

MEDLEY:
The Siren's Song
A Handful Of Stars
Love In Bloom
The Birth Of The Blues
Bugle Call Rag
Moonlight Serenade (Theme)

8 August, 1940 (THUR): Victor Studios, New York City, New York

Same personnel as for May 31st.

055501-1   BB 10845-A
            The Call Of The Canyon (arr BF)-voc Ray Eberle
               (Billy Hill)
            Ts, Beneke

055502-1   BB 10845-B, HMVSp GY 584, HMV 7EG 8241, Vi
               LPM/LSP-3657, RCA RD/SF-7842, RCA G LPM/LSP-
               3657, RD 3/4-64, RCA F 440.727
            Our Love Affair-voc Ray Eberle
               From the MGM film "Strike Up The Band"
               (Arthur Freed-Roger Edens)

055503-1   BB 10832-A, HMVAu EA-2872
            Crosstown-voc Jack Lathrop
               (James Cavanaugh-John Redmond-Nat Simon)
               Ts, Beneke

055504-1   BB 10832-B, HMVAu EA-2685, Vi LPM/LSP-3657, RCA
               RD/SF-7842, RCA G LPM/LSP-3657, RCA F 440.727
            What's Your Story, Morning Glory-voc Tex Beneke
               (Mary Lou Williams-Jack Lawrence-Paul Webster)
               Ts, Beneke; tpt, Best

            "Our Love Affair" 2 takes; all other tunes 1 take.
            (RCA Victor)
            This session lasted from 11:15 A.M. to 3:15 P.M.
            (RCA Victor)

8 August, 1940 (THUR): New York City, New York (CHESTERFIELD SHOW)
*   CBS   10:00-10:15 P.M.*

The announcer for this program is Paul Douglas.

            Moonlight Serenade (Theme)
            Mister Meadowlark
            Outside Of That I Love You
            A Million Dreams Ago

(Broadcast continued on next page)

V-4086 WR-1008 <u>GMMS 31/79</u>, GMMS 45/93
    Int GM   (3:35) <u>Tuxedo Junction</u> (arr JG)
       & PD   (William Johnson-Julian Dash-
                                Erskine Hawkins-Buddy Feyne)
                                Muted tpt, McMickle; open tpt, Best;
                                muted tpt, McMickle; p, MacGregor

                    <u>Moonlight Serenade</u> (Theme)

9 August, 1940 (FRI)

                  Glenn Miller and His Orchestra played at the
                  K. of C. Auditorium, Rochester, New York, from
                  10:00-2:00 A.M. D.S.T. (G.M.D.; BB, July 20, 1940)
                  The promoter for this dance was Max Kearson of
                  Scranton, Pa. 4,000 attended (Met. Oct. 1940)
                  but another magazine stated that 5,200 attended
                  (DB, Oct. 1, 1940)

10 August, 1940 (SAT)

                  Glenn Miller and His Orchestra played at the Pier
                  Ballroom in Celeron Park, Celeron, New York, from
                  10:00-2:00 A.M. E.S.T., and drew 3,800 people.
                  (G.M.D.; BB, July 6, 1940; BB, Aug. 24, 1940)

11 August, 1940 (SUN)

                  Glenn Miller and His Orchestra played at the Pier
                  Ballroom, Geneva On The Lake, Ohio, from 9:00-
                  1:00 A.M. (G.M.D.; BB, July 20, 1940)

12 August, 1940 (MON)

                  Glenn Miller and His Orchestra played at Lakewood
                  Park, Mahoney City, Pennsylvania, from 8:30-
                  12:30 A.M. E.S.T., and drew 5,000 people. (G.M.D.;
                  BB, Aug. 24, 1940; Pottsville Pa. Evening Re-
                  publican, Aug. 10, 1940)

13 August, 1940 (TUES): New York City, New York (CHESTERFIELD SHOW)
                      CBS   10:00-10:15 P.M.

                      <u>Moonlight Serenade</u> (Theme)
                      <u>Old Black Joe</u>
                      <u>Boog-It</u>
                      <u>Sierra Sue</u>
                      <u>Pennsylvania Six-Five Thousand</u>
                      <u>Moonlight Serenade</u> (Theme)

14 August, 1940 (WED): New York City, New York (CHESTERFIELD SHOW)
CBS   10:00-10:15 P.M.

Moonlight Serenade *(Theme)*

V-4086 WR-1007 GMMS 30/78, GMMS 49/97, AFRS P-2242
       (3:04) Solitude
                    (Eddie DeLange-Irving Mills-
                    Duke Ellington)
                    Ts, Beneke; tpt, Best

V-4086 WR-1007 GMMS 30/78
       Int GM   (1:24) Be Happy (arr BF)-voc Marion Hutton
                    (Nemo-Prima-Battle)

V-4086 WR-1007 GMMS 30/78, AFRS P-2252
       Int GM   (2:34) I'm Stepping Out With A Memory Tonight-
                    voc Ray Eberle
                    (Herb Magidson-Allie Wrubel)
                    No saxophone solo

V-4086 WR-1007 GMMS 30/78
       Int GM   (3:36) My Blue Heaven (arr BF)
                    (George Whiting-Walter Donaldson)
                    Tbn, Miller; ts, Beneke; ts, Klink;
                    d, Purtill

Moonlight Serenade *(Theme)*

          Once again Miller has departed from his usual
          Wednesday night format of playing a medley and
          this medley turns up on the Thursday night show.
          From now on until the end of December, 1940, the
          medley nights are heard on different nights each
          week.

14 August, 1940 (WED): Victor Studios, New York City, New York

          Same personnel as for May 31st.

055515-1   BB 10860-B, HMVAu EA-2634
               Fifth Avenue (arr JG)-voc Marion Hutton (and
                    Tex Beneke)
                    From the 20th Century-Fox film
                    "Young People"
                    (Mack Gordon-Harry Warren)
                    Ts, Beneke

(Session continued on next page)

055516-1   BB 10860-A
            I Wouldn't Take A Million-voc Ray Eberle
                From the 20th Century-Fox film "Young People"
                (Mack Gordon-Harry Warren)

055517-1   BB 10893-A, HMV MH 181, HMVSw JK-2134, Vi 20-3563
                (Vi P-255), AFRS P-1445, RD 3/4-64
            A Handful Of Stars (arr BF)-voc Ray Eberle
                From the MGM film "Hullabaloo"
                (Jack Lawrence-Ted Shapiro)
                Ts, Beneke

055518-1   BB 10913-B, HMV 7EG 8077, ViJ 1101, Cam Cal/Cas-
                2128, RCA G Cas-2128
            Old Black Joe (arr GM & ChM)
                (Stephen Foster)
                P, MacGregor

            "A Handful Of Stars" 2 takes; all other tunes
            1 take. (RCA Victor)
            This session lasted from 11:00 P.M. to 2:00
            A.M. and 3:00 A.M. to 5:00 A.M. (RCA Victor)

15 August, 1940 (THUR): New York City, New York (CHESTERFIELD SHOW)
*   CBS 10:00-10:15 P.M.*

                Moonlight Serenade (Theme)
                Crosstown
                MEDLEY:
                    Moon Over Miami
                    A Million Dreams Ago
                    Aloha
                    The Honolulu Blues
                Wham
                Moonlight Serenade (Theme)

16 August, 1940 (FRI)

            Glenn Miller and His Orchestra played at
            Narragansett Pier Casino, Narragansett, Rhode
            Island, from 9:00-1:00 A.M. (G.M.D.)

17 August, 1940 (SAT)

            Glenn Miller and His Orchestra played for two
            days (17th and 18th) at the Steel Pier, Atlantic
            City, New Jersey. (BB, June 22, 1940; The
            Philadelphia Inquirer, Aug. 18, 1940)

19 August, 1940 (MON)

        Glenn Miller and His Orchestra played at Fern-
brook Pavilion a few miles out of town, Wilkes
Barre, Pennsylvania, from 9:00-1:00 A.M. (G.M.D.;
Wilkes Barre Record, Aug. 15, 1940)
       "With a 4,000 draw at a buck a head for the
Buddy Club (Karl Strohl and Max Kearson), Glenn
Miller last month cracked a record at the Fernbrook
Pavillion..." (DB, Oct. 1, 1940)
       "Glenn Miller sets record for attendance
formerly held by Guy Lombardo at Fernbrook park by
playing to 3,200 persons." (Met. Oct. 1940)

20 August, 1940 (TUES): New York City, New York (CHESTERFIELD SHOW)
               CBS   10:00-10:15 P.M.

         Moonlight Serenade (Theme)
         A Cabana In Havana
         MEDLEY:
           Say It Isn't So (arr JG)
             (Irving Berlin)
           The Call Of The Canyon (arr BF)
           Bye Low (arr JG) (borrowed from Freddy
              Martin)
           (
           Blue And Sentimental (arr JG)
             (Mack David-Jerry Livingston-
             Count Basie)
         Anchors Aweigh
         Moonlight Serenade (Theme)

21 August, 1940 (WED): New York City, New York (CHESTERFIELD SHOW)
               CBS   10:00-10:15 P.M.

    The announcer for this program is Paul Douglas.

         Moonlight Serenade (Theme)
          In The Gloaming
          The Gentleman Needs A Shave

V-4086 WR-1011 GMMS 34/82, AFRS P-2250
      Int PD (3:17) The Nearness Of You (arr BF)-voc Ray Eberle
                     (Ned Washington-Hoagy Carmichael)
                     Ts, Beneke

V-4086 WR-1011 GMMS 34/82
      Int GM (2:52) Runnin' Wild (arr BF)
                     (Joe Grey-Leo Wood-Harrington Gibbs)
                     Ts, Beneke; clt, Caceres; ts, Beneke;
                     d, Purtill

         Moonlight Serenade (Theme)

22 August, 1940 (THUR): New York City, New York (CHESTERFIELD SHOW)
                    CBS   10:00-10:15 P.M.

                    Moonlight Serenade (Theme)

V-4086 WR-1009 GMMS 32/80, AFRS P-2249
    Int GM (2:48) What's Your Story, Morning Glory-voc
                    Tex Beneke
                    (Mary Lou Williams-Jack Lawrence-
                    Paul Webster)
                    Ts, Beneke; tpt, Best

V-4086 WR-1009 GMMS 32/80, AFRS P-2249
    Int GM (2:07) Wanna Hat With Cherries-voc Marion Hutton
                    (Larry Clinton-Jo Carringer-Betty Lynn)

V-4086 WR-1009 GMMS 32/80, AFRS P-2249
    Int GM (2:54) Fools Rush In (Where Angels Fear To Tread)-
                    voc Ray Eberle
                    (Johnny Mercer-Rube Bloom)

V-4086 WR-1009 GMMS 32/80, AFRS P-2246
    Int GM (2:32) Solid As A Stonewall, Jackson (arr JG)
                    (Jerry Gray-John Chalmers MacGregor)
                    As, Caceres; ts, Beneke

                    Moonlight Serenade (Theme)

23 August, 1940 (FRI)

            The band was on vacation from August 23rd to
            (and including) August 26th. (G.M.D.)

27 August, 1940 (TUES): New York City, New York (CHESTERFIELD SHOW)
                    CBS   10:00-10:15 P.M.

                    Moonlight Serenade (Theme)

V-4086 WR-980 GMMS 20/68, AFRS P-2245
    Int GM (1:56) Jeannie With The Light Brown Hair (arr JG)
                    (Stephen Foster)

V-4086 WR-980 GMMS 20/68, AFRS P-2244
    Int GM (2:32) I Never Took A Lesson In My Life (arr JG)-
                    voc Marion Hutton and Tex Beneke
                    (Lawrence-Foore)
                    D, Purtill; ts, Beneke

(Broadcast continued on next page)

V-4086 WR-980 <u>GMMS 20/68</u>, AFRS P-2244
    Int GM (3:12) <u>When The Swallows Come Back To Capistrano</u>
                (arr BF)-voc Ray Eberle
                (Leon Rene)

V-4086 WR-980 <u>GMMS 20/68</u>, AFRS P-2245
        (3:01) <u>I Want To Be Happy</u> (arr ED)
                From the musical production "No, No,
                Nanette"
                (Irving Caesar-Vincent Youmans)
                Tpt, Best; ts, Beneke; tbn, Miller;
                d, Purtill

        (0:27) <u>Moonlight Serenade</u> (Theme)
                <u>(Mitchell Parish-Glenn Miller)</u>

28 August, 1940 (WED): New York City, New York (CHESTERFIELD SHOW)
             CBS 10:00-10:15 P.M.

     The announcer for this program is Paul Douglas

        <u>Moonlight Serenade</u> (Theme)

V-4086 WR-1010 <u>GMMS 33/81</u>, AFRS P-2242
        (3:05) <u>Little Brown Jug</u> (arr BF)-Chant by Band
                (Traditional)
                Ts, Beneke; tpt, Frankhauser?;
                tbn, Miller

V-4086 WR-1010 <u>GMMS 33/81</u>, AFRS P-2249
    Int GM (2:44) <u>I Wouldn't Take A Million</u>-voc Ray Eberle
                From the 20th Century-Fox film
                "Young People"
                (Mack Gordon-Harry Warren)

V-4086 WR-1010 <u>GMMS 33/81</u>, Vi LPM-6100, RCA RD 27145, RCA G LPM
                6100, RCA G LPM-9852, AFRS P-2249
    Int GM (2:07) A-Tisket A-Tasket-voc Marion Hutton
                and Tex Beneke
                (Ella Fitzgerald-Al Feldman)
                Ts, Beneke; d, Purtill

V-4086 WR-1010 <u>GMMS 33/81</u>, Vi LPT 6700, Vi EPNT 6700 (947-0116),
                Vi PRM-181, Vi SPD-18 (599-9112), HMV RLS 599,
                RCA RD 27068, Vi LPM/LSP-1192, Vi 45 Special-
                1953, AFRS P-2242, Vi It LPM 10011, RCA Vi It
                LJ 50012, RCA F 530243, RCA G LPT 6700, RCA G
                EPC-1192, RCA G LPM/LSP-1192, Vi Arg LPM/LSP-
                1192, RCA F 740.515
    Int GM (3:02) Farewell Blues
                (Elmer Schoebel-Paul Mares-Joseph Leon
                Rappolo)
                Ts, Beneke; tpt, Frankhauser?
(Broadcast continued on next page)

Moonlight Serenade (Theme)

On Vi LPM-6100 the beginning of "A-Tisket A-Tasket"
is cut before the introduction by Glenn Miller. On
Vi LPT 6700 the introduction by Glenn Miller to
"Farewell Blues" is cut.

29 August, 1940 (THUR): New York City, New York (CHESTERFIELD SHOW)
CBS   10:00-10:15 P.M.

The announcer for this program is Paul Douglas.

Moonlight Serenade (Theme)

V-4086 WR-1011 GMMS 34/82, AFRS P-2250
(1:49) Fifth Avenue (arr JG)-voc Marion Hutton
and Tex Beneke
From the 20th Century-Fox film
"Young People"
(Mack Gordon-Harry Warren)
Ts, Beneke

MEDLEY:
Sweet And Lovely
Sierra Sue
The Very Thought Of You
Blue Hawaii

V-4086 WR-1011 GMMS 34/82
Int GM (2:54) In The Mood
(Andy Razaf-Joe Garland)
Ts, Beneke; ts, Al Klink; tpt,
Frankhauser?
(There are two endings to this version)

Moonlight Serenade (Theme)

GMMS on "In The Mood" have taken the introduction
for this tune from the May 2, 1940 introduction
to "In The Mood". Due to this fact it had been
believed that Larry Bruff was the announcer on
this program until verified at RCA Victor.

This was Rowland Bundock's (bassist) last day with
the band.
"Bundoc quits Miller; plans to study more bass
and arranging in a move to insure a brighter future
in music. One of the veterans of the band, the
soft-spoken, bespectacled bassist, left the group
without any semblance of hard feelings. His place

(Continued on next page)

will be taken by Tony Carlson, younger brother of
Woody Herman's drummer. The new bassist has not
played with any name bands, but is considered a
real find by those who have heard him. (Met.
Sept. 1940)

"Bundock quit on his own accord to study
legit music, with an eye toward symphony work."
(DB, Sept. 15, 1940)

"Bundock gave up $250-$400 weekly to study
symphony work!" (Met. Nov. 1940)

30 August, 1940 (FRI)

Trombones	Glenn Miller, Jimmy Priddy, Paul Tanner, Frank D'Annolfo
Trumpets	Charles Frankhauser, Zeke Zarchy, Dale McMickle, Johnny Best
Reeds	Hal McIntyre, as; Ernie Caceres, as, bar & clt; Wilbur Schwartz, clt & as; Tex Beneke, ts; Al Klink, ts
Rhythm	Chummy MacGregor, p; Jack Lathrop, g; TONY CARLSON, b; Maurice Purtill, d
Vocalists	Marion Hutton, Ray Eberle, Jack Lathrop
Band-Boy	Raul Hidalgo

Glenn Miller and His Orchestra played at Convention
Hall, Asbury Park, New Jersey, from 9:00-1:00 A.M.
(G.M.D.)

31 August, 1940 (SAT)

Glenn Miller and His Orchestra played for three
days (31st August, Sept. 1st and Sept. 2nd) at
the Steel Pier, Atlantic City, New Jersey. (The
Philadelphia Inquirer, Aug. 31, Sept. 1, Sept. 2,
1940)

3 September, 1940 (TUES): Victor Studios, New York City, New York

Same personnel as for August 30th.

055579-1   BB 10893-B, HMVSw JK-2134
              Yesterthoughts (arr BF)-voc Ray Eberle
                 (Stanley Adams-Victor Herbert)
              Muted tbn, Miller

(Session continued on next page)

055580-1   BB 10876-B, HMV BD 5651, HMVAu EA-3318, HMVIn
                 BD 5651, Vi LSP-4125, RCA Int. INTS 1002,
                 Vi P8S-1432
             Falling Leaves
                 (Mack David-Frankie Carle)
                 Ts, Beneke

055581-1   BB 10900-A, HMV MH 95
             Shadows On The Sand-voc Ray Eberle
                 (Stanley Adams-Will Grosz)
                 P, MacGregor; ts, Beneke; clt, Schwartz

055582-1   BB 10931-B, HMVAu EA-3351, HMVSw JK-2252, Vi EPA-
                 5094, Cam Cas-2267, RCA G Cas-2267
             Goodbye, Little Darlin', Goodbye-voc Ray Eberle
                 (Johnny Marvin-Gene Autry)

             All tunes 1 take. (RCA Victor)
             This session lasted from 11:00 A.M. to 5:00 P.M.
             (RCA Victor)

3 September, 1940 (TUES): New York City, New York (CHESTERFIELD SHOW)
                    CBS   10:00-10:15 P.M.

             The announcer for this program is Paul Douglas.

                    Moonlight Serenade (Theme)

V-4086 WR-1024 GMMS 35/83, AFRS P-2246
               (1:57) Caprice Viennois (arr JG)
                      (Fritz Kreisler)
                      P, MacGregor

V-4086 WR-1024 GMMS 35/83
       Int GM (2:25) Outside Of That I Love You (arr JG)-
                      voc Marion Hutton and Tex Beneke
                      From the musical comedy "Louisiana
                      Purchase"
                      (Irving Berlin)

V-4086 WR-1024 GMMS 35/83, AFRS P-2250
       Int GM (2:54) Blueberry Hill (arr BF)-voc Ray Eberle
                      (Al Lewis-Larry Stock-Vincent Rose)

V-4086 WR-1024 GMMS 35/83
       Int GM (3:37) Everybody Loves My Baby (But My Baby Don't
                      Love Nobody But Me) (arr JG)
                      (Jack Palmer-Spencer Williams)
                      Tpt, Best?; ts, Beneke; d, Purtill;
                      ts, Klink

                    Moonlight Serenade (Theme)

4 September, 1940 (WED): New York City, New York (CHESTERFIELD SHOW)
                        CBS   10:00-10:15 P.M.

                    Moonlight Serenade (Theme)
                    I Guess I'll Have To Change My Plan
                    MEDLEY:
                        You Tell Me Your Dream
                        Our Love Affair
                        Sleep
                        Alice Blue Gown
                    St. Louis Blues
                    Moonlight Serenade (Theme)

5 September, 1940 (THUR)

              Glenn Miller and His Orchestra played for one week
              (closed Wednesday, September 11th) at the RKO Keith
              Theater, Boston, Massachusetts. (Boston Daily
              Record, Sept. 5 & 11, 1940; BB, July 13, 1940)

                  "As a followup of Lucky Millinder's last week
              the Glenn Miller outfit sounds tame in comparison.
              Although the hefty attendance on opening day is a
              good indication that he has the bigger following,
              musically and technically, the sweet swing Miller
              band is aces.
                  With the exception of Marion Hutton the frantic
              vocalist, and Maurice Purtill, the rough riding
              drummer, there's a decided paucity of pep. Numbers
              like Sunrise Serenade, Danny Boy and the Ray Eberle
              vocals of Nearness of You and I'll Never Smile Again
              plus the lazy daisy leading by Miller seem to over-
              come. In retrospect, the more exciting stuff
              derived from Tiger Ray, In The Mood (the best band
              number on the list).
                  Boys really swing it for Miss Hutton in Boog-It
              and Rumba Jumps. She gives a welcomed contrast to
              the slow moaning of Ray Eberle but each vocalist
              drew extra bows when caught.
                  On the debit side Miller acts too blase to his
              eager audience and has too much blue lighting on
              the show. On the credit side, he never hogs the spot,
              except for a bit of trombone solo, and delivers some
              of the swellest music in the world for radio or
              dance hall consumption." (Variety, Sept. 11, 1940)

                  "MILLER STOPS RIOT A riot by high school jitter-
              bugs was narrowly averted here during Glenn Miller's
              week at the Keith Theater when Miller, assisted by a
              corps of policemen, handed out a mess of autographed
              pix to frantically excited moppets. Police said there
              were more than 1,000 kids in the mob." (DB, Oct. 1,
              1940)

5 September, 1940 (THUR): Boston, Massachusetts (CHESTERFIELD SHOW)
CBS   10:00-10:15 P.M.

> *Moonlight Serenade (Theme)*
> *I Haven't Time To Be A Millionaire*
> *A Million Dreams Ago*
> *Crosstown*
> *Pagan Love Song*
> *Moonlight Serenade (Theme)*

10 September, 1940 (TUES): Boston, Massachusetts (CHESTERFIELD SHOW)
CBS   10:00-10:15 P.M.

> *Moonlight Serenade (Theme)*
> *Wham*
> *MEDLEY:*
> > *S'posin'*
> > *When The Swallows Come Back To Capistrano*
> > *Thanks For The Memory*
> > *Blues In My Heart*
> *Solid As A Stonewall, Jackson*
> *Moonlight Serenade (Theme)*

11 September, 1940 (WED): Boston, Massachusetts (CHESTERFIELD SHOW)
CBS   10:00-10:15 P.M.

> *The announcer for this program is Larry Bruff.*

> *Moonlight Serenade (Theme)*

V-4086 WR-1025 GMMS 36/84, AFRS P-2252
    Int GM (1:58) In The Gloaming
                  (Meta Orred-Annie F. Harrison)
                  P, MacGregor

V-4086 WR-1025 GMMS 36/84, AFRS P-2250
    Int GM (2:33) Five O'Clock Whistle (arr BF)-voc
                  Marion Hutton and Band
                  (Kim Gannon-Joe Myrow-Gene Irwin)
                  Ts, Beneke

V-4086 WR-1025 GMMS 36/84, AFRS P-2250
    Int GM (3:24) Trade Winds (arr JG)-voc Ray Eberle
                  (Cliff Friend-Chas. Tobias)
                  Ts, Beneke

V-4086 WR-1025 GMMS 36/84
    Int GM (2:45) Down For The Count (arr BF)
                  (Bill Finegan)
                  Tpt, Best; ts, Beneke; p, MacGregor

> *Moonlight Serenade (Theme)*

12 September, 1940 (THUR): Victor Studios, New York City, New York

Same personnel as for August 30th.

056106-1   BB 10900-B, Vi LPM/LSP-3657, RCA RD/SF-7842, AFRS
            P-10071, RD 3/4-64, RCA G LPM/LSP-3657, RCA
            F 440.727
            Five O'Clock Whistle (arr BF)-voc Marion Hutton
            (and the Band)
            (Kim Gannon-Joe Myrow-Gene Irwin)
            Ts, Beneke

056107-1   BB 10876-A, HMV BD 5651, Vi LPM-2321, HMVIn BD 5651
            Beat Me Daddy, Eight To A Bar-voc Jack Lathrop
            (and the Band)
            (Don Raye-Hughie Prince-Eleanore Sheehy)
            P, MacGregor; clt, Caceres; p, MacGregor

056108-1   BB 11042-B (gold label)
            Ring Telephone, Ring-voc Ray Eberle
            (Buck Ram-Peter Tinturin)
            Ts, Beneke

056108-2   BB 11042-B (silver label)
            Ring Telephone, Ring-voc Ray Eberle
            (Buck Ram-Peter Tinturin)
            Ts, Beneke

            "Beat Me Daddy, Eight To A Bar" and "Ring
            Telephone, Ring" 2 takes; "Five O'Clock Whistle"
            1 take. (RCA Victor)
            This session lasted from 9:00 A.M. to 1:30 P.M.
            (RCA Victor)

*12 September, 1940 (THUR): New York City, N.Y. (CHESTERFIELD SHOW)
                CBS   10:00-10:15 P.M.*

The announcer for this program is Paul Douglas.

Moonlight Serenade (Theme)

V-4086 WR-1026 GMMS 37/85, AFRS P-2242, Vi LPT 6701, HMV RLS 598,
            Vi EPOT 6701 (947-0179), Vi It LPM-10141,
            Vi It LPM 50020, RCA Vi It LJ 50020, RCA G
            EPOT-6701
            (2:26) Sophisticated Lady
            (Mitchell Parish-Irving Mills-
            Duke Ellington)
            Tpt, Best

(Broadcast continued on next page)

V-4086 WR-1026 <u>GMMS 37/85</u>, AFRS P-2250
   Int PD (2:34) <u>Cowboy From Brooklyn</u>-voc Marion Hutton and
                   Tex Beneke
                   From the Warner Brothers' film
                   "Cowboy from Brooklyn"
                   (Johnny Mercer-Harry Warren)
                   Ts, Beneke

V-4086 WR-1026 <u>GMMS 37/85</u>, AFRS P-2250
            (1:54) <u>The Call Of The Canyon</u> (arr BF)-voc Ray
                   Eberle
                   (Billy Hill)
                   No Beneke sax solo

V-4086 WR-1026 <u>GMMS 37/85</u>, AFRS P-2242
   Int GM (2:26) <u>Pennsylvania Six-Five Thousand</u> (arr JG)-
                   Chant by Band
                   (Carl Sigman-Jerry Gray)
                   Tpt, Best; ts, Beneke

Moonlight Serenade (Theme)

On Vi LPT 6701 "Sophisticated Lady" was incorrectly listed as being broadcast on March
19, 1940.

13 September, 1940 (FRI)

Trombones	Glenn Miller, Jimmy Priddy, Paul Tanner, Frank D'Annolfo
Trumpets	Charles Frankhauser, Zeke Zarchy, Dale McMickle, Johnny Best
Reeds	Hal McIntyre, as; Ernie Caceres, as, bar & clt; Wilbur Schwartz, clt & as; Tex Beneke, ts; Al Klink, ts
Rhythm	Chummy MacGregor, p; Jack Lathrop, g; HERMAN "TRIGGER" ALPERT, b; Maurice Purtill, d
Vocalists	Marion Hutton, Ray Eberle, Jack Lathrop
Band-Boy	Raul Hidalgo

Although we do not have payroll records during this
period we do have the band personnel summary made
by a lawyer for the Miller Estate. It indicates
that Alpert joined the band on September 7th and
that Carlson left the band on September 13th. Of
course, this is incorrect. We know that Carlson
was with the band on September 12th as he is on the
Victor recording session. We also know that the
Payroll Records are made up to cover the period

(Continued on next page)

[214]

from Saturday to Friday of each week. Therefore, for Alpert to appear on the Payroll Records for the week beginning September 7th and ending September 13th would indicate that a pro-rata salary figure was shown beside his name but this was not taken into consideration by the lawyer who did the summary. Since Carlson was with the band on September 12th we assume that Alpert joined the band on September 13th and was paid for the one day. Alpert came from Alvino Rey's band.

Glenn Miller and His Orchestra played for one week (closed Thursday, September 19th) at the Metropolitan Theater, Providence, Rhode Island. (G.M.D.)

17 September, 1940 (TUES): Providence, Rhode Island
(CHESTERFIELD SHOW)
CBS   10:00-10:15 P.M.

> *Moonlight Serenade* (Theme)
> *Star Dust*
> *Five O'Clock Whistle*
> *Blueberry Hill*
> *Anchors Aweigh*
> *Moonlight Serenade* (Theme)

18 September, 1940 (WED): Providence, Rhode Island
(CHESTERFIELD SHOW)
CBS   10:00-10:15 P.M.

> *Moonlight Serenade* (Theme)
> (1:11) *All Through The Night*
> From the musical production
> "Anything Goes"
> (Cole Porter)
> Int GM (2:14) *I Never Took A Lesson In My Life* (arr JG)-
> voc Marion Hutton and Tex Beneke
> (Lawrence-Foore)
> D, Purtill; ts, Beneke
> *A Handful Of Stars*
> (3:35) *Tuxedo Junction* (arr JG)
> (William Johnson-Julian Dash-Erskine
> Hawkins-Buddy Feyne)
> Muted tpt, McMickle; open tpt, Best;
> muted tpt, McMickle; p, MacGregor
> *Moonlight Serenade* (Theme)

19 September, 1940 (THUR): Providence, Rhode Island
                    (CHESTERFIELD SHOW)
                 .   *CBS   10:00-10:15 P.M.*

        Moonlight Serenade (Theme)
        Be Happy
        MEDLEY:
          Please
            From the Paramount film "The Big
            Broadcast"
            (Leo Robin-Ralph Rainger)
          Yesterthoughts
          Thanks (borrowed from Bing Crosby)
            (Sam Coslow - Arthur Johnston)
          Am I Blue?
            From the Warner Bros. film "On
            With The Show"
            (Grant Clarke-Harry Akst)
        Beat Me Daddy, Eight To A Bar
        Moonlight Serenade (Theme)

20 September, 1940 (FRI)

    Glenn Miller and His Orchestra played for one week (closed Thursday, September 26th) at the Hippodrome Theater, Baltimore, Maryland. Also on the same bill were Tommy Trent and the Berry Bros. (G.M.P.R.; Baltimore Sun, Sept. 20 & 26, 1940; BB, July 20 & Oct. 26, 1940)
    "Men Against the Sky" (RKO) and Glenn Miller's Orchestra reaching for a very nice $18,000." (Variety, Sept. 25, 1940)

24 September, 1940 (TUES): Baltimore, Maryland (CHESTERFIELD SHOW)
           CBS   10:00-10:15 P.M.

        Moonlight Serenade (Theme)
        The Old Refrain (arr JG)
          (Fritz Kreisler)
        Outside Of That I Love You
        Trade Winds

E1LVB 3201   Vi LPT-16, Vi EPBT-3025 (947-0025), Vi 42-0110 (Vi PT-25), Vi 27-0110 (Vi WPT-25), Vi EPA-729, Vi LPM-1193, Vi EPB-1193 (547-0823), HMV DLP-1013, Vi TP3-5020, RCA F 130243, E1 WDLP 1013, RCA Int. B-21032, RCA Int. T-21032, RCA G LPM-1193, HMV Norway

(Broadcast continued on next page)

Int GM (2:48) ~~Everybody Loves My Baby (But My Baby Don't~~
Love Nobody But Me) (arr JG)
(Jack Palmer-Spencer Williams)
Tpt, Best; ts, Beneke; d, Purtill

Moonlight Serenade (Theme)

25 September, 1940 (WED): Baltimore, Maryland (CHESTERFIELD SHOW)
CBS   10:00-10:15 P.M.

The announcer for this program is Larry Bruff.

Moonlight Serenade (Theme)

V-4086 WR-1027 GMMS 38/86
(2:38) The Gentleman Needs A Shave (arr JG)- voc
Marion Hutton and Tex Beneke
(Kim Gannon-Guy Wood)
D, Purtill; ts, Beneke

V-4086 WR-1027 GMMS 38/86, AFRS P-2246
(4:56) MEDLEY:
Int LB   Isn't It Romantic? (arr JG)
From the Paramount film "Love Me
Tonight"
(Lorenz Hart-Richard Rodgers)
Ts, Beneke; muted tbn, Miller
Int GM   Shadows On The Sand (arr JG)-voc Ray
Eberle
(Stanley Adams-Will Grosz)
Int GM   Blue Prelude (arr JG) (borrowed from
Woody Herman)
(Gordon Jenkins-Joe Bishop)
Muted tpt, McMickle?

V-4086 WR-1027 GMMS 38/86, Vi LPT-16, Vi EPBT-3025 (947-0024)
Vi 42-0110 (Vi PT-25), Vi 27-0110
(Vi WPT-25), Vi LPM-1193, Vi EPB-1193
(547-0823), HMV DLP-1021, Vi It LPM-10141,
Vi TP3-5020, RCA Int. T-21032, RCA Int.
B-21032, RCA Vi It LJ 50020, El WDLP 1021,
RCA G LPM 9852, RCA G LPM-1193, Vi It LPM
50020, HMV Norway, RCA G LPM/LSP-9944
Int LB & GM (2:42) Tiger Rag (arr ED)
(Tony Sbarbaro-Eddie Edwards-Henry
Ragas-Larry Shields-Nick LaRocca-
Henry DeCosta)
Ts, Klink; d, Purtill

Moonlight Serenade (Theme)

(Continued on next page)

"Blue Prelude" in the medley served as both the "borrowed" and the "blue" tune. The Larry Bruff and Glenn Miller introduction to "Tiger Rag" (on GMMS 38/86) has been omitted from the other releases. Although the soloists on "Tiger Rag" are the same as when it was originally broadcast on November 26th, 1939, the arrangement has been considerably shortened.

26 September, 1940 '(THUR): Baltimore, Maryland (CHESTERFIELD SHOW)
                    CBS   10:00-10:15 P.M.

> *Moonlight Serenade (Theme)*
> *Boog-It*
> *The Call Of The Canyon*
> *Crosstown*
> *{3:29} My Blue Heaven (arr BF)*
> *   (George Whiting-Walter Donaldson)*
> *   Tbn, Miller; ts, Beneke; ts, Klink;*
> *   d, Purtill*
> *Moonlight Serenade (Theme)*

The band took the Greyhound buslines from Baltimore to Washington. (G.M.P.R.)

27 September, 1940 (FRI)

Glenn Miller and His Orchestra played for one week (closed Thursday, October 3rd) at Warner Brothers Earle Theater, Washington, D.C. Also on the same bill were Roy Davis and the Berry Bros. (Ananyas, James and Warren). (G.M.P.R.; Evening Star, Sept. 27 & Oct. 3, 1940)

Approximately 1 October, 1940

Marion Hutton was married to Jack Philbin, Johnny Long's personal manager, in Washington, D.C. (DB, Oct. 15, 1940)

1 October, 1940 (TUES): Wardman Park Hotel, Washington, D.C.
                    (CHESTERFIELD SHOW)
                    CBS   10:00-10:15 P.M.

The announcer for this program is Larry Bruff.

(Broadcast continued on next page)

                        Moonlight Serenade (Theme)
                        MEDLEY:
                        Moon Over Miami
                        A Million Dreams Ago
            (0:16)   _Aloha_ (arr JG) (borrowed from Hawaii)
                                (Princess Liliuokalani)
        Int LB (1:30)   _The Honolulu Blues_ (arr JG)
                                (Grant Clarke-Jimmie Monaco)
                                Ts, Beneke; tpt, Best
            (2:49) _Bugle Call Rag_ (arr GM)
                                (Jack Pettis-Billy Meyers-Elmer
                                Schoebel)
                                Tbn, Miller; ts, Beneke; clt,
                                Caceres;tbn, Miller; ts, Beneke;
                                d, Purtill
            (0:38) _Moonlight Serenade_ (Theme)
                                (Mitchell Parish-Glenn Miller)

        Information is missing on the first tune played
        on this program.

2 October, 1940 (WED): Wardman Park Hotel, Washington, D.C.
                        (CHESTERFIELD SHOW)
                        CBS   10:00-10:15 P.M.

                        Moonlight Serenade (Theme)
                        Goin' Home
                        Five O'Clock Whistle
                        Indian Summer
                        Down For The Count
                        Moonlight Serenade (Theme)

3 October, 1940 (THUR): Wardman Park Hotel, Washington, D.C.
                        (CHESTERFIELD SHOW)
                        CBS   10:00-10:15 P.M.

                        Moonlight Serenade (Theme)
                        A Cabana In Havana
                        Yesterthoughts
                        Mister Meadowlark
                        Pennsylvania Six-Five Thousand
                        Moonlight Serenade (Theme)

4 October, 1940 (FRI)

        Glenn Miller and His Orchestra played at Hecla
        Park, Bellfonte, Pennsylvania, from 9:00-1:00 A.M.
        E.S.T. (G.M.D.; Variety, Sept. 4, 1940)

5 October, 1940 (SAT)

> Glenn Miller and His Orchestra played at
> Convention Hall, (34th & Spruce) Philadelphia,
> Pennsylvania, from 9:00-1:00 A.M. (G.M.D.;
> Variety, Sept. 4, 1940)
>   "Longhairs will mingle with cats Oct. 13
> when the Philadelphia La Scala Opera Co., throws
> its annual benefit at Convention Hall, Atlantic
> City.
>   There'll be no Martinellis or Tibbetts on
> hand to entertain, however. That choice assign-
> ment goes to Glenn Miller's band, said to be a
> great favorite of the opera-singing crowd."
> (DB, Oct. 1, 1940)
>
>   "The Philly La Scala Opera Company has
> hired Glenn Miller's band to play at a benefit
> of the operatic organization at Atlantic City's
> Convention Hall October 13, 1940.
>   This believed the first time that a group
> representing serious lyric drama has turned to a
> swing outfit to help raise funds. The contract
> with Miller's band was signed yesterday (Monday)
> at the Steel Pier, where Miller is currently
> booked.
>   Date is the nite before Miller goes back
> into his second stand at the Pennsylvania Hotel,
> N.Y.C." (Variety, Sept. 4, 1940)
>
>   "Glenn Miller La Scala date changed from
> October 13, 1940 to October 5, 1940 to conform
> with band's opening at Hotel Pennsylvania."
> (Variety, Sept. 11, 1940)
>
>   Contrary to the location shown in various
> magazine articles the G.M.D. states that the
> location was Philadelphia.

6 October, 1940 (SUN)

> Off. (G.M.D.)

7 October, 1940 (MON): Cafe Rouge, Hotel Pennsylvania,
>   New York City, N.Y.
>   NBC Red
>
> Glenn Miller and His Orchestra opened at the
> "Cafe Rouge" of the Hotel Pennsylvania, New York
> City, New York. Other bandleaders present:

(Continued on next page)

Les Brown, Johnny Long, Sonny Burke, Woody
Herman, Jan Savitt, Gray Gordon, Eddie DeLange
and Cecil Golly. Leonard Joy, Victor executive,
showed up with both of his Bluebird singing
stars, Dinah Shore and Yvette. The band did
not play on Sundays. (G.M.D.)

> *Moonlight Serenade (Theme)*
> ~~*Pennsylvania Six-Five Thousand*~~   ALP
> *The Call Of The Canyon*
> *The Gentleman Needs A Shave*
> *A Handful Of Stars*
> *Moonlight Serenade*
> *On Brave Old Army Team*
> *When The Swallows Come Back To Capistrano*
> *Down For The Count*
> *Slumber Song (Theme)*

We do not know whether "Moonlight Serenade" was
played in full after "A Handful Of Stars" or
whether it was played in part to mark the half-
way point in the program.

G.M.P.R. show that there were two sustaining
programs this evening from the Hotel Pennsylvania.

8 October, 1940 (TUES): New York City, New York (CHESTERFIELD SHOW)
CBS   10:00-10:15 P.M.

The announcer for this program is Paul Douglas.

> *Moonlight Serenade (Theme)*
> (2:09) *Jeannie With The Light Brown Hair* (arr JG)
> *(Stephen Foster)*
> *I Never Took A Lesson In My Life*
> *Our Love Affair-voc RE*
> (4:14) *St. Louis Blues* (arr ED)
> *(William C. Handy)*
> *Tpt, Best; ts, Beneke; p, MacGregor;*
> *tbn, Miller; tpt, Best; d, Purtill*
> (0:27) *Moonlight Serenade (Theme)*
> *(Mitchell Parish-Glenn Miller)*

9 October, 1940 (WED): New York City, New York (CHESTERFIELD SHOW)
CBS   10:00-10:15 P.M.

The announcer for this program is Paul Douglas.

> (0:46) *Moonlight Serenade (Theme)*
> *(Mitchell Parish-Glenn Miller)*

(Broadcast continued on next page)

```
Int GM (3:00) Beat Me Daddy, Eight To A Bar-voc Jack
                   Lathrop and The Band
                   (Don Raye-Hughie Prince-Eleanore Sheehy)
                   P, MacGregor; clt, Caceres; p, MacGregor
              Blueberry Hill
              You've Got Me This Way
       (3:01) Farewell Blues
                   (Elmer Schoebel-Paul Mares-Joseph Leon
                   Rappolo)
                   Ts, Beneke; tpt, Best?
       (0:37) Moonlight Serenade (Theme)
                   (Mitchell Parish-Glenn Miller)
```

```
9 October, 1940 (WED): Cafe Rouge, Hotel Pennsylvania,
                        New York City, N.Y.
                        NBC-Blue  11:30-12:00 Midnight
```

G.M.P.R. show that there was one sustaining
program this evening from the Hotel Pennsylvania.

```
10 October, 1940 (THUR): New York City, New York (CHESTERFIELD SHOW)
                         CBS  10:00-10:15 P.M.
```

```
              Moonlight Serenade (Theme)
              Wham
       (4:35) MEDLEY:
                   Coquette (arr JG)
                   (Gus Kahn-Carmen Lombardo-John W. Green)
       Int GM  I'll Never Smile Again (arr JG)-voc Ray
                   Eberle
                   (Ruth Lowe)
       Int GM  Does Your Heart Beat For Me? (arr JG)
                   (borrowed from Russ Morgan)
                   (Mitchell Parish-Russ Morgan-Arnold
                   Johnson)
                   P, MacGregor
       Int GM  Blue Hawaii (arr JG)
                   From the Paramount film "Waikiki
                   Wedding"
                   (Leo Robin-Ralph Rainger)
              Runnin' Wild
              Moonlight Serenade (Theme)
```

Since October 10th 1940 all bands broadcasting on
Mutual, CBS or NBC have been ordered to play two
public domain or non-ASCAP (Ed.-meaning, BMI)
songs for every 15-minute broadcast. That means
four for a half-hour shot, which most sustainers
are. (DB, Nov. 1, 1940)

11 October, 1940 (FRI): Victor Studios, New York City, New York

> Same personnel as for September 13th except that
> THE MODERNAIRES (Chuck Goldstein, Bill Conway,
> Hal Dickinson, and Ralph Brewster) were added for
> this one recording session.

056479-1   BB 10913-A, ViJ 1101, RD 3/4-64
            Make Believe Ballroom Time (arr JG)-voc The Four
                Modernaires
                (Martin Block-Harold Green-Mickey Stoner)
                Tpt, Best?; d, Purtill; ts, Beneke

056479-2   Vi EPA-5035, HMV 7EG 8077, RCA RCX 1034
            Make Believe Ballroom Time (arr JG)-voc The Four
                Modernaires
                (Martin Block-Harold Green-Mickey Stoner)
                Tpt, Best?; d, Purtill; ts, Beneke

056480-1   BB 10906-B, HMV BD 5670, HMV 7EG 8224
            You've Got Me This Way (arr JG)-voc Marion Hutton
                From the RKO film "You'll Find Out"
                (Johnny Mercer-Jimmy McHugh)

056481-1   BB 10931-A, HMV BD 5850, HMV MH 142, HMVSw JK-
                2354, HMV DLP 1049, Cam Cal/Cas-2128, RCA G
                Cas-2128, Vi LSP-4125, RCA Int. INTS 1002,
                Vi P8S-1432, HMVAu DLP 1049, RCA Br. INTS 1019
            A Nightingale Sang In Berkeley Square (arr BF)-
                voc Ray Eberle
                From the London Musical Success "New Faces"
                (Eric Maschwitz-Manning Sherwin)
                Clt, ??;ts, Beneke;clt, ??

056481-2   Vi PR-125
            A Nightingale Sang In Berkeley Square (arr BF)-
                voc Ray Eberle
                From the London Musical Success "New Faces"
                (Eric Maschwitz-Manning Sherwin)
                Clt, ??; ts, Beneke; clt, ??

056482-1   BB 10906-A, HMV BD 5670, HMV 7EG 8224
            I'd Know You Anywhere (arr BF)-voc Ray Eberle
                From the RKO film "You'll Find Out"
                (Johnny Mercer-Jimmy McHugh)

> "Make Believe Ballroom Time" was recorded as the
> new theme for Martin Block's radio show "Make
> Believe Ballroom".
>   "At his own expense, Glenn Miller had his
> band record the number, with a vocal chorus

(Continued on next page)

contributed gratis by the Modernaires."
(Met. Nov. 1940)
The Four Modernaires were hired for this one
tune and joined Miller permanently at a later
date. They had been singing with Paul Whiteman
and His Orchestra.

"You've Got Me This Way" 1 take; all other tunes
2 takes. (RCA Victor)
This session lasted from 1:45 P.M. to 4:55 P.M.
(RCA Victor)

11 October, 1940 (FRI): Cafe Rouge, Hotel Pennsylvania,
New York City, N.Y.
NBC-Red 12:30-12:57 A.M.

G.M.P.R. show that there was one sustaining
program this evening from the Hotel Pennsylvania.

12 October, 1940 (SAT)

New York--Polly Davis, secretary to Glenn Miller,
was married Oct. 12 to Don Haynes, one-nighter
booker for General Amusement Corp. Glenn and
Helen Miller, along with Mike Nidorf and "Bullets",
Miller's left-hand man, were "in" on the ceremony.
(DB Nov. 1, 1940)

12 October, 1940 (SAT): Cafe Rouge, Hotel Pennsylvania,
New York City, N.Y.
NBC-Blue 12:05-12:30 A.M.

(2:20) Down For The Count (arr BF)
(Bill Finegan)
Tpt, Best; ts, Beneke
Blueberry Hill-voc RE
(1:32) On Brave Old Army Team (arr JG)
(Philip Egner)
Tpt, Best; d, Purtill; clt, Caceres
(1:56) Tiger Rag (arr ED)
(Tony Sbarbaro-Eddie Edwards-Henry
Ragas-Larry Shields-Nick LaRocca-
Harry DeCosta)
D, Purtill
(1:28) Slumber Song(Theme)
(Saul Tepper-John Chalmers MacGregor)

The above listing of tunes is only part of a 25
minute program. Other tunes played are unknown.

(Continued on next page)

The arrangement on "Slumber Song" is slightly
different from the recorded version.

According to G.M.P.R. this was Zeke Zarchy's
(trumpet) last day with the band. He was paid
for two days at the Hotel Pennsylvania for the
week ending October 17th. His replacement,
Phil Rommel, joined the band on October 14th
(the Hotel Pennsylvania was closed on Sundays)
and was paid for four days (out of six) for the
week ending October 17th.

G.M.P.R. show that there was one sustaining
program this evening from the Hotel Pennsylvania.

14 October, 1940 (MON): Cafe Rouge, Hotel Pennsylvania,
New York City, N.Y.
NBC-Red 7:30-8:00 P.M.

Trombones	*Glenn Miller, Jimmy Priddy, Paul Tanner, Frank D'Annolfo*
Trumpets	*Charles Frankhauser, PHIL ROMMEL, Dale McMickle, Johnny Best*
Reeds	*Hal McIntyre, as; Ernie Caceres, as, bar & clt; Wilbur Schwartz, clt & as; Tex Beneke, ts; Al Klink, ts*
Rhythm	*Chummy MacGregor, p; Jack Lathrop, g; Herman "Trigger" Alpert, b; Maurice Purtill, d*

G.M.P.R. show that there was one sustaining
program this evening from the Hotel Pennsylvania.

15 October, 1940 (TUES): New York City, N.Y. (CHESTERFIELD SHOW)
CBS 10:00-10:15 P.M.

The announcer for this program is Paul Douglas.

    Moonlight Serenade (Theme)
    Boog-It-voc MH & Band
    When The Swallows Come Back To Capistrano
    Anvil Chorus
    Moonlight Serenade (Theme)

This version of the "Anvil Chorus" is very slow.

16 October, 1940 (WED): New York City, N.Y.   (CHESTERFIELD SHOW)
                    CBS   10:00-10:15 P.M.

> Moonlight Serenade *(Theme)*
> Long Time No See, Baby
> MEDLEY:
>   The Siren's Song
>   A Handful Of Stars
>   Love In Bloom
>   The Birth Of The Blues
> Limehouse Blues
> Moonlight Serenade *(Theme)*

16 October, 1940 (WED): Cafe Rouge, Hotel Pennsylvania,
                    New York City, N.Y.
                    NBC-Blue   11:36-12:00 Midnight

G.M.P.R. show that there was one sustaining
program this evening from the Hotel Pennsylvania.

17 October, 1940 (THUR): New York City, N.Y. (CHESTERFIELD SHOW)
                    CBS   10:00-10:15 P.M.

The announcer for this program is Paul Douglas.

(0:48) Moonlight Serenade *(Theme)*
                    (Mitchell Parish-Glenn Miller)
Int GM (1:48) Drink To Me Only With Thine Eyes
                    (Ben Jonson)
                    P, MacGregor
            Five O'Clock Whistle
            A Nightingale Sang In Berkeley Square
(3:19) By The Waters Of Minnetonka *(arr GM)-*
                    Chant by the Band
                    (Indian Love Song)
                    (J.M. Cavanass-Thurlow Lieurance)
                    Ts, Beneke; clt, Caceres; muted tpt,
                    ??; d, Purtill
(0:32) Moonlight Serenade *(Theme)*
                    (Mitchell Parish-Glenn Miller)

18 October, 1940 (FRI): Cafe Rouge, Hotel Pennsylvania,
                    New York City, N.Y.
                    NBC-Red   12:30-12:57 A.M.

> Moonlight Serenade *(Theme)*
> Pennsylvania Six-Five Thousand

(Broadcast continued on next page)

Yesterthoughts
Beat Me Daddy, Eight To A Bar

PPRM-5337   Vi LPM/LSP-2768 (Vi LPM/LSP-6101), RCA RD/SF-7611,
             RCA Au LPM 2768
             (2:56) A Handful Of Stars (arr BF)-voc Ray Eberle
                 From the MGM film "Hullabaloo"
                 (Jack Lawrence-Ted Shapiro)
                 Ts, Beneke

Anvil Chorus

PPRM-5334   Vi LPM/LSP-2767 (Vi LPM/LSP-6101), RCA RD/SF-7610,
             RCA Au LPM 2767
             (3:10) The Gentleman Needs A Shave (arr JG)-voc
                 Marion Hutton and Tex Beneke
                 (Kim Gannon-Guy Wood)
                 D, Purtill; ts, Beneke

PPRM-5334   Vi LPM/LSP-2767 (Vi LPM/LSP-6101), RCA RD/SF-7610,
             RCA Au LPM 2767
             (2:11) Slumber Song (Theme)
                 (Saul Tepper-John Chalmers MacGregor)
                 Ts, Beneke

        G.M.P.R. show that there was one sustaining
        program this evening from the Hotel Pennsylvania.

18 October, 1940 (FRI)

        According to G.M.P.R. John O'Leary replaced Eak
        Kenyon as road manager on this date.

19 October, 1940 (SAT): Cafe Rouge, Hotel Pennsylvania,
                        New York City, N.Y.
                        NBC-Red 12:05-12:30 A.M.

        G.M.P.R. show that there was one sustaining
        program this evening from the Hotel Pennsylvania.

21 October, 1940 (MON): Cafe Rouge, Hotel Pennsylvania,
                        New York City, N.Y.
                        NBC-Blue 7:30-8:00 P.M.

        G.M.P.R. show that the program planned for
        this evening was cancelled.

22 October, 1940 (TUES): New York City, N.Y. (CHESTERFIELD SHOW)
                    CBS   10:00-10:15 P.M.

   The announcer for this program is Paul Douglas.

     <u>*Moonlight Serenade*</u> *(Theme)*
     <u>*You've Got Me This Way*</u>
     MEDLEY:
      <u>*Let's Fall In Love*</u> *(arr JG)*
        From the film "Let's Fall In Love"
        (Ted Koehler-Harold Arlen)
      <u>*Along The Santa Fe Trail*</u>
      <u>*Indian Love Call*</u> *(arr JG) (borrowed from*
        (From the musical comedy "Rose-Marie"
        (Oscar Hammerstein, 2nd-Otto Harbach-
        Rudolph Friml)
      <u>*Haunting Blues*</u> *(arr JG)*
        (
    (3:37) <u>*Oh So Good*</u> *(arr JG)-Chant by Band*
      (Jerry Gray)
      Tpt, ??; p, MacGregor; ts, Beneke;
      tbn, Miller; tpt, ??; d, Purtill;
      clt, Caceres
   (0:11) <u>*Moonlight Serenade*</u> *(Theme)*
      (Mitchell Parish-Glenn Miller)

23 October, 1940 (WED): New York City, N.Y. (CHESTERFIELD SHOW)
                    CBS   10:00-10:15 P.M.

     <u>*Moonlight Serenade*</u> *(Theme)*
     <u>*In A Sentimental Mood*</u>
     <u>*Fifth Avenue*</u>
     <u>*The Call Of The Canyon*</u>
     <u>*Down For The Count*</u>
     <u>*Moonlight Serenade*</u> *(Theme)*

23 October, 1940 (WED): Cafe Rouge, Hotel Pennsylvania,
                    New York City, N.Y.
                    NBC-Blue   11:36-12:00 Midnight

   The announcer for this program is Lyle Van.

   According to G.M.P.R. this was Phil Rommel's
   (trumpet) last day with the band. He is paid
   for the Chesterfield program and night at the
   Hotel Pennsylvania. G.M.P.R. show that he was
   paid for five days out of six (Not including
   Sunday) at the Hotel Pennsylvania and for two

(Continued on next page)

Chesterfield programs for the week ending October
24th. Max Kaminsky joined the band the next day
and G.M.P.R. shows that he was paid just for the
one day (both the Chesterfield program and the
night at the Hotel Pennsylvania) for the week ending October 24th.

G.M.P.R. show that there was one sustaining
program this evening from the Hotel Pennsylvania.

(1:45) *Long Time No See, Baby* (arr JG)-voc
Marion Hutton
(Jack Lathrop)
D, Purtill; ts, Beneke
(1:55) *A Handful Of Stars* (arr BF)-voc Ray Eberle
From the MGM film "Hullabaloo"
(Jack Lawrence-Ted Shapiro)
(3:04) *On Brave Old Army Team* (arr JG)
(Philip Egner)
D, Purtill; ts, Klink; tpt, Best;
d, Purtill; clt, Caceres
(1:19) *Slumber Song* (Theme)
(Saul Tepper-John Chalmers MacGregor)
Ts, Beneke

24 October, 1940 (THUR): New York City, N.Y. (CHESTERFIELD SHOW)
CBS 10:00-10:15 P.M.

Trombones   Glenn Miller, Jimmy Priddy, Paul
Tanner, Frank D'Annolfo
Trumpets   Charles Frankhauser, MAX KAMINSKY,
Dale McMickle, Johnny Best
Reeds   Hal McIntyre, as; Ernie Caceres, as,
bar & clt; Wilbur Schwartz, clt & as;
Tex Beneke, ts; Al Klink, ts
Rhythm   Chummy MacGregor, p; Jack Lathrop, g;
Herman "Trigger" Alpert, b; Maurice
Purtill, d

Moonlight Serenade (Theme)
Carry Me Back To Old Virginny
Fresh As A Daisy
Yesterthoughts
Int GM (2:57) *Everybody Loves My Baby (But My Baby Don't*
& PD   *Love Nobody But Me)* (arr JG)
(Jack Palmer-Spencer Williams)
Tpt, Best; ts, Beneke; d, Purtill
Moonlight Serenade (Theme)

25 October, 1940 (FRI): Cafe Rouge, Hotel Pennsylvania,
New York City, N.Y.
NBC-Red 12:30-12:57 A.M.

> *Moonlight Serenade (Theme)*
> *Solid As A Stonewall, Jackson*
> *A Nightingale Sang In Berkeley Square*
> *You've Got Me This Way*
> *When The Swallows Come Back To Capistrano*
> *Oh So Good*
> *A Handful Of Stars*

E4VP 8202   ~~Vi LPT 6701,~~ Vi EPOT 6701 (947-0183), HMV RLS 598,
RD 3/4-64, RCA G EPOT-6701
~~(2:08)~~ Crosstown-voc Jack Lathrop
(James Cavanaugh-John Redmond-Nat Simon)
No sax solo

> *Anchors Aweigh*
> *Slumber Song (Theme)*

G.M.P.R. show that there was one sustaining
program this evening from the Hotel Pennsylvania.

26 October, 1940 (SAT): Cafe Rouge, Hotel Pennsylvania,
New York City, N.Y.
NBC-Red 12:05-12:30 A.M.

G.M.P.R. show that there was one sustaining
program this evening from the Hotel Pennsylvania.

28 October, 1940 (MON): Cafe Rouge, Hotel Pennsylvania,
New York City, N.Y.
NBC-Red

G.M.P.R. show that there was one sustaining
program this evening from the Hotel Pennsylvania.

29 October, 1940 (TUES): New York City, N.Y. (CHESTERFIELD SHOW)
CBS 10:00-10:15 P.M.

> *Moonlight Serenade (Theme)*
> *Five O'Clock Whistle*
> *A Million Dreams Ago*
> *Anvil Chorus*
> *Moonlight Serenade (Theme)*

There were only three tunes played on this
broadcast due to the length of time "Anvil
Chorus" took to perform. This occurs on a
number of occasions.

30 October, 1940 (WED): New York City, N.Y. (CHESTERFIELD SHOW)
                    CBS   10:00-10:15 P.M.

                    Moonlight Serenade (Theme)
                    Yes, My Darling Daughter
                    MEDLEY:
                      I'll Never Be The Same (arr JG)
                        (Gus Kahn-Matty Malneck-
                            Frank Signorelli)
                      Helpless
       (0:50)   *Street Of Dreams* (arr JG) (borrowed from ?)
                      (Sam M. Lewis-Victor Young)
    Int GM (2:00)   *Washboard Blues* (arr JG)
                      (Fred Callahan-Mitchell Parish-
                      Hoagy Carmichael)
                      Muted tpt, ??; open tpt, ??
                    Beat Me Daddy, Eight To A Bar
                    Moonlight Serenade (Theme)

30 October, 1940 (WED): Cafe Rouge, Hotel Pennsylvania,
                    New York City, N.Y.
                    NBC-Blue   11:36-12:00 Midnight

        G.M.P.R. show that there was one sustaining
        program this evening from the Hotel Pennsylvania.

31 October, 1940 (THUR): New York City, N.Y. (CHESTERFIELD SHOW)
                     CBS   10:00-10:15 P.M.

                    Moonlight Serenade (Theme)
                    Danny Boy
                    Long Time No See, Baby
                    Our Love Affair
                    Tuxedo Junction
                    Moonlight Serenade (Theme)

        According to G.M.P.R. this was Max Kaminsky's
        (trumpet) last day with the band. He was paid
        for the Chesterfield program and we presume he
        was present for the night at the Hotel
        Pennsylvania even though G.M.P.R. do not indicate
        this. His replacement, Ray Anthony, joined the
        next day and is paid for six days at the Hotel
        Pennsylvania for the week ending November 7th.

1 November, 1940 (FRI): Cafe Rouge, Hotel Pennsylvania,
New York City, N.Y.
NBC-Red 12:30-12:57 A.M. EST

Trombones	*Glenn Miller, Jimmy Priddy, Paul Tanner, Frank D'Annolfo*
Trumpets	*Charles Frankhauser, RAY ANTHONY, Dale McMickle, Johnny Best*
Reeds	*Hal McIntyre, as; Ernie Caceres, as, bar & clt; Wilbur Schwartz, clt & as; Tex Beneke, ts; Al Klink, ts*
Rhythm	*Chummy MacGregor, p; Jack Lathrop, g; Herman "Trigger" Alpert, b; Maurice Purtill, d*

G.M.P.R. show that there was one sustaining
program this evening from the Hotel Pennsylvania.

> *Moonlight Serenade*
> *Oh So Good*
> *Along The Santa Fe Trail*
> *You've Got Me This Way*
> *Helpless*
> *Anvil Chorus*
> *The Call Of The Canyon*
> *Slumber Song* (Theme)

2 November, 1940 (SAT): Cafe Rouge, Hotel Pennsylvania,
New York City, N.Y.
NBC-Blue 12:05-12:30 A.M.

G.M.P.R. show that there was one sustaining
program this evening from the Hotel Pennsylvania.

4 November, 1940 (MON): Cafe Rouge, Hotel Pennsylvania,
New York City, N.Y.
NBC-Blue

Trombones	*Glenn Miller, Jimmy Priddy, Paul, Tanner, Frank D'Annolfo*
Trumpets	*BILLY MAY, Ray Anthony, Dale McMickle, Johnny Best*
Reeds	*Hal McIntyre, as; Ernie Caceres, as, bar & clt; Wilbur Schwartz, clt & as; Tex Beneke, ts; Al Klink, ts*
Rhythm	*Chummy MacGregor, p; Jack Lathrop, g; Herman "Trigger" Alpert, b; Maurice Purtill, d*

(Continued on next page)

G.M.P.R. show that Billy May was paid for four
days at the Hotel Pennsylvania (November 4, 5,
6 & 7) for the week ending November 7th as well
as being paid for the three Chesterfield
programs of November 5, 6 & 7. However, to con-
fuse matters, G.M.P.R. also show that Charles
Frankhauser was paid for the same number of days
as May at the Hotel Pennsylvania as well as the
three Chesterfield programs. We can only assume
that there is an error here and that Frankhauser
left the band on November 3rd and that perhaps
he was paid a full week's salary for giving a
week's notice. There is no explanation on G.M.P.R.
regarding this overlap but since G.M.P.R. is so
definite about the date of May joining the band
(and his salary is pro rated) we have excluded
Frankhauser from the above personnel listing.

G.M.P.R. show that there was one sustaining
program this evening from the Hotel Pennsylvania.

4 November, 1940-25 November, 1940 (MON): Cafe Rouge, Hotel
                    Pennsylvania, New York City, N.Y.
                    NBC-

        (0:46) Moonlight Serenade (Theme)
                    (Mitchell Parish-Glenn Miller)
        (3:08) Midnight On The Nile
                    (
                    Muted tpt, McMickle?; ts, Beneke;
                    muted tpt, McMickle?
        (2:26) Shadows On The Sand-voc Ray Eberle
                    (Stanley Adams-Will Grosz)
                    Clt, Schwartz; ts, Beneke
        (2:42) Fresh As A Daisy (arr JG)-voc Marion
                    Hutton, Jack Lathrop, Tex Beneke
                    (From the musical production
                    "Panama Hattie"
                    (Cole Porter)
        (2:50) Yesterthoughts (arr BF)-voc Ray Eberle
                    (Stanley Adams-Victor Herbert)
                    Muted tbn, Miller
        (1:33) Solid As A Stonewall, Jackson (arr JG)
                    (Jerry Gray-John Chalmers MacGregor)
                    As, Caceres; ts, Beneke
        (2:06) Isn't That Just Like Love (arr BF)-voc
                    Jack Lathrop
                    From the Paramount film "Love Thy
                    Neighbor"
                    (Johnny Burke-Jimmy Van Heusen)
                    Ts, Beneke

(Broadcast continued on next page)

(5:37) <u>*I Dreamt I Dwelt In Harlem*</u> *(arr JG)*
    (Robert Wright-Ben Smith-Leonard Ware-
    Jerry Gray)
    Ts, Klink; tpt, May; tbn, Miller;
    b, Alpert;clt, Caceres; p, MacGregor;
    muted tpt, May
(0:46) <u>*Slumber Song*</u> *(Theme)*
    (Saul Tepper-John Chalmers MacGregor)

The actual broadcast date for this program is unknown except that the announcer mentions that it
is a Monday. The above program would have to be
one of the following dates: November 4th (May is
on this program so this excludes any October
date), November 11 or November 25th. November
18th is excluded from this list as we have a program
listing for this date. Any date in December 1940
and January 1941 would have to be excluded as Glenn
was using "Slumber Song" as his opening theme because the ASCAP ban went into effect December 1st.

5 November, 1940 (TUES): New York City, N.Y. (CHESTERFIELD SHOW)
    CBS 10:00-10:15 P.M. EST.

  G.M.P.R. show that there wasn't a Chesterfield
  program this evening as it was election night.

6 November, 1940 (WED): New York City, N.Y. (CHESTERFIELD SHOW)
    CBS 10:00-10:15 P.M. EST.

   <u>*Moonlight Serenade*</u> *(Theme)*
   <u>*Star Dust*</u>
   <u>*The Gentleman Needs A Shave*</u>
   <u>*A Nightingale Sang In Berkeley Square*</u>
   <u>*Solid As A Stonewall, Jackson*</u>
   <u>*Moonlight Serenade*</u> *(Theme)*

6 November, 1940 (WED): Cafe Rouge, Hotel Pennsylvania,
    New York City, N.Y.
    NBC-Blue 11:36-12:00 Midnight EST.

  G.M.P.R. show that there was one sustaining
  program this evening from the Hotel Pennsylvania.

  (1:40) <u>*Moonlight Serenade*</u> *(Theme)*
     (Mitchell Parish-Glenn Miller)
  (2:25) <u>*Down For The Count*</u> *(arr BF)*
     (Bill Finegan)
     Tpt, Best; Ts, Beneke

(Broadcast continued on next page)

(3:19) _Blueberry Hill_ (arr BF)-voc Ray Eberle
      (Al Lewis-Larry Stock-Vincent Rose)
(2:00) _Long Time No See, Baby_ (arr JG)-voc
      Marion Hutton
      (Jack Lathrop)
      D, Purtill; ts, Beneke
(2:33) _Shadows On The Sand_-voc Ray Eberle
      (Stanley Adams-Will Grosz)
      Clt, Schwartz; ts, Beneke
(2:58) _Limehouse Blues_ (arr JG)
      (Douglas Furber-Philip Braham)
      Tpt, Best; ts, Beneke; clt, Caceres;
      d, Purtill; ts, Beneke & Klink;
      d, Purtill
(3:02) _A Handful Of Stars_ (arr BF)-voc Ray Eberle
      From the MGM film "Hullabaloo"
      (Jack Lawrence-Ted Shapiro)
      Ts, Beneke
(2:10) _Crosstown_-voc Jack Lathrop
      (James Cavanaugh-John Redmond-Nat Simon)
      No saxophone solo
(5:03) _Tiger Rag_ (arr ED)
      (Tony Sbarbaro-Eddie Edwards-Henry Ragas-
      Larry Shields-Nick LaRocca-Harry DeCosta)
      Ts, Klink; tpt, May; ts, Beneke;
      d, Purtill
(3:13) _Slumber Song_ (Theme)
      (Saul Tepper-John Chalmers MacGregor)
      Ts, Beneke

7 November, 1940 (THUR): _New York City, N.Y._ (CHESTERFIELD SHOW)
      CBS 10:00-10:15 P.M. EST.

      Moonlight Serenade (Theme)
      Fresh As A Daisy
      MEDLEY:
        Please
        Yesterthoughts
        Thanks
        Am I Blue?
      In The Mood
      Moonlight Serenade (Theme)

7 November, 1940 (THUR)

      G.M.P.R. for the week ending November 7th show
      that Billy May arranged "Lights Out! Hold Me
      Tight!"

8 November, 1940 (FRI): Victor Studios, New York City, New York

        Same personnel as for November 4th.

057610-1   BB 10959-B, HMV MH 95, HMVAu EA-3345, HMVSw JK-2269
          Fresh As A Daisy (arr JG)-voc Marion Hutton, Jack Lathrop, Tex Beneke
             From the musical production "Panama Hattie"
             (Cole Porter)

057611-1   BB 10936-B
          Isn't That Just Like Love (arr BF)-voc Jack Lathrop
             From the Paramount film "Love Thy Neighbor"
             (Johnny Burke-Jimmy Van Heusen)
             Ts, Beneke

057612-1   BB 10970-A, HMVAu EA-2787, HMVSw JK-2199, Vi 20-1529, HMV DLP 1122, Vi LPM/LSP-3377, Vi TP3-5044, Vi P8S-5061, RD 3/4-64, RCA G LPM/LSP-3377, HMVIn NE 779, RCA G Cas 10231, AFRS G.I. Jive H-12-2208
          Along The Santa Fe Trail-voc Ray Eberle
             From the Warner Bros. film "Along The Santa Fe Trail"
             (Al Dubin-Edwina Coolidge-Will Grosz)

057613-1   BB 10936-A
          Do You Know Why (arr BF)-voc Ray Eberle
             From the Paramount film "Love Thy Neighbor"
             (Johnny Burke-Jimmy Van Heusen)
             As, McIntyre?

        All tunes 1 take. (RCA Victor)
        This session lasted from 1:30 P.M. to 4:30 P.M. (RCA Victor)

8 November, 1940 (FRI): Cafe Rouge, Hotel Pennsylvania,
                New York City, N.Y.
                NBC-Red 12:30-12:57 A.M. EST.

        G.M.P.R. show that there was one sustaining program this evening from the Hotel Pennsylvania.

9 November, 1940 (SAT)

        Al Klink married Patricia Mooreland, a model.
        (DB, Dec. 1, 1940)

9 November, 1940 (SAT): Cafe Rouge, Hotel Pennsylvania,
                       New York City, N.Y.
                       NBC-Blue 12:05-12:30 A.M. EST.

     G.M.P.R. show that there was one sustaining
     program this evening from the Hotel Pennsylvania.

11 November, 1940 (MON): Cafe Rouge, Hotel Pennsylvania,
                        New York City, N.Y.
                        NBC-Blue

     G.M.P.R. show that there was one sustaining
     program this evening from the Hotel Pennsylvania.

12 November, 1940 (TUES): New York City, N.Y. (CHESTERFIELD SHOW)
                         CBS 10:00-10:15 P.M. EST.

     The announcer for this program is Paul Douglas.

               Moonlight Serenade (Theme)
               Goin' Home
               Yes, My Darling Daughter
               Along The Santa Fe Trail
Int GM (3:25) *St. Louis Blues* (arr ED)
                  (William C. Handy)
                  Tpt, Best; ts, Beneke; p, MacGregor;
                  tpt, Best; d, Purtill
               Moonlight Serenade (Theme)

13 November, 1940 (WED): New York City, N.Y. (CHESTERFIELD SHOW)
                        CBS 10:00-10:15 P.M. EST.

     The announcer for this program is Paul Douglas.

               Moonlight Serenade (Theme)
               You've Got Me This Way
               MEDLEY:
     (0:06)   *How Deep Is The Ocean?* (arr JG)
                  (Irving Berlin)
Int GM (1:19) *I'd Know You Anywhere* (arr BF)-voc
                  Ray Eberle
                  From the RKO film "You'll Find Out"
                  (Johnny Mercer-Jimmy McHugh)
Int GM (0:43) *It's A Wonderful World* (arr JG) (borrowed
                  from Jan Savitt)
                  (Jan Savitt-Johnny Watson-Harold
                  Adamson)
                  Tpt, Best

(Broadcast continued on next page)

        Int PD (0:38)   *My Blue Heaven (arr JG)*
                              (George Whiting-Walter Donaldson)
                          I Dreamt I Dwelt In Harlem
                          Moonlight Serenade (Theme)

13 November, 1940 (WED): Cafe Rouge, Hotel Pennsylvania,
                          New York City, N.Y.
                          NBC-Blue 11:36-12:00 Midnight EST.

        G.M.P.R. show that there was one sustaining
        program this evening from the Hotel Pennsylvania.

        (2:21) Five O'Clock Whistle (arr BF)-voc
                  Marion Hutton and The Band
                  (Kim Gannon-Joe Myrow-Gene Irwin)
                  Ts, Beneke
        (3:11) Oh So Good (arr JG)-Chant by Band
                  (Jerry Gray)
                  Tpt, Best; p, MacGregor; ts, Beneke;
                  tbn, Miller; tpt, May; d, Purtill;
                  clt, Caceres
        (3:46) I Dreamt I Dwelt In Harlem (arr JG)
                  (Robert Wright-Ben Smith-Leonard Ware-
                  Jerry Gray)
                  As, Caceres; muted & open tpt, May;
                  b, Alpert; clt, Caceres; p, MacGregor

14 November, 1940 (THUR): New York City, N.Y. (CHESTERFIELD SHOW)
                          CBS 10:00-10:15 P.M. EST.

            Moonlight Serenade (Theme)
            Sophisticated Lady
            Lights Out! Hold Me Tight!
            Our Love Affair
            Sleep (partial)
            Tuxedo Junction
            Moonlight Serenade (Theme)

        A review of this program appeared in "His Master's
        Voice" newspaper, January, 1941 issue. The title
        of the article was "Fast Work Creates Clockwork As
        'They Satisfy' Via Miller":

            "The time is 9:35 p.m. Thursday. The place
        New York. Glenn Miller and his band pile into
        taxis at the Hotel Penn and dash up to CBS Play-
        house No. 2 on 45th Street, near Broadway.
            They rush in the backstage entrance, with
        Glenn bordered by autograph hounds pulling in the
        rear. The Chesterfield movie is being shown out

(Continued on next page)

front in the remodeled theatre. A modernistic
stage is capped by a large white blackboard
reaching from the top of the curtain to the roof.
It throws the sound.

Drummer starts tuning behind curtain, pre-
suming that the movie sound will drown him out.
Crowd hears it and starts applauding. As if en-
couraged, the brass takes a few toots. Glenn
gives last minute instructions with seven minutes
to go.

In This Corner

Curtain rises at 9:55. Applause by gathered
youth--and oldsters, too--only small roar.

Announcer: 'Not enough, put it down.'
Laughter as curtain dips. Introduces: 'The head
man--Mr. Miller.' Ovation sounds like winning
touchdown at the big game.

Big female sigh as Ray Eberle is introduced.
Masculine ovation, with roar and whistles, for
Marion Hutton.

Announcer holds up hand. Big clock shows
seven second to go. At the dot of 10, 'Moonlight'
blows the opening whistle. Glenn says hello to
radio audience, then holds script in his teeth as
he goes over to give the band the finish beat.

On the Air

Indirect lighting effects of pastel crimson
and violet for 'Lady.' Saxes stand for their
chorus. Trombones rise and Miller walks over to
make it a foursome. Wilbur Schwartz, lead
clarinet, keeps seated until it's time to make
the music Millerish. Reeds soar.

Glenn becomes one-man show. Gives downbeat,
rushes over to mike to announce 'Lights Out, Hold
Me Tight.' Dashes back, picks up trombone, holds
it in one hand, and leads with other. Predominant
instrumental sections stand for turns.

Miller flips horn as he plays last note.
Brass up for finish of 'Our Love Affair' sit down
as saxes rise for 'Sleep' like see saw. Miller
adds the Fred Waring theme to his collection with
special ceremony, as Chesterfield's other maestro
suddenly appears.

Guest Artist

Waring takes podium, and gives salute downbeat for 'Tuxedo Junction.' He then retires to

(Continued on next page)

right wing, and carries on a long-distance jitter-
bug session with Marion Hutton, who is sitting on
the left. Announcer has to hush crowd as
laughter at their antics becomes an uproar.
'Junction' rocks out.
    Three of the four trumpets and the reed
section stand for 'Moonlight' with military precision on the last note of 'Junction.' Autograph
books and pencils fly from pockets as the crowd
dashes for the exits to get Miller as he leaves."

14 November, 1940 (THUR)

        G.M.P.R. for the week ending November 14th show
        that Bill Moore arranged "Ode To A Butterfly".

15 November, 1940 (FRI): Victor Studios, New York City, New York

        Same personnel as for November 4th.

057648-1   BB 10959-A, HMVAu EA-2880, HMVSw JK-2269
                Somewhere (arr JG)-voc Ray Eberle
                        From the musical production "Ice Capades of
                        1941"
                        (John Latouche-Peter DeRose)

057649-1   BB 10970-B, HMV BD 5683, HMV MH 140, HMVAu EA-
                        2787, HMVSw JK-2199, Vi PRM-181, HMVAus GA-
                        5082, RD 3/4-64, HMVIn BD 5683
                Yes, My Darling Daughter (arr JG)-voc Marion
                        Hutton and Chorus (The Band)
                        (Jack Lawrence)
                        Ts, Klink

        Both tunes 1 take. (RCA Victor)
        This session lasted from 1:45 P.M. to 4:45 P.M.
        (RCA Victor)

15 November, 1940 (FRI): Cafe Rouge, Hotel Pennsylvania,
                        New York City, N.Y.
                        NBC-Red 12:30-12:57 A.M.

16 November, 1940 (SAT): Cafe Rouge, Hotel Pennsylvania,
                        New York City, N.Y.
                        NBC-Blue 12:05-12:30 A.M.   EST.

        G.M.P.R. show that there was one sustaining
        program this evening from the Hotel Pennsylvania.

(Broadcast continued on next page)

Moonlight Serenade (Theme)
Yes, My Darling Daughter
A Million Dreams Ago

E4VP 8201   ~~Vi LPT 6701,~~ Vi EPOT 6701 (947-0180), HMV RLS 598,
          ~~RCA G EPOT-6701~~
       (2:05) ~~Isn't That Just Like Love~~ (arr BF)-voc
             Jack Lathrop
             From the Paramount film "Love Thy
             Neighbor"
             (Johnny Burke-Jimmy Van Heusen)
             Ts, Beneke

      ~~(3:42)~~ *Tiger Rag* (arr ED)
             (Tony Sbarbaro-Eddie Edwards-Henry
             Ragas-Larry Shields-Nick LaRocca-
             Harry DeCosta)
             Ts, Klink; tpt, May; ts, Beneke;
             d, Purtill
        A Handful Of Stars
        Anvil Chorus
        Slumber Song (Theme)

18 November, 1940 (MON)

       Glenn Miller and His Orchestra played at Manhattan
Center, New York City, for local 802's medical
fund along with Goodman, Lunceford, Basie,etc.
Each band performed for 15 minutes. The entire
show was broadcast over WNEW and Martin Block
emceed the show. Over 6,000 attended. "Almost
as riotous an ovation greeted Glenn Miller's boys
when they finished their stint, a session which
featured some brilliant trumpeting by Bill May."
(Metronome Dec. 1940) The Miller band played at
2:30 A.M. (G.M.D.)

18 November, 1940 (MON): Cafe Rouge, Hotel Pennsylvania,
                          New York City, N.Y.
                          NBC-Blue

       G.M.P.R. show that there was one sustaining
program this evening from the Hotel Pennsylvania.

           Moonlight Serenade (Theme)
           Solid As A Stonewall, Jackson
           Along The Santa Fe Trail

(Broadcast continued on next page)

PPRM-5333   Vi LPM/LSP-2767 (Vi LPM/LSP-6101).RCA RD/SF-7610,
               RCA Au LPM 2767
          (2:13) Yes, My Darling Daughter (arr JG)-voc
                  Marion Hutton and The Band
                  (Jack Lawrence)
                  Ts, Klink

E4VP 8201   Vi LPT 6701, Vi EPOT 6701 (947-0179), HMV RLS 598,
               Vi SPA-7-4, RCA G EPOT-6701
          (3:58) In A Sentimental Mood (arr JG)
                  (Manny Kurtz-Irving Mills-Duke
                  Ellington)
                  Ts, Beneke; open tpt, Best; muted
                  tpt, May?

PPRM-5337   Vi LPM/LSP-2768 (Vi LPM/LSP-6101), RCA RD/SF-7611,
               RCA Au LPM 2768
          (2:55) Beat Me Daddy, Eight To A Bar-voc Jack
                  Lathrop and The Band
                  (Don Raye-Hughie Prince-Eleanore Sheehy)
                  P, MacGregor; clt, Caceres; p, MacGregor

PPRM-5333   Vi LPM/LSP-2767 (Vi LPM/LSP-6101), RCA RD/SF-7610,
               RCA Au LPM 2767
          (2:30) A Nightingale Sang In Berkeley Square
                  (arr BF)-voc Ray Eberle
                  From the London Musical Success "New
                  Faces"
                  (Eric Maschwitz-Manning Sherwin)
                  Clt, ?? (no saxophone solo)

PPRM-5337   Vi LPM/LSP-2768 (Vi LPM/LSP-6101), RCA RD/SF-7611,
               RCA Au LPM 2768
          (1:49) You've Got Me This Way (arr JG)-voc
                  Marion Hutton
                  From the RKO film "You'll Find Out"
                  (Johnny Mercer-Jimmy McHugh)

                  I Dreamt I Dwelt In Harlem

                  Slumber Song (Theme)

19 November, 1940 (TUES): New York City, N.Y. (CHESTERFIELD SHOW)
                CBS 10:00-10:15 P.M. EST.

      The announcer for this program is Larry Bruff.

V-4086 WR-   GMMS 106
          (0:31) Moonlight Serenade (Theme)
               (Mitchell Parish-Glenn Miller)

(Broadcast continued on next page)

V-4086 WR-   GMMS 106
    Int GM   (2:33) Five O'Clock Whistle (arr BF)-voc Marion
                          Hutton and The Band
                          (Kim Gannon-Joe Myrow-Gene Irwin)
                          Ts, Beneke

V-4086 WR-   GMMS 106
            (6:11) MEDLEY:
    Int GM   The Siren's Song (arr JG)
                    From the musical comedy "Leave It
                    To Jane"
                    (P.G. Wodehouse-Jerome Kern)
        Int GM   A Handful Of Stars (arr BF)-voc Ray Eberle
                    From the MGM film "Hullabaloo"
                    (Jack Lawrence-Ted Shapiro)
        Int GM   Love In Bloom (arr JG) (borrowed from Jack
                    Benny)
                    From the Paramount film "She Loves
                    Me Not"
                    (Leo Robin-Ralph Rainger)
                    P, MacGregor
            The Birth Of The Blues (arr JG)
                    From "George White's Scandals"
                    (B.G. De Sylva-Lew Brown)
                    Tpt, Best; ts, Beneke

V-4086 WR-   GMMS 106
            (3:03) Beat Me Daddy, Eight To A Bar-voc Jack
                    Lathrop and The Band
                    (Don Raye-Hughie Prince-Eleanore
                    Sheehy)
                    P, MacGregor; clt, Caceres;
                    p, MacGregor

V-4086 WR-   GMMS 106
            (0:11) Moonlight Serenade (Theme)
                    (Mitchell Parish-Glenn Miller)

        Note that the timings of the theme (opening and
        closing) are not complete due to their being
        edited on the transcription.

        On listening to the medley at RCA Victor it was
        noted that Larry Bruff's introduction to "The
        Birth Of The Blues" was edited on GMMS 106.

20 November, 1940 (WED): New York City, N.Y. (CHESTERFIELD SHOW)
CBS   10:00-10:15 P.M. EST.

Moonlight Serenade (Theme)
Jeannie With The Light Brown Hair

(Broadcast continued on next page)

Long Time No See, Baby
Is This Our Last Night Together (arr BF)-
     voc Ray Eberle
     (Pauline Boshard)
I Dreamt I Dwelt In Harlem
Moonlight Serenade (Theme)

20 November, 1940 (WED): Cafe Rouge, Hotel Pennsylvania,
     New York City, N.Y.
     NBC-Blue 11:30-12:00 Midnight EST.

G.M.P.R. show that there was one sustaining
program this evening from the Hotel Pennsylvania.

Lights Out! Hold Me Tight!
Do You Know Why
A Million Dreams Ago
Isn't That Just Like Love
St. Louis Blues
Oh So Good

This program was reviewed in the December, 1940
issue of Metronome and, although two other tunes
were mentioned, we believe that the above are
the tunes that were actually played. The rest of
the tunes on the program are unknown.

"Something is happening to lighten the Miller
music's tendency to heaviness. Maybe it's the
presence of ex-Charlie Barnet trumpeter Billy May,
for one thing.

The alternating between largo and molto
allegro tempos is likewise being modified, thus
giving the men more chance to unrap their feelings.
This was evidenced by Marion Hutton's easier-
voiced solo in Lights Out, Hold Me Tight, and by a
moderately paced Do You Know Why?, in which vocalist
Ray Eberle did not have to perform his usual
incredible feats of breathing. (i.e., Yester-
thought.)

Tex Beneke's tenor solos are the real boot in
the band. Whether Beneke soars out fast and fluid,
or persuades the notes along in that soft, full
tone of his, he tells the story right. Especially
noteworthy were his choruses on A Million Dreams
Ago, Isn't That Just Like Love,and St. Louis Blues.

Whereas St. Louis exhibited the new lighter
touch, with beautiful sax team phrasing and a clean
MacGregor piano chorus, the arrangement would have

(Continued on next page)

had more punch had it been cut in half. The
rhythm was in this, as in most tunes, not
under the band. That may explain the frequent
descent of numbers like Oh, So Good into mere
instrumental calisthenics, instead of ascent
into a rhythmic ride.

Maurice Purtill's drumming has too often
the effect of bullets spurting from a machine-
gun.

Size alone, without taking into account
smoothness of performance and sophistication
of arrangements, would make the Miller band
impressive. However, size and performance do
not live music make, necessarily. Glenn's is
an appeal to the head rather than to the heart
of the listener.

As an aggregation that has been rehearsed
until every bar of every tune is perfect, the
Miller men probably have no rivals. For
precision, attack, shading, and blend, the
band cannot be topped.

But is letter-perfect playing worth the
inevitable sacrifice of natural feeling?--LEE"

21 November, 1940 (THUR): New York City, N.Y. (CHESTERFIELD SHOW)
CBS   10:00-10:15 P.M. EST

> *Moonlight Serenade (Theme)*
> *In A Sentimental Mood*
> *Fresh As A Daisy*
> *Yesterthoughts*
> *Watcha Know Joe*
> *Moonlight Serenade (Theme)*

22 November, 1940 (FRI): Victor Studios, New York City, New York

Same personnel as for November 4th.

057661-1   BB 11063-B
A Stone's Throw From Heaven (arr BF)-voc Ray Eberle
(Bob Ray-Jan Burton-Irving Green)
Ts, Beneke

057662-1   Vi 20-1600-A
Helpless (arr JG)-voc Ray Eberle
(Jack Lathrop)

(Session continued on next page)

057663-1   Vi 20-1563-B, HMV DLP 1122
            Long Time No See, Baby (arr JG)-voc Marion Hutton
                (Jack Lathrop)
                D, Purtill; ts, Beneke

057664-1   BB 11020-B
            You Are The One (arr BF)-voc Ray Eberle
                (Carroll Carroll-John Scott Trotter)

            The two Victor issues were released some time
            during 1943-44. Usually records were released
            about two months after they were recorded. The
            reason for the late release is unknown and these
            two tunes may have remained unissued if Glenn
            Miller had not disbanded his orchestra in
            September, 1942.

            "Long Time No See, Baby" 2 takes; all other
            tunes 1 take. (RCA Victor)
            This session lasted from 1:30 P.M. to 4:30 P.M.
            (RCA Victor)

22 November, 1940 (FRI): Cafe Rouge, Hotel Pennsylvania,
                         New York City, N.Y.
                         NBC-Red 12:30-12:57 A.M. EST.

            G.M.P.R. show that there was one sustaining
            program this evening from the Hotel Pennsylvania.

                Moonlight Serenade (Theme)
                Pennsylvania Six-Five Thousand

E4VP 8201   Vi LPT 6701, Vi EPOT 6701 (947-0178), HMV RLS 598,
            RCA G EPOT-6701
            (3:00) Along The Santa Fe Trail-voc Ray Eberle
                From the Warner Bros. film "Along The
                Santa Fe Trail"
                (Al Dubin-Edwina Coolidge-Will Grosz)

                Yes, My Darling Daughter
                I'd Know You Anywhere
                Anvil Chorus
                A Nightingale Sang In Berkeley Square
                Down For The Count
                Slumber Song (Theme)

23 November, 1940 (SAT): Cafe Rouge, Hotel Pennsylvania,
New York City, N.Y.
NBC-Blue 12:05-12:30 A.M. EST.

G.M.P.R. show that there was one sustaining
program this evening from the Hotel Pennsylvania.

Moonlight Serenade (Theme)
Little Brown Jug
Our Love Affair

PPRM-5338   Vi LPM/LSP 2768 (Vi LPM/LSP 6101), RCA RD/SF-7611,
                RCA Au LPM 2768
                (2:16) Lights Out! Hold Me Tight! (arr BM)-voc
                        Marion Hutton
                        From the University of Pennsylvania
                        Mask and Wig Club Revue
                        (Bickley Reichner-Clay Boland)
                        Ts, Klink

E4VP 8202   Vi LPT 6701, Vi EPOT 6701 (947-0182), HMV RLS 598,
                RCA G-EPOT-6701
                (2:32) A Million Dreams Ago (arr BF)-voc Ray Eberle
                        (Lew Quadling-Eddy Howard-Dick Jurgens)
                        Ts, Beneke

                Limehouse Blues
                Do You Know Why
                I Dreamt I Dwelt In Harlem
                Slumber Song (Theme)

25 November, 1940 (MON): Cafe Rouge, Hotel Pennsylvania,
New York City, N.Y.
NBC-Blue

G.M.P.R. show that there was one sustaining
program this evening from the Hotel Pennsylvania.

November, 1940

Jack Lathrop married Barbara Jane Mitchell,
a secretary. (DB-Dec. 1, 1940)

26 November, 1940 (TUES): New York City, N.Y. (CHESTERFIELD SHOW)
CBS 10:00-10:15 P.M. EST.

Moonlight Serenade (Theme)
Drink To Me Only With Thine Eyes
Dig It

(Broadcast continued on next page)

A Nightingale Sang In Berkeley Square
Oh So Good
Moonlight Serenade (Theme)

27 November, 1940 (WED): New York City, N.Y. (CHESTERFIELD SHOW)
CBS 10:00-10:15 P.M. EST.

The announcer for this program is Paul Douglas.

(0:04) *Moonlight Serenade* (Theme)
        (Mitchell Parish-Glenn Miller)
(2:19) *Slumber Song* (arr BF)
        (Saul Tepper-John Chalmers MacGregor)
        Ts, Beneke
Lights Out! Hold Me Tight!
Along The Santa Fe Trail
(3:27) *Tiger Rag* (arr ED)
        (Tony Sbarbaro-Eddie Edwards-Henry
        Ragas-Larry Shields-Nick LaRocca-
        Harry DeCosta)
        Ts, Klink; tpt, May; ts, Beneke;
        d, Purtill
(0:43) *Moonlight Serenade* (Theme)
        (Mitchell Parish-Glenn Miller)

27 November, 1940 (WED): Cafe Rouge, Hotel Pennsylvania,
New York City, N.Y.
NBC-Blue 11:36-12:00 Midnight EST.

G.M.P.R. show that there was one sustaining
program this evening from the Hotel Pennsylvania.

(2:07) *Down For The Count* (arr BF)
        (Bill Finegan)
        Tpt, Best; ts, Beneke; d, Purtill
(3:02) *When The Swallows Come Back To Capistrano*
        (arr BF)-voc Ray Eberle
        (Leon Rene)
(3:12) *Tiger Rag* (arr ED)
        (Tony Sbarbaro-Eddie Edwards-Henry
        Ragas-Larry Shields-Nick LaRocca-
        Henry DeCosta)
        Ts, Klink; tpt, May; ts, Beneke;
        d, Purtill
(2:55) *Do You Know Why* (arr BF)-voc Ray Eberle
        From the Paramount film "Love Thy
        Neighbor"
        (Johnny Burke-Jimmy Van Heusen)

(Broadcast continued on next page)

(2:48) *Limehouse Blues* (arr JG)
   (Douglas Furber-Philip Braham)
   Tpt, Best; ts, Beneke; clt, Caceres;
   d, Purtill; ts, Beneke; d, Purtill
(2:03) *Slumber Song* (Theme)
   (Saul Tepper-John Chalmers MacGregor)
   Ts, Beneke

28 November, 1940 (THUR): New York City, N.Y. (CHESTERFIELD SHOW)
     CBS 10:00-10:15 P.M. EST.

    Moonlight Serenade (Theme)
    Yes, My Darling Daughter

E3VP 5240 Vi LPT 6700, Vi EPNT 6700 (947-0129), Vi SPD-18
     (599-9108), HMV RLS 599, RCA G LPT 6700
   (4:25) MEDLEY:
   Int GM Moon Over Miami (arr JG)
       (Edgar Leslie-Joe Burke)
       Ts, Beneke
   Int GM A Million Dreams Ago (arr BF)-voc
       Ray Eberle
       (Lew Quadling-Eddy Howard-Dick Jurgens)
   Int GM Aloha (arr JG)(borrowed from Hawaii)
       (Princess Liliuokalani)

    The Honolulu Blues

    Everybody Loves My Baby
    Moonlight Serenade (Theme)

On Vi LPT 6700 the medley was incorrectly listed
as being broadcast on January 29, 1940. The
timing for this medley does not include "The
Honolulu Blues" as it was not issued by RCA
Victor.

Glenn Miller and His Orchestra played a benefit
at Madison Square Garden, New York City, New
York, at 10:30 P.M. (G.M.D.)

29 November, 1940 (Fri): Cafe Rouge, Hotel Pennsylvania,
      New York City, N.Y.
      NBC-Red 12:30-12:57 A.M. EST.

   G.M.P.R. show that there was one sustaining
   program this evening from the Hotel Pennsylvania.

(Broadcast continued on next page)

(4:08) My Blue Heaven (arr JG)
(George Whiting-Walter Adamson)
Tbn, Miller; ts, Beneke; ts, Klink;
d, Purtill
(1:20) Slumber Song (Theme)
(Saul Tepper-John Chalmers MacGregor)

30 November, 1940 (SAT): Cafe Rouge, Hotel Pennsylvania,
New York City, N.Y.
NBC-Blue 12:05-12:30 A.M. EST.

G.M.P.R. show that there was one sustaining
program this evening from the Hotel Pennsylvania.

December, 1940

"Starting Dec. 1, only non-ASCAP music may
be played on sustaining remotes over the three
major networks. Although the contract with ASCAP
doesn't expire until Dec. 31, the webs have
placed the demand on orchestras heard over their
systems a month in advance.

This will enable the broadcasters to experi-
ment with a complete BMI program schedule and try
to get the public used to non-ASCAP music even
before the deadline.

Last minute preparations are being made
among all bandleaders, whose themes belong in the
ASCAP files, to change their signatures. Some
bands already have introduced their new themes
over the air.

Glenn Miller is using his own composition,
"Slumber Song," instead of "Moonlight Serenade."
(Metronome--Dec., 1940)

It must be noted that on the back of the jacket
for LPM-2767 "Slumber Song" is shown as an ASCAP
tune. Perhaps it was a BMI tune at the time.

Our first "official" record of "Slumber Song" being
used as a closing theme is the "Cafe Rouge" broadcast of October 12th, 1940. It would appear from
the preceeding article that as of December 1st
"Slumber Song" was used as the opening and closing
theme on the sustaining shows from the "Cafe
Rouge" and this is further borne out by the
December 7th program. However, on the commercial

(Continued on next page)

show for Chesterfield, we have aircheck evidence
that, as late as December 18th, Miller was using
"Moonlight Serenade" as his theme and presume
that he continued to use it as his theme right
up to and including December 31st.

The dispute between the broadcasters and ASCAP
(American Society of Composers, Authors and
Publishers) was brought about by the fact that
ASCAP wanted to charge a higher fee for the
privilege of playing music in the catalogs con-
trolled by the performance-rights society. Radio
refused to pay, and beginning at midnight on
December 31, 1940, it became an infringement for
any radio station to broadcast any ASCAP music
over American air-waves. Fortunately for radio,
the National Association of Broadcasters had for-
seen this problem and had begun preliminary meetings starting as early as 1938. The groundwork
was sketched for the formation of a rival
performance-rights society in the likely event that
ASCAP would present its outrageous demands for more
money before the expiration of contracts on
December 31, 1940. On October 14, 1939, Broadcast
Music, Inc. (BMI), was organized and from the
spring of 1940 on until the deadline in December
BMI songs were aired throughout each broadcast,
skipping in and out among new and old ASCAP tunes.
And so, until a truce was declared 10 months after
the December 31st deadline, the American public
heard music through BMI, SESAC and public-domain
compositions (such as "Jeannie With The Light Brown
Hair").

Some time in December Glenn Miller signed with 20th
Century-Fox and the earliest reference to this
appeared in the December 15th issue of Down Beat:
"New York--Glenn Miller and his band have been
signed by 20th Century-Fox to appear in a coming
movie pic which will star Sonja Henie, ice queen.
Miller and crew are to receive a reported $100,000
for its work, which will take eight weeks, it was
said.

Deal was set by General Amusement Corp., with
Mike Nidorf in charge of dickering. Miller has
long been rumored for movie work but he was never
satisfied with offers until the Henie pic deal was
brought to a head. Miller, now at Hotel Pennsylvania, leaves there Jan. 19 and will take to the

(Continued on next page)

road heading west, winding up in Hollywood in the
early spring. Miller is holding the period of
March 1 to April 15 wide open for his film work,
which will be the first he has done."

1 December, 1940 (SUN): New York City, New York

> *Lights Out! Hold Me Tight!*
> *In The Mood*

This listing was supplied to us by the Miller
Estate but since this is a Sunday date we believe
that the date is probably incorrect.

3 December, 1940 (TUES): New York City, N.Y. (CHESTERFIELD SHOW)
        CBS   10:00-10:15 P.M. EST.

> *Moonlight Serenade (Theme)*
> *Wham*
> *A Nightingale Sang In Berkeley Square*
> *Anvil Chorus*
> *Moonlight Serenade (Theme)*

4 December, 1940 (WED): New York City, N.Y. (CHESTERFIELD SHOW)
        CBS   10:00-10:15 P.M. EST.

The announcer for this program is Paul Douglas.

> *Moonlight Serenade (Theme)*
> *Long Time No See, Baby*
> {4:42} *MEDLEY:*
> > *Shine On, Harvest Moon (arr JG)*
> >   *From "The Follies of 1908"*
> >   *(Jack Norworth-Nora Bayes)*
> Int GM *Helpless (arr JG)-voc Ray Eberle*
> >   *(Jack Lathrop)*
> Int GM *Rose Room (borrowed from Phil Harris)*
> >   *(Harry Williams-Art Hickman)*
> >   *Tpt, Best; ts, Beneke*
> Int PD *Blue Moon*
> >   *(Lorenz Hart-Richard Rodgers)*

E2VL 4420   Vi LPT-30, Vi 42-0154 (Vi PT-39), Vi 27-0154
             (Vi WPT-39), Vi EPBT-3026 (947-0027),
             Vi LPT 6701, HMV RLS 598, Vi EPOT 6701
             (947-0188), Vi LPM-1189, Vi It LPM-10141,
             RCA F 430228, RCA G EPC-1189, RD 3/4-64,
             RCA G EPOT-6701, RCA G EPBT-3026, El WDLP

(Broadcast continued on next page)

                         1012, HMV DLP 1012, RCA Vi It LJ 50020,
                         RCA Au L 11021, RCA Vi It LPM 50020, HMVAu
                         ODLP 1012, RCA G LPT-30
        Int PD (2:46) Limehouse Blues (arr JG)
                         (Douglas Furber-Philip Braham)
                         Tpt, Best; ts, Beneke; clt, Caceres;
                         d, Purtill; ts, Beneke & Klink;
                         d, Purtill

                 (0:32) *Moonlight Serenade* (Theme)
                         (Mitchell Parish-Glenn Miller)

                 On Vi LPT 6701 "Limehouse Blues" was incorrectly
                 listed as being broadcast on March 27, 1942.

5 December, 1940 (THUR): New York City, N.Y. (CHESTERFIELD SHOW)
                 CBS   10:00-10:15 P.M. EST.

                         Moonlight Serenade (Theme)
                         Old Black Joe
                         Five O'Clock Whistle
                         Yesterthoughts
                         I Dreamt I Dwelt In Harlem
                         Moonlight Serenade (Theme)

5 December, 1940 (THUR)

                 G.M.P.R. for the week ending December 5th show
                 that Billy May arranged 2 originals, Nos. 505
                 (No title shown) and Nos. 510 (Measure For
                 Measure) in the books.

7 December, 1940 (SAT): Cafe Rouge, Hotel Pennsylvania,
                 New York City, N.Y.
                 NBC-Blue

PPRM-5333   Vi LPM/LSP 2767 (Vi LPM/LSP 6101), RCA RD/SF-7610,
                         RCA Au LPM 2767
                 (1:17) Slumber Song (Theme) (arr BF)
                         (Saul Tepper-John Chalmers MacGregor)

E4VP 8202   Vi LPT 6701, Vi EPOT 6701 (947-0182), HMV RLS 598,
                         RCA G EPOT-6701
                 (4:17) Daisy Mae (arr BM)
                         (Arletta May-Hal McIntyre)
                         Ts, Klink; tpt, May; as, Caceres

(Broadcast continued on next page)

PPRM-5337   Vi LPM/LSP 2768 (Vi LPM/LSP 6101), RCA RD/SF-7611,
                        RCA Au LPM 2768
                   (3:01) There I Go (arr JG)-voc Ray Eberle
                        (Hy Zaret-Irving Meiser)
                        Ts, Beneke

                   Song Of The Volga Boatmen

E4VP 8202   Vi LPT 6701, Vi EPOT 6701 (947-0183), HMV RLS 598,
                        RD 3/4-64, RCA G EPOT-6701
                   (3:25) Falling Leaves
                        (Mack David-Frankie Carle)
                        Ts, Beneke

                   Down For The Count
                   You Walk By
                   I Dreamt I Dwelt In Harlem
                   Slumber Song (Theme)

All of the issued tunes shown above were broadcast
on December 17th according to Victor. However,
December 17th is a Tuesday, and as far as we know,
the band did not broadcast from the "Cafe Rouge"
on that night during this period. Also note that
the announcer introduces the program as being "on
a Saturday evening". We have been supplied with
this list of tunes on this date by the Miller
Estate and presume that Victor's date is incorrect,
due perhaps to a typist error in adding a one before the seven.

A word or two needs to be said about the tune
"Daisy Mae". Arletta May, who is listed as one of
the composers, is Billy May's wife, but we suspect
that Billy May is in fact the composer as well as
the arranger. When Hal McIntyre left the Miller
band in October, 1941, to go on his own, Miller
gave McIntyre several of his band's arrangements.
"Daisy Mae" was one of those tunes and McIntyre
recorded it later on for Victor.

This is the first indication that we have that
"Slumber Song" was being used as the opening theme
on the "Cafe Rouge" broadcasts.

10 December, 1940 (TUES): New York City, N.Y. (CHESTERFIELD SHOW)
CBS   10:00-10:15 P.M. EST.

                   Moonlight Serenade (Theme)
                   Lights Out! Hold Me Tight!

(Broadcast continued on next page)

        MEDLEY:
          Isn't It Romantic?
          Along The Santa Fe Trail
          Blue Prelude
        Bugle Call Rag
        Moonlight Serenade (Theme)

11 December, 1940 (WED): *New York City, N.Y.* (CHESTERFIELD SHOW)
             CBS   10:00-10:15 P.M. EST.

        Moonlight Serenade (Theme)
        In A Sentimental Mood
        Yes, My Darling Daughter
        Do You Know Why
        Watcha Know Joe
        Moonlight Serenade (Theme)

12 December, 1940 (THUR): *New York City, N.Y.* (CHESTERFIELD SHOW)
             CBS   10:00-10:15 P.M. EST.

        Moonlight Serenade (Theme)
        Danny Boy
   (2:49) *Dig It* (arr JG)-voc Tex Beneke and
            Marion Hutton
            (Hal Borne-Johnny Mercer)
            Tpt, May
   (0:04) *A Handful Of Stars* (arr BF)-voc Ray Eberle
            From the MGM film "Hullabaloo"
            (Jack Lawrence-Ted Shapiro)
        St. Louis Blues
        Moonlight Serenade (Theme)

13 December, 1940 (FRI): Victor Studios, New York City, New York

     Same personnel as for November 4th.

058172-1   BB 10982-A, HMV BD 5671, HMV MH 183, HMVAu EA-2911,
             Vi 20-1495, ViJ 1082, RCA RCX 1062, Vi 447-
             0034, Vi LPT-3002, Vi EPBT-3002 (947-0038),
             Vi EPA-5149, HMV DLP 1081, Vi SP-33-90,
             Vi LPM-1190, RD 3/4-64, Vi EPB-1190 (547-
             0828), Vi LPM/LSP-3377, Vi TP3-5044, RCA
             Int. B-21040, RCA Int. T-21040, Vi P8S-5061,
             RCA G (Teldec) LPM-1190, RCA G (Teldec)
             LPM/LSP-3377, HMVIr I.P. 1093, AFRS G.I. Jive
             H-12-761, AFRS G.I. Jive H-12-865, RCA G
             LPT-3002, RCA Br. GM-1, Vi VPM-6019, RCA G
             Cas 10231, RCA Br. RD-8094 (unissued)

(Session continued on next page)

Anvil Chorus (Part 1) (arr JG)
　　From "Il Trovatore"
　　(Guiseppe Verdi)
　　Ts, Beneke; tpt, May; d, Purtill

058173-1　　BB 10982-B, HMV BD 5671, HMV MH 183, HMVAu EA-2911,
　　　　　　Vi 20-1495, ViJ 1082, RCA RCX 1062, Vi 447-
　　　　　　0034, Vi LPT-3002, Vi EPBT-3002 (947-0038),
　　　　　　Vi EPA-5149, HMV DLP 1081, Vi SP-33-90, Vi LPM-
　　　　　　1190, RD 3/4-64, Vi EPB-1190 (547-0828), Vi
　　　　　　LPM/LSP-3377, Vi TP3-5044, RCA Int. B-21040,
　　　　　　RCA Int. T-21040, Vi P8S-5061, RCA G(Teldec)
　　　　　　LPM-1190, RCA G(Teldec) LPM/LSP-3377, HMVIr I.P.
　　　　　　1093, RCA G LPT-3002, RCA Br. GM-1, RCA Br. RD-
　　　　　　8094, Vi VPM-6019, RCA G Cas 10231
Anvil Chorus (Part 2) (arr JG)
　　From "Il Trovatore"
　　"Guiseppe Verdi)
　　D, Purtill; clt, Caceres; tpt, May

058173-2　　BB 10982-B (Canadian Gold Label-not on all)
Anvil Chorus (Part 2) (arr JG)
　　From "Il Trovatore"
　　(Guiseppe Verdi)
　　D, Purtill; clt, Caceres; tpt, May

058174-1　　BB 10994-A, HMV BD 5678, HMVSw JK-2323, ViJ 1099,
　　　　　　RD 3/4-64, ViI EPA-30-078, HMVIn BD 5678
Frenesi (arr BF)
　　(Ray Charles-S.K. Russell-Albert Dominguez)
　　Ts, Beneke; tpt, Best; muted tpt, ??

Both tunes 2 takes. (RCA Victor)
This session lasted from 1:30 P.M. to 5:50 P.M.
(RCA Victor)

The original 78 of "Anvil Chorus" was a 2-sided
10" disc while the later EP & LP reissues have
made it into a continuous number. The label on
the 78 issue erroneously shows Glenn Miller as
the arranger.
　　"Glenn Miller, after three previous attempts
which left him dissatisfied, finally got his two-
sided, six minute jump version of The Anvil Chorus
on records. The day he made it was Friday, the
13th!" (DB, Jan. 1, 1941) Some of the takes
mentioned in this article may have been destroyed.
The apparent difference on the Canadian issue is
the trumpet mistake near the end of Part 2.

An interesting point about the lyricist-composer
credits for "Frenesi" is that Vi LPT 6701 credits

(Continued on next page)

Alberto Dominguez-Leonard Whitcup which is different from the credits on the Bluebird issue.
Variety Music Cavalcade, a book published in 1952,
gives the following information: Spanish words and
music, Albert Dominguez. English words, Ray
Charles and S.K. Russell. On the other hand, a
book published in 1948, A History of Popular Music
in America, credits Alberto Dominguez with Spanish
words and music but mentions "an English version
by Leonard Whitcup".

16 December, 1940 (MON)

G.M.P.R. shows that Glenn Miller arranged "Let's
Conga Gate" on this date.

17 December, 1940 (TUES): New York City, N.Y. (CHESTERFIELD SHOW)
CBS   10:00-10:15 P.M. EST.

The announcer on this program is Paul Douglas.

Moonlight Serenade (Theme)
Star Dust

E3VP 5254   Vi LPT 6700, Vi EPNT 6700 (947-0125), Vi SPD-18
(599-9106), HMV RLS 599, RCA G
LPT 6700
(2:24) Fresh As A Daisy (arr JG)-voc Marion Hutton,
Jack Lathrop, Tex Beneke (Glenn Miller
and Paul Douglas)
From the musical production "Panama
Hattie"
(Cole Porter)

The Mem'ry Of A Rose
(2:40) *On Brave Old Army Team (arr JG)*
West Point Football Song
(Philip Egner)
D, Purtill; ts, Klink; tpt, Best;
d, Purtill; clt, Caceres
(0:21) *Moonlight Serenade (Theme)*
(Mitchell Parish-Glenn Miller)

On "Fresh As A Daisy" it is Glenn Miller and Paul
Douglas who say: "Mild as a Chesterfield, they
sure taste great!" This comment was not in the
original recording. The introduction to this tune
has been edited due to Miller introducing the title
after the song had begun.

18 December, 1940 (WED): New York City, N.Y.   (CHESTERFIELD SHOW)
CBS   10:00-10:15 P.M. EST.

The announcer for this program is Paul Douglas.

(0:08) Moonlight Serenade (Theme)
(Mitchell Parish-Glenn Miller)

E1LVB 3200   Vi LPT-16, Vi 42-0108 (Vi PT-25), Vi 27-0108
(Vi WPT-25), Vi EPBT-3025 (947-0024),
Vi EPA-729, Vi LPM-1193, Vi EPB-1193 (547-
0822), Vi TP3-5020, Vi It LPM-10141, RCA
Int. B-21032, RCA Int. T-21032, RCA G LPT
16, RCA G LPM-1193, RCA Vi It LJ 50020,
RCA Vi It LPM 50020
(2:14) Goin' Home
Adapted from the Largo of Anton
Dvorak's "New World Symphony"
(William Arms Fisher)

Keep An Eye On Your Heart
Our Love Affair
Tuxedo Junction
Moonlight Serenade (Theme)

19 December, 1940 (THUR): New York City, N.Y.   (CHESTERFIELD SHOW)
CBS   10:00-10:15 P.M. EST.

The announcer for this program is Paul Douglas.

Moonlight Serenade (Theme)
Wham

K2PP-0044   Vi LPM-6100, RCA RD 27146, RCA G LPM-6100,
RCA Au L 11024
(3:25) MEDLEY:
Int GM Sweet Leilani
From the Paramount film "Waikiki
Wedding"
(Harry Owens)
Int GM Yesterthoughts (arr BF)-voc Ray Eberle
(Stanley Adams-Victor Herbert)
Smoke Rings (borrowed from Glen Gray)
(Gene Gifford-Ned Washington)
E3VP 5245   Vi LPT 6700, Vi EPNT 6700 (947-0117), Vi SPD-18
(599-9105), HMV RLS 599, RCA G LPT-6700
(1:41) Under A Blanket Of Blue
(Marty Symes-Al. J. Neiburg-Jerry
Levinson)
Ts, Beneke

(Broadcast continued on next page)

In The Mood
Moonlight Serenade (Theme)

The introduction of "Smoke Rings" by Paul Douglas
has been edited in Vi LPM-6100 etc. "Under A
Blanket Of Blue" was issued independently from
the rest of the medley.

*19 December, 1940 (THUR): Cafe Rouge, Hotel Pennsylvania,
New York City, N.Y.*

We suspect that this date may be incorrect as it
does not appear that Miller was broadcasting from
the Cafe Rouge during this period.

*(2:57) A Stone's Throw From Heaven (arr BF)-voc
Ray Eberle
(Bob Ray-Jay Burton-Irving Green)
Ts, Beneke*

*20 December, 1940 (FRI): Cafe Rouge, Hotel Pennsylvania,
New York City, N.Y.
NBC-Blue*

*(4:30) Anvil Chorus (arr JG)
From "Il Trovatore"
(Guiseppe Verdi)
Ts, Beneke; tpt, May; d, Purtill;
(Note: no clarinet solo at this point);
tpt, May*

The remainder of the tunes played on this program
are unknown.

*21 December, 1940 (SAT): Cafe Rouge, Hotel Pennsylvania,
New York City, N.Y.
NBC-Blue 12:05-12:30 A.M.*

*Slumber Song (Theme)
Daisy Mae
Helpless
Song Of The Volga Boatmen
Falling Leaves
Slumber Song*

E4VP 8202   Vi LPT 6701, Vi EPOT 6701 (947-0181), HMV RLS 598,
RCA G EPOT-6701

(Broadcast continued on next page)

Chesterfield program in New York, December 1940. Paul Douglas is standing in front of the band. Trigger Alpert is on bass, Jack Lathrop is on guitar. (*Photo courtesy Glenn Miller Estate*)

Latin-American number at Cafe Rouge, November 1940–January 1941. Left to right, front row: Eberle, May, Klink, Schwartz, Lathrop, Hutton, Caceres, McIntyre. Middle row: Tanner, Priddy, D'Annolfo, Miller. Back row: Best, Anthony (hidden), Mc-Mickle, Purtill, Alpert. (*Photo courtesy Glenn Miller Estate*)

(2:37) Are You Jumpin' Jack (arr BF)
    (Bill Finegan)
    Ts, Beneke; tpt, May; tbn, Miller;
    as, Caceres

I Do, Do You?
Slumber Song (Theme)

The "Slumber Song" which appears midway in this
program may have been a theme to end the first
part of the program.

24 December, 1940 (TUES): New York City, N.Y. (CHESTERFIELD SHOW)
CBS 10:00-10:15 P.M. EST.

    Moonlight Serenade (Theme)
    Beat Me Daddy, Eight To A Bar
    Along The Santa Fe Trail

K2PP-0047   Vi LPM-6100, RCA RD 27147, RCA G LPM-6100, RCA Au
    L 11025
    (2:41) Dig It (arr JG)-voc Tex Beneke and
    Marion Hutton
    (Hal Borne-Johnny Mercer)
    Tpt, May

    Farewell Blues
    Moonlight Serenade (Theme)

25 December, 1940 (WED): New York City, N.Y. (CHESTERFIELD SHOW)
CBS 10:00-10:15 P.M. EST.

    Moonlight Serenade (Theme)
    Falling Leaves
    Five O'Clock Whistle
    Do You Know Why
    Pennsylvania Six-Five Thousand
    Moonlight Serenade (Theme)

26 December, 1940 (THUR): New York City, N.Y. (CHESTERFIELD SHOW)
CBS 10:00-10:15 P.M. EST.

The announcer for this program is Paul Douglas.

    Moonlight Serenade (Theme)
    Little Brown Jug

(Broadcast continued on next page)

```
        +4:40+ MEDLEY:
        Int GM   You Tell Me Your Dream (I Had A Dream, Dear)
                         (arr JG)
                         (Seymour A. Rice-Al H. Brown-Charles N.
                         Daniels)
        Int GM   A Nightingale Sang In Berkeley Square
                         (arr BF)-voc Ray Eberle
                         From the London Musical Success
                         "New Faces"
                         (Eric Maschwitz-Manning Sherwin)
        Int PD   Sleep (arr JG) (borrowed from Fred Waring)
                         (Earl Lebieg)
                         Whistle by ?
                 Alice Blue Gown (arr JG)
                 Yes, My Darling Daughter
                 Moonlight Serenade (Theme)
```

The timing for this medley does not include
"Alice Blue Gown".

26 December, 1940 (THUR)

G.M.P.R. for the week ending December 26th show that
Billy May arranged "Swingin' At The Seance".

27 December, 1940 (FRI): Victor Studios, New York City, New York

Same personnel as for November 4th.

058805-1   BB 11011-A
             The Mem'ry Of A Rose-voc Ray Eberle
                 (Jimmy Kennedy-Richard Young)

058806-1   BB 11020-A
             I Do, Do You? (Do You Believe In Love) (arr BF)-
                 voc Ray Eberle
                 (Lew Quadling)
                 Ts, Beneke

058807-1   BB 11029-B, HMV MH 102, HMVSw JK-2324
             Chapel In The Valley-voc Ray Eberle
                 (Leon Rene-Johnny Lange-Lew Porter)

058808-1   BB 11011-B, HMVAu EA-3556
             Prairieland Lulluby (arr BF)-voc Ray Eberle
                 From the Paramount film "Arizona Sketches"
                 (Frank Loesser-Victor Young)

             All tunes 1 take. (RCA Victor)
             This session lasted from 1:00 P.M. to 4:00 P.M.
             (RCA Victor)

27 December, 1940 (FRI): Cafe Rouge, Hotel Pennsylvania,
New York City, N.Y.
NBC-Blue 12:05-12:30 A.M.

28 December, 1940 (SAT): Cafe Rouge, Hotel Pennsylvania,
New York City, N.Y.
NBC-Blue 12:05-12:30 A.M.

E4VP 8202   Vi LPT 6701, Vi EPOT (947-0181). HMV RLS 598, RCA
G(Teldec) EPOT-6701, AFRS "America's Pop
Music" 72
    (3:25) You Walk By-Ray Eberle
(Ben Raleigh-Bernie Wayne)

E4VP 8201   Vi LPT 6701, Vi EPOT 6701 (947-0180), HMV RLS 598,
RCA G(Teldec) EPOT-6701
    (4:48) I Dreamt I Dwelt In Harlem (arr JG)
(Robert Wright-Ben Smith-Leonard Ware-
Jerry Gray)
Ts, Klink; tpt, May; tbn, Miller;
b, Albert; clt, Caceres; p, MacGregor;
muted tpt, May

Since we only have the two tunes listed for this
date we suspect that these two tunes are from the
December 7th broadcast.

30 December, 1940 (MON): Cafe Rouge, Hotel Pennsylvania,
New York City, N.Y.
NBC-Blue 12:05-12:30 A.M.

31 December, 1940 (TUES): New York City, N.Y. (CHESTERFIELD SHOW)
CBS 10:00-10:15 P.M.

The announcer for this program is Paul Douglas.

Moonlight Serenade (Theme)
The Mem'ry Of A Rose-voc RE
Lights Out! Hold Me Tight!
Prairieland Lullaby-voc RE
Anchors Aweigh
Moonlight Serenade (Theme)

January 1941

"Glenn Miller intends using Dorothy Claire
in place of Marion Hutton, who is retiring to a
life of domesticity as Mrs. Jack Philbin.
Glenn's hiring of the brilliant, young
songstress, has its complications, however. One
is her still being bound by a three-year contract
to Bobby Byrne, with whose band she has been
singing.
Miss Hutton, who is expecting an heir, was
to have remained with the band a while longer,
but a gossip columnist's ill-timed scoop made it
impossible for her to continue comfortably."
(Metronome--Jan., 1941).

Later Byrne sued Miller: "Charging Glenn Miller
with 'conspiracy, connivance, coercion and
intimidation,' representatives of Bobby Byrne,
young trombone-playing leader, last week filed
suit for $25,000 against Miller, whose band is
about to wind up a long run at Hotel Pennsylvania.
Miller was said to have offered Claire $250
a week. She's been getting $75 with Byrne, plus
evening clothes, extra for recordings and extras
for special broadcasts. David Mackay, Miller's
attorney, declared Claire's contract with Byrne
'didn't mean a thing' because she is under age.
'Therefore any contract she has entered into
isn't binding in the eyes of the law,' said he.
Court hearing on the suit is expected later this
month. Both Miller and Byrne are booked by
General Amusement Corp." (DB--Jan. 15, 1941).

"Glenn Miller signed a new 3-year contract
with RCA-Victor which will bring Miller $750 a
side($1500 a record) guarantee against an indivi-
dual record sale royalty. The new agreement--by
far the 'fattest' record contract ever signed--
is more than double the terms of Miller's old
contract." (DB--Feb. 1, 1941)

"Mutual Music Society, Inc., publishers of
Glenn Miller's original songs and copyrighted
arrangements of public domain songs, has entered
into a contract with BMI for the next three years.
Action means that Miller's Slumber Song, Are You
Rusticating, Daisy May, Are You Jumpin', Jack and
Down For The Count, among others, may be performed
over the radio networks. The society will be paid
2 cents per performance per station. Mutual is
Miller's own firm." (DB--Feb. 1, 1941). As

(Continued on next page)

previously mentioned, "Slumber Song" was an ASCAP song and this "contract" enabled Glenn to use it as his theme during the ban on ASCAP music.

1 January, 1941 (WED): New York City, N.Y. (CHESTERFIELD SHOW)
CBS   10:00-10:15 P.M. EST.

> *Slumber Song (Theme)*
> *Frenesi*

WPRS-0975   Vi LSP-3981, RCA Br RD/SF-7982
(2:07) Keep An Eye On Your Heart (arr JG)-voc
> Marion Hutton
> (Henry Manners-Milton Leeds-Shirl)
> Ts, Klink

> *A Stone's Throw From Heaven*
> *Song Of The Volga Boatmen*
> *Slumber Song (Theme)*

1 January, 1941 (WED)-12 March, 1942 (THUR): (CHESTERFIELD SHOWS)

> We have one GMMS tune that we were unable to find a date, but since it is from the Chesterfield material it must be from the period shown above.

V-4086 WR-1028 GMMS 39/87, GMMS 49/97
(3:29) Song Of The Volga Boatmen (arr BF)
> (Russian Folk Song)
> Muted tpt, May; as, Caceres; ts,
> Beneke; tpt, ??

1 January, 1941 (WED): Cafe Rouge, Hotel Pennsylvania,
New York City, N.Y.
NBC-Blue 12:05-12:30 A.M.

2 January, 1941 (THUR): New York City, N.Y. (CHESTERFIELD SHOW)
CBS   10:00-10:15 P.M. EST.

> *The announcer for this program is Paul Douglas.*

> *Slumber Song (Theme)*
> *Swingin' At The Seance*
> *The Morning After*
> *Anvil Chorus*
> *Slumber Song (Theme)*

2 January, 1941 (THUR)

G.M.P.R. for the week ending January 2nd show
that Glenn Miller arranged "Let's Conga Gate"
and Billy May arranged "Ida".

4 January, 1941 (SAT): Cafe Rouge, Hotel Pennsylvania,
                       New York City, N.Y.
                       NBC-Blue 12:05-12:30 A.M.

G.M.P.R. show that there was one sustaining
program this evening from the Hotel Pennsylvania.

6 January, 1941 (MON): Cafe Rouge, Hotel Pennsylvania,
                       New York City, N.Y.
                       NBC-Blue 12:05-12:30 A.M.

G.M.P.R. show that there was one sustaining
program this evening from the Hotel Pennsylvania.

7 January, 1941 (TUES): Cafe Rouge, Hotel Pennsylvania,
                        New York City, N.Y.
                        NBC-Blue 7:30-7:45 P.M.

G.M.P.R. show that there was one sustaining
program this evening from the Hotel Pennsylvania.

7 January, 1941 (TUES): New York City, N.Y. (CHESTERFIELD SHOW)
                        CBS 10:00-10:15 P.M. EST.

The announcer for this program is Paul Douglas.

Slumber Song (Theme)

K2PP-0044   Vi LPM-6100, RCA RD 27146, RCA G LPM-6100, RCA
                     Au L 11024
                 (2:45) Sarong (arr JG)
                        (Jerry Gray)
                        Ts, Beneke

V-4086 WR-981   GMMS 21/69, AFRS P-2248
      Int GM   (2:12) Bugle Woogie (arr BF)-voc Marion Hutton
                        (Gordon Andrews-Floria Vestoff)
                        Dedicated to the boys at Chanute
                        Field, Illinois
                        Tpt, ??; p, MacGregor; tpt, ??

(Broadcast continued on next page)

```
V-4086 WR-984    GMMS 24/72, GMMS 52/100, AFRS P-2248
       Int GM    (3:14) High On A Windy Hill (arr BF)-voc
                         Ray Eberle
                         (Alex Kramer-Joan Whitney)
                         Muted tpt, McMickle

V-4086 WR-981    GMMS 21/69, GMMS 50/98, AFRS P-2241
                 (3:11) Oh So Good (arr JG)-Chant by Band
                         (Jerry Gray)
                         Tpt, ??; p, MacGregor; ts, Beneke;
                         tpt, May; d, Purtill; clt, Caceres
```

Slumber Song (Theme)

*8 January, 1941 (WED): New York City, N.Y. (CHESTERFIELD SHOW)
              CBS   10:00-10:15 P.M. EST.*

The announcer for this program is Paul Douglas.

Slumber Song (Theme)

```
V-4086 WR-981    GMMS 21/69, GMMS 51/99, AFRS P-2241
                 (1:42) Largo (Goin' Home)
                         Adapted from the Largo of Anton
                         Dvorak's "New World Symphony"
                         (William Arms Fisher)

UPRM-6315        Vi LPM/LSP-3873, RCA Br. RD/SF-7932, RCA G LSP-
                         3873
                 (2:34) Long Time No See, Baby (arr JG)-voc
                         Marion Hutton
                         (Jack Lathrop)
                         D, Purtill; ts, Beneke

V-4086 WR-981    GMMS 21/69, GMMS 49/97, AFRS P-GL-78, AFRS P-2248
       Int GM    (3:21) You Walk By-voc Ray Eberle
                         (Ben Raleigh-Bernie Wayne)

       Int PD    (3:04) Solid As A Stonewall, Jackson (arr JG)
                         (Jerry Gray-John Chalmers MacGregor)
                         As, Caceres; ts, Beneke
                 (0:34) Slumber Song (Theme)
                         (Saul Tepper-John Chalmers MacGregor)
```

That evening, at the "Cafe Rouge", George Simon
in his article "The Diary Of Our Own Jimmy
Bracken" reported:
    "Then down to Miller's to hear Dorothy
Claire open with the band--she's going to fit

(Continued on next page)

fine." (Met. Feb. 1941)
G.M.P.R. show that Dorothy Claire joined the
band on this date and sang only at the "Cafe
Rouge" on January 8th and 9th. "Hutton has
been singing on Miller's Chesterfield show
only." (DB, Jan. 15, 1941)

8 January, 1941 (WED): Cafe Rouge, Hotel Pennsylvania,
                        New York City, N.Y.
                        NBC-Blue 12:05-12:30 A.M.

G.M.P.R. show that there was one sustaining
program this evening from the Hotel Pennsylvania.

9 January, 1941 (THUR): New York City, N.Y. (CHESTERFIELD SHOW)
                        CBS 10:00-10:15 P.M. EST.

The announcer for this program is Paul Douglas.

(0:15) Slumber Song (Theme)
*   (Saul Tepper-John Chalmers MacGregor)*

E4VP 8207   Vi LPT 6701, Vi EPOT 6701 (947-0189), HMV RLS
                   598, RCA G EPOT-6701
                   (3:43) Georgia On My Mind (arr JG)
                        (Stuart Gorrell-Hoagy Carmichael)
                        Ts, Beneke; tpt, Best; muted tpt, ??

                   Sentimental Me (arr JG)-voc MH
                   From the Stage Musical "Garrick
                   Gaieties"
                   (Lorenz Hart-Richard Rodgers)
        Int GM (2:34) I Close My Eyes-voc Ray Eberle
                        (   )
                   Are You Jumpin' Jack?
                   Slumber Song (Theme)

On Vi LPT 6701 "Georgia On My Mind" was incorrectly listed as being broadcast on March 22,
1940.

This was the last Chesterfield program that
Marion Hutton sang on (and it was also her last
day with the band) until she rejoined the band
on August 15th, 1941. (G.M.P.R.)

The tune "Sentimental Me" is sometimes known
as "Sentimental Me And Romantic You".

11 January, 1941 (SAT): Cafe Rouge, Hotel Pennsylvania,
                        New York City, N.Y.
                        NBC-Blue 12:05-12:30 A.M. EST.

        G.M.P.R. show that there was one sustaining
program this evening from the Hotel Pennsylvania.

        Slumber Song (Theme)
        Daisy Mae
        You Walk By

E4VP 8201   Vi LPT 6701, Vi EPOT 6701 (947-0178), HMV RLS 598,
        RCA G EPOT-6701
        (3:07) Swingin' At The Seance (arr BM)-voc
            Dorothy Claire
            (Avey-Stone-Carnice)
            Tpt, May

E4VP 8201   Vi LPT 6701, Vi EPOT 6701 (947-0179), HMV RLS 598,
        Vi It LPM-10141, RCA Vi It LJ 50020, RCA
        G EPOT-6701, RCA Vi It LPM 50020
        (3:46) Frenesi (arr BF)
            (Ray Charles-S.K. Russell-Albert
            Dominguez)
            Ts, Beneke; tpt, Best; muted tpt, ??

        Anvil Chorus
        Slumber Song (Theme)

        It would appear from this listing of tunes that
there are one or two tunes lacking if this was
a 30 minute program.

        Vi LPT 6701 incorrectly lists Marion Hutton on
vocal instead of Dorothy Claire on "Swingin'
At The Seance".

13 January, 1941 (MON): Cafe Rouge, Hotel Pennsylvania,
                        New York City, N.Y.
                        NBC-Blue 12:05-12:30 A.M.

        G.M.P.R. show that there was one sustaining
program this evening from the Hotel Pennsylvania.

        The Four Modernaires (Ralph Brewster, William
Conway, Harold Dickinson, Charles Joseph
Goldstein) joined the band permanently on this
date.
        "The Modernaires, who were rehearsing with
Goodman last week, started with Glenn tonight."
(Met. Feb. 1941) G.M.P.R. show that the

(Continued on next page)

Modernaires were paid for their services on the
13th, 14th, 15th and 16th.

"Plenty of band leaders at Glenn Miller's
tonight--Woody Herman, Les Brown, Charlie
Spivak, Sammy Kaye and Larry Clinton helped to
inaugurate some gorgeous stands." (Met., Feb.
1941). The new bandstand front was made of
stainless steel and was designed by Col. E.J.W.
Ragsdale, chief engineer of the Budd company who
invented the "shotweld" process of fabricating
stainless steel, which made possible the stream-
lining effect applied on trains. A picture of
the "christening ceremonies" appeared in the
February 15th, 1941 issue of Down Beat.

14 January, 1941 (TUES): New York City, N.Y. (CHESTERFIELD SHOW)
CBS   10:00-10:15 P.M. EST.

The announcer for this program is Paul Douglas.

Slumber Song (Theme)
There'll Be Some Changes Made

E4VP 8208   Vi LPT 6701, Vi EPOT 6701 (947-0185), HMV RLS
598, RCA G EPOT-6701
(3:00) A Stone's Throw From Heaven (arr BF)-
voc Ray Eberle
(Bob Ray-Jay Burton-Irving Green)
Tpt, ??; ts, Beneke

Anvil Chorus
Slumber Song (Theme)

On Vi LPT 6701 "A Stone's Throw From Heaven"
was incorrectly listed as being broadcast on
February 26, 1942.

14 January, 1941 (TUES): Cafe Rouge, Hotel Pennsylvania,
New York City, N.Y.
NBC

G.M.P.R. show that there was one sustaining
program this evening from the Hotel Pennsylvania.

15 January, 1941 (WED): New York City, N.Y. (CHESTERFIELD SHOW)
CBS   10:00-10:15 P.M. EST.

The announcer for this program is Paul Douglas.

(Broadcast continued on next page)

New streamlined bandstand front used by Miller sax section in January 1941. Joining in the christening ceremonies at the Cafe Rouge are, left to right: Miller, Bob Burns (Tommy Dorsey's manager), Charlie Spivak, Les Brown, Larry Clinton, Woody Herman, Sammy Kaye. (*Photo courtesy Glenn Miller Estate*)

Third date at Paramount, January–February 1941. Band is playing without music stands. Trumpeter at far right is Billy May. Third trumpeter from right is Ray Anthony.

From the 20th Century-Fox Film *Sun Valley Serenade*, March–May 1941. Paula Kelly is the vocalist surrounded by Ray Eberle and the Modernaires. (*20th Century-Fox*)

From *Sun Valley Serenade*. Band is playing *In the Mood*. Trumpet soloist is Billy May, with John Payne at the piano. (*20th Century-Fox*)

Slumber Song (Theme)
Drink To Me Only With Thine Eyes

E3VP 5244   Vi LPT 6700, Vi EPNT 6700 (947-0120), Vi SPD-18
             (599-9105), HMV RLS 599, RCA G LPT 6700
        (2:06) Naughty Sweetie Blues (arr JG)-voc
                    Dorothy Claire
                    (Meyer)
                    Ts, Klink

                There I Go
  Int GM & PD (4:00) *Song Of The Volga Boatmen (arr BF)*
                    (Russian Folk Song)
                    B, Alpert; muted tpt, May; as,
                    Caceres; ts, Beneke; tpt, ??
        (0:29) *Slumber Song (Theme)*
                    (Saul Tepper-John Chalmers MacGregor)

        "Naughty Sweetie Blues" is better known as "The
        Blues My Naughty Sweetie Taught Me".

15 January, 1941 (WED): Cafe Rouge, Hotel Pennsylvania,
                    New York City, N.Y.
                    NBC-Blue 12:05-12:30 A.M.

        G.M.P.R. show that there was one sustaining
        program this evening from the Hotel Pennsylvania.

16 January, 1941 (THUR): New York City, N.Y.(CHESTERFIELD SHOW)
                    CBS 10:00-10:15 P.M. EST.

        The announcer for this program is Paul Douglas.

        (0:13) *Slumber Song (Theme)*
                    (Saul Tepper-John Chalmers MacGregor)
        (3:04) *Ida! Sweet As Apple Cider (arr BM)-*
                    voc Tex Beneke
                    (Eddie Leonard)
                    Ts, Beneke; p, MacGregor
        (2:40) *Swingin' At The Seance (arr BM)-voc*
                    Dorothy Claire
                    (Avey-Stone-Carnice)
                    Tpt, May
                The Morning After
        (2:39) *Measure For Measure (arr BM)*
                    (Arletta May)
                    As, Caceres; ts, Beneke; tpt, May
        (0:28) *Slumber Song (Theme)*
                    (Saul Tepper-John Chalmers MacGregor)

16 January, 1941 (THUR): Cafe Rouge, Hotel Pennsylvania,
New York City, N.Y.
NBC-Blue   12:05-12:30 A.M.

G.M.P.R. show that there was one sustaining
program this evening from the Hotel Pennsylvania.

Later in the evening Tex Beneke recorded in the
Metronome All-Star Band: "And Glenn Miller also
came through and let Tex run over before the final
set at the Pennsylvania....Just like last year,
Glenn refused to make the date, insisting that he
wasn't good enough to take over the hot chair."
(Met., Feb. 1941)

G.M.P.R. for the week ending January 16th show
that Billy May arranged "Harlem Chapel Bells" and
"In A Jam".

17 January, 1941 (FRI): Victor Studios, New York City, New York

Same personnel as for November 4th except that
DOROTHY CLAIRE has replaced Marion Hutton as
vocalist and the FOUR MODERNAIRES have been
added.

058884-1   BB Test Pressing
                Ida! Sweet As Apple Cider (arr BM)-voc Tex Beneke
                (Eddie Leonard)
                Ts, Beneke (solo differs from take 2);
                p, MacGregor

058884-2   BB 11079-B, HMVAu EA-3253, Vi 20-2510, Vi 420-0040,
                Vi 447-0040, Vi LPT-3067, Vi EPBT-3067
                (947-0199), Vi LPT 6700, Vi EPNT 6700
                (947-0124), HMV DLP 1062, Vi 45 Special-1953,
                Vi SPD-18 (599-9106), HMV RLS 599, AFRS P-
                1118, RD 3/4-64, RCA G LPT 6700, RCA F
                130211, RCA G LPT 3067, RCA G EPBT-3067,
                AFRS G.I. Jive H-12-1919, AFRS G.I. Jive
                H-12-2026
                Ida! Sweet As Apple Cider (arr BM)-voc Tex Beneke
                (Eddie Leonard)
                Ts, Beneke; p, MacGregor

058885-1   BB 11029-A, HMV BD 5798, HMV MH 138, HMVSw JK-
                2324, Vi 20-1564 (Vi P-148), Vi 27-0004
                (Vi WPT-2), Vi 47-2852 (Vi WP-148), Vi 420-
                0033, Vi 447-0033, Vi EPA-148, Vi EPAT-2,
                Vi EPA-5103, HMV DLP 1062, Vi LPT-2, Vi LPM
                31, Vi LPT 3067, Vi SP-33-90, Vi LPM/LSP-

(Session continued on next page)

3377, RCA Int. 20003, RCA Int. 21019,
Vi 7" LP, RCA G EPA-148, AFRS P-1542, AFRS
P-NAV-2, RD 3/4-64, El G EG 7685, RCA F
85243, RCA G 447-0033, Vi TP3-5044, AFRS
G.I. Jive H-12-1053, RCA G LPT-3067, AFRS
G.I. Jive H-12-1001, Vi P8S-5061, RCA G
LPM 9852, RCA G LPM/LSP-3377, RCA F 130211,
HMVIn BD 5798, AFRS H-62-43, Vi VPM-6019,
AFRS G.I. Jive H-12-979, AFRS G.I. Jive
H-12-1699, AFRS G.I. Jive H-12-1616, RCA
Br. RD-8094, RCA Br. GM-1, RCA G LPM/LSP-
9944, RCA G Cas 10231
Song Of The Volga Boatmen (arr BF)
(Russian Folk Song)
B, Alpert; muted tpt, May; as, Caceres;
tpt, ??

058886-1   BB 11110-A, HMV BD 5698, HMVSw JK-2325, HMVIr
I.P. 1104, HMVIn BD 5698
The One I Love (Belongs To Somebody Else) (arr JG)-
voc Ray Eberle and The Modernaires
(Gus Kahn-Isham Jones)

058887-1   BB 11042-A, HMV DLP-1145, Vi LPM-2080, RD 3/4-64
You Stepped Out Of A Dream-voc Ray Eberle and The
Modernaires
From the MGM film "Ziegfeld Girl"
(Gus Kahn-Nacio Herb Brown)

058888-1   BB 11063-A, HMV BD 5817, HMV MH 143, HMVAu EA-
2988, El G (Test), HMVIn BD 5817, VdP HN
2983, VdP 7EPQ 542
I Dreamt I Dwelt In Harlem (arr JG)
(Robert Wright-Ben Smith-Leonard Ware-
Jerry Gray)
Ts, Klink; tpt, May; b, Alpert; clt,
Caceres; p, MacGregor; muted tpt, May

058889-1   BB 11110-B, HMV BD 5817, HMV MH 143, HMVAu EA-
2863, HMVSw JK-2304, HMV 7EG 8204, HMV RLS
599, Vi LPT 6700, Vi EPNT 6700 (947-0129),
Vi SPD-18 (599-9111), El G (Test), Vi EPA-
5149, Vi 45 Special-1953, Vi It LPM-10141,
RCA Vi It LJ 50020, RCA G LPT 6700, RCA G
LPM-9852, VdP HN 2983, VdP 7EPQ 542, HMVAus
GA 5029, Vi It LPM 50020, HMVIn BD 5817,
RCA G LPM/LSP-9944, AFRS G.I. Jive H-12-912
Sun Valley Jump (arr JG)
(Jerry Gray)
Tpt, May; ts, Klink; tpt, May; clt,
Caceres; d, Purtill; tpt, ??

(Session continued on next page)

"Ida! Sweet As Apple Cider" 2 takes; all other
tunes 1 take. (RCA Victor)
This session lasted from 1:00 P.M. to 5:00 P.M.
(RCA Victor)

18 January, 1941 (SAT): Cafe Rouge, Hotel Pennsylvania,
New York City, N.Y.
NBC-Blue 12:05-12:30 A.M.

G.M.P.R. show that there was one sustaining
program this evening from the Hotel Pennsylvania.

Glenn Miller and His Orchestra closed at the
"Cafe Rouge" of the Hotel Pennsylvania, New York
City, New York. (DB, Feb. 1, 1941; G.M.P.R.)

19 January, 1941 (SUN)

Glenn Miller and His Orchestra played at Lowell,
Massachusetts (played three shows--G.M.D.). The
band travelled by the New York-New Haven Hartford
RR from New York to Boston, then we presume by
bus to Lowell and then Lowell to New York.
(G.M.P.R.)

20 January, 1941 (MON)

Off. (G.M.D.)

21 January, 1941 (TUES): New York City, N.Y. (CHESTERFIELD SHOW)
CBS 10:00-10:15 P.M. EST.

The announcer for this program is Paul Douglas.

   Slumber Song (Theme)
(1:47) *Old Black Joe (arr GM & ChM)*
       (Stephen Foster)
       P, MacGregor
   Sentimental Me-voc DC
(3:31) *These Things You Left Me (arr JG)-voc*
       Ray Eberle and The Modernaires
       (Hal Dickinson-Sidney Lippman)
(2:51) *Sun Valley Jump (arr JG)*
       (Jerry Gray)
       Tpt, May; ts, Klink; tpt, May;
       clt, Caceres; d, Purtill; tpt, ??
(0:30) *Slumber Song (Theme)*
       (Saul Tepper-John Chalmers MacGregor)

22 January, 1941 (WED): New York City, N.Y. (CHESTERFIELD SHOW)
CBS 10:00-10:15 P.M. EST.

    The announcer for this program is Paul Douglas.

        (0:40) Slumber Song (Theme)
            (Saul Tepper-John Chalmers MacGregor)
Int PD (2:44) Frenesi (arr BF)
            (Ray Charles-S.K. Russell-Albert
            Dominguez)
            Ts, Beneke; tpt, Best, muted tpt, ??
      (2:15) La Cucaracha-voc Dorothy Claire and The
            Modernaires
            (Mexican Folk Song)
Int GM (2:00) I Close My Eyes-voc Ray Eberle
Int GM & PD (3:21) Boulder Buff (arr FN)
            (Eugene Novello-Fred Norman)
            P, MacGregor; tpt, ??; ts, Klink
        Slumber Song (Theme)

    "La Cucaracha" was arranged (1) as a fox-trot by
Hawley Ades, American adaption by Juan Y. D'Lorah,
and introduced in the film "La Cucaracha", Irving
Berlin, Inc., cop. 1934; (2) as a song, words by
Stanley Adams, Edward B. Marks Music Corp., cop.
1934; words by Carl Field, M.M. Cole Pub. Co.,
Chicago, cop. 1935; etc. (Variety Music Cavalcade,
1952). There were probably other adaptations of
this tune and in this case The Modernaires may
have added some of their own words and arranging
ideas. It is known that The Modernaires arranged
many of the "special" vocal numbers in which they
were involved.

23 January, 1941 (THUR): New York City, N.Y. (CHESTERFIELD SHOW)
CBS 10:00-10:15 P.M. EST.

    The announcer for this program is Paul Douglas.

        Slumber Song (Theme)
ALP *So You're The One-voc The Modernaires*
        ( )
        Bugle Woogie
        High On A Windy Hill
        I Dreamt I Dwelt In Harlem
        Slumber Song (Theme)

24 January, 1941 (FRI)

    Glenn Miller and His Orchestra played for four
(Continued on next page)

days (closed Monday, January 27th) at the State
Theater, Hartford, Connecticut. Cass Daley and
Bobby Lane (Lane & Ward) were on the same bill.
Miller bought some rhumba equipment from
Perlmutter Inc., 36 Allyn St., Hartford,
Connecticut. (G.M.P.R.)

28 January, 1941 (TUES)

Glenn Miller and His Orchestra opened at the
Paramount Theater, New York City, New York.
(DB, Jan. 15, 1941; New York Times, Jan. 28, 1941;
G.M.P.R.)

"Glenn Miller's band started regular run today, Wednesday following benefit preem last night
(Tuesday.)." (Variety, Jan. 29, 1941) The film
was "Virginia".

*28 January, 1941 (TUES): New York City, N.Y. (CHESTERFIELD SHOW)
CBS 10:00-10:15 P.M. EST.*

The announcer for this program is Paul Douglas.

Slumber Song (Theme)
Georgia On My Mind
Int GM (2:21) Cheer Up-voc Dorothy Claire and The
Modernaires
(   )
You Walk By
Measure For Measure
Slumber Song (Theme)

*29 January, 1941 (WED): New York City, N.Y. (CHESTERFIELD SHOW)
CBS 10:00-10:15 P.M. EST.*

Slumber Song (Theme)
Watcha Know Joe
Naughty Sweetie Blues
The Morning After
The Spirit Is Willing
Slumber Song (Theme)

*30 January, 1941 (THUR): New York City, N.Y. (CHESTERFIELD SHOW)
CBS 10:00-10:15 P.M. EST.*

The announcer for this program is Paul Douglas.

(Broadcast continued on next page)

Slumber Song (Theme)
Ida!

E3VP 5240   Vi LPT 6700, Vi EPNT 6700 (947-0128), Vi SPD-18
            (599-9109), HMV RLS 599, RCA G LPT 6700
            (2:47) There'll Be Some Changes Made (arr JG)-
            voc Dorothy Claire
            (Billy Higgins-W.B. Overstreet)
            Tpt, Best; ts, Beneke; as, Caceres;
            tpt, Best

K2PP-0043   Vi LPM-6100, RCA RD 27145, RCA G LPM-6100, RCA
            Au L 11023
      Int PD (2:24) I Hear A Rhapsody-voc Ray Eberle and The
            Modernaires
            (George Fragos-Jack Baker)

Oh So Good
Slumber Song (Theme)

30 January, 1941 (THUR)

      G.M.P.R. for the week ending January 30th show
      that Billy May arranged "Trigger's Tune" and
      "I Know That You Know".

31 January, 1941 (FRI)

      Glenn Miller and His Orchestra were reviewed
      Friday evening on stage at the Paramount Theater.
      Here is part of the review (pertaining to the
      Miller band's participation): "Aided by judicious
      lighting and good vocal and instrumental stand-
      outs, each number held close attention. The band
      theme won immediate recognition and then went
      into Tuxedo Junction, followed by a swell Frenesi.
      The Modernaires, male quartet, step off the band-
      stand to warble Make Believe Ballroom Time, and
      then the band's new vocalist, Dorothy Claire,
      sings I'm in Love, followed by a special version
      of La Cucaracha with the Modernaires. She's
      okeh. The Modernaires warble again and smoothly,
      and then Ray Eberle baritones The Nightingale
      Sang in Berkeley Square pleasantly enough, and
      joins the Modernaires for The One I Love. The
      band's final number is Anvil Chorus, played in
      tricky, showmanly style that had the patrons
      clapping in rhythm. The band as a whole once
      more impresses as a superb dance band that relies
      entirely on musicianship and which shuns indivi-
      dual personality stuff, comedians, and novelty
      effects." (The Billboard--Feb. 8, 1941)

4 February, 1941 (TUES): New York City, N.Y.   (CHESTERFIELD SHOW)
                    CBS   10:00-10:15 P.M. EST.

      The announcer for this program is Paul Douglas.

               Slumber Song (Theme)
               Daisy Mae
               MEDLEY:
                    Vilia
    (1:08)   *You Walk By-voc Ray Eberle*
                      (Ben Raleigh-Bernie Wayne)
    Int GM   *Adios (borrowed from Enrico Madriguera)*
                    Blue Afterglow
    (0:45)   *Ciri-Biri-Bin (arr JG)-voc Dorothy Claire*
                    and The Modernaires
                    (Harry James-Jack Lawrence-
                    A. Pestalozza)
             Slumber Song (Theme)

      This version of "Ciri-Biri-Bin" is a different
      arrangement from the Bluebird release.

4 February, 1941 (TUES)

      Glenn Miller and His Orchestra completed their
      first week at the Paramount: "Show ended its
      first week last night (Tuesday) at a very cocky
      $60,000. This included special opener Tuesday,
      Jan. 28, 1941 with most of the house sold out
      at regular scale to the Maple Leaf Fund."
      (Variety, Feb. 5, 1941)

5 February, 1941 (WED): New York City, N.Y. (CHESTERFIELD SHOW)
                    CBS   10:00-10:15 P.M. EST.

      The announcer for this program is Paul Douglas.

               Slumber Song (Theme)
               Oysters In June (arr JG)-voc 4M
                       (   )
    AuP   *Sentimental Me*
               High On A Windy Hill
               Song Of The Volga Boatmen
               Slumber Song (Theme)

6 February, 1941 (THUR): New York City, N.Y. (CHESTERFIELD SHOW)·
                    CBS   10:00-10:15 P.M. EST.

      The announcer for this program is Paul Douglas.

(Broadcast continued on next page)

Slumber Song (Theme)
(2:23) *Swingin' At The Seance (arr BM)-voc*
Dorothy Claire
(Avey-Stone-Carnice)
Tpt, May
These Things You Left-voc RE & 4M

At this point in the program, Martin Block, of
station WNEW (NYC) awarded Glenn for the third
time as the top band in the Make Believe Ballroom Poll.

Anvil Chorus
Slumber Song (Theme)

7 February, 1941 (FRI)

Glenn Miller and His Orchestra played a club
date (for the St. Johns' College Junior Prom--
G.M.D.) at the Hotel Biltmore, New York City,
New York (starting time immediately following
the last show at the Paramount--G.M.D.).
(G.M.P.R.)

11 February, 1941 (TUES): New York City, N.Y. (CHESTERFIELD SHOW)
CBS   10:00-10:15 P.M. EST.

Slumber Song (Theme)
Largo
Breakfast For Two (arr JG)-voc Dorothy
Claire, Tex Beneke and The Modernaires
(Joe McKiernan-Art Wilson-Merrill
Knighton)
I Close My Eyes
Sun Valley Jump
Slumber Song (Theme)

11 February, 1941 (TUES)

Glenn Miller and His Orchestra completed their
second week at the Paramount: "Socking through
like a Joe Louis is the Paramount show of
Virginia and Glenn Miller. Finishing the
second week last night (Tuesday) at a powerful
$46,000." (Variety, Feb. 12, 1941)

The same issue of Variety (Feb. 12, 1941) reported that the Miller band was due to check
into 20th Century-Fox February 24, 1941 to

(Continued on next page)

start on the film "The Great American Broadcast" and as far as we know, Miller did not
appear in this film as the band was doing
theater dates at this time.

12 February, 1941 (WED): New York City, N.Y. (CHESTERFIELD SHOW)
                    CBS   10:00-10:15 P.M. EST.

                    Slumber Song (Theme)
                    Frenesi
                    La Cucaracha
                    I Do, Do You?
                    I Dreamt I Dwelt In Harlem
                    Slumber Song (Theme)

13 February, 1941 (THUR): New York City, N.Y. (CHESTERFIELD SHOW)
                    CBS   10:00-10:15 P.M. EST.

                    Slumber Song (Theme)
                    Sarong

WPRS-0976   Vi LSP-3981, RCA Br. RD/SF-7982
                    (1:48) Bugle Woogie (arr BF)-voc Dorothy Claire
                          (Gordon Andrews-Floria Vestoff)
                          Tpt, ??; p, MacGregor; tpt, ??

                    I Hear A Rhapsody
                    Boulder Buff
                    Slumber Song (Theme)

13 February, 1941 (THUR)

          G.M.P.R. for the week ending February 13th show
          that Billy May arranged "Music Makers".

17 February, 1941 (MON)

          The night before Glenn Miller left the Paramount
          Theater to head west towards the coast on one-
          nighters he was presented two trophies. One was
          Down Beat's trophy given Miller after readers
          voted him to have the greatest "sweet band" in
          the land. The second was a scroll presented
          Miller by Martin Block of WNEW who conducted a
          poll which also revealed Miller to be tops.
          (DB--March 15, 1941).

(Continued on next page)

Approximately at this time in the month Miller
renewed his contract with Chesterfield: "New
York--Although his current contract on the
Chesterfield commercial doesn't expire until
the end of this month, Glenn Miller two weeks
ago was signed for another year by the same
sponsor. For the three shows a week, plus rebroadcasts, Miller will get $4,850." (DB--
March 1, 1941).

18 February, 1941 (TUES): New York City, N.Y. (CHESTERFIELD SHOW)
CBS   10:00-10:15 P.M. EST.

The announcer for this program is Paul Douglas.

Slumber Song (Theme)
Sunrise Serenade
Naughty Sweetie Blues
It Was Wonderful Then-voc RE & 4M
Song Of The Volga Boatmen
Slumber Song (Theme)

It's rather surprising to see "Sunrise Serenade"
appear on this program as it is an ASCAP tune.

18 February, 1941 (TUES)

Glenn Miller and His Orchestra closed at the
Paramount Theater, New York City, New York.
(New York Times, Feb. 18, 1941; G.M.P.R.)

"Glenn Miller band stage show nifty $38,000.
third final week and $144,000.00 for three weeks
plenty profit." (Variety, Feb. 19, 1941)

19 February, 1941 (WED): Victor Studios, New York City, New York

Same personnel as for November 4th with vocal
additions and changes as noted on the January
17th recording session.

060911-1   BB 11069-B, HMVSw JK-2304, Vi Arg 68-0691
            When That Man Is Dead And Gone (arr JG)-voc Tex
                Beneke and The Modernaires
                (Irving Berlin)
                As, Caceres; tpt, ??; d, Purtill

060912-1   BB 11135-A, HMVAu EA-2863, HMV 7EG 8031, Vi EPAT-
                428, Vi LPT-1031, RD 3/4-64, RCA G EPAT-
                428, RCA G LPT-1031

(Session continued on next page)

                    The Spirit Is Willing (arr JG)
                        (Jerry Gray)
                        Muted tpt, May; tpt, ??; muted tpt, ??;
                        tpt, May; muted tpt, ??; muted tpt, May;
                        tpt, ??; muted tpt, May; tpt, ??; muted
                        tpt, May

060913-1   BB 11069-A, HMV MH 102
                    A Little Old Church In England-voc Ray Eberle,
                        Dorothy Claire and The Modernaires
                        (Irving Berlin)

060914-1   BB 11095-A, HMV BD 5698, HMVSw JK-2268, HMVAus
                        GA-5010, VdP AV-695, Vi 20-2412 (Vi P-189),
                        Vi 42-0157, Vi 27-0157, Vi 420-0035, Vi
                        447-0035, Vi EPAT-430, HMV DLP 1049, Vi LPT-
                        1016, El G EG 7905, RD 3/4-25, RCA Int.
                        11015, RD Br. RDS 6099, RD Br. RDS 6172,
                        RCA G LPT 1016, RCA F 130211, Vi DJ 27-0157,
                        VdP 7EPQ 541, HMVIr I.P. 1104, Vi LSP-4125,
                        Vi P8S-1432, HMVIn BD 5698, RCA Int. INTS
                        1002, Vi VPM-6019, RCA Br. RD-8094, RCA Br.
                        GM-1, AFRS G.I. Jive H-12-1788, AFRS G.I.
                        Jive H-12-1826, AFRS G.I. Jive H-12-1857,
                        HMVAu DLP 1049, RCA G EPAT-430
                    Perfidia-voc Dorothy Claire and The Modernaires
                        (Milton Leeds-Alberto Dominguez)

                    All tunes 1 take. (RCA Victor)
                    This session lasted from 10:00 A.M. to 2:00 P.M.
                    (RCA Victor)

19 February, 1941 (WED): New York City, N.Y. (CHESTERFIELD SHOW)
                    CBS 10:00-10:15 P.M. EST.

                    The announcer for this program is Paul Douglas.

                    (0:11) Slumber Song (Theme)
                            (Saul Tepper-John Chalmers MacGregor)
                    (3:14) Daisy Mae (arr BM)
                            (Arletta May-Hal McIntyre)
                            Ts, Klink; muted tpt, May; as,
                            Caceres
        Int GM (1:51) Cheer Up-voc Dorothy Claire and The
                            Modernaires
                            (   )
        Int GM (2:23) A Stone's Throw From Heaven (arr BF)-
                            voc Ray Eberle
                            (Bob Ray-Jay Burton-Irving Green)
                            Ts, Beneke
                        Are You Jumpin' Jack?
                        Slumber Song (Theme)

20 February, 1941 (THUR): Victor Studios, New York City, New York

    Same personnel as for November 4th with vocal additions and changes as noted on the January 17th recording session.

060915-1   BB 11079-A, HMVSw JK-2252, HMV 7EG 8241, HMV DLP 1145, RD 3/4-25, RD Br. RDS 6094
It's Always You (arr BF)-voc Ray Eberle
From the Paramount film "Road To Zanzibar"
(Johnny Burk-Jimmy Van Heusen)

060916-1   BB 11095-B, HMVSw JK-2268, VdP AV-695
Spring Will Be So Sad (When She Comes This Year)
(arr JG)-voc Ray Eberle and The Modernaires
(Margaret Bonds-Harold Dickinson)
Ts, Beneke; clt, ??

060917-1   BB 11135-B
The Air Minded Executive (arr JG)-voc Tex Beneke
and Dorothy Claire (and The Band)
(Johnny Mercer-Bernie Hanighen)
Ts, Beneke

060918-1   BB 11235-B, HMVAu EA-2931, HMV 7EG 8254
Below The Equator-voc Ray Eberle and The Modernaires
(Charlie Tobias-Cliff Friend)

The flutter tongue (airplane effect) that begins "The Air Minded Executive" anticipated the same idea for "Keep 'Em Flying".

"Spring Will Be So Sad" 2 takes; all other tunes 1 take. (RCA Victor)
This session lasted from 10:00 A.M. to 2:00 P.M. (RCA Victor)

20 February, 1941 (THUR): New York City, N.Y. (CHESTERFIELD SHOW) CBS 10:00-10:15 P.M. EST.

The announcer for this program is Paul Douglas.

Slumber Song (Theme)
(3:09) The Spirit Is Willing (arr JG)
(Jerry Gray)
Muted tpt, May; tpt, ??; muted tpt, ??; tpt, May; muted tpt, ??; muted tpt, May; tpt, ??; muted tpt, May; tpt, ??; muted tpt, May

(Broadcast continued on next page)

> *Perfidia*
> (1:40) ~~The Morning After~~-voc *Ray Eberle*
> *(Robert Sour-Lee Wainer)*
>
> Int PD & GM (2:28) *Measure For Measure (arr BM)*
> *(Arletta May)*
> As, *Caceres;* ts, *Beneke;* tpt, *May*
> *Slumber Song (Theme)*

The band took the NY Central RR from New York to Cleveland. (G.M.P.R.)

21 February, 1941 (FRI)

Glenn Miller and His Orchestra played for one week (closed Thursday, February 27th) at the Palace Theater, Cleveland, Ohio. (DB, Feb. 15, 1941; The Cleveland Plain Dealer, Feb. 21 & 27, 1941; Variety, Feb. 19, 1941; G.M.P.R.)

The Chesterfield shows were broadcast from the stage. Also on the same bill was Paul Regan and the Three Arnolds. The film was "Night Train". Theater schedule for the band was as follows: 11:49, 2:30, 5:21, 8:02, 10:33.

"Miller's fans jammed the house for the first show yesterday, and the votaries of rhythmic cacophony repeated the performance they always give when one of their favorite band leaders comes to town.
Whistles, applause in time, stomping, and all those outward expressions of great joy were heard again from the Palace audience during the show.
For the most part Miller's band, with its restless trombones, is fairly muted and pleasantly tuneful in a jive sort of way. What it does to 'Moonlight Serenade,' 'In the Mood,' 'Frenesi,' 'Perfidia,' 'Tuxedo Junction' and some other numbers seems to put the children in the closer rows into ecstasy.
Miller has a good male quartet with him, a pleasing novelty singer in Dorothy Claire, with Ray Eberle ballading okay, Toots.
Miller also introduces Irving Berlin's 'A Little Old Church in England.' I hope none of them left standing is as weak as this song is silly and mawkish." (Review by W. Ward Marsh from The Cleveland Plain Dealer, Feb. 22, 1941)

"Glenn Miller and 'Night Train' were whammers great $24,500.00" (Variety, March 5, 1941)

After 21 February, 1941

      "Glenn Miller heads for Hollywood where on March 24 he and his band start working on their first picture, produced by 20th Century-Fox. Starred with the band will be Sonja Henie and Jack Oakie. Rumors to the effect that the band will play while ice-skating have been denied from all quarters. 'A sliphorn is enough; I don't want a slip-anything-else,' explained Glenn." (Met. March 1941) Jack Oakie did not appear in the film.

      "Ralph Brewster, a member of the Four Modernaires, vocal quartet with the band, henceforth will literally double in brass. He has taken over Ray Anthony's trumpet chair." (Met. March 1941)

      "New York--Ray Anthony, young Cleveland trumpeter, has been replaced in Glenn Miller's band by Ralph Brewster, a member of the Modernaires vocal group, who plays horn as well as he sings, in the opinion of Miller." (DB, March 1, 1941)

G.M.P.R. do not indicate that Anthony left the band during this period but does indicate that Anthony was only paid for two days at the Palace Theater and was paid for two Chesterfield broadcasts. G.M.P.R. do not supply the dates Anthony missed and no explanation is given for the reduction in salary. We can only assume that it was during this period that Brewster <u>substituted</u> for Anthony as G.M.P.R. do not indicate that Brewster played trumpet during this period. "Substituted" would appear to be the correct word as Anthony is paid in full for the next week and until he actually left the band in early July, 1941. Anthony played and appeared in the film. There is a picture of Brewster playing trumpet on the 20th Century-Fox set (he is the fifth trumpet) and it is quite possible that Miller used five trumpets during this period. If he did, G.M.P.R. do not indicate which broadcasts had five trumpets.

25 February, 1941 (TUES): Palace Theater, Cleveland, Ohio
                          (CHESTERFIELD SHOW)
                          CBS 10:00-10:15 P.M. EST.

                Slumber Song (Theme)
                Georgia On My Mind

(Broadcast continued on next page)

Ciri-Biri-Bin-voc DC & 4M
High On A Windy Hill
I Dreamt I Dwelt In Harlem
Slumber Song (Theme)

26 February, 1941 (WED): Palace Theater, Cleveland, Ohio
(CHESTERFIELD SHOW)
CBS   10:00-10:15 P.M. EST.

The announcer for this program is Larry Bruff.

Slumber Song (Theme)
Adios
There'll Be Some Changes Made
I Do, Do You?
Whatcha Know Joe
Slumber Song (Theme)

27 February, 1941 (THUR): Palace Theater, Cleveland Ohio
(CHESTERFIELD SHOW)
CBS   10:00-10:15 P.M. EST.

Slumber Song (Theme)
Ida!
Keep An Eye On Your Heart
Spring Will Be So Sad
Oh So Good
Slumber Song (Theme)

The band took the NY Central RR from Cleveland
to Cincinnati. (G.M.P.R.)

28 February, 1941 (FRI)

Glenn Miller and His Orchestra played for one
week (closed Thursday, March 6th) at the
Shubert Theater, Cincinnati, Ohio. (DB--Feb.
15, 1941). "It was a complete sell-out for the
Shubert Theatre with Glenn Miller and his band
for the week of first. Standing room only."
(DB--April 1, 1941).
    "Glenn Miller is linked with "Lessons from
La Zonga", is topping the burg currently and
setting a season's high for that stand. Squeezed
in a sixth performance Sunday, March 2, 1941 to
care for Miller rooters only such schedule for a
stage show here this season. Miller stompers

(Continued on next page)

jamming the house for its season's tops at
$18,000.00" (Variety, March 5, 1941)
Also on the same bill were Paul Regan and
Lorraine and Rognan. (G.M.P.R.)

4 March, 1941 (TUES): Shubert Theater, Cincinnati, Ohio
                     (CHESTERFIELD SHOW)
                     CBS 10:00-10:15 P.M.

                        Slumber Song (Theme)
                        Frenesi
                        La Cucaracha
                        A Stone's Throw From Heaven
                        Song Of The Volga Boatmen
                        Slumber Song (Theme)

5 March, 1941 (WED): Shubert Theater, Cincinnati, Ohio
                     (CHESTERFIELD SHOW)
                     CBS 10:00-10:15 P.M.

                        Slumber Song (Theme)
                        Perfidia
                        The Spirit Is Willing
                        Spring Will Be So Sad
                        Sun Valley Jump
                        Slumber Song (Theme)

6 March, 1941 (THUR): Shubert Theater, Cincinnati, Ohio
                     (CHESTERFIELD SHOW)
                     CBS 10:00-10:15 P.M.

                        Slumber Song (Theme)
                        Old Black Joe
                        Bugle Woogie
                        I Hear A Rhapsody
                        Anvil Chorus
                        Slumber Song (Theme)

            The band took the NY Central RR from Cincinnati
            to Columbus. (G.M.P.R.)

7 March, 1941 (FRI)

            Glenn Miller and His Orchestra played for one
            week (closed Thursday, March 13th) at the Palace
            Theater, Columbus, Ohio. (Variety, Feb. 19, 1941;
            G.M.P.R.) Also on the same bill were Paul Regan
            and Lorraine & Rognan. (G.M.P.R.)

11 March, 1941 (TUES): Palace Theater, Columbus, Ohio
(CHESTERFIELD SHOW)
CBS   10:00-10:15 P.M.

Slumber Song (Theme)
Sarong
Breakfast For Two
I Do, Do You?
I Dreamt I Dwelt In Harlem
Slumber Song (Theme)

12 March, 1941 (WED): Palace Theater, Columbus, Ohio
(CHESTERFIELD SHOW)
CBS   10:00-10:15 P.M.

Slumber Song (Theme)
Goin' Home
Swingin' At The Seance
It Was Wonderful Then
Boulder Buff
Slumber Song (Theme)

13 March, 1941 (THUR): Palace Theater, Columbus, Ohio
(CHESTERFIELD SHOW)
CBS   10:00-10:15 P.M.

Slumber Song (Theme)
Georgia On My Mind
Cheer Up
High On A Windy Hill
Measure For Measure
Slumber Song (Theme)

The band took the Penn. RR from Columbus to
St. Louis. (G.M.P.R.)

13 March, 1941 (THUR)

G.M.P.R. for the week ending March 13th show
that Billy May arranged "Gabby Goose".

14 March, 1941 (FRI)

Glenn Miller and His Orchestra played for one
week (closed Thursday, March 20th) at the Fox
Theater, St. Louis Missouri. (Variety, Feb. 19,
1941; G.M.P.R.) Also on the same bill were Paul
Regan and Lorraine & Rognan. (G.M.P.R.) The
film was "Meet the Chump."

(Continued on next page)

Here is an undated review of the band:
"Despite the Lenten season lag elsewhere
Glenn Miller and his tooters are generating plenty
of box office activity. Current show ranks with
the best offered this season and at session caught
huge first floor was brimful. This is Miller's
last public appearance in flicker house as at the
end of the current engagement, Thursday March 20,
1941, he takes the band to Hollywood to continue
his three a week network broadcasts for Chesterfields and preps for work in "Sun Valley", a
flicker in which Sonja Henie will be starred.
Show begins with Glenn Miller and his lads
doing their themer Moonlight Serenade behind the
closed curtains and finishing with the stage fully
exposed. The sax section and Miller with his
trombone are spotlighted for portions of the ditty.
Before the customers stopped palm pounding the
tooters continued right on with In the Mood and
Frenesi. The Modernaires (4) next present their
version of a novelty number Whatcha Know Joe? with
Tex Beneke, tenor sax contributing some vocal.
Dot Claire, tiny looker with the band possesses
smart pipes and socks over Perfidia and La Cucaracha
with the Modernaires. The band scores with Tuxedo
Junction and Ray Eberle's baritone won a nice hand
from the mob with his Berkley Square and I Hear A
Rhapsody with the Modernaires chiming in for
chorus.
The 53 minute session wound up with band
presenting Anvil Chorus from 'Il Trovatore with the
brasses carrying the load. Miller acts as M.C. and
keeps up the speedy tempo." (Variety, March 19,
1941)

18 March, 1941 (TUES): Fox Theater, St. Louis, Missouri
(CHESTERFIELD SHOW)
CBS 9:00-9:15 P.M.

Slumber Song (Theme)
The Spirit Is Willing
Naughty Sweetie Blues
Walking By The River
Oh So Good
Slumber Song (Theme)

19 March, 1941 (WED): Fox Theater, St. Louis, Missouri
(CHESTERFIELD SHOW)
CBS 9:00-9:15 P.M.

(Broadcast continued on next page)

Slumber Song (Theme)
Daisy Mae
Perfidia
Sweet Dreams-voc Ray Eberle
(
Are You Jumpin' Jack?
Slumber Song (Theme)

Later that night the band broadcast over CBS
(KMOX) for Washington University Night and St.
Louis University Night.

20 March, 1941 (THUR): Fox Theater, St. Louis, Missouri
(CHESTERFIELD SHOW)
CBS (KMOX) 9:00-9:15 P.M.

Slumber Song (Theme)
(2:38) *Sun Valley Jump* (arr JG)
(Jerry Gray)
Tpt, May; ts, Klink; tpt, May;
clt, Caceres; d, Purtill; tpt, ??
Slumber Song (Theme)

Information is missing on the other three tunes.
This was Dorothy Claire's last day with the band.
Paula Kelly joined the band in St. Louis but
officially replaced Dorothy Claire on the 21st.
(G.M.P.R.)

"Miller-Byrne feud over; Dorothy Claire
returns to Bobby's band, after the two leaders,
who had been at odds ever since Glenn took the
singer from Byrne, met in a hotel here late in
March. They reached an amicable agreement, up-
shot of which was the return of the young singing
star to the band with which she had previously
been spotted.
Miller immediately took on Paula Kelly,
former Al Donahue warbler and wife of Hal
Dickinson, one of Miller's Modernaires. Kay
Little, whom Dorothy replaces with Byrne, was
rumored at press-time to be joining Del Courtney's
orchestra.--COLUMBUS, OHIO." (Met. April 1941)
Evidently the agreement was made in a Columbus
hotel but the article is incorrect in stating that
it was late March as the Miller band was in
Columbus from March 7 to 13.

The band took the Missouri Pacific RR from St.
Louis to Los Angeles. (G.M.P.R.)

20 March, 1941 (THUR)

> G.M.P.R. for the week ending March 20th show
> that Billy May arranged "Carmen".

21 March, 1941 (FRI)

> En route to Hollywood. (G.M.D.)

22-23 March, 1941 (SAT & SUN)

> En route to Hollywood. (G.M.D.)

24 March, 1941 (MON)

> Band arrived in Hollywood and started picture.
> (G.M.D.)

24 March (MON)-3 May (SAT), 1941: 20th Century-Fox Studios,
                            Hollywood, California

> Glenn Miller and His Orchestra start work on
> the film "Sun Valley Serenade" at the 20th
> Century-Fox Studios, Hollywood, California.
> (Met. March 1941; G.M.P.R.) The film was pro-
> duced by Milton Sperling and directed by H. Bruce
> Humberstone. Lyrics by Mack Gordon and words by
> Harry Warren. Starring in the film (along with
> the Miller band) were Sonja Henie, John Payne,
> Milton Berle, Lynn Bari, Joan Davis, the Nicholas
> Brothers and Dorothy Dandridge. The Nicholas
> Brothers and Dorothy Dandridge were featured in
> a specialty dance routine during "Chattanooga
> Choo Choo". There appears to be some confusion
> as to who ghost-vocalled for Lynn Bari. There
> is mention of Lorraine Elliot but the October 1st,
> 1942 issue of Down Beat reported that Pat Friday,
> who did the vocal selections for Lynn Bari in
> "Orchestra Wives" also sang for Lynn Bari in "Sun
> Valley Serenade".
>
> During this period several numbers were recorded
> for the film and several issues of the numbers
> have been made. In all cases there is no evid-
> ence of alternate takes being issued as the film
> numbers are the same versions as the recordings.
> Several tunes were issued in edited form for
> promotional discs (eg. a 15 minute radio preview

(Continued on next page)

16" transcription was made for "Sun Valley
Serenade"--issue number is unknown) and some
were issued without the dubbed in sounds (such
as tap dancing) that were on the film. In
September 1954 R.C.A. Victor released a 10" LP
containing some of the selections from the film
sound track. "The Kiss Polka" was not included
in this issue but three tunes, although not used
in the completed film, were nevertheless recorded at the time for the film ("Sun Valley
Jump", "Measure For Measure" and "The Spirit Is
Willing") and were released by R.C.A. Victor.

Film
(0:54) The Kiss Polka (arr JG) (Instrumental)
          From the 20th Century-Fox film
          "Sun Valley Serenade"
          (Mack Gordon-Harry Warren)
          Tpt, May

Film, Preview, TCF TCF-70
(0:47) Moonlight Serenade
          (Mitchell Parish-Glenn Miller)

E4VL 5050   Vi LPT 3064, Film,Preview, Vi EPBT-3064 (947-
                   0201), HMV DLP 1104, Emb EMB 3318, TCF
                   TCF-100-2. TR 35/023, MTM 71018/MTS
                   72018, TCF F 3021, TCF TCF-70/71, TCF F
                   1001, RD 3/4-64, TCF TFM 3160/TFS 4160,
                   Emb EMB 4526, MT G MTS 4008, Cl Sp 18-
                   1115, TCF Int. LP 60004, RCA G LSP-9901,
                   RCA G EPBT-3064, Bert. Schall. 71003,
                   Ar 31052, TCF Arg FE 4160, RCA G SRS 560,
                   WRC T./ST. 252, TCF Au TL 31128
         (4:31) I Know Why (arr JG & BF)-voc Lorraine
                   Elliot?, John Payne and The
                   Modernaires
                   From the 20th Century-Fox film "Sun
                   Valley Serenade"
                   (Mack Gordon-Harry Warren)
                   Ts, Beneke; tbn, Miller

Film
(0:34) The Farmer In The Dell
          (

E4VL 5049   Vi LPT 3064, Film, Preview, Vi EPBT-3064 (947-
                   0201), HMV DLP 1104, Emb EMB 3318, TCF
                   TCF-100-2, TR JKR 8019, TR RX 3004, RD
                   3/4-64, TCF F 1001, TCF F 3020, TCF TFM
                   3159/TFS 4159, Emb EMB 4500, MTM 71003/
                   MTS 72003, MT G MTS 4004, Ar 31052,

(Film session continued on next page)

TCF Int. LP 60004, Bert. Schall. 71003,
Cl Sp 18-1114, RCA G EPBT-3064, TCF Arg
FE 4159, TCF Au TL 31127, TCF Au TL
31590, WRC TP/STP 223

(3:15) In The Mood
       (Andy Razaf-Joe Garland)
       Ts, Beneke; ts, Klink; tpt, May

E4VL 5049   Vi LPT 3064, Film, Preview, Vi EPBT-3064 (947-
0201), HMV DLP 1104, Emb EMB 3324, Emb
EMB 4500, TCF TCF-100-2. TR JKR 8019,
TCF TFM 3159/TFS 4159, RD 3/4-64, TCF F
3020, TCF F 1001, TCF TCF-77, MTM 71018/
MTS 72018, TR RX 3004, MT G MTS 4008,
Bert. Schall. 71003, RCA G EPBT-3064,
Cl Sp 18-1115, TCF Arg FE 4159, WRC TP/
STP 223, TCF Au TL 31127, TCF Au TL
31590

(2:09) It Happened In Sun Valley (arr BF)-voc
       Six Hits And A Miss and The Band
       From the 20th Century-Fox film
       "Sun Valley Serenade"
       (Mack Gordon-Harry Warren)

Film, TCF TCF-76
(1:50) The Kiss Polka-voc ??
       From the 20th Century-Fox film
       "Sun Valley Serenade"
       (Mack Gordon-Harry Warren)

E4VL 5049   Vi LPT 3064, Film, Preview, Vi EPBT-3064 (947-
0202), HMV DLP 1104, Emb EMB 3324, Emb
EMB 4500, Ar 31052, TCF TCF-100-2. TR TR
5003, Vi LPM-1190, Vi PR-114, TCF TFM
3159/TFS 4159, TCF F 3020, TCF F 1001,
RD 3/4-64, MTM 71003/MTS 72003, TR RX
3004, WRC TP 238, MT G MTS 4004, Cl Sp
18-1114, TCF Int. LP 60004, Bert. Schall.
71003, RCA G EPC-1190, RCA G LPM-1190,
RCA G EPBT-3064, TCF TCF-74/75, TCF Arg
FE 4159, TCF Au TL 31127, TCF Au TL 31590,
WRC TP/STP 223

(7:42) Chattanooga Choo Choo (arr JG)-voc Tex
       Beneke, Paula Kelly, The Modernaires,
       Nicholas Brothers and Dorothy
       Dandridge
       From the 20th Century-Fox film
       "Sun Valley Serenade"
       (Mack Gordon-Harry Warren)
       Ts, Beneke; p, MacGregor; muted tpt,
       May; open tpt, May; ts, Beneke;
       clt, Caceres

(Film session continued on next page)

E4VL 5049   Vi LPT 3064, Film, Vi EPBT-3064 (947-0202),
                HMV DLP 1104, RCA RCX 1062, Vi LPM-1190,
                Vi EPB-1190 (547-0829), RD 3/4-64, TCF
                TCF-72/73, RCA G EPBT-3064, RCA G EPC-
                1190, RCA G LPM-1190

            (4:56) At Last (arr JG & BF)-voc Lorraine Elliot?
                    and John Payne
                    Originally written for the film "Sun
                    Valley Serenade" but featured in the
                    20th Century-Fox film "Orchestra
                    Wives"
                    (Mack Gordon-Harry Warren)

E4VL 5050   Vi LPT 3064, Vi EPBT-3064 (947-0201), HMV DLP
                1104, Ar 31052, Emb EMB 3324, Emb EMB
                4512, TCF TCF-100-2, TCF F 3021, RCA RCX
                1062, Vi LPM-1190, TCF TFM 3160/TFS 4160,
                TR 35/023, RD 3/4-64, MTM 71003/MTS
                72003, MTM 71018/MTS 72018, MT G MTS 4004,
                MT G MTS 4008, Bert. Schall. 71003, RCA G
                EPBT-3064, RCA G LPM-1190, TCF Int. LP
                60004, Cl Sp 18-1114, Cl Sp 18-1115, WRC
                T./ST.252, TCF Arg FE 4160, TCF Au TL
                31128

           (2:26) Sun Valley Jump (arr JG)
                    (Jerry Gray)
                    Tpt, May; clt, Caceres; d, Purtill;
                    tpt, ??

E4VL 5050   Vi LPT 3064, Vi EPBT-3064 (947-0202), HMV DLP
                1104, Emb EMB 3324, Emb EMB 4512, TCF TCF-
                100-2, TR JKR 8019, TCF TFM 3159/TFS 4159,
                TCF F 3020, TR RX 3004, MTM 71018/MTS
                72018, MT G MTS 4008, Bert. Schall. 71003,
                Cl Sp 18-1115, TCF Arg FE 4159, TCF Au TL
                31127, WRC TP/STP 223, TCF Au TL 31590

           (2:35) Measure For Measure (arr BM)
                    (Arletta May)
                    As, Caceres; ts, Beneke; tpt, May

E4VL 5050   Vi LPT 3064, Vi EPBT-3064 (947-0202), HMV DLP
                1104, Emb EMB 3318, TCF TCF-100-2, Emb
                EMB 4525, TCF F 3021, MTM 71018/MTS 72018,
                TR 35/023, TCF TFM 3160/TFS 4160, MT G
                MTS 4008, Bert. Schall. 71003, WRC T./ST.
                252, Cl Sp 18-1115, TCF Arg FE 4160,
                TCF Au TL 31128

           (3:24) The Spirit Is Willing (arr JG)
                    (Jerry Gray)
                    Muted tpt, May; tpt, ??;muted tpt,
                    ??; tpt, May; muted tpt, ??; muted
                    tpt, May; tpt, ??; muted tpt, May;
                    tpt, ??; muted tpt, May

(Film Session continued on next page)

TCF TCF-76
(1:54) _The World Is Waiting To Waltz Again_
           (arr BF)-voc John Payne
           From the 20th Century-Fox film
           "Sun Valley Serenade"
           (Mack Gordon-Harry Warren)

Now, just a note on some of the edited differences between the film and the commercial
releases:
Miller's trombone can be heard in the film at
the end of "In The Mood". The TCF issue of "I
Know Why" has had John Payne's vocal and Miller's
trombone solo edited. The TCF issue of "It
Happened In Sun Valley" has a repeated "again" at
the end of the tune and this is believed to be a
recording error. In the film, Lorraine Elliot,
John Payne, Sonja Henie and Milton Berle sing
(voices dubbed in) during "It Happened In Sun
Valley". The commercial releases of "Chattanooga
Choo Choo" lack the tap dancing. The TCF issue
of "Chattanooga Choo Choo" is cut short and ends
before the Nicholas Brothers and Dorothy Dandridge
begin to sing. "At Last" is not heard in its
entirety in the film but it is heard in the background after "In The Mood" has ended in the film
and the band begins the introduction to "At Last"
after having played "Chattanooga Choo Choo" in
the film.
Finally, it might be pointed out that in the film,
after the band has played "Moonlight Serenade"
there is a piano run into "I Know Why". Part of
this run is heard on the TCF release but none is
heard on the original Victor release.

According to G.M.P.R. work on the film ended May
3rd, 1941. Metronome, April 1941, reported that
work on the film ended May 4th but we believe that
G.M.P.R. is more accurate.

25 March, 1941 (TUES): Hollywood, California (CHESTERFIELD SHOW)
                CBS 10:00-10:15 P.M.

     The announcer for this program is Larry Bruff.

           Slumber Song (Theme)
(2:00) _La Cucaracha_-voc Paula Kelly and The
                Modernaires
                (Mexican Folk Song)

(Broadcast continued on next page)

Int GM (1:48) *A Love Song Hasn't Been Sung* (arr JG)-
voc Ray Eberle
(Harold Dickinson-Bill Conway-
Jerry Gray)

K2PP-0045   Vi LPM-6100, RCA RD 27146, RCA G LPM-6100,
RCA Au L 11024
(2:30) Solid As A Stonewall, Jackson (arr JG)
(Jerry Gray-John Chalmers MacGregor)
As, Caceres; ts, Beneke

Slumber Song (Theme)

Information is missing on the opening tune. On
this program Miller introduced Paula Kelly to
the studio audience as it was her first appearance on the Chesterfield program.

This arrangement of "A Love Song Hasn't Been Sung"
is slightly different from the one used on the
Chesterfield broadcast of May 8, 1941.

26 March, 1941 (WED): Hollywood, California (CHESTERFIELD SHOW)
CBS   10:00-10:15 P.M.

Slumber Song (Theme)
Adios
There'll Be Some Changes Made
Spring Will Be So Sad
Song Of The Volga Boatmen
Slumber Song (Theme)

27 March, 1941 (THUR): Hollywood, California (CHESTERFIELD SHOW)
CBS   10:00-10:15 P.M.

WPRS-0975   Vi LSP-3981, RCA Br. RD/SF-7982
(0:48) Slumber Song (Theme)
(Saul Tepper-John Chalmers MacGregor)

WPRS-0975   Vi LSP-3981, RCA Br. RD/SF-7982
Int GM (3:13) Watcha Know Joe-voc Tex Beneke and The
Band
(James Young)
As, Caceres

WPRS-0976   Vi LSP-3981, RCA Br. RD/SF-7982
Int GM (3:10) It Was Wonderful Then (And It's Wonderful
Now)-voc Ray Eberle and The
Modernaires
(Berkeley Graham-Carley Mills)

I Dreamt I Dwelt In Harlem
Slumber Song (Theme)

28 March, 1941 (FRI)

        Glenn Miller and His Orchestra played for the
U.C.L.A. (University of California at Los
Angeles) Junior Prom (Kerlahoff Hall, 402 West-
wood Blvd., West Los Angeles), Los Angeles,
California, and are paid $2,000.00 (the highest
price ever paid by the University). (Met. April
1941; G.M.P.R.; G.M.C.)

1 April, 1941 (TUES): Hollywood, California (CHESTERFIELD SHOW)
*   CBS 10:00-10:15 P.M.*

*   The announcer for this program is Larry Bruff.*

*   (0:45) Slumber Song (Theme)*
*   (Saul Tepper-John Chalmers MacGregor)*
*   (3:15) The Spirit Is Willing (arr JG)*
*   (Jerry Gray)*
*   P, MacGregor; muted tpt, May; tpt, ??;*
*   muted tpt, ??; tpt, May; muted tpt,*
*   ??; muted tpt, May;tpt, ??;muted tpt,*
*   May; tpt, ??; muted tpt, May*
Int LB (1:35) Bugle Woogie (arr BF)-voc Paula Kelly
*   (Gordon Andrews-Floria Vestoff)*
*   Tpt, ??; p, MacGregor; tpt, ??*
Int GM (2:04) These Things You Left Me (arr JG)-voc
*   Ray Eberle and The Modernaires*
*   (Hal Dickinson-Sidney Lippman)*
*   Boulder Buff*
*   Slumber Song (Theme)*

2 April, 1941 (WED): Hollywood, California (CHESTERFIELD SHOW)
*   CBS 10:00-10:15 P.M.*

*   The announcer for this program is Larry Bruff.*

*   Slumber Song (Theme)*

UPRM-6315   ~~Vi LPM/LSP-3873,~~ RCA Br. RD/SF-7932, RCA G LSP-
                 ~~3873~~
*   Int LB (2:44)* ~~Harlem Chapel Bells~~ *(arr BM)*
*   (   )*
           P, MacGregor; as, Caceres; tpt, Best

*   Breakfast For Two*
*   I Do, Do You?*
*   Measure For Measure*
*   Slumber Song (Theme)*

3 April, 1941 (THUR): Hollywood California (CHESTERFIELD SHOW)
                        CBS   10:00-10:15 P.M.

              The announcer for this program is Larry Bruff.

                    Slumber Song (Theme)
                    Georgia On My Mind
                    Keep An Eye On Your Heart
                    Walking By The River-voc RE & 4M
                    Anvil Chorus
                    Slumber Song (Theme)

3 April, 1941 (THUR)

              G.M.P.R. for the week ending April 3rd show
              that Billy May arranged "I Take To You".

4 April, 1941 (FRI)

              Glenn Miller and His Orchestra played for U.S.C.
              (University of Southern California) dance held
              at the Hotel Biltmore, Los Angeles, California
              and are paid $2,000.00 (the highest price ever
              paid by the university). (Met. April, 1941;
              G.M.P.R.) It must be noted here that Met.
              April, 1941 shows March 29th as being the date
              of this dance but there is no mention of a dance
              being held on this date by G.M.P.R. until April
              4th. The final answer to this date is on the
              Chesterfield show of April 3rd in which Miller,
              as he signs off, says that the band will be play-
              ing for the University of Southern California
              Junior Prom at the Blue Room of the Biltmore
              Hotel. The band played from 9:00-1:00 A.M.
              (G.M.D.)

8 April, 1941 (TUES): Hollywood, California (CHESTERFIELD SHOW)
                        CBS   10:00-10:15 P.M.

                    Slumber Song (Theme)
                    Sarong
                    Naughty Sweetie Blues

WPRS-0975   Vi LSP-3981, RCA Br. RD/SF-7982
          Int GM (3:04) Spring Will Be So Sad (When She Comes
                        This Year)
                        (arr JG)-voc Ray Eberle and The
                        Modernaires
                        (Margaret Bonds-Harold Dickinson)
                        Ts, Beneke; clt, ??
(Broadcast continued on next page)

Sun Valley Jump
Slumber Song (Theme)

9 April, 1941 (WED): Hollywood, California (CHESTERFIELD SHOW)
            CBS   10:00-10:15 P.M.

                    Slumber Song (Theme)

K2PP-0045   Vi LPM-6100, RCA RD 27146, RCA G LPM-6100,
                   RCA Au L 11024
       Int GM (2:49) Blue Afterglow (arr JG)
                        (Glover-Hall)
                    Ts, Beneke; tpt, Best; ts, Beneke

                    I Take To You (arr BM)-voc Paula Kelly
                    (
                    A Love Song Hasn't Been Sung
                    Are You Rusty, Gate?
                    Slumber Song (Theme)

10 April, 1941 (THUR): Hollywood, California (CHESTERFIELD SHOW)
            CBS   10:00-10:15 P.M.

                    Slumber Song (Theme)

K2PP-0043   Vi LPM-6100, RCA RD 27145, RCA G LPM-6100,
                   RCA G LPM/LSP-9944, RCA Au L 11023
           (2:55) Gabby Goose (arr BM)
                        (Arletta May)
                        Muted tpt, May; clt, Caceres;
                        muted tpt, May; clt, Caceres;
                        muted tpt, May; clt, Caceres;
                        muted tpt, May

                    Perfidia
                    High On A Windy Hill
                    Oh So Good
                    Slumber Song (Theme)

15 April, 1941 (TUES): Hollywood, California (CHESTERFIELD SHOW)
            CBS   10:00-10:15 P.M.

                    Slumber Song (Theme)
                    Frenesi
                    Ciri-Biri-Bin
                    I Do, Do You?
                    Solid As a Stonewall, Jackson
                    Slumber Song (Theme)

16 April, 1941 (WED): Hollywood, California (CHESTERFIELD SHOW)
             CBS 10:00-10:15 P.M.

               Slumber Song (Theme)
               Adios
               Cheer Up
               The Morning After
               Are You Jumpin' Jack?
               Slumber Song (Theme)

17 April, 1941 (THUR): Hollywood, California (CHESTERFIELD SHOW)
             CBS 10:00-10:15 P.M.

               Slumber Song (Theme)

K2PP-0044   Vi LPM-6100, RCA RD 27146, RCA G LPM-6100,
                   RCA G LPM 9852, RCA G LPM/LSP-9944, RCA
                   Au L 11024
          Int GM (2:12) Rockin' Chair (arr JG)-voc Tex Beneke
                   (Hoagy Carmichael)
               Tpt, Best

               Swingin' At The Seance
               It Was Wonderful Then
               Song Of The Volga Boatmen
               Slumber Song (Theme)

19 April, 1941 (SAT): Hollywood Palladium, Hollywood, California
             NBC-Red 12:30 A.M. EST.

               Slumber Song (Theme)
               Song Of The Volga Boatmen
               I Do, Do You?
               The Booglie Wooglie Piggy
               Spring Will Be So Sad
               Here We Go Again
               Adios
               Swing Low, Sweet Chariot
               Slumber Song (Theme)

               According to G.M.P.R. Miller opened at the
Hollywood Palladium May 2nd so we're not quite
sure how this program fits in with the scheme
of things unless the date is incorrect. Information on this program is from a review of
"Dance Bands on the Air", Metronome, June 1941:

               "The Glenn Miller sustainings continue to
be exemplary displays of showmanship and polish.

(Continued on next page)

Not only does Glenn order his programs to the
fullest advantage of his caravan of musicians
and singers, but the latter come through with
some of the most radio-receptive playing around.
   Whatever else may be true of the Miller
manuscript, it is not simple, and it doesn't
get simpler. Which is not to say that the music
these men play is complicated beyond listening
pleasure. On the contrary, in such things on
this program as the Ravel-like introduction to
Spring Will Be So Sad, the strident contrasts of
Adios and the brass canon of the opening Volga
Boatmen, the true distinction of this band was
clearly indicated. For Glenn leads a band that
reflects his own diversified musical interests,
his love for rich, almost lush orchestration,
and his continuing jazz kick, his affection for
beautiful balladizing and for sinuous swing.
   After the opening in gloomy Russia, with
The Volga Boatmen impressing that gloom in a
chanted "Who-oooo-oooooo," and Billy May adding
a poignant note of growled trumpet, the band
got around to a happier climate in I Do, Do You.
This was pleasantly short. Ray Eberle sang the
lyrics, the orchestra struck a good dance beat,
and that was that.
   Tapped then were the novelty talents of Tex
Beneke, Paula Kelly and the Modernaires, for the
amusing plays-on-words that riffle through
Boogily, Woogily, Piggy, with logically enough,
some b.w. figures at its base. Trouble here was
a troublesome mike, or a troublesome Tex, or a
ditto engineer. Anyway, Tex didn't come through
the speaker as if he were in the same room with
the rest of the band. He sounded long away and
far ago.
   Paula Kelly didn't sound at all. She
pitched a few notes out of the Modernaires-Beneke
voicing on the Piggy piece and then was heard no
more. That was the only lapse of showmanship on
the program. But there most definitely could and
should have been some womanly warbling.
   One more ballad popped up among the next and
last four numbers. This was the affecting Spring
Will Be So Sad This Year (How could she be glad
when she reaches here), which the Modernaires and
Ray Eberle sing with the restrained religious
fervor of an Armenian come-all-ye. And that's
good enough. The lovely tune and the strikingly
simple lyrics are thereby incisively imbedded in
your head.

(Continued on next page)

Here We Go Again showed how much the
precision playing and the crisp dynamics of the
Miller men could do to routine riffs in a routine
arrangement. The sforzando kick in the last
chorus is especially illustrative, changing a
typical Miller jazz softening into a powerful
climax.

Adios, a charming arrangement of the Enric
Madriguera theme, preceded the riff rides, while
some able swing stuff ended the program. The
able swing stuff was constructed around Swing Low,
Sweet Chariot, which boasted of a good beat, best
of the evening in fact, some clean arranging that
strode effectively in and out of a Basie-like
piano-rhythm interlude, and was highspotted by a
swell chorus of growl trumpeting by Billy May's
Ellington-educated horn. The Chariot's climax
built around infectious figures that we shall
probably hear more of.

In sum, the airing was pleasing for good
playing, nimble arrangements and a series of
climaxes, hot and sweet, that might have been
leavened a step higher by the inclusion of a
female voice, but which nonetheless left the
listener fighting the sentiment expressed by the
Glenn Miller theme, Slumber Song.--ULANOV."

22 April, 1941 (TUES): Hollywood, California (CHESTERFIELD SHOW)
                CBS 10:00-10:15 P.M.

                Slumber Song (Theme)
                There'll Be Some Changes Made
                Walking By The River
                I Dreamt I Dwelt In Harlem
                Slumber Song (Theme)

23 April, 1941 (WED): Hollywood, California (CHESTERFIELD SHOW)
                CBS 10:00-10:15 P.M.

        The announcer for this program is Larry Bruff.

                Slumber Song (Theme)
                Breakfast For Two-voc PK, TB & 4M
                A Love Song Hasn't Been Sung
                Swing Low, Sweet Chariot
                Slumber Song (Theme)

24 April, 1941 (THUR): Hollywood, California (CHESTERFIELD SHOW)
CBS   10:00-10:15 P.M.

> *Slumber Song (Theme)*
> *Ida!*
> *Keep An Eye On Your Heart*
> *These Things You Left Me*
> *Measure For Measure*
> *Slumber Song (Theme)*

24 April, 1941 (THUR)

> G.M.P.R. for the week ending April 24th show
> that Billy May arranged "Sweeter Than The
> Sweetest".

29 April, 1941 (TUES): Hollywood, California (CHESTERFIELD SHOW)
CBS   10:00-10:15 P.M.

> *Slumber Song (Theme)*
> *Goin' Home*
> *Naughty Sweetie Blues*
> *Spring Will Be So Sad*
> *Anvil Chorus*
> *Slumber Song (Theme)*

30 April, 1941 (WED): Hollywood, California (CHESTERFIELD SHOW)
CBS   10:00-10:15 P.M.

> *Slumber Song (Theme)*
> *Blue Afterglow*

E3VP 5245   Vi LPT 6700, Vi EPNT 6700 (947-0117), HMV RLS
             599, Vi SPD-18 (599-9104), RCA G LPT
             6700
     (1:45) Just A Little Bit South Of North
             Carolina (arr JG)-voc Paula Kelly
             (Sonny Skylar-Arthur Shaftel-Bette
             Cannon)
             Tpt, Best

> *It Was Wonderful Then-voc RE & 4M*
> *Sun Valley Jump*
> *Slumber Song (Theme)*

Vi LPT 6700 lists the vocalist on "Just A
Little Bit South of North Carolina" as Dorothy
Claire but the vocalist is Paula Kelly.

1 May, 1941 (THUR): Hollywood, California (CHESTERFIELD SHOW)
        CBS   10:00-10:15 P.M.

        The announcer for this program is Larry Bruff.

                    Slumber Song *(Theme)*
                    Amapola-*voc PK & 4M*
                    Dancing In A Dream With You
                        Muted tpt, Best; ts, Beneke
                    Boulder Buff
                    Slumber Song *(Theme)*

2 May, 1941 (FRI)

            Glenn Miller and His Orchestra opened at the
            Hollywood Palladium, Hollywood, California for
            a three week engagement. (G.M.P.R.)

                "Glenn Miller's opening at the Palladium
            (May 2) broke all previous box-office records
            here. Palladium management didn't give out
            official figures but experienced observers esti-
            mated the total admissions as being in excess of
            7,000.
                The Palladium's 750 table reservations were
            completely sold out well in advance of the open-
            ing. Several hundred were taken by movie
            celebs. A big representation came from 20th
            Century-Fox where Miller has been working on a
            picture deal.
                The big turn-out for the Miller opening was
            strictly in the cards, inasmuch as it was the
            band's first public appearance here but many had
            figured that the two college dates and the radio
            broadcasts played here prior to the Palladium
            opening might take the edge off the occasion."
            (DB, May 15, 1941)

                "The Palladium announced that during Glenn
            Miller's engagement the entire 'free list' would
            be suspended. Ruling applied to passes of all
            types, including season 'courtesy' cards issued
            to newsmen, writers, etc. Biggest howl came
            from those who had been hoarding publicity dept.
            passes handed out in return for favors received.
            Maddest of all was 'Hank, the Night Watchman,'
            KFVD's disc flipper, who has been awarding
            Palladium tickets to winners of band-guessing
            contests. When the kids who had been saving
            these tickets for Miller learned that they were
            duds--well, you can imagine!" (DB, May 15, 1941)

(Continued on next page)

G.M.P.R. indicate that there was a Glenn Miller party at the Palladium on May 2nd.

"Despite the hottest May weather in 50 years Glenn Miller took out $7,800. as his share for the first of a three week engagement at the Palladium. It's top coin for the dancery.
He's in for a guarantee of $4,000.00 against 50% at the door." (Variety, May 14, 1941)

The band played from 8:00-2:00 A.M. 7 nights a week and from 2:00-6:00 P.M. Saturday afternoons. (G.M.D.)

3 May, 1941 (SAT)

Glenn Miller and His Orchestra wind up their work on the film "Sun Valley Serenade". (G.M.P.R.)

G.M.P.R. for the week ending May 3rd show that Billy May arranged a "Montage" in the film (10 Pages).

6 May, 1941 (TUES): Hollywood, California (CHESTERFIELD SHOW)
CBS   10:00-10:15 P.M.

The announcer for this program is Larry Bruff.

> *Slumber Song (Theme)*
> *Sweeter Than The Sweetest*
> *High On A Windy Hill*
> ALP *Song Of The Volga Boatmen*
> *Slumber Song (Theme)*

7 May, 1941 (WED): Victor Studios, Hollywood, California

Same personnel as for November 4th except that PAULA KELLY has replaced Dorothy Claire (who replaced Marion Hutton) as vocalist.

061243-1   BB 11163-A, HMV BD 5711, HMVAu EA-2988, HMV
              7EG 8204, Vi LPT 6700, Vi EPNT 6700
              (947-0118), HMV RLS 599, Vi SPD-18 (599-
              9108), RCA RD 27068, Vi LPM/LSP-1192,
              Vi 45 Special-1953, RCA G LPT 6700,
              RD 3/4-64, RCA F 530243, RCA G LPM/LSP-
              1192, Vi Arg LPM/LSP-1192, RCA F 740.515

(Session continued on next page)

Boulder Buff (arr FN)
(Eugene Novello-Fred Norman)
P, MacGregor; muted tpt, May; ts, Klink

061244-1 BB 11163-B, HMV BD 5711, HMVAu EA-2882, RD 3/4-64,
The Booglie Wooglie Piggy (arr JG)-voc Tex Beneke
and The Four Modernaires (and Paula Kelly)
(Roy Jacobs)
P, MacGregor; ts, Beneke; tpt, May

061245-1 BB 11230-B, HMV BD 5720, HMVAu EA-2999,
AFRS G.I. Jive H-12-2002,
AFRS G.I. Jive H-12-1589, HMVF
7EMF11, HMVSw JK-2357, Vi 20-2410 (Vi P-189),
Vi 42-0026, Vi 27-0026, Vi 420-0039, Vi 447-
0039, Vi 20-2972, Vi 47-2858, Vi EPAT-401,
Vi EPA-529, Vi EPA-5081, RCA RCX 1035, HMV
DLP 1024, Vi LPT 1016, Vi LPM-3182, Vi LOP-
1509, Vi LPM/LSP-3377, RD Br. RDS 6098, RD
Br. RDS 6172, HMVAus VDLP 302, El WDLP 1024,
Vi 83872-B, RD 3/4-25, El G EG 7541, AFRS
P-S-15, AFRS "Jukebox USA" 154, AFRS "Juke-
box USA" 252, AFRS P-1118, HMVAus GA-5012,
El 7MW 643, RCA Int. 11002, RCA G LPM 9801,
RCA It 45NO899, RCA It EPA 30-078, Vi P8S-
5061, Vi VLP 3377, RCA G 447-0039, RCA G
EPAT-401, RCA G LPT 1016, Vi EPB 1072, Vi
TP3-5044, Vi LPM 1072, Vi VPM-6019, RCA G
LPM 1072, RCA G LPM/LSP-3377, RCA G LSP-
9901, RCA Int. CT 20124, HMVIr I.P. 932,
Vi PRM-261, RD 8-5013, RCA Vi Arg 3AE-3342,
AFRS G.I. Jive EN-12-2349, AFRS G.I. Jive
EN-12-2305, AFRS G.I. Jive EN-12-2263, AFRS
G.I. Jive H-12-1826, AFRS G.I. Jive H-12-
1837, AFRS G.I. Jive H-12-1867, AFRS G.I.
Jive H-12-753, AFRS G.I. Jive H-12-866,
AFRS G.I. Jive H-12-937, AFRS G.I. Jive
H-12-1006, RCA Br. RD-8094, RCA Br. GM-1,
AFRS G.I. Jive H-12-1063, AFRS G.I. Jive
H-12-1086, AFRS G.I. Jive H-12-1113, AFRS
G.I. Jive H-12-1146, AFRS G.I. Jive H-12-
1174, RCA G Cas 10231, RCA G SRS 560, AFRS
G.I. Jive H-12-1258, AFRS G.I. Jive H-12-
1339, AFRS G.I. Jive H-12-1399, AFRS G.I.
Jive H-12-1708, AFRS G.I. Jive H-12-1460,
AFRS G.I. Jive H-12-1504, AFRS G.I. Jive
H-12-1553, AFRS G.I. Jive H-12-1802, AFRS
G.I. Jive H-12-1804, AFRS G.I. Jive
H-12-1586, AFRS G.I. Jive H-12-2053
Chattanooga Choo Choo (arr JG)-voc Tex Beneke and
The Four Modernaires (and Paula Kelly)
From the 20th Century-Fox film "Sun Valley
Serenade"
(Mack Gordon-Harry Warren)

(Session continued on next page)

061246-1   BB 11230-A, HMV BD 5720, HMVSw JK-2357, HMV DLP
           1024, El G EG 7541, HMVAus GA-5012, HMVAus
           VDLP 302, El WDLP 1024, El 7MW 643, HMVAus
           BA 765, HMVIr I.P. 932, AFRS G.I. Jive
           H-12-1001, AFRS G.I. Jive H-12-1803, AFRS
           G.I. Jive H-12-1284, AFRS G.I. Jive H-12-
           1643, AFRS G.I. Jive H-12-1842 (incomplete)
       I Know Why (arr JG & BF)-voc Paula Kelly and The
           Four Modernaires
           From the 20th Century-Fox film "Sun Valley
           Serenade"
           (Mack Gordon-Harry Warren)

       "I Know Why" 3 takes; all other tunes 2 takes
       (RCA Victor)
       This session lasted from 1:00 P.M. to 5:00 P.M.
       (RCA Victor)
       Although Jerry Gray is shown as the arranger on
       "Chattanooga Choo Choo" it must be noted that this
       was for the band portion only and that for the
       vocal part Bill Conway arranged the harmony and Hal
       Dickinson arranged the verse.

7 May, 1941 (WED): Hollywood, California (CHESTERFIELD SHOW)
           CBS   10:00-10:15 P.M.

               Slumber Song (Theme)
               Sing And Be Gay-voc PK

K2PP-0047   Vi LPM-6100, RCA RD 27147, RCA G LPM-6100, RCA Au
               L 11025
       Int GM (2:55) Walking By The River (arr JG)-voc Ray Eberle
                   and The Modernaires
                   (Robert Sour-Una Mae Carlisle)

               Oh So Good
               Slumber Song (Theme)

       On Vi LPM-6100 "Walking By The River" was in-
       correctly listed as being broadcast on March 7,
       1941.

8 May, 1941 (THUR): Hollywood, California (CHESTERFIELD SHOW)
           CBS   10:00-10:15 P.M.

       The announcer for this program is Larry Bruff.

               Slumber Song (Theme)
               I Take To You-voc PK & 4M

(Broadcast continued on next page)

K2PP-0046 ~~Vi LPM-6100,~~ RCA RD 27147, RCA G LPM-6100, RCA Au
~~L 11025~~
~~(3:00) A Love Song Hasn't Been Sung~~ (arr JG)-voc
Ray Eberle
(Harold Dickinson-Bill Conway-Jerry Gray)

Swing Low, Sweet Chariot
Slumber Song (Theme)

13 May, 1941 (TUES): Hollywood, California (CHESTERFIELD SHOW)
CBS   10:00-10:15 P.M.

(0:45) Slumber Song (Theme)
(Saul Tepper-John Chalmers MacGregor)
Int GM (3:10) The Booglie Wooglie Piggy (arr JG)-voc Tex
Beneke, Paula Kelly and The Modernaires
(Roy Jacobs)
P, MacGregor; ts, Beneke; tpt, May
Int GM (3:15) You Walk By-voc Ray Eberle
& RE (Ben Raleigh-Bernie Wayne)
Here We Go Again
Slumber Song (Theme)

14 May, 1941 (WED): Hollywood, California (CHESTERFIELD SHOW)
CBS   10:00-10:15 P.M.

The announcer for this program is Larry Bruff.

Slumber Song (Theme)
Gabby Goose
Just A Little Bit South Of North Carolina
It Was Wonderful Then-voc RE & 4M
Are You Rusty, Gate?
Slumber Song (Theme)

15 May, 1941 (THUR): Hollywood,California (CHESTERFIELD SHOW)
CBS   10:00-10:15 P.M.

The announcer for this program is Larry Bruff.

Slumber Song (Theme)
Perfidia
Dancing In A Dream With You
I Dreamt I Dwelt In Harlem
Slumber Song (Theme)

15 May, 1941 (THUR)

> G.M.P.R. for the week ending May 15th show that
> Billy May arranged "Friday Afternoon" and
> "Dolores".

20 May, 1941 (TUES): Victor Studios, Hollywood, California

Trombones	Glenn Miller, Jimmy Priddy, Paul Tanner, Frank D'Annolfo
Trumpets	Billy May, Ray Anthony, Dale McMickle, HARRY GELLER
Reeds	Hal McIntyre, as; Ernie Caceres; as, bar & clt; Wilbur Schwartz, clt & as; Tex Beneke, ts; Al Klink, ts
Rhythm	Chummy MacGregor, p; Jack Lathrop, g; Trigger Alpert, b; Maurice Purtill, d
Vocalists	Paula Kelly, Ray Eberle and The Four Modernaires

061253-1   BB 11183-A, HMV MH 93, HMVAu EA-2872, El G EG 7432
Don't Cry, Cherie (arr BF)-voc Ray Eberle
                   (Lew Brown-Ray Henderson)

061254-1   BB 11203-B, HMV BD 5733, HMV MH 137, HMVIn BD 5733
Cradle Song (arr HGC)-voc Ray Eberle and Chorus
                   (J. Brahms-Arr. by H.G. Chapman)

061255-1   BB 11183-B, HMV MH 93, Vi LPM 2080, El G EG 7432,
                   RD 3/4-64, RCA G EPA-9019, HMVSc X 7524,
                   Vi P8S-1432, Vi LSP-4125, RCA Int. INTS 1002
Sweeter Than The Sweetest (arr BM)-voc Paula Kelly
                   and The Four Modernaires
                   (Neil Lawrence-Willie (The Lion) Smith)
                   Ts, Klink

All tunes 2 takes. (RCA Victor)
This session lasted from 12:00 Noon to 3:00 P.M.
(RCA Victor)

According to G.M.P.R. Harry Geller substituted for
Johnny Best on this date only for: the record
session, the Chesterfield program, and this one
night at the Palladium. Best, who must have been
ill, rejoined the band on May 23rd.

20 May, 1941 (TUES): Hollywood, California (CHESTERFIELD SHOW)
*   CBS 10:00-10:15 P.M.*

(Broadcast continued on next page)

Slumber Song (Theme)
Boulder Buff
La Cucaracha
A Stone's Throw From Heaven
Sun Valley Jump
Slumber Song (Theme)

21 May, 1941 (WED): *Hollywood, California (CHESTERFIELD SHOW)*
         CBS   10:00-10:15 P.M.

Trombones	*Glenn Miller, Jimmy Priddy, Paul Tanner, Frank D'Annolfo*
Trumpets	*Billy May, Ray Anthony, Dale McMickle, JOE MEYER*
Reeds	*Hal McIntyre, as; Ernie Caceres, as, bar & clt; Wilbur Schwartz, clt & as; Tex Beneke, ts; Al Klink, ts*
Rhythm	*Chummy MacGregor, p; Jack Lathrop, g; Trigger Alpert, b; Maurice Purtill, d*

Slumber Song (Theme)
Adios
Keep An Eye On Your Heart-voc PK
Walking By The River-voc RE & 4M
Anvil Chorus
Slumber Song (Theme)

According to G.M.P.R. Joe Meyer substituted for Johnny Best on this Chesterfield program. No mention is made of who substituted for Best at the Palladium this evening but we assume that Meyer would probably be the substitution.

22 May, 1941 (THUR): *Hollywood, California (CHESTERFIELD SHOW)*
         CBS   10:00-10:15 P.M.

The announcer for this program is Larry Bruff.

Trombones	*Glenn Miller, Jimmy Priddy, Paul Tanner, Frank D'Annolfo*
Trumpets	*Billy May, Ray Anthony, Dale McMickle, LEONARD ARLO MACH*
Reeds	*Hal McIntyre, as; Ernie Caceres, as, bar & clt; Wilbur Schwartz, clt & as; Tex Beneke, ts; Al Klink, ts*
Rhythm	*Chummy MacGregor, p; Jack Lathrop, g; Trigger Alpert, b; Maurice Purtill, d*

Slumber Song (Theme)

(Broadcast continued on next page)

WPRS-0976   Vi LSP-3981, RCA Br. RD/SF-7982
            (2:56) Amapola (Pretty Little Poppy) (arr JG)-
                   voc Paula Kelly and The Modernaires
                   (Joseph M. Lacalle-Albert Gamse)

            A Love Song Hasn't Been Sung
            Swing Low, Sweet Chariot
            Slumber Song (Theme)

            According to G.M.P.R. Leonard Arlo Mach substituted
            for Johnny Best on this Chesterfield program. No
            mention is made of who substituted for Best at the
            Palladium this evening but we assume that Mach
            would probably be the substitution.

22 May, 1941 (THUR): Hollywood Palladium, Hollywood, California
                     NBC-Red

            Glenn Miller and His Orchestra closed at the
            Hollywood Palladium, Hollywood, California (G.M.P.R.)

            (2:40) Amapola (Pretty Little Poppy) (arr JG)-
                    voc Paula Kelly and The Modernaires
                    (Joseph M. Lacalle-Albert Gamse)
            (1:39) It Was Wonderful Then (And It's Wonderful
                    Now)-voc Ray Eberle and The Modernaires
                    (Berkeley Graham-Carley Mills)
            (3:24) Swing Low, Sweet Chariot (arr BF)
                    (Spiritual)
                    Ts, Beneke; p, MacGregor, muted tpt, May

            This was Jack Lathrop's last day with the band.
            G.M.P.R. show that he was paid for the Chesterfield
            shows of May 20th, 21st and 22nd. He sold his
            guitar to Bill Conway.

23 May, 1941 (FRI): Hollywood, California

            Jack Lathrop, guitarist, left the band on May 22nd.
            Until his permanent successor, Bobby Hackett,
            arrived on July 10th, Bill Conway of the Modernaires
            was the guitarist.

            Trombones   Glenn Miller, Jimmy Priddy, Paul
                         Tanner, Frank D'Annolfo
            Trumpets   Billy May, Ray Anthony, Dale McMickle,
                         JOHNNY BEST
            Reeds   Hal McIntyre, as; Ernie Caceres, as,
                         bar & clt; Wilbur Schwartz, clt & as;
                         Tex Beneke, ts; Al Klink, ts
            Rhythm   Chummy MacGregor, p; BILL CONWAY, g;
                         Trigger Alpert, b; Maurice Purtill, d

23 May, 1941 (FRI)

> Glenn Miller and His Orchestra played at the Civic
> Auditorium, Fresno, California, from 9:00-1:00 A.M.
> The band stayed at the Hotel Fresno. (G.M.P.R. &
> G.M.D.)

24 May, 1941 (SAT)

> Glenn Miller and His Orchestra played at the
> Cocoanut Grove Ballroom, Manteca, California, from
> 10:00-2:00 A.M. (G.M.P.R. & G.M.D.)

25 May, 1941 (SUN)

> Glenn Miller and His Orchestra played at the Sweets
> Ballroom, Oakland, California, from 10:00-2:00 A.M.,
> and drew 3,200. (G.M.P.R.; G.M.D.; Variety, June
> 4, 1941)

26 May, 1941 (MON)

> Glenn Miller and His Orchestra played at the Civic
> Auditorium, San Jose, California, and drew 2,000.
> (G.M.P.R.; Variety, June 4, 1941)

27 May, 1941 (TUES)

> G.M.P.R. show this as being an open date which
> means that the band returned to Hollywood to do
> the Chesterfield program.

27 May, 1941 (TUES): Hollywood, California (CHESTERFIELD SHOW)
CBS   10:00-10:15 P.M.

> *The announcer for this program is Larry Bruff.*

> *Slumber Song (Theme)*
> *Sweeter Than The Sweetest*

UPRM-6315   Vi LPM/LSP-3873, RCA G LSP-3873, RCA Br. RD/SF-7932
        Int GM (3:10) High On A Windy Mill (arr BF)-voc Ray Eberle
                    (Alex Kramer-Joan Whitney)
                    Muted tpt, McMickle

> *Oh So Good*
> *Slumber Song (Theme)*

(Continued on next page)

The band played the Chesterfield program in
Hollywood and played a dance date at the Civic
Auditorium, San Bernardino, California, from
9:00-1:00 A.M. (G.M.D.)

28 May, 1941 (WED): Victor Studios, Hollywood, California

Same personnel as for May 23rd.

061265-1   BB 11187-A, HMV 7EG 8097, RCA RCX 1034, Vi EPA-
            5035, RD 3/4-25, RD Br. RDS 6098
            I Guess I'll Have To Dream The Rest-voc Ray Eberle
            and The Modernaires
            (Mickey Stoner-Martin Block-Harold Green)
            Ts, Beneke

061266-1   BB 11187-B, HMV BD 5829, HMV 7EG 8031, Vi EPAT-
            428, Vi LPT-1031, Vi LPM/LSP-3564, El G EG
            7965, AFRS "America's Pop Music" 72, Vi TP3-
            5044, Vi P8S-5061, RCA G LPT 1031, RCA G
            EPAT-428, VdP HN 2494, VdP 7EPQ 542, HMVHu
            HUC 114, Vi Arg LPM 3564
            Take The "A" Train (arr BM)
            (Billy Strayhorn)
            Muted tpt, May; ts, Beneke

061267-1   BB 11203-A, Vi Braz 82-0023, Vi Arg 68-1344
            Peekaboo To You (arr JG)-voc The Four Modernaires
            (and Paula Kelly)
            (Johnny Mercer-Carl Sigman-Joseph Meyer)
            As, Caceres; tpt, Best

061268-1   BB 11215-B, RD 3/4-64
            The Angels Came Thru-voc Ray Eberle
            (Al Dubin-Ernesto Lecuona)
            Muted tpt, ??; ts, Beneke

            All tunes 2 takes. (RCA Victor)
            This session lasted from 11:00 A.M. to 3:30 P.M.
            (RCA Victor)

28 May, 1941 (WED): Hollywood, California (CHESTERFIELD SHOW)
            CBS   10:00-10:15 P.M.

            Slumber Song (Theme)
            Goin' Home
Int GM (2:20) Sing And Be Gay-voc Paula Kelly
            (
                Ts, Klink
            It Was Wonderful Then
            Measure For Measure
            Slumber Song (Theme)

29 May, 1941 (THUR)

> Glenn Miller and His Orchestra played at the
> Rendezvous Ballroom, Balboa, California, from
> 9:00-1:00 A.M., and drew 2,492. (G.M.P.R.;
> G.M.D.; Variety, June 11, 1941)

> G.M.P.R. for the week ending May 29th show that
> Billy May arranged "Take The 'A' Train".

29 May, 1941 (THUR): Hollywood, California (CHESTERFIELD SHOW)
CBS   10:00-10:15 P.M.

> *The announcer for this program is Larry Bruff.*

> > *Slumber Song (Theme)*
> > *The Booglie Wooglie Piggy*
> > *Dancing In A Dream With You*
> > *Here We Go Again*
> > *Slumber Song (Theme)*

30 May, 1941 (FRI)

> Glenn Miller and His Orchestra played at the
> Armory, Santa Barbara, California, from 9:00-
> 1:00 A.M., and drew 2,563. (G.M.P.R.; G.M.D.;
> Variety, June 4, 1941)

31 May, 1941 (SAT)

> Glenn Miller and His Orchestra played in
> Sacramento, California. (G.M.P.R.)

1 June, 1941 (SUN)

> Glenn Miller and His Orchestra played an after-
> noon (3:00-6:00 P.M.) and evening (10:00-2:00
> A.M.) engagement at Sweets Ballroom, Oakland,
> California. The band took the SO Pacific RR from
> Oakland to Los Angeles. (G.M.P.R. & G.M.D.)

2 June, 1941 (MON)

> Glenn Miller and His Orchestra played at the
> Shrine Auditorium, Los Angeles, California, from
> 9:00-1:00 A.M. (G.M.P.R. & G.M.D.)

3 June, 1941 (TUES)

> Glenn Miller and His Orchestra played for three
> days (closing Thursday, June 5th) at the Pacific
> Square Ballroom, San Diego, California. The
> band stayed at the El Cortez Hotel while in San
> Diego. (G.M.P.R.)

3 June, 1941 (TUES): Pacific Square Ballroom, San Diego,
California (CHESTERFIELD SHOW)
CBS   10:00-10:15 P.M.

> . *The announcer for this program is Larry Bruff.*

E3VP 5236   Vi LPT 6700, Vi EPNT 6700 (947-0116), HMV RLS 599,
               Vi SPD-18 (599-9103), RCA G LPT 6700
               (0:29)Slumber Song (Theme)
                         (Saul Tepper-John Chalmers MacGregor)

E3VP 5236   Vi LPT 6700, Vi EPNT 6700 (947-0116), HMV RLS 599,
               Vi SPD-18 (599-9103), RCA G LPT 6700
        Int GM (3:19)Perfidia-voc Paula Kelly and The Modernaires
                         (Milton Leeds-Alberto Dominguez)

> *I Do, Do You?-voc RE*
> *Swing Low, Sweet Chariot*
> *Slumber Song (Theme)*

On Vi LPT 6700 "Perfidia" (and the theme) were
incorrectly listed as being broadcast on July 3,
1941.

4 June, 1941 (WED): Pacific Square Ballroom, San Diego,
California (CHESTERFIELD SHOW)
CBS   10:00-10:15 P.M.

> *The announcer for this program is Larry Bruff.*

> *Slumber Song (Theme)*
> *Ida!*
> *I Guess I'll Have To Dream The Rest*
> *I Dreamt I Dwelt In Harlem*
> *Slumber Song (Theme)*

5 June, 1941 (THUR): Pacific Square Ballroom, San Diego,
California (CHESTERFIELD SHOW)
CBS   10:00-10:15 P.M.

> *Slumber Song (Theme)*

(Broadcast continued on next page)

[314]

> *Amapola*
> *A Love Song Hasn't Been Sung*
> *Twenty-Four Robbers*
> *Song Of The Volga Boatmen*
> *Slumber Song* (Theme)

The band took the Union Pacific RR from Los
Angeles to Chicago with several stops en route.
(G.M.P.R.)

6 June, 1941 (FRI)

> G.M.P.R. show that this date was open as the
> band was en route to Salt Lake City but G.M.D.
> indicate that the band played a concert at the
> Naval Base, San Diego.

7 June, 1941 (SAT)

> Glenn Miller and His Orchestra played at Salt
> Aire, Salt Lake City, Utah, from 9:00-1:00 A.M.,
> and drew 4,389. (G.M.P.R.; G.M.D.; Variety,
> June 18, 1941)
> "Glenn Miller suffered from inadequate
> parking space, which turned many away but still
> drew good 4,389 at $1.12 in 7,000 capacity spot."
> (Variety, June 18, 1941)

8 June, 1941 (SUN)

> G.M.P.R. show that this date was open as the
> band was en route to Cedar Rapids.

9 June, 1941 (MON)

> Glenn Miller and His Orchestra played at Dance-
> land, Cedar Rapids, Iowa, from 9:00-1:00 A.M.,
> and drew 2,600. (G.M.P.R.; G.M.D.; Variety,
> June 18, 1941)

10 June, 1941 (TUES)

> Glenn Miller and His Orchestra arrived in
> Chicago. (G.M.P.R.)

10 June, 1941 (TUES): Chicago, Illinois (CHESTERFIELD SHOW)
                     CBS   10:00-10:15 P.M.

                 Slumber Song (Theme)
                 The Spirit Is Willing
                 Naughty Sweetie Blues
                 Spring Will Be So Sad
                 Anvil Chorus
                 Slumber Song (Theme)

11 June, 1941 (WED): Chicago, Illinois (CHESTERFIELD SHOW)
                    CBS   10:00-10:15 P.M.

                 Slumber Song (Theme)
         (2:40) Sweeter Than The Sweetest (arr BM)-voc
                     Paula Kelly and The Modernaires
                     (Neil Lawrence-Willie (The Lion)
                     Smith)
                     No Klink sax solo
V-4086 WR-985   GMMS 25/73, AFRS P-2248
     Int GM (2:09) Dancing In A Dream With You (arr BF)-voc
                     Ray Eberle
                     (Jack Miller-Tony Gale-Al Douglas)

V-4086 WR-985   GMMS 25/73, GMMS 50/98, AFRS P-2248, AFRS P-GL-78
              (2:38) Whatcha Know Joe-voc Tex Beneke and The
                     Band
                     (James Young)
                     As, Caceres

V-4086 WR-985   GMMS 25/73, AFRS P-2245
     Int GM (2:42) Are You Rusty, Gate? (arr JG)
                     (Jerry Gray)
                     Ts, Beneke; clt, Caceres; muted tpt,
                     May

                 Slumber Song (Theme)

12 June, 1941 (THUR): Chicago, Illinois (CHESTERFIELD SHOW)
                     CBS   10:00-10:15 P.M.

                 Slumber Song (Theme)
                 Sunrise Serenade
                 Keep An Eye On Your Heart
                 I Guess I'll Have To Dream The Rest
                 Here We Go Again
                 Slumber Song (Theme)

13 June, 1941 (FRI)

Glenn Miller and His Orchestra played for one
week (closed Thursday, June 19th) at the
Chicago Theater, Chicago, Illinois. The film
was "One Night in Lisbon" while the accompany-
ing acts were Lorraine & Rognan and Paul Regan.
(G.M.P.R.; Chicago Times, June 13 & 19; Met.
June, 1941; DB, June 1, 1941; BB, May 28 &
July 5, 1941)

"Glenn Miller topped the band parade week
ended June 19 by drawing $46,000 at the Chicago.
He has been an annual ace for some three years
now, altho some of his past grosses have been
better." (BB, July 5, 1941)

This was bassist "Trigger" Alpert's last day
with the band (he was inducted into the armed
forces) and he was replaced the next day by
Myer Rubin. G.M.P.R. show that Alpert was paid
for the three Chesterfield programs of June 10,
11 and 12 as well as one full day at the Chicago
Theater (the 13th).

14 June, 1941 (SAT)

Trombones	Glenn Miller, Jimmy Priddy, Paul Tanner, Frank D'Annolfo
Trumpets	Billy May, Ray Anthony, Dale McMickle, Johnny Best
Reeds	Hal McIntyre, as; Ernie Caceres, as, bar & clt; Wilbur Schwartz, clt & as; Tex Beneke, ts; Al Klink, ts
Rhythm	Chummy MacGregor, p; Bill Conway, g; MYER RUBIN, b; Maurice Purtill

17 June, 1941 (TUES): Chicago, Illinois (CHESTERFIELD SHOW)
              CBS   10:00-10:15 P.M.

                    Slumber Song (Theme)
                    Perfidia
                    Do I Worry?
                    Song Of The Volga Boatmen
                    Slumber Song (Theme)

18 June, 1941 (WED): Chicago Theater, Chicago, Illinois
                     4:20 P.M. Show

> Glenn Miller and His Orchestra were reviewed on
> stage at the Chicago Theater. Here is part of
> the review:
> "The Miller show was more like a drill than
> an entertainment. Everyone was on stage at once--
> the band, the Modernaires, Paula Kelly, and Ray
> Eberle. The band opened, of course, with <u>Moon-
> light Serenade</u>,and proceeded from there into <u>Anvil
> Chorus</u>, followed by <u>Stardust</u>. The transition from
> the blare of the <u>Anvil</u> to the slow-mooded <u>Stardust</u>
> was a striking effect. The use of a darkened
> stage with bright stars on the brass section's
> hats, and a spot on Beneke for his tenor solo on
> <u>Stardust</u>, was basically all right, but the stars
> stole attention.
> Paula Kelly sang <u>Amapola</u> with the Modernaires;
> Ray Eberle sang <u>Do I Worry</u>, and joined the Modern-
> aires for <u>The One I Love Belongs to Somebody Else</u>.
> The Modernaires have plenty to sell. Unfortunately
> they weren't given a chance.
> The other band numbers were strictly flag-
> wavers." (Metronome--July 1941).

18 June, 1941 (WED): Chicago, Illinois (CHESTERFIELD SHOW)
*   CBS 10:00-10:15 P.M.*

The announcer for this program is Larry Bruff.

> *Slumber Song (Theme)*
> *The Booglie Wooglie Piggy-voc PK, TB & 4M*
> *The Things I Love-voc RE*

K2PP-0047   Vi LPM-6100, RCA RD 27147, RCA G LPM-6100, RCA Au
                     L 11025
                   (5:25) Swing Low, Sweet Chariot (arr BF)-hum by
                     The Band
                     (Spiritual)
                     B, Rubin; ts, Beneke; p, MacGregor;
                     muted tpt, May; p, MacGregor

> *Slumber Song (Theme)*

19 June, 1941 (THUR): Chicago, Illinois (CHESTERFIELD SHOW)
*   CBS 10:00-10:15 P.M.*

> *Slumber Song (Theme)*

(Broadcast continued on next page)

Twenty-Four Robbers
High On A Windy Hill
Just A Little Bit South Of North Carolina
Sun Valley Jump
Slumber Song (Theme)

20 June, 1941 (FRI)

> Glenn Miller and His Orchestra played a one
> nighter at the University of Michigan, Ann Arbor,
> Michigan, from 10:00-2:00 A.M. (played one hour
> overtime). (G.M.P.R.; G.M.D.; Variety, May 28,
> 1941)

21 June, 1941 (SAT)

> Glenn Miller and His Orchestra played at the
> I.M.A. Auditorium, Flint, Michigan, from 9:00-
> 1:00 A.M. (G.M.P.R.; G.M.D.; Variety, May 28,
> 1941)

22 June, 1941 (SUN)

> Glenn Miller and His Orchestra played a one
> nighter at the Modernistic Ballroom, Milwaukee,
> Wisconsin, from 8:30-12:30 A.M. C.S.T., and drew
> 5,500. (G.M.P.R.; G.M.D.; Variety, May 28 &
> June 25, 1941)
> "After negotiating for nearly two years in
> an effort to reach mutually agreeable terms Glenn
> Miller and his band are to play Modernistic Ball-
> room at the Wisconsin State Fair Park here on
> Sunday night June 22, 1941 with the leader practi-
> cally running the place for the occasion. Contract
> is said to be the toughest ever signed by C.S.
> Rose, manager of the suburban dancery.
> Miller dictates the admission fee to be
> charged and refuses to do the broadcast usually
> heard from Park Ballroom over W.T.M.J., any airing
> of his music being confined strictly to his
> regularly weekly commercials. No second band or
> artist may be used without the visiting bandsmen's
> approval, although in this case Steve Swedish and
> His Orchestra, the house band for the last five
> seasons was ok'd without argument.
> Admission fee set by Miller for the local
> date is $1.10 per person or double the usual 55¢.
> Sunday nite gate at this resorts the touring leader

(Continued on next page)

taking full advantage of his first personal
appearance in the Milwaukee area. And the free
list is out!

Just to make sure he gets his way Miller
is said to have been given a guarantee of close
to $2,000.00 for the night against more than 50%
of the gross. What this may amount to may be
gauged by the fact that Kay Kyser, holder of the
Modernistic Record, played to 8,500 people on a
date there! (Variety, June 11, 1941)

23 June, 1941 (MON)

Glenn Miller and His Orchestra played a one
nighter at Electric Park, Waterloo, Indiana,
from 9:00-1:00 A.M. This was originally to have
been a four day stay. (G.M.P.R.; G.M.D.; DB,
June 15, 1941; Variety, May 28, 1941)

According to G.M.P.R. on this date there was a
trombone substitution for Frank D'Annolfo (sub's
name not listed).

24 June, 1941 (TUES): Chicago, Illinois (CHESTERFIELD SHOW)
CBS   10:00-10:15 P.M.

Trombones	*Glenn Miller, Jimmy Priddy, Paul Tanner, WARREN SMITH*
Trumpets	*Billy May, Ray Anthony, Dale McMickle, Johnny Best*
Reeds	*Hal McIntyre, as; Ernie Caceres, as, bar & clt; Wilbur Schwartz, clt & as; Tex Beneke, ts; Al Klink, ts*
Rhythm	*Chummy MacGregor, p; Bill Conway, g; EDWARD "DOC" GOLDBERG, b; Maurice Purtill, d*

Slumber Song (Theme)
I Guess I'll Have To Dream The Rest-voc
    PK, RE & 4M
Oh So Good
Intermezzo
Slumber Song (Theme)

According to G.M.P.R., Warren Smith, tbn, replaced Frank D'Annolfo on the Chesterfield
programs of June 24th, 25th, 26th and the recording session of June 25th. He was not paid the
general salary for the one nighters earlier in the
week (prior to June 24th). There is a slight
problem here and that is the fact that G.M.P.R.

(Continued on next page)

also show that D'Annolfo was paid for the three
Chesterfield programs of June 24th, 25th and 26th
but not for the record date. We believe that
this is an error and that D'Annolfo was absent
from June 23rd to June 26th.

According to G.M.P.R. Edward "Doc" Goldberg
joined the band on this date replacing Myer Rubin.
Goldberg is paid for the three Chesterfield
programs of June 24th, 25th, 26th and the recording session of June 25th while he is not paid the
general salary for the one nighters.

25 June, 1941 (WED): Victor Studios, Chicago, Illinois

Same personnel as for June 24th broadcast.

064471-1   BB 11219-A, HMV BD 5727, HMVAu EA-3484, HMVIr
              I.P. 972, Cam Cas-2267, RCA G Cas-2267
              Under Blue Canadian Skies (arr BF)-voc Ray Eberle
              (Al Lewis-Larry Stock-Vincent Rose)

064472-1   BB 11235-A, HMV JO 198, Cam Cal/Cas-751, El G EG
              7523, RCA G Cas-751, Pick. Int. CDS 1040,
              Cam Au Cas-751
              The Cowboy Serenade (While I'm Rollin' My Last
              Cigarette)
              (arr BF)-voc Ray Eberle
              (Rich Hall)
              Muted tbn, Miller

064473-1   BB 11215-A, HMV JO 198, El G EG 7523, Vi LPM/LSP-
              3657, RCA RD/SF-7842, RCA G LPM/LSP-3657,
              HMVSc X 6742, RCA F 440.727
              You And I-voc Ray Eberle
              (Meredith Wilson)
              Muted tbn, Miller

064474-1   BB 11219-B, AFR-50, HMV BD 5727, Vi 20-2942, Vi
              420-0031, Vi 447-0031, El G EG 7905, Vi
              LPT-3002, Vi EPA-5094, Vi EPBT-3002 (947-
              0039), Vi EPA-727, RCA RCX 1063, Vi LPM-
              1190, Vi EPB-1190 (547-0828), HMV DLP
              1081, Vi It LPM-10141, RCA Vi It LJ 50020,
              AFRS P-S-15, RD 3/4-64, RCA Int. B-21040,
              RCA Int. T-21040, RCA F 130211, RCA G
              447-0031, RCA G EPC-1190, RCA G LPM-1190,
              HMVIr I.P. 972, Vi VPM-6019, Vi It LPM
              50020, Vi DJ-387, AFRS G.I. Jive EN-12-
              2241, AFRS G.I. Jive EN-12-2265,

(Session continued on next page)

```
                    AFRS G.I. Jive H-12-2034, AFRS G.I. Jive
                    H-12-2073, AFRS G.I. Jive H-12-2204, RCA
                    Br. RD-8094, RCA Br. GM-1, AFRS G.I. Jive
                    H-12-2223, RCA Au 20227, RCA G LPT-3002,
                    AFRS G.I. Jive EN-12-2305
          Adios (arr JG)
                    (Eddie Woods-Enric Madriguera)
                    Muted tpt, McMickle; muted tbn, Miller;
                    muted tpt, McMickle; b, Goldberg
```

"You And I" 1 take; all other tunes 2 takes.
(RCA Victor)
This session lasted from 1:00 P.M. to 4:45 P.M.
(RCA Victor)

25 June, 1941 (WED): Chicago, Illinois (CHESTERFIELD SHOW)
             CBS   10:00-10:15 P.M.

                    Slumber Song (Theme)
                    Adios
                    Sweeter Than The Sweetest
                    The Cowboy Serenade

E2VL 4545   Vi LPT-3001, Vi EPBT-3001 (947-0054), Vi LPM-1193,
                    HMV DLP 1021, Vi TP3-5020, El WDLP 1021,
                    RCA G EPB-3001, RCA G LPM-1193, RCA G LPT-
                    3001
          (2:42) Are You Rusty, Gate? (arr JG)
                    (Jerry Gray)
                    Ts, Beneke; clt, Caceres; muted tpt,
                    May

                    Slumber Song (Theme)

This version of "Are You Rusty, Gate?" is slightly
different from the June 11th broadcast.

26 June, 1941 (THUR): Chicago, Illinois (CHESTERFIELD SHOW)
             CBS   10:00-10:15 P.M.

          (0:23) *Slumber Song (Theme)*
                    (Saul Tepper-John Chalmers MacGregor)
     Int GM (2:11) *Georgia On My Mind (arr JG)*
                    (Stuart Gorrell-Hoagy Carmichael)
                    Ts, Beneke; tpt, Best
          The Hut-Sut Song (arr JG)-voc PK, EC & 4M
                    (Leo V. Killian-Ted McMichael-
                    Jack Owens)

(Broadcast continued on next page)

[322]

E4VP 8210   Vi LPT 6701, Vi EPOT 6701 (947-0179), HMV RLS 598,
              RCA G EPOT-6701
     Int GM (1:54) Dancing In A Dream With You (arr BF)-voc
              Ray Eberle
              (Jack Miller-Tony Gale-Al Douglas)

              The Spirit Is Willing
              Slumber Song (Theme)

     The beginning of "Dancing In A Dream With You" has
     been edited by RCA Victor. The Miller introduction
     to the tune has also been edited but we have an
     aircheck of this version with the introduction but
     the timing we show is the RCA Victor release.

27 June, 1941 (FRI)

     Glenn Miller and His Orchestra played at the
     Lincoln Field House, Wisconsin Rapids, Wisconsin.
     (G.M.P.R.) There was a trumpet substitution for
     Ray Anthony on this date but G.M.P.R. did not state
     the name of the sub.

     Trombones   Glenn Miller, Jimmy Priddy, Paul
                  Tanner, FRANK D'ANNOLFO
     Trumpets   Billy May, UNKNOWN SUB FOR RAY
                  ANTHONY, Dale McMickle, Johnny Best
     Reeds   Hal McIntyre, as; Ernie Caceres, as,
                  bar & clt; Wilbur Schwartz, clt & as;
                  Tex Beneke, ts; Al Klink, ts
     Rhythm   Chummy MacGregor, p; Bill Conway, g;
                  Doc Goldberg, b; Maurice Purtill, d

28 June, 1941 (SAT)

     Glenn Miller and His Orchestra played at the Prom
     Ballroom, St. Paul, Minnesota and drew 5,742.
     (G.M.P.R.; Variety, June 18, 1941; Variety, July
     16, 1941)
          "Glenn Miller gloomed plenty over the draft
     while here at The Prom one nighter (3,000 turned
     away) last month." (DB, Aug. 1, 1941)

     Trombones   Glenn Miller, Jimmy Priddy, Paul
                  Tanner, Frank D'Annolfo
     Trumpets   Billy May, RAY ANTHONY, Dale McMickle,
                  Johnny Best
     Reeds   Hal McIntyre, as; Ernie Caceres, as,
                  bar & clt; Wilbur Schwartz, clt & as;
                  Tex Beneke, ts; Al Klink, ts
     Rhythm   Chummy MacGregor, p; Bill Conway, g;
                  Doc Goldberg, b; Maurice Purtill, d

29 June, 1941 (SUN)

>Glenn Miller and His Orchestra played at the
>Roof Garden Ballroom, Arnolds Park, Iowa.
>(G.M.P.R.; G.M.D.)

30 June, 1941 (MON)

>Glenn Miller and His Orchestra played at the
>Turnpike Casino, Lincoln, Nebraska, from 9:00-
>1:00 A.M., and drew 2,920. (G.M.P.R.; G.M.D.;
>Variety, July 9, 1941)
>   "Glenn Miller pulled nearly 3,000 dancers,
>without room to dance, into the Turnpike Casino
>here June 30. While the official gross was kept
>secret, at a scale of $1.15 and $1.45 advance
>and $1.65 at the door the take must have been
>around $3,500. This shatters records for both
>attendance and shekels." (BB, July 19, 1941)

July, 1941

>   "In a sudden switch of affiliations,
>'Bullets' Durgan of Glenn Miller's troupe last
>week moved over to Tommy Dorsey's band to take a
>job doing record promotion work as an advance man
>on the road.
>   Durgan, a Jersey cat, recently returned to
>New York after spending several months on the
>coast with Miller. Dorsey is said to have pur-
>chased a new station wagon for Durgan's work."
>(DB, July 15, 1941.) The exact date of Durgan
>leaving Miller is unknown. "Bullets" has done
>well since these days and was Jackie Gleason's
>manager more recently.

1 July, 1941 (TUES): Municipal Auditorium, Kansas City, Missouri
                     (CHESTERFIELD SHOW)
                     CBS   10:00-10:15 P.M.

>The announcer for this program is Larry Bruff.
>Glenn announced at the beginning of this program
>that "there are 14,000 folks in the Municipal
>Auditorium."

>>Slumber Song (Theme)
>>Twenty-Four Robbers

(Broadcast continued on next page)

```
V-4086 WR-986     GMMS 26/74, AFRS P-2251
         Int GM  (2:08) A Love Song Hasn't Been Sung (arr JG)-
                        voc Ray Eberle
                        (Harold Dickinson-Bill Conway-
                        Jerry Gray)

V-4086 WR-986     GMMS 26/74, GMMS 52/100, AFRS P-2251, AFRS P-GL-78
         Int GM  (2:05) Just A Little Bit South Of North Carolina-
                        voc Paula Kelly
                        (Sonny Skylar-Arthur Shaftel-Bette
                        Cannon)
                        Tpt, Best

V-4086 WR-986     GMMS 26/74, AFRS P-2245
                  (3:36) Here We Go Again (arr JG)
                        (Jerry Gray)
                        Ts, Klink; tpt, May; clt, Caceres;
                        tpt, Best; d, Purtill; tpt, ??
```

Slumber Song (Theme)

1 July, 1941 (TUES)

        Glenn Miller and His Orchestra played a one nighter at Meadow Acres Ballroom, Topeka, Kansas and drew 2,750. (G.M.P.R.; BB, July 19, 1941; Variety, June 25, 1941)
        "Playing his first date here, Miller broke all records at the two-year-old spot, where Jimmy Dorsey drew the previous top house of 2,360 a year ago last February.
        Despite week-night date, crowd waited patiently till 10 o'clock to start the four-hour sprint. Miller broadcast his regular CBS Chesterfield show at Kansas City, Mo. (70 miles away) same night, and sped here under police escort to start dance on time.
        Practically all tickets went at big $1.75 per person advance sale price (including tax), only 35 customers paying $2.25 levy. Passes were out." (BB, July 19, 1941)
There is a notation on G.M.P.R. that Chummy MacGregor tipped the police escort on their dash from Kansas City to Topeka.

2 July, 1941 (WED)

        G.M.P.R. show that this date was open (no one nighter) but the band did it's Chesterfield program from Kansas City.

2 July, 1941 (WED): Municipal Auditorium, Kansas City,
                    Missouri (CHESTERFIELD SHOW)
                    CBS   10:00-10:15 P.M.

> *Slumber Song (Theme)*
> *Boulder Buff*
> *The Things I Love*
> *I'm Not Much On Looks*
> *Measure For Measure*
> *Slumber Song (Theme)*

3 July, 1941 (THUR)

> Glenn Miller and His Orchestra played at the Frog
> Hop Ballroom, St. Joseph, Missouri. The band
> started at 10:30 P.M. after doing the Chesterfield
> show from Kansas City. (G.M.P.R.; G.M.D.; Variety,
> June 25, 1941)

3 July, 1941 (THUR): Municipal Auditorium, Kansas City,
                     Missouri (CHESTERFIELD SHOW)
                     CBS   10:00-10:15 P.M.

> *Slumber Song (Theme)*
> *Georgia On My Mind*
> *The Booglie Wooglie Piggy*
> *Do I Worry?*
> *Song Of The Volga Boatmen*
> *Slumber Song (Theme)*

4 July, 1941 (FRI)

> Glenn Miller and His Orchestra played at the Forum,
> Witchita, Kansas, from 9:00-1:00 A.M. (G.M.P.R.;
> G.M.D.; Variety, June 25, 1941)
>   "Glenn Miller's Orchestra will play for annual
> Coronation Ball of Witchita Transportation Booster
> Club to be held at the Forum July 4, 1941. Dance
> will be under management of Trocadero." (Variety,
> June 25, 1941)

5 July, 1941 (SAT)

> Glenn Miller and His Orchestra played at the Munici-
> pal Auditorium, Oklahoma City, Oklahoma, from 9:00-
> 1:00 A.M. (G.M.P.R.; G.M.D.; Variety, June 25 & July
> 9, 1941)

(Continued on next page)

"Glenn Miller set an all-time record for
dance attendance--as well as gross receipts--
here when he drew 4,088 persons to the Municipal
Auditorium July 5. Total take for the dance was
$5,653, with Miller taking $2,950 and the
sponsors netting $1,147, exclusive of concessions.
According to T.T. Johnson, aud manager, 2,825
dancers paid $1.25 each advance, and 1,263 more
came in at $1.68, door price." (BB, July 26,
1941)

6 July, 1941 (SUN)

Glenn Miller and His Orchestra played at Crystal
City Park, Tulsa, Oklahoma, from 9:00-1:00 A.M.
(G.M.P.R.; G.M.D.)

7 July, 1941 (MON)

Glenn Miller and His Orchestra played at the
Shrine Mosque, Springfield, Missouri, from 9:00-
1:00 A.M. (G.M.P.R.; G.M.D.)

*8 July, 1941 (TUES): St. Louis, Missouri (CHESTERFIELD SHOW)
CBS 10:00-10:15 P.M.*

Trombones	*Glenn Miller, Jimmy Priddy, Paul Tanner, Frank D'Annolfo*
Trumpets	*Billy May, ALEC FILA, Dale McMickle, Johnny Best*
Reeds	*Hal McIntyre, as; Ernie Caceres, as, bar & clt; Wilbur Schwartz, clt & as; Tex Beneke, ts; Al Klink, ts*
Rhythm	*Chummy MacGregor,p; Bill Conway, g; Doc Goldberg, b; Maurice Purtill, d*

Slumber Song (Theme)
Adios
Sweeter Than The Sweetest
The Cowboy Serenade
Are You Rusty, Gate?
Slumber Song (Theme)

According to G.M.P.R. Alec Fila joined the band
on this date. The payroll records are a little
confusing here as they also indicate that
Anthony was paid for the three Chesterfield
programs of July 8th, 9th and 10th. Since Fila
is paid for the same three shows we suspect that
Anthony's pay for the three programs was really
separation pay. Anthony was paid the general
salary for the one nighters (but Fila was not
paid the general salary).

9 July, 1941 (WED): St. Louis, Missouri (CHESTERFIELD SHOW)
CBS 10:00-10:15 P.M.

Slumber Song (Theme)

E2VL 4546   ~~Vi LPT-3001,~~ Vi EPBT-3001 (947-0055), HMV DLP
1013, El WDLP 1013, Vi LPM 1189, Vi EPB-
1189 (547-0800), Vi It LPM-10141, RCA It
A1OV 0007, RCA It LJ 50020, RCA G EPB-
3001, AFRS P-2666, RCA F 430228, RCA F
130243, RCA G EPC-1189, HMVAu ODLP 1013,
Vi It LPM 50020, RCA Au L 11021, RCA G
LPT-3001

~~(3:40) Intermezzo (arr BF)~~
        (Heinz Provost)
        Ts, Beneke

Keep An Eye On Your Heart
I Guess I'll Have To Dream The Rest
That's Where I Came In (Keep 'Em Flying)
Slumber Song (Theme)

The tune "That's Where I Came In" was later
recorded under the title of "Keep 'Em Flying"
but was announced as shown above during this
period. Since the tune was recorded one day
after Pearl Harbor the title was probably
changed for patriotic reasons.

10 July, 1941 (THUR): St. Louis, Missouri (CHESTERFIELD SHOW)
CBS 10:00-10:15 P.M.

Trombones	*Glenn Miller, Jimmy Priddy, Paul Tanner, Frank D'Annolfo*
Trumpets	*Billy May, Alec Fila, Dale McMickle, Johnny Best*
Reeds	*Hal McIntyre, as; Ernie Caceres, as, bar & clt; Wilbur Schwartz, clt & as; Tex Beneke, ts; Al Klink, ts*
Rhythm	*Chummy MacGregor, p; BOBBY HACKETT, g & cnt; Doc Goldberg, b; Maurice Purtill, d*

Slumber Song (Theme)
The Spirit Is Willing
The Hut-Sut Song
You And I
Anvil Chorus
Slumber Song (Theme)

(Continued on next page)

G.M.P.R. show that Bobby Hackett joined the
band on this date (and he is paid for one
Chesterfield program this week). G.M.P.R. also
show that there was a concert in St. Louis on
this date as well as the Chesterfield program.

Prior to joining Miller, Hackett had been leading his own band in Boston and Providence.

11 July, 1941 (FRI)

Glenn Miller and His Orchestra played at Weco
Pavilion, Lake Wawasee, Indiana, from 9:00-
1:00 A.M. (G.M.P.R.; G.M.D.)

12 July, 1941 (SAT)

Glenn Miller and His Orchestra played at the
Aragon Ballroom, Chicago, Illinois. (G.M.P.R.;
Chicago Times, July 11, 1941)
"Glenn Miller played to more than 6,000
patrons at the Aragon Ballroom here Saturday
(12), running only second to Kay Kyser for this
year's record of a one-nighter in the William
Karzas temple. Kyser on the first Sunday in
February attracted more than 10,000 dancers.
Admission was upped to $1.25 ($1.10 for
ladies). Management rates it as a terrific
date. While it is admitted that Kyser would
have topped Miller anyway, it should be pointed
out that Kyser had the benefit of a Sunday
afternoon during his stay." (BB, Aug. 2, 1941)

"Miller gathered 9,000 admissions at $1.10
beating spot's previous attendance records."
(Variety, July 16, 1941) This article would
appear to be less factual than the Billboard
article.

13 July, 1941 (SUN)

Glenn Miller and His Orchestra played at Valley
Dale, Columbus, Ohio, from 9:00-1:00 A.M. E.S.T.
(G.M.P.R.; G.M.D.)
"Hackett thrills Miller fans at a Valley
Dale, Ohio, date in mid-July. The Bostonian Bix-
like trumpeter, who joined Glenn shortly before
this appearance, doubled on guitar, and on both
the frets and the valves scored a huge success.

(Continued on next page)

Members of the Miller band, obviously as
excited as the dancers, stopped to listen to
Bobby solo. The band drew the season's biggest
crowd for its date." (Met. Aug. 1941)

14 July, 1941 (MON)

Glenn Miller and His Orchestra played at
Russells Point, Indian Lake, Ohio, from 9:00-
1:00 A.M. (G.M.P.R.; G.M.D.)

15 July, 1941 (TUES)

Glenn Miller and His Orchestra played for five
nights (closed Saturday, July 19th) at Eastwood
Gardens, Detroit, Michigan. (G.M.P.R.; International Musicians, May & July 1941; Variety,
May 28, 1941)
"Glenn Miller set an all-time record for a
five-night stand at Eastwood Gardens here with
26,000 admissions last week, according to Manager
Henry Wagner. With admissions at 50 cents,
upping to 75 cents for Saturday, gross was around
$15,000 for the five nights.
Record crowd was on Saturday night, when
6,100 admissions were counted. Spot has a dancing
and seating capacity of 4,900, and some 1,500
standees were provided for without seating being
available. Extra Saturday afternoon matinee was
set for the band, an almost unprecedented step
for Eastwood.
Previous record, totally eclipsed, was said
to have been 16,000,set for for five nights by
Rudy Vallee about four years ago." (BB, Aug. 2,
1941)

"Miller chased every mark at this spot, pulling turnaway biz every night for a total of 26,310
customers in five nights and a matinee." (Variety,
July 23, 1941)

The band played from 9:00-2:00 A.M. nightly.
(G.M.D.)

15 July, 1941 (TUES): Eastwood Gardens, Detroit, Michigan
                      (CHESTERFIELD SHOW)
                      CBS 10:00-10:15 P.M.

                      Slumber Song (Theme)

(Broadcast continued on next page)

Ida!
Perfidia

WPRS-0975   Vi LSP-3981, RCA Br. RD/SF-7982
      Int GM (1:54) Do I Worry?-voc Ray Eberle
                   (Stanley Cowan-Bobby Worth)
                   Muted tbn, Miller

Measure For Measure
Slumber Song (Theme)

16 July, 1941 (WED): Eastwood Gardens, Detroit, Michigan
                 (CHESTERFIELD SHOW)
                 CBS 10:00-10:15 P.M.

The announcer for this program is Larry Bruff.

Slumber Song (Theme)
Sunrise Serenade

E3VP 5243   Vi LPT 6700, Vi EPNT 6700 (947-0122), Vi SPD-18
              (599-9107), HMV RLS 599, RCA G LPT 6700
      Int LB (2:47) Twenty-Four Robbers (arr BF)-voc Paula
                   Kelly, Tex Beneke and The Modernaires
                   (James Young-Ted Buckner)
                   Tpt, May

You And I
Sun Valley Jump
Slumber Song (Theme)

17 July, 1941 (THUR): Eastwood Gardens, Detroit, Michigan
                 (CHESTERFIELD SHOW)
                 CBS 10:00-10:15 P.M.

Slumber Song (Theme)
Largo

UPRM-6314   Vi LPM/LSP-3873, RCA Br. RD/SF-7932, RCA G LSP-
              3873
      Int GM (2:31) The Booglie Wooglie Piggy (arr JG)-voc
                   Tex Beneke and The Modernaires
                   (and Paula Kelly)
                   (Roy Jacobs)
                   Ts, Beneke; tpt, May

The Things I Love
Here We Go Again
Slumber Song (Theme)

17 July, 1941 (THUR)

        G.M.P.R. for the week ending July 17 show that
        Billy May arranged "Daddy".

20 July, 1941 (SUN)

        Glenn Miller and His Orchestra played at Yankee
        Lake in Youngstown, Ohio, from 9:00-1:00 A.M. and
        drew 4,305. (G.M.P.R.; G.M.D.)
            "Miller's band followed swift ringing up
        $4,305.00 with same number of dancers at $1.10."
        (Variety, July 23, 1941)

21 July, 1941 (MON)

        Glenn Miller and His Orchestra played at the
        Sunset Ballroom, Carrolltown, Pennsylvania, from
        9:00-1:00 A.M. (G.M.P.R.; G.M.D.; Variety, June
        18, 1941; International Musicians, July 1941)

22 July, 1941 (TUES)

        Glenn Miller and His Orchestra played for three
        days (22nd, 23rd & 24th) in Washington, D.C. doing
        the Chesterfield program only. (G.M.P.R.)

22 July, 1941 (TUES): Riverside Stadium, Washington, D.C.
            (CHESTERFIELD SHOW)
            CBS 10:00-10:15 P.M.

     The announcer for this program is Larry Bruff.

     (0:25) Slumber Song (Theme)
            (Saul Tepper-John Chalmers MacGregor)
  Int GM (2:51) Adios (arr JG)
            (Eddie Woods-Enric Madriguera)
            Muted tpt, McMickle; muted tbn, Miller;
            muted tpt, McMickle; b, Goldberg
  Int GM (3:31) Daddy (arr BM)-voc Paula Kelly, Tex Beneke
            and The Modernaires
            (Robert Troup, Jr.)
  Int GM (1:51) I'm Thrilled (arr BF)-voc Ray Eberle
            (Sylvia Dee-Sidney Lippman)
  Int LB (2:30) That's Where I Came In (arr JG)
            (Jerry Gray)
            Ts, Beneke; d, Purtill; clt, Caceres
        Slumber Song (Theme)

23 July, 1941 (WED): Riverside Stadium, Washington, D.C.
(CHESTERFIELD SHOW)
CBS   10:00-10:15 P.M.

> *Slumber Song (Theme)*
> *Georgia On My Mind*
> *Watcha Know Joe*
> *I Guess I'll Have To Dream The Rest*
> *Carmen (arr BM)*
>   *(G. Bizet)*
> *Slumber Song (Theme)*

24 July, 1941 (THUR): Riverside Stadium, Washington, D.C.
(CHESTERFIELD SHOW)
CBS   10:00-10:15 P.M.

The announcer for this program is Larry Bruff.

> *Slumber Song (Theme)*
> *Intermezzo*
> *The Hut-Sut Song*
> *The Cowboy Serenade*
> *Flagwaver*
> *Slumber Song (Theme)*

25 July, 1941 (FRI)

Glenn Miller and His Orchestra played for two days (Friday, July 25th and Saturday, July 26th) at the Surf Beach Club, Virginia Beach, Virginia. The band played a matinee and evening performance on the 26th. (G.M.P.R.; International Musicians, July 1941; Variety, June 18, 1941: BB, July 26, 1941) The band played from 9:30-1:00 A.M. on Friday and from 4:30-6:00 P.M. and 9:00-1:30 A.M. on Saturday. (G.M.D.)

27 July, 1941 (SUN)

The band had this day off. (G.M.P.R.) From this date until August 15th, the band went on a 19-day vacation from one-nighters and stage appearances but continued to do the Chesterfield programs.

28 July, 1941 (MON)

Glenn Miller and His Orchestra arrived in New York. "Miller returned to New York July 28 after six months in the West. His first movie pic, "Sun

(Continued on next page)

Valley Serenade", is set for August 29 release
throughout the nation. The band's next major
location is Hotel Pennsylvania starting in
October." (DB, Aug. 15, 1941)

29 July, 1941 (TUES): New York City, New York (CHESTERFIELD SHOW)
CBS   10:00-10:15 P.M.

> *Slumber Song (Theme)*
> ɟ2:12ɬ *Uncle Tom   (arr BF)*
> ( )
> *Ts, Klink*
> *I'm Not Much On Looks*
> *Do I Worry?*
> *Solid As A Stonewall, Jackson*
> *Slumber Song (Theme)*

"Uncle Tom" was later recorded (May 28, 1946) by
Tex Beneke and His Orchestra under the title
"Texas Tex".

30 July, 1941 (WED): New York City, New York (CHESTERFIELD SHOW)
CBS   10:00-10:15 P.M.

The announcer for this program is Paul Douglas.

> *Slumber Song (Theme)*
> *The Booglie Wooglie Piggy-voc PK, TB & 4M*
> *Cradle Song-voc RE & Ch*
> *Anvil Chorus*
> *Slumber Song (Theme)*

31 July, 1941 (THUR): New York City, New York (CHESTERFIELD SHOW)
CBS   10:00-10:15 P.M.

> *Slumber Song (Theme)*

WPRS-0975   Vi LSP-3981, RCA Br. RD/SF-7982
                 (3:12) The Spirit Is Willing (arr JG)
                              (Jerry Gray)
                         Muted tpt, May; tpt, ??; muted tpt, ??;
                         tpt, May; muted tpt, ??; muted tpt, May;
                         tpt, ??; muted tpt, May; tpt, ??;
                         muted tpt, May

> *Amapola*
> *I'm Thrilled*
> *Here We Go Again*
> *Slumber Song (Theme)*

1 August, 1941 (FRI)

> G.M.P.R. indicate that the band took a vacation
> from August 1st to (and including) August 4th.

5 August, 1941 (TUES): New York City, New York (CHESTERFIELD SHOW)
CBS   10:00-10:15 P.M.

> *Slumber Song (Theme)*
> *Intermezzo*
> *Sweeter Than The Sweetest*
> *The Things I Love*
> *Introduction To A Waltz*
> *Slumber Song (Theme)*

6 August, 1941 (WED): New York City, New York (CHESTERFIELD SHOW)
CBS   10:00-10:15 P.M.

> *The announcer for this program is Paul Douglas.*

> *Slumber Song (Theme)*
> *Daddy-voc PK, TB & 4M*
> *Cradle Song*
> *Boulder Buff*
> *Slumber Song (Theme)*

7 August, 1941 (THUR): New York City, New York (CHESTERFIELD SHOW)
CBS   10:00-10:15 P.M.

> *Slumber Song (Theme)*
> *Vilia*
> *Twenty-Four Robbers*
> *The Cowboy Serenade*
> *Keep 'Em Flying*
> *Slumber Song (Theme)*

> The Miller Estate begins to list "Keep 'Em
> Flying" under this title from this date onward.

7 August, 1941 (THUR)

> G.M.P.R. for the week ending August 7th show that
> Billy May arranged "Delilah".

8 August, 1941 (FRI)

> G.M.P.R. indicate that the band took a vacation
> from August 8th to (and including) August 11th
> (except for the recording session on this last
> date).

Ray Eberle watches Glenn blow.

Band returns to New York in late July 1941. Glenn uses two guitarists at this CBS rehearsal, Conway and Hackett. Doc Goldberg is on bass, and trumpet section now comprises Best (eyes bandaged), Fila, McMickle and May (dark glasses).

Left to right: Larry Bruff (announcer), Glenn and Gene Hight (producer) go over the script and music of an upcoming Chesterfield program.

Glenn rehearsing the band for a Chesterfield program. At right is bassist Doc Goldberg. Seated at right is Modernaire Chuck Goldstein.

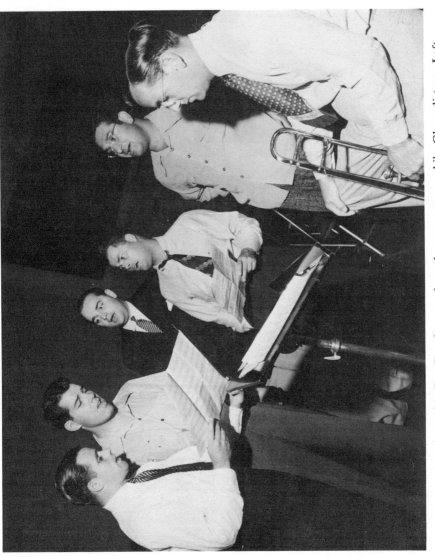

The Modernaires with Tex Beneke run through a new tune while Glenn listens. Left to right: Bill Conway, Tex, Hal Dickinson, Ralph Brewster, Chuck Goldstein and Glenn.

Glenn Miller and Chummy MacGregor going over the scores of *Delilah* and *The Things I Love*.

Arranger Jerry Gray, Glenn and deejay Jerry Lawrence review music for Jerry's theme song, *The Man in the Moon*.

Three key men in the Miller success story: Cy Shribman, Boston band-builder and financier who operated a string of ballrooms; Don Haynes, personal manager for the Miller band; and George B. Evans, press agent.

PR man George Evans goes over some photos with Glenn.

Glenn and announcer Paul Douglas check script.

Glenn practices his broadcast spiel.

Coffee break for Marion Hutton.

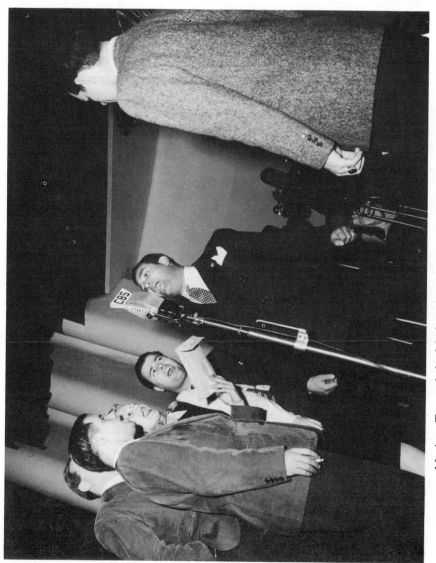

Marion, Tex and the Modernaires try out a new tune at rehearsal.

Glenn adds some unmusical effects behind the singing of the Modernaires, Marion and Tex.

11 August, 1941 (MON): Victor Studios, New York City, New York

Same personnel as for July 10th broadcast.

067625-1   BB 11263-A, HMV MH 17, RCA RCX 1034, Vi EPA-5035
            It Happened In Sun Valley (arr BF)-voc Paula Kelly,
                    Ray Eberle, Tex Beneke, and The Modernaires
                    (and The Band)
                    From the 20th Century-Fox film "Sun Valley
                    Serenade"
                    (Mack Gordon-Harry Warren)
                    Ts, Klink

067626-1   BB 11287-B, HMV DLP 1145
            I'm Thrilled (arr BF)-voc Ray Eberle
                    (Sylvia Dee-Sidney Lippman)
                    Ts, Beneke

067627-1   BB 11263-B, HMV MH 17, El G EG 7647, HMVAus GA-5046
            The Kiss Polka (arr JG)-voc Paula Kelly, Ernie
                    Caceres and The Modernaires
                    From the 20th Century-Fox film "Sun Valley
                    Serenade"
                    (Mack Gordon-Harry Warren)
                    Maraccas, Eberle (per G.M. Club Bulletin,
                    March 1942)

067628-1   BB 11274-B, HMV BD 1216, Vi 20-2942, Vi EPAT 429,
                    Vi LPT-3067, Vi EPBT-3067 (947-0200), HMV
                    DLP 1062, RCA G LPT-3067, RCA G EPAT-429,
                    RCA G EPBT-3067, Vi LSP-4125, Vi P8S-1432,
                    RCA Int. INTS 1002, Vi DJ-386, AFRS G.I.
                    Jive H-12-1990
            Delilah (arr BM)-voc Tex Beneke and The Modernaires
                    (Jimmy Shirl-Henry Manners)

067629-1   BB 11287-A, HMVAu EA-3139, HMV DLP 1145
            From One Love To Another (Danza Lucumi) (arr BF)-
                    voc Ray Eberle
                    (Albert Gamse-Ernesto Lecuona)
                    Cnt, Hackett

067630-1   BB 11274-A, HMV BD 5733, HMV MH 137, HMVAu EA-2999,
                    Vi 20-3185, Vi 420-0041, Vi 447-0041, RCA RCX
                    1040, Vi EPAT 429, Vi SP-45-28, Vi EPA-5008,
                    Vi LPT-1016, Cam Cal/Cas-829, Vi LPM/LSP-
                    3546, RD 3/4-64, AFRS G.I. Jive H-12-746,
                    AFRS G.I. Jive H-12-1282, AFRS G.I. Jive
                    H-12-1553, AFRS G.I. Jive H-12-1053, AFRS
                    "Jill's Jukebox" 118, AFRS "Jukebox USA" 90,
                    AFRS P-8996, RCA F 130210, RCA G LPT 1016,

(Session continued on next page)

RCA G EPAT-429, RCA G Cas-829, Vi P8S-5061,
Vi TP3-5044, RCA G EPA-5008, HMVIn BD 5733,
AFRS G.I. Jive H-12-1631, AFRS G.I. Jive
H-12-1307, AFRS G.I. Jive H-12-2194, AFRS
G.I. Jive H-12-1536, AFRS G.I. Jive
H-12-841, RCA Cam Fr 900.028, RCA Cam Arg
Cal-3138, Pick Int. CDS 1004, Vi Arg LPM-
3564, Vi DJ-589, Vi VPM-6019, Vi RCA G
LPM/LSP-9944, RCA Br. RD-8094, AFRS G.I. Jive
H-12-1374, AFRS G.I. Jive H-12-1410, AFRS
G.I. Jive H-12-1479, RCA Br. GM-1, AFRS G.I.
Jive H-12-2089, AFRS G.I. Jive H-12-1972,
AFRS G.I. Jive H-12-1779, AFRS G.I. Jive
H-12-1613, AFRS G.I. Jive H-12-1229,
AFRS G.I. Jive H-12-1429

Elmer's Tune (arr JG)-voc Ray Eberle and The
        Modernaires
        (Elmer Albrecht-Sammy Gallop-Dick Jurgens)
        Ts, Beneke; muted tpt, ??; muted tbn, Miller

"The Kiss Polka" 2 takes; all other tunes 1 take.
(RCA Victor)
This session lasted from 1:00 P.M. to 7:00 P.M.
(RCA Victor)

12 August, 1941 (TUES): New York City, New York (CHESTERFIELD SHOW)
*   CBS   10:00-10:15 P.M.*

            Slumber Song (Theme)
            Adios
            The Booglie Wooglie Piggy
            From One Love To Another
            Flagwaver
            Slumber Song (Theme)

13 August, 1941 (WED): New York City, New York (CHESTERFIELD SHOW)
*   CBS   10:00-15 P.M.*

    The announcer for this program is Paul Douglas.

            Slumber Song (Theme)

E1VLB 3201   Vi LPT-16, HMV B10235, Vi 42-0109 (Vi PT-25),
              HMV DLP 1013, Vi 27-0109 (Vi WPT-25), Vi
              EPBT-3025 (947-0025), Vi EPA-729, Vi LPM-
              1193, Vi EPB-1193 (547-0823), Vi TP3-5020,
              RCA It LPM 10011, RCA It LJ 50012, RCA Int.
              B-21032, RCA Int. T-21032, HMVAus GA-5091,

(Broadcast continued on next page)

```
                    E1 WDLP 1013, RCA G LPM-1193, HMVAu ODLP
                    1013, RCA F 130243, RCA G LPT-16
            (2:33) Georgia On My Mind (arr JG)
                        (Stuart Gorrell-Hoagy Carmichael)
                        Ts, Beneke; tpt, Best

WPRS-0975      Vi LSP-3981, RCA Br. RD/SF-7982
    Int GM (2:17) Delilah (arr BM)-voc Tex Beneke and The
                        Modernaires
                        (Jimmy Shirl-Henry Manners)

            You and I-voc RE & PK
            I Dreamt I Dwelt In Harlem
            Slumber Song (Theme)
```

```
14 August, 1941 (THUR): New York City, New York (CHESTERFIELD SHOW)
                    CBS   10:00-10:15 P.M.

          (0:11) Slumber Song (Theme)
                        (Saul Tepper-John Chalmers MacGregor)
          (2:36) A String Of Pearls (arr JC)
                        (Jerry Gray)
                        As, Caceres; tpt, May; p, MacGregor
                 The Hut-Sut Song
   Int GM (2:18) I'm Thrilled (arr BF)-voc Ray Eberle
                        (Sylvia Dee-Sidney Lippman)
                        Ts, Beneke
                 Sun Valley Jump
                 Slumber Song (Theme)
```

This was Paula Kelly's last broadcast with the band. (G.M.P.R.)

15 August, 1941 (FRI)

Marion Hutton rejoined the band replacing Paula Kelly. Marion had given birth to a boy on May 26th. Up until she rejoined there had been many rumors that she would return to the bandstand. (G.M.P.R.; BB, Aug. 9, 1941; Met. Sept. 1941)
    "Miss Kelly, also a mother, in private life is the wife of Hal Dickinson of the four singing Modernaires, also featured with the Miller band. She was undecided whether she'd continue singing." (DB, Aug. 15, 1941)

    "Glenn Miller's band will sport five trumpets and three guitars when it reorganizes this week after a 19-day vacation, the first Glenn and his men have taken in more than three years.

(Continued on next page)

Bobby Hackett, Miller told the <u>Beat</u>, will be featured on jazz guitar prominently, possibly even more than cornet. Hackett's soft, delicately-phrased horn will be featured in specialty numbers however, Miller disclosed.

Alec Fila is in the brass section on trumpet. None of the regular Miller trumpeters are leaving. Miller already has two guitar players within his band and Hackett will make three." (DB, Aug. 15, 1941)

One of the guitar players with the band was Bill Conway, one of the Modernaires. Who the other guitar player was is not known. We are not quite sure who the fifth trumpet player was unless it was Ralph Brewster, another member of the Modernaires. This is a rather unusual article and as far as we know Miller continued to use four trumpets and one guitar on recording sessions and broadcasts.

Glenn Miller and His Orchestra played at Danceland, Sylvan Beach, New York. (G.M.P.R.; Variety, July 30, 1941) The band played from 9:30-1:30 A.M. D.S.T. (G.M.D.)

16 August, 1941 (SAT)

Glenn Miller and His Orchestra played in the Dream-land Ballroom at Conneaut Lake Park, Conneaut, Pennsylvania. (G.M.P.R.; Variety, July 30, 1941)

17 August, 1941 (SUN)

Glenn Miller and His Orchestra played at Summit Beach Park, Akron, Ohio. (G.M.P.R.; Cleveland Plain Dealer, Aug. 17, 1941) The band played from 9:00-1:00 A.M. (G.M.D.)

"Playing his only one-nighter this season, Glenn Miller and his ork attracted 4,300 paid customers, most of them at $1 advance but plenty at $1.25 at the box office Sunday night, August 17, at Summit Beach Park here. Ticket lines an hour before starting time extended to all corners of the park, and police were necessary to keep the ticket buyers in line.

Miller was a guest at the national soapbox derby finals in the afternoon, acknowledged his presence at the mike, and received a big ovation.

Lew Platt, manager of the park pavilion, said the Miller band gross was the best at the local spot

(Continued on next page)

for any band in the five years Summit Beach Inc.,
has operated the spot." (BB, Aug. 30, 1941)

"Lou Platt, operator of the ballroom in Summit
Beach Park in Akron, Ohio, was jailed Sunday night
August 17, 1941 for running a dance on the Sabbath.
Platt had booked Glenn Miller's band for that evening
with the okay of the City Council but apparently the
cops and the council didn't see eye to eye on the one
night infraction of the town's blue laws. Platt
spent the night in the jug and the following morning
was fined $50.00 and given a thirty day jail
sentence which was suspended.
Fine was a drop in the bucket. However, Miller
drew approximately 3,100 people at $1.35 a ticket and
walked out with $2,200.00 as his end of the evenings
take. Draw cracked the spot's record." (Variety,
Aug. 20, 1941)

18 August, 1941 (MON)

Glenn Miller and His Orchestra played at Memorial
Park, Williamsport, Pennsylvania. (G.M.P.R.)
"Glenn Miller's refusal to go through with a
one nighter for which he twice set dates has Richard
Guinan, owner, and Howard Hobbs, operator of Lakewood
Park, Mahoney City, Pa., up in arms and seeking the
advisability of legal action. Rumpus began when
Miller cancelled out of an appearance during the
latter part of July setting it back to August 18,
1941 because he wanted a vacation, then refusing to
play the spot at all. Both appearances were heavily
advertised. Miller played at Williamsport, Pa. on
August 18, 1941 about 90 miles from Lakewood.
According to Guinan, Miller's actions stem from
a disagreement between them last year. Lakewood
Park, he claims, admits some people at lower prices
on courtesy passes issued for various reasons (dis-
playing window cards) etc. Miller objected to anyone being admitted under the $1.00 per person that
was being levied for his date and claimed that
Guinan owed him $111.00 which was 60% of the differ-
ence between 75¢ and $1.00 on the no. people admitted
on passes.
Guinan wouldn't pay the money then but did so
this year; he claims when he was informed that Miller
wouldn't play for him unless the $111.00 was forth-
coming. Much of Guinan's yelp is that the prestige
of Lakewood Park was considerably injured after Miller
was twice advertised and then didn't show at all."
(Variety, Aug. 27, 1941) The band played from 9:00-
1:00 A.M. E.S.T. (G.M.D.)

19 August, 1941 (TUES)

   Glenn Miller and His Orchestra arrived in Washington,
   D.C. to do three Chesterfield programs. (G.M.P.R.)

19 August, 1941 (TUES): Washington, D.C. (CHESTERFIELD SHOW)
      CBS   10:00-10:15 P.M.

    Slumber Song (Theme)
    Ida!
    Just A Little Bit South Of North Carolina
    I Guess I'll Have To Dream The Rest
    Keep 'Em Flying
    Slumber Song (Theme)

20 August, 1941 (WED): Washington, D.C. (CHESTERFIELD SHOW)
      CBS   10:00-10:15 P.M.

   The announcer for this program is Larry Bruff.

    Slumber Song (Theme)
    Goin' Home
    I'm Not Much On Looks
    Cradle Song
    Introduction To A Waltz
    Slumber Song (Theme)

21 August, 1941 (THUR): Washington, D.C. (CHESTERFIELD SHOW)
      CBS   10:00-10:15 P.M.

    Slumber Song (Theme)
    Daddy
    The Things I Love
    Anvil Chorus
    Slumber Song (Theme)

21 August, 1941 (THUR)

   G.M.P.R. for the week ending August 21st show that
   Billy May arranged "Summer Shadows".

22 August, 1941 (FRI)

   Glenn Miller and His Orchestra played at Wheeling
   Park, Wheeling, West Virginia. (G.M.P.R.; Variety,
   July 30 & Aug. 13, 1941)

(Continued on next page)

"Miller drew 2,085 at Wheeling Park, Wheeling,
West Virginia with 1,122 tickets at $1.35 advance
and 963 tickets at $1.75 at the gate." (Variety, Aug.
27, 1941). The band played from 9:00-1:00 A.M.
D.S.T. (G.M.D.)

23 August, 1941 (SAT)

Glenn Miller and His Orchestra played at Casa Loma
Park, Charleston, West Virginia. (G.M.P.R.; Variety,
July 30 & Aug. 13, 1941)
"Miller set another new record mark here with
2,089 with 1,634 at $1.75 (tickets) advance and 455
at $2.25 (tickets) at the gate." (Variety, Aug. 27,
1941) The band played from 9:30-1:30 A.M. E.S.T.
(G.M.D.)

24 August, 1941 (SUN)

Glenn Miller and His Orchestra played at Dreamland
Park, Kenova, West Virginia. (G.M.P.R.; Variety,
Aug. 13, 1941) G.M.P.R. mentions Huntington, West
Virginia, but we suspect that this is the town where
the union fee was sent. Kenova is a small town not
far from Huntington. The band played from 10:00-
2:00 A.M. (G.M.D.)

25 August, 1941 (MON)

Glenn Miller and His Orchestra played at the
Roanoke Auditorium, Roanoke, Virginia. (G.M.P.R.;
Variety, Aug. 13, 1941)
"Glenn Miller knocked off a record $4,679.40
here August 25 at the Roanoke Auditorium. There
were 3,679 persons packed into the hall, 2,580 of
them dancers. B.O. admish was $1.50 for the
hoofers, 980 of whom paid $1.25 for advance sale
tickets. Balcony seats went at $1.10 at the gate
and 75 cents in advance." (BB, Sept. 13, 1941)
The band played from 10:00-2:00 A.M. (G.M.D.)

26 August, 1941 (TUES)

The band returned to Washington, D.C. to do three
Chesterfield programs. (G.M.P.R.)

26 August, 1941 (TUES): Washington, D.C. (CHESTERFIELD SHOW)
            CBS   10:00-10:15 P.M.

> *Slumber Song (Theme)*
> *Vilia*
> *Sweeter Than The Sweetest*
> *From One Love To Another-voc RE*
> *Song Of The Volga Boatmen*
> *Slumber Song (Theme)*

27 August, 1941 (WED): Washington, D.C.   (CHESTERFIELD SHOW)
            CBS   10:00-10:15 P.M.

> *Slumber Song (Theme)*
> *The Nickel Serenade*

UPRM-6314   ~~Vi LPM/LSP-3873~~, RCA Br. RD/SF-7932, RCA G LSP-3873
    Int GM ~~(3:36) Blue Champagne~~ (arr JG)-voc Ray Eberle
                (Grady Watts-Frank Ryerson)

> *Boulder Buff*
> *Slumber Song (Theme)*

28 August, 1941 (THUR): Washington, D.C.   (CHESTERFIELD SHOW)
            CBS   10:00-10:15 P.M.

> *Slumber Song (Theme)*
> *A String Of Pearls*
> *The Booglie Wooglie Piggy*
> *'Til Reveille*
> *Flagwaver*
> *Slumber Song (Theme)*

28 August, 1941 (THUR)

> G.M.P.R. for the week ending August 28th show that
> Billy May arranged "Nothin'"

29 August, 1941 (FRI)

> This was an open date according to G.M.P.R. The
> band hired a Greyhound bus in Washington on this
> date to travel to Atlantic City, then to Hershey
> (Sept. 1st) and then to New York City (Sept. 2nd)
> --a total of 509 miles. (G.M.P.R.)

30 August, 1941 (SAT): Steel Pier, Atlantic City, New Jersey
(SUNSET SERENADE)
NBC-Blue 5:00-6:00 P.M.

Glenn Miller and His Orchestra played for two days (Saturday, August 30th and Sunday, August 31st) at the Steel Pier, Atlantic City, New Jersey. Alex Bartha was the house band. (G.M.P.R.; BB, July 5, 1941; DB, July 1, 1941; Variety, June 18, July 30 & Aug. 13, 1941)

On August 30th the band broadcast the first of many "Sunset Serenades" on Saturday afternoons. These were hour long programs presented over NBC at Glenn's own expense. Part of each program was a salute to the men in service and each week a poll was conducted among five different service camps to determine the favorite song of the men in each camp. When the camps were chosen they automatically received 50 recordings of America's favorite artists (none of Miller). After Miller played the five tunes selected, the home audience chose their favorite tune and the top tune determined the camp that would receive a radio-phonograph combination. There were times when all five camps chose the same tune and so Miller got stuck for five radio-phonograph combinations. The radio-phonograph combinations were sent to the USO (United Service Organizations) club room at the camps.

The following program is not complete as it is only half an hour in length. Information on the other parts of this program is missing. The announcer for this program is Don ??.

5:00-5:15 P.M. Portion

(0:52) *Slumber Song (Theme)*
(Saul Tepper-John Chalmers MacGregor)
Int GM (3:38) *Here We Go Again (arr JG)*
(Jerry Gray)
Ts, Klink; tpt, May; clt, Caceres;
tpt, Best; d, Purtill; tpt, ??
Int GM (2:51) *The Cowboy Serenade (While I'm Rollin' My Last*
Cigarette (arr BF)-voc Ray Eberle
(Rich Hall)
Muted tbn, Miller
Int GM (2:30) *The Booglie Wooglie Piggy (arr JG)-voc Tex*
Beneke, Marion Hutton and The
Modernaires)
(Roy Jacobs)
Ts, Beneke; tpt, May

(Broadcast continued on next page)

```
    Int GM (3:13) Georgia On My Mind (arr JG)
                        (Stuart Gorrell-Hoagy Carmichael)
                        Ts, Beneke; tpt, Best; muted tpt, ??
          (0:32) Slumber Song (Theme)
                        (Saul Tepper-John Chalmers MacGregor)


                  5:30-5:45 P.M. Portion

          (0:48) Slumber Song (Theme)
                        (Saul Tepper-John Chalmers MacGregor)
    Int GM (0:52) It's Great To Be An American-voc The
                        Modernaires
                        (Ray Muffs-Jimmie Crane)
    Int GM (2:26) 'Til Reveille (arr BF)-voc Ray Eberle
                        (Stanley Cowan-Bobby Worth)
    Int GM (3:25) Daddy (arr BM)-voc Marion Hutton, Tex Beneke
                        and The Modernaires
                        (Robert Troup, Jr.)
    Int GM (3:15) The Things I Love-voc Ray Eberle
                        (Harold Barlow-Lew Harris)
    Int GM (3:51) Intermezzo (arr BF)
                        (Heinz Provost)
                        Ts, Beneke
          (0:32) Slumber Song (Theme)
                        (Saul Tepper-John Chalmers MacGregor)
```

Early September, 1941

>   Don Haynes, manager of Miller, Spivak, Thornhill
>   (and the soon-to-be-formed band of Hal McIntyre)
>   left General Amusement Corporation to form his own
>   personal management office. The new personal
>   managership tie-up did not affect Miller's bookings
>   as they were still being handled through the G.A.C.
>   office. (DB, Oct. 15, 1941; Met. Nov. 1941)

1 September, 1941 (MON)

>   Glenn Miller and His Orchestra played at the
>   Hershey Park Ballroom, Hershey, Pennsylvania.
>   (G.M.P.R.; Variety, July 30, 1941) The band played
>   from 8:30-12:30 A.M. D.S.T. (G.M.D.)
>   "Glenn Miller and his ork grossed $3,566 at
>   Hershey Park Ballroom Labor Day (1), with gate of
>   3,692 admishs at $1.10 for dancers, 55 cents for
>   spectators." (BB, Sept. 13, 1941)
>
>   "Miller did alright here pulling 3,682 admission
>   totalling $3,566.00 gross." (Variety, Sept. 10, 1941)

2 September, 1941 (TUES)

> The band returned to New York City to do the
> Chesterfield programs. (G.M.P.R.)

2 September, 1941 (TUES): New York City, New York
> *(CHESTERFIELD SHOW)*
> *CBS   10:00-10:15 P.M.*

> > *Slumber Song (Theme)*
> > *Intermezzo*
> > *Amapola*
> > *You And I*
> > *Measure For Measure*
> > *Slumber Song (Theme)*

3 September, 1941 (WED): Victor Studios, New York City, New York

> Same personnel as for July 10th broadcast except
> that Marion Hutton has replaced Paula Kelly as
> vocalist.

067741-1   BB 11315-B, HMVAu EA-2940, Cam Cas-2267, RCA G
                Cas-2267
           Says Who? Says You, Says I!-voc Marion Hutton,
                Tex Beneke and The Modernaires
                From the Warner Bros. film "Blues In The
                Night"
                (Johnny Mercer-Harold Arlen)

067742-1   BB 11326-B, AFRS Swingtime 53
           Orange Blossom Lane (arr JG)-voc Ray Eberle
                (Peter DeRose-Mitchell Parish-Nick Kenny)
                As, McIntyre; tpt, Best; muted tbn, Miller;
                ts, Beneke

067743-1   BB 11326-A
           Dear Arabella (arr JG)-voc Marion Hutton, Tex
                Beneke and The Modernaires
                (Stanley Joseloff-Sidney Lippman)
                Tpt, May

067744-1   BB 11299-A, Cam Cal/Cas-751, RCA G Cas-751, Pick.
                Int. CDS 1040, Cam Au Cas-751
           The Man In The Moon (arr JG)-voc Ray Eberle
                (Jerry Lawrence-Jerry Gray-John Benson Brooks)
                Ts, Beneke; tpt, Best

(Session continued on next page)

```
067745-1        BB 11299-B, HMV MH 99
                Ma-Ma-Maria (Fee-dle, ee-dle-lee, Fee-dle, ee-dle-la)
                    (arr BF)-voc Ray Eberle and The Modernaires
                    (Lewis-Stock-Rose)

067746-1        BB 11315-A
                This Time The Dream's On Me (arr BF)-voc Ray Eberle
                    From the Warner Bros. film "Blues In The Night"
                    (Johnny Mercer-Harold Arlen)
                    As, McIntyre; cnt, Hackett

                All tunes 1 take. (RCA Victor)
                This session lasted from 9:00 A.M. to 3:00 P.M.
                (RCA Victor)
```

3 September, 1941 (WED): New York City, New York
                (CHESTERFIELD SHOW)
                CBS 10:00-10:15 P.M.

Slumber Song (Theme)

```
E4VP 8207       Vi LPT 6701, Vi EPOT 6701 (947-0187), HMV RLS 598,
                    RCA G EPOT-6701
                (3:37) Daddy (arr BM)-voc Marion Hutton, Tex Beneke
                    and The Modernaires
                    (Robert Troup, Jr.)
```

The Things I Love

```
E3VP 5240       Vi LPT 6700, Vi EPNT 6700 (947-0127), HMV RLS 599,
                    Vi SPD-18 (599-9110), RCA G LPT 6700,
                    Vi 45 Special-1953
          Int GM (3:38) Oh So Good (arr JG)-Chant by Band
                    (Jerry Gray)
                    Tpt, Best; p, MacGregor; ts, Beneke;
                    tbn, Miller; tpt, May; d, Purtill;
                    clt, Caceres
```

Slumber Song (Theme)

```
                On Vi LPT 6701 "Daddy" was incorrectly listed as
                being broadcast on March 27, 1942.  On Vi LPT 6700
                "Oh So Good" was incorrectly listed as being broad-
                cast on September 5, 1941.
```

4 September, 1941 (THUR): New York City, New York
                (CHESTERFIELD SHOW)
                CBS 10:00-10:15 P.M.

Slumber Song (Theme)

(Broadcast continued on next page)

Adios
I'm Not Much On Looks
I'm Thrilled
Here We Go Again
Slumber Song (Theme)

The band took the NY-New Haven RR from New York
to Boston. (G.M.P.R.)

5 September, 1941 (FRI)

Glenn Miller and His Orchestra played for one week
(closed Thursday, September 11th) at the RKO Keith
Theater, Boston, Massachusetts. (G.M.P.R.; BB,
July 19, 1941; Variety, July 30 & Aug. 20, 1941;
Boston Daily Record, Sept. 5 & 11, 1941)
       "Glenn Miller and his band topped its last
season's gross at the RKO-Boston Theater (3,212
seats) during week ended September 11. Last season
Miller and the band drew $26,000 for one-week at
this house.
       This year's gross hit $32,000.
       During both stands the regular house prices
were raised to 44 cents, 55 cents and 65 cents.
       Also on the bill were Sibyl Bowan, Wally and
Verdyn Stapleton. Pic was "Hurry, Charlie, Hurry."
       Miller's gross was the highest since the
season began three weeks ago." (BB, Sept. 20, 1941)

       "It was just a year ago that Glenn Miller's
brassy band played this stand and in that interim
his local popularity has perked up along with
musical calibre of the organization. If the opening day mobs are good indicators, he has a chance
of bettering a big box office mark he chalked up
last season. As soon as the opening bars of his
theme song seeps through the curtains and as long
as Miller's crew are in sight the heps are out of
this world. With the entertainment concentrated into a well packaged sample of the stuff youngsters
want from his orchestra Miller hands 'em a commend-
able chunk of band how.
       Not only do they roar at every announcement but
they anticipate most of the numbers by interrupting
the bandleader's intros. The Modernaires (4) are
in and out with the soloists providing accompanying
vocals. Marion Hutton is a peppy asset in the sound
department and an eyeful besides. She and Tex Beneke
assisted by Modernaires have a good time on Nickel
Serenade sauced up with tricky caricatures of Sammy

(Continued on next page)

Kaye and Charlie Barnet. One of this show's highlights Ray Eberle registers okay in I Guess I'll
Have To Dream the Rest but his bawling of Braham's
Lullaby is something like a dirge.
   Chattanooga Choo Choo sung by Marion Hutton,
Tex Beneke and the Modernaires is a whizzer for the
jivers and Booglie Wooglie Piggy as a follow up also
hits their mental groove. Anvil Chorus for the
opener with Adios featuring one of the trumpets and
Miller on trombone plus Bugle Call Rag next to the
close are the best straight band numbers. Finish
with the National Anthem played with a zest that
could be copied to advantage by thousands of brass
bands throughout the United States. Incidentally,
the band has a unique set that carries some of the
atmosphere of a streamlined train and the costuming
in two shades of green rates tops." (Variety,
Sept. 10, 1941)

While in Boston the band stayed at Hotel Touraine.
(G.M.P.R.)

6 September, 1941 (SAT): Boston, Massachusetts (SUNSET SERENADE)
NBC-Red 5:00-6:00 P.M.

9 September, 1941 (TUES): Keith Theater, Boston, Massachusetts
(CHESTERFIELD SHOW)
CBS 10:00-10:15 P.M.

Slumber Song (Theme)
Sweeter Than The Sweetest
Just A Little Bit South Of North Carolina
Blue Champagne
Flagwaver
Slumber Song (Theme)

10 September, 1941 (WED): Keith Theater, Boston, Massachusetts
(CHESTERFIELD SHOW)
CBS 10:00-10:15 P.M.

The announcer for this program is Larry Bruff.

Slumber Song (Theme)
The Nickel Serenade-voc MH, TB & 4M
Cradle Song-voc RE
Keep 'Em Flying
Slumber Song (Theme)

(Continued on next page)

Miller introduced the second tune under both titles, "Brahm's Lullaby" and "Cradle Song".

11 September, 1941 (THUR): Keith Theater, Boston, Massachusetts
                          (CHESTERFIELD SHOW)
                          CBS   10:00-10:15 P.M.

Information is missing on the tunes played on this program.

The band took the NY Central RR from Boston to Albany. (G.M.P.R.)

12 September, 1941 (FRI)

Glenn Miller and His Orchestra played for four days (closed Monday, September 15th) at the Palace Theater, Albany, New York. Also on the same bill were Wally & Verdun Stapleton and Sibyl Bowan. The band took a Greyhound bus from Albany to Schenectady. (G.M.P.R.; Variety, Aug. 20, 1941; BB, Aug. 23, 1941)

13 September, 1941 (SAT): Albany, New York (SUNSET SERENADE)
                         NBC-Red   5:00-6:00 P.M.

> *Moonlight Serenade (Theme)*
> *The Cowboy Serenade*
> *Introduction To A Waltz*
> *It's Great To Be An American*
> *Intermezzo*
> *Maria Elena (arr BF)-voc RE*
>   *From "Down Mexico Way"*
>   *(Lorenzo Barcelata-S.K. Russell)*
> *The Booglie Wooglie Piggy*
> *'Til Reveille*
> *I Dreamt I Dwelt In Harlem*
> *It's So Peaceful In The Country (arr BF)*
>   *(Alec Wilder)*
> *Twenty-Four Robbers*
> *Do I Worry?*
> *Keep 'Em Flying*
> *Slumber Song (Theme)*

16 September, 1941 (TUES)

Glenn Miller and His Orchestra played for three days (closed Thursday, September 18th) at Proctor's

(Continued on next page)

Theater, Schenectady, New York. Also on the same
bill were Wally & Verdun Stapleton and Sibyl Bowan.
(G.M.P.R.; Variety, Aug. 20, 1941; BB, Aug. 23 &
Sept. 20, 1941)

16 September, 1941 (TUES): Schenectady, New York
                    (CHESTERFIELD SHOW)
                    CBS   10:00-10:15 P.M.

   The announcer for this program is Larry Bruff

          Slumber Song (Theme)
          Vilia
          The Booglie Wooglie Piggy
          From One Love To Another
          I Dreamt I Dwelt In Harlem
          Slumber Song (Theme)

17 September, 1941 (WED): Schenectady, New York
                    (CHESTERFIELD SHOW)
                    CBS   10:00-10:15 P.M.

          Slumber Song (Theme)
          Rockin' Chair (arr BF)
                Cnt, Hackett
          Sweeter Than The Sweetest
          I'm Thrilled
          Measure For Measure
          Slumber Song (Theme)

This version of "Rockin' Chair" is an instrumental
(an entirely different arrangement from the April
17, 1941 broadcast) and features Bobby Hackett on
cornet throughout the tune. It is hoped that RCA
Victor will issue this version.

18 September, 1941 (THUR): Schenectady, New York
                    (CHESTERFIELD SHOW)
                    CBS   10:00-10:15 P.M.

          Slumber Song (Theme)
          Daddy
          The Cowboy Serenade
          Anvil Chorus
          Slumber Song (Theme)

The band took the NY Central RR from Schenectady
to Philadelphia. (G.M.P.R.)

19 September, 1941 (FRI)

> Glenn Miller and His Orchestra played for one week
> (closed Thursday, September 25th) at the Earle
> Theater, Philadelphia, Pennsylvania. Also on the
> same bill were Wally & Verdun Stapleton and Sibyl
> Bowan. (G.M.P.R.; The Philadelphia Inquirer, Sept.
> 19 & 25; DB, Sept. 15, 1941; BB, Sept. 20 & 27,
> 1941; Variety, Aug. 20, 1941)
>   "Glenn Miller remains high in realm of the hep-
> cats. Everything he says, every note his lads play
> got a bombardment of applause that probably made the
> manager of the Earle wish the walls were made of
> rubber when this reviewer caught the show.
>   Band in third trip here tees off with a bouncy
> version of Anvil Chorus with the individual members
> of Miller's aggregation getting a chance to shine.
>   There's plenty of handclapping down front when
> the Miller gang goes into its latest hit Chattanooga
> Choo Choo (from Sun Valley Serenade) with Marion
> Hutton and Modernaires along with Tex Beneke handling
> the zingy vocalizing. Also getting the kudos from
> the assembled alligators is Booglie Wooglie Piggy and
> Cowboy Serenade with the Modernaires and Miss Hutton
> on deck.
>   Ray Eberle continues to evoke sighs from the
> femme pewholders crooning The Things I love,
> Indian Summer, and I Guess I'll Have To Dream The
> Rest with the Modernaires joining." (Variety, Sept.
> 24, 1941)

>   "Colossal $34,000.00 racked up by "Pittsburgh
> Kid" and Glenn Miller band last week. Latter take
> tied all-time band gross at this house." (Variety,
> Oct. 1, 1941)

20 September, 1941 (SAT): Philadelphia, Pennsylvania
                (SUNSET SERENADE)
                NBC-Red 5:00-6:00 P.M.

> *Moonlight Serenade* (Theme)
> *You And I*
> *Daddy*
> *Sunrise Serenade*
> *The Spirit Is Willing*
> *Carmen*
> *Perfidia*
> *Green Eyes* (arr JG)-voc MH & 4M
>   (Nilo Menendez-Adolfo Utrera-Rivera-
>   Woods)
> *Intermezzo*
> *Slumber Song* (Theme)

23 September, 1941 (TUES): Earle Theater, Philadelphia, Penn.
                            (CHESTERFIELD SHOW)
                            CBS   10:00-10:15 P.M.

                Slumber Song (Theme)
                A String Of Pearls
                The Hut-Sut Song
                The Things I Love
                Oh So Good
                Slumber Song (Theme)

24 September, 1941 (WED): Earle Theater, Philadelphia, Penn.
                          (CHESTERFIELD SHOW)
                          CBS   10:00-10:15 P.M.

    The announcer for this program is Paul Douglas.

                Slumber Song (Theme)
                Adios
                Just A Little Bit South Of North Carolina
                I Guess I'll Have To Dream The Rest
                Keep 'Em Flying
                Slumber Song (Theme)

25 September, 1941 (THUR): Earle Theater, Philadelphia, Penn.
                           (CHESTERFIELD SHOW)
                           CBS   10:00-10:15 P.M.

                Slumber Song (Theme)
                Song Of The Volga Boatmen
                I'm Not Much On Looks
                You And I
                Flagwaver
                Slumber Song (Theme)

26 September, 1941 (FRI)

        Glenn Miller and His Orchestra played for one week
(closed Thursday, October 2nd) at the Stanley
Theater, Pittsburg, Pennsylvania. (G.M.P.R.;
Pittsburg Post Gazette, Sept. 26 & Oct. 2, 1941;
BB, Sept. 20 & 27, 1941; Variety, Aug. 20, Oct. 1 &
8, 1941)
        "Glenn Miller and orchestra, headlining bill
that included Sibyl Bowan and the Stapletons, piled
up near-record $32,500 at Stanley. . . . Presenting
five shows daily and six Saturday, instead of usual
four and five, Miller also broadcast three CBS

(Continued on next page)

Chesterfield programs from stage. On the screen, reckoned little help, <u>Parachute Battalion</u> (RKO).
    Only band to top Miller at Stanley has been Kyser, who neared $36,000 several years ago."
(BB, Oct. 11, 1941)

27 September, 1941 (SAT): Pittsburg, Pennsylvania (SUNSET SERENADE)
                    NBC-Red   5:00-6:00 P.M.

28 September, 1941 (SUN)

Glenn Miller and His Orchestra played at Steubenville, Ohio on this date as the Stanley Theater was closed on Sunday. (G.M.P.R.)

30 September, 1941 (TUES): Stanley Theater, Pittsburg, Penn.
                    (CHESTERFIELD SHOW)
                    CBS   10:00-10:15 P.M.

> *Slumber Song (Theme)*
> *Georgia On My Mind*
> *The Nickel Serenade*
> *Do I Worry?*
> *Introduction To A Waltz*
> *Slumber Song (Theme)*

October, 1941

While in California Glenn Miller acquired a 55-acre ranch which produced oranges. Miller named his ranch "Tuxedo Junction". (DB, July 15, 1941)

When Miller attempted to build a home on this property he ran into union problems.
    "Los Angeles--Glenn Miller is in a bit of hot water here over building of a home with non-union labor.
    Situation was called to the attention of Local 47 authorities by the Los Angeles Building Trades Council and an investigation was made by John Boyd, new Local 47 trustee. Boyd reported that Miller had purchased 20 acres near Pomona, California and that construction had been started on the home under a non-union contractor who was the son of the former owner of the property. Boyd stated that Miller had been notified of the situation and that he was confident Miller would take steps to put himself back in the good graces of the Building Trades Council." (DB, Oct. 1, 1941)

[354]

*1 October, 1941 (WED): Stanley Theater, Pittsburg, Pennsylvania
(CHESTERFIELD SHOW)
CBS   10:00-10:15 P.M.*

> *Slumber Song* (Theme)
> *The Spirit Is Willing*
> *La Cucaracha*
> *Cradle Song*
> *Here We Go Again*
> *Slumber Song* (Theme)

*2 October, 1941 (THUR): Stanley Theater, Pittsburg, Pennsylvania
(CHESTERFIELD SHOW)
CBS   10:00-10:15*

> *Slumber Song* (Theme)
> *The Booglie Wooglie Piggy*
> *The Man In The Moon-voc RE*
> *Anvil Chorus*
> *Slumber Song* (Theme)

3 October, 1941 (FRI)

> Glenn Miller and His Orchestra played a one-nighter
> at A.J. Perry's Empire Ballroom, Allentown,
> Pennsylvania. The band took a Greyhound bus from
> Allentown to White Plains. (G.M.P.R.; The Morning
> Call, Oct. 3, 1941; BB, Sept. 20 & 27, 1941)
>   "Miller hit slightly over 4,000 at $1.00 and
> $1.25 big. Operator, Andy Perry said draw was cut
> by 1,500 by bad weather and fogged mountain roads."
> (Variety, Oct. 8, 1941)
> The band played from 9:00-1:00 A.M. E.S.T. (G.M.D.)

*4 October, 1941 (SAT): White Plains, New York (SUNSET SERENADE)
NBC-Red   5:00-6:00 P.M.*

4 October, 1941 (SAT)

> Glenn Miller and His Orchestra played a one-nighter
> at the County Center, White Plains, New York. The
> band took a Greyhound bus from White Plains to New
> York City. (G.M.P.R.; Variety, Oct. 1, 1941)
>
>   "Westchester Arena for big dances on a one-
> night (Saturday) basis instead of all-week oper-
> ation like the Madison Square Garden Dance
> Carnival after which the White Plains County
> Center shindigs will be patterned. Glenn Miller

(Continued on next page)

opens the series on October 4, with other top name
bands planned for the huge ballroom, enlarged to
accommodate 7,500, with a new $15,000 dance floor
covering an area of 25,000 square feet, as large
as the aforementioned Garden.
      A regular relief band will be on regular duty
from week to week at the spot, and the affairs will
have the policy of regular stage, screen and radio
star guests as well as the bands for entertainment.
Admission will be $1.10, with increased prices for
lodge seats." (Met. Oct. 1941)

After all this buildup how did the Miller band do?
      "Next night band took one of its few brodies
at White County Center in White Plains, New York
opening a dance policy. Miller drew 1,850 at $1.10.
Center's capacity of five to six thousand has never
made a dance policy stick. This was heavily
advertised--loss big!" (Variety, Oct. 8, 1941)
The band played from 9:00-1:00 A.M. (G.M.D.)

5 October, 1941 (SUN)

      Open. (G.M.D.)

6 October, 1941 (MON): Cafe Rouge, Hotel Pennsylvania,
                        New York City, N.Y.
                        NBC-   12:05-12:30 A.M. EST.

Glenn Miller and His Orchestra opened at the "Cafe
Rouge" of the Hotel Pennsylvania, New York City,
New York. (G.M.P.R.; DB, Sept. 1, Oct. 1 & 15, 1941)

A number of other bands began long runs at New York
City hotels during this period. The most notable
competitor was Benny Goodman who opened at the New
Yorker Hotel on October 9th but other bands offered
varying amounts of competition. Sammy Kaye was at
the Essex House, Horace Heidt at the Biltmore,
Xavier Cugat at the Waldorf-Astoria, and Vaughn
Monroe at the Commodore. (DB, Sept. 1 & Oct. 1,
1941) The "Cafe Rouge" was closed on Sundays.
(G.M.P.R. & G.M.D.)

This was Hal McIntyre's last day with the band be-
fore he was to strike out on his own with a band.
Benny Feman, formerly with Larry Clinton, joined the
band the next day on saxophone. G.M.P.R. show that
McIntyre was paid for four days (week ending
October 9th) which meant that he was with the band on

(Continued on next page)

Oct. 3,4,5, & 6. Feman was paid for three days at
the Hotel Pennsylvania which meant that he was with
the band on Oct. 7,8, & 9.
    "The opening, as you'd suspect, was stupendous.
This was Hal McIntyre's last night with the band,
which, to those who have been close to the outfit
since its beginning (Hal's been with it since then)
made this a very sentimental occasion." (Met. Nov.
1941)

Miller sponsored McIntyre's new band financially
and also gave McIntyre about 40 arrangements.
McIntyre stated: "But they are tunes--mostly
standards--which Glenn never played and which aren't
styled in Glenn's 'clarinet above saxes' fashion."
(DB, Nov. 1, 1941) One of these tunes was "Daisy
Mae" which McIntyre later recorded.

Miller's broadcast schedule in early October (as
per Music & Rhythm, Nov. 1941) ran as follows:

CBS--Tuesdays, Wednesdays, Thursdays, 10:00 P.M.
    Chesterfield Show

NBC--Mondays, Thursdays, 12:05 A.M. Cafe Rouge
NBC--Fridays, 7:30 P.M. Cafe Rouge
NBC--Saturdays, 5:00 P.M. Cafe Rouge "Sunset Serenade"

G.M.P.R. show that there was one sustaining program
this evening from the Hotel Pennsylvania.

6-15 October, 1941: Cafe Rouge, Hotel Pennsylvania,
                    New York City, N.Y.

        Here is an undated review of the Miller
        band at the Cafe Rouge:

        "This is Glenn Miller's third straight, fall
season at the Pennsylvania Hotel's Cafe Rouge Room
which was closed for the last part of the summer.
The band he is leading is essentially the same and
its pulling power indicated by his summer one niters
is just as strong so there's no reason to expect
other than a good stay.
        There's only one fault to be found with
Miller's 4 trumpet, 4 tram (with leader), 5 sax,
4 rhythm combo, and that's that occasionally those
8 brasses get a bit deafening. That's much more of
the problem presently than a year ago. Today, big

(Continued on next page)

Hal McIntyre leaves Miller organization to form his own band in October 1941.

A gathering of Glenn's friends at the Cafe Rouge. Left to right: Sy Shribman, George Evans, Helen Miller, Glenn, Charlie Spivak, Don and Polly Haynes.

Glenn Miller and his Orchestra open at the Cafe Rouge on October 6, 1941—Hal McIntyre's last night with the band.

The Modernaires with Marion and Tex.

Trumpeters Best, Fila, McMickle, May.

Bobby Hackett and his tender-toned cornet.

Bobby Hackett's usual chair in the band was in the rhythm section, on guitar.

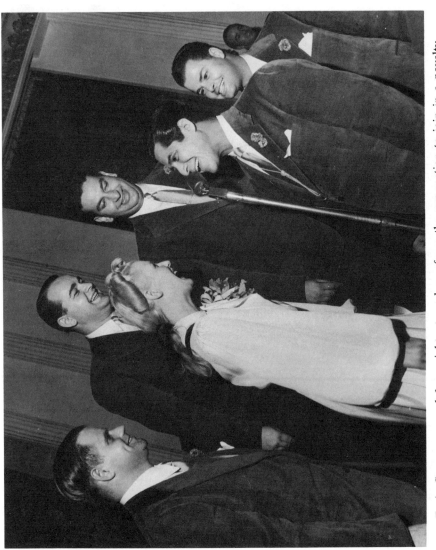

Ernie Caceres, second from right, steps down from the sax section to join in a novelty vocal.

Glenn gets into the singing act too.

Glenn on trombone.

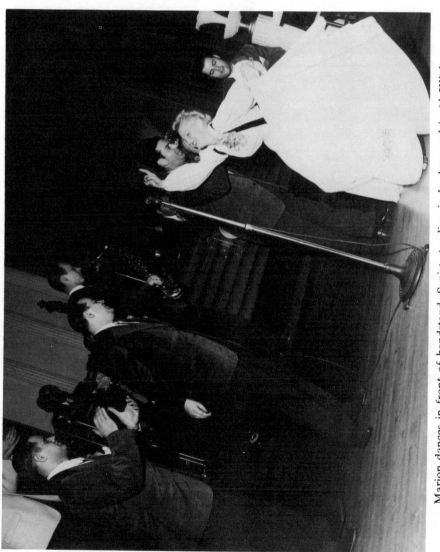

Marion dances in front of bandstand. Saxist standing in background is Al Klink.

Glenn and comic Joe E. Brown.

bands spotted in such spots are leaning backward to
avoid blasting. Miller apparently doesn't. Of
course he gets a lot of kids (they were fairly
plentiful when caught) who demand to have their heads
blown off but there's a lot more trade at the Cafe
which maybe don't agree.

The Pennsylvania is trying something new this
year. The band, with one dance act, puts on a
dinner show using the outfit's extremely tasty
muted arrangements to build a fine response. It
doesn't disturb dining because the interlude is 90%
sweet music. Miller conducts from the floor and
uses Marion Hutton, Ray Eberle and Modernaires to
good advantage. Ray Eberle however could find something better than 'These Are The Things I Love' to
open.

The Cherney Twins are dancers.
Miller is bucking strong name competition this
year from nearby New Yorker, which has Benny Goodman
and an ice show." (Variety, Oct. 15, 1941)

7 October, 1941 (TUES): New York City, N.Y. (CHESTERFIELD SHOW)
CBS 10:00-10:15 P.M.

Trombones	*Glenn Miller, Jimmy Priddy, Paul Tanner, Frank D'Annolfo*
Trumpets	*Billy May, Alec Fila, Dale McMickle, Johnny Best*
Reeds	*BENNY FEMAN, as; Ernie Caceres, as, bar & clt; Wilbur Schwartz, clt & as; Tex Beneke, ts; Al Klink, ts*
Rhythm	*Chummy MacGregor, p; Bobby Hackett, g & cnt; Doc Goldberg, b; Maurice Purtill, d*

Slumber Song (Theme)
Intermezzo
Jack And Jill (arr JG)-voc MH, TB & 4M
    (Roy Jacobs-Martin Block)
I Don't Want To Set The World On Fire
Measure For Measure
Slumber Song (Theme)

8 October, 1941 (WED): New York City, N.Y. (CHESTERFIELD SHOW)
CBS 10:00-10:15 P.M.

Slumber Song (Theme)
Goin' Home
Twenty-Four Robbers
Do You Care?
Sun Valley Jump
Slumber Song (Theme)

9 October, 1941 (THUR): New York City, N.Y. (CHESTERFIELD SHOW)
             CBS   10:00-10:15 P.M.

     The announcer for this program is Paul Douglas.

> *Slumber Song (Theme)*
> *A String Of Pearls*
> *'Til Reveille-voc RE, 4M, & MH*[1]
> *Flagwaver*
> *Slumber Song (Theme)*

  [1]This is a rather extended version of this tune which
changes to an up-tempo treatment about half way with
vocals by The Modernaires and Marion Hutton to
another tempo change started by Purtill, and then a
solo by Beneke, and then a cornet solo by Hackett
with The Modernaires in the background, and then
finally the whole tune slows down to its original
beginning with a vocal (once again) by Ray Eberle.
The timing is approximately 4:22. (Heard at RCA
Victor)

9 October, 1941 (THUR)

    G.M.P.R. for the week ending October 9th show that
Billy May arranged "Checkin' With Chuck" (later
recorded as "Long Tall Mama"). Chuck Goldstein was
interested in radio production and Glenn used to let
him help Glenn make up programs and keep a time
check and so he always had a stop watch and was
giving a "go" sign. The band used to say "before
anything happens we'd better check with Chuck."
(from Tom Zak's interview with Ralph Brewster)

11 October, 1941 (SAT): Cafe Rouge, Hotel Pennsylvania,
             New York City, N.Y.
             (SUNSET SERENADE)
             NBC-Blue   5:00-6:00 P.M. EST.

    I Don't Want To Set The World On Fire

    "Glenn Miller will inaugurate a Saturday after-
noon series of tea dances at the Pennsylvania Hotel
N.Y.C. beginning Oct. 11, 1941 for which an admission
of one Defense Savings Stamp will be charged. Latter
are sold in various denominations but the lowest
(25¢) will be accepted. As well as helping Stamp
Sales the idea is to provide an audience for Miller's

(Continued on next page)

Glenn Miller's Saturday U.S.O. matinee at Cafe Rouge, October 1941.

Inside the Cafe Rouge. Since Benny Feman (third sax to right of Glenn) is in band this photo dates from either the 11th or 18th of October 1941.

The saxophone section in October 1941: Schwartz, Klink, Feman, Caceres, Beneke.

Ray Eberle.

Climax of "Sunset Serenade" broadcast. Miller presents soldiers from lucky army camp with radio-phonograph.

Glenn Miller autographing record at CBS.

Saturday five to six P.M. full hour sustaining show
on the N.B.C. Blue Network which donates 250 record-
ings and one or more radio phono combination to
Army Camps.
      Dances will last two hours 4:15-6:15 P.M.
Admission will cover only the privilege of listen-
ing or dancing to the band and seeing the broadcast.
Drinks etc. will of course be extra." (Variety,
Sept. 17, 1941)

14 October, 1941 (TUES): New York City, N.Y. (CHESTERFIELD SHOW)
                    CBS   10:00-10:15 P.M.

> *Slumber Song (Theme)*
> *Tschaikowsky's Piano Concerto*
> *Daddy*
> *Maria Elena (arr BF)-voc RE*
>   *From "Down Mexico Way"*
>   *(Lorenzo Barcelata-S.K. Russell)*
>
> *Slumber Song (Theme)*

Information on one of the tunes is missing.

15 October, 1941 (WED): New York City, N.Y. (CHESTERFIELD SHOW)
                    CBS   10:00-10:15 P.M. EST.

> *Slumber Song (Theme)*
> *Rockin' Chair*
> *I'm Not Much On Looks*
> *I'm Thrilled*
> *Keep 'Em Flying*
> *Slumber Song (Theme)*

This version of "Rockin' Chair" is an instrumental
and features Bobby Hackett on cornet throughout
the tune.

16 October, 1941 (THUR): New York City, N.Y. (CHESTERFIELD SHOW)
                    CBS   10:00-10:15 P.M. EST.

> *Slumber Song (Theme)*

E2VL 4420   Vi LPT-30, HMV MH 172, Vi 42-0155 (Vi PT-39),
               Vi EPA-726, Vi 27-0155 (Vi WPT-39), Vi EPBT-
               3026 (947-0027), Vi LPM-1189, Vi EPB-1189
               (547-0800), HMV DLP-1012, Vi It LPM-10141,
               E1 WDLP 1012, RCA Vi It LJ 50020, HMVAus GA-

(Broadcast continued on next page)

5113, RCA F 430228, RCA G EPBT-3026, RCA G
EPC-1189, Vi It LPM 50020, RCA Au L 11021,
HMVAu ODLP 1012, RCA G LPT-30

(2:29) Vilia (arr BF)
From the musical production "The Merry
Widow"
(Franz Lehar)
Muted tpt, McMickle; ts, Beneke; cnt,
Hackett

Just A Little Bit South Of North Carolina
Cradle Song
Song Of The Volga Boatmen
Slumber Song (Theme)

16 October, 1941 (THUR)

G.M.P.R. for the week ending October 16th show
that Billy May arranged "B-1-By".

18 October, 1941 (SAT): Cafe Rouge, Hotel Pennsylvania,
New York City, N.Y.
(SUNSET SERENADE)
NBC-Blue 5:00-6:00 P.M. EST.

I Don't Want To Set The World On Fire
V Hop

19 October, 1941 (SUN)

Glenn Miller and His Orchestra played between halves
of a Brooklyn Dodgers football game at Ebbetts
Stadium, Brooklyn, New York. (G.M.P.R.; DB, Nov.
15, 1941)
"On a deal that was started during the making
of 20th century-Fox Sun Valley Serenade Glenn Miller
will take his band and singing troupe to Ebbetts
Field, N.Y.C. next Sunday October 19, 1941 to give a
between halves concert at the Dodgers-Pittsburgh
football game. Dan Topping, owner of the Dodgers is
Sonja Henie's husband. Miss Henie is starred in Sun
Valley Serenade.
Topping is building a large portable bandstand,
which will be wheeled to mid field for the show.
The grid intermission will be longer than usual to
allow Miller plenty time to give a performance.

(Continued on next page)

Miller band plays at Ebbetts Field, Brooklyn, between halves of Dodger football game, October 19, 1941.

Only Marion is protected against the autumn chill.

Another photo of the band from Ebbetts Field.

American Patrol—just the arrangement for this occasion.

Looks grim for the Dodgers. Miller, football player in high school, watches intently.

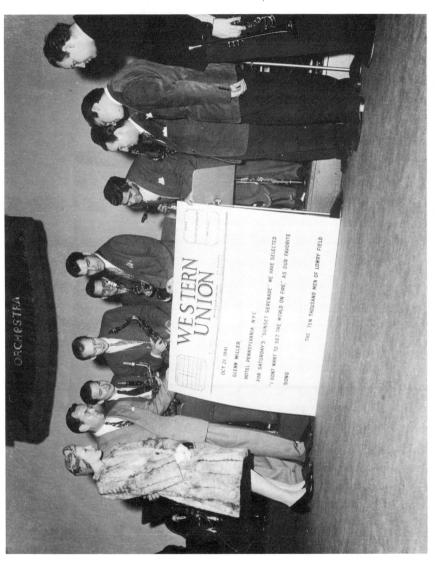

Left to right: Hutton, Miller, Schwartz, Klink, Purtill, Beneke, Caceres, Hackett, Eberle, May.

Miller is currently playing six days a week at the Pennsylvania Hotel and usually local 802 of the A.F.M. doesn't allow the seven days work. They gave Miller permission, however, and in addition Topping has hired a twenty-five piece military band composed of local's musicians. Miller's crew is, of course, also on salary." (Variety, Oct. 15, 1941)

"Glenn Miller took his outfit into Ebbetts Field in Brooklyn a few weeks ago to play between halves of the Dodgers and Chicago Cardinal's football game on Oct. 19, 1941 Sunday. Glenn Miller and his Orchestra entertained the 12,054 onlookers between halves." (Variety, Nov. 5, 1941)

"The Brooklyns lost anyway." (DB, Nov. 15, 1941)

20 October, 1941 (MON): Victor Studios, New York City, New York

Same personnel as for October 7th.

071190-1   BB 11342-A, HMV DLP 1122, RD 3/4-64
Dreamsville, Ohio (arr JG)-voc Ray Eberle and The
         Modernaires
         (Craig Lee-Al Rinker-Judy Freeland)
         Cnt, Hackett

071191-1   BB 11342-B, HMV DLP 1122
Papa Niccolini (The Happy Cobbler)-voc Ray Eberle,
         Tex Beneke and The Modernaires
         (Anne and Jean Edwards-Don George)

071192-1   BB 11353-A, AFR-112, HMV BD 5789, HMV MH 57, HMVSw
         JK-2433, HMVAus GA-5020, Vi 20-2510, AFRS
         "Jukebox USA" 77, AFRS "Jukebox USA" 147, AFRS
         Swingtime 53, RD 3/4-57, HMVIr I.M. 1023,
         HMVHu HUC 113, AFRS Jill's Juke Box Series
         H-46: 220, 36, 58, 201, HMVAu E.A. 3404, AFRS
         G.I. Jive Series H-12: 838, 1014, 1139
Jingle Bells (arr GM & BF)-voc Tex Beneke, Ernie
         Caceres and The Modernaires
         (Harold Dickinson-Bill Conway)
         P, MacGregor; muted tpt, May

071193-1   BB 11369-B, HMV BD 5749, HMV MH 126, HMV DLP 1049,
         Vi LPM 2080, HMVIn BD 5749
This Is No Laughing Matter-voc Ray Eberle
         (Van Loman-Martin Block-Al Frisch)

(Continued on next page)

"Jingle Bells" was not written by Harold Dickinson and Bill Conway as the label reads. They supplied the new words and arrangement for the vocal portion of the tune. The tune was originally written in 1857 by J.S. Pierpont. The reverse side of Bluebird 11353 was not Miller but Alvino Rey and His Orchestra playing "Santa Claus Is Comin' To Town." This was a special Xmas record issued by Victor.

The Martin Block in the composer-lyricist credits for "This Is No Laughing Matter" is the very well-known Disc Jockey who ran the popular radio program "Make Believe Ballroom" over WNEW in New York City.

All tunes 1 take. (RCA Victor)
This session lasted from 1:45 P.M. to 4:15 P.M.
(RCA Victor)

20 October, 1941 (MON): Cafe Rouge, Hotel Pennsylvania,
New York City, N.Y.
NBC- 12:05-12:30 A.M. EST.

G.M.P.R. show that there was one sustaining program this evening from the Hotel Pennsylvania.

21 October, 1941 (TUES): New York City, N.Y. (CHESTERFIELD SHOW)
CBS 10:00-10:15 P.M.

> *Slumber Song (Theme)*
> *Ida!*
> *Amapola*
> *Blue Champagne*
> *Oh So Good*
> *Slumber Song (Theme)*

According to G.M.P.R. this was Benny Feman's last day with the band. He was paid for the Tuesday Chesterfield program and the night at the Hotel Pennsylvania.

22 October, 1941 (WED): New York City, N.Y. (CHESTERFIELD SHOW)
CBS 10:00-10:15 P.M. EST.

> *Trombones*   *Glenn Miller, Jimmy Priddy, Paul*
> *Tanner, Frank D'Annolfo*
> *Trumpets*   *Billy May, Alec Fila, Dale McMickle,*
> *Johnny Best*

(Broadcast continued on next page)

Reeds	*Tex Beneke, as (lead alto); Ernie Caceres, as, bar & clt; Wilbur Schwartz, clt & as; IRVING "BABE"RUSSIN, ts; Al Klink, ts*
Rhythm	*Chummy MacGregor, p; Bobby Hackett, g & cnt; Doc Goldberg, b; Maurice Purtill, d*

Slumber Song (Theme)
A String Of Pearls
To All Of You-voc MH
     (
Papa Niccolini
Largo
Slumber Song (Theme)

According to G.M.P.R. "Babe" Russin joined the band on this date for both the Chesterfield program and the job at the Hotel Pennsylvania.

"Babe Russin moved into Glenn Miller's reed section at Hotel Pennsylvania two weeks ago, giving up his hopes of becoming a successful band leader, and Gordon (Tex) Beneke switched to lead alto. Miller made the switch after temporarily using Ben Feman in the chair vacated by Hal McIntyre, who now has his own band on tour in New England.

Miller will give Russin most of the tenor solo passages, splitting them with Al Klink, while Beneke holds down the all-important first chair. Russin had his own band for nearly a year but never enjoyed much success. He is considered by many to be one of the greatest white tenor men in the field." (DB. Nov. 15, 1941)

23 October, 1941 (THUR): New York City, N.Y. (CHESTERFIELD SHOW)
CBS   10:00-10:15 P.M.

Slumber Song (Theme)
Drink To Me Only With Thine Eyes
ALP *Jack And Jill*
Tschaikowsky's Piano Concerto
Anvil Chorus
Slumber Song (Theme)

23 October, 1941 (THUR): Cafe Rouge, Hotel Pennsylvania,
New York City, N.Y.
NBC-   12:05-12:30 A.M. EST.

G.M.P.R. show that there was one sustaining program this evening from the Hotel Pennsylvania.

24 October, 1941 (FRI): Cafe Rouge, Hotel Pennsylvania,
New York City, N.Y.
NBC-   7:30-8:00 P.M. EST.

G.M.P.R. show that there was one sustaining program
this evening from the Hotel Pennsylvania.

25 October, 1941 (SAT): Cafe Rouge, Hotel Pennsylvania
New York City, N.Y. (SUNSET SERENADE)
NBC-Blue 5:00-6:00 P.M. EST.

Georgia On My Mind
I Don't Want To Set The World On Fire
Are You Rusty, Gate?
Dear Arabella
You And I

27 October, 1941 (MON): Cafe Rouge, Hotel Pennsylvania,
New York City, N.Y.
NBC-   12:05-12:30 A.M. EST.

G.M.P.R. show that there was one sustaining program
this evening from the Hotel Pennsylvania.

28 October, 1941 (TUES): New York City, N.Y. (CHESTERFIELD SHOW)
CBS   10:00-10:15 P.M.

Slumber Song (Theme)
Adios
Dear Arabella
I'm Thrilled
Are You Jumpin' Jack?
Slumber Song (Theme)

29 October, 1941 (WED): New York City, N.Y. (CHESTERFIELD SHOW)
CBS   10:00-10:15 P.M.

Slumber Song (Theme)
Sunrise Serenade
Pin Ball Paul
Humpty Dumpty Heart
Measure For Measure
Slumber Song (Theme)

30 October, 1941 (THUR): New York City, N.Y. (CHESTERFIELD SHOW)
                    CBS   10:00-10:15 P.M.

> *Moonlight Serenade* (Theme)
> *Star Dust*
> *Chattanooga Choo Choo*
> *This Is No Laughing Matter*
> *One O'Clock Jump*
> *Slumber Song* (Theme)

The ASCAP-radio war was resolved late Wednesday night, October 29 and on Thursday, October 30, ASCAP music returned to the air. The theme songs of major bands and major programs returned to pre-BMI normal. On this program we have a number of ASCAP tunes. This was the first broadcast of "Chattanooga Choo Choo" since it was recorded May 7th, and from this point on the tune began its spectacular rise to becoming a million copy seller.

30 October, 1941 (THUR)

G.M.P.R. for the week ending October 30th show that Billy May arranged "Valse Triste".

30 October, 1941 (THUR): Cafe Rouge, Hotel Pennsylvania,
                    New York City, N.Y.
                    NBC-   12:05-12:30 A.M.

G.M.P.R. show that there was one sustaining program this evening from the Hotel Pennsylvania.

31 October, 1941 (FRI): Cafe Rouge, Hotel Pennsylvania,
                    New York City, N.Y.
                    NBC-   7:30-8:00 P.M. EST.

G.M.P.R. show that there was one sustaining program this evening from the Hotel Pennsylvania.

Miller's broadcast schedule was slightly altered at this time and we assume that this change (from Music & Rhythm, Dec. 1941) applied to the month of November. The only change is that the Mondays and Thursdays broadcasts from the Cafe Rouge were moved down to 11:30 P.M.

1 November, 1941 (SAT): Cafe Rouge, Hotel Pennsylvania,
New York City, N.Y. (SUNSET SERENADE)
NBC-Blue 5:00-6:00 P.M. EST.

I Don't Want To Set The World On Fire
I Guess I'll Have To Dream The Rest

3 November, 1941 (MON): Victor Studios, New York City, N.Y.

Same personnel as for October 22nd broadcast.

068066-1   BB 11369-A, HMV BD 5749, HMV MH 126, HMVIn BD 5749
Humpty Dumpty Heart (arr JG)-voc Ray Eberle
From the RKO-Radio picture "Playmates"
(Johnny Burke-Jimmy Van Heusen)
Clt, ??

068066-2   Cam Cal/Cas-751, RCA G Cas-751, Pick. Int. CDS 1040,
Cam Au Cal/Cas-751
Humpty Dumpty Heart (arr JG)-voc Ray Eberle
From the RKO-Radio picture "Playmates"
(Johnny Burke-Jimmy Van Heusen)
Clt, ??

068067-1   BB 11365-A, Vi LPM/LSP-3657, RCA RD/SF-7842, AFRS P-
10071, RCA G LPM/LSP-3657, RCA F 440.727,
HMVAu E.A. 3383
Ev'rything I Love (arr JG)-voc Ray Eberle and Choir
From the musical production "Let's Face It"
(Cole Porter)
As, Beneke

068068-1   BB 11382-B, HMV BD 5927, HMVSw JK-2412, Vi 20-1552
(Vi P-146), Vi 20-4086, Vi 27-0085 (Vi WPT-
12), Vi 420-0043, Vi 447-0043, Vi 47-2858, Vi
47-4086, Vi LPT-3036, Vi EPBT-3036 (947-0090),
Vi EPBT-3029, Vi EPA-5032, HMV DLP 1024, Vi
LPT-12, Vi SP-33-90, Vi LPM/LSP-3564, RCA G
447-0043, Vi P8S-5061, RD 3/4-45, RCA Int.
10004, RCA G EPA-5032, El G EG 7562, AFRS
"Jukebox USA" 159, AFRS "Jukebox USA" 230,
AFRS "Jukebox USA" 299, Vi 83872-A, HMVAus GA-
5070, HMVAus VDLP 302, Vi LPM-1070, AFRS G.I.
Series H-12 No. 1053, US Marine Corps. "Music
You Like" HD7 MM 10353, El WDLP 1024, RCA G
LPM 1070, RCA RCX 1003, Vi TP3-5044, Vi P8S-
1253, HMVIr I.P. 923, AFRS H-62-138 (82)
Phonograph Album No. 138 (82), RD 3/4-64
(Production albums only), Vi Arg LPM 3564,

(Session continued on next page)

AFRS G.I. Jive H-12-1180 (partial only),
AFRS G.I. Jive Series H-12: 716, 743, 776,
839, 858, 914, 956, 1007, 1029, 1053, 1158,
1179, 1965, 1208, 1233, 1286, 1309, 1457,
2120, 2060, 1736, 1610, 1338, 1507, 1219,
2019, 1429, 1524, 1886, 1751, 1998, 1627,
RCA Br. RD-8094, RCA Br. GM-1, Vi VPM-6019,
ViJ S-18, RCA Au 20048, Fe Au MX-10583, RCA
Au VPM-6019, AFRS G.I. Jive EN-12-2342, AFRS
Jill's Juke Box Series H-46: 18, 39, 45, 49,
157, 85, 150, 200, 205, 86
A String Of Pearls (arr JG)
(Jerry Gray)
As, Caceres; two bar alto sax exchanges between Caceres and Beneke; followed by another
challenge on tenors between Klink and Russin;
cnt, Hackett; p, MacGregor

068069-1 BB 11365-B, HMV 7EG 8241
Baby Mine (arr BF)-voc Ray Eberle and Choir
From the Walt Disney production "Dumbo"
(Ned Washington-Frank Churchill)

068070-1 Vi 27943-B, HMV 7EG 8031, Vi EPAT-428, Vi LPT 1031,
RCA G EPAT-428, RD 3/4-45, RCA G LPT-1031,
AFRS G.I. Jive H-12-919, AFRS Soundoff H-25-
Long Tall Mama (arr BM)
(Arletta May)
As, Beneke; clt, Caceres; tpt, May; ts, Russin

068071-1 BB 11382-A
Day Dreaming (arr BF)-voc Ray Eberle and The
Modernaires
(Gus Kahn-Jerome Kern)

"Humpty Dumpty Heart" 2 takes; all other tunes 1
take. (RCA Victor)
This session lasted from 12:00 noon to 5:30 P.M.
(RCA Victor)

The Arletta May mentioned on the composer credit for
"Long Tall Mama" is Billy May's wife and it is quite
possible that May is also the composer (instead of
his wife) and used her name, perhaps for income tax
purposes. This tune was not issued by Victor until
August, 1942.

The "Choir" shown as part of the vocal credit for
"Ev'rything I Love" and "Baby Mine" was just the full
band plus all the vocalists.

3 November, 1941 (MON): Cafe Rouge, Hotel Pennsylvania,
New York City, N.Y.
NBC-   11:30-12:00 Midnight

"A Salute to the Trinidad Army Base"

The announcer for this program is Allan Prescott.

(0:51) *Moonlight Serenade* (Theme)
         (Mitchell Parish-Glenn Miller)
(3:23) *Dear Arabella* (arr JG)-voc Marion Hutton,
         Tex Beneke and The Modernaires
         (Stanley Joseloff-Sidney Lippman)
         Tpt, May
(2:31) *'Til Reveille* (arr BF)-voc Ray Eberle
         (Stanley Cowan-Bobby Worth)
(3:11) *Chattanooga Choo Choo* (arr JG)-voc Marion
         Hutton, Tex Beneke and The Modernaires
         From the 20th Century-Fox film "Sun
         Valley Serenade"
         (Mack Gordon-Harry Warren)
(3:15) *Song Of The Volga Boatmen* (arr BF)
         (Russian Folk Song)
         B, Goldberg; muted tpt, May; as,
         Caceres; tpt, ??

At this part in the program Glenn talks to Allan
Prescott and describes the idea of the "Sunset
Serenade" program.

(3:05) *Keep 'Em Flying* (arr JG)
         (Jerry Gray)
         As, Beneke; tpt, May; d, Purtill;
         clt, Caceres
(2:02) *The One I Love (Belongs To Somebody Else)*
         (arr JG)-voc Ray Eberle and The
         Modernaires
         (Gus Kahn-Isham Jones)

At this part in the program General Irving Philipson,
Commanding General of the Second Corps area, spoke
about the Trinidad Army Base.

(3:04) *In The Mood*
         (Andy Razaf-Joe Garland)
         As, Beneke; ts, Klink; tpt, May
         (Two endings)
(0:44) *Slumber Song* (Theme)
         (Saul Tepper-John Chalmers MacGregor)

There may have been other tributes to other bases
but this one is the only one that we know of at the
moment.

(Continued on next page)

Miller showmanship. Playing *In the Mood*, trombone section tosses horns up so that top part of instruments move up the slide.

Something amuses Ray, Marion and Glenn.

G.M.P.R. show that there was one sustaining program
this evening from the Hotel Pennsylvania.

4 November, 1941 (TUES): New York City, N.Y. (CHESTERFIELD SHOW)
CBS   10:00-10:15 P.M. EST.

> *Moonlight Serenade (Theme)*
> *Little Brown Jug*
> *Five O'Clock Whistle*
> *Elmer's Tune*
> *V For Victory Hop*
> *Slumber Song (Theme)*

"V For Victory Hop" also went under the titles of
"V Hop" and "The Hop".

5 November, 1941 (WED): New York City, N.Y. (CHESTERFIELD SHOW)
CBS   10:00-10:15 P.M. EST.

> *Moonlight Serenade (Theme)*
> *Jingle Bells*
> *MEDLEY:*
> > *Sweet And Lovely*
> > *This Time The Dream's On Me*
> > *The Very Thought Of You*
> > *Blue Hawaii*
> > *Introduction To A Waltz*
> *Slumber Song (Theme)*

6 November, 1941 (THUR): New York City, N.Y. (CHESTERFIELD SHOW)
CBS   10:00-10:15 P.M. EST.

> *Moonlight Serenade (Theme)*
> ~~*Take The "A" Train*~~ ALP
> *It Happened In Sun Valley*
> *I'm Thrilled*
> *Runnin' Wild*
> *Slumber Song (Theme)*

6 November, 1941 (THUR): Cafe Rouge, Hotel Pennsylvania,
New York City, N.Y.
NBC-   11:30-12:00 Midnight

G.M.P.R. show that there was one sustaining program
this evening from the Hotel Pennsylvania.

7 November, 1941 (FRI): Cafe Rouge, Hotel Pennsylvania,
*   New York City, N.Y.*
*   NBC-   7:30-8:00 P.M. EST.*

          G.M.P.R. show that there was one sustaining
          program this evening from the Hotel Pennsylvania.

8 November, 1941 (SAT): Cafe Rouge, Hotel Pennsylvania,
*   New York City, N.Y. (SUNSET SERENADE)*
*   NBC-Blue 5:00-6:00 P.M. EST.*

          Moonlight Serenade (Theme)
          Song Of The Volga Boatmen
          The Man In The Moon
          Jingle Bells
          Dreamsville, Ohio
          V For Victory Hop

PPRM-5342   Vi LPM/LSP-2769 (Vi LPM/LSP-6101), RCA RD/SF-7612,
            RCA Au LPM/LSP-2769
      Int GM (2:38) Pin Ball Paul (arr JG)-voc Tex Beneke and
                The Modernaires (and Marion Hutton?)
                (Harold Dickinson-Spragge-Bill Conway)
                Tpt, May

PPRM-5338   Vi LPM/LSP-2768 (Vi LPM/LSP-6101), RCA RD/SF-7611,
            RCA Au LPM/LSP-2768
      Int GM (3:18) This Time The Dream's On Me (arr BF)-voc
                Ray Eberle
                From the Warner Bros. film "Blues In
                The Night"
                (Johnny Mercer-Harold Arlen)
                As, Beneke; cnt, Hackett

ALP   Int GM (3:32) A String Of Pearls (arr JG)
                (Jerry Gray)
                As, Caceres; two bar alto sax exchanges
                between Caceres and Beneke; followed
                by another challenge on tenors between
                Klink and Russin; cnt, Hackett;
                p, MacGregor
          (0:57) *Moonlight Serenade (Theme)*
                (Mitchell Parish-Glenn Miller)
              Moonlight Serenade (Theme)
ALP   *Star Dust*
          (0:53) *It's Great To Be An American*-voc The
                Modernaires
                (Ray Muffs-Jimmie Crane)
      Int GM (2:46) *You And I*-voc Ray Eberle
                (Meredith Wilson)
                Muted tbn, Miller; cnt, Hackett

(Broadcast continued on next page)

Int GM (3:32) Tschaikowsky's Piano Concerto (arr BF)
            (Peter I. Tschaikowsky)
            P, MacGregor; as, Beneke

PPRM-5333   Vi LPM/LSP-2767 (Vi LPM/LSP-6101), RCA RD/SF-
                7610, RCA Au LPM/LSP-2767
    Int GM (3:26) I Don't Want To Set The World On Fire
                (arr JG)-voc Ray Eberle
                (Eddie Seiler-Sol Marcus-Bennie
                Benjemen-Eddie Durham)
                Cnt, Hackett

        (0:45) It's Great To Be An American
                (Ray Muffs-Jimmie Crane)
    Int GM (3:12) Papa Niccolini (The Happy Cobbler)-voc Ray
                Eberle, Tex Beneke and The Modernaires
                (and Marian Hutton)
                (Anne and Jean Edwards-Don George)
    Int GM (2:01) I'm Thrilled (arr BF)-voc Ray Eberle
                (Sylvia Dee-Sidney Lippman)
                No Beneke solo
    Int GM (4:00) Anvil Chorus (arr JG)
                From "Il Trovatore"
                (Guiseppe Verdi)
                D, Purtill; as, Beneke; tpt, May;
                d, Purtill; tpt, ??

10 November, 1941 (MON): Cafe Rouge, Hotel Pennsylvania
                New York City, N.Y.
                NBC-   11:30-12:00 Midnight

        G.M.P.R. show that there was one sustaining
        program this evening from the Hotel Pennsylvania.

11 November, 1941 (TUES): New York City, N.Y. (CHESTERFIELD SHOW)
                CBS 10:00-10:15 P.M. EST.

        No Chesterfield program on this date and no
        reason is given by G.M.P.R.

12 November, 1941 (WED): New York City, N.Y. (CHESTERFIELD SHOW)
                CBS 10:00-10:15 P.M. EST.

            Moonlight Serenade (Theme)
            Tschaikowsky's Piano Concerto
            I Know Why
            Ev'rything I Love
            Sun Valley Jump
            Slumber Song (Theme)

13 November, 1941 (THUR): New York City, N.Y. (CHESTERFIELD SHOW)
CBS   10:00-10:15 P.M. EST.

The announcer for this program is Paul Douglas.

> *Moonlight Serenade* (Theme)
> *Dear Arabella*
> MEDLEY:
>   *How Deep Is The Ocean?*
>   *Hereafter* (arr JG)-voc RE
>   (Alan Courtney-John Jacob Loeb)
>   *It's A Wonderful World*
>   *My Blue Heaven*
> *Oh So Good*
> *Slumber Song* (Theme)

According to G.M.P.R. this was Fila's and Russin's
last day with the band. Both received full
salaries for the week ending November 13th and both
were paid for the Chesterfield programs of
November 12th and 13th. Fila was replaced the next
day by Bobby Hackett and Bill Conway moved into the
guitar chair. Russin was replaced by Skippy Martin
from the Benny Goodman orchestra.

"Goodman, Miller swap; Fila ill; swap a flop
for Benny, at least, who found he couldn't use the
brilliant young trumpeter from Glenn's band because
the lad's lip had suddenly gone completely sour.
Neither could Glenn.

The Miller band got first saxist Skippy Martin
from the Goodman ranks. Tex Beneke was temporarily
on first chair with Babe Russin tentatively on
tenor. Babe left when Skippy came in and Tex went
back to his original seat.

As for Fila, he has retired for the time being,
hoping the rest will bring back his lip." (Met.
Dec. 1941)

"Russin left to reorganize his own little jam
band, set at the Famous Door for a long engagement."
(DB, Dec. 1, 1941)

"Bobby Hackett dropped his guitar and moved
into Glenn Miller's brass section at the Hotel
Pennsylvania to fill the chair vacated by Alec
Fila, who has left the band.

Taking Hackett's gitbox chair was Bill Conway,
of the singing Four Modernaires. Miller emphasized
the change was 'working out nicely' but indicated
it was merely a temporary move, and that Hackett--
famed Bix-like cornetist--would return to the
guitar slot once Miller found a trumpet player
suited to the band." (DB, Jan. 1, 1942)

13 November, 1941 (THUR): Cafe Rouge, Hotel Pennsylvania,
New York City, N.Y.
NBC-   11:30-12:00 Midnight

G.M.P.R. show that there was one sustaining
program this evening from the Hotel Pennsylvania.

14 November, 1941 (FRI): Cafe Rouge, Hotel Pennsylvania,
New York City, N.Y.
NBC-   7:30-8:00 P.M. EST.

G.M.P.R. show that there was one sustaining
program this evening from the Hotel Pennsylvania.

Trombones	*Glenn Miller, Jimmy Priddy, Paul Tanner, Frank D'Annolfo*
Trumpets	*Billy May, BOBBY HACKETT, Dale McMickle, Johnny Best*
Reeds	*LLOYD "SKIPPY" MARTIN, as; Ernie Caceres, as, bar & clt; Wilbur Schwartz, clt & as; Tex Beneke, ts; Al Klink, ts*
Rhythm	*Chummy MacGregor, p; BILL CONWAY, g; Doc Goldberg, b; Maurice Purtill, d*

"Hackett isn't featured much as a cornetist,
Billy May and John Best getting most of the play,
but at dinner sessions Glenn likes to have Bobby
play soft stuff, old jazz classics at slow tempo,
which diners as well as musicians and cats enjoy.
Skippy Martin is working out 'swell' as first
chair alto saxist, Glenn said." (DB, Jan. 1,
1942)

15 November, 1941 (SAT): Cafe Rouge, Hotel Pennsylvania,
New York City, N.Y. (SUNSET SERENADE)
NBC-Blue 5:00-6:00 P.M. EST.

"Glenn Miller digs deep into his own pockets
and spends nearly $1,000 every Saturday afternoon
putting his 'Sunset Serenade' broadcast on the air
from Hotel Pennsylvania.
Charging a 25-cent admish fee, Miller turns
the entire proceeds from the one-hour show over to
the United Service Organizations. Figuring that
Miller must pay for the combination radio-phonograph he gives away every week, and that he buys
200 new records also as gifts to soldiers, plus
salaries for his musicians and union taxes, the
total Miller expenditure comes to $900. Fre-
quently, however, Miller finds himself giving away
more than one phonograph-radio set, as was the case

(Continued on next page)

Nov. 1 when he distributed _five_ sets (each
valued at more than $100) to army camps scattered
throughout the nation.
 Miller, admittedly no philanthropist at heart,
figures the airtime (more than 100 NBC outlets) and
the general good-will he arouses are worth far
more than the grand he shells out. Thousands of
pieces of mail are received by Miller every week
from soldiers and friends of men in the service re-
questing songs. The requests determine which camp
or camps receive the radio-phonographs and stacks
of records. Miller buys the records from Macy's
store here just like anyone else would and he mixes
'em up--only a few Miller discs are included in the
pile of 200 which Glenn ships away every Saturday
night!" (DB, Nov. 15, 1941)

 "Glenn Miller and executives of the Pennsylvania are to huddle this week to set a limit on the
number of admissions to Miller's Saturday afternoon USO benefit concerts in the hotel's Cafe
Rouge. Hotel is objecting to the increasing mobs
the sessions are drawing pointing out that furniture
and other appointments in the rooms are being mis-
handled and the returns to the hotel itself don't
square it up.
 Miller plays from 4:00 to 6:00 P.M. each week
charging admission of one defense stamp (25¢) which
goes to the USO. From 5:00-6:00 P.M. (NBC) he
broadcasts a sort of soldier's hit parade of popular tunes awarding recordings and a combination
radio phonograph to USO canteen in Army Camps
throughout the country. People admitted to the
concerts are not obliged to drink or dine.
 Past week for instance Miller played to 1,340
people in a room that normally seats up for about
400 patrons but can close up tables' ranks to handle
625. This meant that guards had to be stationed
around the bandstand to keep crowd at safe dis-
tance. First week Miller tried idea (Oct. 11,
1941) he played to 449 admissions, following Saturday was 569, then 631, 643 and 901." (Variety,
Nov. 19, 1941)

15 November, 1941 (SAT): New York City, New York
 NBC

 "NBC's 15th Anniversary Show"

(Broadcast continued on next page)

*Int GM (3:02) Chattanooga Choo Choo (arr JG)-voc Marion
                    Hutton, Tex Beneke and The
                    Modernaires
                    From the 20th Century-Fox film "Sun
                    Valley Serenade"
                    (Mack Gordon-Harry Warren)*

        This broadcast is probably from the "Cafe Rouge"
        and may have been part of the "Sunset Serenade".

*17 November, 1941 (MON): Cafe Rouge, Hotel Pennsylvania,
                    New York City, N.Y.
                    NBC-   11:30-12:00 Midnight EST.*

        G.M.P.R. show that there was one sustaining
        program this evening from the Hotel Pennsylvania.

*18 November, 1941 (TUES): New York City, N.Y. (CHESTERFIELD SHOW)
                    CBS   10:00-10:15 P.M. EST.*

                    *Moonlight Serenade (Theme)
                    Jingle Bells
                    MEDLEY:
                        Please
                        Humpty Dumpty Heart
                        Thanks
                        Am I Blue?
                    Measure For Measure
                    Slumber Song (Theme)*

*19 November, 1941 (WED): New York City, N.Y. (CHESTERFIELD SHOW)
                    CBS   10:00-10:15 P.M. EST.*

                    *Moonlight Serenade (Theme)
                    A String Of Pearls
                    Chattanooga Choo Choo
                    I'm Thrilled
                    Tuxedo Junction
                    Slumber Song (Theme)*

*20 November, 1941 (THUR): New York City, N.Y. (CHESTERFIELD SHOW)
                    CBS   10:00-10:15 P.M. EST.*

                    *Moonlight Serenade (Theme)
                    Ida!
                    Wham
                    Below The Equator
                    Keep 'Em Flying
                    Slumber Song (Theme)*

20 November, 1941 (THUR): Cafe Rouge, Hotel Pennsylvania,
New York City, N.Y.
NBC-   11:30-12:00 Midnight EST.

> G.M.P.R. show that there was one sustaining
> program this evening from the Hotel Pennsylvania.

> G.M.P.R. for the week ending November 20th show
> that Billy May arranged "Blues In The Night".

21 November, 1941 (FRI): Cafe Rouge, Hotel Pennsylvania,
New York City, N.Y.
NBC-   7:30-8:00 P.M. EST.

> G.M.P.R. show that there was one sustaining
> program this evening from the Hotel Pennsylvania.

22 November, 1941 (SAT): Cafe Rouge, Hotel Pennsylvania,
New York City, N.Y. (SUNSET SERENADE)
NBC-Blue 5:00-6:00 P.M. EST.

> *Moonlight Serenade (Theme)*
> *Tuxedo Junction*
> *Dreamsville, Ohio*
> *Chattanooga Choo Choo*
> *MEDLEY:*
> > *I Know Why*
> > *It Happened In Sun Valley*

PPRM-5337   Vi LPM/LSP 2768 (Vi LPM/LSP 6101), RCA RD/SF-7611,
              RCA Au LPM/LSP-2768
       Int GM (2:12) I Guess I'll Have To Dream The Rest-voc
              Ray Eberle and The Modernaires
              (Mickey Stoner-Martin Block-Harold
              Green)
              No saxophone solo

PPRM-5338   Vi LPM/LSP 2768 (Vi LPM/LSP 6101) RCA RD/SF-7611,
              RCA Au LPM/LSP-2768
       Int GM (2:37) Do You Care? (arr JG)-voc Ray Eberle
              (Jack Elliot-Lew Quadling)
              Ts, Beneke; tpt, Best

> ALP *Tchaikovsky's Piano Concerto*
> ALP *Ev'rything I Love*
> *V Hop*
> *Moonlight Serenade (Theme)*
> *Moonlight Serenade (Theme)*
> *In A Sentimental Mood*

(Broadcast continued on next page)

                    It's Great To Be An American
(1:26) *'Til Reveille (arr BF)-voc Ray Eberle*
                    (Stanley Cowan-Bobby Worth)
Int GM *I Don't Want To Set The World On Fire*
                    Papa Niccolini
(2:39) *In The Mood*
                    (Andy Razaf-Joe Garland)
                        Ts, Beneke; ts, Klink; tpt, May
                    Slumber Song (Theme)

22 November, 1941 (SAT): New York City, N.Y. (COKE'S SPOTLIGHT BAND)
                MBS   10:15-10:45 P.M. EST.

        The announcer for this program is Al Halfor.

        (0:48) *Waltz Theme (Coca Cola Theme) (arr JG)*
                    (Joy)
        (0:49) *Moonlight Serenade (Theme)*
                    (Mitchell Parish-Glenn Miller)
        (3:19) *In The Mood*
                    (Andy Razaf-Joe Garland)
                        Ts, Beneke; ts, Klink; tpt, May
                    (Four endings)

        At this point in the program Al Halfor presents
        to Glenn Miller the Coca Cola trophy (a facsimile
        of the platter itself) fashioned in silver and
        suitably inscribed. The best band selling record
        in the land was "Chattanooga Choo Choo".

ALP   (3:13) *Elmer's Tune (arr JG)-voc Ray Eberle and*
                    The Modernaires
                    (Elmer Albrecht-Sammy Gallop-Dick
                    Jurgens)
                        Ts, Beneke; muted tpt, ??; muted tbn,
                    Miller
        (0:20) *On Brave Old Army Team (arr JG)*
                    West Point Football Song
                    (Philip Egner)
                        D, Purtill

        The above tune acts as a theme and at this point
        in the program there was a salute to the football
        hero of the day.

        (1:52) *The Kiss Polka (arr JG)-voc Marion Hutton,*
                    Ernie Caceres and The Modernaires
                    From the 20th Century-Fox film "Sun
                    Valley Serenade"
                    (Mack Gordon-Harry Warren)

(Broadcast continued on next page)

(4:30) MEDLEY:
        To You
                (Tommy Dorsey-Ted Shapiro-Benny Davis)
        Indian Summer-voc Ray Eberle
                (Al Dubin-Victor Herbert)
        Sunrise Serenade
                Frankie Carle-Jack Lawrence)
                Ts, Beneke; p, MacGregor
(2:29) Keep 'Em Flying (arr JG)
                (Jerry Gray)
                Ts, Beneke; d, Purtill; clt, Caceres
(1:57) I'm Thrilled (arr BF)-voc Ray Eberle
                (Sylvia Dee-Sidney Lippman)
                No Saxophone solo
(0:04) Waltz Theme (Coca Cola Theme) (arr JG)
                (Joy)

Now the band plays the tune chosen as the best
selling record in the land according to Coke's
survey.

(3:00) Chattanooga Choo Choo (arr JG)-voc Marion
                Hutton, Tex Beneke and The Modernaires
                From the 20th Century-Fox film "Sun
                Valley Serenade"
                (Mack Gordon-Harry Warren)
(0:39) Moonlight Serenade (Theme)
                (Mitchell Parish-Glenn Miller
(0:30) Waltz Theme (Coca Cola Theme) (arr JG)
                (Joy)

This program is on a thin-vinylite 12" transcription by World Broadcasting Systems Inc. split into
two parts. 31152-A22 matrix Plain white label
dark blue printing. A Red, White and Blue Program
Compliments of the Coca Cola Company. This record
is the property of the War Department of the United
States Government and is not to be broadcast.
Program No. 1 Part 1   33 1/3 RPM Outside Start
"Spotlight Bands" presents Glenn Miller as Spotlight Champion of Champions (other side same except
Part 2).

24 November, 1941 (MON): Victor Studios, New York City, New York

        Trombones   Glenn Miller, Jimmy Priddy, Paul
                     Tanner, Frank D'Annolfo
        Trumpets   Billy May, REUBEN "ZEKE" ZARCHY,
                     Dale McMickle, Johnny Best
        Reeds   Lloyd "Skippy" Martin, as; Ernie
                     Caceres, as, bar & clt; Wilbur

(Session continued on next page)

                         Schwartz, clt & as; Tex Beneke, ts;
                         Al Klink, ts
           Rhythm   Chummy MacGregor, p; Bobby Hackett,
                         g; Doc Goldberg, b; Maurice Purtill, d

068418-1   BB 11386-A, HMV BD 5768, HMVSw JK-2338, Vi LSP-
              4125, AFRS Swingtime 53, VdP HN 2358, RCA F
              130210, Vi P8S-1432, RCA Int. INTS 1002, Vi
              Braz 82-0023, AFRS Jill's Juke Box H-46-163
            Moonlight Sonata (arr BF)
              (Ludwig Beethoven)
              P, MacGregor; ts, Beneke; p, MacGregor

068419-1   BB 11386-B, HMV BD 5834, HMVSw JK-2338, El G EG
              7628, RD 3/4-64, RD 3/4-76
            Slumber Song (arr BF)-humming by The Modernaires
              (Saul Tepper-John Chalmers MacGregor)
              Ts, Beneke

068420-1   BB 11397-A, HMV DLP 1049, Cam Cas-2267, RCA G Cas-
              2267
            (There'll Be Blue Birds Over) The White Cliffs of
              Dover (arr JG)-voc Ray Eberle
              (Nat Burton-Walter Kent)
              Ts, Beneke

068421-1   BB 11397-B
            We're The Couple In The Castle-voc Ray Eberle
              From the Paramount Cartoon "Mr. Bug Goes
              To Town"
              (Frank Loesser-Hoagy Carmichael)

068422-1   BB 11416-B, Vi 20-2536, Vi EPAT-430, HMV DLP 1145
              RCA G EPAT-430, AFRS G.I. Jive H-12-2027,
              HMVAu E.A. 3383
            It Happened In Hawaii (arr JG)-voc Ray Eberle and
              The Modernaires
              (Al Dubin-Mabel Wayne)
              Ts, Beneke

            "Moonlight Sonata" 2 takes; all other tunes 1
            take. (RCA Victor)
            This session lasted from 12:00 Noon to 6:00 P.M.
            (RCA Victor)

            According to the Glenn Miller Payroll Records
            Zarchy was paid for this one record session and
            therefore, Hackett would revert back to the
            cornet (Conway back on guitar) for the job at the
            Hotel Pennsylvania and Chesterfield broadcasts.
            Miller probably called in Zarchy to replace

(Continued on next page)

Hackett in the brass section to add more power on
the record date. "But from a technical point of
view (and Miller has always laid much emphasis
upon that technical point of view), his pretty
but weak blowing doesn't fill out the trumpet
quartet the way it should." (see Simon's review,
Met. Jan. 1942)

Although "Slumber Song" was primarily the band's
closing theme it became the band's opening theme
during the ASCAP ban.

24 November, 1941 (MON): Cafe Rouge, Hotel Pennsylvania,
                         New York City, N.Y.
                         NBC-   11:30-12:00 Midnight EST.

G.M.P.R. show that there was one sustaining
program this evening from the Hotel Pennsylvania.

Trombones   *Glenn Miller, Jimmy Priddy, Paul*
              Tanner, Frank D'Annolfo
Trumpets   *Billy May, BOBBY HACKETT, Dale*
              McMickle, Johnny Best
Reeds   *Lloyd "Skippy" Martin, as; Ernie*
              Caceres, as, bar & clt; Wilbur
              Schwartz, clt & as; Tex Beneke, ts;
              Al Klink, ts
Rhythm   *Chummy MacGregor, p; BILL CONWAY, g;*
              Doc Goldberg, b; Maurice Purtill, d

25 November, 1941 (TUES): New York City, N.Y. (CHESTERFIELD SHOW)
                          CBS   10:00-10:15 P.M. EST.

Moonlight Serenade (Theme)
Moonlight Sonata
Chattanooga Choo Choo
Orange Blossom Lane

E3VP 5239   Vi LPT 6700, Vi EPNT 6700 (947-0126), Vi SPD-18
                 (599-9105), HMV RLS 599, RCA G LPT 6700
                 (2:22) Bugle Call Rag (arr GM)
                        (Jack Pettis-Billy Meyers-Elmer
                        Schoebel)
                        D, Purtill; tbn, Miller; ts, Beneke;
                        clt, Caceres; tbn, Miller; ts, Beneke;
                        d, Purtill

                 Slumber Song (Theme)

26 November, 1941 (WED): New York City, N.Y. (CHESTERFIELD SHOW)
CBS   10:00-10:15 P.M. EST.

Moonlight Serenade (Theme)

K2PP-0044   Vi LPM-6100, RCA RD 27146, RCA G LPM-6100, RCA Au
                  L 11023
              (3:42) The Nickel Serenade (arr JG)-voc Tex Beneke,
                  Marion Hutton and The Modernaires
                  (Del Sharbutt-Axel Remark-Frank
                  Stanton)
                  Ts, Beneke

MEDLEY:
Sweet Leilani
I'm Thrilled
Smoke Rings
Under A Blanket Of Blue
Song Of The Volga Boatmen
Slumber Song (Theme)

"The Nickel Serenade" was a forerunner of "Juke Box
Saturday Night" and Beneke's later version of
"Blues Of The Record Man". Although Jerry Gray is
shown as the arranger on "The Nickel Serenade" it
must be noted that this was for the band portion
only and that for the vocal part Bill Conway
arranged the harmony and Hal Dickinson arranged the
verse. Vi LPM-6100 gave the title as "Nickel
Serenade" but the title as shown above is the
correct one. It is Glenn Miller who says "Hi Ya
All" in imitating Kay Kyser.

27 November, 1941 (THUR): New York City, N.Y. (CHESTERFIELD SHOW)
CBS   10:00-10:15 P.M. EST.

Moonlight Serenade (Theme)
On Brave Old Army Team
Five O'Clock Whistle
Elmer's Tune
Anchors Aweigh
Slumber Song (Theme)

27 November, 1941 (THUR): Cafe Rouge, Hotel Pennsylvania,
New York City, N.Y.
NBC-   11:30-12:00 P.M. EST.

G.M.P.R. show that there was one sustaining
program this evening from the Hotel Pennsylvania.

28 November, 1941 (FRI): Cafe Rouge, Hotel Pennsylvania,
                        New York City, N.Y.
                        NBC-   7:30-8:00 P.M. EST.

                G.M.P.R. show that there was one sustaining
                program this evening from the Hotel Pennsylvania.

29 November, 1941 (SAT): Cafe Rouge, Hotel Pennsylvania,
                        New York City, N.Y. (SUNSET SERENADE)
                        NBC-Blue 5:00-6:00 P.M. EST.

                Moonlight Serenade (Theme)
                Flagwaver
                This Is No Laughing Matter

PPRM-5334   Vi LPM/LSP-2767 (Vi LPM/LSP-6101), RCA RD/SF-7610,
                RCA Au LPM/LSP-2767
        Int GM (2:40) I'm Not Much On Looks (arr JG)-voc Tex
                        Beneke, Marion Hutton and The
                        Modernaires
                        (Leah Worth-Jean Barry)

PPRM-5338   Vi LPM/LSP-2768 (Vi LPM/LSP-6101), RCA RD/SF-7611,
                RCA Au LPM/LSP-2768
              (2:55) Dreamsville, Ohio (arr JG)-voc Ray Eberle
                        and The Modernaires
                        (Craig Lee-Al Rinker-Judy Freeland)
                        Cnt, Hackett

                The Nickel Serenade
                Moonlight Serenade (Theme)
                Moonlight Serenade (Theme)
                Georgia On My Mind
                It's Great To Be An American
                Tschaikowsky's Piano Concerto
                Elmer's Tune
                Chattanooga Choo Choo

PPRM-5341   Vi LPM/LSP-2769 (Vi LPM/LSP-6101), RCA RD/SF-7612,
                RCA Au LPM/LSP-2769
        Int GM (3:04) Papa Niccolini (The Happy Cobbler) -voc
                        Ray Eberle, Marion Hutton, Tex Beneke
                        and The Modernaires
                        (Anne and Jean Edwards-Don George)

                Keep 'Em Flying
                Slumber Song (Theme)

1 December, 1941 (MON): Cafe Rouge, Hotel Pennsylvania,
New York City, N.Y.
NBC-Blue   11:30-12:00 Midnight, EST.

G.M.P.R. show that there was one sustaining
program this evening from the Hotel Pennsulvania.

2 December, 1941 (TUES): New York City, N.Y. (CHESTERFIELD SHOW)
CBS   10:00-10:15 P.M. EST.

No Chesterfield program on this date due to a
foreign correspondence program. (G.M.C.)

3 December, 1941 (WED): New York City, N.Y. (CHESTERFIELD SHOW)
CBS   10:00-10:15 P.M. EST.

> *Moonlight Serenade (Theme)*
> *Jingle Bells*
> *MEDLEY:*
> *In The Mood (?)*
> *Papa Niccolini*
> *The Waltz You Saved For Me*
> *Blue Danube*
> *Anvil Chorus*
> *Slumber Song (Theme)*

We suspect that "In The Mood" was not played in
this medley and if we refer back to June 19th,
1940 the old tune was "The Touch Of Your Hand".
The tunes are shown as listed by the Miller
Estate and we were unable to listen to the medley
as the original record had been broken before it
could be taped.

4 December, 1941 (THUR): New York City, N.Y. (CHESTERFIELD SHOW)
CBS   10:00-10:15 P.M. EST.

> *Moonlight Serenade (Theme)*
> *Moonlight Sonata*
> *The Kiss Polka*
> *This Time The Dream's On Me*
> *Keep 'Em Flying*
> *Slumber Song (Theme)*

4 December, 1941 (THUR): Cafe Rouge, Hotel Pennsylvania,
New York City, N.Y.
NBC-Blue   11:30-12:00 Midnight EST.

G.M.P.R. show that there was one sustaining
program this evening from the Hotel Pennsylvania.

5 December, 1941 (FRI): Cafe Rouge, Hotel Pennsylvania,
New York City, N.Y.
NBC-Blue 7:30-8:00 P.M. EST.

G.M.P.R. show that there was one sustaining
program this evening from the Hotel Pennsylvania.

6 December, 1941 (SAT): Cafe Rouge, Hotel Pennsylvania,
New York City, N.Y. (SUNSET SERENADE)
NBC-Blue 5:00-6:00 P.M. EST.

Information is missing on the tunes played on
this program.

6 December, 1941 (SAT): New York City, N.Y. (COKE'S SPOTLIGHT BAND)

G.M.P.R. indicate that this was a half hour
program. The announcer for this program is
Al Halfor.

(3:03) Moonlight Sonata (arr BF)
(Ludwig Beethoven)
P, MacGregor; ts, Beneke; p, MacGregor
(0:20) California Here I Come (arr JG)
From the musical production "Big Boy"
(Al Jolson-Bud DeSylva-Joseph Meyer)
(2:50) Jingle Bells (arr GM & BF)-voc Tex Beneke,
Marion Hutton, Ernie Caceres and
The Modernaires
(Harold Dickinson-Bill Conway)
P, MacGregor; muted tpt, May
(3:13) Tuxedo Junction (arr JG)
(Buddy Fegne-William Johnson-Julian
Dash-Erskine Hawkins)
Muted tpt, McMickle; open tpt, Best;
muted tpt, McMickle; p, MacGregor

8 December, 1941 (MON): Victor Studios, New York City, N.Y.

Trombones	Glenn Miller, Jimmy Priddy, Paul Tanner, Frank D'Annolfo
Trumpets	Billy May, REUBEN "ZEKE" ZARCHY, Dale McMickle, Johnny Best
Reeds	Lloyd "Skippy" Martin, as; Ernie Caceres, as, bar & clt; Wilbur Schwartz, clt & as; Tex Beneke, ts; Al Klink, ts
Rhythm	Chummy MacGregor, p; Bill Conway, g; Doc Goldberg, b; Maurice Purtill, d

(Session continued on next page)

068456-1   BB 11401-A, HMV BD 5834, HMVIn NE-673, Vi 20-2536,
                Vi 420-0046, Vi 447-0046, Vi EPAT-430,
                Vi EPA-530, Vi EPA-5008, RCA RCX 1040, El G
                EG 7628, Vi LPM 3183, Vi LPT-1016, RD 3/4-25,
                RD Br. RDS 6097, RD Br. RDS 6173, Vi LPM/LSP-
                3564, AFRS G.I. Jive H-12-1189, AFRS P-S-15,
                AFRS H-62-1 Phonograph Album No. 1, AFRS
                P-1118, RCA G LPT 1016, Vi TP3-5044, RCA G
                EPA 5008, RCA G 447-0046, Vi P8S-5061,
                AFRS Remember H-54-138, RCA Int. CT 20126,
                Vi Arg LPM 3564, Vi VPM-6019, AFRS Jill's
                Juke Box H-46-8, RCA G EPAT-430, RCA Au
                VPM-6019, AFRS G.I. Jive Series H-12: 807,
                1836, 1849, 1870, 1929, 1970, 2027, 2056,
                RCA Br. GM-1, RCA Br. RD-8094, AFRS G.I.
                Jive EN-12-2268
            Moonlight Cocktail (arr JG)-voc Ray Eberle and
                The Modernaires
                (Kim Gannon-Lucky Roberts)
                P, MacGregor; ts, Beneke

068457-1   BB 11401-B, HMVAu EA-3139, HMVIn NE-673, Vi LPM/
                LSP-3657, RCA RD/SF-7842, AFRS P-10071,
                Vi Arg 68-1061,RD 3/4-76, RCA F 440.727,
                AFRS Jill's Juke Box Series H-46:107, 123
            Happy In Love (arr JG)-voc Marion Hutton
                From the musical production "Sons O' Fun"
                (Jack Yellen-Sam E. Fain)
                Muted tpt, McMickle; ts, Beneke

068458-1   BB 11416-A
            Fooled (arr JG)-voc Ray Eberle
                (Bob Russell-Ros Metzger-Frank Lavere)
                Ts, Beneke

068459-1   BB 11443-B, HMV DLP 1122, Vi LPM-6702
            Keep 'Em Flying (arr JG)
                (Jerry Gray)
                Ts, Beneke; d, Purtill; tpt, May; p,
                MacGregor; d, Purtill; clt, Caceres

068460-1   BB 11450-B, HMV BD 5784, HMV MH 141, Vi LPT 6700,
                Vi EPNT 6700 (947-0123), Vi SPD-18 (599-
                9112), HMV RLS 599, RCA G LPT 6700
            Chip Off The Old Block
                (Al Young)
                Ts, Klink

068461-1   BB 11462-A, HMV BD 5768, HMVAu EA-3222, Vi 20-
                3561 (Vi P-255), HMV 7EG 8043, Vi EPAT-
                426, Vi LPT 1031, AFRS P-1445, RD 3/4-64,
                AFRS "America's Pop Music" 72, VdP HN 2358,
                RCA G LPT-1031

(Session continued on next page)

The Story Of A Starry Night (arr BF)-voc Ray Eberle
    Adapted from Tschaikowsky's "Pathetique
    Symphony"
    (Al Hoffman-Mann Curtis-Jerry Livingston)

All tunes 1 take. (RCA Victor)
This session lasted from 12:00 Noon to 5:30 P.M.
(RCA Victor)

Since the Japanese struck at Pearl Harbor on
December 7th this may have been the reason for
Miller finally recording "Keep 'Em Flying". This
tune had been broadcast as far back as July 9th,
1941 under its original title of "That's Where I
Came In".

According to the G.M.P.R. Bobby Hackett did not
play on this date and he was not paid for this
session. G.M.P.R. show that Zarchy was paid for 3
days at the Hotel Pennsylvania: December 8th, 17th
and 18th and he was also paid for two Chesterfield
Programs: December 17th and 18th. Since Hackett is
paid for the Chesterfield programs of December 10th,
11th,16th, 17th and 18th as well as nights at
the Hotel Pennsylvania (December 8th, 9th, 10th,
11th, 12th, 13th, 15th, 16th, 17th and 18th we must
assume that he was on guitar on the three nights
and two Chesterfield programs that Zarchy played.
The other nights and Chesterfield programs would
probably have Hackett on cornet and Conway on
guitar. Since Conway's salary is grouped in with
the Modernaires it is not easy to determine when he
played guitar. No reason is given for Hackett not
playing on this recording session and this is
contrary to RCA Victor's listing as they show
Hackett on guitar. However, we believe that the
G.M.P.R. must be our prime basis for determining
the personnel.

8 December, 1941 (MON): Cafe Rouge, Hotel Pennsylvania,
                        New York City, N.Y.
                        NBC-Blue

Trombones	*Glenn Miller, Jimmy Priddy, Paul Tanner, Frank D,Annolfo*
Trumpets	*Billy May, Reuben "Zeke" Zarchy, Dale McMickle, Johnny Best*
Reeds	*Lloyd "Skippy" Martin, as; Ernie Caceres, as, bar & clt; Wilbur Schwartz, alt & as; Tex Beneke, ts; Al Klink, ts*

(Broadcast continued on next page)

```
Rhythm        Chummy MacGregor, p; BOBBY HACKETT, g;
              Doc Goldberg, b; Maurice Purtill, d
```

G.M.P.R. show that there were <u>two</u> sustaining
programs this evening from the Hotel Pennsylvania.

9 December, 1941 (TUES): New York City, N.Y. (CHESTERFIELD SHOW)
*   CBS   10:00-10:15 P.M. EST.*

No Chesterfield program on this date but no
reason is given by G.M.P.R. Not on due to FDR's
fireside chat. (G.M.D.)

The personnel for the evening at the Hotel
Pennsylvania:

```
Trombones     Glenn Miller, Jimmy Priddy, Paul
              Tanner, Frank D'Annolfo
Trumpets      Billy May, BOBBY HACKETT, Dale
              McMickle, Johnny Best
Reeds         Lloyd "Skippy" Martin, as; Ernie
              Caceres, as, bar & clt; Wilbur
              Schwartz, clt & as; Tex Beneke, ts;
              Al Klink, ts
Rhythm        Chummy MacGregor, p; BILL CONWAY, g;
              Doc Goldberg, b; Maurice Purtill, d
```

This personnel remains the same until December
17, 1941.

10 December, 1941 (WED): New York City, N.Y. (CHESTERFIELD SHOW)
*   CBS   10:00-10:15 P.M. EST.*

The announcer for this program is Larry Bruff.

```
              Moonlight Serenade (Theme)
              Dear Arabella
     (5:51)   MEDLEY:
              Goodnight, Sweetheart (arr JG)
                   Introduced in: "Earl Carroll's
                   Vanities"
                   (Ray Noble-James Campbell-Reg.
                   Connelly)
                   clt, ??
     Int GM   (There'll Be Blue Birds Over) The White
                   Cliffs Of Dover (arr BF)-voc
                   Ray Eberle
                   (Nat Burton-Walter Kent)
```

(Broadcast continued on next page)

            Int LB   When My Baby Smiles At Me (arr JG)
                        (borrowed from Ted Lewis)
                        (Andrew B. Sterling-Ted Lewis-
                        Bill Munro)
                        Ts, Beneke
            Int GM   A Blues Serenade (arr JG)
                        (Mitchell Parish-Frank Signorelli)
                        P, MacGregor
                   Oh So Good
                   Slumber Song (Theme)

11 December, 1941 (THUR): New York City, N.Y. (CHESTERFIELD SHOW)
                    CBS   10:00-10:15 P.M. EST.

                   Moonlight Serenade (Theme)
                   A String Of Pearls
                   Chattanooga Choo Choo
                   Ev'rything I Love

E3VP 5232   Vi LPT 6700, Vi EPNT 6700 (947-0119), Vi SPD-18
                        (599-9104), HMV RLS 599, RCA G LPT 6700
                   (2:37) Introduction To A Waltz (arr JG)
                        (Hal Dickinson-Glenn Miller-Jerry
                        Gray)
                        P, MacGregor; ts, Beneke; tpt, May;
                        as, Caceres; tpt, May; p, MacGregor;
                        d, Purtill

                   Slumber Song (Theme)

            "Introduction To A Waltz" has quite an intro-
            duction--187 bars to be exact, with 8 bars of
            'waltz' near the end of the tune.

11 December, 1941 (THUR): Cafe Rouge, Hotel Pennsylvania,
                    New York City, N.Y.
                    NBC-Blue   11:30-12:00 Midnight EST.

            G.M.P.R. show that there was one sustaining
            program this evening from the Hotel Pennsylvania.

12 December, 1941 (FRI): New York City, N.Y.

            Dean Kincaide joined the band as staff arranger
            from December 12, 1941 to January 15, 1942.
            (G.M.P.R.) None of his arrangements were recorded,
            and it is doubtful if any were used on broadcasts.

12 December, 1941 (FRI): Cafe Rouge, Hotel Pennsylvania,
New York City, N.Y.
NBC-Blue 7:30-8:00 P.M. EST.

G.M.P.R. show that there was one sustaining
program this evening from the Hotel Pennsylvania.

13 December, 1941 (SAT): Cafe Rouge, Hotel Pennsylvania,
New York City, N.Y. (SUNSET SERENADE)
NBC-Blue 5:00-6:00 P.M. EST.

Tune picked by the sailors of the Naval Training
Station at Pensacola, Florida.

Chattanooga Choo Choo-voc Marion Hutton,
Tex Beneke and The Modernaires

15 December, 1941 (MON): Cafe Rouge, Hotel Pennsylvania,
New York City, N.Y.
WJZ 11:30 P.M.-12:00 Midnight NBC-Blue

G.M.P.R. show that there was one sustaining
program this evening from the Hotel Pennsylvania
and we have an air check of one of the tunes
played.

(3:04) The Story Of A Starry Night (arr BF)-voc
Ray Eberle
Adapted from Tschaikowsky's "Pathetique
Symphony"
(Al Hoffman-Mann Curtis-Jerry
Livingston)

16 December, 1941 (TUES): New York City, N.Y. (CHESTERFIELD SHOW)
CBS 10:00-10:15 P.M. EST.

Moonlight Serenade (Theme)
Moonlight Sonata
It Happened In Sun Valley
A Dream And I (arr JG)-voc RE
(
V Hop
Slumber Song (Theme)

16 December, 1941 (TUES): Cafe Rouge, Hotel Pennsylvania,
New York City, N.Y.
NBC

G.M.P.R. show that there was one sustaining
program this evening from the Hotel Pennsylvania.

17 December, 1941 (WED): New York City, N.Y. (CHESTERFIELD SHOW)
CBS   10:00-10:15 P.M. EST.

Trombones	*Glenn Miller, Jimmy Priddy, Paul Tanner, Frank D'Annolfo*
Trumpets	*Billy May, REUBEN "ZEKE" ZARCHY, Dale McMickle, Johnny Best*
Reeds	*Lloyd "Skippy" Martin, as; Ernie Caceres, as, bar & clt; Wilbur Schwartz, clt & as; Tex Beneke, ts; Al Klink, ts*
Rhythm	*Chummy MacGregor, p; BOBBY HACKETT, g; Doc Goldberg, b; Maurice Purtill, d*

This personnel remains the same for the Hotel Pennsylvania broadcast this evening as well as the Chesterfield and Hotel Pennsylvania broadcasts of December 18th.   (G.M.P.R.)

> *Moonlight Serenade* (Theme)
> *Happy In Love*
> *MEDLEY:*
> *Shine On, Harvest Moon*
> *The Story Of A Starry Night*
> *Rose Room*
> *Blue Moon*

E4VP 8209   Vi LPT 6701, Vi EPOT 6701 (947-0181), HMV RLS 598, RCA G EPOT-6701
(2:38) Measure For Measure (arr BM)
(Arletta May)
As, Caceres; ts, Beneke; tpt, May; p, MacGregor

> *Slumber Song* (Theme)

On Vi LPT 6701 "Measure For Measure" was incorrectly listed as being broadcast on February 10, 1942.

17 December, 1941 (WED): Cafe Rouge, Hotel Pennsylvania,
New York City, N.Y.
NBC

G.M.P.R. show that there was one sustaining program this evening from the Hotel Pennsylvania.

18 December, 1941 (THUR): New York City, N.Y. (CHESTERFIELD SHOW)
CBS   10:00-10:15 P.M. EST.

> *Moonlight Serenade* (Theme)

(Broadcast continued on next page)

This Is No Laughing Matter

K2PP-0042   Vi LPM 6100, RCA RD 27145, RCA G LPM 6100, RCA
            G LPM 9852, RCA G LPM/LSP-9944, RCA Au
            L 11023

FFT   Int GM (4:28) Blues In The Night (arr BM)-voc Marion
                     Hutton, Tex Beneke and The Modernaires
                     From the Warner Bros. film "Blues In
                     The Night"
                     (Johnny Mercer-Harold Arlen)
                     Ts, Beneke; muted tpt, May

Angels Of Mercy
Keep 'Em Flying
Slumber Song (Theme)

18 December, 1941 (THUR): Cafe Rouge, Hotel Pennsylvania,
                              New York City, N.Y.
                              NBC-Blue 11:30-12:00 Midnight EST.

     G.M.P.R. show that there was one sustaining
program this evening from the Hotel Pennsylvania.

19 December, 1941 (FRI): Cafe Rouge, Hotel Pennsylvania,
                         New York City, N.Y.

        Trombones   *Glenn Miller, Jimmy Priddy, Paul*
                      Tanner, Frank D'Annolfo
        Trumpets   *Billy May, BOBBY HACKETT, Dale*
                      McMickle, Johnny Best
        Reeds   *Lloyd "Skippy" Martin, as; Ernie*
                      Caceres, as, bar & clt; Wilbur
                      Schwartz, clt & as; Tex Beneke, ts;
                      Al Klink, ts
        Rhythm   *Chummy MacGregor, p; BILL CONWAY, g;*
                      Doc Goldberg, b; Maurice Purtill, d

     G.M.P.R. show that there was one sustaining
program this evening from the Hotel Pennsylvania.

     Miller wrote to the commander of Fort Harrison
and arranged for a ten day furlough for Trigger
Alpert to come to New York over Christmas--all
expenses on Miller. Trigger Alpert guested on
some of the Miller broadcasts during this
period. (DB, Dec. 15, 1941)

     Miller also tried unsuccessfully to get a
furlough for his former band boy, Raul Hidalgo.

22 *December, 1941 (MON): Cafe Rouge, Hotel Pennsylvania,*
New York City, N.Y.
NBC-Blue   11:30-12:00 Midnight EST.

G.M.P.R. show that there was one sustaining
program this evening from the Hotel Pennsylvania.

23 *December, 1941 (TUES): New York City, N.Y. (CHESTERFIELD SHOW)*
CBS   10:00-10:15 P.M. EST.

The announcer for this program is Paul Douglas.

Moonlight Serenade (Theme)
The Story Of A Starry Night[1]
Happy In Love
Elmer's Tune
Oh So Good
Slumber Song (Theme)

[1] Glenn announces the opening tune as "the beautiful theme of Tschaikowsky's 'Pathetique'
Symphony". This is a non vocal version and is a
different arrangement.

23 *December, 1941 (TUES): Cafe Rouge, Hotel Pennsylvania,*
New York City, N.Y.
NBC-

G.M.P.R. show that there was one sustaining
program this evening from the Hotel Pennsylvania.

24 *December, 1941 (WED): New York City, N.Y. (CHESTERFIELD SHOW)*
CBS   10:00-10:15 P.M. EST.

The announcer for this program is Paul Douglas.

Moonlight Serenade (Theme)

GMMS 105
ALP Int GM & PD (3:15) Jingle Bells (arr GM & BF)-voc Tex Beneke,
Ernie Caceres and The Modernaires
(Harold Dickinson-Bill Conway-J.S.
Pierpont)
Muted tpt, May

(Broadcast continued on next page)

Cafe Rouge, Christmas 1941. The Modernaires with Ray and Marion.

Cafe Rouge, Christmas 1941. Left to right, front row: Eberle, Dickinson, Goldstein, Brewster, Hutton. Middle row: Tanner, Priddy, D'Annolfo, Miller (trombones); Schwartz, Klink, Martin, Caceres, Beneke (saxophones). Back row: Hackett, Best, McMickle, May (trumpets); Conway (guitar); Goldberg (bass); Purtill (drums).

```
          GMMS 105
Int GM (2:06) The Story Of A Starry Night (arr BF)-voc
                    Ray Eberle
                    Adapted from Tschaikowsky's
                    "Pathetique Symphony"
                    (Al Hoffman-Mann Curtis-Jerry
                    Livingston)

          GMMS 105
Int GM (2:40) Nobody Ever Wants Me (arr BM)-voc Trigger
                    Alpert and The Band
                    (Harold Dickinson)
                    B, Alpert

          GMMS 105
       (2:35) Sun Valley Jump (arr JG)
                    (Jerry Gray)
                    Tpt, May; ts, Klink; tpt, May;
                    clt, Caceres; d, Purtill; tpt, ??

          GMMS 105
       (0:20) Slumber Song (Theme)
                    (Saul Tepper-John Chalmers MacGregor)
```

"The Story Of A Starry Night" has a rather abrupt
jump into the vocal which indicates editing.
"Nobody Ever Wants Me" was also known as "Trigger's
Tune" and on this tune Trigger Alpert (who was a
guest on this show) hums along with his bass playing a la Slam Stewart.

24 December, 1941 (WED): Cafe Rouge, Hotel Pennsylvania,
*   New York City, N.Y.*
*   NBC-*

G.M.P.R. show that there was one sustaining
program this evening from the Hotel Pennsylvania.

25 December, 1941 (THUR): New York City, N.Y. (CHESTERFIELD SHOW)
*   CBS 10:00-10:15 P.M. EST.*

The announcer for this program is Paul Douglas.

Moonlight Serenade (Theme)

E3VP 5242   Vi LPT 6700, Vi EPNT 6700 (947-0124), Vi SPD-18
                   (599-9111), HMV RLS 599, RCA G LPT 6700
             (3:15) Flagwaver (arr JG)
                    (Jerry Gray)
                    D, Purtill; ts, Beneke; tpt, May;
                    p MacGregor

(Broadcast continued on next page)

Moonlight Cocktail
Chattanooga Choo Choo
Slumber Song (Theme)

The Queen from Chattanooga was present on this
program and this accounts for only three tunes
being played due to the conversation content.

25 December, 1941 (THUR): Cafe Rouge, Hotel Pennsylvania,
New York City, N.Y.
NBC-Blue 11:30-12:00 Midnight EST.

G.M.P.R. show that there was one sustaining
program this evening from the Hotel Pennsylvania.

G.M.P.R. for the week ending December 25th show
that Billy May got paid for arranging "I Said No"
and"I Got Rhythm".

26 December, 1941 (FRI): Cafe Rouge, Hotel Pennsylvania,
New York City, N.Y.
NBC-Blue 7:30-8:00 P.M.

G.M.P.R. show that there was one sustaining
program this evening from the Hotel Pennsylvania.

27 December, 1941 (SAT): New York City, N.Y.

"Glenn Miller and his band were renewed for the
umpteenth time by the makers of Chesterfield
Cigarets last week, meaning that Miller will
continue to broadcast for the smoke firm on
Tuesdays, Wednesdays and Thursdays on CBS at
least for the first half of 1942. Miller
started the series in December of '39.
     Ninety-nine CBS stations carry Miller's
programs. The renewal was one of the first to
be made by a major air advertiser since the war
started. Band currently is at Hotel Pennsylvania,
New York." (DB--January 1, 1942)

An article from The Billboard: "Hollywood, Dec.
27.--Glenn Miller will be immortalized in film
by a 20th Century Fox epic to be entitled Melody
Man. Miller will play the title role in the pic,
which is to be based on the maestro's life.

(Continued on next page)

Story will be written by Stanley Rauh, direction
by Bryan Foy. Betty Grable will co-star with
Miller, who also have his entire band in the
film." (BB--January 3, 1942) There is no further
mention made of this planned film. Perhaps
"Orchestra Wives" was an offshoot of this idea.

27 December, 1941 (SAT): Cafe Rouge, Hotel Pennsylvania,
New York City, N.Y. (SUNSET SERENADE)
NBC-Blue 5:00-6:00 P.M. EST.

The announcer for this program is Bill Abernathy.

(0:50) *Moonlight Serenade (Theme)*
(Mitchell Parish-Glenn Miller)
Int GM (3:43) *Here We Go Again (arr JG)*
(Jerry Gray)
Ts, Klink; tpt, May; clt, Caceres;
tpt, Best; d, Purtill; tpt, May
Int GM (3:10) *(There'll Be Blue Birds Over)*
The White Cliffs Of Dover
(arr JG)-voc Ray Eberle
(Nat Burton-Walter Kent)
Ts, Beneke
"The White Cliffs Of Dover" was interrupted twice
by Station Identifications.
Int GM (3:15) *Jingle Bells (arr GM & BF)-voc Tex Beneke,*
Ernie Caceres and The Modernaires
(Harold Dickinson-Bill Conway-
J.S. Pierpont)
Muted tpt, May
Int GM (2:50) *Introduction To A Waltz (arr JG)*
(Hal Dickinson-Glenn Miller-Jerry Gray)
P, MacGregor; ts, Beneke; tpt, May;
as, Caceres; tpt, May; p, MacGregor;
d, Purtill
Int GM (3:12) *This Is No Laughing Matter-voc Ray Eberle*
(Van Loman-Martin Block-Al Frisch)

At this point in the program Glenn was presented
a scroll by Herman Finkus of Motion Picture Daily
for "having been voted the best swing orchestra
by over six hundred radio editors throughout the
United States and Canada in the sixth annual radio
poll conducted by Motion Picture Daily and Fame."

Int GM (2:30) *Oh So Good (arr JG)*
(Jerry Gray)
Tpt, Best; p, MacGregor; tpt, May;
d, Purtill

(Broadcast continued on next page)

"Oh So Good" is cut short as this was the half-way mark in the program.

(0:45) Moonlight Serenade (Theme)
(Mitchell Parish-Glenn Miller)
Int GM *(3:43) Tuxedo Junction (arr JG)*
(William Johnson-Julian Dash-
Erskine Hawkins-Buddy Feyne)
Muted tpt, McMickle; open tpt, Best;
muted tpt, McMickle
(0:50) It's Great To Be An American-voc The
Modernaires
(Ray Muffs-Jimmie Crane)

All five camps chose "Chattanooga Choo Choo" as their favorite tune so that Miller had to give away five radios. The camps were: Camp Waelders, Texas; Fort Casey, Washington; Pine Camp, New York; Camp Forest, Tennessee; and the U.S. Marine Corps at Norfolk, Virginia.

Int GM *(3:00) Chattanooga Choo Choo (arr JG)-voc Marion*
Hutton, Tex Beneke and The Modernaires
From the 20th Century-Fox film "Sun
Valley Serenade"
(Mack Gordon-Harry Warren)
(0:40) It's Great To Be An American
(Ray Muffs-Jimmie Crane)
Int GM *(3:17) Papa Niccolini (The Happy Cobbler)-voc*
Ray Eberle, Tex Beneke and
The Modernaires
(Anne and Jean Edwards-Don George)
Int GM *(2:10) This Time The Dream's On Me (arr BF)-voc*
Ray Eberle
From the Warner Bros. film "Blues In
The Night"
(Johnny Mercer-Harold Arlen)
No as or cnt solos
Int GM *(3:08) Dear Arabella (arr JG)-voc Marion Hutton,*
Tex Beneke and The Modernaires (and
the Audience)
(Stanley Joseloff-Sidney Lippman)
Tpt, May
Int GM *(3:47) Elmer's Tune (arr JG)-voc Ray Eberle and*
The Modernaires (and the Audience)
(Elmer Albrecht-Sammy Gallop-Dick
Jurgens)
Ts, Beneke; muted tpt, ??; muted
tbn, Miller

(Broadcast continued on next page)

At this point in the program Miller had Trigger
Alpert (guest) announce the camp (Naval Training
Station at Pensacola, Florida) that had chosen
the favorite tune, "Chattanooga Choo Choo" from
the December 13th show. There was no December
20th program.

Int GM (2:51) *Keep 'Em Flying (arr JG)*
                  (Jerry Gray)
                  Ts, Beneke; d, Purtill; tpt, May;
                  p, MacGregor; d, Purtill; alt,
                  Caceres
      (1:09) *Slumber Song (Theme)*
                  (Saul Tepper-John Chalmers MacGregor)

29 December, 1941 (MON): Cafe Rouge, Hotel Pennsylvania,
                    New York City, N.Y.
                    NBC-Blue 11:30-12:00 Midnight EST.

        G.M.P.R. show that there was one sustaining
        program this evening from the Hotel Pennsylvania.

30 December, 1941 (TUES): New York City, N.Y.(CHESTERFIELD SHOW)
                    CBS   10:00-10:15 P.M. EST.

            Moonlight Serenade (Theme)
            Star Dust

E3VP 5242   Vi LPT 6700, Vi EPNT 6700 (947-0126), Vi SPD-18
             (599-9110), HMV RLS 599, Vi It LJ 50012,
             Vi It LPM 10011, RCA It A1OV 0007, RCA
             G LPT 6700, AFRS "America's Pop Music" 67
         (2:57) Chattanooga Choo Choo (arr JG)-voc Marion
                  Hutton, Tex Beneke and The Modernaires
                  From the 20th Century-Fox film "Sun
                  Valley Serenade"
                  (Mack Gordon-Harry Warren)

            Elmer's Tune
            Keep 'Em Flying
            Slumber Song (Theme)

30 December, 1941 (TUES): Cafe Rouge, Hotel Pennsylvania,
                    New York City, N.Y.
                    NBC-

        G.M.P.R. show that there was one sustaining
        program this evening from the Hotel Pennsylvania.

31 December, 1941 (WED): New York City, N.Y. (CHESTERFIELD SHOW)
CBS   10:00-10:15 P.M. EST.

The announcer for this program is Paul Douglas.

Moonlight Serenade (Theme)
The White Cliffs Of Dover
The Nickel Serenade
ALP - *In The Mood*
Slumber Song (Theme)

31 December, 1941 (WED): Cafe Rouge, Hotel Pennsylvania,
New York City, N.Y.
NBC-

G.M.P.R. show that there was one sustaining
program this evening from the Hotel Pennsylvania.

Moonlight Serenade (Theme)
Blues In The Night

1 January, 1942 (THUR): New York City, N.Y. (CHESTERFIELD SHOW)
CBS   10:00-10:15 P.M. EST.

The announcer for this program is Paul Douglas.

Moonlight Serenade (Theme)

E2VL 4419   Vi LPT-30, Vi 42-0154 (Vi PT-39), Vi 27-0154
            (Vi WPT-39),Vi EPBT-3026 (947-0026),
            Vi LPM-1189, RD 3/4-64, Vi EPB-1189
            (547-0799), HMV DLP 1012, E1 WDLP 1012,
            HMVSw JK-2804, RCA F 430228, RCA G EPC-
            1189, RCA G EPBT-3026, RCA G LPM 6000,
            Vi LPM 6000, Vi EPF 6000?, RCA G LPM/LSP-
            9944, HMVAu ODLP 1012, RCA G LPT-30,
            RCA Au L 11021
     (3:35) I Got Rhythm (arr BM)
                From the musical production "Girl
                Crazy"
                (Ira Gershwin-George Gershwin)
                B, Goldberg; muted tpt, May; ts, Klink;
                as, Martin?; tpt, May

            Ev'rything I Love-voc RE & Ch
            Dear Arabella -voc MH, TB & 4M
            Are You Rusty, Gate?
            Slumber Song (Theme)

1 January, 1942 (THUR): Cafe Rouge, Hotel Pennsylvania,
New York City, N.Y.
NBC-Blue   11:30-12:00 P.M. EST.

       G.M.P.R. show that there was one sustaining
program this evening from the Hotel Pennsylvania.

2 January, 1942 (FRI): Cafe Rouge, Hotel Pennsylvania,
New York City, N.Y.
NBC-Blue   7:30-8:00 P.M. EST.

       G.M.P.R. show that there was one sustaining
program this evening from the Hotel Pennsylvania.

3 January, 1942 (SAT): Cafe Rouge, Hotel Pennsylvania,
New York City, N.Y. (SUNSET SERENADE)
NBC-Blue   5:00-6:00 P.M. EST.

       Moonlight Serenade (Theme)
I Got Rhythm
Elmer's Tune
It's Great To Be An American
Chattanooga Choo Choo
Papa Niccolini
Ev'rything I Love
Boulder Buff
Happy In Love
Tschaikowsky's Piano Concerto

5 January, 1942 (MON): Victor Studios, New York City, N.Y.

Trombones	Glenn Miller, Jimmy Priddy, Paul Tanner, Frank D'Annolfo
Trumpets	Billy May, REUBEN "ZEKE" ZARCHY, Dale McMickle, Johnny Best
Reeds	Lloyd "Skippy" Martin, as; Ernie Caceres, as, bar & clt; Wilbur Schwartz, clt & as; Tex Beneke, ts; Al Klink, ts
Rhythm	Chummy MacGregor, p; BOBBY HACKETT, g; Doc Goldberg, b; Maurice Purtill, d

068833-1   BB 11429-A
            At The President's Ball (arr BM)-voc Marion Hutton
                and The Modernaires
                (Irving Berlin)

(Session continued on next page)

068834-1   BB 11429-B
               Angels Of Mercy-voc Ray Eberle and Chorus
                   Written for and Dedicated to The American
                   Red Cross
                   (Irving Berlin)

068836-1   BB 11480-A
               On The Old Assembly Line (arr JG)-voc Tex Beneke,
                   Marion Hutton and The Modernaires
                   (Bud Green-Ray Henderson)
                   Ts, Beneke

068837-1   BB 11450-A, HMV BD 5784, HMV MH 141, AFRS G.I.
                   Jive H-12-923
               Let's Have Another Cup O' Coffee (arr JG)-voc
                   Marion Hutton, Ernie Caceres and The
                   Modernaires
                   From the musical production "Face The Music"
                   (Irving Berlin)

See January 8, 1942 recording session for missing
matrix 068835-1.

According to the Glenn Miller Payroll Records
Zarchy was paid for this recording session only
and was not on any of the Chesterfield or sustaining broadcasts during this period.

Some copies of "At The President's Ball" are
titled "The President's Birthday Ball". This
occurs on both American and Canadian issues. "At
The President's Ball" was a tune written especially for the President's Birthday Ball which was
held on January 30th in Washington, D.C. Glenn
Miller and His Orchestra were supposed to play at
this ball, but due to theater commitments, had to
cancel out. All royalties from the sale of "At
The President's Ball" went to the Infantile Paralysis
Fund. Miller served as National Chairman of the
Dance Band Leaders' Division of the campaign. Johnny
Long and His Orchestra took Miller's place at the
ball. (Met. Feb. 1942; DB, Feb. 1, 1942)

"On The Old Assembly Line" 2 takes; all others 1
take. (RCA Victor)
This session lasted from 12:00 Noon to 5:30 P.M.
(RCA Victor)

5 January, 1942 (MON): Cafe Rouge, Hotel Pennsylvania,
                   New York City, N.Y.
                   NBC-Blue 11:30-12:00 Midnight

     G.M.P.R. show that there was one sustaining
     program this evening from the Hotel Pennsylvania.

(Broadcast continued on next page)

The personnel from now until the January 8th
recording session is as follows:

Trombones	Glenn Miller, Jimmy Priddy, Paul Tanner, Frank D'Annolfo
Trumpets	Billy May, BOBBY HACKETT, Dale McMickle, Johnny Best
Reeds	Lloyd "Skippy" Martin, as; Ernie Caceres, as, bar & clt; Wilbur Schwartz, clt & as; Tex Beneke, ts; Al Klink, ts
Rhythm	Chummy MacGregor, p; BILL CONWAY, g; Doc Goldberg, b; Maurice Purtill, d

6 January, 1942 (TUES): New York City, N.Y. (CHESTERFIELD SHOW)
                        CBS   10:00-10:15 P.M. EST.

        The announcer for this program is Paul Douglas.

              Moonlight Serenade (Theme)
              A String Of Pearls
Int GM (2:29) The Kiss Polka (arr JG)-voc Marion Hutton,
                  Ernie Caceres and The Modernaires
                  From the 20th Century-Fox film "Sun
                  Valley Serenade"
                  (Mack Gordon-Harry Warren)
              Humpty Dumpty Heart
              Measure For Measure
              Slumber Song (Theme)

6 January, 1942 (TUES): Cafe Rouge, Hotel Pennsylvania,
                        New York City, N.Y.
                        NBC-

        G.M.P.R. show that there was one sustaining
        program this evening from the Hotel Pennsylvania.

7 January, 1942 (WED): New York City, N.Y. (CHESTERFIELD SHOW)
                       CBS   10:00-10:15 P.M. EST.

        The announcer for this program is Paul Douglas.

              Moonlight Serenade (Theme)
              On The Old Assembly Line-voc MH, TB & 4M
              MEDLEY:
                  Peg O' My Heart
                  Fooled
                  Mood Indigo
                  Blue Orchids
              V Hop
              Slumber Song (Theme)

7 January, 1942 (WED): Cafe Rouge, Hotel Pennsylvania,
New York City, N.Y.
NBC-

      G.M.P.R. show that there was one sustaining
      program this evening from the Hotel Pennsylvania.

      Glenn Miller and His Orchestra closed at the
      "Cafe Rouge" of the Hotel Pennsylvania, New York
      City, New York. Charlie Spivak succeeded Glenn
      Miller on January 8th at the Hotel Pennsylvania.
      (Met. Jan. 1942)

      During his final week at the Hotel Pennsylvania
      Miller attracted 3,987 covers. (BB, Jan. 24, 1942)

8 January, 1942 (THUR): Victor Studios, New York City, N.Y.

Trombones	Glenn Miller, Jimmy Priddy, Paul Tanner, Frank D'Annolfo
Trumpets	Billy May, BILL GRAHAM, Dale McMickle, Johnny Best
Reeds	Lloyd "Skippy" Martin, as; Ernie Caceres, as, bar & clt; Wilbur Schwartz, clt & as; Tex Beneke, ts; Al Klink, ts
Rhythm	Chummy MacGregor, p; BOBBY HACKETT, g; Doc Goldberg, b; Maurice Purtill, d
Vocalists	Ray Eberle and The Modernaires

068789-1   BB 11462-B, HMV DLP 1122, AFRS G.I. Jive Series
                   H-12: 758, 921, 1429
            Skylark (arr BF)-voc Ray Eberle
                   (Johnny Mercer-Hoagy Carmichael)
                   Clt, ??

068789-2   Vi LSP-4125, Vi P8S-1432, RCA Int. INTS 1002,
                   Vi VPM-6019, RCA Br. RD-8094, RCA Br. GM-1,
            RCA Au VPM-6019
            Skylark (arr BF)-voc Ray Eberle
                   (Johnny Mercer-Hoagy Carmichael)
                   Clt, ??

068835-1   BB 11443-A, HMVAu EA-3167
            Dear Mom (arr JG)-voc Ray Eberle and The Modernaires
                   (Maury Coleman Harris)
                   Ts, Beneke; bass clt, Klink; ts, Beneke

(Session continued on next page)

068790-2   BB 11438-A, HMV 7EG 8097
When The Roses Bloom Again (arr JG)-voc Ray Eberle
          (Nat Burton-Walter Kent)
          Muted tpt, McMickle; ts, Beneke

068791-1   BB 11438-B, HMVAu EA-3035, Vi LPT 6700, HMV RLS
          599, Vi EPNT 6700 (947-0117), Vi SPD-18
          (599-9104), RCA G LPT 6700, AFRS Jill's
          Juke Box H-46-99
Always In My Heart (arr BM)-voc Ray Eberle
          From the Warner Bros. film "Always In My
          Heart"
          (Kim Gannon-Ernesto Lecuona)
          Ts, Beneke

All tunes 2 takes. (RCA Victor)
This session lasted from 12:00 Noon to 4:20 P.M.
and 5:00 P.M. to 6:00 P.M. (RCA Victor)

According to G.M.P.R. Graham was paid for this
recording session only and was not on any of the
Chesterfield or sustaining broadcasts during this
period.

The matrix for "Dear Mom" would appear to be out
of sequence and fit into the recording session of
January 5th. However, Brad McCuen of RCA Victor
has informed us that there is no record of anything rejected and that the file does not indicate
that "Dear Mom" was recorded prior to January 8th.

8 January, 1942 (THUR): New York City, N.Y. (CHESTERFIELD SHOW)
*   CBS   10:00-10:15 P.M. EST.*

Trombones	*Glenn Miller, Jimmy Priddy, Paul Tanner, Frank D'Annolfo*
Trumpets	*Billy May, BOBBY HACKETT, Dale McMickle, Johnny Best*
Reeds	*Lloyd "Skippy" Martin, as; Ernie Caceres, as, bar & clt; Wilbur Schwartz, clt & as; Tex Beneke, ts; Al Klink, ts*
Rhythm	*Chummy MacGregor, p; BILL CONWAY, g; Doc Goldberg, b; Maurice Purtill, d*

Moonlight Serenade (Theme)
Boulder Buff
At The President's Ball
The Story Of A Starry Night
In The Mood
Slumber Song (Theme)

The band took the New York Central R.R. System
to Cleveland. (G.M.P.R.)

9 January, 1942 (FRI)

Glenn Miller and His Orchestra played for one week
(closed Thursday, January 15th) at the Palace
Theater, Cleveland, Ohio. (BB, Jan. 3, 1942;
Cleveland Press, Jan. 9 & 15, 1942; G.M.P.R.)

"Glenn Miller's ork gave the RKO Palace (3,200
seats) one of the heftiest weeks in recent years,
a huge $31,000. Overage clause in the contract
enabled Miller to carry out an extra $2,000." (BB,
Jan. 24, 1942) Miller also carried along the
Lorraine-Rognan (Roy Rognan and Jeannie Lorraine)
comedy act. The film shown at the theater was
"Blues in the Night."

A review of the stage show appeared in the Saturday,
January 10th issue of the Cleveland Plain Dealer:
"MILLER BAND GETS CHEERS FROM PALACE'S JITTER-
BUGS" by W. Ward Marsh.
"There must be many nice things to be said
about Glenn Miller and his famous orchestra, who
came to the RKO-Palace stage a little late yesterday afternoon due to delayed trains.
But to one who is getting around to the place
where Miller's opening number, 'In the Mood,' is
just beginning to mean something--heaven knows
what--I find it rather difficult to repeat all the
cheers and 'yeah man' shouts which I heard in the
theater.
If there were not more to it than cheers and
'yeah man' outbursts, it would be simple enough to
take proper care of the talented leader and his
equally talented reeds, brasses, piano, bull fiddle
and drums.
But the frenzy and the ecstasy he created in
the auditorium are as far beyond me as they always
are when the boys and girls get into the groove a
popular band digs for them.
It is obviously something elemental if for no
other reason than it is at once impolite and in-
considerate. It seems to be a case of every
emotion for itself, and the more vocally responsive
that emotion, the more it stirs other emotions as
well as other individuals to be up and doing--and
shouting.
To repeat, I can now get some of the qualities
of 'In the Mood.' That trick ending, which is, of
course, repeated until one is quite sure there is
no ending, really does stir something within me.
To tell you exactly what it is would be, I am sure,
rather uncivil.

(Continued on next page)

Then Miller does 'String of Pearls,' which ripple beautifully from reed to brass and back again.

Ray Eberle, who hadn't much of a voice from where I sat, and the four Modernaires do 'The White Cliffs of Dover,' 'Elmer's Tune' and 'Ev'ry-thing I Love'--all quite to the delight of the crowd.

Three more numbers come under the almost cake-walk ministrations of Marion Hutton and again the lilting Modernaires. Rather unhappily, I felt, they did 'Blues in the Night,' and only the Lunceford version is worth the ozone which carries it. I liked Miss Hutton's 'Chattanooga Choo Choo' and 'Nickel Serenade,' and Miller's accompaniment is something over which to have a fresh ectasy in the theater."

10 January, 1942 (SAT): Cleveland, Ohio (SUNSET SERENADE)
Mutual 5:00-6:00 P.M. EST.

Information is missing on the tunes played on this program.

"Reportedly dissatisfied because his 'Sunset Serenade' broadcasts were being cancelled due to the lengthy run of Metropolitan Opera pickups, Glenn Miller has switched the series from NBC to Mutual. On tour now, Miller aired the first show on Mutual from Cleveland Jan. 10 and Detroit will be the originating point, Jan. 17." (DB-- January 15, 1942)

13 January 1942 (TUES): RKO Palace Theater, Cleveland, Ohio
(CHESTERFIELD SHOW)
CBS 10:00-10:15 P.M. EST.

Moonlight Serenade (Theme)
Sunrise Serenade
Happy In Love
Moonlight Cocktail
Chip Off The Old Block
Slumber Song (Theme)

This broadcast was dedicated to the Bond Festival organized by students of Bergen Junior College, Teaneck, New Jersey, to be held at the Meadowbrook, January 14th. This school no longer exists as it was taken over by Fairleigh Dickinson University.

[406]

14 January, 1942 (WED): RKO Palace Theater, Cleveland, Ohio
(CHESTERFIELD SHOW)
CBS   10:00-10:15 P.M. EST.

> *Moonlight Serenade (Theme)*
> *It Happened In Sun Valley*
> *MEDLEY:*
> > *My Reverie (arr JG)*
> > *'Tis Autumn-voc RE*
> > > *(Nemo)*
> > *Snowfall (arr JG) (borrowed from Claude*
> > > *Thornhill)*
> > > *(Claude Thornhill)*
> > *Blue Champagne (arr JG)*
> *Keep 'Em Flying*
> *Slumber Song (Theme)*

15 January, 1942 (THUR): RKO Palace Theater, Cleveland, Ohio
(CHESTERFIELD SHOW)
CBS   10:00-10:15 P.M. EST.

> *The announcer for this program is Larry Bruff.*

> *Moonlight Serenade (Theme)*
> *Tschaikowsky's Piano Concerto*
> *At The President's Ball*
> *Skylark*
> *Flagwaver*
> *Slumber Song (Theme)*

15 January, 1942 (THUR)

> According to G.M.P.R. this was Dean Kincaide's last day as staff arranger with the band.

> G.M.P.R. for the week ending January 15th show that Billy May got paid for arranging "Pushin' Along" and "Always In My Heart".

> The band took the New York Central R.R. System from Cleveland to Detroit. (G.M.P.R.)

16 January, 1942 (FRI)

> Glenn Miller and His Orchestra played for one week (closed Thursday, January 22nd) at the Michigan Theater, Detroit, Michigan. (BB--January 3, 1942)

(Continued on next page)

Opening day drew $7,200 topping the Bob Hope record
opener of $5,200. (BB--January 24, 1942)

Here is part of the evening show January 16th from
Variety, January 16, 1942:
    "Miller must be taking it for granted that it
is his regular following out in front for he isn't
bothering with any identification of his tunes
which is a little hard on the strays. He mixes it
up hot and sweet from the beginning medley of 'In
the Mood', 'Sunrise Serenade', and 'Little Brown
Jug'.
    First one sells the audience pronto with the
kids practically getting out of hand. It needed
smoothed voice Eberle to quiet them down with
'White Cliffs' before increasing tempo again with
the Modernaires in 'Elmer's Tune'. The five stay
on with 'Ev'rything I Love.'
    Miller lets his music speak for him nicely
blending the sweet and then letting out the polished
brass registering big with numbers such 'Dear Mom'
or 'One O'Clock Jump'. Marion Hutton seems to have
forsaken solo choruses singing mostly with the
Modernaires in 'Nickel Serenade' and 'Chattanooga
Choo Choo'. Her personality impresses none the less.
Also gaining recognition was Tex Beneke as feature
sax and with impersonations of Sully Mason."

The film at this theater was <u>Sullivan's Travels</u>.
Lorraine and Rognan were also on the bill.
"Michigan Theater which still is sweeping out the
jitterbugs after hanging up a new record of
$55,900.00" (Variety, Jan. 21, 1942)

17 January, 1942 (SAT): Detroit, Michigan (SUNSET SERENADE)
                Mutual 5:00-6:00 P.M. EST.

    Information is missing on the tunes played on
this program.

20 January, 1942 (TUES): Michigan Theater, Detroit, Michigan
                (CHESTERFIELD SHOW)
                CBS 10:00-10:15 P.M. EST.

        <u>*Moonlight Serenade*</u> *(Theme)*
        <u>*A String Of Pearls*</u>
        <u>*On The Old Assembly Line*</u>
        <u>*Elmer's Tune*</u>
        <u>*In The Mood*</u>
        <u>*Slumber Song*</u> *(Theme)*

[408]

21 January, 1942 (WED): *Michigan Theater, Detroit, Michigan*
                       (CHESTERFIELD SHOW)
                       CBS   10:00-10:15 P.M. EST.

                  Moonlight Serenade (Theme)
                  Chattanooga Choo Choo
                  MEDLEY:
                     The Siren's Song
                     When The Roses Bloom Again
                     Love In Bloom
                     The Birth Of The Blues
                  Boulder Buff
                  Slumber Song (Theme)

22 January, 1942 (THUR): *Michigan Theater, Detroit, Michigan*
                        (CHESTERFIELD SHOW)
                        CBS   10:00-10:15 P.M. EST.

                  Moonlight Serenade (Theme)
                  Moonlight Sonata
                  At The President's Ball
                  The Story Of A Starry Night
                  Keep 'Em Flying
                  Slumber Song (Theme)

   "Shortly after copping top spot for sweet bands
in the '42 'Beat' poll, the Miller man proved there
is no priority on sweet. The Michigan theater's
gate was smashed to the tune of $55,000. Never in
eleven years has so much sugar been shoved across a
Wheelburg window for danceband ducats. Being
strictly Miller, Glenn gave each cat a cut of fifty
clams for the week.
   John O'Leary, the ork's road manager, took a
beating with international complications so that
Miller could do a nite apiece in London and Toronto,
Canada. O'Leary spent about two days with US
officers from the customs, immigration and other
federal departments, going over instrument listings,
salaries, etc. Rush letters were sent to Frankie
D'Annolfo's wife, ill in Conn., in order to obtain
papers in a Long Island vault, necessary to his
crossing the border with the band. All personal
radios, cameras, etc., were left in Detroit to
facilitate the Canadian jump." (DB, Feb. 15, 1942)

The Billboard estimated that Glenn Miller's gross
at the Michigan Theater was around $42,000. (BB,
Jan. 31, 1942) Billboard eventually got things
straightened out when it reported "broke the house
record for a sizzling $55,000." (BB, Feb. 7, 1942)

(Continued on next page)

The band took the Canadian Pacific R.R. Company
System from Detroit to Toronto. (G.M.P.R.)

23 January, 1942 (FRI)

Glenn Miller and His Orchestra drew 6,000 for a
one-nighter at the Mutual Street Arena, Toronto,
Ontario. Miller was interviewed on CBY and a
transcription was made (whereabouts unknown).

"Glenn Miller and His Chattanooga Choo-Choo
hit town last night and for three and one-half
hours gave 6,000 persons one of the swingiest
sweet programs ever heard in the city.
Appearing at the Mutual Street Arena in his
record-breaking tour, for one night only, Glenn
also broke all city dance crowd records when the
complete ticket sale was sold out four days before his scheduled appearance.
Although arena officials and police alike
took all precautions to avoid it, ticket scalping
developed into a profitable proposition with some
people paying as high as $5 for a $1.50 ticket.
So intent was the throng in not missing anything, that they 'ganged up' in front of the band
stand during the whole program." (Evening Telegram--
January 24, 1942)

24 January, 1942 (SAT): London Arena, London, Ontario, Canada
(SUNSET SERENADE)

The announcer for this program is Elwood Glover.

"To-day the band played in London, Ontario, in
the afternoon, where their weekly radio broadcast
to all the United States army camps would be 'aired.'
Members of the RCAF stationed at London were the
guests of honor. At night the band was playing for
London and district residents.
"And on Sunday we are going to take a rest,"
Glenn said, "and don't think we don't need it after
playing six times a day while in Detroit." (Evening
Telegram, January 24, 1942)

The band took the Pennsylvania R.R. Company System
to Washington. (G.M.P.R.)

25 January, 1942 (SUN)

The band spent the day travelling to Washington
by train. (G.M.D.)

26 January, 1942 (MON)

> Glenn Miller and His Orchestra played a one-nighter (originally planned for a one-week engagement but for a previous commitment to play the Paramount Theater, New York) at the opening night of a new room at the Roosevelt Hotel, Washington, D.C. Tony Pastor and His Orchestra opened the next night. (BB--January 24, 1942) The band played from 10:00-2:00 A.M. (G.M.D.)
>
> The band took the Pennsylvania R.R. Company System from Washington to New York City. (G.M.P.R.)

27 January, 1942 (TUES): New York City, N.Y. (CHESTERFIELD SHOW)
               CBS   10:00-10:15 P.M. EST.

Trombones	*Glenn Miller, Jimmy Priddy, Paul Tanner, Frank D'Annolfo*
Trumpets	*Billy May, STEVE LIPKINS, Dale McMickle, Johnny Best*
Reeds	*Lloyd "Skippy" Martin, as; Ernie Caceres, as, bar & clt; Wilbur Schwartz, clt & as; Tex Beneke, ts; Al Klink, ts*
Rhythm	*Chummy MacGregor, p; BOBBY HACKETT, g & cnt; Doc Goldberg, b; Maurice Purtill, d*

> *Moonlight Serenade (Theme)*
> *Chip Off The Old Block*
> *We're The Couple In The Castle*
> *Blues In The Night*
> *V Hop*
> *Slumber Song (Theme)*

According to the G.M.P.R. Steve Lipkins (until recently first trumpeter with Artie Shaw) joined the band on this date. He was not paid for the Toronto, London or Washington dates and he is first paid for this Chesterfield broadcast. He became the permanent replacement for Alec Fila, who left in November, 1941. Bobby Hackett reverted back to the guitar with occasional cornet solos.

28 January, 1942 (WED): Paramount Theater, New York City, N.Y.

Glenn Miller and His Orchestra opened at the
Paramount Theater, New York City, New York (BB--
January 24). If Miller had played at the President's
Birthday Ball the opening would have been February
4th. As a result of Miller opening on the 28th the
stay at the Paramount was for three weeks instead of
the usual two.

Glenn Miller and His Orchestra were reviewed Wednesday Evening, January 28th, on stage at the Paramount
Theater.
    "The Miller band, with its bevy of star vocal-
ists and instrumentalists, showed up as better than
ever. Stripped of the usual tricky and very often
corny arrangements used by many big crews today,
Miller paces his outfit thru a show library that is
perfectly balanced and uniquely played. Plays such
stuff as A String of Pearls and In The Mood with a
pulsating rhythm and tonal restraint that are send-
ing for even the uninitiated.
    On the pop side, and to display the vocal
talent, ork comes forth with White Cliffs of Dover,
Dear Mom, Blues in the Night and the famous
Chattanooga Choo Choo. Ray Eberle pipes the first
one solo and joins with the Modernaires on the Mom
ballad. Marion Hutton and tenor saxist Tex Beneke
vocalize the last two numbers, with the Modernaires
furnishing a background. All turn in good jobs,
backed by the band's very nifty and sharp rhythm."
(BB--February 7, 1942)

    Also on the bill were Lorraine and Rognan, a
comedy dance team, and a girl juggler known as
Trixie. There are pictures from the Paramount at
this time showing these acts with the Miller band
in the background. (New York Daily News, Jan. 28,
1942)

The Miller band did 36 shows this week (week ending
Feb. 3rd) (G.M.P.R.)

28 January, 1942 (WED): New York City, N.Y. (CHESTERFIELD SHOW)
              CBS 10:00-10:15 P.M. EST.

       (0:39) Moonlight Serenade (Theme)
                    (Mitchell Parish-Glenn Miller)

(Broadcast continued on next page)

Int GM (0:30) *Let's Have Another Cup O' Coffee* (arr JG)-
voc Marion Hutton, Ernie Caceres and
The Modernaires
From the musical production "Face The
Music"
(Irving Berlin)
MEDLEY:
Sweet And Lovely
This Time The Dream's On Me
The Very Thought Of You
Blue Hawaii
To The Shores Of Tripoli (The Marine's
Hymn) (arr JG)
(L.Z. Phillips)
Slumber Song (Theme)

29 January, 1942 (THUR): New York City, N.Y. (CHESTERFIELD SHOW)
CBS   10:00-10:15 P.M. EST.

Moonlight Serenade (Theme)
Goin'Home
At The President's Ball
Dear Mom
Anvil Chorus
Slumber Song (Theme)

30 January, 1942 (FRI): Waldorf Astoria Hotel, New York City, N.Y.

The millionth record of Miller's Chattanooga Choo
Choo was auctioned off during the President's Birthday Ball at the Waldorf Astoria. Miller's band was
replaced by Johnny Long's as theater commitments
cancelled out Miller. Miller was awarded a silver
platter for selling a million copies. This was the
first time that an artist had done this since Gene
Austin's record of My Blue Heaven. (DB--February 1,
1942)

Contrary to what the above article states Miller was
at the Waldorf Astoria for the President's Birthday
Ball Salute but G.M.D. does not make it clear
whether it was Miller alone or Miller with his band.

31 January, 1942 (SAT): New York City, N.Y. (SUNSET SERENADE)
Mutual 5:00-6:00 P.M. EST.

Fourth and final date at the Paramount, January–February 1942. From the way the trombones are pointing, the band is probably playing *In the Mood*. New trumpeter Steve Lipkins can be seen between Priddy and D'Annolfo.

Marion Hutton, Glenn Miller and unknown announcer examine silver platter awarded for top-selling *Chattanooga Choo Choo*. (*Photo courtesy Glenn Miller Estate*)

3 February, 1942 (TUES): New York City, N.Y. (CHESTERFIELD SHOW)
                CBS 10:00-10:15 P.M. EST.

        The announcer for this program is Paul Douglas.

           Moonlight Serenade (Theme)
           Fooled-voc RE
           On The Old Assembly Line
           Angels Of Mercy-voc RE & 4M
           Sun Valley Jump
           Slumber Song (Theme)

4 February, 1942 (WED): New York City, N.Y. (CHESTERFIELD SHOW)
                CBS 10:00-10:15 P.M. EST.

           Moonlight Serenade (Theme)
           Blues In The Night
           MEDLEY:
              The Touch Of Your Hand
              Papa Niccolini
              The Waltz You Saved For Me
              Blue Danube
           Keep 'Em Flying
           Slumber Song (Theme)

5 February, 1942 (THUR): New York City, N.Y. (CHESTERFIELD SHOW)
                CBS 10:00-10:15 P.M. EST.

           Moonlight Serenade (Theme)
           A String Of Pearls
           Dreamsville, Ohio
           Happy In Love
           Introduction To A Waltz
           Slumber Song (Theme)

7 February, 1942 (SAT): New York City, N.Y. (SUNSET SERENADE)
              Mutual 5:00-6:00 P.M. EST.

10 February, 1942 (TUES): New York City, N.Y. (CHESTERFIELD SHOW)
                CBS 10:00-10:15 P.M. EST.

        The announcer for this program is Paul Douglas.

           Moonlight Serenade (Theme)
           Marching Along Together (arr JG)
              (Edward Pola-Franz Steininger-
              Mort Dixon)

(Broadcast continued on next page)

At this point in the program, Wally Early, a top RCA Victor executive, presented Glenn Miller with the _first_ gold (gold-plated) record, which has now become symbolic for a million-record seller. "Chattanooga Choo Choo" had just passed the 1,200,000 mark in sales.

ALP _Chattanooga Choo Choo_
When The Roses Bloom Again
Measure For Measure
Slumber Song (Theme)

"Marching Along Together" was presented on this program as a salute to the Boy Scouts of America on their 32nd anniversary. The tune is quite short.

The band did 31 shows this week (week ending Feb. 10th) at the Paramount Theater. (G.M.P.R.)

11 February, 1942 (WED): Paramount Theater, New York City, N.Y.

There is a stage show review of the 7:15 p.m. show.

"Glenn Miller is an institution on the stage of the Paramount Theater. He devoted this show to a resume of the reasons why he is such an institution.
In the Mood, It Happened In Sun Valley and Chattanooga Choo Choo were the Miller standards that opened and closed the show. In between, there were such tried and true devices with this band as the Something Old, Something New, Something Borrowed, Something Blue medley (Sweet and Lovely, This Time The Dream's On Me, The Very Thought Of You, Blue Hawaiian Waters), a couple of Ray Eberle numbers (one with the assistance of the Modernaires) and a Jerry Gray jazz instrumental.
The Gray jazz, String of Pearls, was certainly the musical high spot of the show. Duets between altoists Skippy Martin and Ernie Caceres and tenorists Al Klink and Tex Beneke were easy to listen to and smart showmanship. Bobby Hackett's brief cornet piece was neatly essayed and the intermittent bars of MacGregor piano were effective.
Effective is the word too, for the effervescent delivery of Marion Hutton in Sun Valley, and the running entrances and exits of the Modernaires, who pranced around as if they were at a party of kindergarten kids. The audience ate it up.

(Continued on next page)

Chattanooga Choo Choo passes 1,200,000 mark in sales and Glenn gets gold-plated record from RCA-Victor executive Wally Early as announcer Paul Douglas looks on. Presentation was made on February 10, 1942 Chesterfield program. (*Photo courtesy Glenn Miller Estate*)

Opening scene from *Orchestra Wives*, March–May 1942. Band is playing *People Like You and Me*. (*20th Century-Fox*)

In this closing scene from *Orchestra Wives*, Marion Hutton, Tex Beneke and the Modernaires sing *Kalamazoo*. That's Jackie Gleason on bass, Cesar Romero on piano and George Montgomery on trumpet (fourth from right). (*20th Century-Fox*)

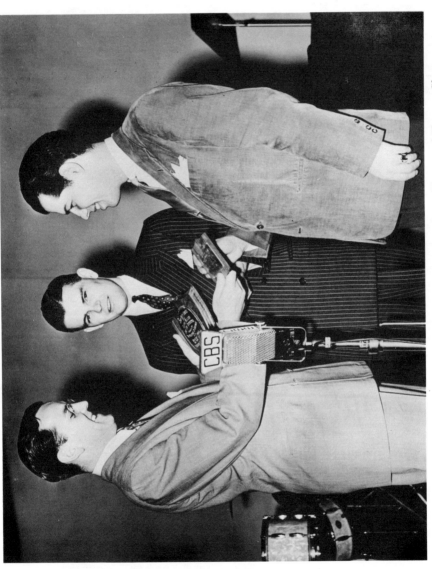

Dave Dexter, Jr. of *Down Beat* magazine presents awards to Glenn and Tex on Chesterfield program of February 18, 1942. (*Photo courtesy Glenn Miller Estate*)

When Glenn announced <u>Chattanooga Choo Choo</u>,
with a retreating train on the big backdrop, the
audience roared. When it was over, and the band
was dropping into the pit, the audience roared
again." (Met.--March 1942)

11 February, 1942 (WED): New York City, N.Y. (CHESTERFIELD SHOW)
CBS   10:00-10:15 P.M. EST.

> <u>*Moonlight Serenade*</u> *(Theme)*
> <u>*Star Dust*</u>
> <u>*When Johnny Comes Marching Home*</u>
> <u>*Always In My Heart*</u>
> <u>*By The Waters Of Minnetonka*</u>
> <u>*Slumber Song*</u> *(Theme)*

12 February, 1942 (THUR): New York City, N.Y. (CHESTERFIELD SHOW)
CBS   10:00-10:15 P.M. EST.

> <u>*Moonlight Serenade*</u> *(Theme)*
> <u>*Dear Arabella*</u>
> *MEDLEY:*
> > <u>*To You*</u>
> > <u>*Moonlight Cocktail*</u>*-voc RE & 4M*
> > <u>*The Story Of A Starry Night*</u> *(borrowed*
> > *   from Tschaikowsky)*
> > <u>*Rhapsody In Blue*</u>
> <u>*Oh So Good*</u>
> <u>*Slumber Song*</u> *(Theme)*

14 February, 1942 (SAT): New York City, N.Y. (SUNSET SERENADE)
Mutual   5:00-6:00 P.M. EST.

17 February, 1942 (TUES): New York City, N.Y. (CHESTERFIELD SHOW)
CBS   10:00-10:15 P.M. EST.

> <u>*Moonlight Serenade*</u> *(Theme)*
> <u>*A String Of Pearls*</u>
> <u>*Day Dreaming*</u>
> <u>*The Kiss Polka*</u>

E2VL 4420   <u>Vi LPT-30</u>, Vi 42-0152 (Vi PT-39), Vi 27-0152
(Vi WPT-39), Vi EPBT-3026 (947-0027), Vi
LPM 1189, HMV DLP 1012, Vi EPB-1189 (547-
0800), E1 WDLP 1012, HMVSw JK-2803, RCA F
430228, RCA G EPBT-3026, HMVAu ODLP 1012,
RCA G EPC-1189, RCA Au L 11021, RCA G LPT-
30

(Broadcast continued on next page)

(2:49) On Brave Old Army Team (arr JG)
West Point Football Song
(Philip Egner)
D, Purtill; ts, Klink; ts, Beneke;
tpt, Best; tpt, May; d, Purtill;
clt, Caceres

Slumber Song (Theme)

Victor lists "On Brave Old Army Team" as "On Army
Team" but the former title is correct for this
West Point Football Song.

17 February, 1942 (TUES): Paramount Theater, New York City, N.Y.

Glenn Miller and His Orchestra closed at the
Paramount Theater, New York City, New York. Alvino
Rey and the King Sisters opened the next day. (New
York Daily News, Feb. 17, 1942; G.M.P.R.)
"Glenn Miller's first week at the Paramount
wound up with a boom $73,000; the second week
$52,000; and the third and final week $42,000."
(BB--February 28, 1942)

While in New York Glenn Miller and a number of
other name bandleaders made a series of "spot"
recordings in the WMCA studios to promote the sale
of defense bonds and stamps. Each leader paid
about $100. New idea was under the direction of
Bob Bach of WMCA. (DB--March 1, 1942)

18 February, 1942 (WED): Victor Studios, New York City, N.Y.

Same personnel as for January 27th broadcast.

071860-1   BB 11493-B
            Shhh, It's A Military Secret (arr JG)-voc Marion
                Hutton, Tex Beneke and The Modernaires
                (Alan Courtney-Earl Allvine-Walter Bishop)

071861-1   BB 11474-B, HMV B10662, Vi 420-0042, Vi 447-0042,
                HMV 7M195, Vi LPT 3067, Vi EPBT-3067 (947-
                0199), Vi EPA-5049, RCA RCX 1024, HMV DLP
                1062, El 7MW 117, Vi LPM/LSP-3377, RD 3/4-21,
                RD Br. RDS 6173, Vi PR-125, Vi TP3-5044,
                RCA G LPM/LSP-3377, RCA G EPBT-3067, RCA G
                LPT-3067, RCA F 130211, Vi P8S-5061, HMVIr
                I.P. 887, Vi VPM-6019, AFRS G.I. Jive
                Series H-12: 793, 940, 1192, RCA Au 20037,

(Session continued on next page)

RCA G Cas 10231, Vi Arg 68-1344, RCA Br.
GM-1, RCA Br. RD-8094, RCA Au VPM-6019,
AFRS Jill's Juke Box Series H-46: 6, 78,
105
Don't Sit Under The Apple Tree (With Anyone Else
But Me)-voc Marion Hutton, Tex Beneke and
The Modernaires
(Lew Brown-Charlie Tobias-Sammy Stept)

071862-1   BB 11493-A, HMVAu EA-3337
She'll Always Remember-voc Ray Eberle and The
Modernaires
(Eddie Pola-Johnny Marks)
Muted tpt, McMickle; ts, Beneke

071863-1   BB 11474-A, Vi LPT 6700, Vi EPNT 6700 (947-0116),
Vi SPD-18 (599-9105), HMV RLS 599, HMV DLP
1122, Vi PR-114, Vi LPM/LSP-3564, RD 3/4-64,
Vi TP3-5044, Vi P8S-5061, RCA G LPT 6700,
Vi Arg LPM 3564, AFRS G.I. Jive Series H-12:
1063, 1178, 1251, AFRS Jill's Juke Box
H-46-66
The Lamplighter's Serenade-voc Ray Eberle and The
Modernaires
(Paul Francis Webster-Hoagy Carmichael)
Ts, Beneke

071864-1   BB 11480-B, HMV BD 5798, HMV MH 138, HMVAu EA-3087,
Vi 20-1600, HMV 7EG 8254, Vi LPM/LSP-3657,
RCA RD/SF-7842, AFRS Phonograph Album No. 1
(H-62-1), El G EG 7685, AFRS P-10071, RD 3/4-
64, HMVIn BD 5798, RCA G LPM/LSP-3657, RCA F
440.727, AFRS G.I. Jive Series H-12: 757,
1014, 1454, 1505, 1709, AFRS Jill's Juke Box
Series H-46: 3, 75, 165, 213, 237
When Johnny Comes Marching Home (arr BF)-voc Tex
Beneke, Marion Hutton and The Modernaires
(Lyrics and Adaptation by: Harold Dickinson-
Bill Conway-Bill Finegan)
(Patrick Sarsfield Gilmore)
Ts, Klink

"She'll Always Remember" 2 takes; all others 1 take.
(RCA Victor)
This session lasted from 10:00 A.M. to 4:00 P.M.
(RCA Victor)

This was the band's last recording session on
Victor's 35¢ Bluebird label. For the next recording session the band moved to the higher-priced
50¢ Victor label.

[418]

18 February, 1942 (WED): New York City, N.Y. (CHESTERFIELD SHOW)
                    CBS   10:00-10:15 P.M. EST.

> *Moonlight Serenade* (Theme)
> *We're The Couple In The Castle-voc* RE

At this part in the program Dave Dexter, Jr., from
Down Beat magazine, presented awards to Miller and
Beneke. Miller's band won <u>Down Beat's</u> "sweet"
band poll and Beneke won a seat on the All-American
band. The presentation was heard over more than
100 CBS stations from New York to Hawaii. (DB,
March 15 & April 1, 1942)

> *(2:31) Blues In The Night (arr BM)-voc Marion*
> *   Hutton, Tex Beneke and The Modernaires*
> *   From the Warner Bros. film "Blues In*
> *   The Night"*
> *   (Johnny Mercer-Harold Arlen)*
> *   Muted tpt, May*
> *Angels Of Mercy-voc* RE
> *In The Mood*
> *Slumber Song* (Theme)

19 February, 1942 (THUR): New York City, N.Y. (CHESTERFIELD SHOW)
                    CBS   10:00-10:15 P.M. EST.

> *Moonlight Serenade* (Theme)
> *On The Old Assembly Line*
> *MEDLEY:*
> *   How Deep Is The Ocean?*
> *   Always In My Heart*
> *   It's A Wonderful World*
> *   My Blue Heaven*
> *Chip Off The Old Block*
> *Slumber Song* (Theme)

20 February, 1942 (FRI)

> The band was on vacation from February 20th until
> (and including) February 23rd. (G.M.D.)
>
> "VACATION RAMBLES. The band 'took off' for
> four days after closing at the Paramount with the
> following results: Ray Eberle spent most of his
> time at Glen Island, with Hal McIntyre, who, by
> the way, did a swell job pinch-hitting for Glenn
> on Sunset Serenade; Modernaire Ralph Brewster, to
> the dentist, ouch! 'Doc' Goldberg to his name-
> sake for medical attention. Marion Hutton to the
> dressmaker--you'll see the results in 'Orchestra
> Wife'; Tex Beneke to the famous 'Choo-Choo'

(Continued on next page)

country and back by train and plane--Miller him-
self--to Pinehurst, N.C., where he whacked a
mighty 3-iron shot into the wind and wound up with
a hole in one--wow!--Whatta vacation!"
(Glenn Miller Club Bulletin Vol. 1 No. 2--March,
1942)

21 February, 1942 (SAT)

According to the Glenn Miller files on the Sunset
Serenades there was a Hal McIntyre broadcast for
Glenn Miller on Sunset Serenade on this date.

*24 February, 1942 (TUES): New York City, N.Y. (CHESTERFIELD SHOW)
CBS   10:00-10:15 P.M. EST.*

The announcer for this program is Paul Douglas.

Moonlight Serenade (Theme)

E2VL 4545   Vi LPT-3001, Vi EPBT-3001 (947-0054), Vi LPM-1193,
Vi EPB-1193 (547-0822), Vi It LPM-10141,
Vi TP3-5020, Vi It LJ 50020, RCA G EPB 3001,
Vi It LPM 50020, RCA G LPM-1193, RCA G LPT-
3001
(3:11) Tschaikowsky's Piano Concerto (arr BF)
(Peter I. Tschaikowsky)
P, MacGregor; ts, Beneke

The Lamplighter's Serenade
Happy In Love
Introduction To A Waltz
Slumber Song (Theme)

*25 February, 1942 (WED): New York City, N.Y. (CHESTERFIELD SHOW)
CBS   10:00-10:15 P.M. EST.*

Moonlight Serenade (Theme)
Shhh, It's A Military Secret
MEDLEY:
Stairway To The Stars (arr BF)
She'll Always Remember
*Star Dreams (arr BF) (borrowed from
Charlie Spivak)
(Sylvia Dee-Charlie Spivak-Sonny
Burke)*
Blue Evening (arr BF)
Keep 'Em Flying
Slumber Song (Theme)

26 February, 1942 (THUR): New York City, N.Y. (CHESTERFIELD SHOW)
CBS   10:00-10:15 P.M. EST.

> *Moonlight Serenade* (Theme)
> *Moonlight Sonata*
> *Don't Sit Under The Apple Tree*
> *Skylark*

E4VP 8210   Vi LPT 6701, Vi EPOT 6701 (947-0178), HMV RLS 598,
             RCA G EPOT-6701
             (2:13) V For Victory Hop (arr JG)
                   (Ray Conniff)
                   Tpt, May; clt, Caceres; ts, Beneke;
                   tpt, ??

> *Slumber Song* (Theme)

The band took the Pennsylvania R.R. Company from
New York to Altoona, Pennsylvania and then a Blue
& White Lines Inc. bus to Altoona State College
and return. (G.M.P.R.)

G.M.P.R. for the week ending February 26th show
that Billy May got paid for his arrangement of
"Me & Melinda".

27 February, 1942 (FRI)

> Glenn Miller and His Orchestra played at the
> Recreation Hall of the Pennsylvania State College,
> State College, Pennsylvania, from 10:00-2:00 A.M.
> (BB, Feb. 7, 1942; G.M.P.R.; G.M.D.)
> The band took the Pennsylvania R.R. Company to
> Philadelphia (27th). While in Philadelphia the
> band stayed at the Ben Franklin Hotel. (G.M.P.R.)

28 February, 1942 (SAT)

> Glenn Miller and His Orchestra played at the
> Sunnybrook Ballroom, Pottstown, Pennsylvania, from
> 8:30-12:30 A.M., and drew 7,125. State troopers
> had to be called to preserve order. (BB, Feb. 7
> & March 14, 1942; Variety, March 4, 1942;
> G.M.P.R.; G.M.D.)

28 February, 1942 (SAT): Pottstown, Pennsylvania? (SUNSET SERENADE)
Mutual   5:00-6:00 P.M. EST.

1 March, 1942 (SUN)

       Glenn Miller and His Orchestra played at the
Masonic Temple, Scranton, Pennsylvania, from
9:00-1:00 A.M., and drew 4,700. This dance
was for the Elks War Fund. The band stayed at
the Hotel Casey. (BB. March 14, 1942; Variety,
March 4, 1942; G.M.P.R.; G.M.D.)

2 March, 1942 (MON)

       Glenn Miller and His Orchestra played at the
George F. Pavilion, Johnson City, New York,
from 9:00-1:00 A.M., and drew 4,222. (BB, March
14, 1942; Variety, March 4, 1942; G.M.P.R.;
G.M.D.)

4 March, 1942 (WED): New York City, N.Y. (CHESTERFIELD SHOW)
               CBS 10:00-10:15 P.M. EST.

       The Chesterfield series changed its opening night
from Tuesdays to Wednesdays on this date.
     "Chesterfield gets away next week from Bob
Hope's opposition to its Tuesday night Glenn
Miller stanza. The cig account has dropped the
latter period and substituted a Friday quarter
hour. This makes the new Chesterfield schedule
Wednesday, Thursday, and Friday from 10:00 to
10:15 P.M. (Variety, Feb. 25, 1942)

          Moonlight Serenade (Theme)
          Little Brown Jug
          Dear Arabella
          Moonlight Cocktail
          Here We Go Again
          Slumber Song (Theme)

       The band took the Pennsylvania R.R. Company from
New York to Washington. (G.M.P.R.)

5 March, 1942 (THUR)

       Glenn Miller and His Orchestra played for one
week (closed Wednesday, March 11th) at Loew's
Capitol Theater, Washington, D.C. (BB, Jan. 17,
1942; DB, April 1, 1942; The Evening Star,
March 5, 1942; G.M.P.R.) Lorraine and Rognan
were on the same bill at Loew's Capitol (F at
14th St.). The band stayed at the Raleigh Hotel
while in Washington.

5 *March, 1942 (THUR): Capitol Theater, Washington, D.C.*
                               (CHESTERFIELD SHOW)
                               CBS   10:00-10:15 P.M. EST.

                               Moonlight Serenade (Theme)
                               Largo
                               Let's Have Another Cup O' Coffee
                               When The Roses Bloom Again
                               Tuxedo Junction
                               Slumber Song (Theme)

6 *March, 1942 (FRI):   Capitol Theater, Washington, D.C.*
                               (CHESTERFIELD SHOW)
                               CBS   10:00-10:15 P.M. EST.

                               Moonlight Serenade (Theme)
                               When Johnny Comes Marching Home
                               MEDLEY:
                                    Shine On, Harvest Moon
                                    The Story Of A Starry Night
                                  Rose Room
                                  Blue Moon
                               Everybody Loves My Baby
                               Slumber Song (Theme)

Earlier in the day (afternoon) Glenn Miller and
His Orchestra played on the steps of the U.S.
Treasury Building (in overcoats) to help the drive
for sale of Defense Bonds and Stamps.
(Met. April 1942; Variety, March 4, 1942)

7 *March, 1942 (SAT): Washington, D.C.   (SUNSET SERENADE)*
                               Mutual 5:00-6:00 P.M. EST.

11 *March, 1942 (WED): Capitol Theater, Washington, D.C.*
                               (CHESTERFIELD SHOW)

                  The announcer for this program is Larry Bruff.

                               Moonlight Serenade (Theme)
                               Chip Off The Old Block
                               On The Old Assembly Line
                               The White Cliffs Of Dover
                               Anvil Chorus
                               Slumber Song (Theme)

11 March, 1942 (WED): Washington, D.C.

        Glenn Miller and His Orchestra broke all house
records during their week's work at Loew's Capitol
Theater. (DB--April 1, 1942)

        One night during this week Bobby Hackett and Wilbur
Schwartz took off to play at the Turkish Embassy
for the Ambassador's son, Neshui Ertegun, and were
present for a record session. (Met.--April 1942)

        George (The Fox) Williams joined Miller as a full-
time staff arranger. Williams left Sonny Dunham's
Orchestra to accept Miller's offer. "Miller said
Williams also would help score the movie flicker
which the band is now making in Hollywood for 20th
Century-Fox" (DB--April 1, 1942)

        "Glenn Miller's recall to the Coast by 20th
Century-Fox has necessitated cancellation of his
vaude dates. Houses affected are the Central,
Passaic, March 12 (12-18); Metropolitan, Providence,
March 20; Plymouth, Worcester, March 24; State,
Hartford, March 27, and the Buffalo, April 10.
Miller has resigned for Passaic, to open September
24. Miller's usual theater contracts have been
carrying a rider permitting cancellations should he
be called upon to fill a film commitment." (BB--
February 28, 1942)

        The band took the Chicago and Northwest R.R. Co.
from Washington to Chicago. (G.M.P.R.)

12 March, 1942 (THUR)

        Glenn Miller and His Orchestra played for two nights
(Thursday, March 12th and Friday, March 13th) at the
Civic Opera House, Chicago, Illinois.

        WBBM received 25,000 requests for tickets to
Miller's concert and broadcast and only 9,000 seats
were available for both nights. (BB, March 21, 1942;
G.M.P.R.) According to G.M.P.R. concerts of 35
minutes were played both nights as well as the
Chesterfield broadcasts.

12 March, 1942 (THUR): Civic Opera House, Chicago, Illinois
                    (CHESTERFIELD SHOW)
                    CBS 10:00-10:15 P.M.

        The announcer for this program is Larry Bruff.
(Broadcast continued on next page)

Moonlight Serenade (Theme)
Papa Niccolini-voc MH, TB & 4M
MEDLEY:
> *You Leave Me Breathless*-voc RE
> *The Lamplighter's Serenade* (Instrumental)
> *Racing With The Moon*-voc RE & 4M (borrowed
>   from Vaughn Monroe)
>   (Watson-Monroe-Pope)
> *Blues In The Night*
Song Of The Volga Boatmen
Moonlight Serenade (Theme)

The Ray Eberle vocal on "Papa Niccolini" (and the
slow part of the tune) has been omitted from this
version.

13 March, 1942 (FRI): Civic Opera House, Chicago, Illinois
              (CHESTERFIELD SHOW)
              CBS   10:00-10:15 P.M.

Moonlight Serenade (Theme)
Don't Sit Under The Apple Tree
A String Of Pearls
Fooled
Keep 'Em Flying
Slumber Song (Theme)

The band took the Chicago and Northwest R.R. Co.
from Chicago to Los Angeles. (G.M.P.R.)

14 March, 1942 (SAT)

According to the Glenn Miller files on the Sunset
Serenades there was a Charlie Spivak broadcast for
Glenn Miller on Sunset Serenade on this date.

14 March, 1942 (SAT)

According to G.M.D. the band was en route to
California on March 14th, 15th, and 16th. G.M.D.
state that the band arrived in Hollywood on
March 17th.

18 March, 1942 (WED): Hollywood, California (CHESTERFIELD SHOW)
CBS 10:00-10:15 P.M.

Trombones	*Glenn Miller, Jimmy Priddy, Paul Tanner, Frank D'Annolfo*
Trumpets	*Billy May, Steve Lipkins, Dale McMickle, Johnny Best*
Reeds	*Lloyd "Skippy" Martin, as; Ernie Caceres, as, bar & clt; Wilbur Schwartz; clt & as; ROY PARKINSON, ts; Al Klink, ts*
Rhythm	*Chummy MacGregor, p; Bobby Hackett, g; Doc Goldberg, b; Maurice Purtill, d*

Moonlight Serenade (Theme)
Dear Arabella
Happy In Love
This Is No Laughing Matter
V For Victory Hop
Slumber Song (Theme)

According to G.M.P.R. ROY PARKINSON subbed for Tex Beneke on this broadcast only.

19 March, 1942 (THUR)

Barney McDevitt, publicity director of the Hollywood Palladium, worked on publicity for the Miller band while in Hollywood, from March 19th to May 24th. (G.M.P.R.)

19 March, 1942 (THUR): Hollywood, California (CHESTERFIELD SHOW)
CBS 10:00-10:15 P.M.

Trombones	*Glenn Miller, Jimmy Priddy, Paul Tanner, Frank D'Annolfo*
Trumpets	*Billy May, Steve Lipkins, Dale McMickle, Johnny Best*
Reeds	*Lloyd "Skippy" Martin, as; Ernie Caceres, as, bar & clt; Wilbur Schwartz, clt & as; TEX BENEKE, ts; Al Klink, ts*
Rhythm	*Chummy MacGregor, p; Bobby Hackett, g; Doc Goldberg, b; Maurice Purtill, d*

The announcer for this program is Don Wilson.

Moonlight Serenade (Theme)
Shhh, It's A Military Secret

(Broadcast continued on next page)

                    MEDLEY:
                        The Siren's Song
                        When The Roses Bloom Again
                        Love In Bloom
                        The Birth Of The Blues
                    Here We Go Again
                    Slumber Song (Theme)

20 March, 1942 (FRI): Hollywood, California (CHESTERFIELD SHOW)
                    CBS   10:00-10:15 P.M.

                        Moonlight Serenade (Theme)
                        Little Brown Jug
                        It Happened In Sun Valley
                        Always In My Heart

E2VL 4546   Vi LPT-3001, Vi EPBT-3001 (947-0055), HMV DLP 1013,
                    RCA G EPB 3001, AFRS P-2666, RCA F 130243,
                    E1 WDLP 1013, HMVAu ODLP 1013, RCA G LPT-
                    3001
                    (2:25) Introduction To A Waltz (arr JG)
                        (Hal Dickinson-Glenn Miller-Jerry Gray)
                        P, MacGregor; ts, Beneke; tpt, May;
                        p, MacGregor; d, Purtill

                    Slumber Song (Theme)

21 March, 1942 (SAT): Hollywood, California (SUNSET SERENADE)
                    Mutual

23 March (MON) - 22 May (FRI), 1942: 20th Century-Fox Studios,
                                Hollywood, California.

        Glenn Miller and His Orchestra began work on their
        second (and last) film for 20th Century-Fox,
        "Orchestra Wives", produced by William LeBaron and
        directed by Archie Mayo. Featured were George
        Montgomery, Ann Rutherford, Lynn Bari, Carole
        Landis, Mary Beth Hughes, Cesar Romero, Jackie
        Gleason and Henry Morgan. The Nicholas Brothers
        were featured in a specialty dance routine during
        "Kalamazoo". Lyrics by Mack Gordon and music by
        Harry Warren. Pat Friday did the vocal selections
        for Lynn Bari. Chummy MacGregor plays piano for
        Cesar Romero, Doc Goldberg plays bass for Jackie
        Gleason and Johnny Best plays trumpet for George
        Montgomery.

(Continued on next page)

During this period several numbers were recorded for the film (some were not used), and several issues of the numbers have been made. In all cases (except the theme "Moonlight Serenade") there is no evidence of alternate takes being issued as the film numbers are the same versions as the recordings. Several tunes were issued in edited form for promotional discs (eg. a 15 minute radio preview 16" transcription was made for "Orchestra Wives"--TCF-150, and a 12" recording of "Kalamazoo"--TCF-137 and TCF-138) and some were issued without the dubbed in sounds (such as tap dancing, etc.) that were on the film.

Film, TCF TCF-150
(0:45) Moonlight Serenade (Theme)
          (Mitchell Parish-Glenn Miller)

J8OP 9908   TCF TCF-100-2, Emb EMB 3318, Emb EMB 4526, MTM
            1003/MTS 2003, MTM 71018/MTS 72018, MTM
            71003/MTS 72003, TR 35/023, TCF F 1001,
            TCF F 3021, TCF G LP 60004, TCF TFM
            3160/TFS 4160, MT G MTS 4004, MT G MTS
            4008, Ar 31052, Cl Sp 18-1114, Cl Sp 18-
            1115, TCF Arg FE 4160, WRC T./ST. 252,
            TCF Au TL 31128, TCF Au TL 31590
(1:01) Moonlight Serenade (Theme)
          (Mitchell Parish-Glenn Miller)
          With harp introduction

Film
(0:39) Chattanooga Choo Choo (arr JG)
          From the 20th Century-Fox film
          "Sun Valley Serenade"
          (Mack Gordon-Harry Warren)

E4VL 5048   Vi LPT-3065, Film, Vi EPBT-3065 (947-0203), TCF
            TCF-150, TCF TCF-100-2, Emb EMB 3318, Emb
            EMB 4526, TR 35/023, HMV DLP 1059, TCF F
            3021, TCF TCF-127, TCF TFM 3160/TFS 4160,
            MTM 71018/MTS 72018, RD 3/4-64, Cl Sp 18-
            1115, MT G MTS 4008, Bert Schall. 71003
            Vi LPC-101 (Edited) TCF Arg FE 4160, WRC
            T./ST. 252, TCF Au TL 31128, TCF Au TL
            31590
(3:42) People Like You And Me (arr GW or JG-2
          scores available)-voc Marion Hutton,
          Ray Eberle, Tex Beneke and The
          Modernaires
          From the 20th Century-Fox film
          "Orchestra Wives"
          (Mack Gordon-Harry Warren)
          Tpt, Best; p, MacGregor

(Film continued on next page)

J8OP 9905   TCF TCF-100-2, Film, Emb EMB 3318, Emb EMB 4526,
TR 45-JAR 114, TR 78-JAR 114, TR RX 3004,
TCF 7" 45, TCF TFM 3159/TFS 4159, MTM
71018/MTS 72018, TCF 45-122, TCF F 3020,
TCF G LP 60004, MT G MTS 4008, Ar 31052,
Bert. Schall. 71003, Cl Sp 18-1115, TCF Arg
FE-4159, WRC TP/STP 223, TCF Au TL 31127
(2:31) Boom Shot (arr GW)
        (Glenn Miller-Arletta May)
        Tpt, Best; muted tpt, May; as, Caceres;
        tbn, Miller

J8OP 9907   TCF TCF-100-2. Film, TCF TCF-150, Emb EMB 3324, Emb
EMB 4511, MTM 1003/MTS 2003, MTM 71003/MTS
72003, TR 35/023, TCF F 3021, TCF TFM 3160/
TFS 4160, MT G MTS 4004, TCF TCF-129, Cl
Sp 18-1114, Bert. Schall. 71003, TCF Arg FE-
4160, WRC T./ST. 252, TCF Au TL 31128, TCF
Au TL 31590
(4:21) At Last (arr JG & BF)-voc Pat Friday and
      Ray Eberle
        From the 20th Century-Fox film
        "Orchestra Wives"
        (Mack Gordon-Harry Warren)
        Tpt, Best

E4VL 5047   Vi LPT-3065, Film Vi EPBT-3065 (947-0203), Emb
EMB 3318, Emb EMB 4500, MTM 1003/MTS 2003,
WRC T.223, HMV DLP 1059, TCF TCF-100-2, TCF
F 1001, TCF F 3021, MTM 71003/MTS 72003,
TR 35/023, MT G MTS 4004, TCF G LP 60004,
Ar 31052, Cl Sp 18-1114, Bert. Schall.
71003, TCF Arg FE 4160, TCF TFM 3160/TFS
4160, RD 3/4-64, WRC T./ST. 252, TCF Au TL
31128, TCF Au TL 31590
(3:36) American Patrol (arr JG)
      (F.W. Meacham)
        D, Purtill; tpt, May

E4VL 5048   Vi LPT-3065, Film, Vi EPBT-3065 (947-0204), Emb
EMB 3318, Emb EMB 4525, HMV DLP 1059, MTM
1003/MTS 2003, MTM 71003/MTS 72003, TR JKR
8019, TR RX 3004, TCF TCF-100-2, TCF TFM
3159/TFS 4159, TCF F 1001, TCF F 3020,
RD 3/4-64, MT G MTS 4004, Bert. Schall.
71003, TCF TCF-135, TCF Arg FE-4159, Cl Sp
18-1114, WRC TP/STP 223, TCF Au TL 31127
(2:47) Bugle Call Rag (arr GM)
      (Jack Pettis-Billy Meyers-Elmer
      Schoebel)
        D, Purtill; tbn, Miller; ts, Beneke;
        clt, Caceres; tbn, Miller; ts, Beneke,
        d, Purtill

(Film continued on next page)

E4VL 5047   Vi LPT-3065, Film, Vi EPBT-3065 (947-0203),
                 Emb EMB 3318, Emb EMB 4525, HMV DLP 1059,
                 MTM 1003/MTS 2003, MTM 71003/MTS 72003,
                 TR TR 5003, TR RX 3004, TCF TCF-150, TCF
                 TCF-100-2, RCF F 1001, TCF F 3020, TCF
                 TFM 3159/TFS 4159, RD 3/4-64, MT G MTS
                 4004, Bert. Schall. 71003, Cl Sp 18-1114,
                 TCF TCF-131/132, TCF Arg FE 4159, WRC TP/
                 STP 223, TCF Au TL 31127
         (5:47) Serenade In Blue (arr BM & BF)-voc Pat
                 Friday, Ray Eberle and The Modernaires
                 From the 20th Century-Fox film
                 "Orchestra Wives"
                 (Mack Gordon-Harry Warren)
                 Cnt, Hackett; ts, Beneke

E4VL 5048   Vi LPT-3065, Film, Vi EPBT-3065 (947-0204), Emb.
                 EMB 3324, Emb EMB 4511, MTM 1003/MTS 2003,
                 HMV DLP 1059, RCA RD 27068, MTM 71003/MTS
                 72003, TR 35/023, TCF TCF-150, TCF TCF-
                 100-2, Vi PR-114, Vi LPM/LSP-1192, TCF
                 TCF-137/138, TCF F 1001, TCF F 3021, TCF
                 TFM 3160/TFS 4160, RCA It LPM 10011, RCA
                 It LJ 50012, RD 3/4-64, RCA F 530243, RCA
                 G LPM/LSP-1192, RCA G EPC-1192, TCF G LP
                 60004, MT G MTS 4004, Ar 31052, Bert.
                 Schall. 71003, Cl Sp 18-1114, TCF Arg FE-
                 4160, TCF TCF-136, Vi Arg LPM/LSP-1192,
                 WRC T./ST. 252, TCF Au TL 31128, TCF Au
                 TL 31590, RCA F 740.515
         (8:52) (I've Got A Gal In) Kalamazoo (arr JG)-
                 voc Marion Hutton, Tex Beneke, The
                 Modernaires and The Nicholas Brothers
                 From the 20th Century-Fox film
                 "Orchestra Wives"
                 (Mack Gordon-Harry Warren)
                 Muted tpt, May; ts, Beneke; d, Purtill

         Film, TCF TCF-150
         (1:09) (I've Got A Gal In) Kalamazoo (arr JG)
                 From the 20th Century-Fox film
                 "Orchestra Wives"
                 (Mack Gordon-Harry Warren)
                 D, Purtill (No vocal--wind-up to film)

         The remaining tunes were not featured in the film
         although it has been rumored that "Moonlight
         Sonata" and "That's Sabotage" were shown in some
         countries, including Canada, but this has never
         been verified.

(Film continued on next page)

E4VL 5047   Vi LPT-3065, Vi EPBT-3065 (947-0204), Emb EMB
3324, Emb EMB 4512, HMV DLP 1059, TCF TCF-
100-2, TCF TFM 3160/TFS 4160, MTM 71018/
MTS 72018, TCF F 3021, TR 35/023, MT G MTS
4008, Cl Sp 18-1115, Bert. Schall. 71003,
TCF TCF-128, TCF Arg FE-4160, WRC T./ST.
252, TCF Au TL 31128, TCF Au TL 31590
(2:37) That's Sabotage-voc Marion Hutton
           From the 20th Century-Fox film
           "Orchestra Wives"
           (Mack Gordon-Harry Warren)
           Ts, Klink

E4VL 5047   Vi LPT-3065, Vi EPBT-3065 (947-0203), Emb EMB
3324, Emb EMB 4512, HMV DLP 1059, MTM 1003/
MTS 2003, TCF TCF-100-2, Vi LPM-1189, Vi
EPB-1189 (547-0799), MTM 71003/MTS 72003,
TR RX 3004, TCF TFM 3159/TFS 4159, TCF F
3020,RD 3/4-64, TCF G LP 60004, MT G MTS
4004, Vi 447-0444, Cl Sp 18-1114, RCA G
EPC-1189, Ar 31052, Bert. Schall. 71003,
RCA F 430228, Vi EPA-5133, TCF Arg FE-4159
RCA Au EPA-5133, TCF Au TL 31127, RCA Au
L 11021, WRC TP/STP 223
(3:47) Moonlight Sonata (arr BF)
           (Ludwig Beethoven)
           P, MacGregor; ts, Beneke; p, MacGregor

J80P 9906   TCF TCF-100-2, Emb EMB 3324, Emb EMB 4511, TR 45-
JAR 114, TR 78-JAR 114, TR RX 3004, MTM
71018/MTS 72018, TCF F 3020, TCF TFM 3159/
TFS 4159, TCF 7" 45, TCF 45-122, MT G MTS
4008, WRC TP/STP 223, Bert. Schall. 71003,
Cl Sp 18-1115, TCF Arg FE-4159, TCF Au TL
31127
(2:24) You Say The Sweetest Things, Baby
           From the 20th Century-Fox film "Tin
           Pan Alley"
           (Mack Gordon-Harry Warren)
           Tpt, May; clt, ??; ts, Beneke; tpt,
           May
           By sextet from the band

Now, just a note on some of the edited differences
between the film and the commercial releases:
"Boom Shot" on the film has the opening trumpet
solo by Best edited out. The film version of "At
Last" is slightly longer than the commercial releases as these latter issues have had a muted
trombone passage edited out just before the vocal.
"American Patrol" is only heard in part in the film.

(Continued on next page)

The long introduction to "Serenade In Blue" and
the Ray Eberle vocal are not heard in the film
version. "Kalamazoo" is slightly edited in the
film in that some of the music before and after
the vocal is omitted. However, there is a short
drum solo heard on the film version to introduce
the tune that is not on the commercial issues.
The TCF-100-2 issue and other British issues do
not have the tap dance vocal and are, therefore,
shorter versions. You can hear Miller counting
time on the Victor issues of "Kalamazoo" just
before the tune gets going.

The release date for "Orchestra Wives" was
September 4th, 1942. (BB, Aug. 29, 1942)

While the band was in Hollywood making this film
many of the Chesterfield broadcasts were done
from the Sound Stage.

25 March, 1942 (WED): Hollywood, California (CHESTERFIELD SHOW)
CBS 10:00-10:15 P.M.

The announcer for this program is Don Wilson.

> *Moonlight Serenade* (Theme)
> *A String Of Pearls*
> *Chattanooga Choo Choo*
> *When The Roses Bloom Again*

E2VL 4419   Vi LPT-30, Vi 42-0152 (Vi PT-39), Vi 27-0152
(Vi WPT-39), Vi EPBT-3026 (947-0026),
Vi EPA-726, Vi LPT 6701, Vi EPOT 6701
(947-0183), Vi LPM-1189, E1 WDLP 1012,
Vi EPB-1189 (547-0799), HMV RLS 598, HMV
DLP 1012, HMVAus GA-5113, RCA G LSP-9901,
RCA G EPBT-3026, RCA G EPOT-6701, RCA G
EPC-1189, RCA G SRS 560, RCA F 430228,
RCA Au L 11021, HMVAu ODLP 1012, RCA G
LPT-30

(1:55) Anchors Aweigh
(Alfred H. Miles-R. Lovell-Charles A.
Zimmerman)
D, Purtill; clt, Caceres; muted tpt,
May

> *Slumber Song* (Theme)

Glenn Miller announced on this program that the
band started work on the film "Orchestra Wives"
this day. According to G.M.P.R. the band began
work on the 22nd (which is a Sunday) and G.M.D.
stated that the band began work on the 23rd

(Continued on next page)

(which is a Monday). We've decided to accept
March 23rd as being the first day of work on the
film due to the fact that the contract that was
drawn up between the Miller Orchestra and 20th
Century-Fox stated that the band would start
work on the 23rd.

*26 March, 1942 (THUR): Hollywood, California (CHESTERFIELD SHOW)
CBS 10:00-10:15 P.M.*

> *Moonlight Serenade (Theme)*
> *Don't Sit Under The Apple Tree*
> *MEDLEY:*
>> *Peg O' My Heart*
>> *Fooled*
>> *Mood Indigo*
>> *Blue Orchids*
> *Keep 'Em Flying*
> *Slumber Song (Theme)*

*27 March, 1942 (FRI): Hollywood California (CHESTERFIELD SHOW)
CBS 10:00-10:15 P.M.*

> *The announcer for this program is Don Wilson.*

>> *Moonlight Serenade (Theme)*
>> *When Johnny Comes Marching Home*
>> *Moonlight Cocktail*
>> *American Patrol*
>> *Slumber Song (Theme)*

A close listening to this version of "American
Patrol" indicates that a slightly different
chart was used and this is most evident in the
"middle" of the tune.

*28 March, 1942 (SAT): Hollywood, California (SUNSET SERENADE)
Mutual*

Early April, 1942

"Glenn Miller's Sunset Serenade was ordered
off the air indefinitely along with all remote
broadcasts on Mutual as the result of a union
controversy with stations in Louisville and
Nashville.
The Miller Sunset Serenade program, an hour
show on Saturday afternoons, has been presented

(Continued on next page)

at Miller's own expense for the benefit of
soldiers in Army camps. The bandleader paid his
orchestra men out of his own pocket for their
services.
     When the ARM edict cancelling all remote
broadcasts from the Mutual net came through it
was interpreted as including Miller's show, even
though he presented it in the studio of the local
Mutual outlet, KHJ." (DB, April 15, 1942)

Although the "Sunset Serenades" were cancelled
Miller continued to give away radios and records
to the camps now on the Chesterfield show.

According to the Glenn Miller files the "Sunset
Serenades" were broadcast until May 30th so that
the above mentioned "order" may not have become
effective until May 30th.

1 April, 1942 (WED)

     "Glenn Miller's cigaret show has been re-
newed for another 13 weeks, bringing it up to
June 29. Now heard Wednesdays, Thursdays and
Fridays, the sponsor is endeavoring to change the
time (on CBS) to two 30-minute programs a week.
Miller went on the program in December, 1939, and
has held the job without a miss ever since."
(M & R, May, 1942)

*1 April, 1942 (WED): Hollywood, California (CHESTERFIELD SHOW)
             CBS 10:00-10:15 P.M.*

The announcer for this program is Don Wilson.

          Moonlight Serenade (Theme)
          Adios
          Deep In The Heart Of Texas
          I Don't Want To Walk Without You
          Quartermasters Song (arr JG)-voc TB & 4M
               (Edward Fox-Major D.G. Paston-LC. H.
               Orenstein)
               D, Purtill
          Slumber Song (Theme)

Glenn Miller announced the last tune as "We're
The Gang That Keeps Things Moving" but it is
properly known as the "Quartermasters Song".
This tune was dedicated to (it is also the
official song of) the US Quartermaster's Corps.

2 April, 1942 (THUR): Victor Studios, Hollywood, California

Same personnel as for March 19th broadcast.

072230-1   Vi 27873-A, HMV BD 5789, HMV BD 5942, HMV MH 57,
AFRS P-1542, HMVAu EA-3253, HMVSw JK-2433,
Vi 20-1564 (Vi P-148), Vi 47-2852 (Vi WP-
148), Vi EPA-148, Vi EPA-5081, RCA RCX
1035, RCA 1096 (78), RCA 1096 (45), HMV
DLP 1021, HMV DLP 1024, Vi LPM-31, Vi SP
33-90. Vi LPM/LSP-3564, El G EG 7465, RCA
It LPM 60001, RCA It EPA 30-153, AFRS P-
NAV-2, HMVAus GA-5070, El 7MW 644, HMVAus
VDLP 302, El WDLP 1021, RCA Int. 20003,
RCA G EPA-148, El WDLP 1024, AFRS P-9980,
Vi 7" LP, AFRS "Jukebox USA" 207, AFRS
"Jukebox USA" 276, HMVHu HUC 131, HMVHu
HUC 113, Vi TP3-5044, Vi P8S-5061, RCA F
85243, HMVIr I.M. 1189, HMVIr I.M. 1023,
VdP HN 2253, VdP 7EPQ 541, AFRS H-62-43,
Vi Arg LPM-3564, Vi VPM-6019, RCA Br.
GM-1, HMV F BD 5942, AFRS G.I. Jive Series
H-12: 965, 818, 868, 995, 1069, 1148. 1186,
1307, 1396, 1479, 1518, 1553, 1589, 1745,
1809, 1854, RCA Br. RD-8094, RCA Au VPM-
6019, RCA Au 20020, Fe Au MX-10584, AFRS
Jill's Juke Box Series H-46: 63, 114, 129,
193
American Patrol (arr JG)
      (F.W. Meacham)
      D, Purtill; tpt, May

072231-1   Vi 27873-B, HMVAu EA-3175
Soldier, Let Me Read Your Letter (arr BM)-voc
      Ray Eberle and The Modernaires
      (Pvt. Pat Fallon-Pvt. Tim Pasma-Sidney
      Lippman)

072232-1   Vi 27879-B, HMV BD 5779, HMV MH 127, Cam Cas-2267,
      RCA G Cas-2267
Sleep Song (arr GW)-voc Ray Eberle and The
      Modernaires
      (Henry Tobias-Don Reid)

072233-1   Vi 27879-A, HMV BD 5779, HMV MH 127, HMVAu EA-
3177, Vi LPT 6700, Vi EPNT 6700 (947-
0119), HMV RLS 599, Vi SPD-18 (599-9108),
El G EG 7647, RCA G LPT 6700
Sweet Eloise (arr JG)-voc Ray Eberle and The
      Modernaires
      (Mack David-Russ Morgan)
      Cnt, Hackett

All tunes 1 take. (RCA Victor)
This session lasted from 8:00 A.M. to 12:30 P.M.
(RCA Victor)

2 April, 1942 (THUR): Hollywood, California (CHESTERFIELD SHOW)
CBS   10:00-10:15 P.M.

> *The announcer for this program is Don Wilson.*

> > *Moonlight Serenade (Theme)*
> > *Papa Niccolini*
> > *MEDLEY:*
> > > *To You*
> > > *Moonlight Cocktail-voc RE & 4M*
> > > *The Story Of A Starry Night*
> > > *Rhapsody In Blue*
> > *On Brave Old Army Team*
> > *Slumber Song (Theme)*

3 April, 1942 (FRI): Hollywood, California (CHESTERFIELD SHOW)
CBS   10:00-10:15 P.M.

> *The announcer for this program is Don Wilson.*

> > *Moonlight Serenade (Theme)*
> > *Take The "A" Train*
> > *On The Old Assembly Line*
> > *She'll Always Remember*
> > *Sun Valley Jump*
> > *Slumber Song (Theme)*

4 April, 1942 (SAT): Hollywood, California (SUNSET SERENADE)
Mutual

5 April, 1942 (SUN)

> G.M.P.R. for the week ending April 5th show that
> Billy May got paid for arranging "Soldier, Let
> Me Read Your Letter"; that Cecil Stover got paid
> for copying arrangement (arranger unknown) "Texas
> After Taps" and that Arthur Schutt got paid for
> an arrangement (tune unknown).

8 April, 1942 (WED): Hollywood, California (CHESTERFIELD SHOW)
CBS   10:00-10:15 P.M.

> *The announcer for this program is Don Wilson.*

> > *Moonlight Serenade (Theme)*

(Broadcast continued on next page)

[436]

E4VP 8209   Vi LPT 6701, Vi EPOT 6701 (947-0182), HMV RLS 598,
             RCA G EPOT-6701
             (3:00) Let's Have Another Cup O' Coffee (arr JG)-
                         voc Marion Hutton, Ernie Caceres and
                         The Modernaires
                         From the musical production "Face The
                         Music"
                         (Irving Berlin)

                    Sweet Eloise-voc RE & 4M
                    American Patrol
                    Slumber Song (Theme)

             On Vi LPT 6701 "Let's Have Another Cup O' Coffee"
             was incorrectly listed as being broadcast on
             August 25, 1942.

9 April, 1942 (THUR): Hollywood, California (CHESTERFIELD SHOW)
             CBS   10:00-10:15 P.M.

                    Moonlight Serenade (Theme)

V-4086 WR-962 GMMS 14/62, GMMS 42/90, AFRS P-2238
               (3:13) Sunrise Serenade
                         (Frankie Carle)
                         Ts, Beneke

                    Shhh, It's A Military Secret

V-4086 WR-962 GMMS 14/62, GMMS 45/93, AFRS P-2252
      Int GM   (1:56) The Story Of A Starry Night (arr BF)-voc
                         Ray Eberle
                         Adapted from Tschaikowsky's
                         "Pathetique Symphony"
                         (Al Hoffman-Mann Curtis-Jerry
                         Livingston)

V-4086 WR-962 GMMS 14/62
               (2:16) In The Mood
                         (Andy Razaf-Joe Garland)
                         Ts, Beneke; ts, Klink; tpt, May
                         (Two endings)

                    Slumber Song (Theme)

10 April, 1942 (FRI): Hollywood, California (CHESTERFIELD SHOW)
             CBS   10:00-10:15 P.M.

                    Moonlight Serenade (Theme)
                    Papa Niccolini

(Broadcast continued on next page)

```
                    MEDLEY:
E3VP 8208    Vi LPT 6701, Vi EPOT 6701 (947-0181), HMV RLS 598,
                    RCA G EPOT-6701
             (1:35)  How Deep Is The Ocean? (arr JG)
                       (Irving Berlin)
                    Ts, Beneke; muted tpt, McMickle

                    Always In My Heart
                    It's A Wonderful World
                    My Blue Heaven

E3VP 5243    Vi LPT 6700, Vi EPNT 6700 (947-0121), HMV RLS 599,
                    Vi SPD-18 (599-9106), RCA G LPT 6700
             (2:36)  The Hop (arr JG)
                       (Ray Conniff)
                    Tpt, May; clt, Caceres; ts, Beneke;
                    tpt, May

                    Slumber Song (Theme)
```

The last three tunes in this medley were not
issued on any of the commercial issues shown above.

11 April, 1942 (SAT): Hollywood, California (SUNSET SERENADE)
Mutual

On The Old Assembly Line
Tschaikowsky's Piano Concerto
When Johnny Comes Marching Home
Always In My Heart
Dear Mom

15 April, 1942 (WED)

Glenn Miller and His Orchestra drew 7,300 people
at the Hollywood Palladium, for the first military
ball in twenty years. Stacked with movie stars,
the ball was a benefit for an Army hospital.
(DB, May 15, 1942; G.M.P.R.)
Apparently this was Miller's only appearance at
the Hollywood Palladium during this trip to the
coast as "Palladium and Glenn Miller couldn't get
together on dates and dough so Miller will not
play the big Sunset Blvd. dine and dancer on this
trip." (DB, May 15, 1942)

15 April, 1942 (WED): Hollywood, California (CHESTERFIELD SHOW)
CBS   10:00-10:15 P.M.

The announcer for this program is Don Wilson.

(Broadcast continued on next page)

Moonlight Serenade (Theme)
Star Dust
Happy In Love
Soldier, Let Me Read Your Letter
Here We Go Again
Slumber Song (Theme)

16 April, 1942 (THUR): Hollywood, California (CHESTERFIELD SHOW)
CBS   10:00-10:15 P.M.

Moonlight Serenade (Theme)
Papa Niccolini
MEDLEY:
The Touch Of Your Hand
To The Shores Of Tripoli (Marine Hymn)
Blue Danube
The Nickel Serenade
Slumber Song (Theme)

The information pertaining to this program appears
to be mixed up. Possibly the opening tune was
"The Nickel Serenade", followed by the medley (with
the new tune being "Papa Niccolini" and the
borrowed tune being "The Waltz You Saved For Me" as
per June 19, 1940 medley) and then the final tune
in the program would be "To The Shores Of Tripoli"
(see January 28, 1942 program).

17 April, 1942 (FRI): Hollywood, California (CHESTERFIELD SHOW)
CBS   10:00-10:15 P.M.

Moonlight Serenade (Theme)
Little Brown Jug
Skylark
Deep In The Heart Of Texas
Introduction To A Waltz
Slumber Song (Theme)

18 April, 1942 (SAT): Hollywood, California (SUNSET SERENADE)
Mutual

19 April, 1942 (SUN)

G.M.P.R. for the week ending April 19th show that
Billy May got paid for arranging a Medley insert
(tunes not stated); and that Clyde Balsley got
paid for copying arrangements (George Williams)
of "Just Plain Lonesome" and an original (tune
not stated) by George Williams.

22 April, 1942 (WED): Hollywood, California (CHESTERFIELD SHOW)
CBS   10:00-10:15 P.M.

Moonlight Serenade (Theme)
Moonlight Serenade
On The Old Assembly Line
I Don't Want To Walk Without You
Keep 'Em Flying
Slumber Song (Theme)

23 April, 1942 (THUR): Hollywood, California (CHESTERFIELD SHOW)
CBS   10:00-10:15 P.M.

The announcer for this program is Don Wilson.

Moonlight Serenade (Theme)

E4VP 8207   Vi LPT 6701, Vi EPOT 6701 (947-0187), Vi SPA-7-4,
              HMV RLS 598, RCA G EPOT 6701
     (2:36) Deep In The Heart Of Texas (arr JG)-voc
              Marion Hutton, Tex Beneke and The
              Modernaires
              (June Hershey-Don Swandler)
              Ts, Beneke

Sweet Eloise-voc RE & 4M

E3VP 5239   Vi LPT 6700, Vi EPNT 6700 (947-0124), HMV RLS 599,
              Vi SPD-18 (599-9110), Vi LPT-3057, RCA RD
              27068, Vi EPBT-3057 (947-0136), Vi LPM/LSP-
              1192, Vi EPB-1192 (547-0809), Vi 45 Special-
              1953, RCA It LPM 10011, USA RS HO7H-1761,
              Vi EPBT-1192, RCA G LPM 9801, RCA G LPT 6700,
              RCA G EPC-1192, RCA G LPM/LSP-1192, RCA G
              LSP-9901, RCA It LJ 50012, RCA F 230201,
              RCA F 530243, Vi 420-0033, Vi 447-0033, RCA
              G 447-0033, Vi Arg LPM/LSP-1192, RCA G SRS
              560, RCA F 740.515
     (3:39) American Patrol (arr JG)
              (F.W. Meacham)
              D, Purtill; tpt, May

Slumber Song (Theme)

On Vi LPT 6701 "Deep In The Heart Of Texas" was
incorrectly listed as being broadcast on May 18,
1942.

24 April, 1942 (FRI): Hollywood, California (CHESTERFIELD SHOW)
                      CBS 10:00-10:15 P.M.

            The announcer for this program is Don Wilson.

                    Moonlight Serenade (Theme)
                    Don't Sit Under The Apple Tree
                    MEDLEY:
                        My Reverie
                        Soldier, Let Me Read Your Letter
                        Snowfall
                        Blue Champagne
                    Quartermasters Song-voc TB & 4M
                    Slumber Song (Theme)

25 April, 1942 (SAT): Hollywood, California (SUNSET SERENADE)
                      Mutual

29 April, 1942 (WED): Hollywood, California (CHESTERFIELD SHOW)
                      CBS 10:00-10:15 P.M.

            The announcer for this program is Don Wilson.

                    Moonlight Serenade (Theme)
                    Shhh, It's A Military Secret

        At this point in the program the Hollywood Editor
        of Radio Mirror Magazine, Elaine Osterman, pre-
        sented Glenn with the original copy of a photo
        that appeared in the June, 1942 issue and, an
        engraved cigaret case. Radio Mirror Magazine,
        June, 1942 issue named Glenn Miller as America's
        favorite dance band.

                    Sweet Eloise-voc RE & 4M
                    By The Waters Of Minnetonka
                    Slumber Song (Theme)

30 April, 1942 (THUR): Hollywood, California (CHESTERFIELD SHOW)
                       CBS 10:00-10:15 P.M.

            The announcer for this program is Don Wilson.

                    Moonlight Serenade (Theme)
                    Jeep Jockey Jump (arr JG)
                        (Jerry Gray)
                    Always In My Heart-voc RE
                    Dear Arabella-voc MH, TB & 4M
                    Everybody Loves My Baby
                    Slumber Song (Theme)

1 May, 1942 (FRI): Hollywood, California (CHESTERFIELD SHOW)
                    CBS 10:00-10:15 P.M.

    The announcer for this program is Don Wilson.

> *Moonlight Serenade (Theme)*
> *Chattanooga Choo Choo*
> *Sleep Song*
> *American Patrol*
> *Slumber Song (Theme)*

    "Starting May 5, Glenn Miller's <u>Moonlight Serenade</u> on CBS will jump down from 10 P.M. Tuesdays through Thursdays to 7:15." (DB, May 1, 1942) Not only was there a time change but the band reverted back to its old Tuesdays, Wednesdays, and Thursdays schedule.

1 May, 1942 (FRI)

    Glenn Miller and His Orchestra played for the University of Southern California Prom at the "Cocoanut Grove" in the Ambassador Hotel, Los Angeles, California. (G.M.D. & G.M.P.R.)

April-May 1942: Hollywood, California

    The announcer for this program is Edward G. Robinson.

> *(0:17) Moonlight Serenade (Theme)*
>   *(Mitchell Parish-Glenn Miller)*
> *Int GM (3:15) A String Of Pearls (arr JG)*
>   *(Jerry Gray)*
>   *As, Caceres; two bar alto sax exchanges between Caceres and Martin; followed by another challenge on tenors between Klink and Beneke; cnt, Hackett; p, MacGregor*

> *(0:26) American Patrol (arr JG)*
>   *(F.W. Meacham)*

2 May, 1942 (SAT): Hollywood, California (SUNSET SERENADE)
                    Mutual

3 May, 1942 (SUN)

        G.M.P.R. for the week ending May 3rd show that
        Billy May got paid for arranging an "original"
        (tune not stated).

5 May, 1942 (TUES): Hollywood, California (CHESTERFIELD SHOW)
        CBS 7:15-7:30 P.M.

        Moonlight Serenade (Theme)
        A String Of Pearls
        The Lamplighter's Serenade
        Happy In Love
        V For Victory Hop
        Slumber Song (Theme)

        "Four stations have been added to the Glenn
Miller program on Columbia, effective Tuesday (5).
Stations added are WCAX, Burlington, Vt.; WKNE,
Keene, N.H.; WKBN, Youngstown, and KROD, El Paso.
Total hook-up is 101 stations. Newell-Emmett
handles the program for Chesterfield." (BB, May 9,
1942)

6 May, 1942 (WED): Hollywood, California (CHESTERFIELD SHOW)
        CBS 7:15-7:30 P.M.

        Moonlight Serenade (Theme)
        Goin' Home
        When Johnny Comes Marching Home
        Moonlight Cocktail
        Introduction To A Waltz
        Slumber Song (Theme)

7 May, 1942 (THUR): Hollywood, California (CHESTERFIELD SHOW)
        CBS 7:15-7:30 P.M.

        The announcer for this program is Don Wilson.

        Moonlight Serenade (Theme)
        Chip Off The Old Block
        She'll Always Remember

E3VP 5243   Vi LPT 6700, Vi EPNT 6700 (947-0123), Vi SPD-18
        (599-9109), HMV RLS 599, Vi 45 Special-
        1953, Vi PR-114, RCA G LPT 6700
        (2:04) Don't Sit Under The Apple Tree (With Anyone
                Else But Me)-voc Marion Hutton, Tex
                Beneke and The Modernaires
                (Lew Brown-Charlie Tobias-Sammy Stept)

(Broadcast continued on next page)

On Brave Old Army Team
Slumber Song (Theme)

9 May, 1942 (SAT): Hollywood, California (SUNSET SERENADE)
Mutual

I Don't Want To Walk Without You
Blues In The Night
Deep In The Heart Of Texas
The Story Of A Starry Night

10 May, 1942 (SUN)

G.M.P.R. for the week ending May 10th show that
Jerry Gray arranged a medley (tunes not stated).

12 May, 1942 (TUES): Hollywood, California (CHESTERFIELD SHOW)
CBS   7:15-7:30 P.M.

The announcer for this program is Don Wilson.

Moonlight Serenade (Theme)
Star Dust
Deep In The Heart Of Texas
Skylark
Keep 'Em Flying
Slumber Song (Theme)

13 May, 1942 (WED): Hollywood, California (CHESTERFIELD SHOW)
CBS   7:15-7:30 P.M.

The announcer for this program is Don Wilson.

Moonlight Serenade (Theme)
The Lamplighter's Serenade
Happy In Love
Angels Of Mercy
American Patrol
Slumber Song (Theme)

14 May, 1942 (THUR): Hollywood, California (CHESTERFIELD SHOW)
CBS   7:15-7:30 P.M.

Moonlight Serenade (Theme)

Shhh, It's A Military Secret
I Don't Want To Walk Without You

(Broadcast continued on next page)

Slumber Song (Theme)

Information on two of the tunes is missing.

16 May, 1942 (SAT): *Hollywood, California (SUNSET SERENADE)*
Mutual WRUL

    I Don't Want To Walk Without You
    Sweet Eloise
    In The Mood

16 May, 1942 (SAT)

    Glenn Miller and His Orchestra played a one-
    nighter at the Long Beach Civic Auditorium, Long
    Beach, California, from 10:00-1:30 A.M. (G.M.P.R.)

17 May, 1942 (SUN)

    G.M.P.R. for the week ending May 17th show that
    Billy May was paid for arranging an "original"
    (tune not stated); and Cecil Stover was paid for
    copying arrangements (arranger unknown) of "My
    Ideal" and "Something To Remember You By".

19 May, 1942 (TUES): *Hollywood, California (CHESTERFIELD SHOW)*
CBS 7:15-7:30 P.M.

    Moonlight Serenade (Theme)
    Georgia On My Mind
    Don't Sit Under The Apple Tree
    Sweet Eloise
    Introduction To A Waltz
    Slumber Song (Theme)

20 May, 1942 (WED): Victor Studios, Hollywood, California

    Same personnel as for March 19th broadcast.

072283-1   Vi 27934-A, HMV BD 5808, HMVAu EA-3171, HMVF
    7EMF11, HMVSw JK-2422, Vi 42-0026, Vi 420-
    0039, Vi 447-0039, Vi 27-0026, Vi EPAT-401,
    Vi EPA-530, Vi EPA-5081, RCA RCX 1035, Vi
    LPT-1016, Vi LPM 3183, El G EG 7819, Vi
    LPM/LSP-3564, AFRS "America's Pop Music" 67,
    RCA Int. CT20126, RCA Int. 11002, RCA G
    447-0039, RCA G EPAT-401, Vi TP3-5044,

(Session continued on next page)

Vi P8S-5061, Vi P8S-1253, HMVIn NE. 650,
Vi Arg LPM-3564, RCA Vi Arg 3AE-3342,
AFRS G.I. Jive Series H-12: 916, 805, 855,
1168, 1181, 1307, 1361, 1406, 1421, 1586,
1603, 1807, RCA Br. RD-8094, RCA Au VPM-
6019, AFRS Jill's Juke Box Series H-46:
67, 71, 153, 169, RCA Br. GM-1, Vi VPM-6019
(I've Got A Gal In) Kalamazoo (arr JG)-voc Tex Beneke,
Marion Hutton and The Modernaires
From the 20th Century-Fox film "Orchestra
Wives"
(Mack Gordon-Harry Warren)
Muted tpt, May; ts, Beneke

072284-1   Vi 27935-A, HMV BD 5808, HMVAu EA-3171, HMVSw JK-
                2329, HMVIn NE-651, Vi 20-2889, Vi 420-0037,
                Vi 447-0037, VdP AV-721, Vi EPAT-430, Vi
                EPA-727, Vi EPA-5049, Vi LPT-1016, Vi LPC-
                101, Vi LPM/LSP-3564, RD 3/4-25, Vi LPM-1190,
                Vi EPB-1190 (547-0829), RCA RCX 1024, RD Br.
                RDS 6096, RD Br. RDS 6174, AFRS P-1118,
                HMVAus GA-5013, HMVAus BA 764, RCA G LPT 1016,
                Vi P8S-5061, Vi TP3-5044, RCA G EPC-1190,
                RCA G LPM-1190, VdP 7EPQ 541, Vi DJ-338,
                RD 8-5013, AFRS G.I. Jive Series H-12: 1145,
                1659, 1897, 1880, 2027, 2172, 2177, 2345, 1968,
                AFRS Jill's Juke Box Series H-46: 34, 56, 176,
                228, Vi Arg LPM-3564, Vi VPM-6019, RCA Br.
                GM-1, RCA Au 20037, RCA Au VPM-6019, RCA Br.
                RD-8094, RCA G EPAT-430
                Serenade In Blue (arr BM & BF)-voc Ray Eberle and
                The Modernaires
                From the 20th Century-Fox film "Orchestra
                Wives"
                (Mack Gordon-Harry Warren)
                Cnt, Hackett

072285-1   Vi 27934-B, HMV BD 5811, HMVAu EA-3177, HMVSw JK-
                2329, Vi 42-0157, Vi 27-0157, Vi 420-0035,
                Vi 447-0035, Vi EPAT-429, Vi EPA-5103, VD 12,
                HMV DLP 1024, Vi LPT-1016, RD 3/4-21, RD R/
                SYM, RD Br. RDS 6175, El G EG 7747, RCA Int.
                11015, El WDLP 1024, Vi P8S-1432, HMVAus
                VDLP 302, RCA G EPAT-429. RCA G LPT 1016,
                HMVSc X7106, Vi LSP-4125, AFRS H-62-43, RCA
                F 130211, AFRS G.I. Jive Series H-12: No.
                1053, HMVIn NE. 650, VdP AV-691, VdP 7EPQ
                518, RCA Int. INTS 1002, AFRS G.I. Jive
                Series H-12: 540, 590, 707, 867, 980, 1030,
                1342, 1131, 1147, 1209, 1420, 1478, AFRS
                Jill's Juke Box Series H-46: 5, 35, 52, 95,
                Vi VPM-6019, RCA Br. RD-8094, RCA Au VPM-
                6019, RCA Br. GM-1, RCA Au-20020

(Session continued on next page)

At Last (arr JG & BF)-voc Ray Eberle
                From the 20th Century-Fox film "Orchestra
                Wives"
                (Mack Gordon-Harry Warren)

072286-1   Vi 27894-B, HMV DLP 1122, HMVIn NE. 669, HMVAu EA
                    3539
                Lullaby Of The Rain-voc Ray Eberle and The
                    Modernaires
                    (Barbs Furman-Lou Ricca)
                    G, Hackett

072287-1   Vi 27894-A, HMVIn NE. 669
                Knit One, Purl Two (arr JG)-voc Marion Hutton and
                    The Modernaires
                    (Flossy Frills and Ben Lorre)
                    (Edited by Glenn Miller)

                All tunes 1 take. (RCA Victor)
                This session lasted from 9:00 A.M. to 3:35 P.M.
                (RCA Victor)

                Although Jerry Gray is shown as the arranger on
                "Kalamazoo" it must be noted that this was for the
                band portion only and that for the vocal part Bill
                Conway arranged the harmony and Hal Dickinson
                arranged the verse.

                The long introduction to "Serenade In Blue" was
                arranged by Billy May while the rest of the tune
                was arranged by Bill Finegan.

                Flossy Frills, shown as one of the writers of "Knit
                One, Purl Two", was a fictional cartoon character
                that appeared in the Hearst chain of newspapers.
                Hearst, apparently on a patriotic kick, decided to
                have Flossy Frills ask Glenn Miller to help her
                write a tune and, therefore, her name is included
                on the label as being a composer. Ben Lorre is
                probably the only writer on this tune.

20 May, 1942 (WED): Hollywood, California (CHESTERFIELD SHOW)
*   CBS 7:15-7:30 P.M.*

                Moonlight Serenade (Theme)
                On The Old Assembly Line
                MEDLEY:
                    The Touch Of Your Hand
                    Papa Niccolini
                    The Waltz You Saved For Me
                    Blue Danube

(Broadcast continued on next page)

Bugle Call Rag
Slumber Song (Theme)

20 May, 1942 (WED)

Glenn Miller threw a party at the Beverly Wilshire Hotel, Hollywood, California. The California Rhythm Rascals Orchestra performed. 235 buffet suppers were ordered. (G.M.P.R.)

21 May, 1942 (THUR): *Hollywood California (CHESTERFIELD SHOW)* *CBS 7:15-7:30 P.M.*

The announcer for this program is Don Wilson.

Moonlight Serenade (Theme)
The Story Of A Starry Night

The Lamplighter's Serenade

Slumber Song (Theme)

Information on two of the tunes is missing.

This is the same instrumental version of "The Story Of A Starry Night" that was played on the December 23, 1941 program.

"Moonlight Serenade, the Glenn Miller broadcast, winds up its Hollywood stay May 21. Miller takes off for Chicago for a three-week stand." (BB, May 23, 1942)

22 May, 1942 (FRI): 20th Century-Fox Studios, Hollywood, California

According to G.M.D. the band wound up its work on the 20th Century-Fox film "Orchestra Wives" on this date. G.M.P.R. differs slightly in that it states that the band wound up its work on May 23rd but the contract between the Miller Orchestra and 20th Century-Fox stated that the band would wind up its work on the film on May 22nd.

23 May, 1942 (SAT): *Hollywood, California (SUNSET SERENADE)* *Mutual WRUL*

Boulder Buff
Skylark
A String Of Pearls

(Continued on next page)

After this broadcast the band took the Union
Pacific RR from Los Angeles to Chicago. (G.M.P.R.)
G.M.D. states that the band spent three days (May
23rd, 24th and 25th) travelling from Hollywood to
Chicago.

26 May, 1942 (TUES): Great Lakes Naval Training Station, Illinois
(CHESTERFIELD SHOW)
CBS 7:15-7:30 P.M.

The announcer for this program is Larry Bruff.

> *Moonlight Serenade (Theme)*
> *Deep In The Heart Of Texas-voc MH, TB & 4M*
> *Lullaby Of The Rain-voc RE & 4M*

V-4086 WR-965   GMMS 17/65, GMMS 46/94, AFRS P-2239, Vi LPT 6700,
Vi PR-112, Vi EPNT 6700 (947-0129), Vi SPD-
18 (599-9111), Vi LPT-3057, Vi EPBT-3057
(947-0137), Vi EPA-733, Vi LPM/LSP-1192,
Vi EPB-1192 (547-0810), Vi EPBT-1192, HMV
RLS 599, RCA RD 27068, El G EG 8048, RCA It
LPM 10011, RCA It LJ 50012, Vi 45 Special-
1953, RCA G LPM 9801, RCA G EPC-1192, El
7MW 648, RCA G LPT 6700, RCA G LSP-9901,
RCA G LPM/LSP-1192, RCA F 230201, RCA F
530243, RCA Vi Arg 3AE-3286, Vi Arg LPM/LSP-
1192, RCA G SRS 560, RCA F 740.515, Vi
Promotion Disc 10" 78 (E3-CB-3369)
(3:11) A String Of Pearls (arr JG)
(Jerry Gray)
As, Caceres; two bar alto sax exchanges
between Caceres and Martin; followed by
another challenge on tenors between
Klink and Beneke; cnt, Hackett;
p, MacGregor

> *Anchors Aweigh*
> *Slumber Song (Theme)*

On Vi LPT 6700 "A String Of Pearls" was incorrectly
listed as being broadcast on May 5, 1942.

Note: Immediately preceding opening theme the
trumpet section blows opening bars of bugle call
"Assembly".

27 May, 1942 (WED): Navy Pier, Chicago, Illinois (CHESTERFIELD SHOW)
CBS   7:15-7:30 P.M.

       The announcer for this program is Larry Bruff.

         Moonlight Serenade (Theme)
         When Johnny Comes Marching Home
         Moonlight Cocktail
         American Patrol
         Slumber Song (Theme)

28 May, 1942 (THUR): Fort Sheridan, Illinois (CHESTERFIELD SHOW)
CBS   7:15-7:30 P.M.

       The announcer for this program is Larry Bruff.

         Moonlight Serenade (Theme)

E2VL 4546   Vi LPT-3001, Vi EPBT-3001 (947-0055), HMV DLP-
1013, Vi LPM-1189, Vi It LPM-10141, RCA It
A1OV 0007, RCA It LJ 50020, AFRS "America's
Pop Music" 72, El WDLP 1013, RCA G EPB
3001, AFRS P-2666, RCA G EPC-1189, RCA F
430228, RCA F 130243, Vi It LPM-50020, RCA
Au L 11021, HMVAu ODLP 1013, RCA G LPT-
3001
(2:11) Sleepy Lagoon (arr BF)
       (Jack Lawrence-Eric Coates)
       As, Martin?; clt, ??; ts, Beneke
       (twice); as, Martin?

        Don't Sit Under The Apple Tree
        At Last-voc RE
        Keep 'Em Flying
        Slumber Song (Theme)

When Bill Finegan arranged for Tommy Dorsey in
the late 1940's he took his arrangement of
"Sleepy Lagoon" with him and the Dorsey band
played almost the same arrangement.

The band took the Rock Island RR Lines from
Chicago to Omaha. (G.M.P.R.)

29 May, 1942 (FRI)

Glenn Miller and His Orchestra played at the
Chermot Ballroom, Omaha, Nebraska, from 9:30-
1:30 A.M., and collected $1,900. (BB, June
13, 1942; G.M.P.R.; G.M.D.)

The band took the C.B. & Q. RR. Co. from Omaha
to Kansas City. (G.M.P.R.)

30 May, 1942 (SAT): Kansas City, Kansas (SUNSET SERENADE)
                    Mutual

> According to the Glenn Miller files this was the
> 38th and last week of the "Sunset Serenades".

30 May, 1942 (SAT)

> Glenn Miller and His Orchestra played at the
> Municipal Auditorium, Kansas City, Kansas, from
> 9:00-1:00 A.M., and drew 9,004. This was not
> only the biggest one-nighter in Kansas City's
> history but it was also the biggest one-nighter
> gross in the band's history and Miller's share
> of the box-office take was $5,616.31. (BB, June
> 13, 1942; Variety, May 13, 1942; DB, June 15,
> 1942; G.M.P.R.; G.M.D.)

31 May, 1942 (SUN)

> Glenn Miller and His Orchestra played at the Val
> Air Ballroom, Des Moines, Iowa, from 9:00-1:00
> A.M., and earned $2,800. (BB, June 13, 1942;
> Variety, May 13, 1942; G.M.P.R.; G.M.D.)

1 June, 1942 (MON)

> Glenn Miller and His Orchestra played at the Prom
> Ballroom, St. Paul, Minnesota, from 9:00-1:00
> A.M., and drew 6,500. Miller earned $3,300.
> (BB, June 13, 1942; DB, July 15, 1942; G.M.P.R.;
> G.M.D.)

> For these four one-nighters Glenn Miller earned
> $13,616.31 which was considered Miller's
> biggest take for four consecutive nights. All
> dates were for 60 per cent from the first dollar.
> (BB, June 13, 1942)

> Around this time Glenn Miller was in Chicago and
> indicated to reporters that he might join the
> navy later in the year. (BB, June 13, 1942)

2 June, 1942 (TUES): Great Lakes Naval Training Station, Ill.
                     (CHESTERFIELD SHOW)
                     CBS 7:15-7:30 P.M.

> *The announcer for this program is Larry Bruff.*

(Broadcast continued on next page)

Moonlight Serenade (Theme)

E3VP 5238   Vi LPT 6700, Vi EPNT 6700 (947-0121), Vi LPT 3057,
             Vi EPBT 3057 (947-0137), Vi LPM/LSP-1192,
             Vi EPB-1192 (547-0809), Vi SPD-18 (599-
             9112), Vi 45 Special-1953, RCA It LPM 10011,
             RCA It LJ 50012, Vi Promotion Disc 10" 78
             (E3-CB-3370), RCA F 230201, RCA F 530243,
             RCA G LSP-9901, HMV RLS 599, RCA G LPM/LSP-
             1192, RCA G LPM 9801, RCA G LPT 6700, RCA G
             EPC-1192, Vi EPBT-1192, RCA RD 27068, E1 G
             EG 8048, E1 7MW 648, RCA Vi Arg 3AE-3286.
             RCA F 740.515, RCA G SRS 560, Vi Arg LPM/LSP-
             1192
(2:53) Little Brown Jug (arr BF)
             (Traditional)
             Ts, Beneke; cnt, Hackett

Don't Sit Under The Apple Tree
Always In My Heart
Serenade (arr BF) ??
             (From "The Student Prince"
             (Sigmund Romberg)
Slumber Song (Theme)

On Vi LPT 6700 "Little Brown Jug" was incorrectly
listed as being broadcast on June 2, 1940.

Victor list "Serenade" as being one of the tunes
on this program. However, since this disc is
broken (and was not put on tape) we are unable to
check further. There is an arrangement of this
tune on file. This tune was also listed by
Victor as being played on the April 30, 1942
program, but in checking this out the tune was
discovered to actually be "Everybody Loves My
Baby". Because of this fact and since Miller
usually wound up his programs with a fast tune we
suspect that "Serenade" was not played.

3 June, 1942 (WED): Camp Grant, Rockford, Illinois
             (CHESTERFIELD SHOW)
             CBS 7:15-7:30 P.M.

Moonlight Serenade (Theme)

E1LVB 3201   Vi LPT-16, HMV B-10235, Vi 42-0108 (Vi PT-25),
             E1 WDLP 1013, Vi 27-0108 (Vi WPT-25), Vi
             EPBT-3025 (947-0025), HMV DLP 1013, Vi LPM-
             1193, Vi It LPM-10141, RCA It LJ 50020,

(Broadcast continued on next page)

El G EG 7795, Vi TP3-5020, HMVAus GA-
5091, RCA Int. G-21032, RCA Int. T-21032,
RCA G LPM-1193, RCA F 130243, HMVAu ODLP
1013, Vi It LPM 50020, RCA G LPT-16, RD
3/4-76

(2:06) Jersey Bounce (arr JG)
(Bobby Plater-Tiny Bradshaw-
Edward Johnson-Robert B. Wright)
Ts, Beneke; open tpt, Best; muted tpt,
May

Shhh, It's A Military Secret
Moonlight Cocktail
Introduction To A Waltz
Slumber Song (Theme)

4 June, 1942 (THUR): Fort Custer, Battle Creek, Michigan
(CHESTERFIELD SHOW)
CBS   7:15-7:30 P.M.

The announcer for this program is Larry Bruff.

Moonlight Serenade (Theme)
On The Old Assembly Line
Skylark
Don't Sit Under The Apple Tree   (few bars
of last week's winning tune)
In The Mood
Slumber Song (Theme)

5 June, 1942 (FRI)

Glenn Miller and His Orchestra played at the
Trianon Ballroom, Toledo, Ohio, from 9:00-1:00
A.M. Miller cracked the attendance mark set by
Guy Lombardo nine years ago. With tickets $1.25
in advance and $1.50 at the door, Miller netted
$2,838. for himself. (BB, June 20, 1942; G.M.P.R.;
G.M.D.)

6 June, 1942 (SAT)

Glenn Miller and His Orchestra played at Lakeside
Park, Dayton, Ohio, from 9:00-1:00 A.M., and
drew 3,200. Patrons paid $2.50 per head to give
the spot the highest gross in its history. In
addition, it was the highest admission price
ever played to by the Miller crew. Miller's
share there was $4,168. (BB, June 20, 1942:
G.M.P.R.; G.M.D.)

The band travelled by car to Canton. (G.M.P.R.)

7 June, 1942 (SUN)

> Glenn Miller and His Orchestra played at Meyers
> Lake Park, Canton, Ohio, from 9:00-1:00 A.M.,
> and drew 4,496 at $1.25 each. (BB, June 20,
> 1942; G.M.P.R.; G.M.D.)

> On these three successive one-nighters set by
> Howard Sinnott, of General Amusement Corporation
> in Cincinnati, Glenn Miller set new attendance
> and money marks, coming away with around $9,700
> for his own share. (BB, June 20, 1942)

8 June, 1942 (MON)

> Glenn Miller and His Orchestra played at the Sun-
> set Ballroom, Carrolton, Pennsylvania, from
> 9:00-1:00 A.M. (G.M.P.R.; G.M.D.)

9 June, 1942 (TUES): New York City, N.Y. (CHESTERFIELD SHOW)
CBS 7:15-7:30 P.M.

> Moonlight Serenade (Theme)
> Skylark
> A String Of Pearls
> Deep In The Heart Of Texas
> Keep 'Em Flying
> Slumber Song (Theme)

10 June, 1942 (WED): New York City, N.Y. (CHESTERFIELD SHOW)
CBS 7:15-7:30 P.M.

> Moonlight Serenade (Theme)
> Don't Sit Under The Apple Tree
> Knit One, Purl Two
> I Don't Want To Walk Without You
> Anchors Aweigh
> Slumber Song (Theme)

11 June, 1942 (THUR): New York City, N.Y. (CHESTERFIELD SHOW)
CBS 7:15-7:30 P.M.

The announcer for this program is Gil Newsome.

> Moonlight Serenade (Theme)
> The Story Of A Starry Night

(Broadcast continued on next page)

> *Don't Sit Under The Apple Tree*
> *Skylark (few bars of last week's*
> *winning tune)*
> *American Patrol*
> *Slumber Song (Theme)*

12 June, 1942 (FRI)

> Glenn Miller and His Orchestra played a one-
> nighter at Sun Valley, Shrewsbury, Massachusetts
> (Junction of Route 9 & 20, Worcester Pike).
> (Boston Daily Record, June 12, 1942; Boston Post,
> June 12, 1942; G.M.P.R.) The band played from
> 9:00-1:00 A.M. (G.M.D.)

13 June, 1942 (SAT)

> Glenn Miller and His Orchestra played a one-
> nighter at the City Hall Auditorium, Portland,
> Maine. (Boston Daily Record, June 12, 1942;
> G.M.P.R.) The band played from 8:00-12:00
> Midnight. (G.M.D.)

14 June, 1942 (SUN)

> Glenn Miller and His Orchestra played a one-
> nighter at Lake Compounce, Bristol, Connecticut.
> (G.M.P.R.) The band played from 9:00-1:00 A.M.
> (G.M.D.)
> G.M.P.R. for the week ending June 14th show that
> Billy May was paid for arranging "One Dozen Roses";
> that Harold O'Brien was paid for copying arrange-
> ments (Jerry Gray) of "Jersey Bounce" and "Some-
> body Else Is Taking My Place"; and that Don Brown
> was paid for copying the arrangement (George
> Williams) of "Miss You". (G.M.P.R.)

15 June, 1942 (MON)

> Glenn Miller and His Orchestra played a one-
> nighter at Rhodes, Providence, Rhode Island.
> (Boston Daily Record, June 12, 1942; Boston Post,
> June 15, 1942; G.M.P.R.) The band played from
> 9:00-1:00 A.M. (G.M.D.)

16 June, 1942 (TUES): New York City, N.Y. (CHESTERFIELD SHOW)
CBS 7:15-7:30 P.M.

(Broadcast continued on next page)

Moonlight Serenade (Theme)
Serenade In Blue-voc RE
Don't Sit Under The Apple Tree
Sleepy Lagoon
Bugle Call Rag
Slumber Song (Theme)

17 June, 1942 (WED): Victor Studios, New York City, New York

      Same personnel as for March 19th broadcast.

075090-1   Vi 27935-B, HMVAu EA-3175, HMVIn NE-651, VdP AV-
         721, VdP 7EPQ 541
    That's Sabotage-voc Marion Hutton
         From the 20th Century-Fox film "Orchestra
         Wives"
         (Mack Gordon-Harry Warren)
         Ts, Klink

075091-1   Vi 27943-A, HMV DLP 1122
    Conchita, Marquita, Lolita, Pepita, Rosita,
         Juanita Lopez
         (arr JG)-voc Marion Hutton, Tex Beneke and
         The Modernaires (and Ernie Caceres)
         From the Paramount film "Priorities On
         Parade"
         (Herb Magidson-Jule Styne)
         Ts, Klink

075092-1   Vi 27933-B, HMVAu EA-3191, HMVIn NE-736, Vi Arg
         68-1546
    The Humming-Bird (arr JG)-voc Marion Hutton, Tex
         Beneke and The Modernaires
         (Harold Adamson-E. Di Lazzaro)
         Muted tpt, May

075093-1   Vi 27933-A, HMVIn NE-736, Vi Arg 68-1546
    Yesterday's Gardenias-voc Ray Eberle and The
         Modernaires
         (Robertson-Cogane-Mysels)
         Muted tpt, ??; ts, Beneke

        All tunes 1 take. (RCA Victor)
        This session lasted from 10:00 A.M. to 3:15 P.M.
        (RCA Victor)

17 June, 1942 (WED): New York City, N.Y. (CHESTERFIELD SHOW)
*   CBS 7:15-7:30 P.M.*

        Moonlight Serenade (Theme)
        That's Sabotage

(Broadcast continued on next page)

        Deep In The Heart Of Texas
ALP   *At Last*
        On Brave Old Army Team
        Slumber Song (Theme)

18 June, 1942 (THUR): White Plains, New York (CHESTERFIELD SHOW)
        CBS 7:15-7:30 P.M.

    The announcer for this program is Gil Newsome.

        Moonlight Serenade (Theme)
        Knit One, Purl Two
        A String Of Pearls

At this point in the program Allan Courtney presented Glenn with an award. Glenn was chosen as
the favorite bandleader of the WOV 1280 club.
Courtney gave Glenn a plaque.

        Kalamazoo
        Slumber Song (Theme)

There was also a cigarette dance later on in the
evening. (G.M.P.R.)

19 June, 1942 (FRI)

    G.M.P.R. indicate that the band was off on June
    19th, 20th, 21st (no mention of June 22nd) and
    that the band was on vacation June 23-26-27-28.
    Of course, the band continued to do its
    Chesterfield program.

23 June, 1942 (TUES): New York City, N.Y. (CHESTERFIELD SHOW)
        CBS 7:15-7:30 P.M.

    The announcer for this program is Gil Newsome.

        Moonlight Serenade (Theme)

UPRM-6314   ~~Vi LPM/LSP-3873,~~ RCA G LSP-3873, RCA Br. RD/SF-
        7932
    (2:03) ~~Something To Remember You By~~

        From the revue "Three's A Crowd"
        (Howard Dietz-Arthur Schwartz)
        Cnt, Hackett; ts, Beneke; muted tpt,
        McMickle?

        ~~*One Dozen Roses*~~
        ~~*Moonlight Cocktail*~~
        ~~*Oh So Good*~~
        Slumber Song (Theme)

24 June, 1942 (WED): New York City, N.Y. (CHESTERFIELD SHOW)
              CBS 7:15-7:30 P.M.

                    Moonlight Serenade (Theme)
                    Star Dust
                    Kalamazoo

UPRM-6315   Vi LPM/LSP-3873, RCA G LSP-3873, RCA Br. RD/SF-
                    7932
                 (2:15) Skylark (arr BF)-voc Ray Eberle
                              (Johnny Mercer-Hoagy Carmichael)
                              Clt, ??

                    Keep 'Em Flying
                    Slumber Song (Theme)

25 June, 1942 (THUR): New York City, N.Y. (CHESTERFIELD SHOW)
              CBS 7:15-7:30 P.M.

           The announcer for this program is Gil Newsome.

           (0:48) *Moonlight Serenade (Theme)*
                         (Mitchell Parish-Glenn Miller)
     Int GM (3:02) *People Like You And Me (arr GW or JG)-voc*
                         Marion Hutton, Ray Eberle, Tex Teneke
                         and The Modernaires
                         From the 20th Century-Fox film
                         "Orchestra Wives"
                         (Mack Gordon-Harry Warren)
     Int GM (3:23) *I Don't Want To Walk Without You-voc Ray*
                         Eberle
                         From the Paramount film "Sweater Girl"
                         (Frank Loesser-Jule Styne)
                         Tpt, Best; p, MacGregor
     Int GM (0:13) *A String Of Pearls (arr JG)*
                         (Jerry Gray)
     Int GM (2:50) *V For Victory Hop (arr JG)*
                         (Ray Conniff)
                         Tpt, May; clt, Caceres; ts, Beneke;
                         tpt, May
           (0:45) *Slumber Song*
                         (Saul Tepper-John Chalmers MacGregor)

           "A String Of Pearls" was last week's winning tune
           and was only played for a few bars.

28 June, 1942 (SUN)

           G.M.P.R. for the week ending June 28th show that
           Billy May was paid for arranging "Cheek To Cheek".

30 June, 1942 (TUES): New York City, N.Y. (CHESTERFIELD SHOW)
CBS   7:15-7:30 P.M.

The announcer for this program is Gil Newsome.

Moonlight Serenade *(Theme)*
St. Louis Blues
    (William C. Handy)
        Cnt, Hackett; ts, Beneke
Shhh, It's A Military Secret
Skylark
Bugle Call Rag
Slumber Song *(Theme)*

This version of "St. Louis Blues" is quite slow
and is the same arrangement that is on the Jerry
Gray album "A Tribute To Glenn Miller" (Decca
DL 5375). This is probably a Jerry Gray arrangement.

1 July, 1942 (WED): New York City, N.Y. (CHESTERFIELD SHOW)
CBS   7:15-7:30 P.M.

Moonlight Serenade *(Theme)*
Sleepy Lagoon
I Left My Heart At The Stage Door Canteen
    (arr GW)-voc TB, MH & 4M
        From the musical production "This
        Is The Army"
        (Irving Berlin)
        Ts, Beneke
Skylark
Anchors Aweigh
Slumber Song *(Theme)*

2 July, 1942 (THUR)

G. Kunstmann, bandboy, was with the band from
July 2nd to August 13th. (G.M.P.R.)

2 July, 1942 (THUR): New York City, N.Y. (CHESTERFIELD SHOW)
CBS   7:15-7:30 P.M.

The announcer for this program is Gil Newsome.

Moonlight Serenade *(Theme)*
Jersey Bounce
Sweet Eloise

(Broadcast continued on next page)

Moonlight Cocktail-voc RE *(few bars of*
   last week's winning tune)
Kalamazoo
Slumber Song *(Theme)*

3 July, 1942 (FRI)

> Glenn Miller and His Orchestra played a one-
> nighter at the Sports Arena, Rochester, New York.
> The band travelled by railroad from New York to
> Rochester. (BB June 20 & July 4, 1942; Variety,
> June 24, 1942; G.M.P.R.) The band played from
> 9:00-1:00 A.M. (G.M.D.)

4 July, 1942 (SAT)

> Glenn Miller and His Orchestra played a one-
> nighter at Waldameer Park, Erie, Pennsylvania.
> (G.M.P.R.) The band played from 9:00-1:00 A.M.
> (G.M.D.)

5 July, 1942 (SUN)

> Glenn Miller and His Orchestra played a one-
> nighter at Yankee Lake, Brookfield, Ohio. (BB,
> June 20 & July 4, 1942; G.M.P.R.) The band
> played from 9:00-1:00 A.M. (G.M.D.)

6 July, 1942 (MON)

> Glenn Miller and His Orchestra played a one-
> nighter at Sandy Beach Park, Russells Point,
> Ohio. (BB, June 27 & July 4, 1942; G.M.P.R.)
> The band played from 9:30-1:30 A.M. (G.M.D.)

7 July, 1942 (TUES)

> Glenn Miller and His Orchestra opened at the
> "Panther Room" of the Hotel Sherman in Chicago,
> Illinois, for a ten day stay (through to July
> 16th). Miller broadcast his Chesterfield show
> from the hotel. (BB, May 9, 1942; DB, July 1,
> 1942; M & R, July 1942; G.M.P.R.; Variety, June
> 24, 1942) On Tuesdays, Wednesdays, Thursdays,
> and Fridays the band played from 7:30-10:00 P.M.
> and 10:45-1:30 A.M. On Saturdays the band played
> from 7:30-10:00 P.M. and 10:45-2:30 A.M. (G.M.D.)

7 July, 1942 (TUES): Panther Room, Hotel Sherman, Chicago, Ill.
            (CHESTERFIELD SHOW)
            CBS   7:15-7:30 P.M.

       The announcer for this program is Larry Bruff.

           Moonlight Serenade (Theme)
           At Last-voc RE
           Conchita, Marquita, Lolita, Pepita, Rosita,
              Juanita Lopez
           Sleepy Lagoon
           Introduction To A Waltz
           Slumber Song (Theme)

8 July, 1942 (WED): Panther Room, Hotel Sherman, Chicago, Ill.
            (CHESTERFIELD SHOW)
            CBS   7:15-7:30 P.M.

           Moonlight Serenade (Theme)
           Serenade In Blue-voc RE
           Jersey Bounce
           The Humming-Bird-voc MH, TB & 4M
           American Patrol
           Slumber Song (Theme)

9 July, 1942 (THUR): Panther Room, Hotel Sherman, Chicago, Ill.
            (CHESTERFIELD SHOW)
            CBS   7:15-7:30 P.M.

       The announcer for this program is Larry Bruff.

           Moonlight Serenade (Theme)
           Kalamazoo
           Always In My Heart-voc RE
           Jersey Bounce (few bars of last week's
              winning tune)
           One O'Clock Jump
           Slumber Song (Theme)

12 July, 1942 (SUN)

       Ray Eberle was discharged from the Miller band
this evening and Miller hired Skip Nelson, a
20-year-old Pittsburg boy who was singing with
the Chico Marx band in New York. Nelson arrived
in Chicago by air from New York in less than 24
hours after Eberle's departure. Nelson, besides
singing, played piano.

(Continued on next page)

"Due to many acts of misconduct on his part over an extended period of time, I was forced to terminate Ray's engagement with my orchestra," Miller said. (M & R--August, 1942; DB--August 1, 1942)

Eberle eventually went with Gene Krupa and His Orchestra.

13 July, 1942 (MON)

The payroll records show that Skip Nelson worked for the orchestra from July 13th (first day of work actually was July 14th) until the orchestra disbanded on September 27, 1942. (G.M.P.R.) The band was off work this day. (G.M.D.)

14 July, 1942 (TUES): Victor Studios, Chicago, Illinois

Same personnel as for March 19th broadcast except that SKIP NELSON (SCIPIONE MIRABELLA), vocalist, replaces Ray Eberle.

074736-1   Vi 27953-A, HMV DLP 1122, Cam Cas-2267, RCA G
            Cas-2267, AFRS Jill's Juke Box Series
            H-46: 54, 91, 111
            Dearly Beloved (arr JG)-voc Skip Nelson (and
            chorus)
            From the Columbia film "You Were Never
            Lovelier"
            (Johnny Mercer-Jerome Kern)

074737-1   Vi 20-1520-B, HMVAu EA-3057, VD 12, HMV 7EG 8077,
            RD 8-5012, AFRS H-62-138 (82) Phonograph
            Album No. 138 (82), RD 3/4-25, RD Br. RDS
            6175, RD Br. RDS 6095, AFRS G.I. Jive
            H-12-620, AFRS G.I. Jive H-12-1014
            Moonlight Mood (arr JG)-voc Skip Nelson and The
            Modernaires
            (Harold Adamson-Peter De Rose)
            Tpt, ??

074738-1   Vi 20-1536-B, HMV BD 5833, El G EG 7819, Vi LPT
            6700, Vi EPNT 6700 (947-0118), Vi SPD-18
            (599-9108), HMV RLS 599, RD 3/4-64, RCA G
            LPT 6700, AFRS G.I. Jive Series H-12:
            1021, 1254, 1515, 1300, 715, 755, 1220,
            804, 854, 1641, 1722, AFRS Jill's Juke
            Box Series H-46: 74, 122

(Session continued on next page)

Caribbean Clipper (arr JG)
(Jerry Gray)
Ts, Beneke; tpt, May; d, Purtill

074739-1   Vi 20-1563-A, HMV 7EG 8077, Vi LPT 6700, HMV RLS
599, Vi EPNT 6700 (947-0118), Vi SPD-18
(599-9109), RCA G LPT 6700, AFRS G.I.
Jive Series H-12: 794, 845, 918, 961,
1140, 1223, AFRS Jill's Juke Box H-46-133
Here We Go Again (arr JG)
(Jerry Gray)
Ts, Klink; tpt, May; d, Purtill; tpt, ??

All tunes 1 take. (RCA Victor)
This session lasted from 11:00 A.M. to 2:40 P.M.
(RCA Victor)

14 July, 1942 (TUES): Panther Room, Hotel Sherman, Chicago, Ill.
(CHESTERFIELD SHOW)
CBS 7:15-7:30 P.M.

The announcer for this program is Larry Bruff.

ALP

Moonlight Serenade (Theme)
Moonlight Cocktail-voc SN & 4M
Jersey Bounce
I Left My Heart At The Stage Door Canteen
Keep 'Em Flying
Slumber Song (Theme)

15 July, 1942 (WED): Victor Studios, Chicago, Illinois

Same personnel as for March 19th broadcast except that SKIP NELSON, vocalist, replaces Ray
Eberle.

074740-1   Vi 20-1523-A, HMV BD 5811, HMVF 7EMF 11, HMVSw
JK-2326, El G EG 7747, Vi 20-1560 (Vi P-
147), Vi 42-0035, Vi 27-0035, Vi 420-0044,
Vi 447-0044, Vi 27-0089, Vi 42-0089, Vi
EPAT-401, Vi EPA-5103, Vi LPT 13, Vi LPT-
1016, Cam Cal/Cas-751, RD 3/4-25, RD Br.
RDS 6095, AFRS H-62-138 (82) Phonograph
Album No. 138 (82), RD Br. RDS 6176, RCA
Int. T-21028, AFRS P-2412, RCA G LPT
1016, RCA G Cas-751, Vi LPM 1704, RCA G
447-0044, RCA G EPAT-401, HMVIn NE. 705,
RCA Au VPM-6019, AFRS Jill's Juke Box
Series H-46: 10, 48, 71, 92, 117, 148,
167, 199, 217, Pick. Int. CDS 1040, Vi
VPM-6019, RCA Br. RD-8094, RCA Br. GM-1,

(Session continued on next page)

Cam Au Cal/Cas-751, AFRS G.I. Jive Series
H-12: 1774, 2092, 1822, 601, 843, 983,
1014, 1234, 1624

That Old Black Magic-voc Skip Nelson and The
Modernaires
From the Paramount film "Star Spangled
Rhythm"
(Johnny Mercer-Harold Arlen)

074741-1   Vi 20-1520-A, HMVAu EA-3035, HMV 7EG 8067, Vi
EPAT-427, Vi EPA-5133, Vi LPT-1031, Cam
Cal/Cas-751, AFRS H-62-138 (82) Phonograph
Album No. 138 (82), RCA G Cas-751, RCA G
LPT-1031, Pick. Int. CDS 1040, RCA Au EPA-
5133, Cam Au Cal/Cas-751, AFRS Jill's Juke
Box Series H-46: 41, 71

Moonlight Becomes You-voc Skip Nelson and The
Modernaires
From the Paramount film "Road To Morocco"
(Johnny Burke-Jimmy Van Heusen)
Muted tpt, ??

074742-1   Vi 20-1509-A, HMV BD 5876, HMVAu EA-3063, HMVF
7EMF 11, Vi 20-3185, Vi 42-0035, Vi 27-
0035, Vi 420-0044, Vi 447-0044, Vi EPAT-
401, Vi EPA-5035, RCA RCX 1034, Cam Cal/
Cas-751, Vi LPT-1016, Vi LPM/LSP-3377,
AFRS H-62-70 Phonograph Album No. 70, RD
3/4-49, AFRS H-12 G.I. Jive Program No.
1023, RCA G Cas-751, El G EG 7787, AFRS
"Jukebox USA" 179, RCA G LPT 1016, RCA G
LPM/LSP-3377, Vi TP3-5044, RCA G 447-
0044, RCA G EPAT-401, Vi P8S-5061, Vi VPM-
6019, AFRS G.I. Jive H-12-1001, Pick. Int.
CDS 1040, RCA Br. GM-1, AFRS G.I. Jive
Series H-12:795, 1594, 958, 976, 1126,
2205, 1879, 2045, 1477, 1180, 911, 824,
593, 682, 690, Cam Au Cal/Cas-751, AFRS
G.I. Jive 308 (BB34936 A22L), RCA G Cas
10231, Vi VLP 3377, RCA Br. RD-8094,
RCA Au VPM-6019, AFRS Jill's Juke Box
Series H-46: 137, 176, AFRS Jill's Juke
Box EN-243

Juke Box Saturday Night (arr JG)-voc Marion
Hutton, Tex Beneke and The Modernaires
From the musical production "Stars On Ice"
(Albert Stillman-Paul McGrane)
Tpt, Best

074743-1   Vi 20-1546-A, HMV BD 5847, HMVSw JK-2339, AFRS
Jill's Juke Box EN-46-239, AFRS G.I. Jive

(Session continued on next page)

Series H-12: 566, 1005, 2053, 2002,
It Must Be Jelly ('Cause Jam Don't Shake Like
That) (arr GW)-voc The Modernaires
(George Williams-John Chalmers MacGregor)
P, MacGregor; ts, Klink; tpt, Best; tpt,
May; as, Martin; d, Purtill

All tunes 1 take. (RCA Victor)
This session lasted from 11:00 A.M. to 3:15 P.M.
(RCA Victor)

Victor almost did not release "Juke Box Saturday
Night" because of possible offense to coin
machine operators. (DB, Sept. 15, 1942) Ralph
Brewster did both of the Ink Spots' imitations
with Hal Dickinson singing the high voice when
Brewster was singing the deep voice. Bill
Conway arranged the harmony.

15 July, 1942 (WED): Panther Room, Hotel Sherman, Chicago, Ill.
(CHESTERFIELD SHOW)
CBS 7:15-7:30 P.M.

> *Moonlight Serenade (Theme)*
> *Rhapsody In Blue*

K2PP-0047   Vi LPM-6100, RCA RD 27147, RCA G LPM 6100, RCA
                Au L 11024
        (2:19) One Dozen Roses (arr BM)-voc Marion
               Hutton, Tex Beneke and The Modernaires
               (Roger Lewis-Country Washburn-Dick Jurgens-
               Walter Donovan)

> *Skylark-voc SN*
> *Caribbean Clipper*
> *Slumber Song (Theme)*

This version of "Rhapsody In Blue" has a different introduction than on the recording.

On Vi LPM-6100 "One Dozen Roses" was incorrectly
listed as being broadcast on July 14, 1942.

16 July, 1942 (THUR): Victor Studios, Chicago, Illinois

Same personnel as for March 19th broadcast except that SKIP NELSON, vocalist, replaces Ray
Eberle.

(Session continued on next page)

074744-1 Vi 27953-B, HMV 7EG 8224, AFRS Jill's Juke Box
     H-46-80, RD 3/4-64 (Test albums only),
     Cam Cas-2267, RCA G Cas-2267
  I'm Old Fashioned-voc Skip Nelson
     From the Columbia film "You Were Never
     Lovelier"
     (Johnny Mercer-Jerome Kern)

074745-1 Vi 20-1523-B, HMV 7EG 8224, RD 3/4-25, HMVIn NE.
     705, AFRS H-62-70 Phonograph Album No. 70,
     RD Br. RDS 6174, RD Br. RDS 6094, AFRS G.I.
     Jive H-12-1796
  A Pink Cocktail For A Blue Lady (arr JG)-voc Skip
     Nelson
     (Herb Magidson-Ben Oakland)
     Ts, Beneke; clt, ??

074746-1 Vi 20-1546-B, HMV BD 5847, HMVSw JK-2339, HMV
     7EG 8031, Vi EPAT-428, Vi LPT-1031, HMV
     RLS 599, Vi LPT 6700, Vi EPNT 6700 (947-
     0121), Vi SPD-18 (599-9108), RCA G LPT
     6700, AFRS "America's Pop Music" 72, RCA G
     EPAT-428, RCA G LPT-1031, AFRS G.I. Jive
     Series H-12: 2002, 2053, AFRS G.I. Jive
     EN-12-2349, AFRS G.I. Jive H (EN)-12-2220
  Rainbow Rhapsody
     (Benny Carter)
     Cnt, Hackett; ts, Beneke

074747-1 Vi 20-1509-B, HMV BD 5876, HMVAu EA-3063, HMVSw
     JK-2396, VD 201, Vi LPT 6700, Vi EPNT
     6700 (947-0125), Vi SPD-18 (599-9111),
     HMV RLS 599, El G EG 7787, RCA G LPT 6700,
     AFRS G.I. Jive Series H-12: 702, 1266
  Sleepy Town Train
     (Allan Roberts-Bill Fontaine)
     Muted tpt, May; as, Martin; muted tpt, May;
     ts, Beneke

074748-1 Vi 20-1529-A, HMV BD 5833, HMVAu EA-3222, Vi EPA-
     5149, Vi LPT 6700, Vi EPNT 6700 (947-0119),
     RD 3/4-64, Vi SPD-18 (599-9110), HMV RLS
     599, Vi SP 33-90, HMV DLP 1145, HMVAus GA-
     5011, Vi It LPM-10141, AFRS P-2463, Vi It
     LJ-50020, RCA G LPT 6700, Vi It LPM 50020,
     AFRS "America's Pop Music" 67, HMVIn NE
     779, AFRS G.I. Jive H-12-1021, AFRS Jill's
     Juke Box H-46-236
  Rhapsody In Blue (arr BF)
     (George Gershwin)
     Cnt, Hackett; ts, Beneke; muted tpt, ??

(Continued on next page)

All tunes 1 take. (RCA Victor)
This session lasted from 11:00 A.M. to 3:45 P.M.
(RCA Victor)

This was the last recording session by the Miller
civilian band due to the dispute between the
American Federation of Musicians and the recording
companies. A ban on recording was imposed by the
Union on its members as of August 1, 1942, and
this continued until November 22, 1944 for RCA
Victor and Columbia. Decca and several other new
companies began recording in October of 1943.
Since Miller was well aware of this upcoming ban
on recording, the above "slew" of recordings over
a three day period was the result. Some of these
tunes were released by Victor as late as January,
1944.

16 July, 1942 (THUR): Panther Room, Hotel Sherman, Chicago, Ill.
                      (CHESTERFIELD SHOW)
                      CBS   7:15-7:30 P.M.

                      Moonlight Serenade (Theme)
                      Sweet Eloise-voc SN & 4M
                      Jersey Bounce
                      Kalamazoo
                      Slumber Song (Theme)

16 July, 1942 (THUR)

Glenn Miller and His Orchestra closed at the
"Panther Room" of the Hotel Sherman in Chicago,
Illinois. The management bought no outside acts
with the Miller band staging the entire show.
They established a new gross attendance record
during the 10 day run. Duke Ellington and His
Orchestra followed Miller on the 17th. (DB,
July 15, 1942; BB, Aug. 1, 1942; Variety, July
15, 1942; G.M.P.R.)
      "Miller closed short stay last Thursday,
July 16, 1942, and smashed spot's records closing
its doors each night at eight to keep the crowds
out. Miller played to around 6,700 people on the
final week." (Variety, July 22, 1942)

The band took the New York Central RR from
Chicago to Detroit. (G.M.P.R.)

17 July, 1942 (FRI)

        Glenn Miller and His Orchestra played for one
week (closed Thursday, July 23rd) at Eastwood
Gardens, Detroit, Michigan. (BB, July 25, 1942;
Variety, June 24, 1942; Variety, July 15, 1942;
G.M.P.R.) The band played from 9:00-2:00 A.M.
nightly and from 3:00-6:00 P.M. Saturday.
(G.M.D.)

19 July, 1942 (SUN)

        Glenn Miller and His Orchestra played a Tea
Dance at Eastwood Gardens, Detroit, Michigan.
(G.M.P.R.)

21 July, 1942 (TUES): Eastwood Gardens, Detroit, Michigan
        (CHESTERFIELD SHOW)
        CBS 7:15-7:30 P.M.

    The announcer for this program is Larry Bruff.

        Moonlight Serenade (Theme)
        Sleepy Town Train
        Don't Sit Under The Apple Tree
        Always In My Heart-voc SN

        Slumber Song (Theme)

    Information on one of the tunes is missing.

22 July, 1942 (WED): Eastwood Gardens, Detroit, Michigan
        (CHESTERFIELD SHOW)
        CBS 7:15-7:30 P.M.

        Moonlight Serenade (Theme)
        Sleepy Lagoon
        Juke Box Saturday Night
        At Last-voc SN
        It Must Be Jelly
        Slumber Song (Theme)

23 July, 1942 (THUR): Eastwood Gardens, Detroit, Michigan
        (CHESTERFIELD SHOW)
        CBS 7:15-7:30 P.M.

    The announcer for this program is Larry Bruff.

(Broadcast continued on next page)

Moonlight Serenade (Theme)
Little Brown Jug
    Tpt, May (instead of Hackett)
I Don't Want To Walk Without You—voc SN
Jersey Bounce *(few bars of last week's*
    winning tune)
Kalamazoo
Slumber Song (Theme)

The band took the New York Central RR from Detroit
to Buffalo. (G.M.P.R.)

24 July, 1942 (FRI)

Glenn Miller and His Orchestra played for one
week (closed Thursday, July 30th) at Shea's
Buffalo Theater, Buffalo, New York. (BB, May 16,
1942; BB, June 27, 1942; BB July 25, 1942; BB
Aug. 1, 1942; Variety, June 24, 1942; Variety,
July 15, 1942; Buffalo Courier Express, July 24 &
30, 1942; G.M.P.R.)
    "In the face of sizzling temperatures Glenn
Miller at the Buffalo with Magnificent Dope is
jamming the house for probably the bumper session
this summer." (Variety, July 29, 1942)
    "Last week Glenn Miller's Orchestra on stage
hit tallest tally in many seasons at $31,000.00"
(Variety, Aug. 5, 1942)

Dean Murphy was also on the same bill. (G.M.P.R.)

28 July, 1942 (TUES): Shea's Buffalo Theater, Buffalo, New York
(CHESTERFIELD SHOW)
CBS 7:15-7:30 P.M.

Moonlight Serenade
Juke Box Saturday Night
Jersey Bounce
Sweet Eloise—voc SN & 4M
American Patrol
Slumber Song (Theme)

29 July, 1942 (WED): Shea's Buffalo Theater, Buffalo, New York
(CHESTERFIELD SHOW)
CBS 7:15-7:30 P.M.

Moonlight Serenade (Theme)
Sleepy Lagoon

(Broadcast continued on next page)

I Left My Heart At The Stage Door Canteen
Yesterday's Gardenias-voc SN & 4M
It Must Be Jelly
Slumber Song (Theme)

30 July, 1942 (THUR): Shea's Buffalo Theater, Buffalo, New York
            (CHESTERFIELD SHOW)
            CBS   7:15-7:30 P.M.

      The announcer for this program is Larry Bruff.

            Moonlight Serenade (Theme)
            Rhapsody In Blue
            Always In My Heart-voc SN
            Sleepy Lagoon (few bars of last week's
                  winning tune)
            Kalamazoo
            Slumber Song (Theme)

      The band took the New York Central RR from
      Buffalo to Akron.   (G.M.P.R.)

31 July, 1942 (FRI)

            Glenn Miller and His Orchestra played for four
            days (closed Monday, August 3rd) at the Palace
            Theater, Akron, Ohio.   (BB, May 16 & June 27,
            1942; DB, Aug. 1, 1942; BB, Aug. 1, 1942;
            Variety, June 24, 1942; G.M.P.R.)
            Amelia Gilmore was also on the same bill.
            (G.M.P.R.)
            Dean Murphy was also on the same bill.   (G.M.P.R.)

            The band took the B & O RR from Akron to
            Youngstown.   (G.M.P.R.)

4 August, 1942 (TUES)

            Glenn Miller and His Orchestra played for three
            days (closed Thursday, August 6th) at the Palace
            Theater, Youngstown, Ohio.   Miller broadcasted
            his Chesterfield show from the theater stage at
            7:15 and a 11:15 P.M. rebroadcast to the West.
            (BB, June 27 & Aug. 1, 1942; DB, Aug. 1 & Aug.
            15, 1942; G.M.P.R.)
            Amelia Gilmore and Dean Murphy were both on the
            same bill.   (G.M.P.R.)

(Continued on next page)

The band took the B & O RR from Youngstown to
Pittsburg; the Pennsylvania RR from Pittsburg
to Hershey; and the Pennsylvania RR from
Hershey to Atlantic City. (G.M.P.R.)

"Reports circulated in the trade yesterday
(Tuesday, August 4th) that Glenn Miller's
Orchestra was about to part with its Chesterfield
commercial after close to three years association.
Don Langen, account executive with Newell-Emmett
Agency and Miller's manager Don Haynes knew
nothing about it." (Variety, Aug. 5, 1942)

4 August, 1942 (TUES): *Palace Theater, Youngstown, Ohio*
                        (CHESTERFIELD SHOW)
                        CBS 7:15-7:30 P.M.

                    Moonlight Serenade (Theme)
                    Tuxedo Junction
                    Conchita, Marquita, Lolita, Pepita,
                          Rosita, Juanita Lopez
                    Skylark-voc SN
                    Keep 'Em Flying
                    Slumber Song (Theme)

5 August, 1942 (WED): *Palace Theater, Youngstown, Ohio*
                       (CHESTERFIELD SHOW)
                       CBS 7:15-7:30 P.M.

                    Moonlight Serenade (Theme)
                    Sleepy Town Train
                    Juke Box Saturday Night
                    The Story Of A Starry Night-voc SN
                    Caribbean Clipper
                    Slumber Song (Theme)

6 August, 1942 (THUR): *Palace Theater, Youngstown, Ohio*
                        (CHESTERFIELD SHOW)
                        CBS 7:15-7:30 P.M.

The announcer for this program is Larry Bruff.

                    Moonlight Serenade (Theme)
                    Serenade In Blue-voc SN & 4M
                    Jersey Bounce
                    Jersey Bounce (few bars of last week's
                        winning tune)
                    Kalamazoo
                    Slumber Song (Theme)

7 August, 1942 (FRI)

>   Glenn Miller and His Orchestra played a one-
>   nighter at Hershey Park Ballroom, Hershey,
>   Pennsylvania. (G.M.P.R.) The band played
>   from 8:30-12:30 A.M. (G.M.D.)

8 August, 1942 (SAT)

>   Glenn Miller and His Orchestra played for two
>   days (Saturday, August 8th and Sunday, August
>   9th) at Hamid's Million Dollar Pier, Atlantic
>   City, New Jersey. The band played afternoons
>   and evenings. (BB, June 27 & Aug. 8, 1942;
>   DB, Aug. 1, 1942; Variety, June 24, 1942;
>   G.M.P.R.) On Saturday the band played from
>   4:00-6:00 P.M. and 10:00-1:00 A.M. On Sunday
>   the band played from 3:00-5:00 P.M. and 9:00-
>   12:00 Midnight. (G.M.D.)

10 August, 1942 (MON)

>   Off. (G.M.D.)

11 August, 1942 (TUES): New York City, N.Y. (CHESTERFIELD SHOW)
*   CBS   7:15-7:30 P.M.*

>   *Moonlight Serenade (Theme)*
>   *Jersey Bounce*
>   *The Humming-Bird*
>   *I'm Old Fashioned*
>   *It Must Be Jelly*
>   *Slumber Song (Theme)*

12 August, 1942 (WED): New York City, N.Y. (CHESTERFIELD SHOW)
*   CBS   7:15-7:30 P.M.*

>   *Moonlight Serenade (Theme)*

E4VP 8210   Vi LPT 6701, Vi EPOT 6701 (947-0180), HMV RLS 598,
RCA G EPOT-6701
(2:22) April In Paris (arr BF)
>   From the stage musical "Walk A Little
>   Faster"
>   (E.Y. "Yip" Harburg-Vernon Duke)
>   Ts, Beneke; cnt, Hackett; ts, Beneke;
>   clt. ??

(Broadcast continued on next page)

I Left My Heart At The Stage Door Canteen

E4VP 8207   ~~Vi LPT 6701~~, Vi EPOT 6701 (947-0188), HMV RLS 598,
             RCA G EPOT-6701
             (2:00) ~~I Don't Want To Walk Without You~~-voc
                    Skip Nelson
                    From the Paramount film "Sweater Girl"
                    (Frank Loesser-Jule Styne)

             American Patrol
             Slumber Song (Theme)

             On Vi LPT 6701 "April In Paris" was incorrectly
             listed as being broadcast on September 1, 1942.
             On Vi LPT 6701 "I Don't Want To Walk Without
             You" was incorrectly listed as being broadcast
             on July 1, 1941.

*13 August, 1942 (THUR): New York City, N.Y. (CHESTERFIELD SHOW)
             CBS   7:15-7:30 P.M.*

             The announcer for this program is Tip Corney.

             Moonlight Serenade (Theme)
             Dearly Beloved
             Jersey Bounce
             Jersey Bounce (few bars of last week's
                     winning tune)
             Kalamazoo
             Slumber Song (Theme)

             The band took the New York-New Haven-Hartford
             RR from New York to Worcester. (G.M.P.R.)

14 August, 1942 (FRI)

             Glenn Miller and His Orchestra played at Sun
             Valley, Shrewsbury, Massachusetts, from 9:00-
             1:00 A.M. (Boston Daily Record, Aug. 14, 1942;
             Boston Post, Aug. 14, 1942; G.M.P.R.; G.M.D.)

             The band took the New York-New Haven-Hartford
             RR from Worcester to Lewiston. (G.M.P.R.)

15 August, 1942 (SAT)

             Glenn Miller and His Orchestra played at the
             City Hall Auditorium, Lewiston, Maine, from
             8:00-12:00 Midnight. (Boston Daily Record,
             Aug. 14, 1942; Boston Post, Aug. 14, 1942;
             G.M.P.R.; G.M.D.)

             The band took the New York-New Haven-Hartford
             RR from Lewiston to Bridgeport. (G.M.P.R.)

16 August, 1942 (SUN)

   Glenn Miller and His Orchestra played at Pleasure
   Beach Ballroom, Bridgeport, Connecticut, from
   9:00-1:00 A.M. (G.M.P.R.; G.M.D.; BB, Aug. 29,
   1942)
    "Making his first appearance there in several
   years, Glenn Miller, in at Pleasure Beach Ballroom
   here Sunday (16), shattered the season's record
   for both attendance and gross, drawing a record
   crowd of 3,502 persons. Without ducats the
   highest ever charged for any dance band in the
   history of Bridgeport, $1.50, gross totalled a
   sweet $5,253. Perry Rodman, managing director of
   the ballroom, stated that if the night had not
   been a stormy one, house would have been sold
   out." (BB, Aug. 29, 1942)

   The band took the New York-New Haven-Hartford RR
   from Bridgeport to Boston. (G.M.P.R.)

17 August, 1942 (MON)

   Glenn Miller and His Orchestra played at Canobie
   Lake Park, Salem, New Hampshire. (G.M.P.R.)

   The band took the New York-New Haven-Hartford RR
   from Boston to New York. (G.M.P.R.)

18 August, 1942 (TUES): New York City, N.Y. (CHESTERFIELD SHOW)
      CBS 7:15-7:30 P.M.

    Moonlight Serenade (Theme)
    Sleepy Lagoon
    Juke Box Saturday Night
    At Last-voc SN
    Caribbean Clipper
    Slumber Song (Theme)

19 August, 1942 (WED): New York City, N.Y. (CHESTERFIELD SHOW)
      CBS 7:15-7:30 P.M.

   The announcer for this program is Mel Allen.

   Moonlight Serenade (Theme)

(Broadcast continued on next page)

E2VL 4419   Vi LPT-30, Vi 42-0153 (Vi PT-39), Vi 27-0153
         (Vi WPT-39), Vi EPBT-3026 (947-0026),
         Vi EPA-726, HMV DLP 1012, Vi LPM-1189,
         Vi EPB-1189 (547-0799), El WDLP 1012,
         HMVSw JK-2803, RCA G EPBT-3026, RCA G
         EPC-1189, RCA F 430228, RCA Au L 11021,
         HMVAu ODLP 1012, RCA G LPT-30
     (2:27) My Buddy (arr BF)
         (Gus Kahn-Walter Donaldson)
         Ts, Beneke; muted tpt, Best?;
         muted tpt, May?

WPRS-0976   Vi LSP-3981, RCA Br. RD/SF-7982
     (1:43) (I've Got Spurs That) Jingle, Jangle,
         Jingle (arr JG)-voc Marion Hutton,
         Tex Beneke and The Modernaires
         From the Paramount film "Forest
         Rangers"
         (Frank Loesser-Joseph J. Lilley)

         Serenade In Blue-voc SN & 4M
         In The Mood
         Slumber Song (Theme)

20 August, 1942 (THUR): New York City, N.Y. (CHESTERFIELD SHOW)
         CBS 7:15-7:30 P.M.

     The announcer for this program is Mel Allen.

         Moonlight Serenade (Theme)
         Sleepy Town Train
         Always In My Heart-voc SN
         Jersey Bounce (few bars of last week's
                  winning tune)
         Kalamazoo
         Slumber Song (Theme)

21 August, 1942 (FRI)

     Glenn Miller and His Orchestra played for one
     week (closed Thursday, August 27th) at the Earle
     Theater, Philadelphia, Pennsylvania. They
     played six or seven 40 minute shows per day. The
     Friday evening program was reviewed in the
     August 29th issue of The Billboard (this was the
     fourth show of the day with two more to go):

         "Tees off with In The Mood and then into a
     dance arrangement of the Rhapsody In Blue theme,
     followed by another swingy dish in a String Of

(Continued on next page)

(Continued on next page)

Pearls. Miller then steps off the bandstand for
the first time, taking to the mike to introduce
Marion Hutton, blonde and lovely in a flowing
chiffon dress, to sing That's Sabotage. Miss
Hutton calls on the Modernaires, male quartet,
and Tex Beneke, out of the sax section, for I've
Got A Gal In Kalamazoo, vocal troupe continuing
with a neat novelty, Juke Box Saturday Night,
which has the band doing a take on Harry James
and the Modernaires adding a comedy punch in
their take on the Ink Spots.

Band continues the fast pace with another
dish of musical jive in Tall, Fat Mama, and for a
change of pace Miller brings on the new male voice
with the band, Skip Nelson, whose romancy baritone
registers for Skylark and, assisted by the
Modernaires, for Sweet Eloise.

Band rings down the rug with Anvil Chorus."

The band grossed $45,800. for the week which was
$900. short of the all-time high set by Tommy
Dorsey. "Such grosses are almost impossible here
considering that it's a six day week at the Earle.
Moreover, it is conceded by the management that
Miller would have topped $50,000 were it not for
his radio commercial broadcasts from the stage
Tuesday, Wednesday and Thursday nights. Crowds
stayed on for the broadcasts and there was
practically no turnover for the radio shows, which
hurt the gate." (BB--July 25; DB--August 15;
BB--August 29; BB--September 5, 1942)

While in Philadelphia Miller failed to appear as
guest conductor at the USO dance on Tuesday night
and was 'too busy' for a backstage interview with
Harold Davis of WDAS. Miller also failed to
appear at the Stage Door Canteen. The result was
that the press attacked his actions. "That
Miller had to do a repeat broadcast for the West
Coast on his three Chesterfield shows precluded
the possibility of any outside personals. However, nobody took the trouble to explain the
situation to the groups involved, with the result
that the maestro pulled out of town in the bad
graces of the townfolk." (BB--September 5, 1942)

The band did 40 shows while at the Earle (closed
on August 23rd-Sunday). Wally Brown was also on
the same bill. (G.M.P.R.)

25 August, 1942 (TUES): *Earle Theater, Philadelphia, Pennsylvania*
(CHESTERFIELD SHOW)
CBS 7:15-7:30 P.M.

Moonlight Serenade (Theme)
(2:37) ~~*She's Funny That Way*~~ *(arr BF)*
(Richard A. Whiting-Neil Moret)
Tpt, Best
(0:02) *It's Great To Be An American*
(Ray Muffs-Jimmie Crane)
Jingle, Jangle, Jingle
Yesterday's Gardenias-voc SN & 4M
I Hear You Screamin'
Slumber Song (Theme)

26 August, 1942 (WED): *Earle Theater, Philadelphia, Pennsylvania*
(CHESTERFIELD SHOW)
CBS 7:15-7:30 P.M.

Moonlight Serenade (Theme)
Something To Remember You By
Jingle, Jangle, Jingle
Sweet Eloise-voc SN & 4M
It Must Be Jelly
Slumber Song (Theme)

27 August, 1942 (THUR): *Earle Theater, Philadelphia, Pennsylvania*
(CHESTERFIELD SHOW)
CBS 7:15-7:30 P.M.

Moonlight Serenade (Theme)
A String Of Pearls
Always In My Heart
Kalamazoo
Slumber Song (Theme)

28 August, 1942 (FRI)

Glenn Miller and His Orchestra played for one
week (closed Thursday, September 3rd) at the Fox
Theater, Brooklyn, New York. The band did 33
shows this week. (DB, Aug. 15, 1942; New York
Times, Aug. 28 & Sept. 3, 1942; G.M.P.R.) The
Miller band did $30,000 worth of business.
(Variety, Sept. 9, 1942)

1 September, 1942 (TUES): New York City, N.Y. (CHESTERFIELD SHOW)
CBS   7:15-7:30 P.M.

>   *Moonlight Serenade (Theme)*
>   *April In Paris*
>   *Conchita, Marquita, Lolita, Pepita, Rosita,*
>   *Juanita Lopez*
>   *Always In My Heart-voc SN*
>   *Keep 'Em Flying*
>   *Slumber Song (Theme)*

2 September, 1942 (WED): New York City, N.Y. (CHESTERFIELD SHOW)
CBS   7:15-7:30 P.M.

>   *Moonlight Serenade (Theme)*

V-4086 WR-984   GMMS 24/72, GMMS 39/87, AFRS P-2237
                   (2:35) My Buddy (arr BF)
                             (Gus Kahn-Walter Donaldson)
                             Ts, Beneke; muted tpt, Best?;
                             muted tpt, May?

>   *Kalamazoo*
                   (1:53) I've Caught Love (arr JG & GW)-voc Skip
                             Nelson and The Modernaires
                             (Naomi Walton-Mort Walton)

V-4086 WR-984   GMMS 24/72, GMMS 40/88
                   (2:08) Caribbean Clipper (arr JG)
                             (Jerry Gray)
                             Ts, Beneke; tpt, May; d, Purtill

>   *Slumber Song (Theme)*

3 September, 1942 (THUR): New York City, N.Y. (CHESTERFIELD SHOW)
CBS   7:15-7:30 P.M.

>   *Moonlight Serenade (Theme)*
>   *On The Old Assembly Line*
>   *Always In My Heart-voc SN*
>   *American Patrol*
>   *Slumber Song (Theme)*

The band took the Pennsylvania RR from New York
to Atlantic City. (G.M.P.R.)

4 September, 1942 (FRI)

Release date for Glenn Miller movie "Orchestra
Wives". (BB, Aug. 29, 1942)

The band was off on this date. (G.M.D.)

5 September, 1942 (SAT)

        Glenn Miller and His Orchestra played for two
days (Saturday, September 5th and Sunday,
September 6th) at Hamid's Million Dollar Pier,
Atlantic City, New Jersey. (BB, Aug. 22, 1942;
DB, Sept. 1, 1942; Variety, Aug. 19 & Sept. 2,
1942; G.M.P.R.) On Saturday the band played
from 4:30-6:00 P.M. and 10:00-1:30 A.M. On
Sunday the band played from 3:00-5:00 P.M. and
10:00-1:00 A.M. (G.M.D.)

        "Hamid had its biggest bill of the season
with Glenn Miller's Orchestra, Reggie Childs
and personal appearance of the Andrews Sisters."
(Variety, Sept. 9, 1942)

7 September, 1942 (MON)

        Glenn Miller and His Orchestra played at Con-
vention Hall, Asbury Park, New Jersey, from
9:00-1:00 A.M. (G.M.P.R.; G.M.D.; Variety,
Sept. 2, 1942)

        "Army takes over the Convention Hall in
Atlantic City after Labor Day September 7, 1942.
Glenn Miller plays final hop Sept. 7, 1942 where
capacity is 6,000." (Variety, Sept. 2, 1942)

8 September, 1942 (TUES): New York City, N.Y. (CHESTERFIELD SHOW)
CBS   7:15-7:30 P.M.

        Moonlight Serenade (Theme)
        Sleepy Lagoon
        Jingle, Jangle, Jingle
        Serenade In Blue-voc SN & 4M
        I Hear You Screamin'
        Slumber Song (Theme)

9 September, 1942 (WED): New York City, N.Y. (CHESTERFIELD SHOW)
CBS   7:15-7:30 P.M.

        The announcer for this program is Mel Allen.

        Moonlight Serenade (Theme)

E3VP 5237   Vi LPT 6700, Vi EPNT 6700 (947-0119), HMV RLS
               599, Vi SPD-18 (599-9104), RCA G LPT
               6700

(Broadcast continued on next page)

A Chesterfield broadcast on the road in 1942. Announcer and location are unknown. Identifiable band members, left to right: Lipkins, Priddy, McMickle, D'Annolfo, May, Miller, Purtill, Schwartz, Martin, Caceres, Beneke, Conway. (*Photo courtesy Glenn Miller Estate*)

Glenn Miller at the door of the recruiting office in New York, just after he traded his baton for the double bars of an army captain. (*Photo courtesy of Glenn Miller Estate*)

(1:59) Make Believe (arr BF)
           From the musical production "Show Boat"
           (Oscar Hammerstein, 2nd-Jerome Kern)
           Ts, Beneke; as, Martin?; ts, Beneke

           Juke Box Saturday Night

E3VP 5242   Vi LPT 6700, Vi EPNT 6700 (947-0125), HMV RLS 599,
                 Vi SPD-18 (599-9104), RCA G LPT 6700,
                 RD 3/4-64
(1:54) My Devotion (arr JG)-voc Skip Nelson and
           The Modernaires
           (Roc Hillman-Johnny Napton)

           Bugle Call Rag
           Slumber Song (Theme)

10 September, 1942 (THUR): New York City, N.Y. (CHESTERFIELD SHOW)
           CBS 7:15-7:30 P.M.

           Moonlight Serenade (Theme)
           In The Mood
           My Devotion-voc SN & 4M
           Kalamazoo
           Slumber Song (Theme)

           On this date Glenn Miller enlisted in the army.
           (BB, Sept. 19, 1942)

           The band took the New York-New Haven Hartford RR
           from New York to Boston. (G.M.P.R.)

11 September, 1942 (FRI)

           Glenn Miller and His Orchestra played for one
           week (closed Thursday, September 17th) at the
           RKO Keith's Boston Theater, Boston, Massachusetts
           (at Washington Street and Essex). Broadcasts
           originated from the stage. The band's gross for
           the week was $46,000 and was the high figure for
           the year. (BB, Sept. 5, 19 & 26, 1942; Boston
           Post, Sept. 11 & 17, 1942; G.M.P.R.)

               "There's nothing to say about this setup
           except that it's terrific, and with weekend
           prices at 85¢ top (the rule at the RKO Boston for
           the last month). Seven two hour shows a day and
           the fact that this is Miller's last appearance be-
           fore becoming a captain in the Army (which division
           manager Harry MacDonald hasn't kept a secret) the

(Continued on next page)

show will come close to nudging Eddie Cantor's
record gross of $50,000 for this stall.
    As stage shows go it hasn't really got much,
but the Miller band packs a staggering punch with
the customers and as Miller is what they want to
hear that's what they get. The band does four
tunes winding up with the inevitable Chattanooga
Choo Choo and spots Marion Hutton, Tex Beneke,
Skip Nelson and the Modernaires in solos and in
combinations.
    Al Bernie gives radio imitations and satires.
The whole show lasts something under 45 minutes
but none of the customers complained. On the contrary they shouted themselves silly." (Variety,
Sept. 16, 1942)

According to G.M.P.R. the band did a total of 37
shows. Glenn Miller stayed at the Hotel Statler
while in Boston. (G.M.P.R.)

15 September, 1942 (TUES): RKO Boston Theater, Boston,Massachusetts
                          (CHESTERFIELD SHOW)
                          CBS 7:15-7:30 P.M.

                    Moonlight Serenade (Theme)
                    Jersey Bounce
                    When Johnny Comes Marching Home
                    Serenade In Blue-voc SN & 4M

E3VP 5238   Vi LPT 6700, Vi EPNT 6700 (947-0122), HMV RLS 599,
                    Vi SPD-18 (599-9112), RCA G(Teldec) LPT
                    6700
                    (3:15) It Must Be Jelly ('Cause Jam Don't Shake
                          Like That)
                          (arr GW)-voc The Modernaires
                          (George Williams-John Chalmers
                          MacGregor)
                          P, MacGregor; ts, Klink; ts, Beneke;
                          ts, Klink; tpt, Best; tpt, May; tpt,
                          Best; as, Martin; d, Purtill

                    Slumber Song (Theme)

16 September, 1942 (WED): RKO Boston Theater, Boston, Massachusetts
                         (CHESTERFIELD SHOW)
                         CBS 7:15-7:30 P.M.

         The announcer for this program is Larry Bruff.

                    Moonlight Serenade (Theme)

(Broadcast continued on next page)

Kalamazoo-voc MH, TB & 4M
My Devotion-voc SN & 4M
American Patrol
Slumber Song (Theme)

17 September, 1942 (THUR): RKO Boston Theater, Boston, Mass.
(CHESTERFIELD SHOW)
CBS 7:15-7:30 P.M.

The announcer for this program is Larry Bruff.

Moonlight Serenade (Theme)
Sleepy Town Train
Every Night About This Time (arr GW)-
voc SN
(
I Left My Heart At The Stage Door Canteen
Caribbean Clipper
Slumber Song (Theme)

The band took the New Haven RR from Boston to New York. (G.M.P.R.)

18 September, 1942 (FRI)

Steve Lipkins, trumpet, left the Miller band and joined Jimmy Dorsey. September 17th was his last day with the band. The result of this move was that Bobby Hackett, once again, moved into the trumpet section and Bill Conway doubled on vocals and guitar. Since the band only had a week to go no replacement was sought. For the three Chesterfield programs of September 22, 23 and 24 G.M.P.R. show that there were only 16 men and leader who paid their dues to Local 802.

Trombones	Glenn Miller, Jimmy Priddy, Paul Tanner, Frank D'Annolfo
Trumpets	Billy May, BOBBY HACKETT, Dale McMickle, Johnny Best
Reeds	Lloyd "Skippy" Martin, as; Ernie Caceres, as, bar & clt; Wilbur Schwartz, clt & as; Tex Beneke, ts; Al Klink, ts
Rhythm	Chummy MacGregor, p; BILL CONWAY, g; Doc Goldberg, b; Maurice Purtill, d

The band was off on this date. (G.M.D.)

19 September, 1942 (SAT)

        The band was also off on September 19th, 20th
        and 21st. (G.M.D.)

22 September, 1942 (TUES): New York City, N.Y. (CHESTERFIELD SHOW)
                CBS 7:15-7:30 P.M.

        The announcer for this program is Mel Allen

          Moonlight Serenade (Theme)

E2VL 4545   Vi LPT-3001, Vi EPBT-3001 (947-0054), Vi EPA-729,
             Vi EPB-1193 (547-0822), Vi LPM-1193,
             HMV DLP 1021, Vi TP3-5020, E1 WDLP 1021,
             RCA G EPB-3001, RCA G LPM-1193, RCA G LPT-
             3001
       (2:23)April In Paris (arr BF)
             From the stage musical "Walk A Little
             Faster"
             (E.Y. "Yip" Harburg-Vernon Duke)
             Ts, Beneke; cnt, Hackett; ts, Beneke;
             clt, ??

          Chattanooga Choo Choo
          My Devotion
      (2:32)I Hear You Screamin' (arr GW)
           (George Williams)
           Ts, Klink; as, Caceres; d, Purtill;
           tpt, May
      (0:26)*Slumber Song (Theme)*
           (Saul Tepper-John Chalmers MacGregor)

23 September, 1942 (WED): New York City, N.Y. (CHESTERFIELD SHOW)
                CBS 7:15-7:30 P.M.

        The announcer for this program is Mel Allen.

          Moonlight Serenade (Theme)
ALP   *Kalamazoo*
          Serenade In Blue-voc SN & 4M
          Keep 'Em Flying
          Slumber Song (Theme)

24 September, 1942 (THUR)

        Glenn Miller and His Orchestra played for four
        days (closed Sunday, September 27th) at the

(Continued on next page)

Central Theater, Passaic, New Jersey. The band
was originally scheduled to play until September
30 but when Miller enlisted in the army he
wanted to cancel the entire engagement and do
only the Chesterfield radio program for his
final civilian week. The theater protested, and
Miller then agreed to work out four days in
Passaic just before his induction. (G.M.P.R.;
BB, Sept. 5 & Oct. 17, 1942; Variety, Sept. 16,
1942)

"Glenn Miller agreed to play four days of a
scheduled week booking at the Central Theater in
Passaic, New Jersey opening Sept. 24, 1942.
Miller tried to cancel the date entirely last
week to take a two week rest before entering the
Army October 7, 1942 but the theater operators
threatened a suit for damages. It's understood
that the house also threatened to secure an
injunction against Miller's playing his last
Chesterfield broadcast which falls on the day he
is to open the theater.
Now the leader is in a bad position with
Chesterfields. Latter went ahead, after being
told the Central was cancelled and distributed
tickets to the broadcast at CBS Playhouse in
NYC. Miller always does his commercials from
the stage during a theater booking and undoubtedly will have to do the one in question from the
Central. He couldn't easily make it into N.Y.C.
from Passaic and back between shows which puts
CBS and Chesterfields in a spot since the tickets
are out.
Thing that riled the Central operators into
forcing Miller to fullfil his date for them was
that last February the leader begged out of playing the house to go to the coast to make a film.
He then signed a contract for the week of Sept.
24, 1942 but wanted to cancel again when his Army
commission came through.
H. Robert Broder, attorney, handled the
action for the Central Theater. He contended
that Miller inasmuch as he appeared free to play
before a free theater audience for Chesterfields,
was in the position to fullfil the theater date.
Central's management agreed to cut the date to
four days figuring that Thursday, Friday, Saturday, and Sunday are the best Box Office days
anyhow." (Variety, Sept. 23, 1942) Also on the
same bill was Wally Brown. The band did 22
shows at the Passaic. (G.M.P.R.)

24 September, 1942 (THUR): Central Theater, Passaic, New Jersey
                        (CHESTERFIELD SHOW)
                        CBS 7:15-7:30 P.M.

    The announcer for this program is Mel Allen.

        Moonlight Serenade (Theme)
(3:09) <u>In The Mood</u>
        (Andy Razaf-Joe Garland)
        Ts, Beneke; ts, Klink; tpt, May
        Always In My Heart-voc SN
(0:06) <u>I Left My Heart At The Stage Door Canteen</u>
        (arr GW)
        From the musical production "This Is
        The Army"
        (Irving Berlin)

ALP (2:55) *Juke Box Saturday Night (arr JG)-voc*
        Marion Hutton, Tex Beneke and The
        Modernaires
        From the musical production "Stars
        On Ice"
        (Albert Stillman-Paul McGrane)
        Tpt, Harry James

After "Juke Box Saturday Night" Miller introduced Harry James to the audience and announced that James would be taking over the Chesterfield program next Tuesday night (Sept. 29th).

Moonlight Serenade (Theme)

"I Left My Heart At The Stage Door Canteen" was a very short version as it was last week's winning tune.

G.M.D. indicates that the early program was broadcast from New York City and that the late program was broadcast from the stage of the Central Theater in Passaic. Since the band was in Passaic it seems rather unusual to broadcast from two different locations. If G.M.D. is correct this would mean that Miller broadcast his Chesterfield show twice each evening (once for the east coast and once for the west coast). As yet we do not have substantial proof to support this view, although there has been mention of rebroadcasts during this period (see August 4, 1942).

26 September, 1942 (SAT): Central Theater, Passaic, New Jersey
(COKE SPOTLIGHT BAND)
NBC-Blue   9:30-10:00 P.M.

"Glenn Miller's last civilian radio appearance
for the duration takes place tonight when he
broadcasts from Central Theater, Passaic, N.J.,
as the first Saturday 'honor band' in the new
Coca-Cola Blue Network series." (BB, Oct. 3,
1942; G.M.P.R.)

The announcer for this program is Gil Newsome.

Keep 'Em Flying
(0:55) *Moonlight Serenade (Theme)*
          (Mitchell Parish-Glenn Miller)
(0:14) *Waltz Theme (Coca Cola Theme) (arr JG)*
          (Joy)

Information on the other tunes played on this
program is missing. It might be noted that
Miller was able to play on the Coke Spotlight
Band program only because the Chesterfield
programs were over.

27 September, 1942 (SUN)

"Glenn's last show at the Central Theater
in Passaic, N.J., never finished--the curtain
was rung down while the band was still in the
middle of its theme, with Miller and Marion
Hutton no longer on the stage. Vocalist Hutton
broke down in the middle of Kalamazoo, started
crying and ran off the stage. Most of the brass
section weren't doing much better on the start
of the theme that followed--this was one case
of the 'choke-up' being no alibi. Miller, famed
for his taciturnity, turned away from the band
to keep from cracking up himself--only to face
rows and rows of kids bawling their eyes out.
'I could stand everything, all the heartache of
breaking up things that had taken us years to
build--but I just couldn't face those kids,'
Miller said." (DB--October 15, 1942)

There is a note in G.M.D. which states that the
band went on stage at 10:00 P.M. and played for
the last time together. They played the following tunes:

(Continued on following page)

In The Mood
Rhapsody In Blue
American Patrol
Kalamazoo
Juke Box Saturday Night
At Last
Serenade In Blue
It Must Be Jelly
Star Spangled Banner (arr BF)
      (Francis Scott Key)
Moonlight Serenade

Glenn Miller was scheduled to open at the Hotel Pennsylvania, October 6, 1942.

"Glenn Miller's enlistment in the Army last week threw one of the most sought after location jobs on the open market and started a mad scramble by G.A.C. to pull a replacement out of the hat sadly depleted of top bands by prior bookings.

In joining the Army Miller represents a loss in commissions to G.A.C. of approximately $100,000.00 yearly. If he had continued in front of his band until the end of this year Miller's gross income would have been between $750,000.00 and one million, probably closer to the latter. His band breaks up after September 24, 1942.

Miller goes into the Army as a Captain on October 7, 1942 in Omaha, Nebraska, the Seventh Corp Area. His chores will be musical, though details on his exact duties aren't clear." (Variety, Sept. 16, 1942)

"Glenn Miller's sudden entry into the Army caused the cancellation of his third picture deal with 20th Century-Fox calling for one film annually over a three year stretch.

Company is dickering for another band for the first picture, "Blind Date", slated for autumn production. (Variety, Sept. 16, 1942)

Marion Hutton, Tex Beneke and The Modernaires (Chuck Goldstein dropped out and was replaced) stayed together for a theater tour. Ernie Caceres and Al Klink joined Goodman. Johnny Best went with Bob Crosby. Dale McMickle went into radio. Frank D'Annolfo, Jimmy Priddy and Paul Tanner went as a unit to Charlie Spivak. Bobby Hackett formed a small jazz group. Billy May went with Les Brown as brass and arranger. Doc Goldberg enlisted in the navy. Skip Nelson returned to Chico Marx. Wilbur Schwartz joined the army. Chummy MacGregor went to the coast with Miller and then retired. (Met. Oct. 1942; DB, Oct. 1, 1942).

SUMMARY OF THE BAND'S POSITION IN BAND POLLS CONDUCTED
BY "DOWN BEAT" MAGAZINE AND "METRONOME" MAGAZINE

To shorten the listings no bands are shown after Miller.

DOWN BEAT 1938 POLL

Swing Band
1. Artie Shaw...........2535
2. Benny Goodman........2497
3. Bob Crosby...........1486
4. Count Basie.......... 889
5. Jimmy Dorsey......... 714
6. Tommy Dorsey......... 676
7. Casa Loma............ 618
8. Duke Ellington....... 461
9. Jimmie Lunceford..... 401
10. Gene Krupa........... 304
11. Larry Clinton........ 169
12. GLENN MILLER......... 158

Sweet Band
1. Casa Loma...............1971
2. Hal Kemp...............1660
3. Tommy Dorsey...........1444
4. Kay Kyser.............. 740
5. Guy Lombardo........... 679
6. Wayne King............. 459
7. Larry Clinton.......... 360
8. Russ Morgan............ 326
9. Horace Heidt.......... 229
10. GLENN MILLER........... 222

DOWN BEAT 1939 POLL

Swing Band
1. Benny Goodman........5251
2. GLENN MILLER........3211

Sweet Band
1. Tommy Dorsey............3673
2. GLENN MILLER...........3589

"The first time any band ever placed second in both
divisions, Miller's huge vote total makes him the most all-around
popular bandsman in the land. And it's all the more amazing because the band is so young--not yet two years old.
Miller's band is unique in that his arrangements, most of
them his own products, are 'different' than others. Miller also
stresses fine musicianship in his band, all of which forecasts
a trend toward more subtle swing." (DB, Jan. 1, 1940)

DOWN BEAT 1940 POLL

Swing Band
1. Benny Goodman........2130
2. Duke Ellington.......1841
3. Woody Herman.........1025
4. GLENN MILLER......... 805

Sweet Band
1. GLENN MILLER.............2605

"Just as in 1939, Glenn Miller was high scorer in both
divisions. His first in the sweet and fourth in the swing gave
him the most combined votes of all." (DB, Jan. 1, 1941)

DOWN BEAT 1941 POLL

Swing Band	Sweet Band
1. Benny Goodman.........3207	1. GLENN MILLER.............3543
2. Tommy Dorsey..........2046	
3. Duke Ellington........1882	
4. GLENN MILLER..........1737	

DOWN BEAT 1942 POLL

Swing Band	Sweet Band
1. Duke Ellington........3453	1. Tommy Dorsey.............3708
2. Benny Goodman.........3302	2. GLENN MILLER.............3435
3. Harry James...........2088	
4. Woody Herman..........1674	
5. Count Basie...........1668	
6. Tommy Dorsey..........1635	
7. GLENN MILLER..........1353	

METRONOME'S 1938 DANCE BAND CONTEST (SEE MET. JULY 1938)

Sweet	Swing
1. Hal Kemp..............2962	1. Benny Goodman............3556
2. Casa Loma.............1743	2. Tommy Dorsey.............2142
3. Tommy Dorsey..........1163	3. Bob Crosby...............1208
4. Guy Lombardo..........1152	4. Artie Shaw............... 828
5. Horace Heidt.......... 668	5. Duke Ellington........... 667
6. Wayne King............ 595	6. Casa Loma................ 648
7. Kay Kyser............. 487	7. Jimmie Lunceford......... 501
8. Ray Noble............. 396	8. Jimmy Dorsey............. 449
9. Will Osborne.......... 342	9. Red Norvo................ 390
10. Sammy Kaye............ 324	10. Count Basie.............. 283
11. Ozzie Nelson.......... 176	11. Chick Webb............... 276
12. Jan Garber............ 138	12. Gene Krupa............... 256
13. Jimmy Dorsey.......... 135	13. Bunny Berigan............ 191
14. Red Norvo............. 126	14. Larry Clinton............ 180
15. Freddy Martin......... 118	15. Ozzie Nelson............. 69
16. Russ Morgan........... 96	16. Hal Kemp................. 56
17. Duke Ellington........ 83	17. Jan Savitt............... 44
18. Jimmy Lunceford....... 76	18. GLENN MILLER............. 41
19. Benny Goodman......... 73	
20. George Olsen.......... 69	
21. Isham Jones........... 67	
22. Paul Martin........... 64	
23. Paul Whiteman......... 58	
24. Eddy Duchin........... 54	
25. Blue Barron........... 53	
26. GLENN MILLER.......... 45	

METRONOME'S 1939 DANCE BAND CONTEST (SEE MET. JULY 1939)

Sweet
1. Casa Loma.........2444
2. Tommy Dorsey......1641
3. Hal Kemp..........1061
4. GLENN MILLER....... 845

Swing
1. Benny Goodman...........2870
2. Artie Shaw..............1862
3. Tommy Dorsey............ 803
4. Bob Crosby............. 778
5. GLENN MILLER............ 726

"The biggest sensation, of 1939, according to the musicians of America, is Glenn Miller's band!
The newly organized group, whose broadcasts and records have been causing so much comment, finished like veterans in not one, but in all three divisions of the contest, winding up fifth in Swing, fourth in Sweet and fifth in Favorite of All. It was a magnificent showing for the group that finished far out of the running last year." (Met. July 1939)

METRONOME'S 1940 DANCE BAND CONTEST (SEE MET. AUGUST 1940)

Sweet
1. Tommy Dorsey......1384
2. GLENN MILLER......1192

Swing
1. Benny Goodman..........1703
2. GLENN MILLER............ 740

"Miller hung on tenaciously throughout. Not only did he dog Benny's heels, but he also kept shoving Tommy Dorsey for top sweet honors. When the final smoke had cleared, the popular Glenn was perched on the second rung of all three ladders, the greatest example of all-around showing in the history of the contest." (Met. Aug. 1940)

This was the last Metronome dance band poll.

ADDENDA AND ERRATA

The following are corrections, additional issues and material that was received too late for inclusion in the text:

P. 1 - April 1935 - In a 1964 tape interview with a record collector Smith Ballew claimed that this was his Orchestra (with some additions), and that he suggested to Glenn that they put Glenn's name on the record (as leader) to help his career.
- 25 April, 1935 - This session started at 12:45 A.M.

mx. 17379 - This is take 1 of two takes. Add, AFRS "America's Popular Music" END-390-200.
mx. 17380 - This is take 1 of two takes.
mx. 17381 - This is take 1 of two takes. Add, AFRS "America's Popular Music" END-390-420/602,
Ha HS 11393, and Hall Br. HM 691.
- The above three tunes were completed at 1:30 A.M.
mx. 17382 - This is take 1 of two takes. Add, Ha HS 11393, and Hall Br. HM 691.

P. 3 - 22 March, 1937, mx. 62058 A - BREOE 9169 should read BrE OE 9169. Add, Longines Br. LP (number unknown), DeArg 333270, and AFRS G.I. Jive H-12-2079.
mx. 62060 A - Add, AFRS "America's Popular Music" END-390-420.
mx. 62062 A - Delete, AFRS "America's Pop Music" 67. Add, AFRS "America's Popular Music" END-390-2/67/163/884, Br. 12" LP (details unknown),
DeArg 333270, AFRS G.I. Jive H-12-2075, and AFRS Jill's Juke Box H-46-204.
mx. 62063 A - Add, AFRS "America's Popular Music" END-390-200/603.

P. 5 - 9 June, 1937, mx. B 21234-3 - Co XLP 114353 should read Co P7M/P7S 5121/5122. Add, PhAu B 07738R, AFRS "America's Popular Music" END-390-200/603, and Co G 30009.
mx. B 21235-1 - Add, PhAu B 07738R, and AFRS "America's Popular Music" END-390-163/420.
mx. B 21236-1 - Add, PhAu B 07738R, and AFRS "America's Popular Music" END-390-27.

P. 6 - 9 June, 1937, mx. B 21240-1 - Add, PhAu B 21542H, and PhAu B 07738R.

In a recent discussion with George Simon he stated that he was not on drums on this session and that probably the mid-April 1937 personnel should apply for this recording session.

P. 8 - 29 November, 1937, mx. B 22079-1 - Add, RZAu G 23389 (labelled as "Casino Royal Orchestra"), Ha HS 11393, and Hall Br. HM 691.
mx. B 22080-1 - Add, PhAu B 07738R.

P. 9 - 29 November, 1937, mx. B 22081-1 - Add, PhAu B 07738R, and AFRS "America's Popular Music" END-390-27.
mx. B 22082-1 - Add, Ha HS 11393, and Hall Br. HM 691.

P. 10 - 13 December, 1937 - This date should be shown after the
          recording session of the same date.
P. 10 - 13 December, 1937, mx. B 22135-1 - Add, Ha HS 11393, and
                    Hall Br. HM 691.
                mx. B 22136-1 - Add, Ha HS 11393, and Hall
                    Br. HM 691.
P. 11 - 25 December, 1937 - The Brookline Country Club, Brookline
          is located in Massachusetts and not as shown by G.M.C.
P. 12 - Insert the following before 2 January, 1938:

       GLENN MILLER 1937 BROADCASTS--Other than those mentioned
       in the text. No data available at the moment on the
       tunes played.

Day	Date	Starting Time	Length	Radio Station
Wednesday	24 November, 1937	Midnight	30 minutes	WJZ
Wednesday	1 December, 1937	Midnight	30 minutes	WJZ
Tuesday	7 December, 1937	11:05 P.M.	10 minutes	WJZ
Wednesday	8 December, 1937	11:30 P.M.	30 minutes	WJZ
Tuesday	14 December, 1937	11:05 P.M.	25 minutes	WJZ
Tuesday	14 December, 1937	11:00 P.M.	30 minutes	WOR (same as above?)
Wednesday	15 December, 1937	Midnight	30 minutes	WJZ
Wednesday	22 December, 1937	Midnight	30 minutes	WJZ

P. 14 - 23 May, 1938, mx. B 22972-1 - Add, RZAu G 23612 (labelled
                    as "Casino Royal Orchestra"), Ha HS 11393,
                    and Hall Br. HM 691.
                mx. B 22973-1 - Add, RZAu G 23502 (labelled
                    as "Casino Royal Orchestra"), Lu 60440,
                    Ha HS 11393, and Hall Br. HM 691.
                mx. B 22974-1 - Add, PhAu B 07738R.
                mx. B 22975-1 - Add, PhAu B 07738R, AFRS
                    G.I. Jive H-12-831, and AFRS Jill's Juke
                    Box H-46-22.
P. 15 - 18 June, 1938, mx. PPRM-5333 - Add, RCA Au LPM/LSP-2767,
                    and AFRS "America's Popular Music" END-
                    390-1037//EN-1925.
P. 16 - 20 June, 1938, mx. E4VP 8208 Doin' The Jive - Add, AFRS
                    "America's Popular Music" END-390-50/163/
                    200/603
          25 June, 1938, mx. PPRM-5341 Moonlight Serenade - Add, AFRS
                    "America's Popular Music" END-390-1043,
                    and RCA Au LPM/LSP-2769.
                mx. PPRM-5341 MEDLEY - Add, AFRS "America's
                    Popular Music" END-390-1043, and RCA Au
                    LPM/LSP-2769.
P. 17 - 25 June, 1938, mx. PPRM-5334 - Add, AFRS "America's Popular
                    Music" END-390-1039//EN-1932, and RCA Au
                    LPM/LSP-2767.
          27 June, 1938, mx. E4VP 8208 - Add, AFRS "America's Popular
                    Music" END-390-50

                        mx. PPRM-5334 - Add, AFRS "America's
                        Popular Music" END-390-1038//EN-1932,
                        and RCA Au LPM/LSP-2767.
                        mx. PPRM-5337 - Add, AFRS "America's
                        Popular Music" END-390-1039//EN-1940, and
                        RCA Au LPM/LSP-2768.
P. 18 - 27 June, 1938, mx. PPRM-5334 - Add, AFRS "America's
                        Popular Music" END-390-1038//EN-1928, and
                        RCA Au LPM/LSP-2767.
P. 23 - 27 September, 1938, mx. 027410-1 - Add, AFRS "America's
                        Popular Music" EN-1663.
                        mx. 027411-1 - Add, AFRS "America's Popular
                        Music" END-390-603//EN-1858.
                        mx. 027412-1 - Add, AFRS "America's Popular
                        Music" END-390-603//EN-1858.
P. 25 - 6 October, 1938 - The Brookline Country Club, Brookline is
        located in Massachusetts and not as shown by G.M.C. &
        G.M.P.R.
P. 36 - After December 11, 1938. The correct spelling of Legh Knowles'
        first name is Leigh. This applies to all further listings of
        his name.
P. 39 - 30 December, 1938, mx. PPRM-5338 - Add, AFRS "America's
                        Popular Music" END-390-1042, and RCA Au
                        LPM/LSP-2768.
P. 40 - Insert the following before 31 December, 1938:

        GLENN MILLER 1938 BROADCASTS--Other than those mentioned
        in the text. No data available at the moment on the tunes
        played.

Day	Date		Starting Time	Length	Radio Station
Wednesday	27 April, 1938	(actually 28th)	12:30 A.M.	30 minutes	WJZ
Saturday	30 April, 1938		11:05 P.M.	25 minutes	WJZ
Wednesday	4 May, 1938	(actually 5th)	12:30 A.M.	30 minutes	WJZ
Wednesday	11 May, 1938	(actually 12th)	12:30 A.M.	30 minutes	WJZ
Saturday	14 May, 1938	(actually 15th)	12:30 A.M.	30 minutes	WJZ
Saturday	21 May, 1938		11:00 P.M.	15 minutes	WJZ
Wednesday	25 May, 1938	(actually 26th)	12:30 A.M.	30 minutes	WJZ
Saturday	28 May, 1938		11:15 P.M.	15 minutes	WJZ
Thursday	7 July, 1938		11:30 P.M.	30 minutes	WOR
Saturday	9 July, 1938		6:45 P.M.	15 minutes	WOR
Sunday	10 July, 1938		2:15 P.M.	30 minutes	WOR
Tuesday	12 July, 1938		5:15 P.M.	30 minutes	WOR
Friday	22 July, 1938		11:30 P.M.	30 minutes	WOR
Saturday	23 July, 1938		7:45 P.M.	15 minutes	WOR
Sunday	24 July, 1938		2:15 P.M.	30 minutes	WOR
Tuesday	26 July, 1938		5:15 P.M.	15 minutes	WOR
Saturday	20 August, 1938		5:00 P.M.	30 minutes	WOR
Sunday	21 August, 1938		8:00 P.M.	30 minutes	WOR
Monday	22 August, 1938		8:30 P.M.	30 minutes	WOR
Saturday	1 October, 1938		11:15 P.M.	15 minutes	WABC
Tuesday	4 October, 1938		11:30 P.M.	30 minutes	WABC
Saturday	8 October, 1938		11:15 P.M.	15 minutes	WABC
Tuesday	11 October, 1938		11:30 P.M.	30 minutes	WABC

Day	Date	Starting Time	Length	Radio Station
Saturday	15 October, 1938	11:15 P.M.	15 minutes	WABC
Tuesday	18 October, 1938	11:30 P.M.	30 minutes	WABC
Saturday	22 October, 1938	11:15 P.M.	15 minutes	WABC
Tuesday	25 October, 1938	11:30 P.M.	30 minutes	WABC
Saturday	29 October, 1938	11:15 P.M.	15 minutes	WABC
Tuesday	1 November, 1938	11:30 P.M.	30 minutes	WABC
Wednesday	9 November, 1938	11:30 P.M.	30 minutes	WABC
Saturday	12 November, 1938	11:15 P.M.	15 minutes	WABC
Tuesday	15 November, 1938	11:30 P.M.	30 minutes	WABC
Saturday	19 November, 1938	11:15 P.M.	15 minutes	WABC
Tuesday	22 November, 1938	11:30 P.M.	30 minutes	WABC
Saturday	26 November, 1938	11:15 P.M.	15 minutes	WABC
Tuesday	29 November, 1938	11:30 P.M.	30 minutes	WABC
Tuesday	6 December, 1938	11:30 P.M.	30 minutes	WABC
Saturday	10 December, 1938	11:15 P.M.	15 minutes	WABC
Saturday	17 December, 1938	11:15 P.M.	15 minutes	WABC
Tuesday	20 December, 1938	11:30 P.M.	30 minutes	WABC
Wednesday	21 December, 1938	Midnight	30 minutes	WABC
Tuesday	27 December, 1938	11:30 P.M.	30 minutes	WABC

6 January, 1939, mx. PPRM-5333 - Add, AFRS "America's Popular Music" END-390-1037//EN-1925, and RCA Au LPM/LSP-2767.

P. 50 - 23 March, 1939, mx. PPRM-5341 - Add, AFRS "America's Popular Music" END-390-1044, and RCA Au LPM/LSP-2769.

mx. PPRM-5338 - Add, AFRS "America's Popular Music" END-390-1041, and RCA Au LPM/LSP-2768.

mx. E4VP 8206 - Delete, AFRS "America's Pop Music" 72. Add, AFRS "America's Popular Music" END-390-72/98/135, and RD Br. RDM 2456/RDS 6456.

P. 52 - 31 March, 1939, mx. PPRM-5341 - Add, AFRS "America's Popular Music" END-390-1043, and RCA Au LPM/LSP-2769.

mx. PPRM-5333 - Add, AFRS "America's Popular Music" END-390-1036//EN-1917, and RCA Au LPM/LSP-2767.

P. 53 - 31 March, 1939, mx. E4VP 8206 - Delete, AFRS "America's Pop Music" 72. Add, AFRS "America's Popular Music" END-390-72/98/135.

4 April, 1939, mx. 035699-1 - Add, AFRS "America's Popular Music" EN-1728, and Cam Au Cal/Cas-751

P. 54 - 4 April, 1939, mx. 035701-1 - HMV F M33090 should read HMV F MR 3090. Delete, AFRS "America's Pop Music" 67. Add, RCA G LPM-9901, RCA Au VPM-6019, RD Br. RDM 2451/RDS 6451, RCA Br. RD-8094, RCA Br. GM-1, RD 3/4-76, HMVAu EA 3463, RCA G CS-10258, RCA Au 20020, Fe Au MX-10583,

ViArg 1A-0149, ViArg AGLT-2, ViArg 26955,
RCA Au L 10351, AFRS Jill's Juke Box
H-46-17/62/71/88/89/193, AFRS "America's
Popular Music" END-390-34/67/163/201/229/
234/244/582/1102/1359/1455//EN-1738, RCA
G RCS-3105, AFRS G.I. Jive H-12-725/1072/
1184/1307/1429/1538/1616/1758, AFRS "Hot
Off The Record Press" EN-257-190, and
HMVIn NE. 684.

mx. 035702-1 - RZ Au G 23821 is labelled as
by "Masters Of Rhythm". Add, RD Br. RDM
2452/RDS 6452, AFRS G.I. Jive H-12-1063,
and AFRS "America's Popular Music" EN-
1813.

P. 55 - 4 April, 1939, mx. E4VP 8205 - Delete, AFRS "America's
Pop Music" 67. Add, AFRS "America's
Popular Music" END-390-50/67/163/201/603,
RCA G CS-10258, RCA G RCA 3105, and RCA
G LPM-9901.

mx. PPRM-5342 The Masquerade Is Over - Add,
RCA Au LPM/LSP-2769.

mx. PPRM-5342 Our Love - Add, RCA Au LPM/
LSP-2769.

P. 57 - 10 April, 1939, mx. 035729-1 - Add, AFRS "America's Popular
Music" END-390-201/603.

mx. 035730-1 - Add, Cam Cal-2267 (unissued)

mx. 035731-1 - Delete, AFRS "America's Pop
Music" 72. Add, RCA Au 20049, AFRS Jill's
Juke Box H-46-4/98/121/130, AFRS G.I.
Jive H-12-752/940/1055/1579/1800/1644 (in-
complete)/1830 (incomplete), RCA Au VPM-
6019, RCA G RCS-3105, Fe Au MX-10584,
RCA Br. GM-1, RCA Br. RD-8094 (unissued),
AFRS "America's Popular Music" EN-1663,
HMVIn NE. 684, and RD Br. RDM 2455/RDS
6455.

P. 58 - 10 April, 1939, mx. 035732-1 - Delete, AFRS "Jukebox USA"
199. Add, ViArg 1A-0154, ViArg AGET-1,
RCA G RCS 3105, AFRS Jill's Juke Box
H-46-13/44/71/100/135/172/193, AFRS
"America's Popular Music" END-390-163/
349/409/659, AFRS "Jukebox U.S.A." EN-
106-9/199/325/369, AFRS G.I. Jive H-12-
852/910/1371/1471/1583/1623/1662/1872/
767/1760/2154, RD RD8-5001, RCA PK-1432,
Fe Au MX-10584, RCA Au VPM-6019, RD Br. RDM
2174/RDS 6174, RCA Br. GM-1, RCA Br. RD-
8094 (unissued), and RCA Au 20020.

P. 59 - 18 April, 1939, mx. 035764-1 - Add, RCA Au 20227.

mx. 035765-1 - Add, AFRS "America's Popular
Music" EN-1813.

            mx. 035766-1 - Delete, AFRS "Jukebox USA"
            140. Add, AFRS "Jukebox U.S.A." EN-106-
            140/310, RCA G LPT 3002, RD Br. RDM 2455/
            RDS 6455, ViArg 1A-0154, ViArg AGET-9,
            AFRS G.I. Jive H-12-2009, AFRS Jill's Juke
            Box H-46-175, AFRS "Hot Off The Record Press"
            EN-257-48, and AFRS "America's Popular
            Music" END-390-201/604//EN-1788.
            mx. 035767-1 - Delete, AFRS "Jukebox U.S.A."
            308. Add, AFRS "Jukebox U.S.A." EN-106-15/
            308/359, ViArg 1A-0406, ViArg 68-0685,
            AFRS Jill's Juke Box H-46-151/175, AFRS
            G.I. Jive H-12-335/1740/1789/1826/1853,
            AFRS "America's Popular Music" EN-1658,
            and AFRS "Hot Off The Record Press" EN-257-
            78/120.

P. 60 - 18 April, 1939 - Delete, Mutual 10:30-11:00 P.M. EST and
        add, NBC-Blue 11:30-12:00 Midnight EST.
            mx. PPRM-5342 - Add, RCA Au LPM/LSP-2769,
            and AFRS "America's Popular Music" END-
            390-1044.

P. 63 - 9 May, 1939, mx. 036877-1 - Delete, AFRS "America's Pop
            Music" 72. Add, AFRS "America's Popular
            Music" END-390-72/98//EN-1673, RCA Au
            VPM-6019, RCA Br. GM-1, and RCA Br. RD-
            8094 (unissued).
            mx. 036878-1 - Add, RCA Br. RD-8094 (un-
            issued), RCA Br. GM-1, RCA Au VPM-6019,
            and RD Br. RDM 2451/RDS 6451.

P. 64 - 17 May, 1939 - Add under the date, NBC-Blue 11:30-12:00
            Midnight EST. (WJZ).
            mx. E4VP 8203 - Add, AFRS "America's
            Popular Music" END-390-50/81/116/201/604.
            mx. E4VP 8204 - Delete, AFRS "America's
            Pop Music" 67. Add, AFRS "America's
            Popular Music" END-390-67/163.

P. 66 - 25 May, 1939, mx. 037152-1 - Add, AFRS "America's Popular
            Music" EN-1668, ViArg 1AC-0676, and AFRS
            G.I. Jive H-12-1901/2027.
            mx. 037153-1 - Add, RD Br. RDM 2097.
            mx. 037156-1 - Add, ViArg 1A-0143, and
            ViArg 68-1545.
            mx. 037157-1 - Add, ViArg 1A-0143, ViArg
            68-1545, Cam Au Cal/Cas-751, RCA Au EPA-
            5133, AFRS "America's Popular Music"
            EN-1718, and RD Br. RDM 2455/RDS 6455.

P. 67 - 29 May, 1939, mx. E4VP 8203 My Last Goodbye - Add, AFRS
            "America's Popular Music" END-390-81/116.

P. 68 - 2 June, 1939, mx. 037179-1 - Add, AFRS "America's Popular
            Music" EN-1803.
            mx. 037182-1 - Add, RCA PK-1432.

P. 69 - 2 June, 1939 - Add under the location, WJZ.
       13 June, 1939, mx. PPRM-5338 - Add, RD 3/4-76, RCA Au
                       LPM/LSP-2768, and AFRS "America's
                       Popular Music" END-390-1040.
                   mx. E4VP 8203 - Add, AFRS "America's
                   Popular Music" END-390-81/116.
P. 70 - 19 June, 1939 - Add under the location, WJZ 11:15-11:30
                   P.M.
P. 72 - 22 June, 1939, mx. 037675-1 - Add, RCA Au EPA-5133, and
                   RD Br. RDM 2456/RDS 6456.
P. 73 - 27 June, 1939, mx. 038201-1 - Add, AFRS "America's
                   Popular Music" END-390-604//EN-1818.
                   mx. 038202-1 - Add, HMVAu EA 3473, RD 3/4-
                   76, and AFRS "America's Popular Music"
                   EN-1668.
       30 June, 1939, mx. PPRM-5342 - Add, RCA Au LPM/LSP-2769,
                   and AFRS "America's Popular Music END-
                   390-1044.
                   mx. E4VP 8203 - Add, AFRS "America's
                   Popular Music" END-390-50/81/116.
P. 75 - 12 July, 1939, mx. 038261-1 - Add, AFRS "America's
                   Popular Music" EN-1752.
                   mx. 038262-1 - Add, AFRS "America's
                   Popular Music" EN-1813.
                   mx. 038263-1 - Add, AFRS "America's
                   Popular Music" END-390-201/604.
                   mx. 038264-1 - Add, Cam Cal 2267 (unissued).
       14 July, 1939 - Add under the location, WJZ 11:15-
                   11:30 P.M.
P. 76 - 14 July, 1939, mx. PPRM-5341 - Add, RCA Au LPM/LSP-2769.
       20 July, 1939, mx. E4VP 8203 - Add, AFRS "America's
                   Popular Music" END-390-81/116, and
                   RD 3/4-76.
P. 77 - 26 July, 1939, mx. 038138-1 - Delete, AFRS "America's Pop
                   Music" 72. Add, AFRS "America's Popular
                   Music" END-390-72/98/135.
P. 78 - 26 July, 1939, mx. 038139-1 - Delete, AFRS "America's Pop
                   Music" 72.
                   mx. 038140-1 - Add, HMVAu EA 3473, RD Br.
                   RDM 2455/RDS 6455, and AFRS "America's
                   Popular Music" END-390-27/201/604//
                   EN-1863.
                   mx. 038141-1 - Add, AFRS "America's
                   Popular Music" END-390-844.
                   mx. 038142-1 - Add, AFRS "America's
                   Popular Music" END-390-2/201/380/604,
                   and RD Br. RDM 2455/RDS 6455.
P. 79 - 26 July, 1939, mx. E4VP 8204 - Add, AFRS "America's
                   Popular Music" END-390-72/98/135.
       28 July, 1939, mx. E4VP 8204 - Add, AFRS "America's
                   Popular Music" END-390-72/98/135.

        1 August, 1939, mx. 038170-1 - Delete, AFRS H-12-1000
G.I. Jive, AFRS "America's Pop Music"
67, AFRS "Jukebox USA" 263, and AFRS
"Jukebox USA' 180. ViJ 1044 should
read ViJ A-1044. Add, ViArg 26966,
ViArg 1A-0148, ViArg AGET-1, ViArg
AGLT-2, RCA Au L 10351, RCA Au VPM-
6019, RCA G LPM/LSP-9901,
RCA Cam G CS-10258, RCA G RCS 3105, RD
Br. RDM 2172, RCA Br. GM-1, RCA Br. RD-
8094 (unissued), Vi LSP 2774, RCA F
740.515, Fe Au MX-10583, AFRS Jill's
Juke Box H-46-27/71/110/136/193, AFRS
"Hot Off The Record Press" EN-257-40,
AFRS G.I. Jive H-12-710/723/738/766/
825/848/875/901/940/945/978/1001/1035/
1111/1214/1217/1345/1402/1479/1553/1562/
1571/1608/1629/1747/1869/2149, AFRS
"Jukebox U.S.A." EN-106-1/180/263/325/363,
and AFRS "America's Popular Music" END-
390-12/67/163//EN-1758/1888.

P. 80 - 1 August, 1939, mx. 038171-1 - Add, AFRS G.I. Jive H-12-
1063, and AFRS "America's Popular Music"
EN-1808.

mx. 038173-1 - Add, HMVAu EA 3377.

P. 81 - 1 August, 1939, mx. 038174-1 - Add, AFRS G.I. Jive H-12-
581/1121, RD Br. RDM 2451/RDS 6451, and
AFRS "America's Popular Music" END-390-
606.

mx. 038175-1 - Add, RCA Au 20227, RD Br.
RDM 2451/RDS 6451, and AFRS "America's
Popular Music" END-390-604.

P. 82 - 4 August, 1939 - Add under the location, WJZ 11:15-
11:30 P.M.

mx. PPRM-5334 - Add, RCA Au LPM/LSP-2767,
and AFRS "America's Popular Music"
END-390-1038//EN-1928.

15 August, 1939 - Add under the location, WEAF 6:30-
6:45 P.M.

P. 83 - 18 August, 1939, mx. 041586-1 - Add, AFRS "America's
Popular Music" EN-1853, HMVAu EA 3377,
and RD Br. RDM 2453/RDS 6453.

mx. 038143-1 - Add, AFRS G.I. Jive H-12-
1786/2143, AFRS Jill's Juke Box H-46-
151/175, RCA G LPT 3002, RCA Au 20048,
ViArg 1A-0090, ViArg 68-1595, and AFRS
"America's Popular Music" EN-1783.

mx. 041587-1 - Add, RCA Br. GM-1, RCA Au
VPM-6019, RCA Br. RD-8094 (unissued),
and AFRS "America's Popular Music"
EN-1803.

                    mx. 041588-1 - Add, AFRS "America's
                    Popular Music" EN-1713.
P. 87 - 11 September, 1939, mx. 042662-1 - Add, AFRS "America's
                    Popular Music"EN-1668.
                    mx. 042663-1 - HMVSw JK-5822 should
                    read HMVSw JK-2281.
P. 89 - 25 September, 1939, mx. 042730-1 - Add, Cam Au Cal/Cas-751,
                    and AFRS "America's Popular Music"EN-
                    1733.
P. 90 - 3 October, 1939, mx.042780-1 - Add, AFRS Jill's Juke Box
                    H-46-55/64, AFRS G.I. Jive H-12-754/
                    1021/1195/1975, RD Br. RDM 2092, ViArg
                    20-1536, and AFRS "America's Popular
                    Music" END-390-372.
P. 91 - 6 October, 1939, mx. H2PP-6679 Moonlight Serenade - Add,
                    AFRS "America's Popular Music" END-390-
                    201/605/1531.
                    mx. H2PP-6679 Runnin' Wild - Add, AFRS
                    "America's Popular Music" END-390-201/
                    605/1531.
P. 92 - 6 October, 1939, mx. H2PP-6679 Sunrise Serenade - Add,
                    AFRS "America's Popular Music" END-
                    390-605/1531.
                    mx. H2PP-6679 Little Brown Jug - Add,
                    AFRS "America's Popular Music" END-
                    390-605/1531.
                    mx. H2PP-6679 Stairway To The Stars -
                    Add, AFRS "America's Popular Music"
                    END-390-201/605/1531.
                    mx. H2PP-6679 To You - Add, AFRS
                    "America's Popular Music" END-390-605.
                    mx. H2PP-6679 One O'Clock Jump - Add,
                    AFRS "America's Popular Music" END-
                    390-201/605/1531.
                    mx. H2PP-6680 Londonderry Air - Add,
                    AFRS "America's Popular Music" END-
                    390-201/606.
P. 93 - 6 October, 1939, mx. H2PP-6680 The Jumpin' Jive - Add,
                    AFRS "America's Popular Music" END-
                    390-201/606.
                    mx. H2PP-6680 FDR Jones - Add, AFRS
                    "America's Popular Music" END-390-606.
                    mx. H2PP-6680 Hold Tight - Add, AFRS
                    "America's Popular Music" END-390-606.
                    mx. H2PP-6680 In The Mood - Add, AFRS
                    "America's Popular Music" END-390-201/
                    606/1531.
                    mx. H2PP-6680 Bugle Call Rag - Add, AFRS
                    "America's Popular Music" END-390-606/
                    1531.
                    mx. H2PP-6680 Moonlight Serenade - Add,
                    AFRS "America's Popular Music" END-
                    390-606.

P. 94 - 9 October, 1939, mx. 042924-1 - Add, AFRS "America's
                        Popular Music" END-390-605. Delete,
                        HMVSw JK-2281.
                        mx. 042925-1 - Add, RCA Br. INTS 1019.
P. 97 - 5 November, 1939, mx. 043354-1 - Add, Vi PK-1432, HMVSp
                        GY 702, RCA Au VPM-6019, RCA Br. GM-1,
                        RD 3/4-76, and RCA Br. RD-8094 (un-
                        issued).
                        mx. 043356-1 - Delete, AFRS "Jukebox
                        USA" 151. Add, AFRS G.I. Jive H-12-
                        1826 (partial)/2002//EN-12-2349, AFRS
                        Jill's Juke Box H-46-175, AFRS "America's
                        Popular Music" EN-1778/1798, AFRS "Hot
                        Off The Record Press" EN-257-175, AFRS
                        Downbeat H-7-390, AFRS "Jukebox U.S.A."
                        EN-106-55/151, RCA Au VPM-6019, RCA Br.
                        GM-1, RCA G RCS 3105, RCA Br. RD-8094
                        (unissued), ViArg 1A-0152, RCA Au 20403,
                        and RCA G LPT 3002.
P. 100 - 16 November, 1939, mx. E4VP 8205 - Add, AFRS "America's
                        Popular Music" END-390-81/116.
P. 101 - 18 November, 1939, mx. 043390-1 - Add, AFRS "America's
                        Popular Music" EN-1673, and AFRS Jill's
                        Juke Box H-46-32.
                        mx. 043391-1 - Add, HMVSp GY 702, and AFRS
                        "America's Popular Music" END-390-27.
P. 102 - 24 November, 1939 - Add under the location, WJZ 11:05-
                        12:00 Midnight.
P. 103 - 25 November, 1939, mx. E4VP 8205 - Add, AFRS "America's
                        Popular Music" END-390-81/116.
P. 104 - 26 November, 1939, mx. E4VP 8206 - Add, RCA G RCS 3105, and
                        AFRS "America's Popular Music" END-390-
                        81/116.
P. 105 - 6 December, 1939, mx. 043975-1 - Add, AFRS "America's
                        Popular Music" EN-1698.
P. 106 - 6 December, 1939 - Add under the location, WJZ 12:30-
                        1:00 A.M. (7 December, 1939)
P. 113 - 3 January, 1940, mx. K2PP-0043 - Add, RD Br. RDM 2451/RDS
                        6451, and RCA Au L 11025.
P. 116 - 6 January, 1940, mx. 046084-1 - Add, AFRS "America's
                        Popular Music" END-390-202/606.
P. 117 - 10 January, 1940, mx. E3VP 5242 - Add, ViArg AGET-3000,
                        ViArg AGLT-1, and AFRS "America's
                        Popular Music" END-390-12/202/234/265/
                        606//EN-1838.
P. 118 - 15 January, 1940, mx. 046432-1 - Add, AFRS Jill's Juke Box
                        H-46-175, RCA G RCS 3105, RCA Au 20059,
                        and RCA Br. INTS 1019.
                        mx. 046433-1 - Add, RCA Au 20059, RCA G
                        LPT 3002, ViArg AGET-9, and AFRS
                        "America's Popular Music" END-390-202/
                        305/355/402/607//EN-1788.

P. 119 - 16 January, 1940, mx. K2PP-0042 - Add, RCA Au L 11023,
and AFRS "America's Popular Music"
END-390-301.
P. 121 - 23 January, 1940, mx. K2PP-0046 - Add, AFRS "America's
Popular Music" END-390-301, and RCA
Au L 11024.
        24 January, 1940, mx. E3VP 5237 - Add, ViArg AGET-3000,
and ViArg AGLT-1.
P. 122 - 24 January, 1940, mx. E3VP 5237 - Add, ViArg AGET-3000,
ViArg AGLT-1, AFRS "America's Popular
Music" END-390-47/608.
P. 123 - 26 January, 1940, mx. 046727-1 - Add, ViArg 1A-0090, ViArg
68-1595, Vi PK-1432, and HMVAu EA 2606.
        mx. 046728-1 - Add, ViArg 26973.
P. 124 - 29 January, 1940, mx. 046735-1 - Delete, AFRS "America's
Pop Music" 72, and AFRS "Jukebox USA"
220.   Add, AFRS Jill's Juke Box H-46-
51/97/161/193/216, RCA G RCS 3105,
RCA Cam G CS-10258, ViArg 1A-0151,
ViArg AGET-6, ViArg 26977, RCA Au
VPM-6019, Fe Au MX-10584, AFRS
"America's Popular Music" END-390-72/
135/202/607, AFRS G.I. Jive H-12-751/
877/959/1039/1051/1010/1104/1197/1401/
1461/1479/1718/1743/1766/1787/1827/
1928/1967//EN-12-2344, AFRS "Hot Off
The Record Press" EN-257-25/118, RCA
Br. GM-1, RD Br. RDM 2451/RDS 6451,
RCA G LPM-9901, and AFRS "Jukebox U.S.A."
EN-106-42/220.   RCA Br. RD-8094 should
read as RCA Br. RD-8094 (unissued).
Hurley is shown as the trumpet soloist
on this record.   This information came
from the May 1, 1940 issue of Down
Beat magazine (the record review by
Barrelhouse Dan).   However, according
to an article entitled "Who's Who in
Music" from the Sept. 15, 1940 issue of
Down Beat magazine, John Best is quoted
as having played this solo.
        mx. 046736-1 - Add, RCA Br. INTS 1019,
ViArg 1A-0151, and ViArg 26977.
        mx. 046738-1 - Add, RD Br. RDM 2453/RDS
6453, ViArg 1A-0153, and AFRS "America's
Popular Music" END-390-202/607.
P. 125 - 29 January, 1940, mx. 046739-1 - Add, RD Br. RDM 2099.
P. 126 - 30 January, 1940, mx. K2PP-0042 - Add, AFRS "America's
Popular Music" END-390-81/116/301, RCA
Au L 11023, RD 3/4-76, and RCA G RCS 3105.
        31 January, 1940, mx. K2PP-0044 - Add, RCA Au L 11023, and
AFRS "America's Popular Music" END-390-
301.

P. 128 -   5 February, 1940, mx. 046786-1 - Add, HMVIn BD 5595, and
                          Vi J A-1024.
                          mx. 046786-2 - Delete, Vi EPB-1192,
                          and AFRS "America's Pop Music" 72.
                          Add, RCA Br. GM-1, RCA Au 20403, Fe
                          Au MX-10583, RCA G Cam CS-10258, RCA
                          G RCS 3105, RCA Au L 10351, RD Br.
                          RDM 2176, ViArg 1A-0559, ViArg AGLT-2,
                          RCA Au VPM-6019, AFRS G.I. Jive H-12-
                          777/846/887/1107/1240/1274/1495/1720/
                          2060, AFRS Jill's Juke Box H-46-157/193,
                          AFRS "America's Popular Music" END-
                          390-72/98/135/202/607//EN-1748, RCA G
                          LPM-9901, and RD RD8-5000.
P. 129 -   5 February, 1940, mx. 046787-1 - Add, RCA Br. GM-1, RD Br.
                          2452/RDS 6452, RCA Au 20049, RCA Au
                          VPM-6019, HMVIn BD 5595, ViArg 1A-
                          0152, ViArg AGET-9, RCA G LPT 3002,
                          AFRS "America's Popular Music" EN-
                          1788, and AFRS Jill's Juke Box
                          H-46-90.
P. 130 -   5 February, 1940 - The trumpet solo credit on "Star Dust"
           might be by John Best instead of Hurley (see comments
           regarding record session of January 29, 1940).
P. 131 -   7 February, 1940, mx. K2PP-0042 - Add, RCA Au L 11023,
                          and AFRS "America's Popular Music"
                          END-390-301.
P. 133 - 14 February, 1940, mx. K2PP-0042 - Add, RCA Au L 11023,
                          and AFRS "America's Popular Music"
                          END-390-301.
           16 February, 1940,- Second sentence: where it reads "as a
           number lesser known bands" it should read "as a number of
           lesser known bands".
P. 134 - 19 February, 1940, mx. 047067-1 - Add, AFRS "America's
                          Popular Music" END-390-202/607.
                          mx. 047068-1 - Add, RD Br. RDM 2455/
                          RDS 6455.
                          mx. 047069-1 - Add, ViArg 26973.
P. 135 - 19 February, 1940, mx. 047070-1 - Add, Cam Cal 2267 (un-
                          issued).
           21 February, 1940, mx. K2PP-0045 - Add, RCA Au L 11025.
P. 137 - 24 February, 1940, mx. 047093-1 - Add, RD Br. RDM 2456/
                          RDS 6456, and AFRS "America's Popular
                          Music" EN-1703.
                          mx. 047096-1 - Add, AFRS "America's
                          Popular Music" EN-1708.
                          mx. 047097-1 - Add, AFRS "America's
                          Popular Music" EN-1703.
                          mx. 047098-1 - Delete, AFRS "America's
                          Pop Music" 72. Add, AFRS "America's
                          Popular Music" END-390-72/98/135/
                          202/607, RD Br. RDM 2099, and RD Br.
                          RDM 2176.

P. 139 - 28 February, 1940,   mx. K2PP-0045 - Add, RCA Au L 11025.

P. 145 - 12 March, 1940,   mx. E3VP 5241 - Add, RCA Au L 10351, and AFRS "America's Popular Music" EN-1758.

P. 146 - 13 March, 1940,   mx. K2PP-0047 - Add, RCA Au L 11024, and AFRS "America's Popular Music" END-390-301 (AFRS release applies to first two tunes of medley).

P. 147 - 19 March, 1940,   mx. E2VL 4545 - Add, ViArg 1A-0157, ViArg 68-1609, RCA G LPT 3001, and AFRS "America's Popular Music" END-390-265/607//EN-1673.

P. 149 - 26 March, 1940,   mx. V-4086 RR-17356 Moonlight Serenade - Add, AFRS "America's Popular Music" END-390-98/273 (incomplete).

P. 150 - 30 March, 1940,   mx. 048482-1 - Add, HMVAu EA 3404, and AFRS Jill's Juke Box H-46-20/47.

P. 151 - 30 March, 1940,   mx. 048483-1 - Add, RD Br. RDM 2451/RDS 6451, and AFRS "America's Popular Music" END-390-202/607.

                          mx. 048485-1 - Add, RCA Br. INTS 1019, RCA Au 20048, RD Br. RDM 2452/RDS 6452, and AFRS "America's Popular Music" EN-1823.

P. 152 - 31 March, 1940,   mx. 048488-1 - Add, RCA Br. INTS 1019, RD 3/4-76, Cam Au Cal/Cas-751, and AFRS "America's Popular Music" EN-1723.

                          mx. 048489-1 - Add, RCA Br. INTS 1019, and RD Br. RDM 2452/RDS 6452.

                          mx. 048491-1 - Add, RD Br. RDM 2455/RDS 6455, and AFRS "America's Popular Music" EN-1808.

P. 155 - 4 April, 1940,   mx. E4VP-8209 - Add, AFRS "America's Popular Music" END-390-608.

                          mx. V-4086 WR-960 - Add, AFRS "America's Popular Music" END-390-27/47, and AFRS "Hot Off The Record Press" EN-257-75.

P. 156 - 4 April, 1940,   mx. PPRM-5342 - Add, RCA Au LPM/LSP-2769, and AFRS "America's Popular Music" END-390-1042.

P. 160 - 18 April, 1940,   mx. V-4086 WR-983 Anchors Aweigh - Add, AFRS "Hot Off The Record Press" EN-257-75.

P. 162 - 23 April, 1940,   mx. E2VL 4419 - Add, RCA Au L 11021, HMVAu ODLP 1012, RCA G LPT 30, AFRS "America's Popular Music" EN-1768.

P. 163 - 25 April, 1940,   mx. WR-979 Fanhat Stomp - Add, RCA Au L 11021, HMVAu ODLP 1013, RCA G LPT 3001, RCA Arg AVL-31, and AFRS "America's Popular Music" END-390-609//EN-1773 (incomplete).

```
P. 164 - 28 April, 1940,    mx. 048963-1 - Delete, AFRS "America's
                            Pop Music" 67, and AFRS "Jukebox USA"
                            306.  Add, RCA Au VPM-6019, RCA G CS-
                            10258, RCA G RCS 3105, ViArg 1A-0153,
                            ViArg AGLT-2, ViArg AGET-6, RCA Br.
                            GM-1, RCA Au L 10351, RCA Au 20059,
                            AFRS G.I. Jive H-12-828/1196/1371/1634,
                            AFRS Jill's Juke Box H-46-31/70/76/112/
                            125/193/156, AFRS "America's Popular
                            Music" END-390-67/163/202/608/722/1480//
                            EN-1738, RCA G LPM-9901, AFRS "Jukebox
                            U.S.A." EN-106-306, and RD RD8-5001.
P. 165 - 28 April, 1940,    mx. 048964-1 - Delete, AFRS "Jukebox USA"
                            209.  Add, AFRS "Jukebox U.S.A." EN-
                            106-209, AFRS G.I. Jive H-12-1808/1826/
                            2016, AFRS Jill's Juke Box H-46-175, and
                            AFRS "America's Popular Music"EN-1798.
                            mx. 048965-1 - Delete, AFRS "America's
                            Pop Music" 72.  Add, AFRS "America's
                            Popular Music" END-390-72/98, RD Br.
                            RDM 2456/RDS 6456, and RCA Br. INTS
                            1019.
                            mx. 048967-1 - Add, RD 3/4-76, and HMVAu
                            EA 3463.
                            mx. 048968-1 - Add, RCA Br. INTS 1019, and
                            AFRS G.I. Jive H-12-927.
P. 168 -  2 May, 1940,      mx. V-4086 WR-1030 In The Mood - Add, AFRS
                            "Hot Off The Record Press" EN-257-75.
P. 169 -  8 May, 1940,      mx. E1LVB 3200 - Add, RCA G LPT 16, HMVAu
                            EA 4054, and AFRS "America's Popular
                            Music" END-390-265//EN-1678.
P. 171 - 15 May, 1940,      mx. E1LVB 3200 - Add, RCA G LPT 16, ViArg
                            AGLT-2, RCA Au L 10351, and AFRS
                            "America's Popular Music" END-390-2/12/
                            15/199/265/1271//EN-1678/1748.
P. 172 - 16 May, 1940,      mx. E4VP 8209 - Add, RCA G CS-10258, and
                            RCA G LPM-9901.
P. 176 - 28 May, 1940,      mx. V-4086 WR-966 Conversation Piece -
                            Add, RCA Au L 11025.
         29 May, 1940,      mx. UPRM-6315 - Add, AFRS "America's
                            Popular Music" EN-1878.
P. 177 - 30 May, 1940,      mx. K2PP-0046 Some Of These Days - Add,
                            RCA Au L 11024.
                            mx. K2PP-0046 Memphis Blues - Add, RCA
                            Au L 11024.
P. 178 -  4 June, 1940,     mx. V-4086 WR-959 - Add, ViArg 1A-0146,
                            ViArg 68-1509, ViArg AGET-3000, ViArg
                            AGLT-1, and AFRS "Hot Off The Record
                            Press" EN-257-75.
P. 179 -  4 June, 1940,     mx. V-4086 WR-959 My Blue Heaven - Add,
                            AFRS "America's Popular Music" END-390-
                            47/265/575//EN-1693, HMVAu 4054, HMVAu
                            ODLP 1013, and RCA G LPT 16.
```

P. 181 - 11 June, 1940,   mx. V-4086 WR-953 <u>T'Ain't No Use At All</u> - Add, RCA Au L 11024, and AFRS "America's Popular Music" END-390-301.

P. 182 - 13 June, 1940,   mx. 053130-1 - Add, AFRS "America's Popular Music" EN-1808.

mx. 053132-1 - Add, RD Br. RDM 2098, RD Br. RDM 2171, AFRS G.I. Jive H-12-830/940, AFRS Jill's Juke Box H-46-12, and AFRS "America's Popular Music" END-390-608.

P. 183 - 13 June, 1940,   mx. 053135-1 - Add, AFRS "America's Popular Music" END-390-608.

13 June, 1940,   mx. K2PP-0043 - Add, RCA Au L 11025, and RCA G RCS 3105.

P. 187 - 2 July, 1940,   mx. UPRM-6314 - Add, AFRS "America's Popular Music" EN-1868.

P. 189 - 9 July, 1940,   mx. V-4086 WR-960 <u>On Brave Old Army Team</u> - Add, AFRS "Hot Off The Record Press" EN-257-75.

P. 190 - 10 July, 1940,   mx. V-4086 WR-953 - Add, RCA Au L 11024, RD Br. RDM 2453/RDS 6453, and AFRS "America's Popular Music" END-390-301.

P. 191 - 11 July, 1940,   mx. V-4086 WR-956 <u>On The Alamo</u> - Add, RCA G LPT 30, RCA Au L 11021, HMVAu ODLP 1012, and AFRS "America's Popular Music" END-390-2/27/202/549/609.

mx. V-4086 WR-956 <u>I'll Never Smile Again</u> - Add, AFRS "America's Popular Music" END-390-202/607.

P. 192 - 17 July, 1940,   mx. UPRM-6314 - Add, AFRS "America's Popular Music" EN-1873.

P. 194 - 23 July, 1940,   mx. V-4086 WR-961 <u>Outside Of That I Love You</u> - Add, AFRS "America's Popular Music" EN-1883.

P. 195 - 24 July, 1940,   mx. V-4086 WR-955 - Add, ViArg 1A-0145, ViArg AGET-3000, ViArg AGLT-1, and AFRS "America's Popular Music" END-390-608.

P. 197 - 31 July, 1940,   mx. V-4086 WR-936 <u>MEDLEY</u> - Add, ViArg AGET-3000, and ViArg AGLT-1.

P. 200 - 8 August, 1940,   mx. 055502-1 - Add, RD Br. RDM 2452/RDS 6452, and AFRS "America's Popular Music" EN-1708.

mx. 055504-1 - Add, AFRS "America's Popular Music" EN-1703.

P. 203 - 14 August, 1940,   mx. 055517-1 - Add, RD Br. RDM 2451/RDS 6451, and AFRS "America's Popular Music" END-390-608.

mx. 055518-1 - Add, RCA Br. INTS 1019.

P. 206 - 28 August, 1940,   mx. V-4086 WR-1010 <u>A-Tisket A-Tasket</u> - Add, RCA G LPM/LSP-9944, and RCA Au L 11025.

mx. V-4086 WR-1010 <u>Farewell Blues</u> - Add, RCA Au L 10351, AFRS "America's Popular Music" END-390-27 (partial)//EN-1753, and AFRS "Hot Off The Record Press" EN-257-75.

P. 209 - 3 September, 1940, mx. 055580-1 - Add, Vi PK-1432, and
                                   AFRS "America's Popular Music" END-
                                   390-72/98/135.
                            mx. 055582-1 - Add, Cam Cal 2267 (un-
                            issued).
P. 211 - 11 September, 1940, mx. V-4086 WR-1025 In The Gloaming -
                                   Add, AFRS "Hot Off The Record Press"
                                   EN-257-75.
P. 212 - 12 September, 1940, mx. 056106-1 - Add, RD Br. RDM 2451/
                                   RDS 6451, and AFRS "America's
                                   Popular Music" EN-1708.
         12 September, 1940, mx. V-4086 WR-1026 - Add, AFRS "Hot
                                   Off The Record Press" EN-257-75.
P. 213 - 12 September, 1940, mx. V-4086 WR-1026 Pennsylvania Six-
                                   Five Thousand - Add, AFRS "Hot Off
                                   The Record Press" EN-257-75.
         13 September, 1940, - Following the listing of personnel ...
         3rd line - "...summary made by a lawyer for the Miller
         Estate." Please note that this lawyer was not David
         Mackay. It was a lawyer working for another law firm
         who looked over the payroll records for David Mackay.
P. 215 - 19 September, 1940 - "Thanks" is from the Paramount film
         "Too Much Harmony".
         24 September, 1940, mx. E1LVB 3201 - Add, HMVAu EA 4023,
                                   HMVAu ODLP 1013, RCA G LPT 16, and
                                   AFRS "America's Popular Music"
                                   EN-1688.
P. 216 - 25 September, 1940, mx. V-4086 WR-1027 Tiger Rag - Add,
                                   RCA G LPT 16, HMVAu EA 4023, and
                                   AFRS "America's Popular Music"
                                   END-390-265//EN-1683.
P. 222 - 11 October, 1940,   mx. 056479-1 - Add, RD Br. RDM 2451/
                                   RDS 6451.
                            mx. 056481-1 - Delete, HMVAu DLP
                            1049. Add, RCA Br. INTS 1002, and
                            Vi PK-1432.
P. 226 - 18 October, 1940,   mx. PPRM-5337 - Add, RCA Au LSP-2768,
                                   and AFRS "America's Popular Music"
                                   END-390-1039//EN-1940.
                            mx. PPRM-5334 The Gentleman Needs A
                            Shave - Add, RCA Au LSP-2767, and
                            AFRS "America's Popular Music" END-
                            390-1039.
                            mx. PPRM-5334 Slumber Song - Add, RCA
                            Au LSP-2767, and AFRS "America's
                            Popular Music" EN-1832.
P. 229 - 25 October, 1940,   mx. E4VP 8202 - Add, RD Br. RDM 2456/
                                   RDS 6456.
P. 235 - 8 November, 1940,   mx. 057612-1 - Add, RD Br. RDM 2453/
                                   RDS 6453, ViArg 1A-0150, ViArg 20-
                                   1529, and AFRS Jill's Juke Box
                                   H-46-232.

[506]

P. 239 - 15 November, 1940, mx. 057649-1 - Add, RD Br. RDM 2456/
RDS 6456.
P. 241 - 18 November, 1940, mx. PPRM-5333 - Add, RCA Au LSP-2767,
and AFRS "America's Popular Music"
END-390-1036//EN-1917.
mx. E4VP 8201 - Add, RD 3/4-76, and
AFRS "America's Popular Music" END-
390-211.
mx. PPRM-5337 - Add, RCA Au LSP-2768,
and AFRS "America's Popular Music"
EN-1940//END-390-1040.
mx. PPRM-5333 - Add, RCA Au LSP-2767,
and AFRS "America's Popular Music"
END-390-1037//EN-1925.
mx. PPRM-5337 - Add, RCA Au LSP-2768,
and AFRS "America's Popular Music"
END-390-1040.
P. 243 - 20 November, 1940 - After listing of tunes - 12th line -
unrap should be unwrap.
P. 244 - 21 November, 1940 - "Watcha Know Joe" should be "Whatcha
Know Joe".
P. 245 - 22 November, 1940, mx. 057663-1 - Add, AFRS "America's
Popular Music" END-390-377.
22 November, 1940, mx. E4VP 8201 - Add, AFRS "America's
Popular Music" END-390-81/116.
P. 246 - 23 November, 1940, mx. PPRM-5338 - Add, RCA Au LSP-2768,
and AFRS "America's Popular Music"
END-390-1042.
P. 248 - 28 November, 1940, mx. E3VP 5240 - Add, ViArg AGET-3000,
ViArg AGLT-1, and AFRS "America's
Popular Music" END-390-265.
P. 251 - 4 December, 1940, mx. E2VL 4420 - Add, RD Br. RDM 2456/
RDS 6456, and AFRS "America's
Popular Music" END-390-2/50/81/116/
204/335/613.
P. 252 - 7 December, 1940, mx. PPRM-5333 - Add, RCA Au LSP-2767,
and AFRS "America's Popular Music"
EN-1917.
P. 253 - 7 December, 1940, mx. PPRM-5337 - Add, RCA Au LSP-2768,
and AFRS "America's Popular Music"
END-390-1040.
mx. E4VP 8202 - Add, RD Br. RDM 2453/
RDS 6453, and AFRS "America's Popular
Music" END-390-202/608.
P. 254 - 11 December, 1940 - "Watcha Know Joe" should be "Whatcha
Know Joe".
13 December, 1940, mx. 058172 - Delete the word Teldec as
shown in issues RCA G LPM-1190, and
RCA G LPM/LSP-3377. Add, RCA Au VPM-
6019, RD Br. RDM 2451/RDS 6451, RCA
G RCS 3105, AFRS Jill's Juke Box
H-46-15, and AFRS "America's Popular
Music" END-390-211/609//EN-1778.

P. 255 - 13 December, 1940, mx. 058173-1 - Delete the word Teldec
                            as shown in issues RCA G LPM-1190,
                            and RCA G LPM/LSP-3377. Add, RCA Au
                            VPM-6019, RD Br. RDM 2451/RDS 6451,
                            RCA G RCS 3105, and AFRS "America's
                            Popular Music" END-390-211/609//EN-
                            1778. RCA Br. RD-8094 should read
                            as RCA Br. RD-8094 (unissued).
                            mx. 058174-1 - Add, AFRS Jill's Juke
                            Box H-46-29, and RD Br. RDM 2453/
                            RDS 6453.
P. 257 - 18 December, 1940, mx. E1LVB 3200 - Add, AFRS "America's
                            Popular Music" END-390-265//EN-1678.
         19 December, 1940, mx. K2PP-0044 - Delete, RCA Au L 11024.
                            Add, RCA Au L 11023, and AFRS
                            "America's Popular Music" END-390-
                            301.
                            mx. E3VP 5245 - Add, ViArg 68-1509, RD
                            3/4-76, ViArg AGET-3000, ViArg 1A-
                            0146, and ViArg AGLT-1.
P. 258 - 19 December, 1940 - Third line ..."the Cafe Rouge during
         this period"... should read ..."the Cafe Rouge on
         Thursday nights".
P. 258 - 21 December, 1940, mx. E4VP 8202 - Add, AFRS "America's
                            Popular Music" END-390-81/116/609.
P. 259 - 24 December, 1940, mx. K2PP-0047 - Delete, RCA Au L 11025.
                            Add, RCA Au L 11024, and AFRS
                            "America's Popular Music" END-390-301.
P. 260 - 27 December, 1940, mx. 058806 - Add, HMVAu EA 3506.
P. 261 - 28 December, 1940, mx. E4VP 8202 - Delete the word Teldec
                            as shown in issue RCA G EPOT-6701.
                            Delete, AFRS "America's Pop Music"
                            72. Add, AFRS "America's Popular
                            Music" END-390-72/81/98.
                            mx. E4VP 8201 - Delete the word Teldec
                            as shown in issue RCA G EPOT-6701.
                            Add, AFRS "America's Popular Music"
                            END-390-202/609.
P. 264 - 7 January, 1941, mx. K2PP-0044 - Delete, RCA Au L 11024.
                            Add, RCA Au L 11023, and AFRS
                            "America's Popular Music" END-390-
                            301.
P. 265 - 8 January, 1941, mx. UPRM-6315 - Add, AFRS "America's
                            Popular Music" EN-1878.
P. 266 - 9 January, 1941, mx. E4VP 8207 - Add, RD 3/4-76.
P. 267 - 11 January, 1941, mx. E4VP 8201 Swingin' At The Seance -
                            Add, AFRS "America's Popular Music"
                            END-390-50/81/116.
P. 270 - 17 January, 1941, mx. 058884-2 - Add, RD Br. RDM 2452/
                            RDS 6452, RCA Au 20049, AFRS
                            "America's Popular Music" END-390-
                            203/610, AFRS Jill's Juke Box H-46-
                            11/163/181, and AFRS Jukebox U.S.A."
                            EN-106-350.

                                    mx. 058885-1 - Add, AFRS "Jukebox
                                    U.S.A." EN-106-25, ViArg 1A-0406,
                                    RCA Au VPM-6019, ViArg 68-0685, ViArg
                                    AGET-1, RCA Au 20403, AFRS "America's
                                    Popular Music" END-390-202/609//EN-
                                    1823, AFRS Jill's Juke Box H-46-26/72/
                                    116/193, and RD Br. RDM 2452/RDS 6452.
                                    RCA Br. RD-8094 should read as RCA Br.
                                    RD-8094 (unissued).
P. 271 - 17 January, 1941,   mx. 058886-1 - Add, AFRS Jill's Juke Box
                                    H-46-50.
                                    mx. 058887-1 - Add, AFRS "America's
                                    Popular Music" EN-1818.
                                    mx. 058888-1 - Add, RD 3/4-76, and HMVSw
                                    JK-2325.
                                    mx. 058889-1 - Add, AFRS "America's
                                    Popular Music" END-390-135/203/355/610.
P. 274 - 29 January, 1941 - "Watcha Know Joe" should be "Whatcha
                                    Know Joe".
P. 275 - 30 January, 1941,   mx. K2PP-0043 - Delete, RCA Au L 11023.
                                    Add, RCA Au L 11025.
P. 277 - 6 February, 1941 - "These Things You Left" should read
                                    "These Things You Left Me".
P. 279 - 19 February, 1941, mx. 060912-1 - Add, RD Br. RDM 2453/RDS
                                    6453, and AFRS "America's Popular
                                    Music" END-390-348/379.
                                    mx. 060914-1 - Delete, HMVAu DLP 1049.
                                    Add, ViArg 1A-0139, ViArg 29885, Vi
                                    PK-1432, RD Br. RDM 2099, RD Br. RDM
                                    2172, AFRS Jill's Juke Box H-46-23/151/
                                    175, AFRS "Hot Off The Record Press"
                                    EN-257-83, AFRS "Jukebox U.S.A." EN-
                                    106-387, and RCA Au VPM-6019. RCA Br.
                                    RD-8094 should read as RCA Br. RD-8094
                                    (unissued).
P. 281 - 20 February, 1941, mx. 060915-1 - Add, RD Br. RDM 2094, and
                                    AFRS "America's Popular Music" END-
                                    390-203/610.
                                    mx. 060916-1 - Add, ViArg 29885.
P. 290 - 24 March-
            3 May, 1941,   mx. E4VL 5050 - Add, TCF Au TL-31590,
                                    WRC TT/ST 985, RD Br. RDM 2454/RDS
                                    6454 (edited), RCA G RCS 3105, AFRS
                                    "America's Popular Music" EN-1912, and
                                    RCA G LPM-9901. RD 3/4-64 should read
                                    as RD 3/4-64 (edited).
                                    mx. E4VL 5049 - Delete, TCF Au TL 31590.
                                    Add, RD Br. RDM 2454/RDS 6454, AFRS
                                    "America's Popular Music" END-390-254//
                                    EN-1888, and WRC TT/ST 984.

P. 291 - 24 March-3 May, 1941, mx. E4VL 5049 <u>It Happened In Sun Valley</u> - Delete, TCF Au TL 31590. Add, AFRS "America's Popular Music" END-390-254//EN-1893, WRC TT/ST 984, and RD Br. RDM 2454/RDS 6454.

         mx. E4VL 5049 <u>Chattanooga Choo Choo</u> - Delete, TCF Au TL 31590. Add, AFRS "America's Popular Music" END-390-203/254/611//EN-1893, WRC TT/ST 984, and RD Br. RDM 2454/RDS 6454.

P. 292 - 24 March-3 May, 1941, mx. E4VL 5049 - Add, AFRS "America's Popular Music" END-390-610//EN-1783, and RD Br. RDM 2454/RDS 6454.

         mx. E4VL 5050 <u>Sun Valley Jump</u> - Add, TCF Au TL-31590, AFRS "America's Popular Music" EN-1903, WRC TT/ST 985, and RD Br. RDM 2454/RDS 6454.

         mx. E4VL 5050 <u>Measure For Measure</u> - Delete, TCF Au TL 31590. Add, AFRS "America's Popular Music" EN-1898, and WRC TT/ST 984.

         mx. E4VL 5050 <u>The Spirit Is Willing</u> - Add, TCF Au TL 31590, WRC TT/ST 985, and AFRS "America's Popular Music" END-390-254//EN-1908.

P. 294 - 25 March, 1941, mx. K2PP-0045 - Delete, RCA Au L 11024. Add, RCA Au L 11025.

      27 March, 1941, mx. WPRS-0975 "Watcha Know Joe" should read as "Whatcha Know Joe".

P. 295 - 2 April, 1941, mx. UPRM-6315 - Add, AFRS "America's Popular Music" EN-1883.

P. 297 - 9 April, 1941, mx. K2PP-0045 - Delete, RCA Au L 11024. Add, RCA Au L 11025.

      10 April, 1941, mx. K2PP-0043 - Delete, RCA Au L 11023. Add, RCA Au L 11025, and RCA G LPM 9852.

P. 298 - 17 April, 1941, mx. K2PP-0044 - Delete, RCA Au L 11024. Add, RCA Au L 11023.

P. 303 - 7 May, 1941, mx. 061243-1 - Add, RD Br. RDM 2453/RDS 6453, RCA Au 10351, and AFRS "America's Popular Music" END-390-356/413/610.

P. 304 - 7 May, 1941, mx. 061244-1 - Add, RD Br. RDM 2456/RDS 6456.

         mx. 061245-1 - Delete, AFRS "Jukebox USA" 154, and AFRS "Jukebox USA" 252. Add, AFRS "Jukebox U.S.A." EN-106-154/252, AFRS Jill's Juke Box H-46-1/7/30/71/120/152/175//EN-46-250, RCA Au VPM-6019, RCA Cam G CS-10258, RD Br. RDM 2098, RD Br. RDM 2172, AFRS "America's

Popular Music" END-390-241, ViArg 1A-
0155, ViArg 29895, RCA G RCS 3105, RCA
Au 20037, and RCA G LPM-9901. RCA Br.
RD-8094 should read as RCA Br. RD-
8094 (unissued).

P. 305 - 7 May, 1941, mx. 061246-1 - Add, AFRS "America's Popular
Music" END-390-241/610, and AFRS Jill's
Juke Box H-46-19/46/61/160.

         7 May, 1941, mx. K2PP-0047 - Delete, RCA Au L 11025.
Add, RCA Au L 11024, RD 3/4-76, and AFRS
"America's Popular Music" END-390-301.

P. 306 - 8 May, 1941, mx. K2PP-0046 - Delete, RCA Au L 11025.
Add, RCA Au L 11024, and AFRS "America's
Popular Music" END-390-301.

P. 307 - 20 May, 1941, mx. 061255-1 - Add, Vi PK-1432, AFRS
"America's Popular Music" EN-1818 (in-
complete), and RD Br. RDM 2455/RDS 6455.

P. 310 - 27 May, 1941, mx. UPRM-6315 - Add, RD 3/4-76, and AFRS
"America's Popular Music" EN-1878.

P. 311 - 28 May, 1941, mx. 061265-1 - Add, AFRS "America's Popular
Music" END-390-203/611, ViArg 1A-0142,
and RD Br. RDM 2098.

                        mx. 061266-1 - Delete, AFRS "America's Pop
Music" 72. Add, AFRS Jill's Juke Box
H-46-38, and AFRS "America's Popular
Music" END-390-72/98/135//EN-1863 (in-
complete).

                        mx. 061267-1 - Add, ViArg 1A-0144.

                        mx. 061268-1 - Add, RD Br. RDM 2453/RDS
6453.

P. 312 - 1 June, 1941 - The "SO" in "SO Pacific RR" stands for
Southern.

P. 313 - 3 June, 1941, mx. E3VP 5236 - Add, AFRS "America's
Popular Music" END-390-2/27/609.

P. 317 - 18 June, 1941, mx. K2PP-0047 - Delete, RCA Au L 11025.
Add, RCA Au L 11024.

P. 320 - 25 June, 1941, mx. 064471-1 - Add, Cam Cal-2267 (unissued),
and ViArg 29919.

                        mx. 064472-1 - Add, Cam Au Cal-751, and
AFRS "America's Popular Music" EN-1733.

                        mx. 064473-1 - Add, AFRS "America's Popular
Music" EN-1713.

                        mx. 064474-1 - Add, AFRS "Jukebox U.S.A."
EN-106-54/325, RCA Au VPM-6019, RD Br.
RDM 2455/RDS 6455, ViArg 29919, AFRS
Jill's Juke Box H-46-160/202//EN-46-250,
AFRS "America's Popular Music" END-390-
611//EN-1793, AFRS "Hot Off The Record
Press" EN-257-10, ViArg 1A-0166, ViArg
68-1278, and ViArg AGET-9. RCA Br. RD-
8094 should read as RCA Br. RD-8094
(unissued).

P. 321 - 25 June, 1941, mx. E2VL 4545 - Add, AFRS "America's
Popular Music" END-390-265//EN-1693.
P. 325 - 3 July, 1941 - The Frog Hop Ballroom job should come
after the Chesterfield program of the same date.
4 July, 1941 - Witchita should read as Wichita.
P. 327 - 9 July, 1941, mx. E2VL 4546 - Add, ViArg 1A-0157, Vi
Arg 68-1609, and AFRS "America's
Popular Music" END-390-335/611//EN-1773.
- The title of the tune "That's Where I
Came In" changed to "Keep 'Em Flying" on the August 7th
Chesterfield program - 4 months before the recording
date on December 8th - which indicates that the title
was not changed for patriotic reasons after Pearl Harbor.
P. 330 - 17 July, 1941, mx. UPRM-6314 - Add, AFRS "America's Popular
Music" EN-1873.
P. 332 - 23 July, 1941 - "Watcha Know Joe"should read as "Whatcha
Know Joe".
P. 335 - 11 August, 1941, mx. 067625-1 - Add, AFRS "America's
Popular Music" END-390-610
mx. 067627-1 - Add, AFRS "America's
Popular Music" END-390-610, ViArg 1A-
0155, and ViArg 29895.
mx. 067628-1 - Add, Vi PK-1432, AFRS
Jill's Juke Box H-46-194, and ViArg 1AC-
0676.
mx. 067629-1 - Add, AFRS "America's
Popular Music" END-390-203/612.
mx. 067630-1 - Delete, AFRS "Jill's Juke-
box" 118, and AFRS "Jukebox USA" 90.
Add, AFRS "Jukebox U.S.A." EN-106-45/90/
170, RCA Au VPM-6019, RCA Au 20049, RCA
G RCS 3105, RD Br. RDM 2453/RDS 6453,
AFRS Jill's Juke Box H-46-2/37/69/118/
177/194, AFRS "America's Popular Music"
END-390-203/611/1149//EN-1658, and AFRS
"Hot Off The Record Press" EN-257-140.
RCA Br. RD-8094 should read as RCA Br.
RD-8094 (unissued).
P. 342 - 27 August, 1941, mx. UPRM-6314 - Add, AFRS "America's
Popular Music" EN-1868.
P. 345 - 3 September, 1941, mx. 067741-1 - Add, Cam Cal-2267 (un-
issued).
mx. 067744-1 - Add, Cam Au Cal-751, and
AFRS "America's Popular Music" EN-1728.
P. 346 - 3 September, 1941, mx. E4VP 8207 - Add, AFRS "America's
Popular Music" END-81/613.
mx. E3VP 5240 - Add, AFRS "America's
Popular Music" END-390-612.
P. 349 - 13 September, 1941 - Information on this program came
from a source outside of the Miller Estate. We sus-
pect that the opening theme was "Slumber Song" and not
"Moonlight Serenade".

P. 351 - 20 September, 1941 - Same comments here for opening theme
as for program of September 13th.

P. 355 - 4 October, 1941 - Eleventh line from top - lodge should
be loge. Twelfth line from top - buildup
should be build-up.

P. 359 - 16 October, 1941, mx. E2VL 4420 - Add, ViArg 1A-0147.

P. 360 - 19 October, 1941 - First paragraph, 3rd line - Stadium
should be Field as it was Ebbetts Field,
not Ebbetts Stadium. The article from
Down Beat did mention Stadium.

P. 361 - 20 October, 1941, mx. 071190-1 - Add, AFRS "America's
Popular Music" END-390-612, and RD Br.
RDM 2455/RDS 6455.
mx. 071192-1 - Delete, AFRS "Jukebox
USA" 77, and AFRS "Jukebox USA" 147.
Add, AFRS "Jukebox U.S.A." EN-106-14/
77/148, RD RD8-5043, and RD Br. RDM
2304/RDS 6304.
mx. 071193-1 - Add, AFRS "America's
Popular Music" EN-1803, and HMVAu EA
3506.

P. 364 - 25 October, 1941 - The rest of the tunes played on this
broadcast are unknown.

P. 366 - 3 November, 1941, mx. 068066-2 - Add, AFRS "America's
Popular Music" EN-1718.
mx. 068067-1 - Add, AFRS "America's
Popular Music" EN-1713.
mx. 068068-1 - Delete, AFRS "Jukebox
USA" 159, AFRS "Jukebox USA" 230, AFRS
"Jukebox USA" 299, and AFRS G.I. Series
H-12 No. 1053 (this is a duplication).
Add, AFRS "Jukebox U.S.A." END-106-159/
230/299/325, AFRS "America's Popular
Music" END-390-203/612/442/508/986/
1099, AFRS "Hot Off The Record Press"
EN-257-13 (incomplete)/50/93/185, RCA
G RCS 3105, and ViArg 1A-0559. RCA Br.
RD-8094 should read as RCA Br. RD-8094
(unissued).

P. 367 - 3 November, 1941, mx. 068070-1 - Add, ViArg 1A-0006.

P. 370 - 8 November, 1941 - Under the location add the radio
station, WJZ.
mx. PPRM-5342 - Add, AFRS "America's
Popular Music" END-390-1044.
mx. PPRM-5338 - Add, AFRS "America's
Popular Music" END-390-1041.

P. 371 - 8 November, 1941, mx. PPRM-5333 - Add, AFRS "America's
Popular Music" END-390-1036//EN-1917.
11 November, 1941 - Possibly no broadcast due to the fact
that the day is (was) Armistice Day and there might have
been something special on the air.

P. 376 - 22 November, 1941, mx. PPRM-5337 - Add, AFRS "America's
                        Popular Music" END-390-1040.
                        mx. PPRM-5338 - Add, AFRS "America's
                        Popular Music" END-390-1042.
P. 379 - 24 November, 1941, mx. 068418-1 - Add, Vi PK-1432.
                        mx. 068419-1 - Add, RD Br. RDM 2452/
                        RDS 6452, and AFRS "America's
                        Popular Music" END-390-204 (partial).
                        mx. 068420-1 - Add, Cam Cal-2267 (un-
                        issued).
                        mx. 068422-1 - Add, AFRS "America's
                        Popular Music" END-390-203/612.
P. 381 - 26 November, 1941, mx. K2PP-0044 - Add, AFRS "America's
                        Popular Music" END-390-301.
P. 382 - 29 November, 1941, mx. PPRM-5334 - Add, AFRS "America's
                        Popular Music" END-390-1038//EN-1928.
                        mx. PPRM-5338 - Add, AFRS "America's
                        Popular Music" END-390-1041.
                        mx. PPRM-5341 - Add, AFRS "America's
                        Popular Music" END-390-1043.
P. 384 - 6 December, 1941 - Add under the location, 8:15-8:45 P.M.
                        EST.
P. 385 - 8 December, 1941, mx. 068456-1 - Add, AFRS "America's
                        Popular Music" END-390-135/203/241/
                        612//EN-1858, RD Br. RDM 2173, RCA
                        Au 20059, RD Br. RDM 2097, and AFRS
                        "Jukebox U.S.A." EN-106-219. RCA Br.
                        RD-8094 should read as RCA Br. RD-
                        8094 (unissued).
                        mx. 068457-1 - Add, AFRS "America's
                        Popular Music" EN-1698.
                        mx. 068459-1 - Add, AFRS "America's
                        Popular Music" END-390-203 (partial)/
                        612.
                        mx. 068460-1 - Add, AFRS "America's
                        Popular Music" END-390-613.
                        mx. 068461-1 - Delete, AFRS "America's
                        Pop Music" 72. Add, AFRS "America's
                        Popular Music" END-390-72/98/135/204/
                        613, and RD Br. RDM 2453/RDS 6453.
P. 388 - 11 December, 1941, mx. E3VP 5232 - Add, AFRS "America's
                        Popular Music" END-390-47/203/612.
P. 390 - 17 December, 1941, mx. E4VP 8209 - Add, AFRS "America's
                        Popular Music" END-390-204/613.
P. 391 - 18 December, 1941, mx. K2PP-0042 - Add, AFRS "America's
                        Popular Music" END-390-301.
P. 397 - 30 December, 1941, mx. E3VP 5242 - Delete, AFRS "America's
                        Pop Music" 67. Add, AFRS "America's
                        Popular Music" END-390-2/67/163.
P. 398 - 1 January, 1942, mx. E2VL 4419 - Add, RCA G RCS 3105,
                        RD Br. RDM 2456/RDS 6456, and AFRS
                        America's Popular Music" END-390-
                        203/611/265 (incomplete)//EN-1763.

P. 402 - 8 January, 1942, mx. 068789-2 - Add, Vi PK-1432. RCA Br.
                                RD-8094 should read as RCA Br. RD-
                                8094 (unissued).
                            mx. 068835-1 - Add, AFRS "America's
                                Popular Music" END-390-204/613.
P. 415 - 17 February, 1942,mx. E2VL 4420 - Add, AFRS "America's
                                Popular Music" EN-1773.
P. 416 - 18 February, 1942,mx. 071861-1 - Delete, RCA Au 20037.
                                Add, RD RD8-5000, ViArg 1A-0144, RD
                                Br. RDM 2173, and AFRS "America's
                                Popular Music" END-390-204/613/1477.
                                RCA Br. RD-8094 should read as RCA
                                Br. RD-8094 (unissued).
                            mx. 071863-1 - Add, RD Br. RDM 2455/
                                RDS 6455, and AFRS "America's Popular
                                Music" END-390-27//EN-1853.
                            mx. 071864-1 - Add, AFRS "America's
                                Popular Music" END-390-613/594//EN-
                                1698, and RD Br. RDM 2452/RDS 6452.
P. 419 - 24 February, 1942,mx. E2VL 4545 - Add, AFRS "America's
                                Popular Music" END-390-265//EN-1693.
P. 426 - 20 March, 1942,   mx. E2VL 4546 - Add, ViArg 1A-0056, and
                                ViArg 68-1564.
P. 427 - 23 March-22 May, 1942, mx. J80P 9908 - Add, Bert. Schall.
                                71003, WRC ST/TT 985, and AFRS
                                "America's Popular Music" END-390-
                                254//EN-1912.
                            mx. E4VL 5048 - Delete, Vi LPC 101
                                (Edited). Add, WRC ST/TT 985, RD Br.
                                RDM 2454/RDS 6454, and AFRS "America's
                                Popular Music" EN-1908.
P. 428 - 23 March-22 May, 1942, mx. J80P 9905 - Add, WRC ST/TT 984,
                                and AFRS "America's Popular Music"
                                EN-1888.
                            mx. J80P 9907 - Add, WRC ST/TT 985, and
                                AFRS "America's Popular Music" END-
                                390-254.
                            mx. E4VL 5047 - Add, WRC ST/TT 985, RD
                                Br. RDM 2454/RDS 6454, and AFRS
                                "America's Popular Music" END-390-254//
                                EN-1908.
                            mx. E4VL 5048 - Add, AFRS "America's
                                Popular Music" END-390-254//EN-1888,
                                WRC ST/TT 984, and RD Br. RDM 2454/
                                RDS 6454.
P. 429 - 23 March-22 May, 1942, mx. E4VL 5047 - Add, WRC ST/TT 984,
                                RD Br. RDM 2454/RDS 6454, and AFRS
                                "America's Popular Music" END-390-254//
                                EN-1898.
                            mx. E4VL 5048 - Add, WRC ST/TT 985, RD
                                Br. RDM 2454/RDS 6454, RCA Au L 10351,
                                and AFRS "America's Popular Music"
                                END-390-254//EN-1743/1903.

P. 430 - 23 March-22 May, 1942, mx. E4VL 5047 <u>That's Sabotage</u> - Add,
WRC ST/TT 985, and AFRS "America's
Popular Music" EN-1912.

    mx. E4VL 5047 <u>Moonlight Sonata</u> - Add,
WRC ST/TT 984, AFRS "America's Popular
Music" EN-1768, and RD Br. RDM 2454/
RDS 6454.

    mx. J8OP 9906 - Add, WRC ST/TT 984, and
AFRS "America's Popular Music" END-
390-254//EN-1893.

P. 431 - 25 March, 1942,   mx. E2VL 4419 - Add, ViArg 1A-0149, RCA
Cam G CS-10258, RCA G LPM-9901, and
AFRS "America's Popular Music" END-
390-265/336//EN-1763.

P. 434 - 2 April, 1942,   mx. 072230-1 - Delete, AFRS "Jukebox
USA" 207, and AFRS "Jukebox USA" 276.
Add, ViArg 1A-0166, ViArg 68-1278,
ViArg AGET-1, and AFRS "Jukebox U.S.A."
EN-106-207/276/322. RCA Br. RD-8094
should read as RCA Br. RD-8094 (un-
issued).

    mx. 072232-1 - Add, Cam Cal-2267 (un-
issued).

    mx. 072233-1 - Add, AFRS "America's
Popular Music" END-390-614.

P. 436 - 8 April, 1942,   mx. E4VP 8209 - Add, AFRS "America's
Popular Music" END-390-204/615.

P. 439 - 23 April, 1942,   mx. E4VP 8207 - Add, AFRS "America's
Popular Music" END-390-50/613.

    mx. E3VP 5239 - Add, RCA Cam G CS-10258,
RCA G RCS 3105, RCA Au L 10351, ViArg
AGLT-2, AFRS "America's Popular Music"
END-390-12, and RCA G LPM-9901.

P. 444 - 20 May, 1942   mx. 072283-1 - Delete, AFRS "America's
Pop Music" 67. Add, AFRS "America's
Popular Music" END-390-67/204/615,
ViArg 1A-0142, ViArg 27934, and RCA
Au 20037. RCA Br. RD-8094 should read
as RCA Br. RD-8094 (unissued).

P. 445 - 20 May, 1942,   mx. 072284-1 - Add, RD Br. RDM 2096, RD
Br. RDM 2174, RCA G RCS 3105, and AFRS
"America's Popular Music" END-390-204/
241/614//EN-1793. RCA Br. RD-8094
should read as RCA Br. RD-8094 (unissued).

    mx. 072285-1 - Add, RD Br. RDM 2175, Vi
PK-1432, ViArg 1A-0139, ViArg 27934,
AFRS "Hot Off The Record Press" EN-
257-185, AFRS "America's Popular Music"
END-390-204/614, HMVSp GY 669, AFRS
"Jukebox U.S.A." EN-106-386, and RD
RD8-5000. RCA Br. RD-8094 should read
as RCA Br. RD-8094 (unissued).

P. 448 - 26 May, 1942,   mx. V-4086 WR-965 - Add, RCA Cam G
CS-10258, ViArg AGLT-2, RCA Au L
10351, RCA G LPM-9901, and AFRS
"America's Popular Music" END-390-
312//EN-1748.

P. 449 - 28 May, 1942,   mx. E2VL 4546 - Delete, AFRS "America's
Pop Music" 72. Add, AFRS "America's
Popular Music" END-390-72/98//EN-
1768, ViArg 1A-0056, and ViArg 68-
1564.

P. 451 - 2 June, 1942,   mx. E3VP 5238 - Add, RCA Cam G CS-10258,
ViArg AGLT-2, RCA Au L 10351, RCA G
LPM-9901, and AFRS "America's
Popular Music" END-390-47/316/501//
EN-1753.

    3 June, 1942,   mx. E1LVB 3201 - Add, AFRS "America's
Popular Music" END-390-265//EN-1688.

P. 455 - 17 June, 1942,   mx. 075090-1 - Add, AFRS "America's
Popular Music" END-390-204/614.
mx. 075092-1 - Add, ViArg 1A-0439.
mx. 075093-1 - Add, ViArg 1A-0439, and
AFRS "America's Popular Music" END-
390-614.

P. 457 - 24 June, 1942,   mx. UPRM-6315 - Add, AFRS "America's
Popular Music" EN-1883.

P. 461 - 14 July, 1942,   mx. 074736-1 - Add, Cam Cal-2267 (un-
issued), and AFRS "America's Popular
Music" END-390-614.
mx. 074737-1 - Add, RD Br. RDM 2095, and
RD Br. RDM 2175.
mx. 074738-1 - Add, ViArg 20-1536, AFRS
"America's Popular Music" END-390-2,
RD Br. RDM 2456/RDS 6456, and AFRS
G.I. Jive Series H-12: 1975/2082.

P. 462 - 14 July, 1942,   mx. 074739-1 - Add, AFRS "America's
Popular Music" END-390-204/420/615.

    15 July, 1942,   mx. 074740-1 - Add, AFRS "Hot Off The
Record Press" EN-257-95/180, AFRS
"America's Popular Music" END-390-
135/615//EN-1622/1723, ViArg AGET-6,
HMVSp GY 669, ViArg 20-1523, RD Br.
RDM 2095, and RD Br. RDM 2176. RCA
Br. RD-8094 should read as RCA Br.
RD-8094 (unissued).

P. 463 - 15 July, 1942,   mx. 074741-1 - Add, ViArg 1A-0006, and
AFRS "America's Popular Music" END-
390-615//EN-1728.
mx. 074742-1 → Delete, AFRS "Jukebox USA"
179, and AFRS Jill's Juke Box EN 243.
Add, ViArg AGET-6, RCA Au 20403, RD
Br. RDM 2353/RDS 6353, AFRS "America's
Popular Music" END-390-204/615/764//
EN-1718, RCA Au 20037, AFRS "Jukebox

U.S.A." EN-106-1/179, and AFRS Jill's
Juke Box EN-46-243. RCA Br. RD-8094
should read às RCA Br. RD-8094 (unissued).
mx. 074743-1 - Add, ViArg 20-1546, and
AFRS G.I. Jive EN-12-2349.

P. 465 - 16 July, 1942, mx. 074744-1-Add,Cam Cal-2267 (unissued),
and RD Br. RDM 2456/RDS 6456.
mx. 074745-1 - Add, ViArg 20-1523, RD
Br. RDM 2094, and RD Br. RDM 2174.
mx. 074746-1 - Delete, AFRS "America's
Pop Music" 72. Add, AFRS "America's
Popular Music" END-390-72/98/135, and
ViArg 20-1546.
mx. 074748-1 - Delete, AFRS "America's
Pop Music" 67. Add, AFRS "America's
Popular Music" END-390-67/163/615//
EN-1823, ViArg 1A-0150, RD Br. RDM
2455/RDS 6455, and ViArg 20-1529.

P. 471 - 12 August, 1942, mx. E4VP 8210 - Add, RD 3/4-76.
P. 472 - 12 August, 1942, mx. E4VP 8207 - Add, AFRS "America's
Popular Music" END-390-116.
P. 474 - 19 August, 1942, mx. E2VL 4419 - Add, AFRS "America's
Popular Music" END-390-265//EN-1763,
and ViArg 1A-0148.
P. 478 - 9 September, 1942, mx. E3VP 5237 - Add, RD 3/4-76.
P. 479 - 9 September, 1942, mx. E3VP 5242 - Add, ViArg AGET-3000,
ViArg AGLT-1, RD Br. RDM 2456/RDS
6456, and ViArg 1A-0145.
P. 480 - 15 September, 1942, mx. E3VP 5238 - Delete the word Teldec
as shown in issue RCA G LPT 6700.
Add, AFRS "America's Popular Music"
END-390-615.
P. 482 - 22 September, 1942, mx. E2VL 4545 - Add, AFRS "America's
Popular Music" END-390-47/265/382//
EN-1683.
P. 483 - 24 September, 1942 - Lines 7 and 17 up from the bottom of
the page: fullfil should be fulfil or fulfill.

The following are corrections and arranger additions to the
Index of Tune Titles and the Text that were received too late for
inclusion in these sections. Rather than refer to each page in
the Text where these changes apply we have decided to refer to
the Index of Tune Titles section in order to shorten this listing
as follows:

1.   Individual Tunes

Anything But Love. Note that this is an unfinished score.
Are You Jumpin' Jack? Original score reads as Are Ya Jumpin' Jack?
(The) Blues My Sweety Gave To Me. Original score reads as The Blues
My Naughtie Sweetie Gives Me.

Butcher Boy. Original score reads as (The) Butcher Boy.

Daisy Mae. Original score reads as Daisy May.

Dancing In A Dream With You. Victor list this tune as Dancing In A Dream but our title is taken from the original score. Johnny Best had a short solo before the vocal began.

Dig It. Original score reads as I Ain't Hep To That Step.

Do I Worry? Add arranger credit, (arr JG).

Dolores. Original score indicates this tune featured Chuck Goldstein on vocal.

Down For The Count. Original score indicates that tentative title was In Your Hat!

Enlisted Men's Mess. Original score showed other titles to this tune and they were Bum's Away or Bye Bye Benito.

Fools Rush In. Add arranger credit, (arr JG).

Get Ready-Set-Jump. Original score indicates that this tune was originally titled as Getting In The Groove.

Green Eyes. Note that there are two Jerry Gray scores in file.

Hornpipe. The original score indicates that this was incidental music behind the Chesterfield commercial.

I Close My Eyes. The writing credits for this tune are (Van Alexander-Steve Graham).

I Don't Want To Walk Without You. Add arranger credit (only probable because of handwriting), (arr GW?)

I Dreamt I Dwelt In Harlem. Original score indicates that this tune was originally titled as Rhythm In My Dreams.

I Fall In Love Every Day. Original score indicates that full title should read as I Fall In Love With You Every Day.

I Know. This score may be You Know That I Know since they are both arranged by Eddie Durham.

I Never Took A Lesson In My Life. Original score reads as Never Took A Lesson In My Life.

Is This Our Last Night Together. Original score reads as (Is This) Our Last Night Together. The complete writer credit is (Pauline Bouchard-Sam Coslow).

It Happened In Sun Valley. The Jerry Gray score of this tune indicates that just part of the arrangement was done by Gray-- copied rest from Finegan.

I've Caught Love. We show the arrangers as being Jerry Gray and George Williams. Actually, there are two separate scores--one by Jerry Gray and one by George Williams--and it is impossible for us to say which score was used on the broadcast of September 2, 1942.

Jingle, Jangle, Jingle. Note that there are two Jerry Gray scores in file.

Joseph, Joseph. Original score reads as Joesph! Joseph!

Kasaras. Note that this tune was written by Ernie Caceres.

Make Believe Ballroom Time. Original score reads as It's Make Believe Ballroom Time.

(The) Marine's Hymn. This tune is listed in the text under the title To The Shores of Tripoli since this is the way the Miller Estate listed this tune. However, the actual title is The Marine's Hymn.

Me & Melinda. We believe that the actual title of this tune should be Me & My Melinda.

<u>Missouri Waltz</u>. Original score indicates that Pat Forester is the
   arranger but this is unconfirmed.
<u>Oh So Good</u>. Original score reads as <u>Oh! So Good!</u>
<u>On Brave Old Army Team</u>. Original score reads as <u>On, Brave Old Army
   Team</u>.
<u>Opus #1</u>. Note that this is not the Tommy Dorsey version. This
   tune is written by Willie Moore.
<u>Pagan Love Song</u>. Add arranger credit, (arr GM).
<u>People Like You And Me</u> (#746). Note that this version is arranged
   by Jerry Gray and not by Jerry Gray and George Williams.
<u>Prelude In C# Major</u>. Original score reads as <u>(Ray Conniff's)
   Prelude In C# Major</u>.
<u>Quartermasters Song</u>. Original score reads as <u>The Quartermaster Song</u>.
<u>Sarong</u>. Original score indicates that this tune was originally
   titled <u>Gray Turning Blue</u>.
<u>Solid As A Stonewall, Jackson</u>. Original score does not show comma
   after Stonewall.
<u>Star Spangled Banner</u>. Original score reads as <u>The Star Spangled
   Banner</u>.
<u>(The) Story Of A Starry Night</u> (Instrumental) (#687). Original score
   reads as <u>Tschaikowsky 1st Movement From Pathetique (6th Symphony)</u>.
   This score has 12 pages.
<u>Sunrise Serenade</u>. Add arranger credit, (arr BF).
<u>Sun Valley Jump</u>. Original score indicates that this tune was
   originally titled <u>Give 'N Take</u>.
<u>Surprisin' Papa Haydn</u>. This tune was taken from Haydn's <u>Surprise
   Symphony</u>. Perhaps this arrangement is similar to the one used
   later by Tex Beneke and His Orchestra.
<u>Sweet Sue</u>. Note that this is an unfinished score.
<u>Swingin' The Triads</u>. Original score indicates that Buddy Stanton
   is the arranger but other information states that Eddie Barefield
   <u>is</u> the arranger.
<u>T'Ain't No Use At All</u>. Original score indicates that Elton LeRoy
   Hill is the arranger but other information states that Bill
   Finegan <u>is</u> the arranger.
<u>Tea For Two</u>. Note that this is an unfinished score.
<u>Texas After Taps</u>. The word "Texas" is not shown on the original
   score.
<u>Trigger's Tune</u>. Original score reads as <u>Trigger's Tune "Nobody
   Ever Wants Me"</u>.
<u>Uncle Tom</u>. On original score under this title are the words <u>Get
   With It</u> which may be the original title.
<u>V.M.I. Spirit</u>. There is some doubt as to whether this is a score
   for the original Miller band as there are some Beneke and McKinley
   scores scattered throughout the original Miller scores.
<u>Walking By The River</u>. Original score reads as <u>Walkin' By The River</u>.
<u>Weekend Of A Private Secretary</u>. Original score reads as <u>The Weekend
   Of A Private Secretary</u>.
<u>Well, All Right</u>. Original score reads as <u>Well, All Right Then</u>.
<u>Well Conga</u>. This might be <u>Let's Conga Gate</u>. Original score reads
   as <u>Well Jazz Conga</u> with the word "Jazz" crossed out.
<u>We're The Couple In The Castle</u>. Add arranger credit, (arr BF).
<u>What Goes On Here In My Heart?</u> Original score reads as <u>What Goes
   On Here (In My Heart)</u>?

What's The Matter With Me. Add arranger credit, (arr JG).
(The) White Cliffs Of Dover. In the Index of Tune Titles there are
  two arrangements shown. When we did the text we only knew of the
  Jerry Gray arrangement. It is quite possible that the recorded
  arrangement is Bill Finegan's.

2. Medleys

My Gal Sal/You're A Lucky Guy/When Summer Is Gone/Wabash Blues. Add
  arranger credit, (arr JG).
A Pretty Girl Is Like A Melody/Shake Down The Stars/Some Of These
  Days/Memphis Blues. Add arranger credit, (arr JG).
(The) Siren's Song/When The Roses Bloom Again/Love In Bloom/Birth Of
  The Blues. Original score indicates that arranger is Deane
  Kincaide but we fail to see how this could be since Jerry Gray
  arranged the original medley. Perhaps Kincaide was responsible
  for choosing the "new" tune as there is a notation on the score
  "copy C to F of Roses Bloom"--"before D of Medley 443".
To You/Moonlight Cocktail/The Story Of A Starry Night/Rhapsody In
  Blue. Original score reads as To You/Moonlight Cocktail/ Pathetique/
  Rhapsody In Blue. The borrowed tune is an instrumental and is
  probably a shortened version of the tune listed as "The Story Of A
  Starry Night" on page 392 of the text.
When Irish Eyes Are Smiling/Confuscius Say/Rose Room/Wang Wang Blues.
  The last tune of this medley should read as The Wang, Wang Blues.

     The following material was received too late for inclusion in
the text:

     We learn of the discovery of a 2 hour broadcast and 1/2 hour
interview of Miller from Columbus, Ohio (date unknown). So far, no
further details are available.

     There is a Glenn Miller - Tex Beneke interview from either 1939
or 1940 on the Andy Mansfield Show #44 (which we believe is an AFRS
Transcription).

     The author will welcome further additions and corrections to
this work with an eye toward possible dissemination of such information through future supplements to this volume. This information
should be directed to:

                    John Flower,
                    18 Haslemere Road,
                    Toronto 12, Ontario,
                    Canada.

INDEX OF TUNE TITLES

This index is divided into two sections: individual tunes and medleys. The first section lists the individual tunes.

1. Individual Tunes

In order to shorten the index we do not show the full title of the tune (e.g.Wham [Re-Bop-Boom-Bam] is shown as Wham). Basically this decision affects tunes with part of the title in brackets. In the case of the two theme songs, "Moonlight Serenade" and "Slumber Song", we only list the page reference when it was <u>not</u> used as a theme song. In other words, we list the pages where the tune was played in full or is from one of the films.

The words "a", "an" and "the" that begin a tune are bracketed to enable the reader to spot the title.

Tunes from a medley are shown with a reference to the medley or medleys that they are from. The page number(s) are to be found in the medley section. Not all of the tunes from the medleys are shown this way. Regular tunes like "I'll Never Smile Again" which were also used in the medleys but were just copied from the original score are not shown in the above mentioned manner. Only tunes where the arrangement is different from the recording (e.g.Alice Blue Gown) and tunes that were not used outside of the medley (e.g.Aloha) show the reference.

Throughout the index we list alternate titles for some of the tunes (e.g. Londonderry Air refers back to Danny Boy) and the decision to list the page references under one title rather than the other is strictly arbitrary.

In the case of tunes sung by the Andrews Sisters we have shown their name in brackets after the last page reference because, in some instances, Miller recorded, broadcast etc. his own arrangement of the same tune (e.g. Say "Si Si").

The index begins with the tune title (e.g. Adios); the arranger's name (where known) in short form and in brackets (e.g. [arr JG]); the score number (where known) (e.g. [#560]); and then the page number(s) where the tune appears (e.g. 284, 294, etc.). No tune page reference is shown where the tune is listed in a review of a stage show etc. or is part of the comments of a recording session etc. The one exception is the last performance shown on page 486. If a tune appears twice on a page we show (2) after the page reference (e.g. 298[2]). Two exceptions to this rule occur: (a) where a tune is listed twice in the same record session because of two takes being available (e.g. Anvil Chorus) and, (b) when the tune was played twice on the same program (see page 470, August 6, 1942 - Jersey Bounce). There are some "codes" that we have devised to help you find certain recordings or broadcasts faster than having to go through every page reference. These "codes" are as follows:

(AC) Private Air Check	(RS) Recording Session
(GMMS) Glenn Miller Moonlight Serenade Transcription	(ST) Sound Track
	(VI) Commercially Released Air Check

So, using "Adios" as our example we find that the record session
is on page 321 and that we have a private air check on page 331.
Where GMMS has also been issued by Victor we have shown (GMMS/VI).

A word about the score numbers. Some of the scores have been
renumbered so that what we are showing in many cases is the new
number. In very few cases do we know both the original score
number and the new number and where this occurs we have used the
new number to maintain the sequence. With some exceptions, the
score numbers (the renumbered ones) do show a sequence in that
the early numbers are the early scores and the later numbers are
from the last year of the band's existence. Naturally, "Beautiful
Ohio" is not really score number 805 as this is the new number
which we have used since the original score number is unknown. You
will note that there are some tunes without a score number since
there is no score available. There are also many scores that
Miller apparently never used (as far as our records are concerned
as we have no broadcast listing) but they (eg. Ain't Misbehavin')
are shown for completeness. Of course, there are no page references in these cases. There are some tune titles that we list two
or three times (eg. I Got Rhythm) since each arrangement is
different even though the scores have the same number.

Adios (arr JG) (#560), 284, 294, 298(2), 308, 321(RS), 321, 326,
    331(AC), 336, 347, 352, 364, 433
After All (arr JG) (#321), 106(VI)
Ain't Cha Comin' Out? (#257), 72(RS), 74(AC), 82, 103
Ain't Misbehavin' (arr GS) (#73)
(The) Air Minded Executive (arr JG) (#548), 281(RS)
Alabamy Bound (arr JG) (#420)
Alice Blue Gown (arr BF) (#366), 151(RS)
Alice Blue Gown (See Medleys: I Never Knew; Whispering; and
    You Tell Me Your Dream)
Allah's Holiday (#80)
All Ashore (#162)
All For Love (arr DK) (#709)
All The Things You Are (See Medley: If I Had My Way)
All Through The Night, 214(AC)
Aloha (See Medley: Moon Over Miami)
Along The Santa Fe Trail (#442), 231, 235(RS), 236, 240, 245(VI),
    247, 259
Always And Always (#112)
Always In My Heart (arr BM) (#701), 403(RS), 415, 426, 437, 440,
    451, 460, 467, 469, 474, 476, 477(2), 484
Amapola (arr JG) (#595), 302, 309(VI), 309(AC), 314, 333, 345,
    362
America (arr BF)
American Patrol (arr JG) (#742), 428(ST), 432, 434(RS), 436,
    439(VI), 441, 441(AC), 443, 449, 454, 460, 468, 472, 477,
    481, 486

Am I Blue? (See Medley: Please)
Anchors Aweigh, 160(GMMS), 171, 187, 204, 214, 229, 261, 381,
    431(VI), 448, 453, 458
And The Angels Sing (#218), 54(RS), 60, 64(VI)
Angel Child (arr BF) (#390), 183(RS)
(An) Angel In A Furnished Room (#282), 80(RS)
(The) Angels Came Thru, 311(RS)
Angels Of Mercy, 391, 400(RS), 413, 418, 443
Anitra's Dance (arr JG) (#672)
Annie Laurie, 116
Annie's Cousin Fanny (#37)
Anvil Chorus (arr JG), 224, 226, 229, 231, 240, 245, 251, 255(RS),
    258(AC), 263, 267, 268, 277, 285, 296, 301, 308, 315, 327,
    333, 340, 350, 354, 363, 371(AC), 383, 412, 422
Anything But Love (#380)
Anytime, Anyday, Anywhere (#20), 3(RS)
April In Paris (arr BF) (#764), 471(VI), 477, 482(VI)
April Played The Fiddle (arr BF) (#373), 152(RS), 168, 177,
    198(GMMS)
Are You Jumpin' Jack? (arr BF) (#522), 259(VI), 266, 280, 288,
    298, 364
Are You Rusty, Gate? (arr JG) (#518), 297, 306, 315(GMMS),
    321(VI), 326, 364, 398
A-Tisket A-Tasket (#141), 206(GMMS/VI)
At Last (arr JG & BF) (#749), 292(ST), 428(ST), 446(RS), 449,
    456, 460, 467, 473, 486
At Least You Could Say Hello (arr AG) (#513)
At Sundown (#195), 64(VI), 69
At The President's Ball (arr BM) (#702), 399(RS), 403, 406, 408,
    412
At Your Beck And Call (#130), 16
Auld Lang Syne (arr JG) (#707)
Auld Lang Syne (See Medley: Time On My Hands)

Baby Me (arr ED) (#275), 77(AC), 78(RS), 119
Baby Mine (arr BF) (#662), 367(RS)
Back To Back (arr EE) (#237), 68(RS), 69(VI), 70, 73
Basin Street Blues (arr GM) (#47)
Basket Weaver Man (#287), 83(RS)
Beat Me Daddy, Eight To A Bar (#434), 212(RS), 215, 221(AC),
    226, 230, 241(VI), 242(GMMS), 259
Beautiful Ohio (arr JG) (#805), 118(RS)
Beer Barrel Polka (#258), 73(VI), 75
Beer Barrel Polka, 117, 127, 143 (Andrews Sisters)
Begin The Beguine, 127 (Andrews Sisters)
Begin The Beguine (See Medley: Say It With Music)
Be Happy (arr BF) (#400), 180, 182(RS), 184, 189(GMMS/VI),
    202(GMMS), 215
Bei Mir Bist Du Schon, 110 (Andrews Sisters)

Dearly Beloved (arr JG) (#776), 461(RS), 472
Dear Mom (arr JG) (#715), 402(RS), 412, 437
Deep In The Heart Of Texas (arr JG) (#720), 433, 438, 439(VI),
    443(2), 448, 453, 456
Deep Purple (#198), 50(VI), 52
Delilah (arr BM) (#637), 335(RS), 337(VI)
Devil May Care, 151(RS), 171, 180, 188(GMMS)
Devil's Holiday (#85)
Deze Dem Doze (#34)
Dig It (arr JG) (#418), 246, 254(AC), 259(VI)
Ding-Dong! The Witch Is Dead (#264), 75(RS), 84
Dipper Mouth Blues (arr GM) (#101), 14(RS), 16, 36(AC), 40, 41(AC),
    51, 73, 76, 79, 147(VI), 159, 173, 184
(The) Dipsey Doodle (#114), 15
(The) Dipsey Doodle (See Medley: Whispering)
Does Your Heart Beat For Me? (See Medley: Coquette)
Do I Love You? (#301)
Do I Love You?, 144 (Andrews Sisters)
Doin' The Jive (arr GM) (#55), 9(RS), 16(VI)
Do I Worry? (#620), 316, 325, 330(VI), 333, 349, 353
(The) Donkey Serenade, 144(AC), 148(AC) (Andrews Sisters)
Dolores (arr BM) (#591)
Don't Cry, Cherie (arr BF) (#592), 307(RS)
Don't Sit Under The Apple Tree, 417(RS), 420, 424, 432, 440,
    442(VI), 444, 449, 451, 452, 453, 454, 455, 467
Don't Wake Up My Heart (#127), 14(RS), 15, 18(VI)
Don't Want A Thing (arr JG) (#673)
Don't Worry 'Bout Me (#205), 50(VI), 51, 52, 55 56(AC)
Down By The Ohio, 133 (Andrews Sisters)
Down For The Count (arr BF) (#444), 195(GMMS/VI), 199(GMMS),
    211(GMMS), 218, 220, 223(AC), 227, 233(AC), 245, 247(AC), 253
Down South Camp Meetin' (#44), 16(VI), 39
Do You Care? (arr JG) (#642), 357, 376(VI)
Do You Ever Think Of Me (See Medley: Whispering)
Do You Know Why (arr BF) (#488), 235(RS), 243, 246, 247(AC), 254,
    259
(A) Dream And I (arr JG) (#704), 389
Dreamsville, Ohio (arr JG) (#660), 361(RS), 370, 376, 382(VI), 413
Drink To Me Only With Thine Eyes, 119, 145, 167(AC), 181, 192(GMMS),
    225(AC), 246, 269, 363
Durham (#274)

East Side Of Heaven (#215), 56(AC)
(The) Echo Says No (arr DK) (#734)
Elmer's Tune (arr JG), 336(RS), 369, 377(AC), 381, 382, 392,
    396(AC), 397, 399, 407
Enlisted Men's Mess (arr JG) (#579)
Everybody Loves My Baby (arr JG) (#391), 183, 188(GMMS), 196(GMMS),
    209(GMMS), 216(VI), 228(AC), 248, 422, 440

To All Of You, 363
To And Fro (#29)
Too Beautiful To Last (#527)
Too Happy For Words (arr JG) (#541)
Too Romantic (#337), 128(RS), 139, 145(AC), 148, 156, 158
To The Shores Of Tripoli (arr JG), 412
(The) Touch Of Your Hand (See Medley: The Touch Of Your Hand)
To You (arr GM), 63(RS), 69, 70, 92(VI), 110(AC)
To You (See Medley: To You)
Trade Winds (arr JG) (#450), 211(GMMS), 215
Trigger's Tune (See: Nobody Ever Wants Me)
True Confession (#91)
Tschaikowsky's Piano Concerto (arr BF) (#674), 359, 363, 371(AC),
    371, 376, 382, 399, 406, 419(VI), 437
Tuxedo Junction (arr JG) (#328), 127(2), 128(RS), 129(RS), 131(AC),
    132, 138(AC), 139, 146, 147(AC), 156, 161(GMMS), 169, 201(GMMS),
    214(AC), 230, 237, 257, 375, 376, 384(AC), 396(AC), 422, 470
Twenty-Four Robbers (arr BF) (#599), 314, 318, 323, 330(VI), 334,
    349, 357
Twilight Interlude (#270), 80(RS), 81(VI), 84
Two Sleepy People (#168)

Uncle Tom (arr BF) (#641), 333(AC)
Undecided (#200)
Under A Blanket Of Blue (#438)
Under A Blanket Of Blue (See Medley: Sweet Leilani)
Under Blue Canadian Skies (arr BF) (#627), 320(RS)
Unknown Tune, 34(AC)
Unknown Tune, 56(AC)

Vagabond Dreams (#316), 102(RS)
Valse Triste (arr BM) (#675)
(The) Very Thought Of You (See Medley: Sweet And Lovely)
V-Hop (arr JG) (#688), 360, 369, 370, 376, 389, 401, 410, 420(VI),
    425, 437(VI), 442, 457(AC)
V For Victory Hop (See: V-Hop)
Vilia (arr BF), 334, 342, 350, 360(VI)
Vilia (See Medley: Vilia)
V.M.I. Spirit (#431)

Wabash Blues (See Medleys: My Gal Sal and Japanese Sandman)
Wait Until My Heart Finds Out (#153), 30(AC), 38
Walking By The River (arr JG) (#605), 287, 296, 300, 305(VI), 308
Waltz Theme (arr JG) (#700), 377(AC), 378(AC), 485(AC)
(The) Waltz You Saved For Me (See Medley: The Touch Of Your Hand)
(The) Wang, Wang Blues (See Medley: When Irish Eyes Are Smiling)
Wanna Hat With Cherries, 73(RS), 116, 125, 153, 158(GMMS), 205(GMMS)
Washboard Blues (arr JG) (#480)
Washboard Blues (See Medley: I'll Never Be The Same)

2. Medleys

Not all of the medleys shown here are of the "Something Old, Something New, Something Borrowed and Something Blue" type. We suspect that some are individual tunes joined together by a bridge (e.g. Butcher Boy/Marie) and that no editing has been done. As in the case of the individual tunes we have shown medleys that do not appear in the text as we have no broadcast listing of them but as there are scores available they are shown for completeness. The first tune in the medley determines the order of our listing and where we have two or more medleys beginning with the same tune the next tune determines the order of our listing. The medleys are repeated where a new tune was inserted (usually the "new" tune has been changed although in some cases the "blue" tune has been changed). The arranger for the medley is shown at the end of the medley (where known). Note that the arranger quite often copied part of the "new" tune arrangement from another Miller arranger, so, in some cases, only three tunes of the medley were arranged by the one arranger that we show. We didn't discover this fact until late in our work so we may be in error in listing one arranger for some of the medleys (although one arranger would set up the entire medley but would borrow from a previous arrangement).

Butcher Boy/Marie, 17

Coquette/I'll Never Smile Again/Does Your Heart Beat For Me?/
    Blue Hawaii (arr JG), 221(AC)
Coquette/Say It/Does Your Heart Beat For Me?/Blue Hawaii (arr JG)
    (#430), 158(VI), 182

Gershwin Medley (See: Our Love Is Here To Stay)
Goodnight, Sweetheart/I'm Stepping Out With A Memory Tonight/
    When My Baby Smiles At Me/A Blues Serenade (arr JG) (#421),
    160, 190(GMMS/VI)
Goodnight, Sweetheart/The White Cliffs Of Dover/When My Baby Smiles
    At Me/A Blues Serenade (arr JG), 387-388(AC)

Hands Across The Table/Sweet Eloise/I Kiss Your Hand, Madame/St.
    Louis Blues (arr JG) (#753)
How Deep Is The Ocean?/Always In My Heart/It's A Wonderful World/
    My Blue Heaven (arr JG) (#487), 418, 437(VI)
How Deep Is The Ocean?/Hereafter/It's A Wonderful World/My Blue
    Heaven (arr JG), 372
How Deep Is The Ocean?/I'd Know You Anywhere/It's A Wonderful
    World/My Blue Heaven (arr JG) (#487), 236-237(AC)

I Cried For You/And The Angels Sing/Marie/Blue Skies (#228)
I Cried For You/This Changing World/Marie/Blue Skies, 113(VI)
If I Had My Way/All The Things You Are/Oh Johnny! Oh Johnny! Oh!/
    Blue (arr JG) (#353), 135-136(VI)

To You/Indian Summer/Sunrise Serenade, 378(AC)
To You/Moonlight Cocktail/The Story Of A Starry Night/Rhapsody
    In Blue (#508), 415, 435

Vilia/You Walk By/Adios/Blue Afterglow, 276(AC)

(The) Waltz You Saved For Me/Papa Niccolini/Jingle Bells/Blue Danube
Waltz Medley (See: The Touch Of Your Hand)
When Irish Eyes Are Smiling/Confucius Say/Rose Room/Wang Wang
    Blues (arr JG) (#365), 146(VI)
Whispering/Do You Ever Think Of Me/Japanese Sandman (#3)
Whispering/Ooh! What You Said/The Dipsey Doodle/The Birth Of The
    Blues (#377), 126-127
Whispering/Wishing/The Dipsey Doodle/Alice Blue Gown (#509)
Why Do I Love You?/Can't Help Lovin' Dat Man/Make Believe/Ol' Man
    River (#107), 16-17(VI), 38

You Leave Me Breathless/The Lamplighter's Serenade/Racing With
    The Moon/Blues In The Night (#737), 424
You Tell Me Your Dream/Devil May Care/Sleep/Alice Blue Gown (arr JG)
    (#455), 167
You Tell Me Your Dream/A Nightingale Sang In Berkeley Square/Sleep/
    Alice Blue Gown (arr JG), 260(AC)
You Tell Me Your Dream/Our Love Affair/Sleep/Alice Blue Gown
    (arr JG), 210

INDEX TO PERSONNEL

     This index lists the names of all sidemen, vocalists, arrangers, band-boys and road managers who are referred to in the text and in the discographical section as having been actively associated with Glenn Miller either on engagements, broadcasts or recordings. We do not list the copyists, rumoured sidemen or film vocalists. Glenn Miller is not listed as his name appears on most pages. In order to shorten this listing no page reference is given for a solo or vocal credit which is shown on broadcasts and recordings.

Mastren, Al (Alex Mastandrea) (tbn), 13, 20, 23, 25, 26, 28, 29,
    33, 36, 39, 42, 43, 46, 48, 53, 56-58, 60, 65, 68-70, 72, 82,
    85-87, 89, 90, 99, 120, 121
Mastren, Carmen (g), 8
May, Billy (tpt & arr), 231-234, 240, 243, 252, 253, 260, 264, 270,
    275, 278, 286, 289, 296, 299, 300, 301, 303, 307-309, 312, 316,
    319, 322, 326, 327, 331, 334, 340, 342, 357, 358, 360, 362, 365,
    367, 373, 376, 378, 380, 384, 386, 387, 390, 391, 394, 399,
    401-403, 406, 410, 420, 425, 438, 442, 444, 446, 454, 457, 481,
    486
McDonough, Dick (g), 3, 5
McGee, John (tpt), 70
McIntyre, Hal (clt & as), 2-5, 7, 8, 12, 13, 20, 23, 25, 26, 28,
    29, 33, 36, 39, 42, 43, 46, 48, 53, 56-58, 61, 65, 68-70, 72,
    82, 85-87, 89, 90, 99, 122, 124, 126, 129, 132, 134, 164, 172,
    178, 208, 213, 224, 228, 231, 253, 307-309, 316, 319, 322, 326,
    327, 344, 355, 356, 363, 418, 419
McMickle, R. Dale "Mickey" (tpt), 47, 48, 53, 56-58, 60, 65, 68-
    70, 72, 82, 85-87, 89, 90, 99, 122, 123, 126, 132, 134, 172,
    178, 208, 213, 224, 228, 231, 307-309, 316, 319, 322, 326, 327,
    357, 362, 373, 378, 380, 384, 386, 387, 390, 391, 399, 401-403,
    410, 425, 481, 486
Mele, Vi (voc), 4
Meyer, Joe (tpt), 308
Miller, Eddie (ts), 1
Miller, Herbie (rd mgr), 172, 186
Mince, Johnny (clt & as), 1
(The) Modernaires (voc grp), 222, 223, 267, 268, 270, 273, 275,
    283, 287, 288, 299, 307, 317, 337, 338, 347, 348, 351, 357, 358,
    372, 386, 402, 405, 407, 411, 414, 475, 480, 486
Mondello, Toots (as), 2
Moore, Bill (arr), 239
Mucci, Louis (tpt), 20, 23
Nelson, Skip (Scipione Mirabella) (voc), 460-462, 464, 475, 480,
    486
O'Leary, John (rd mgr), 226, 408
Parkinson, Roy (ts), 425
Peck, Bob (tbn), 25, 26, 28
Peterson, Tweet (tpt), 4, 7, 11
Picciano, Andy (d?), 50
Price, Bob (tpt), 7, 8, 12, 13, 20, 21, 23, 25, 26, 28, 29, 33, 36,
    39, 42, 43, 46, 48, 53, 56-58, 60
Priddy, Jimmy (tbn), 132, 134, 163, 172, 177, 208, 213, 224, 228,
    231, 307-309, 316, 319, 322, 326, 327, 357, 362, 373, 378, 380,
    384, 386, 387, 390, 391, 399, 401-403, 410, 425, 481, 486
Purtill, Maurice "Moe" (d), 11, 50, 53, 56, 57, 59, 61, 66, 68-70,
    72, 82, 85-87, 89, 90, 95, 99, 122, 124, 126, 132, 134, 155,
    164, 172, 178, 184, 208, 210, 213, 224, 228, 231, 244, 307-309,
    316, 319, 322, 326, 327, 357, 358, 363, 373, 379, 380, 384, 387,
    390, 391, 399, 401-403, 410, 425, 481
Ralph, Jesse (tbn), 3-5, 7, 8
Rebito, Gasparre (tpt), 13
Reese, Gail (voc), 12, 13, 19

ADDITIONS AND CORRECTIONS

NOTES

NOTES

NOTES

NOTES

NOTES

NOTES

NOTES